"*Puritan Reformed Theology* is a title with a subtle double entendre. It certainly delivers what it promises—*theology* in the *Reformed* tradition mediated especially through the life and writings of the *Puritans*. But it also celebrates the quarter centenary of the *Puritan Reformed Theological Seminary* in Grand Rapids, Michigan, by presenting in one volume the wonderful series of essays its founding president, Dr. Joel R. Beeke, has contributed to the seminary journal.

"In these pages Professor Beeke handles a wide variety of subjects and turns them, one by one, into theological and pastoral gold. The range is extraordinary and yet focused on the main things. The ease of readability pleases the ordinary reader and yet there are footnotes in scholar-satisfying abundance. The sheer size of the book may seem intimidating, yet like a great cathedral it can be appreciated one stone at a time. Here then is a thesaurus of theological and spiritual riches, a veritable Aladdin's cave of intellectual and spiritual pleasures. I feel sure that readers will find themselves frequently returning to *Puritan Reformed Theology* to find in it both theological treasure and spiritual pleasure."

—Sinclair B. Ferguson, chancellor's professor of systematic theology, Reformed Theological Seminary; teaching fellow, Ligonier Ministries

"*Puritan Reformed Theology* is a treasure trove of articles and sermons that reflect godly piety and biblical orthodoxy. Dr. Beeke has once again served us with a valuable work which I gladly recommend."

—John MacArthur, senior pastor-teacher, Grace Community Church, Sun Valley, California

"First, congratulations to Puritan Reformed Theological Seminary on the happy occasion of your twenty-fifth anniversary, and to Dr. Joel Beeke on his completion of a quarter century of teaching there. The Lord is good, and He has shown His goodness in raising up and sustaining a school that is faithful to the Scriptures and Reformed theology. I'm grateful to God for you. Second, thank you to Dr. Beeke for this book, *Puritan Reformed Theology: Historical, Experiential, and Practical Studies for the Whole of Life*. Here is material for those in ministry or preparing for it (especially pastors, professors, missionaries, seminarians, and elders), as we aspire to better serve our flocks. And here is material for all Christians to feed and reflect on as we seek to grow in knowledge, grace, and wisdom. There is plenty here to engage the mind and warm the heart. It's classic Joel: truth for devotion. Enjoy, learn, and grow."

—Ligon Duncan, chancellor and CEO, Reformed Theological Seminary

"Dr. Beeke is one of the world's foremost scholars on Puritanism, and in this volume we have a marvelous collection of chapters covering historical, theological, and practical subjects of substance. I can think of no one I would rather learn from about these matters than Dr. Beeke. This collection contains the highest level of pastoral wisdom and doctrinal reflection through the lens of one of the best theologians and pastors I have ever known."

—Derek W. H. Thomas, senior minister, First Presbyterian Church, Columbia, South Carolina; chancellor's professor, Reformed Theological Seminary; teaching fellow, Ligonier Ministries

"As I look at the title and author of this book, Puritan Reformed Theology by Joel Beeke, each of these words—Puritan, Reformed, Theology, and Joel Beeke—fit together perfectly. Like links forged together on a chain, none can be separated from the others. So it is that Joel Beeke has become virtually synonymous with puritan reformed theology. This collection of articles written by Dr. Beeke and compiled into this one volume, is certain to be a storehouse of theological wealth for all who read it."

—Steven J. Lawson, President, OnePassion Ministries, Dallas, Texas

"It is all here: Puritan, and therefore magnificently Christ-centered. Reformed, and therefore established on the foundations of the Reformation. Theological, and therefore unashamedly confessional. Historical, therefore rehearsing relevantly timeless truths and freshly exposing old errors. Experiential, therefore conveying pathos, warmth, and conviction. Practical, therefore applicatory on almost every page. And finally, massively comprehensive, and therefore suitable for relaxing reading and mind-stretching awe."

—Geoffrey Thomas, emeritus pastor, Alfred Place Baptist Church, Aberystwyth, Wales

"Joel Beeke's commitment to the principle that doctrine is for life makes this collection of articles, along with its variety, a most profitable and joyous read. I cannot commend too highly this treasure trove of biblical, historical, systematic, and experiential theology. No doubt it is a volume to which the heart yearning for communion with God will return time and again."

—David B. McWilliams, senior minister, Covenant Presbyterian Church, Lakeland, Florida

"What a joy it is to congratulate Puritan Reformed Theological Seminary and President Beeke on the achievement of twenty-five years of fruitful ministry. It is certainly the Lord who birthed this seminary, caused her to mature, and has now taken her into full adulthood. This collection of Dr. Beeke's Puritan Reformed Journal articles is a fitting memorial for this celebration, and the sweep of his topics will provide engaging reading for anyone."

—Richard Gamble, professor of systematic theology,
Reformed Presbyterian Theological Seminary, Pittsburgh

"When meditating on the beauty and wonder of Christ, the psalmist confessed that his tongue was 'the pen of a ready writer' (Ps. 45:1). It was his sight and love for Christ that gave energy to his stylus. The same can be said of Joel Beeke. This volume commemorating the twenty-fifth anniversary of PRTS covers a wide range of years and topics and testifies to his passion for Christ and truth that affects all of life. The Lord has given him the 'gift of the pen'—or keyboard—to share that passion with the church and academy."

—Michael Barrett, vice president of academic affairs and professor of Old Testament,
Puritan Reformed Theological Seminary, Grand Rapids, Michigan

"It is a pleasure to commend this wide-ranging compilation of essays explicating the heart of biblical, Reformed Christianity. The range of material is especially impressive, culminating in a section titled 'Contemporary and Cultural Issues.' As with all of

Dr. Beeke's writings, a twin pulse beats and predominates throughout: Christ-centeredness and affectional heart religion. Read and be richly nourished in your faith."

—Ian Hamilton, minister, Evangelical Presbyterian Church of England and Wales

"*Puritan Reformed Theology* by Dr. Joel Beeke offers a precious treasure of truth to readers who are hungry for God's Word. These are edifying articles that open up and apply central biblical doctrines, often as expounded by the great Puritan writers of the past. I recommend this fine new book to all readers who love God's Word, especially to men who have an eye to the ministry. Give this volume to a hungry soul, and you will train up a dwarf to become a giant."

—Maurice Roberts, emeritus minister, Free Church of Scotland (Continuing)

"Dr. Beeke and the Reformed theology of the Puritans are increasingly viewed as nearly synonymous. No other Reformed scholar has been so passionately committed to promoting and publishing the rich heritage of the Puritans as Dr. Beeke. This book affirms his thorough and comprehensive grasp of their Christ-saturated theology. Throughout the history of Puritan Reformed Theological Seminary, Dr. Beeke's students, including myself, have been the grateful recipients of his able transmission of the rich texture of Puritan Reformed theology articulated in this book."

—Bartel Elshout, pastor, Heritage Reformed Congregation, Hull, Iowa

"When the Puritan Reformed Theological Seminary (PRTS) was founded in 1995, there were great joy and thankfulness to God for answering prayer. What Dr. Beeke and his fellow prayer warriors in the Heritage Reformed Congregations had in mind was to establish a theological seminary that combined the best elements of the English Puritan and Dutch Reformed traditions. Beeke's burden was to offer students a curriculum which would emphasize sound biblical and Reformed preaching that was also experiential and practical in its application. In chapter 27 of this commemorative book, titled 'Practical Application in Preaching,' Beeke, looking to Puritans like William Gouge as his model, writes, 'Puritan preachers stressed the need to inform the mind, to prick the conscience, then to bend the will, believing that a sermon must connect with the people, and by the Spirit's grace transform them and their wills. That is the heart of applicatory preaching.' This book's forty-two chapters cover a wide variety of theological, historical, and ethical subjects, thereby offering a good insight into the superb quality of the education provided at PRTS. May God bless this school of the prophets and prepare many more students from around the world there for gospel ministry at a time when worldwide apostasy is growing even as fields are ripening for a worldwide harvest."

—Cornelis (Neil) Pronk, emeritus pastor, Free Reformed Churches of North America

"Although Joel Beeke's father often told him that 'believers sometimes go to the grave with more questions than answers,' if he could have read all the chapters of this magnificent book of his son, he would have said, 'My son, you have supplied many answers to those questions!' *Puritan Reformed Theology* contains much insightful teaching on numerous topics, especially about the great subject of a believer's life: how to serve God 'acceptably with reverence and godly fear.' Having read through this book, I was not only amazed about the knowledge of the author, whom I regard as my brother, but my soul was also repeatedly urged to seek the Lord, to trust Him, and to serve Him; it drove me more than once to the throne of grace. Dr. Beeke informs our mind and convicts our conscience as he seeks to build up God's church by directing us to the biblical doctrine and life of the Puritans."

—Wouter Pieters, pastor, Elspeet, the Netherlands

"*Puritan Reformed Theology* is a resource teeming with exegetical, theological, and pastoral insights. Developed over decades of ministry, Joel Beeke's collection of essays offers readers a resource to be regularly read and referenced for theological enrichment and edification in the service of Christ's church."

—J. V. Fesko, professor of systematic and historical theology, Reformed Theological Seminary, Jackson, Mississippi

"*Puritan Reformed Theology* contains a rich miscellany of informative, fascinating, and edifying articles on a whole range of important subjects, providing the reader with a veritable feast of scholarship and insight. Everything presented in these seven hundred pages of mind-informing, heart-stirring material is well worth reading and will richly repay careful consideration and further study, but I would like to make special mention of 'The Age of the Spirit and Revival'; 'Delighting in God: A Guide to Sabbath-Keeping'; 'Calvin as an Experiential Preacher'; 'Assurance of Salvation: The Insights of Anthony Burgess'; and 'Lessons for Today from the Life of Idelette Calvin.' We are again deeply indebted to Dr. Beeke and his prolific pen. May God bless this excellent material to the good of souls and to the strengthening of His church in this world!"

—Malcolm H. Watts, minister, Emmanuel Church, Salisbury, Wiltshire, England

Puritan Reformed Theology

Puritan Reformed Theology

Historical, Experiential, and Practical Studies for the Whole of Life

Joel R. Beeke

REFORMATION HERITAGE BOOKS
Grand Rapids, Michigan

Reformation Heritage Books
2965 Leonard St. NE
Grand Rapids, MI 49525
616-977-0889
orders@heritagebooks.org
www.heritagebooks.org

Printed in the United States of America
20 21 22 23 24 25/10 9 8 7 6 5 4 3 2

Library of Congress Cataloging-in-Publication Data

Names: Beeke, Joel R., 1952- author.
Title: Puritan reformed theology : historical, experiential, and practical studies for the whole of life / Joel R. Beeke.
Description: Grand Rapids, Michigan : Reformation Heritage Books, 2020. | Contains auhor's articles written for "PRTS's Puritan Reformed Journal in its first decade of publication." | Includes bibliographical references and index.
Identifiers: LCCN 2020021195 (print) | LCCN 2020021196 (ebook) | ISBN 9781601788115 (hardback) | ISBN 9781601788122 (epub)
Subjects: LCSH: Puritans—Doctrines. | Reformed Church—Doctrines.
Classification: LCC BX9323 .B4378 2020 (print) | LCC BX9323 (ebook) | DDC 230/.59—dc23
LC record available at https://lccn.loc.gov/2020021195
LC ebook record available at https://lccn.loc.gov/2020021196

For additional Reformed literature, request a free book list from Reformation Heritage Books at the above regular or email address.

Contents

PRACTICAL THEOLOGY

PASTORAL THEOLOGY AND MISSIONS

CONTEMPORARY AND CULTURAL ISSUES

Introduction:
A Vision for Theological Education

Time flies on eagle's wings. It is hard to believe I am writing this introduction on the occasion of the twenty-fifth anniversary of Puritan Reformed Theological Seminary (PRTS). To mark this special occasion, Reformation Heritage Books (RHB) is publishing in this book the articles that I wrote for PRTS's *Puritan Reformed Journal* in its first decade of publication. I originally agreed to serve as the primary editor for our seminary's journal for one decade, and now I serve as assistant editor to Dr. William VanDoodewaard, who has graciously agreed to be the primary editor. I have the privilege here of presenting my articles from the first decade of the PRJ to a wider audience. I am grateful to both PRTS and RHB for this opportunity.

The goal of my writing ministry has always been to serve the church of Jesus Christ. I feel called strongly to bring Reformed and Puritan theology to bear on all of life through biblical, systematic, historical, experiential, practical, pastoral, and contemporary studies—hence the title and divisions contained in it.

In this introduction, I provide a brief biblical and historical vision for Christian theological education, a short history of the development of theological education at PRTS over the past twenty-five years (forgive me for waxing a bit nostalgic here), and an expression of heartfelt gratitude to those whom God has greatly used for this ministry over the past two and a half decades.[1]

A Biblical Vision for Theological Education

Most Christians view seminaries through the immediate needs of the local church.[2] When a church's pulpit becomes vacant, the congregation must look for a new pastor to faithfully preach God's Word and lead the church. Through

---

1. In a sense, this volume is a companion to my *Puritan Reformed Spirituality* (Grand Rapids: Reformation Heritage Books, 2004), which I published on the occasion of PRTS's tenth anniversary. That book was reprinted in 2006 by Evangelical Press.

2. Thanks to Paul Smalley for assistance on this section of my introduction.

the years, seminaries have been established for this important purpose. How-ever, Scripture presents a larger, grander picture of how Christian theological education fits into God's plan of glorifying His Son through the redemption of the nations. Let's start with the biblical roots found in the writings of the apostle Paul.

If ever there was a strategic, missionary-minded theologian, it was Paul. We see something of his vision for theological education in the only place in Scripture that uses the word "school"—namely, Paul's teaching center in Ephe-sus, recorded in Acts 19:8–10, at the school of Tyrannus. Here is a model of a school that is a center for preaching, resisting, teaching, and sending.

First, a theological school should be *a center for preaching*. Paul's ministry in the synagogue and the school of Tyrannus was characterized by speaking with freedom and confidence, even in the face of enemies of the truth—a confidence given supernaturally by the Spirit. Paul made logical arguments to establish Christian doctrines based on the law and the gospel of Holy Scripture. He labored to convince his hearers and move them to a long-term response of faith and obedience. This is the calling of centers for theological education, that they would be schools where men learn by example and instruction what it is to preach by the power of the Holy Spirit that system of doctrines found in Scrip-ture in a manner that is biblical, doctrinal, experiential, and applicational.

Second, a theological school should be *a center for resisting*. Paul's school in the lecture hall of Tyrannus was born out of persecution and the neces-sity of separation. Though Paul loved his kinsmen according to the flesh, "he departed from them, and separated the disciples" (Acts 19:9), both to preserve the church from false teaching and to protect its witness from compromise by association with unbelievers. A faithful seminary must be countercultural. It must separate itself from worldliness. The gospel wins the elect, but it hardens others. The gospel declares "the kingdom of God" (v. 8) and thus demands that sinners repent and turn back to God (Acts 20:21). Theological education must not be at peace with this world but must threaten its false gods, whether they be the self-righteousness of legalists or the materialism of pagans. We must be prepared to train men for gospel conflict in and against the world.

Third, a theological school must be *a center for teaching*. In the school of Tyrannus, the apostle Paul was "disputing daily," even for "the space of two years" (Acts 19:9–10). Paul poured his time and energy into teaching and reasoning with people from the Holy Scriptures. Although this certainly included evan-gelizing unbelievers, in the context it also reflects Paul's concern to ground "the disciples" of Christ more deeply in biblical truth after they separated from the synagogue. Paul was teaching them Christ from the Word, and he stayed in

Ephesus to invest in this ministry for two years. That is a huge commitment for a man whose ministry ordinarily consisted of traveling to many places to preach the gospel to as many people as possible (Rom. 15:19–21). Paul may have invested fifteen hundred to eighteen hundred hours of teaching in Ephesus, more than many seminary students receive.[3] It is no wonder that Paul's letter to the Ephesian church is one of the most glorious theological gems in the New Testament. All this indicates an intentional and focused time of teaching people the Word of God. Just as the faithful minister must devote himself to prayer and the ministry of the Word (Acts 6:4), so the faithful seminary must devote itself to a rigorous schedule of teaching and academic study.

Fourth, a theological school should be *a center for sending*. The result of Paul's school was not merely that the church in Ephesus became doctrinally grounded or even that Ephesus was reached with the gospel, but "that all they which dwelt in Asia heard the word of the Lord Jesus, both Jews and Greeks" (Acts 19:10). "Asia" here refers to the Roman province of Asia Minor, what is today the western portion of Turkey. The entire region was reached with the gospel. While it is possible that Paul went on preaching tours to some of these towns, other preachers like Epaphras went to other towns (Col. 1:7). In other words, this was not just a school where Paul taught but a school where Paul taught teachers (2 Tim. 2:2). Theological education aims to raise up laborers both to serve existing churches but also to establish new churches.

A Historical Vision for Theological Education

We see this biblical vision played out in history in the Reformed churches. At crucial times in church history such as revival and reformation, seminaries have served as centers for the worldwide spread of the gospel, the growth of the church, and the expansion of the kingdom of God. That was particularly so during the Protestant Reformation. As refugees poured into Geneva, Switzerland, Calvin labored long and hard to furnish them with a "school of Christ" to ground people in the truths of Scripture and the Reformed faith, which they carried back to their homelands in virtually all parts of Europe.

Later, as Reformed and Presbyterian Christians emigrated to North America, they soon realized that Europe's academies, seminaries, and universities could not provide them with more than a trickle of candidates for ministry in the New World. After the American Revolution, that trickle all but ceased.

---

3. The typical seminary student receives about 1,100 to 1,350 hours of teaching in a three-year master of divinity program.

People of faith saw what was needed and began to establish seminaries in the United States. For example, in New York City, John Mitchell Mason (1770–1829) of the Associate Reformed Presbyterian Church and John Henry Livingston (1746–1825) of the Dutch Reformed Church jointly trained generations of ministers for churches in New York, New Jersey, Pennsylvania, and elsewhere. William Tennent (1673–1746), a Presbyterian, organized "Log College" near Philadelphia to supply the needs of churches stirred by the power of the Great Awakening. Alexander Dobbin (1742–1809), a Reformed Presbyterian, and John Anderson (1748–1830) of the Associate Presbyterian Church, headed west to start seminaries under the most primitive of conditions. They too trained several generations of faithful preachers and pastors as well as laymen.

William Proudfit (1732–1802) of the Associate Presbyterian Church in Scotland emigrated from Scotland to London, Ontario, when the city was still being hewn from the forest. He stayed there for almost two decades, planting the Reformed faith deep in the soil of the area. Among his many tasks was to found a seminary, now known as Knox College in Toronto, to train men for gospel outreach throughout the province.

In the nineteenth century, the Second Great Awakening challenged believers to participate in worldwide evangelism and missions. As communication and travel conditions improved, Princeton Theological Seminary in New Jersey was founded in 1812. Its renowned professors Archibald Alexander (1772–1851), Samuel Miller (1769–1850), Charles Hodge (1797–1878), Archibald A. Hodge (1823–1886), and Benjamin B. Warfield (1851–1921) trained nearly six thousand ministers in less than a century to defend Reformed interpretations of Scripture. These professors also provided the intellectual, spiritual, and practical foundations for twentieth-century evangelicalism. Other lesser-known American seminaries became centers of missionary inspiration, information, recruitment, and training. Governing boards reported that large numbers of students were volunteering to go to newly opening mission fields across the world.

As churches grew on these mission fields, native converts were sometimes sent back to American seminaries to be trained for leadership in the infant churches and new colleges. These men then became the mentors of others in their homelands, establishing theological training centers there. Simple addition quickly gave way to multiplication. Though Christ is the builder of His church, orthodox Reformed seminaries have proven to be effective instruments in the hands of Christ under the direction of the Spirit.

A Brief History of Puritan Reformed Theological Seminary

The word "seminary" originally meant a plant nursery where seeds would be grown into plants that would then be transplanted into orchards, fields, and yards where they would flourish and multiply. At Puritan Reformed Theological Seminary in Grand Rapids, God has given us students from thirty different denominations and nearly as many countries, including Canada, England, Scotland, the Netherlands, Lithuania, India, Ethiopia, Egypt, Iran, Iraq, Syria, South Africa, Ghana, Nigeria, Kenya, Tanzania, Australia, the Philippines, Kazakhstan, China, Korea, Malaysia, Myanmar, Mexico, Colombia, and Brazil. One of my great joys is knowing that with each graduation we send out faithful men to the uttermost parts of the earth. Fifty percent of our students come to us from outside of North America. By God's grace, our seminary serves as an arm of the church in fulfilling the Great Commission. This is the high calling and tremendous potential for theological education: to establish centers of preaching, resisting, teaching, and sending (note the acronym of these four words, PRTS) that are seedbeds of leaders for the church among all nations.

Over the past twenty-five years, we have been humbled by and are thankful for the remarkable ways in which the Lord has blessed our ever-growing seminary. PRTS began with me as the sole professor in 1995. The newly birthed Heritage Reformed denomination appointed me to undertake this task along with continuing as pastor of the Heritage Reformed Congregation in Grand Rapids. At that historic classis meeting in Ontario, the question was raised by an elder, "What shall we call the new school?" Another elder quickly replied, "The Heritage Netherlands Reformed Theological Seminary." When I responded that that name was too long and too restrictive because we wanted to reach the world with biblical Reformed teaching and preaching that was confessional, experiential, and practical, I was asked by another delegate what I thought the school should be named. I replied, "I really have no idea. Well, we definitely want to be Reformed, but we also want to stress piety in our training—the kind of piety the Puritans possessed, so I suppose something like Puritan Reformed Theological Seminary." "So moved," said another elder. It was seconded and passed unanimously with no further discussion!

In those early years in the late 1990s, we leaned temporarily on the Protestant Reformed Theological School to teach our students in certain areas, such as exegesis and church order, but help was soon on the way. After a few years the Free Reformed churches expressed an interest in joining our fledgling endeavors and appointed Dr. Gerald Bilkes to the task. And what a godsend he has been to me and this institution for the past two decades! He ably taught many of the Old Testament and New Testament courses and exegesis.

Within ten years of opening its doors, PRTS had outgrown its building. Construction began on our current facility at 2965 Leonard NE in Grand Rapids, and it was dedicated to the Lord's service in the fall of 2004. This first building was twenty thousand square feet and had a price tag of three million dollars. At our regular prayer times each morning, one of our staff prayed often throughout 2004 that the entire building would be paid for by the evening of dedication. I finally felt obliged to inform him that it may not be best to pray for that since it sounded a bit like Gideon putting out his fleece, which is not something we are generally supportive of now that the entire sacred canon is written. Moreover, realistically speaking, this was not going to happen anyway as we were far from our goal. Surprisingly, however, by dedication evening, $2.88 million had been raised, by God's grace, with only $120,000 needed to pay the remainder of the bills. Five minutes before the evening program opened, a friend wanted to speak with me in my study and then put something in my hand and quickly left, saying, "I think you may need this." It was a check for $120,000! When I told the audience that evening that we would not be taking up an offering for the building after all because it was entirely paid for, everyone was astonished. We could actually hear the three hundred attendees inhale then exhale almost in unison in a spontaneous expression of surprise and awe for what God had done!

In October of 2005, Dr. Sinclair Ferguson dedicated our Puritan Research Center (PRC) to God's service. The PRC is a unique part of our library intended to provide people around the world with access to a wide variety of Puritan literature and to foster a deeper appreciation for the Puritan tradition. It is one of the world's largest and most diverse collections of Puritan literature, both in primary and secondary sources. The PRC functions include (1) promoting ground-breaking research, (2) fostering education and publication for Puritan and post-Reformation studies, (3) spawning internationally recognized research centers to strengthen both the church and the academy, (4) promoting primary and secondary resource materials for the majority world and beyond, and (5) bringing distant communities and PRTS together through digital research, education, and publication. Today we have affiliated centers of the PRC located at Hapdong Theological Seminary, South Korea, and the Theological University of Apeldoorn, the Netherlands.

After we entered our new building and established the PRC, the seminary began to grow substantially. In 2007, Dr. David Murray from the Free Church of Scotland (Continuing) joined the faculty as professor of Old Testament and practical theology. He proved to be of immense help as our third full-time professor.

In 2010, Dr. William VanDoodewaard became associate professor of church history at PRTS and assumed all the church history courses that I had been teaching so that I could focus on systematic theology and homiletics. Two years later, PRTS hired Dr. Michael P. V. Barrett as vice president for academic affairs and academic dean and professor of Old Testament, as well as Dr. Mark Kelderman as dean of students and spiritual formation. All these men have been great gifts of God to PRTS and to me in particular and have served our Lord and His church well. Our team of six professors finally was adequate to the task at hand.

However, the seminary was once again becoming too small to hold our increasing student body. Therefore, an extensive addition, effectively doubling the size of the footprint of the original building, plus the addition of a base-ment, was completed in 2014. Regretfully, I told the staff that since the Lord seldom does miracles twice in a row, we should definitely not expect that this time the entire building of $3.6 million would be paid for by the evening of dedication. To the astonishment of us all, however, two days before the Friday dedication $3.54 million had been raised. On that Wednesday a donor called and asked me how much more was needed for the building. I said, "$60,000." "But what about your operation fund?" the donor asked. "Do you have enough to pay your faculty and staff next week at month's end?" "No," I said, "we are near zero." "Well, how much more do you need for that?" the donor asked. "Another $65,000," I said. "Well," the donor replied, "I don't have $125,000 to give just now, but I will call you in a few days to let you know what I can give." Two hours later, that donor called back. "I was able to free up some money," the donor said, "and I want you to know that a $125,000 check is in the mail to you; you should have it by Friday." We received this check four hours before the dedication service. The Lord did it again!

A few years later, PRTS added a PhD program in both historical theol-ogy (2016) and biblical studies (2017). Our long-term vision for this is that we might assist in reaching the goal some decades from now, if Christ tarries, that each nation in the world having a significant Reformed presence would also have at least one thoroughly sound and Reformed seminary where all the professors teach from a biblical, Reformed, confessional, and experiential per-spective. And thus students from these nations would no longer have to leave their native countries to get such a solid education. To support our PhD pro-gram, four additional full-time faculty members were hired: Dr. Adriaan Neele as director of the PhD program and professor of historical theology; Dr. Ste-phen Myers as associate professor of historical theology; Dr. Greg Salazar as assistant professor of historical theology; and Dr. Daniel Timmer as professor of biblical studies (together with assistance from Dr. Barrett). Each of these professors have done well, and under Dr. Neele's able leadership our programs have grown considerably. This fall we are scheduled to open a new PhD degree in systematic theology, of which Dr. Myers will be the primary instructor and I will be the secondary instructor.

The Present Ministry of Puritan Reformed Theological Seminary

Over the years, the seminary also has had over thirty visiting professors/ instructors from around the world to provide module courses and provide assistance for our ten full-time faculty members. And supporting the faculty has been a growing administrative staff. Currently, Dr. Jonathon Beeke serves as registrar and director of admissions and assessment as well as part-time instructor, Marjoleine de Blois as faculty assistant, Darryl Bradford as video producer/editor, Ann Dykema as administrative secretary and finances, Chris Engelsma as director of distance learning, Chris Hanna as director of market-ing and development, Giselle Huang as course designer and TEEC instructor, Seth Huckstead as IT director, Henk Kleyn as vice president for operations, Laura Ladwig and Kim Dykema as librarians, Rod MacQuarrie as Director of UX and Digital Strategy, and Paul Smalley as research/teaching assistant to me. We could not ask for a better, more dedicated, and qualified staff. They are an incredible, foundational, and essential part of the running, stability, and growth of PRTS.

From 1995 until the present, PRTS has grown from 4 students to 224 students. Alumni are serving the church in various ways: preaching and pastor-ing, teaching as seminary presidents or professors, working in international or domestic missions, church planting, and pursuing further education. And in 2018–2019 PRTS felt called to build a dorm complex, so my wife and I now have fifty-three new neighbors—theological students and their wives and chil-dren—literally in our front yard! We love having this little so-called Puritan village in front of our home. And by God's grace, this entire complex is now paid for as well.

The seminary offers four programs designed to meet the needs of church and ministry: the master of divinity (MDiv) degree, the master of arts (religion) degree, the master of theology (ThM) degree, and the doctor of philosophy (PhD) degree. Our programs are demanding and thorough; we believe that there are no shortcuts to proper preparation for ministry. Graduates find that the work done at PRTS is foundational, instructive, and invaluable for the rewarding obligations of their vocation and ministries. As of 2014, PRTS has been fully accredited by the Commission on Accrediting of the Association of Theological Schools in the United States and Canada (ATS) for its MDiv, MA, and ThM degrees, and as of 2018, the PhD degrees have been fully accredited as well. In the near future, we hope with God's help to open a full MA program in counseling—both in-house and long distance—under the leadership of Dr. Kelderman, who has recently acquired his DMin degree in counseling. We also hope to establish a PhD and a DMin degree in homiletics in a few years as the Lord provides.

The vision for a global and worldwide dissemination of the core principles of PRTS was expanded. By God's grace, PRTS has reached many additional students throughout the world with a robust biblical, Reformed, and experiential theological education. The seminary's leadership team, spearheaded by Dr. Neele, has identified strategic regions throughout the world that have been lacking the sort of theological education offered at PRTS. Working closely with like-minded institutional leaders from each of these regions, partnerships have been established with four schools in Cairo (Egypt), London (UK), São Paulo (Brazil), and Taipei (Taiwan), where PRTS and local faculty work together to offer an accredited PRTS master of theology (ThM) degree program in biblical studies, historical theology, and systematic theology. At these sites our faculty teaches 50 percent of the courses, and the partner school's faculty teaches 50 percent of the courses. In each of these locations, as of early this year, the partner school has been assessed by ATS and approved to offer the accredited PRTS degree program. In each case, on completing this degree, students will receive an accredited ThM degree from PRTS. We are grateful to have these four campus extensions for the ThM degree and pray that God will bless all involved with these campuses—faculty, students, and staff alike—to the furtherance of His glory and the growth and maturation of His worldwide church.

As we look to the future in total dependence on the Lord, we are excited about the prospect of training part of the next generation of pastors, theological instructors, missionaries and church planters, and Bible school and seminary presidents. In many parts of the world, Christians are hungry for sound theological instruction that not only grips the mind but also enflames the heart and directs men, women, and children to love the Lord their God with their entire heart, mind, soul, and strength and to love their neighbor as themselves. We at PRTS believe that this sort of Christian understanding and experience can only be fully grasped by growing in appreciation for the richness of the biblical, confessional, experiential, and practical Reformed faith. For more information on PRTS and its programs, please visit us online at https://www.prts.edu.

Acknowledgments

On reaching this anniversary milestone at PRTS, I have many to thank. First, I wish to express my gratitude to God for granting us a faculty that is increasingly becoming known throughout the Reformed, English-speaking world for upholding biblical, Reformed, confessional, experiential, and practical truth and principles—and for teaching God's truth ably and humbly, without shame or capitulation to man-centered desires. I thank God for the giftedness of my esteemed fellow professors and for the spirit in which we can co-labor as brothers in Christ to God's glory and for the good of souls. In dependency on the Spirit, let us continue to train our students faithfully so that God may be glorified, the church of Christ edified, and sinners around the world called to repent of their sins and to seek and find forgiveness, comfort, and joy in the King of glory, the Son of God.

Huge heartfelt gratitude also goes to our gifted staff for all your zealous work for God's church and kingdom. Your diligent work and tireless efforts have not gone unnoticed. I certainly would not trade our staff at PRTS for any other seminary staff in the world. I thank especially Henk Kleyn for his loving management of staff and for the Christlike, peaceable spirit of unity that exudes from you all. A special thanks personally from me to all of you. I know that my work would not be nearly as effective without you. Thanks so much for making your gifts available to me and to the faculty above and beyond the call of duty.

And where would we be without our students! Again, I would not trade our student body for any other in the world. Students, thank you for being you and for entrusting your education to us! You are very special to the entire faculty—more special than you know. Nearly every adjunct faculty member who teaches a module class at PRTS says to me at some point something like this: "You have a remarkable student body here. They are so interested, so godly, ask so many good questions—they are just a joy to teach!" And they are right! We love you and pray that God will use you greatly for His glory, the upbuilding of His church, and the tearing down of the strongholds of Satan throughout your lives.

Chris Hanna and I—and everyone in our seminary—also owe a tremendous debt of gratitude to our donors. Without you, these facilities and this ministry would not exist. A double thanks to those of you who give sacrificially because you believe so much in what we are trying to do, and you understand that seminaries are, in many ways, the backbone of the entire Christian enterprise. Generally speaking, without good training, few servants of God will excel in their callings to God's glory and the good of souls. It has always impressed me that our most generous donors almost always respond to my thanks with servant-hearted responses like this: "Please don't feel a need to thank me; this money really doesn't even belong to me. I am just a channel through which God's gifts pass on to you." That is so very humbling. Many, many thanks, dear donors, first of all for your prayer support but also for your financial support.

To the board of trustees: we owe a hearty thank-you to you—ministers and elders from the Heritage Reformed Congregations (HRC) and the Free Reformed Churches (FRC) who commit your precious time and energy so willingly and faithfully to the betterment of this worthy cause. Please continue to pray for us as well that we as faculty, staff, and students would not stray from or compromise the precious biblical doctrines of sovereign grace bequeathed to us but may remain faithful to our God to the end. In the last decade in particular, under able leadership, you have ramped up your knowledge of and involvement in the seminary and have been a huge help to me and to all of us in organizing and running it. And to our chairman, Dr. Jonathan Engelsma: we are going to grieve to see you relinquish your chairmanship this August as you complete the two allotted four-year terms. Thanks so much for your wisdom and help throughout these years.

Many thanks also to the ministers, elders, deacons, and members of the Heritage Reformed Congregations (HRC) and the Free Reformed Churches (FRC) for your prayerful and financial support. I thank you for the strong church governance of PRTS as we co-labor for theological education *of* the church, *by* the church, and *for* the church denominationally and worldwide. I thank you as well for your respective seminary committees that shoulder the care of your denominational students: the Theological Seminary Committee of the HRC and the Theological Education Committee of the FRC. Your work is deeply appreciated.

And to our many volunteers: thanks so much for your invaluable service in the food bank and in countless other ways. This seminary would not be the same without you. "Let us not be weary in well doing: for in due season we shall reap, if we faint not" (Gal. 6:9). If not for the loving commitment of churches and individuals alike, giving of their time, talent, and treasure, much of what the Lord has allowed us to accomplish would not have happened.

On a personal level, there are two more people I need to express appreciation for who have assisted me immensely behind the scenes in the past quarter century at PRTS with their stellar wisdom and experience in matters that are spiritual, educational, and practical. The first is, in memoriam, Dr. James Grier (1932–2013), who served across the street from us for sixteen years as executive vice president and academic dean of Grand Rapids Theological Seminary. Dr. Grier became one of my closest friends and was always willing to give his incredibly wise advice on all things educational, spiritual, and practical. Humble to a fault, he always had a huge servant's heart. He was the best teacher I have ever known. I sat in on nearly every course he taught for us. I also owe to him much of the little knowledge I have about serving as president of an institution like PRTS. Early on, he embraced then expanded my worldwide vision for PRTS, encouraging me to pursue full ATS accreditation for PRTS as well as to press on to offer PhD degrees. The second is my older brother, James Beeke, who has spent a lifetime in education—teaching at nearly every grade level himself, then becoming inspector of hundreds of schools in British Columbia on behalf of the government, and ultimately helping to start and administrate numerous English-speaking schools in China. The wisdom he has acquired, by God's grace, over these decades of educational experience has been a huge help to me. And his assistance in helping PRTS obtain ATS accreditation status has been invaluable. Never in all these years has he turned down my many requests for advice.

To all of you, please receive my heartfelt gratitude for your prayers, loyalty, and hard and able work during the past twenty-five years, for helping to establish and grow, by God's grace, an international Reformed seminary that, despite our and my shortcomings, promotes biblical, confessional, experiential, and practical ministry. Our prayer is that the day may yet come before Christ returns on the clouds that every city in the world will have at least one Reformed experiential preacher and congregation so that people will no longer have to grieve that they cannot find a solid Reformed church in their vicinity. I love you all and am grateful to all of you and pray that God may continue to use you and all of us for the furtherance of His kingdom here on earth in anticipation of His eternally perfect kingdom hereafter.

Finally, with regard to this book, these pages would never have seen the light of day without my dear wife, Mary, who lovingly and encouragingly gives me time and space to fulfill my calling to write and whose praises I cannot sing highly enough; and Paul Smalley, my faithful and able research/teaching assistant, who is also my daily prayer partner. In addition to providing me invaluable assistance on several chapters in this book, Paul coauthored with me chapters 5–6, 14, 17–20, 22–23, 25, 28, and 34–35. I am convinced that I have the world's best TA! Thanks as well to David Murray, who coauthored chapter 27 with me.

I also express heartfelt gratitude to Samuel Caldwell, Ray Lanning, Rod MacQuarrie, Wouter Pieters, and Liz Smith for ably editing these chapters, and to Linda den Hollander for her stellar typesetting. Many thanks to Jay Collier, Steve Renkema, and David Woollin from Reformation Heritage Books (RHB) for all the friendship, wisdom, and assistance you provide me. Each of you, together with the employees and the ministry of RHB itself, mean far more to me than you know.

Above all, I thank the triune God for communing with me at times in unforgettable ways while writing these chapters. Having felt called to write edifying works since my teenage years, I am profoundly grateful to the Holy Spirit that I often experience fellowship with the Father and the Son more intimately when writing about God and His truth than by any other spiritual discipline in which I engage. Consequently, despite my many shortcomings, I feel compelled to write in order to know and live God's truth better and more fully. It is my prayer that as you read this book, it might move you to know and live God's truth more fully as well: biblically, confessionally, experientially, and practically. *Soli Deo gloria!*

—JRB

BIBLICAL STUDIES

Chapter 1

The Age of the Spirit and Revival

The night on which He was betrayed, Jesus spoke to His disciples about the dawn of a new day that would be heralded by the Holy Spirit coming to dwell in them (John 14:17). Jesus says in John 16:8, "When he is come, he will reprove the world of sin, and of righteousness, and of judgment."[1]

This new day is the period of time in which God the Holy Spirit dwells in believers and the church in the full measure of His divine person and in abundant demonstration of His divine power. Sent by the Father and poured out by the Son, the Spirit's commission is to sanctify believers to be members of Christ, dwelling in them and applying to them what they already have in Christ, namely, the washing away of their sins, the daily renewing of their lives, and all the other benefits purchased for them by Christ's redemptive sacrifice on the cross.

Ten days after Christ's ascension to heaven, the Holy Spirit was poured out on the disciples gathered in Jerusalem on the feast day of Pentecost. Christ had prepared the apostles for what would happen to the church. So now, as the sound of a mighty, rushing wind filled the meeting place and tongues of fire appeared to hover over every head, believers knew that they were being filled with the Spirit. They began to speak in many languages "out of every nation under heaven" (Acts 2:5).

The prophetic words of Christ were being fulfilled: the church was baptized with the Holy Spirit, and its members received power from on high. The age of the Spirit had begun! To understand this phenomenon, let us examine the age of the Spirit from three perspectives: the Spirit's work in prior ages, the Spirit's work in this present age, and the Spirit's work particularly in revival.

---

1. This article is the substance of an address given for the Philadelphia Conference of Reformed Theology (PCRT), 2010, in Sacramento, California, and Greenville, South Carolina.

The Spirit's Work in Prior Ages

A superficial reading of the New Testament might lead some to conclude that the presence of the Spirit in the church and in the world was something new. The same mistake is often made regarding what Christ calls "the new covenant in my blood." It is easy to separate the New Testament from the Old and conclude that a great gulf exists between the two. Some Christians speak of Pentecost as "the birthday of the church," as if there were no visible church in the world prior to that time. Worse yet, some speak of the Jewish church of the Old Testament as something radically different from the Christian church of the New, as though each had nothing to do with the other.

That is simply not so, for the person and work of the Spirit are introduced to us already at the dawn of time. The earth was shrouded in darkness and a flood of great waters, but Moses tells us, in Genesis 1:2, "The Spirit of God moved upon the face of the waters." The verb "moved upon" can be translated as "hovering" in the sense of shaking or fluttering, like a bird hovering over its nest. In fact, Deuteronomy 32:10–11 uses the same verb when it speaks of an eagle hovering over its young, tending to their every need. In His capacity as "Lord and Giver of Life," the Spirit was fully present and active at the beginning to enact the astonishing results demanded by the various creative "fiats" of God. Psalm 104:30 says, "Thou sendest forth thy spirit, they are created: and thou renewest the face of the earth." In particular, the Spirit filled the earth, the seas, and the dry land with all kinds of living things. We may thus speak of the biosphere, or realm of life and living things that cover the earth, as the great creation of God the Holy Spirit (cf. Job 26:13).

In our creation, the Spirit was also present as the "Breath of Life," or the breath of God that proceeded from the Father and the Son. When breathed into the nostrils of the divinely-sculpted but lifeless form of man, the Spirit transformed a creature of dust and earth into a living being (Gen. 2:7). Job 33:4 says, "The spirit of God hath made me, and the breath of the Almighty hath given me life." Thus we owe our life and the life of every other living thing as much to the power and creativity of the Holy Spirit as we do to the hand of our Maker and Father in heaven.

Man is a created being and therefore has no life in himself. He cannot beget himself, nor can he generate or sustain his development to maturity. He cannot keep himself alive or deliver himself from the power of death. For all this we must depend on the grace of God and, in particular, on the work of the Holy Spirit. When God withholds His grace, we decline and die; when He sends forth His life-giving Spirit, we and all living things are quickened again and flourish by the same power that gave us life at the beginning (Ps. 104:30).

So wherever there is life, the Holy Spirit is at work. David lived in a world pervaded by the omnipotent presence of the Holy Spirit, for he says in Psalm 139:7, "Whither shall I go from thy Spirit? Or whither shall I flee from thy presence?" But the Spirit is more than power. As a person, He possesses the intelligence and the wisdom of God. As the source of "all holy desires, all good counsels, and all just works," He is at work in the minds and hearts of human beings everywhere. All valid insights into the nature of things, philosophical or scientific; all skills, whether manual, mechanical, or creative; all discoveries, inventions, or works of art; and everything that blesses the life of mankind reveal the presence and work of the Holy Spirit throughout history. The Spirit distributes gifts of statesmanship and craftsmanship that extend beyond man's natural capacity. Consider the remarkable leadership skills He imparted to Joseph, which Pharaoh recognized (Gen. 41:38), and to Daniel, which the kings of Babylon acknowledged (Dan. 4:8–9, 5:11–14). Exodus 31:3–5 tells us that the Holy Spirit filled Bezaleel with knowledge and wisdom to do "all manner of workmanship" for constructing and furnishing the tabernacle. The Holy Spirit also provided some of the early kings of Israel with special capabilities (1 Sam. 16:13), spoke directly to prophets (Ezek. 2:2), and inspired the Old Testament Scriptures through a divine out-breathing and Spirit-bearing influence (2 Tim. 3:16–17; 2 Peter 1:21). All these things are gifts of God, which are distributed among us by the work of the Holy Spirit. Without His light, human beings would produce anarchy and self-destruct and be condemned to utter darkness.

As the Spirit of holiness, the Spirit also labors in the world as the moral agent of God, "striving with man" to sustain whatever remains of the light of conscience, to restrain the destructive excesses of human depravity, and to mitigate the effects of the evil that people commit against one another. When we are overwhelmed by reports of the terrible things that humans do, we should consider how much worse it would be without the gracious work of the Spirit. His absence did not bode well for the people who lived in the world before the flood, whom God warned, "My spirit shall not always strive with man" (Gen. 6:3). Withdrawing His Spirit from a man, a church, a nation, or the world is a sure sign of God's hot displeasure.

It follows, then, that the Spirit so values the world that He does much more than create political entities and provide Israel with a theocracy. The Spirit also works progressively and cumulatively through historical redemptive revelation, both corporately and individually. Sinclair Ferguson writes, "Isaiah 63:7–14 clarifies this with its reflections on the Exodus, the great paradigmatic redemptive act of the Old Testament. (1) The Spirit is associated with the activity of Moses in working miracles (see Ex. 8:19).... He is the divine witness-bearer to the redemptive activity of God (Isa. 63:11–12). (2) The Spirit leads and guides the people into the benediction of covenant fulfillment (Isa. 63:14).... (3) The Spirit is the executive of the Exodus-redemption wrought by God the Saviour (Isa. 63:8)."[2]

The Spirit has an essential role in the redemptive life of each individual believer. Knowing that true faith is worked in our hearts by the Holy Spirit who uses the Word of God as His chosen instrument, we can say that wherever prophecy and revelation exist and wherever the Word of God is received by faith, the Holy Spirit is at work. The fruit of the Spirit delineated in Galatians 5:22–23 was already manifest in Old Testament believers. Whether it be Adam, Noah, Abraham, Moses, David, the heroes of faith, the martyrs of God, His servants, the prophets, or the believing remnant of the house of Israel, the work of the Holy Spirit was evident in what they believed and how they lived. David said the Holy Spirit was the treasure of his life. Fearing that he might lose this treasure, he earnestly prayed, "Take not thy holy spirit from me" (Ps. 51:11).

Where there is life, the Spirit is at work. Where there is light, the Spirit is at work. Wherever the might of human sin and evil is limited by divine providence, the Spirit strives with men. Where there is faith, the Spirit is at work in the hearts of men, fulfilling both individually and corporately a variety of goals in redemptive history that will lead to His fuller ministry in the Lord Jesus Christ and the present New Testament age.

The Spirit's Work in This Present Age

If the Spirit has been present in the world from the beginning, and if He has done such powerful and important work since then, how is the present age any different? What is so new about the New Testament? Viewed in one light, the answer is: *nothing!* The promises of God are as old as the covenant of grace. The way of justification is the same under both testaments. The principles and laws of God's dealings with mankind remain the same. The purpose of God in exalting His Son and saving His people is unaltered.

But viewed in another light, the answer is: *everything!* When Christ entered the world to be "delivered for our offenses and raised again for our justification" (Rom. 4:25), the Spirit's presence was pervasive and powerful. The Spirit was present in the beginning of His incarnate existence (Luke 1:35), at His baptism (Mark 1:10), at His temptations in the wilderness (Mark 1:12), during His

---

2. Sinclair Ferguson, *The Holy Spirit* (Downers Grove, Ill.: InterVarsity Press, 1995), 24.

teaching (Luke 4:14), in His miracles (Matt. 12:28), throughout His emotional life (Luke 10:17, 21), and behind His resurrection from the dead (Rom. 8:11). But when Christ's Spirit was poured out on the church at Pentecost (Acts 2:1–4), the ground moved underfoot. Ferguson writes, "Pentecost publicly marks the transition from the old to the new covenant.... It is the threshold of the last days, and inaugurates the new era in which the eschatological life of the future invades the present evil age.... Thus, from the New Testament's standpoint, the 'fulfilment [or end] of the ages had dawned' on those who, through the gift of the Spirit, are 'in Christ' (1 Cor. 10:11). That which is 'new' in the new covenant ministry of the Spirit is therefore inextricably related to the significance of the Pentecost event."[3] What was a promise now is fulfilled. What was a hope, expressed in "types and shadows," now is revealed as a body of substance and a new reality for us to enter and take hold of by faith. What was so long hidden, unknown, and unacknowledged is now revealed and proclaimed to the ends of the earth. What for so long was the privilege of a few blessed souls is now offered to whoever believes on the name of the only begotten Son of God. The outpouring of the Spirit ushers in a new era of character and nature as well as of scope or magnitude.

In this new age, the Spirit continues to do all His great works but in more profound ways and on a much larger scale. As the Spirit of Christ, He affects many more people with a more definite focus. The light showers of the pre-Pentecostal Spirit are transformed into the heavy showers of the post-Pentecostal Spirit, bringing about the conversion of millions over the centuries.

Having sustained the bodily life of man for so long, the Holy Spirit now more abundantly works inwardly in human hearts that were dead in trespasses and sins. His first work in this age of the gospel is to quicken the souls of the elect and prepare the soil of their hearts to receive the good seed of the Word of Christ.

The Spirit who for so many ages worked with man to restrain human sin and evil now bombards the consciences of men with convicting power. He crushes resistance to the gospel, puts to flight the lies and errors of the devil, overthrows the citadels of unbelief, and provides the way for the gospel to do its work as the power of God in saving all who savingly believe.

What amazing multitasking the Spirit does in the elect in uniting them to Christ and working out within them the order of salvation! Consider only some of A. W. Pink's chapter titles in his book on the Holy Spirit: the Spirit

---

3. Ferguson, *The Holy Spirit*, 57–58.

regenerates, quickens, enlightens, convicts, comforts, draws, works faith, unites to Christ, indwells, teaches, cleanses, leads, assures, witnesses, seals, assists, intercedes, transforms, preserves, confirms, fructifies, and endows (chaps. 10–31). We ought to appreciate and treasure the Spirit's ministry within us far more than we are prone to do!

Moreover, the Spirit, who for so long has distributed the gifts of God to mankind in general, now takes special care to distribute the gifts of Christ among all the members of His body, the church. He furnishes the church with ministers, elders, and deacons; empowers the means of grace; and equips the people of God to minister to one another and to the needs of a hurting, broken world in the name of Christ. He blesses the witness of the church and extends the mission of the church to every part of the world.

For so long the Spirit worked in hidden ways among a chosen few; now He openly demonstrates His power, working powerfully in the lives of many and helping the church to grow as a kingdom of faith and love and holiness that one day will fill the earth. He does all this in the name of Christ—on His behalf, for His glory.

The Spirit inspires joy, peace, righteousness, and the witness of the love of God in our hearts. He labors among the followers of Christ with the joy and abandon of a deer set free. It is as if the Spirit consented so long to work in a limited way in obedience to the Father and the Son but now has that limitation removed. By Christ and under the gospel (particularly when Christ Himself is being gloriously preached), the Spirit now pours Himself out in all His fullness, unleashing His light, His power, His gifts, and His love for the people of God. Truly the age of Christ, the age of the gospel, is the age of the Spirit. And that age is inseparable from revival.

The Spirit's Work in Revival

The Spirit's outpouring at Pentecost resulted in massive revival. The age of the Spirit is the age of revivals. That raises several critical questions:

What is revival?

Iain Murray points out that, among evangelicals today, there are three different views of what revival is. The first view prefers to speak of *renewal* or *continual revival* rather than special seasons of revival. Murray explains: "Revival, they say, is not to be thought of as an extraordinary event which occurs occasionally and periodically, rather it is something which is of the permanent essence of the New Testament age."[4] It is "Pentecost, once and for all."[5] This view, Murray points out, is often promoted in the Dutch Reformed tradition, even by great thinkers like Abraham Kuyper.[6]

The second view regards revival as *conditional upon obedience.* Murray subdivides this view into two groups. First are those "who believe that revival can be secured by intense and prayerful evangelistic effort."[7] They regard a revival "as being virtually the same thing as a period of energetic evangelistic activity."[8] The trailblazer here is Charles G. Finney (1792–1875) who claimed that revival can be identified with certain phenomena that could be produced at any time through the correct use of the right means. According to this view, man can instigate revival; supernatural intervention is not essential. That's why a revivalist could come to my home city of Grand Rapids recently, pictured with a briefcase in hand, with the promise attached that he carries revival with him in his briefcase! Second, and more commonly, are those who stress that repentance and renewed personal holiness are the means that produce revival. Advocates of this view, like Jonathan Goforth and Duncan Campbell, are fond of quoting 2 Chronicles 7:14. They stress that if Christians would only exercise the graces of repentance, submission, consecration, and obedience, revival would automatically follow. Campbell writes, "A full and complete surrender is the place of blessing, but that also is the price of revival."[9]

The third view teaches that revival is the sovereign outpouring of the Holy Spirit in the salvation of sinners in a greater measure than is normally the case. Authentic revivals are not miraculously different from the regular experience of the church. The difference is in degree, not in kind. In an "outpouring of the Spirit," great numbers of people are born again and grow in spiritual maturity in greater measure than usual. Spiritual influence is more widespread, conviction of sin deeper, feelings more intense, the sense of God more overwhelming,

---

4. Iain Murray, "The Necessary Ingredients of a Biblical Revival," *Banner of Truth*, no. 184 (Jan. 1979): 20; cf. Martyn Lloyd-Jones, *The Puritans: Their Origins and Successors; Addresses Delivered at the Puritan and Westminster Conferences, 1959–1978* (Edinburgh: Banner of Truth, 1987), 368.

5. Iain Murray, *Pentecost Today? The Biblical Basis for Understanding Revival* (Edinburgh: Banner of Truth, 1998), 7.

6. Abraham Kuyper, *The Work of the Holy Spirit* (Grand Rapids: Eerdmans, 1956), 127.

7. Murray, *Pentecost Today?*, 8.

8. Murray, "The Necessary Ingredients of a Biblical Revival," 184.

9. Duncan Campbell, *The Price and Power of Revival* (London: Scripture Illustrations, 1956), 30, 53–54, cited in Murray, *Pentecost Today?*, 9.

and love for God and others stronger. All this heightens normal Christianity rather than changes it.[10]

This view teaches that revivals may be accompanied by unscriptural abuses, bizarre phenomena, and spurious conversions, for along with a surge of wheat is a surge of chaff. Hence a winnowing season usually follows revival.[11] Nevertheless, the Spirit of God plays a great and mighty role in authentic revival. And that work is primarily done through preaching that is honored by the Spirit.

This "old-school view," as Murray calls it, views revival as a special, magnificent work of the Holy Spirit. That differs substantially from the first view that does not expect anything unusual in renewal or revival and from the second view that sees little need for supernatural intervention. A diligent study of the book of Acts certainly upholds the old-school view as the most biblical. This view was taught by John Owen, Jonathan Edwards, Samuel Davies, William B. Sprague, Martyn Lloyd-Jones, J. I. Packer, Iain Murray, and scores of other sound theologians from the Reformation until today.[12]

How is genuine revival distinguished from false revival?

Does Scripture give us marks by which we may test the authenticity of revivals? I believe it does, particularly in the early chapters of Acts, which tell about the New Testament church in the midst of its first major, authentic revival. Peter's sermon in Acts 2 describes some of the marks that accompany true revival, confirming that what is poured out on the church is from the Holy Spirit, not some man-made spirit. Let us consider, first, a brief summary of Peter's sermon, then look at several marks Acts 2 offers about authentic revival.

What did Peter convey in his Spirit-anointed sermon?

The New Testament church of 120 believers was multiplied many times over in one day under the preaching of the apostles, of which Peter's sermon serves as an outline. Of the 3,000 who were added to the church, there is no indication of many false conversions, for verse 42 says the new converts continued steadfastly in the apostles' doctrine, fellowship, breaking of bread, and prayers. By conservative estimates, the New Testament church grew from 120 to 20,000 believers in Jerusalem, from Pentecost to the persecution following Stephen's death (Acts 8). If Peter's sermon was typical of apostolic preaching, we should

---

10. Iain Murray, *Revival and Revivalism: The Making and Marring of American Evangelicalism, 1750–1858* (Edinburgh: Banner of Truth, 1994), 23.

11. Murray, *Revival and Revivalism*, 82–85.

12. Murray, "The Necessary Ingredients of a Biblical Revival," 20.

see what it teaches us about preaching and revival during New Testament times as well as today.

In his sermon on Pentecost, Peter rises to vindicate God and his fellow believers and to proclaim the gospel of Christ Jesus. In Acts 2:17–20, he interprets the events of Pentecost in light of the prophecy of Joel 2:28–32, which is now being fulfilled in the outpouring of the Holy Spirit on multitudes of sinners, both Jews and Gentiles. In verse 21, Peter says, "And it shall come to pass, that whosoever shall call on the name of the Lord shall be saved."

Peter then connects the gift of the Holy Spirit with the resurrection and ascension of the Lord Jesus Christ. He sketches the character and life of his Master, speaking of Christ's humanity (v. 22a); His miracles, wonders, and signs (v. 22b); and His crucifixion according to God's plan (v. 23). He then astonishes his audience by testifying that Jesus Christ has risen from the dead (vv. 24–32).

The crowd is amazed as Peter supports his assertion that Jesus has risen from the dead by referring to Psalm 16:8–11, a prophecy all would admit was Messianic, because, though it was written by David, it could not refer to David, for it speaks of descending into the grave and rising from the dead before the body saw corruption. Peter then argues that David did die and saw physical corruption, for his sepulcher is with us to this day. Therefore David could not be speaking about himself but was foreseeing that the Messiah would sit upon his throne. That prophecy was verified in Jesus of Nazareth, Peter says, who rose from the dead, and the apostles are witnesses of His resurrection.

In verse 33, Peter talks about the ascension of Christ and His sitting at the right hand of the Father. He then declares the outpouring of the Holy Spirit from heaven by the Son of God. Peter affirms that because Christ has now ascended into heaven to pour out His Holy Spirit, He is now doing so in the midst of all those gathered at Pentecost.

Peter goes on to say that listeners should not be surprised that he speaks of Christ's ascension, for David also prophesied of it in Psalm 110, saying, "The LORD said unto my Lord, Sit thou at my right hand, until I make thine enemies thy footstool." The psalmist could not be referring to himself in this prophecy because he had not yet ascended into the heavens. He could only be speaking of Jesus, who was exalted by the right hand of God and is now—notwithstanding their crucifixion of Him—both Lord and Christ.

Peter's exposition of a humiliated and exalted Redeemer bears astonishing fruit by the powerful ministry of the Holy Spirit. Thousands of listeners are convicted that they have sentenced to death the Messiah of whom the prophets spoke. They cry out in response to the sermon, "Men and brethren, what shall we do?" (v. 37).

That provides Peter with a wonderful opportunity to press home his exhortation in verses 38–40. He preaches the gospel boldly, bidding his listeners to repent and be converted. He urges them to publicly declare themselves disciples of Christ by being baptized in His name. God has wounded them so that He might heal them, Peter says. His promise is for them and their children. Peter urges his listeners onward to repentance, baptism, the name of Christ, the forgiveness of sin, the gift of the Holy Spirit, the promises of God, covenant faithfulness, election, the need for salvation, and whatever else he addresses in "many other words" (v. 40). He confronts their consciences. And the Holy Spirit blesses his sermon by bringing three thousand people to conversion. Such is the fruit of the first Christian sermon preached after the outpouring of the Holy Spirit in the midst of the New Testament church's first revival.

What are some important marks of revival according to Acts 2?
Let us now look at some of the marks of revival and lessons we can learn about revival from this history.

First, *authentic revival is always a sovereign work of the Holy Spirit.* The existence, depth, timing, and numbers of revival are all determined by God. Revivals are divinely-appointed and God-sent; they occur at the time of God's choosing. Acts 2:24 says, "The Lord added to the church daily such as should be saved." And Acts 13:48 says, "As many as were ordained to eternal life believed."

Authentic revival cannot be planned or manufactured by man. A revival is not the result of certain processes in history; it cannot be produced by human zeal or endeavor. It is, rather, a rending of the heavens, a divine intervention among the affairs of men. Authentic revival is prompted by the same sovereign, mysterious influences of the Holy Spirit that belong to the supernaturalism of the New Testament. How else can we explain why three thousand people were converted in Jerusalem on the day of Pentecost, not in Athens or Rome, or why one preacher was greatly used in one place and not in another? In authentic revivals, the vast and sudden spreading of the gospel follows no observable plan or pattern. With respect to time, place, and instrumentality, all attempts to account for authentic revival in mere human terms break down.

Said another way, *revivals are independent of human support or human sympathy.* Jesus says about the work of God's Spirit, "The wind bloweth where it listeth, and thou hearest the sound thereof, but canst not tell whence it cometh, and whither it goeth" (John 3:8). Because of its sovereign, sudden, wind-like character, revival almost invariably confounds human calculations. It is not anticipated even by the most zealous believer. It is God coming into the midst of His people in such a way that human plans are confounded and men are humbled in the dust. It is accompanied by an all-pervasive consciousness that God has come among His people. By the Spirit's irresistible power, the most improbable events take place. Israel is withered like a valley of dry bones, and Israel is brought out of Babylon as out of their graves. On the day of Pentecost, the men who crucified Jesus Christ are brought into His church. In the sixteenth century, former Roman Catholic leaders such as Luther and Calvin become the very leaders of revival in the church. God does not always do what men expect. And men cannot hinder what God sovereignly works by His decree. A revival is the sovereign work of God.

What a contrast to massive, evangelistic, man-made campaign revivals! Such campaigns are spurious revivals. They represent man-made *revivalism.* They are not dependent on the sovereignty of the Spirit but on man's devices: psychological prayer, the personality of the revivalist, predictions of impending results, emotional preaching, and other gimmicks that make revivalism predictable. That is why promoters of revivalism can boldly announce beforehand when revivals will take place.

Second, *authentic revival is usually, though not always, preceded by a remarkable effusion of prayer.* As in Acts 2 and throughout church history, revivals have often been prompted, under the Spirit's tutelage, by a felt need for prayer, which in turn prompts prayer meetings that are the seeds of revivals. As James says, "The effectual fervent prayer of a righteous man availeth much" (5:16).

The last great revival in the United States began in New York City in 1857. Often referred to as the Third Great Awakening, this movement began with a prayer meeting of six people and concluded the following year with approximately fifty thousand conversions in New York City and two hundred thousand across the Northeast. Prayer was the Spirit's means to germinate the seed of revival. As Matthew Henry said, "When God designs mercy, He stirs up prayer." And William Gurnall wrote, "The cocks crow thickest toward the break of day."[13]

This was true at Pentecost as well, for the meeting began with 120 people gathering regularly to pray for the outpouring of the Holy Spirit. Note that the New Testament believers did not minimize prayer because revival was promised but because the promises of God roused them to more prayer. They acted like a child who has received a promise from her father to get her something she desires. So she meets her father every day when he arrives home from work, asking, "Daddy, did you get it yet?" As true children of God, these believers

---

13. Willaim Gurnall, *The Christian in Compleat Armour* (London, 1669), 405.

waited and prayed, beseeching the Lord to fulfill His promise that they might receive the Holy Spirit according to His Word.

This attitude is sorely needed today as well. Are we pleading for God to send revival to fulfill His promises? Pentecost was a sovereign act of God, but it was preceded by a spirit of prayer and supplication. God is sovereignly pleased to tie together revival and means, especially the means of prayer.

Could lack of prayer be the reason, humanly speaking, why we have witnessed so little revival in the past 160 years? Is our half-hearted prayer a significant part of the problem? We have too easily become accustomed to living without revival and without conversions. When George Whitefield did not hear of any conversions for two weeks under his ministry, he would write in his diary, "Lord, what's wrong?"

Third, *revival usually begins in the church with the reawakening and enlightening of those who have already been born again.* The small group of disciples who were already enlightened were blessed with the Spirit's outpouring, and through them thousands were converted. When we storm the throne of grace for revival, we may mean well, but even believers are prone to think of other people more than ourselves. We are prone to forget that authentic revival necessitates that we forsake our backsliding ways, be filled with fresh love for God, then be willing to be used as clay in God's hands for the welfare of others. As William Taylor wrote, "To have the world converted, we must have the Church purified and ennobled, through the enjoyment of a rich effusion of the Holy Ghost."[14] Revival is a special season of heart-searching when many believers simultaneously experience conviction and renunciation of sin, culminating in a renewal of their dedication to the Lord.

Believers should be ashamed that personal revival is even necessary. By confessing our sins, appropriating by faith our riches in Christ, obeying God's will, and renouncing evil on a daily basis, we could have the highest joy, the deepest peace, and the fullest measure of God's power every day of our lives. Daily life in Christ can be ours in a victorious life of faith, despite our battles with indwelling sin. The problem is that most believers live on a sub-standard level. We leave our first love. We grow spiritually cold. We become powerless. We lose sight of what is eternal and become enamored with the earthly and temporal. God Himself must revive us with childlike faith, heartfelt repentance, unswerving obedience, and loving service. In revival, God uses His means to powerfully bring His children back to what ought to be a daily Christian walk.

---

14. William Taylor, *Peter, the Apostle* (New York: Harper, 1876), 182.

The church's recovery of truth has been compared to a sunrise in a mountainous region. First, the sun shines on the tops of the mountains; then, as the day proceeds, it reaches down into the valleys. So recovery of truth often shines upon the lives of a few leaders; then, through their influence being blessed by the Spirit, it reaches down to the pew. So on Pentecost and in subsequent weeks, God blessed 120 believers and used them to be a blessing for tens of thousands.

Fourth, in authentic revival, *remarkable spiritual growth results from the Spirit joining Himself to the Word of God.* Notice how Peter's sermon conveys his astonishing spiritual growth. What progress he has made in fifty-three days since his Master's death! What a contrast there is between this sermon and what he said prior to Christ's death!

Much of Peter's growth is no doubt due to the extraordinary teaching of Jesus during the forty days between His resurrection and ascension. But even more of this growth can be attributed to the enlightening power of the Holy Spirit, which has just filled Peter. Christ had promised the disciples that the Comforter would bring all things to their remembrance and teach them all things and guide them into all truth. These promises are obviously being fulfilled in Peter's sermon. Twelve of twenty-two verses are quotations from the Psalms and the Prophets. Peter experienced what all believers experience in times of the Spirit's enlightenment: *the Spirit bears witness to the Word.* Scripture testifies, "He sent his word, and healed them" (Ps. 107:20).

The conclusion is obvious: We do not need man-centered gimmicks to produce revival; we need the Word of truth and the Spirit of truth working together. Peter began his sermon with the Word and ended with the Word. Everything he said was biblical. In true preaching, law and gospel are the substance; the Word of God, the instrument; the Spirit of God, the power; the salvation of God, the result; and the glory of God, the end.

Did you notice how Christ-centered Peter's preaching is? Revival preaching is preaching of the Lord Jesus. In revival preaching, fallow ground must be broken up, the law must be proclaimed, and the tragedy of our fall in Adam must be exposed. The necessity of regeneration must be clearly taught, and people must be commanded to repent and believe the gospel, but the heart of all revival preaching is the preaching of the Lord Jesus Christ and the blessed message of redemption. No other name but Christ has the power to set men free. Let us pray, "Oh, Holy Spirit, we beseech Thee, open our eyes that we may see the face of Christ reflected in every Scripture! Help us to see Him as in a mirror, now darkly, but one day face-to-face!

Note, too, that Peter preaches the whole counsel of God. He preaches Christ's death and resurrection for lost sinners through forgiveness and the Holy Spirit. He calls for faith and repentance, based on the testimony of the prophets and the apostles. We must never shortchange the biblical gospel by preaching the New Testament without the Old, by proclaiming the cross without the resurrection, by offering forgiveness without the Spirit, or by calling for faith without repentance. Authentic revival is inseparable from a faithful proclamation of the whole counsel of God revealed in both the Old and New Testaments.

The church of God depends on the Word that the Holy Spirit has put into its hand and heart. Truth leads the way to the church's restoration and revival. In revival, people are made willing to live and die for the truth. Do you search the Word and love the truth? Do you strive, in dependency on the Spirit, to live that truth?

Fifth, Spirit-worked revival is honest with the souls of men, for *the call to repentance must be coupled with the rediscovery of truth*. Church history affirms that God uses preaching that is honest and upright and aims to bring the whole counsel of God's Word to the whole man. This sort of preaching aims for the conscience, demands repentance, and exalts the grace and glory of God. God used such preaching on Pentecost. Peter did not mince any words; he aimed for the conviction of sin. He urged his hearers, "Repent, and be baptized" (Acts 2:38).

Peter used the most important and strongest Greek word for repentance, *metanoia*, meaning to radically change one's mind, to unconditionally return to God, and to do an about-face in the direction of one's life. It means to sorrow over sin, to confess and forsake it, and to cast oneself upon the mercy of God. It means to turn from a self-centered life to a God-centered life. Repentance is both a divine gift and a lifelong commitment.

Peter did not flatter his listeners. He had no soft words for sin. He preached what his hearers were, which was far from what they ought to be. As he preached, he did not flinch as he had before the maidservant prior to Jesus's trial. By the Spirit's grace, Peter was true to his name: he was a rock. He was filled with the Spirit and therefore preached the truth with confidence, authority, and sympathy. He preached faithfully, earnestly, clearly, personally, and powerfully—so powerfully that hell itself trembled. The Spirit opened Peter's mouth so that he lost all fear of people, including those who mocked him. Peter was not fearless prior to the indwelling of the Spirit. He feared drowning in Matthew 14. He feared mockery and feared telling the truth to a servant in John 18. But now Peter did not hesitate to say more than once to his hearers that they had crucified the

Messiah. He said in verse 23, "Him, being delivered by the determinate counsel and foreknowledge of God, ye have taken, and by wicked hands have crucified and slain," and in verse 36, "Therefore let all the house of Israel know assuredly, that God hath made that same Jesus, whom ye have crucified, both Lord and Christ." The religious leaders of his day could not contradict such truth, and the crowd of listeners was amazed.

Pentecost was a turning point in Peter's life. As the Spirit poured into him, the apostle grew. Previously, he had been a mixture of cowardice and confidence, of good impulses and great mistakes. But now, under the Spirit's augmented control, Peter was strong, sober-minded, and courageous. Even the crowd was bewildered at his speech, not just by the phenomena of speaking in other tongues but because of Peter's clear explanation of what Pentecost meant, which, in turn, prompted massive repentance.

Are you also a recipient of Spirit-worked repentance, or are you still an impenitent unbeliever? My friend, we have all slain the Lord of glory with our wicked hands. Peter's listeners did it literally; we have done it spiritually. By nature, we all have the blood of Jesus on our hands. So Peter's message still comes to every unbeliever today: Repent, for you have crucified the Lord of glory.

Finally, *Spirit-worked revival is always accompanied by saving faith.* This is abundantly illustrated on Pentecost (Acts 2:41, 44), in the church's growth in the early chapters of Acts, and throughout the history of revival. Wherever we turn in Scripture, God's people triumph whenever they are given great exploits. They triumph because they believe the promises of God revealed in the gospel. Hebrews 11:33 tells us, "Faith subdued kingdoms, wrought righteousness, obtained promises, stopped the mouths of lions."

Our attitude to revival must not be passive or faint. We must storm the mercy seat, pleading God's promises, and trusting Him who is able to fill the earth with the knowledge of Himself. In the weeks after Pentecost, when the apostles were persecuted and forbidden to preach the name of Christ, they went forward by faith. Let us pray much for the power of faith that lays hold of the promises of God in prayer.

John Bunyan beautifully illustrates this in *The Pilgrim's Progress*, when Christian and Hopeful fall asleep on the grounds of Giant Despair and are taken in chains into Doubting Castle. In that miserable hole, they are terrified by the Giant as he shows them the bones of various pilgrims he has smashed and broken in pieces. "So it shall be with you," he says. Christian and Hopeful are terrified, Bunyan says, until Saturday night, when they begin to pray. They continue to pray through the night. Finally, at dawn, Christian suddenly stands up and says to Hopeful, "What a fool am I, thus to lie in a stinking dungeon, when I may as well walk at liberty? I have a key in my bosom, called *Promise*, that will, I am persuaded, open any lock in *Doubting-Castle*. Then said *Hopeful*, That's good news, good brother, pluck it out of thy bosom and try."[15]

And so they did. Prayer, which preceded the promise, enabled them to take hold of the promise, so that, almost before they knew it, the pilgrims were loosed from their chains and brought through the grim doors of the castle to freedom.

So it is with the church. We are helpless and bereft of strength, but God has commanded us to pray in faith. He has told us that we shall not seek His face in vain. When the church truly prays, it is clothed with the Spirit's fire from heaven.

Conclusions: Assets or Hindrances to Revival

Are you an asset or hindrance to the age of the Spirit, the age of revival?

+ We are hindrances when we are satisfied with mere *tradition*. Tradition can be valuable if it is grounded on Scripture. But if we are satisfied with mere tradition while lacking the life and power of godliness, we are a hindrance to revival. Do we read our Bibles, pray, and attend church as mere form or tradition? Do we use Christianity only to quiet our consciences? Are we content to believe the truth with our mind and let the world walk by our door, traveling onward to hell, without so much as a prayer to God for their repentance? Do we ever evangelize others? Are we filled with grave concern for their salvation? If not, we are a hindrance to revival.

+ We are hindrances when we fail to be *intercessors* for the eternal well-being of others. How self-centered our prayers can be! We so often pray selfishly, seeking to use God in our prayers rather than letting prayer change us. James 4:3 says, "Ye ask, and receive not, because ye ask amiss, that ye may consume it upon your lusts." What obstacles we are to revival when we essentially ask that our will be done rather than God's will! How shameful we are in failing to ask that God's name be hallowed, for His kingdom to come, for His will to be done, and for souls to be saved. Do we ever take the kingdom of heaven by violence as we wrestle for the Spirit's awakening and reviving work in the lives of others?

+ We are hindrances to revival because of our cursed *unbelief*. Few people realize how serious an enemy unbelief is and how contrary it is to revival.

---

15. John Bunyan, *The Pilgrim's Progress* (Edinburgh: Banner of Truth, 1997), 134.

In my years of ministry, I can only recall one man crying out with tears, "Oh, my cursed, cursed unbelief!" I will never forget the impression that made upon me. I fear that many of us use unbelief to shield ourselves from our responsibility to enter into "soul travail" for revival. We are reticent to see unbelief as the monster that it is. We confess with our mouths that unbelief is the mother of all iniquity, but we do not believe that in our hearts. Because of our unbelief we do not expect God to do much. That is why we are content with a small measure of the Spirit and His work, with a trickle of conversions, and with lukewarm faith.

Do you really believe that God can save sinners and that He delights to do so? James W. Alexander wrote, "Unbelief as to the power and willingness of God to [grant revival] is at the bottom of all our neglect and wrong action.... An awakening which should shake the dry bones in all the lowest populations, rousing them from filth and drunkenness, and raising up an exceeding great army to fight the good fight of faith, is more than we dare ask of God. And yet, it is not more than we may reasonably expect on Scriptural grounds, nor more than the eyes of the Church shall joyfully see, in the day when, by the Spirit, [the church] shall rise to the height of faith and entreaty."[16]

Do we ever rise to "the height of faith and entreaty"? Do we truly believe that God is able and willing to work a great revival in the world today? Let us expect great things from a great God, as John Newton wrote:

> Thou art coming to a King,
> Large petitions with thee bring;
> For His grace and power are such,
> None can ever ask too much.

Should we expect another Pentecost? Numbers are not the point, friends. The point is: Do we believe in God? Do we believe the Holy Spirit can do a mighty work? We must not tell God what to do, but we must storm the mercy seat, crying out with the prophet Habakkuk, "O LORD, revive thy work.... In wrath remember mercy" (Hab. 3:2). Let us not leave the Lord alone but cry out, "O God, glorify Thy Name! Save sinners! Revive Thy church! Is not Thy name, Thy cause, Thy glory at stake? Make a name for Thyself in me, among us, and throughout the world, for Thine own glory! Begin with me, Lord! *Revive me!* And let me be used for many others. Open the windows of heaven, and come down with revival blessings!"

---

16. James W. Alexander, *Revival and Its Lessons* (New York: American Tract Society, 1858), 10.

James W. Alexander asked his readers in the midst of the 1857 New York revival:

- Are you an enemy of revival?
- Do you rejoice in revival?
- Are you a subject of revival?
- Do you pray for revival?
- Are you helping forward revival?
- Does your heart care for the fruits of revival?
- Have you sought to honor God in revival?[17]

Do your faith and life show that you are living in the age of the Spirit, an age of potential revival?

---

17. Alexander, *Revival and Its Lessons*, 1–11 [2].

Chapter 2

Trust in the Incarnate Word

Teaching is hard work. When Jesus and His disciples got into a boat after a full day of teaching His disciples, the disciples were not surprised that Jesus fell asleep. The gently rocking waves of the Sea of Galilee might have lulled them to sleep too. But on their way across the big lake, a terrible storm arose.

The southern end of the Sea of Galilee is a deep valley lined by cliffs. Wind can suddenly come roaring into that valley and whip the sea into a storm.[1] Andrew, Peter, James, and John had seen many storms in their lifetime of fishing, but this one overwhelmed them. The wind howled and the waves crashed. The boat began taking on water. It rode lower in the water so that each wave threatened to fill it. Fear gripped the men. Their boat was sinking; would they all die?

They turned to Jesus, who was still sleeping, and shouted over the roaring sea, "Master, carest thou not that we perish?" Jesus stood up and rebuked the wind and the sea. In an instant, wind and sea were stilled. But the men were still terrified. "What manner of man is this, that even the wind and the sea obey him?" they asked (Mark 4:35–41; cf. Pss. 65:7; 89:9).

Why was Jesus asleep in the midst of the storm? Why didn't the storm awaken Him? The obvious answer is because of His humanity. He was tired. He was worn out after a long day's work and needed rest to renew His strength.

How did Jesus calm the storm? Again, the answer is obvious: His deity. Jesus had such power over creation that His words instantly changed the weather. He did not use technology, magic charms, or rituals. Jesus didn't even pray. He just said to the storm, "Peace, be still" (Mark 4:39). Christ has the

---

1. *The Reformation Study Bible*, ed. R. C. Sproul (Orlando: Ligonier, 2005), 1422. Thanks to Paul Smalley for his assistance on this article, which is slightly enlarged from an address I gave for a regional conference of the Philadelphia Conference of Reformed Theology (PCRT) in Quakertown, Pennsylvania on November 12, 2010.

power of God, and His disciples recognized it when they said, "Even the wind and the sea obey him" (v. 41).

But the mystery here is whether Jesus was tired or all-powerful. Was He drained of energy or full of energy? Was Christ limited so He needed restoration, or was He infinite in ruling over creation by His mere word? The answer, according to Scripture, is both. Jesus is both limited in His humanity and infinite in His deity as Lord over creation.

Jesus Christ the God-Man

John 1:14 says, "The Word was made flesh, and dwelt among us, (and we beheld his glory, the glory as of the only begotten of the Father,) full of grace and truth." As is typical of him, John uses simple words to express a very deep truth. *Incarnation* is a Latin word that means "becoming flesh." In the incarnation, God became human flesh. Contrary to the theologian Rudolf Bultmann, this is not "the language of mythology"; instead, as Robert Reymond says, this testimony of John is the language of eye-witnesses reporting what they know to be true. They say, "We beheld his glory" (cf. also 1 John 1:1–3).[2]

The reality of God made flesh in Jesus was experienced by the apostles and portrayed in the gospels. This reality is what compelled the church to affirm Jesus as both God and man. The Bible compelled the Council of Chalcedon (AD 451) to state that Christ is one person with two distinct natures, human and divine. As the Westminster Confession (8.2) says, "Two whole, perfect, and distinct natures, the Godhead and the manhood, were inseparably joined together in one person, without conversion, composition, or confusion. Which person is very God and very man, yet one Christ, the only Mediator between God and man" (cf. Larger Catechism, Q. 54).

In the process of grafting, a person cuts a living twig off a tree. He then cuts into another tree, sometimes of another species, and presses the twig into the tree. The two are sealed together with wax or wrapping. Over time, the twig and the tree grow together into one unity, one living organism. Both the twig and the tree retain their unique genetic codes and their own distinct natures. But now the twig draws its life and bears its fruit from the roots of the tree.[3]

In a similar but more profound way, God grafted human nature into His divine Son. The result was not a hybrid demigod like Hercules or some kind of Superman. Rather, both the divine nature and the human nature retained their

---

2. Robert L. Reymond, *John, Beloved Disciple: A Survey of His Theology* (Ross-shire, U.K.: Christian Focus, 2001), 180–82.

3. Ray R. Rothenbergarand and Christopher J. Starbuck, "Grafting," http://extension2.missouri .edu/g6971, accessed 5-5-20.

individual, essential properties. But now man was joined to God in one living person, Jesus Christ. In Him, believers draw life from the divine root and bear fruit for God's glory. In botanical grafting, two plants of the same genus or of like nature are combined. The miracle of the incarnation is that God grafted the finite into the infinite. Thus, the Infinite One became bone of our bone, flesh of our flesh. The Prince of glory became the Babe in a manger. The Son of God became the Son of Man. The Creator came out of the creature. He who made the world and was above the world came into the world. The Almighty One became a little Child. The immortal Son was clothed in rags of mortality. The Eternal One became a Child of time. God, who made man after His image, was Himself made in man's image. He whose dwelling is in the heavens was let down into the hell of this earth. He who thunders in the heavens cried in the manger. The invisible God was made visible. God took our flesh and dwelt in it with His divine fullness so that our flesh could become more glorious than the angels—and through that flesh God opened up His gospel treasures by being Savior, Redeemer, Kinsman, Elder Brother, and Shepherd of His own. In short, the Son of God became the Son of Man so that the sons of men might become the sons of God. How unsearchable are His ways!

The sheer magnitude of the incarnation is so incomprehensible; we could borrow the language of the apostle Paul that we see it only through a glass darkly. Describing the incarnation in human language is like painting a mountain on a grain of sand. We stand before this abyss of glory and know we can never reach the bottom. Therefore, we must keep our steps on the path of God's revelation and follow the Bible closely as we explore the mystery of this incarnation.

We also must remember that John wrote his Gospel not merely for our understanding but for us to trust in Christ (John 20:31). The purpose of John 1 is that sinners will receive Christ, which means to believe in His name (John 1:7, 11–12) and to behold His glory (John 1:14; 2:11). We will examine John 1:14 for both those who are unbelievers needing to trust in Jesus for the first time, and those who are believers who need to grow in faith in their Savior.

John 1:14 says, "And the Word was made flesh." Let us meditate on this great statement of the Incarnate Word. We will consider, first, "the Word," and second, "flesh." Throughout, we will keep in mind John's focus on our need to trust the Word made flesh for our salvation.

Jesus Christ, the Word of God

"The *Word* was made flesh," John tells us. The Father did not become flesh, nor did the Holy Spirit become flesh. Also, the divine nature did not become flesh. God's essence did not change in the Word, as if He lost His divine attributes;

rather, the eternal and only-begotten Son of God became flesh. The Holy Spirit did not choose to say, "The Son was made flesh," although that is true. The Spirit chose to say, "The Word was made flesh."

The Spirit uses "the Word" in this text to express the greatest thought of the Father's heart. The Word is the great Revealer of God. God calls us to trust Christ as the Word of God, and we trust Him by listening to Him. Many of us are not good listeners. When someone else is speaking, our minds often race ahead to what we want to say in response. To our shame, we then realize we have missed what the other person was saying.

So, listen to the Father's Word. Give Jesus Christ your full attention. Acknowledge His authority above all others. Cultivate quietness before Him. When the living Word speaks through the written Word, let other voices be silent. Even if your traditions, culture, feelings, and opinions contradict the Holy Scriptures, listen to Christ. Do not assume that you already know what it says. Let God speak in Christ. He is God's Word.

The truth that Christ is God's Word leads us back to John 1:1, "In the beginning was the Word, and the Word was with God, and the Word was God." Here are three teachings about the Word who became flesh that illuminate what it means to trust in Christ. Remember them with the keywords *eternal*, *beloved*, and *divine*.

He Is the Eternal Word

"In the beginning was the Word," says John 1:1. This Word already existed when "in the beginning God created the heaven and the earth" (Gen. 1:1). So the Word was not created.[4] There was never a time when the Word was not. He is the eternal Word the Father speaks from everlasting to everlasting. Christ did not begin in Mary's womb but existed as the Word prior to creation. He is not just two thousand years old, for, in John 8:58, He says to His disciples, "Before Abraham was, I am." He did not say, "I was," though claiming to exist two thousand years before Abraham would have been incredible enough. But Jesus says, "I am," meaning He is the One who said to Moses in Exodus 3:14, "I AM THAT I AM.... Thus shalt thou say unto the children of Israel, I AM hath sent me unto you." Jesus is the eternal Creator.

---

4. Note the contrast between the imperfect of the verb "to be" (John 1:1) and the aorist of the verb "to become" (John 1:3, 10, 14). The latter term is clearly associated with creation, including the world and humanity. The former indicates an already continuing existence apart from the creation of the world and mankind. When the world began, He already was. "In short, the Word's pre-existent *being* is antecedently set off against the *becoming* of all created things" (Reymond, *John*, 35).

We must trust in Jesus by being in awe of Him. Psalm 33:6, 8–9 says, "By the word of the LORD were the heavens made; and all the host of them by the breath of his mouth…. Let all the earth fear the LORD: let all the inhabitants of the world stand in awe of him. For he spake, and it was done; he commanded, and it stood fast." Faith in Jesus requires fearing God—trembling in reverence that we are in the presence of the Word of God by whom the mighty mountains were made. Christ was ancient when the galaxies were born. Yet He is ever fresh and lively and new, for He is "I AM," not just "I was." The stars in the night sky make you feel small and insignificant. Likewise, the ancient mountains remind you that you were born only yesterday and will be gone tomorrow. Looking at Jesus should fill you with trembling, awe, and reverence. He is the eternal Word.

He Is the Beloved Word

John 1:1 says, "The Word was with God." Christ enjoyed personal communion with God the Father and the Holy Spirit from the beginning. John 1:18 says Christ "is in the bosom of the Father," in the place closest to His heart.[5] The Father sent us His eternal companion and friend. God gave us the Word whom He delights to hear and to whom He loves to speak.

We see this also in John 1:14 and 18, where Christ is called the Father's "only-begotten," which in Greek (μονογενής) refers to a son or daughter with a unique relationship to his or her father, like that of an only child.[6] Such a child is precious and beloved, as Isaac was to Abraham. John says in verses 12–13 that every lost sinner who trusts in Jesus becomes a child of God. But now he says that Jesus, the Word, is God's "only begotten" Son. It is as if John is saying, "God has many children who are born again through faith in Jesus. But, dear friends, remember that Jesus is God's Son in a unique way. He is more precious to the Father than all the angels of heaven. He is the One whom the Father has sent to you."

I have been married to my wife for more than thirty years. She is my dearest friend. As I reflect on our time together, I see how, in God's grace, we have grown together. Imagine how close a husband and wife might become after being married for sixty years! How close, then, are the Father and Son, who have been loving companions from eternity! They have done everything together. Their hearts are one. They are even one in essence.

---

5. Luke 16:22–23; John 13:23–25.

6. Luke 7:12; 8:42; 9:38; John 1:14, 18; 3:16, 18; Heb. 11:17; 1 John 4:9. Cf. LXX Judges 11:34; Tobit 3:15; 6:10, 14; 8:17; Aquila Gen. 22:2; Prov. 4:3; Jer. 6:26; Symmachus Gen. 22:12; Prov. 4:3; Jer. 6:26. Especially significant in the Greek OT are the times in Gen. 22 that Isaac is called the "only son" of Abraham. Cf. D. A. Carson, *The Gospel According to John* (Grand Rapids: Eerdmans, 1991), 128, n2.

No book in the New Testament highlights the love relationship of the Father and Son as much as the Gospel of John. John includes more than 120 references to the Father/Son relationship, and 8 times the book says that the Father loves His Son (3:35; 5:20; 10:17; 15:9; 15:10; 17:23; 17:24; 17:26). Love, particularly the love of the Father for the Son, is the preeminent motive for all God's divine activity (John 1:18).[7]

So trust in the beloved Christ as the gift of God's love. God so loves people that He has given them the Word who was with Him from all eternity. He has given them His Son, who is the supreme eternal and infinite object of His fatherly love. John 3:16 tells us, "For God so loved the world, that he gave his only begotten Son, that whosoever believeth in him should not perish, but have everlasting life." God loves sinners so much that He gave them the One He loved most; He gave the best He had for the worst He could find—sinners like you and me. Are you trusting that love and abandoning yourself to it? Christ is the beloved Word.

He Is the Fully Divine Word

John 1:1 goes on to tell us that the Word who became flesh "was God." This is not to be translated as "a god" or "godlike" but "God" with a capital G, as the grammar and context make clear.[8] Jehovah's Witnesses argue that since the Greek word for "the" is not present before "God," this verse should be translated as Christ being "a god" or "godlike."[9] But this is a misleading argument. The word God is also used without the Greek word for "the" in John 1:6, 12, 13, and 18. Not even the Jehovah's Witnesses translate those verses as "a god." So John 1:1 plainly refers to God Almighty, not a god, even without the word "the." Greek grammar teaches us that the absence of the article (or "the") only intensifies the noun, making it a categorical assertion. Christ was and is God, as fully divine as the Father.

Furthermore, as Genesis 1:1 says, "In the beginning God," John 1:1 also says, "In the beginning was the Word." This parallel places the Son at the center of the Father's work as Creator, as verse 3 affirms: "all things were made by him." The plan was the Father's, but the voice of command saying, "Let there be…" is the Son's.

---

7. Bartel Elshout, "The Father's Love for His Son," *Puritan Reformed Journal* 2, 2 (July 2010):15–31.

8. On the grammar of John 1:1 and Colwell's rule, cf. Reymond, *John*, 36, esp. note 19.

9. *The Kingdom Interlinear Translation of the Greek Scriptures* (Brooklyn: Watchtower Bible and Tract Society of New York, 1985), 401, 1139.

Christ is therefore the full and comprehensive revelation of His Father. Every attribute we may affirm of the Father is true of the Son. Jesus lovingly rebuked Philip when Philip asked Him to show him the Father by saying, "He that hath seen me hath seen the Father" (John 14:9). Isaiah 9:6 says Christ is "the mighty God" (cf. Isa. 10:20–21). Truly, as John says, we behold in Christ "the glory as of the only begotten of the Father" (John 1:14), for in Christ we behold the very exegesis and exposition of the Father.

Again, this text calls us to trust Jesus and tells us what it means to trust Him. Since the Word who became flesh is fully God, we trust Jesus by worshiping Him as the Son of God. We trust Him in a way that stirs us to adore Him. People can mean different things when they say, "I trust you." They may have historical faith, merely believing that someone is telling them the truth as if it were a reliable news report. They may have functional faith, or the confidence that someone will do a job for them, such as put siding on their house. They may have relational faith, trusting that someone will be a faithful friend or faithful spouse. Such faith is appropriate with human beings. But none of these kinds of faith is sufficient when it comes to Christ.

The Lord calls us to trust Christ as fully God. Saving faith in Christ is an act of worship in which we adore Him with all that we are and abandon ourselves totally to Him as our all in all. Thomas struggled to believe that Jesus had risen from the dead. But when he saw Christ and His wounds, faith broke through doubt and made him cry out, "My Lord and my God" (John 20:28). We, too, must fall down and worship Christ as our Lord and our God. That is saving faith.[10]

We have begun our discussion on "the Word became flesh," by considering that Jesus is the Word of God. On the basis of the Bible, we confess with the Westminster Confession (8.2) that Jesus is "the Son of God, the second person in the Trinity, being very and eternal God, of one substance, and equal with the Father."

We must give our full attention to this Word. We must sit at His feet in reverent awe, rejoicing that the loving Father has sent us His most beloved Son. We must bow down and worship our great God and Savior, Jesus Christ.

---

10. Both before and after Thomas's worship of Christ, the context speaks of believing in Christ (John 20:25, 27, 29, 31), showing that his outburst of worship expressed saving faith.

Jesus Christ, the Word Become Man

"The Word was made *flesh*," John tells us, meaning that He entered completely into the human condition (John 17:2).[11] The Word took on human nature, taking the nature of a servant (Phil. 2:7). The Son of God embraced all that it means to be human. Paul says in Colossians 2:9, "For in him dwelleth all the fulness of the Godhead bodily." Without ceasing to be God, Christ became flesh.

The incarnation is an act of beautiful and astonishing humility. When a person who is great and powerful treats you with kindness and respect, as if you were on the same level with him, you are deeply touched by his humility. Christ's incarnation displays infinitely more humility than the president of the United States might by taking the place of a lowly private in the army. God displayed His greatest glory with the greatest act of humility. The incarnation overthrows all glory-seeking and calls us to be servants (Phil. 2:1–13).

From the outset, John's statement about the Word becoming flesh was scandalous. The Greeks resonated with the term *Word*. In the culture of their day, the Word (or *Logos*) was the principle that ruled the world and brought order out of chaos.[12] The Word was somewhat like logic, and the laws of nature viewed as a divine spirit. But the Greeks would have been shocked to hear that the Word became "flesh," for they sharply divided the spiritual world of ideas from the physical world of things. The two could not mix, like fire and water. In the Greek order, bodies imprisoned spirits like a bird trapped in a cage. So to say that the divine Word became flesh was offensive to them.[13]

Before judging the Greeks, we should realize that our culture also thinks the world is split into two parts, the subjective and the objective. On the one hand, we recognize the personal and private realm of spirit, feelings, values, faith, and religion. On the other hand, we affirm the public realm of science, facts, measurable results, and visible things. The debate of evolution versus creation often reveals that people assume that science and religion cannot mix. They think spirituality is a matter of personal feelings, not objective truth. As a result, many people live schizophrenic lives with faith in one compartment and daily life and work in another.[14]

---

11. Christ's humanity is not fallen humanity but only finite humanity—humanity as God created it at the beginning, "without sin." Sin detracts from our humanity, making us behave as brute beasts.

12. Leon Morris, *The Gospel According to John* (Grand Rapids: Eerdmans, 1995), 102–103.

13. "If the Evangelist had said only that the eternal Word assumed manhood or adopted the form of a body, the reader steeped in the popular dualism of the hellenistic world might have missed the point. But John is unambiguous, almost shocking in the expressions he uses" (Carson, *John*, 126). Then, too, it was no less offensive to Jews to assert that the infinite God could take on finite flesh.

14. Nancy Pearcey, *Total Truth: Liberating Christianity from Its Cultural Captivity* (Wheaton: Crossway, 2004).

But God does not have a divided mind. God is an infinite Spirit. He created and rules the finite world, which consists of spirits and physical matter in close relationship with each other. In the incarnation, the eternal Spirit joined Himself with matter. The Word became flesh. Flesh in the Bible implies three truths, which can be summarized in the keywords: *body*, *soul*, and *death*. Let's look at each of them.

Christ Took on a Human Body

Jesus spoke of His body as "flesh," as in flesh and blood (John 6:51–56). When the Word became flesh, He became physically human with a body. Hebrews 2:14 says, "Forasmuch then as the children are partakers of flesh and blood, he also himself likewise took part of the same; that through death he might destroy him that had the power of death, that is, the devil."

One of the first heresies the Christian church faced was Docetism, which denied Christ's true physical humanity (1 John 4:3; 2 John 7). This heresy said the body of Christ was only an appearance, a fantasy. It was not historical, touchable, visible, woundable flesh and blood. Contrary to this heresy, the incarnation of Christ brings together God and the flesh and blood of our humanity.

The incarnation also challenges our cultural assumptions. The gospel is not concerned simply with ideas but with facts and objects. It enters the world of physics and biology and history. God's Son became as physical as you. He took on our feet, our legs, our chest, our arms, our mouth, our hair, our eyes, our ears. His hands were roughened by the wood of the carpenter's shop; His back was torn by the lash of the scourge. He was truly human. When He died, He was truly dead. His pulse stopped and His brain activity ceased. When He rose from the dead, His physical body rose to new life. He spoke. People touched Him. He ate fish. Jesus was fully human.

Jesus came to "regenerate" all of creation, including our bodies. Like a diver descending into the depths of a sea to bring up lost treasure, Christ came to earth in a body so that He could raise our bodies into glory. His resurrection is the beginning of a new creation that rises like a phoenix from the ashes of the old fallen order. Philippians 3:21 says, "For our conversation [or citizenship] is in heaven; from whence also we look for the Savior, the Lord Jesus Christ: who shall change our vile body, that it may be fashioned like unto his glorious body, according to the working whereby he is able even to subdue all things unto himself."

So trust in Christ as the Resurrection and the Life (John 11:25). Faith in Christ does not just look forward to an afterlife. Paul is insistent in 1 Corinthians 15 that faith in Christ trusts in and looks for the resurrection of the body.

So believers in Christ should not fear death. They should not fear cancer or a car wreck. The Son of God has taken your flesh into glory, and He will glorify your flesh with His one day. Violence, disease, accident, or death can do nothing to you that Jesus will not restore and make whole again.

As a believer, you have the best of both worlds. You have the best of this world because you are united to Christ here and now. You have the best of the world to come because you will be united to Christ in glory forever with a body that will be radically and comprehensively free of all sin. With that body you will praise Immanuel forever! Truly, the best is yet to be!

Christ Took a Human Soul

Flesh refers to the entire person, including the human soul or spirit. The Bible says in Hebrews 2:16–18, "For verily he took not on him the nature of angels; but he took on him the seed of Abraham. Wherefore in all things it behooved him to be made like unto his brethren, that he might be a merciful and faithful high priest in things pertaining to God, to make reconciliation for the sins of the people. For in that he himself hath suffered being tempted, he is able to succor [or help] them that are tempted." He became like us "in all things" except sin—even like us in our sufferings and temptations of the soul.

Ancient heresy also refuted Christ's becoming like us in all things. Apollinarianism denied Christ's human mind and heart. It said the Word took over a human body as if an alien force were operating an android of flesh. But Jesus had real human thoughts, experiences, and feelings. He was human from the inside out.

In the Bible, the word *flesh* can refer to the human way of thinking (John 8:15). Scripture tells us that Jesus grew intellectually from a child to an adult (Luke 2:40, 52). It tells us that Jesus in His human mind did not know the day of His second coming (Mark 13:32). That should not shake our confidence in Christ's teachings, for the Holy Spirit filled Christ's human nature with truth that was without error. But Jesus had a human mind. If you cannot believe that Christ had some mental limitation in His human nature, how can you accept that Christ died? God's nature is immortal. Jesus was truly God, but He was also truly man.

In Scripture, the word *flesh* can also refer to human feelings and desires (John 1:13). Jesus wept, displaying sincere grief, says John 11:35. Jesus also rejoiced (Luke 10:21). As a godly man, Jesus ordinarily experienced the peace of His Father's presence and love (John 8:29). Yet, as Surety of His people, Jesus went further into the black hole of sorrow and despair than any other human being. At Gethsemane, He was amazed, weighed down with sorrow, and afraid. These emotions did not lightly touch Him; He experienced them in horrendous depth. He was terrified of the impending encounter with the wrath of God. On the cross, He went deeper into darkness than any of us have ever known. He was no stoic. He had strong human feelings.

Jesus "dwelt among us" (John 1:14); He came to save sinners (1 Tim. 1:15). He had to experience that "the wages of sin is death" (Rom. 6:23) to be Savior for His own. He came to deal with cosmic sin. The only way our sin could be dealt with was by agony and bloody sweat, by His dying and burial in the grave, by His bearing the essence of hell for us, by experiencing the bottomless pit for us to suffer the wrath of a sin-hating God. The unthinkable happened as God, who could not bear the sight of sin, looked at Calvary. There the Son of God hung in the naked flame of God's holiness as He bore our sin (Isaiah 53).

Have you ever considered what the agony of Golgotha was all about? What do you see when you look at the cross? You see the absence of all that is pleasant and beautiful and refreshing, and the presence of everything that is ugly and atrocious and revolting. Everything about the place is odious. There is no order or harmony or decency at Calvary. It is a place of skulls and bones and putrid flesh. It is a place of crosses stained with blood and victims writhing in pain, compounded by vile insults from people gathered around to watch. Only one person speaks on Jesus's behalf; he is a fellow human being who is being crucified with Him. He is a thief about to die. The devoted women are silent; the disciples are hiding for fear. His friends have forsaken Him, and so has God the Father, who has always loved Him. The Father has now turned away from His Son.

Sin is fearful in the face of Sinai's thunderous lightning, but sin is most bitter in the torn flesh and bleeding soul of Christ's suffering. Have you realized by faith that Christ has taken your sin upon Himself? That the bridegroom has taken all the liabilities of His bride to Himself and is paying the wages of sin for her? He took her place, being separated from all that is good and lovely, so that she may "be made the righteousness of God in him" (2 Cor. 5:21).

Do you truly trust in God's good news as an unworthy sinner? If you remain as you are in your present condition, despite the gospel, Christ's death will do nothing for you. As long as you can live without Jesus Christ as your first love, your exclusive hope, and your only Savior, you do not truly know that you are a sinner. Oh, that you would be pricked in your heart today to know that you are a lost sinner before a holy God! Then this glorious gospel of our blessed God would be good news to you today. Then you will know the wonder that sinners should be the object of God's eternal love.

Then you will also know the wonder of unconditional election. Without election, our salvation would be hopeless. God knew from all eternity that not a single sinner would seek after Him. If God had not taken the initiative to save sinners, the entire human race would have perished. No human merit of man entered into God's decision of sovereign election. Unconditional election is the foundation for an unconditional gospel that declares to you that salvation is available without money and without price and without any human merit or qualifications.

So trust in Jesus Christ for salvation. No matter what you feel or experience, Jesus understands. Jesus is a person with fully human affections. He is able to sympathize with our weaknesses (Heb. 4:15). Pour out your heart to Him as your best friend (Ps. 62:8). He is the most compassionate friend a sinner can have.

A man who wanted to improve his relationship with his wife read in 1 Peter 3:7, "Likewise, ye husbands, dwell with them according to knowledge, giving honour unto the wife." He wondered what it meant to live with his wife "according to knowledge." This man knew nothing about horses, but his wife loved them, and so the couple bought some horses. The husband now decided to learn about horses. He started helping his wife in the barn. She laughed at him because he had no idea of what he was doing. But he kept helping because he loved his wife. So he entered her world, and the couple drew closer together in understanding.

Infinitely more, the Lord of glory also entered our world. Christ pursues emotional intimacy with us more than any person near to us. Trust Jesus, then. Walk with Him daily. He has lowered Himself to meet you where you are. That should fill you with gratitude and joy in His love. He took a soul so that He could be our soul-Savior and soul-mate to wed Himself to us forever.

Christ Took on Human Death

In the Bible, *flesh* implies mortality, or subjection to the power of death.[15] Jesus took on every aspect of our humanity except sin (Heb. 4:15; cf. Rom. 8:3). His humanity therefore involved mortality. God became man in mortal misery, which was the consequence of the sin of the first Adam.

The Son of God became flesh to unite God and man in His person, but also to unite God and sinners in His death. He says in John 6:51, "I am the living bread which came down from heaven: if any man eat of this bread, he shall live for ever: and the bread that I will give is my flesh, which I will give for the

---

15. Ps. 73:26, 78:39; Isa. 31:3, 40:6; 1 Cor. 15:50.

life of the world." The Word became flesh to give His flesh for the world so that He would give life to the world.

The broken covenant between God and man could not be restored until the demands of God's justice were satisfied. The divine Lawgiver, Jesus, was born under the law to redeem us from the curse of the law (Gal. 4:4–6). The incarnate Word willingly became subject to the curse of the written Word (Gal. 3:13–14). He felt the pangs of death (Ps. 116:3) in all their bitterness on the cross, even to the point of being forsaken by God. Through all His suffering, He was fully conscious, sensitized with the purity of His own mortal humanity. What a mystery! But because of Jesus's suffering and accursed death, we may now become the recipients of God's blessing.

A man and his wife flew thousands of miles over land and sea to get to Russia. They spent tens of thousands of dollars and filled out complicated legal paperwork through a translator. They did all that to adopt a child. They wanted to take an orphan into their home so that they could love the child forever. That is what Christ did for us. He went the distance. He paid the price. Without the cost of His death, we would be eternal orphans cut off from God's family. But He satisfied all the demands of the law so that our sins might be forgiven and we might be welcomed into the Father's home.

No wonder John writes, "Behold, what manner of love the Father hath bestowed upon us, that we should be called the sons of God" (1 John 3:1). "Behold!" is John's way of saying, "Look at this!" The apostle is overwhelmed with the wonder of God's adoption of believers. He asks us to gaze with him at this wonder. Have you, by faith, comprehended the magnificent doctrine of adoption?

John's sense of astonishment is more evident in the original Greek, which says, "Behold, from what country or realm does such love as this come?" Matthew 8:27 uses similar words to describe how astonished the disciples were when Jesus calmed the winds and the sea, literally saying, "From what realm does this man come that even the winds and sea obey Him?"

God's adoption of believers is unparalleled. The world does not understand such love, for it is beyond the realm of human experience.

John is astonished because God showed such amazing love while we were still rebelling against Him and His kingdom. God calls us sons of God; He brings us into His family, giving us the name, privileges, and blessings of His own children. He invites us to know Him as Father, to dwell under His protection and care, and to come to Him with all our needs. John is overwhelmed at the thought of being a full member of God's family.

Do you stand in awe of the wonderful love of the Father who gave His own Son for your salvation? I hope you are amazed! You cannot trust the

Incarnate Word unless you trust the crucified Lord. He was born to die. It was not enough to bridge the gap between the infinite and the finite. Christ bridged the gap between the Righteous and the unrighteous. Therefore, trust in Christ as the One who became flesh to die for our sins. Trust in the infinite value of His death, for the person who died was none other than God.

The Synod of Dort (II.3–4) declared, "This death of God's Son is the only and entirely complete sacrifice and satisfaction for sins; it is of infinite value and worth, more than sufficient to atone for the sins of the whole world.... This death is of such great value and worth for the reason that the person who suffered it is, in order for Christ to be our Savior, not only a true and perfectly holy human, but also the only begotten Son of God, of the same eternal and infinite essence with the Father and the Holy Spirit." What more could you ask for as an atonement for your sins? Guilty sinners need no other mediator. Put your trust in the Word who became dying flesh for the sake of dying sinners that they might live in Him.

The Word of God became flesh. On the basis of God's revelation, we confess with the Westminster Confession (8.2), "The Son of God...did, when the fullness of time was come, take upon him man's nature, with all the essential properties and common infirmities thereof; yet without sin." The Son of God took upon Himself body, soul, and even death. This invites us to receive Christ and to trust in Him, for He is the atonement of sins. He is the Friend of sinners. He is the Resurrection and the Life of fallen, frail, dying men. Rest your heart on Him!

Conclusion: God Offers You the God-Man

John concludes in John 1:14 by telling us that the Word made flesh is "full of grace and truth." He who is "the truth" delights to give Himself away to sinners in *grace*—to sinners who have merited only death and hell. What a wonder that He offers Himself graciously to us!

You remember the story of John 4. Jesus left Judea. On the way to Galilee, He and His disciples passed through Samaria. While the disciples went into a city to buy food, Jesus sat down beside a well. It was about noon, and the hot sun was beating down. When a Samaritan woman came to draw water from the well, Jesus asked her for a drink.

At first she was shocked that He would talk to her; Jews and Samaritans hated each other. But Jesus then said something that intrigued her. He offered her living water that would become a spring or fountain welling up within her soul to forever satisfy her thirst. She asked Him for this living water. Jesus then exposed her sins. He told her she had had five husbands and was now living with a man who was not her husband. Then He told her that He was the Christ. She was so amazed that she ran off to tell her friends about the Savior: "Come, see a man, which told me all things that ever I did: is not this the Christ?" (v. 29).

Jesus likewise comes to you, humbly and lowly in heart, in our very nature. He understands what it means to be weary, hot, thirsty, and in need of a helping hand. He knows what it is like to be misunderstood and criticized and opposed by people. He, too, has suffered the miseries of our fall. Indeed, He suffered more than you can understand.

He also comes to you as God. He knows you completely. He knows all about your sins, whether public or private. Yet He offers you full pardon, the peace of God, and access to the Fountain of living waters.

"The Word became flesh." As a man, Jesus, like us, was an empty cup that needed to be filled by God. As God, Jesus is the river of living water (Ps. 46:4) that can satisfy our souls forever. God took the cup of Christ's humanity, filled it with Himself, and now offers this cup to you. God offers Himself to you in Jesus. By the Spirit's grace, receive this cup and drink of God. Trust in Jesus, the Incarnate Word, who in His passive and active obedience fully paid for sin and obeys the law so that God can be fully just in justifying the ungodly who believe in Jesus. Receive His precious gifts of pardon and eternal life. Look to Him to support you and save you in the midst of the storms of life. Submit to His divine authority as He exposes the secrets of your heart and calls you to repentance. Then vow, by God's grace, to live forever in, by, and for this Incarnate Word.

Chapter 3

Our Glorious Adoption:
Trinitarian-Based and Transformed Relationships

Behold, what manner of love the Father hath bestowed upon us, that we should be called the sons of God: therefore the world knoweth us not, because it knew him not. Beloved, now are we the sons of God, and it doth not yet appear what we shall be: but we know that, when he shall appear, we shall be like him; for we shall see him as he is. And every man that hath this hope in him purifieth himself, even as he is pure.

—1 John 3:1–3[1]

The triune God delights in family planning. Unlike most modern human family planning, which is restrictive and limiting, God's plans for His family are expansive and enlarging. Spiritual adoption—the wonderful teaching that every genuine Christian is an adopted child into God's family—is a foundational and vital factor that God uses to fulfill His family planning.

The glorious doctrine of spiritual adoption is addressed several places in the New Testament. Romans 8:14–16 and Galatians 4:4–6 will be the most familiar to us, but adoption is also a frequent theme in 1 John. Particularly in 1 John 3:1–3, the apostle John lays before us the central and major New Testament themes of the fatherhood of God and the corresponding sonship of the believer. We don't have to read far in the New Testament before we realize that this is of critical importance for the entirety of the Christian life. Where there is some degree of spiritual maturity, some realization of our sonship to the heavenly Father, this Father-son relationship will undergird our prayer, indeed, control our entire outlook on life. Much of what Christ taught us can be summarized in the precious doctrine of the salvific fatherhood of God. The

---

1. Portions of this article are adapted from my *The Epistles of John* (Darlington, U.K.: Evangelical Press, 2006), 111–20, and my *Heirs with Christ: The Puritans on Adoption* (Grand Rapids: Reformation Heritage Books, 2008), 75–102. Reprinted with permission from *Reformed Theological Journal* 26 (Nov. 2010): 94–108.

revelation of the fatherhood of God to the believer is in a sense the climax of the Scriptures and one of the greatest benefits of salvation.

In this chapter, I aim to first, show the wonder of our glorious adoption; second, expound its Trinitarian foundation; third, and most extensively, consider particularly in the context of 1 John 3 how a right appropriation of this doctrine will transform all our relationships in life; and finally, conclude with adoption's blessings and responsibilities.

The Wonder of Adoption

John begins the third chapter of 1 John with a call for believers to drop everything and consider the great doctrine of adoption. "Behold!" is John's opening cry; "Look at this!" The apostle is so overwhelmed with the wonder of God's adoption of believers that he is determined to direct everyone's attention there. He asks us to gaze with him upon this wonder: "Behold, what manner of love the Father hath bestowed upon us that we should be called the sons of God!" (v. 1). It is as if John asks, "Do you know the wonder of this precious truth? Have you, by faith, comprehended this magnificent doctrine of adoption?"

John's sense of astonishment is more evident in the original Greek, which implies, "Behold, from what country or realm does such love as this come?" Matthew 8:27 uses similar phraseology to describe how astonished the disciples were when Jesus calmed the winds and the sea: "What manner of man is this [literally, 'from what realm does this man come'] that even the winds and sea obey him!"

God's adoption of believers is something unparalleled in this world, John is saying. This fatherly love has come upon us from another realm. The world does not understand such love, for it has never seen anything like it. It is beyond the realm of human experience.

John is astonished because God showed such amazing love even though we were outcasts, rebels, and enemies against Him and His kingdom. God "calls" us sons of God; that is, He brings us into His family, giving us the name, the privileges, and all the blessings of His own children. He invites us to know Him as Father and to dwell under His protection and care and to come to Him with all our cares and needs. John is overwhelmed at the thought of being a full member of God's family.

Have you ever considered what a stupendous wonder adoption is? Wilhelmus à Brakel put it this way: "From being a child of the devil to becoming a child of God, from being a child of wrath to becoming the object of God's favor, from a child of condemnation to becoming an heir of all the promises and a possessor of all blessings, and to be exalted from the greatest misery to the highest felicity—this is something which exceeds all comprehension and all adoration."[2]

Do you stand in awe at this wonderful love of the Father? Holy wonder and amazement is an important part of Christian experience. One of the devil's tactics is to dull our sense of wonder, convincing us that we only feel such wonder in the initial stages of becoming a Christian. It is true that the sinner experiences a special sense of joy and wonder when he first comes to know Christ. We often refer to that time as one's "first love."

But John is writing here as an elderly man who has been a believer for more than sixty years. Yet his heart is still filled with amazement at being a son of God. He has never gotten over his initial sense of wonder at God's fatherly love. He is still asking the question: "From what realm does this amazing love come that has broken in upon my soul and made me a child of God?"

Has the wonder of your salvation and adoption in Christ Jesus grasped your soul? Do you, too, cry out in amazement:

> And can it be that I should gain
> An interest in the Savior's blood?
> Died He for me, who caused His pain—
> For me, who Him to death pursued?
> Amazing love! How can it be,
> That Thou, my God, shouldst die for me?

The psalters, hymns, and poems of our forefathers, especially in seasons of revival, were often filled with this glorious sense of wonder. Such wonder is the heart's response to the saving truths of the gospel. It is evoked in us through the Spirit's sanctifying grace as we meditate on and embrace the glorious truths of sovereign grace (Ps. 104:34). Often God's people experience too little wonder and awe over the gospel because their lives are so rushed that they do not stop long enough to wait upon the Spirit as they meditate on the glorious truths of the gospel.

We must meditate on Scripture and all that accrues to us in Christ Jesus— including our adoption—if we would have our hearts burn within us. That is what the pilgrims on the way to Emmaus said to each other after Christ had opened Scripture to them. "Did not our heart burn within us, while he talked with us by the way, and while he opened to us the scriptures?" (Luke 24:32) they asked in astonishment.

---

2. Wilhelmus à Brakel, *The Christian's Reasonable Service*, trans. Bartel Elshout, ed. Joel R. Beeke (Grand Rapids: Reformation Heritage Books, 1999), 2:419.

The way to a burning heart is through diligent meditation on the Word of God. Scripture is the primary means of grace that God blesses by His Spirit. Is it any wonder that some believers have lost their sense of wonder and amazement over the gospel when they so seldom study the Bible prayerfully and meditatively?

The Trinitarian Foundation of Adoption

Believers are not sons of God by nature because we have lost the status and privileges of sonship in our tragic fall in Paradise. Adoption is only made possible when God's gracious choice calls us into all the privileges and blessings of being His children. When we are born again, God delivers us from Satan's slavery and, by His astounding grace, transfers us to the Father's sonship. He calls us sons; we are adopted into His family.

Adoption in the time of John usually took place in adolescence or adulthood, not infancy. Under Roman law, adoption was a legal act by which a man chose someone outside of the family to be an heir to his inheritance. Likewise, believers become children of God through the gracious act of God the Father, who chooses them to be His heirs.

Sometimes adoptive parents announce receiving their son with the words "chosen son." God the Father, dear believer, set His heart upon you while you were a stranger and rebel—certainly not a member of His family. He called you, drew you to Himself, brought you into His family, constituted you to be His child, and now reserves for you the eternal inheritance of the kingdom of God.

The story is told of a king who finds a poor man's child, takes him out of the gutter, and makes him a prince in the royal household with all its status and privilege. This gospel story is not fiction, however, for like that king, the almighty God and Father has set His heart upon you, raised you up out of a horrible pit (Ps. 40:2), brought you into His home, and given to you all the privileges and blessings of being His child.

"Beloved, now are we the sons of God," says John in verse 2. This is not merely legal language. We believers are, indeed, God's chosen ones, as Ephesians 1:5–7 says. How astonishing that we as God's adopted children share the same privileges that belong to God's only begotten Son! Have you grasped the incredible truth of what Christ prays in John 17:26: "that the love wherewith thou hast loved me may be in them"? This love is the essence of God's fatherhood. It shows us how far God is willing to go to adopt us into His family.

Now we become children of God; that is, God becomes our Father, by substitution or, as John calls it, propitiation: "Herein is love, not that we loved God, but that he loved us, and sent his Son to be the propitiation for our sins"

(1 John 4:10; cf. 1 John 2:2). *Propitiation* may seem like a strange term to us, but it is a vital term, for it contains the heart of the gospel.

Let me explain. We are not sons and daughters of God by nature. Many live under this false idea. They think that everyone is a child of God, coming from the same Father. It is true, of course, that we are all creatures of the one Creator, but the Bible nowhere tells us that we are all children of God by nature. Rather, it tells us that by nature we are children of wrath. We are the objects of God's wrath, anger, and judgment by nature. As Thomas Watson writes, "We have enough in us to move God to correct us, but nothing to move him to adopt us, therefore exalt free grace, begin the work of angels here; bless him with your praises who hath blessed you in making you his sons and daughters."[3]

God has only one Son by nature, and that Son is the Lord Jesus Christ. Now God's amazing love to sinners lies in the way He makes children of wrath to become the sons of His love. His only begotten Son is the Son of His love. The Father loves the Son, but in the astonishing substitution that God made in the atoning sacrifice of Christ, the wrath of God, which was directed to us, was now poured upon His only begotten Son, who thereby became the propitiation for our sins. The way by which we who were sons of wrath became the sons of love is that the Son of God's love and the Child of His glory became the bearer of His wrath on the cross. All the judgment of God was poured out on Him in order that we, dear believers, might be made the children of God and sons of His love.

This is the astonishing biblical doctrine of substitution. Jesus Christ, who deserved eternal heaven, bore my eternal hell as an ungodly sinner (but now by grace a believer) so that the gates of hell may be eternally closed for me and the gates of heaven be eternally thrown open. Oh, what a price Christ had to pay to accomplish this task! He had to hang in the flame of His Father's wrath and be cast into outer darkness, crying out, "My God, my God, why hast thou forsaken me?"—all so that God could take us, for Christ's sake, who are by nature estranged and rebellious sinners and bring us into the family of God and constitute us as His children.

This is the only way to become a child of God—only through Christ being the propitiation, the sacrifice, the substitute, the atonement of God for our sins. Only for Christ's sake does God become the Father of His people. What country does this love come from—a love that would cause the holy God of all eternity to make this transaction on behalf of poor, hopeless, hell-worthy sinners like we are?

---

3. Thomas Watson, *A Body of Practical Divinity* (London: A. Fullarton, 1845), 160.

How great is the love the Father has lavished on us that we should be called children of God—we who deserve His judgment, dethroned Him from our lives, spurned His love, and defied His laws. We can never earn God's love, yet He graciously lavishes love upon us in Christ. Here, surely, is the great assurance of the child of God, that he was not chosen for any good in him but that God the Father loved him when he was bound for hell. God loved the sinner who had no thought of God in his heart, and God adopted him to be His. Oh, what wonder is the assurance of the Father's words: "I have loved thee with an everlasting love" (Jer. 31:3)!

All the members of the Trinity are involved in our adoption. Adoption is the gracious act of God the Father whereby He chooses us, calls us to Himself, and gives us the privileges and blessings of being His children. God the Son earned those blessings for us through His propitiatory death and sacrifice, by which we become children of God (1 John 4:10). And the Holy Spirit changes us from children of wrath, which we are by nature, into children of God by means of regeneration, or the new birth.

John refers to this new birth in 1 John 2:29, explaining the relationship between regeneration and adoption. If in adoption we would only receive the privilege and status of being God's children, something would still be missing. The adopted child retains the nature of his natural parents, not the nature of the adoptive parents. God, in His amazing grace, not only gives us the status and privileges of being His children by adoption but He also gives us the nature of God, which abides within us by Spirit-worked regeneration. The Holy Spirit implants God's nature within us. As 1 John 3:9 says, "Whosoever is born of God doth not commit sin [i.e., no one born of God goes on committing sin]; for his seed remaineth in him [i.e., for God's nature abides in him]."

Are you a child of God? Do you know what it means to have a new nature that cries out for the living God and lives under His fatherly love, fellowship, and protection? Have you been transferred from Satan's slavery to the Father's sonship by God's astounding grace?

Transformed Relationships Resulting from Adoption

Adoption brings blessings into every part of a believer's life. It affects his relationships to God, to the world, to his future, to himself, and to brothers and sisters in God's family. The biblical doctrine of adoption is central to a proper understanding of every major area of the Christian's life. All relationships are put into proper context only when believers are conscious of their sonship to the Father.

Christ Himself is the best proof of this truth. Jesus's consciousness of His unique sonship with the Father controlled all of Christ's living and thinking. As Jesus says in John 5:30, "I seek not mine own will, but the will of my Father which hath sent me," and in John 10:30, "I and my Father are one." "If I do not the works of my Father, believe me not," Jesus says in John 10:37, and "As my Father hath sent me, even so send I you" (John 20:21). Jesus speaks of "my Father" more than thirty times in the Gospel of John.

Though the close relationship of God the Father and God the Son is an obvious truth in the Gospels, what is not so obvious is how Jesus urges His disciples to let their thoughts and lives be controlled by the conviction that God is now their Father and they are His children. Jesus repeatedly urges kinship with the Father as the foundation of Christian discipleship. He tells His disciples that they are to be examples of trusting their Father, asking them, "Why are you anxious about what you should eat or drink or about your future—your Father knows that you have need of all these things" (see Matt. 6:31–34). Because their whole lives must be directed to do their Father's glory and obey His will, Jesus teaches His disciples to pray: "Our Father which art in heaven, hallowed be thy Name. Thy kingdom come. Thy will be done, in earth as it is in heaven" (Matt. 6:9–10). The child of God is to live his whole life in relation to his Father, remembering that the Father has promised each child His kingdom.

Practically speaking, the significance of adoption has great implications. It transforms the following:

1. *Our relationship to God.* When the gospel breaks in upon us, we are led by the Spirit to discover the amazing truth that God is our Father in Christ Jesus. The heartbeat of daily Christian experience is to live in fellowship with the Father and the Son. A true Christian lives under God's fatherly love, wisdom, care, guidance, and discipline.

People are hungry for security today. They look for it in all kinds of places, but they often go about it the wrong way. The only place in the universe where true security can be found is in the household of the heavenly Father, who is the God and Father of our Lord Jesus Christ. There is no security outside of fellowship with God the Father through the Lord Jesus Christ.

So many people are discovering that the things that once gave them security are now falling apart. They are facing failure in business, jobs, or relationships with family members and friends. They are beset with financial insolvency, terrorism, and war. So much in life is uncertain; so much is crumbling away. The most powerful company on earth may fold in the next recession. We learn that nothing in life is secure except God. He alone does not change (Mal. 3:6).

Are you looking for security in the fatherhood of God? Are you daily being led deeper into His faithfulness as your Father? Jesus taught His disciples this truth in many ways. For example, He urged His followers to think about God's fatherly love by comparing it to the love of a human father. He said in Matthew 7:11, "If ye then, being evil, know how to give good gifts to your children, how much more shall your Father which is in heaven give good things to them that ask him?"

The comparison is between the fatherhood of earthly fathers, who are evil (i.e., they have fallen natures and show flaws and failures and sins) and the fatherhood of God, who is steadfast in love that never falters or changes, even when we sin. God's fatherhood is flawless. I will show you a love, says Jesus, which is expansive and glorious beyond imagination. It is the love of your Father in heaven.

I don't know what your experience of human fatherhood has been. Some of us have had little relationship with our earthly fathers; some have had good experiences, and others have had disappointing, even bitter, experiences. Everything that fails in human fatherhood is corrected in God's fatherhood. Everything good we experience in human fatherhood is a mere shadow of the full and perfect fatherhood of God.

If you are a father, you know how your heart sometimes aches and cries out for your children in love. Imagine multiplying that love by infinity. Then realize how even that falls short of the love of God for His people. Do you succumb to the embrace of your heavenly Father? Oh, that you would allow yourself to partake of His unspeakable fatherly love!

To increase His people's appreciation for God's fatherhood, Jesus urges His people to think of His own relationship to God the Father. We need to ponder the wonder of this, especially in the context of daily afflictions, remembering that Jesus felt His Father's love in the afflictions He underwent. When you are under God's discipline and He is permitting trials to fall upon you, remember that these difficulties are evidence of your Father's love (Heb. 12:5–11). God has a plan, a purpose, a vision for His people as a loving Father that embraces every affliction and heartache.

As parents, we dream of what our children might become when they grow up. Likewise, God also has a vision for His children. He knows precisely what He wants them to be. He knows how He will mold and train them according to His plan, and inevitably, that involves discipline because God will not permit His believers to be less than what He intends them to be. He uses His fatherly discipline for their welfare (Lam. 3:31–33). If we are born-again believers, we must ask for wisdom to see everything in our life as a blessing from God our Father, who adopts us as His own.

2. *Our relationship to the world.* The believer's adoption by God the Father also affects his relationship to the world. First John 3:1 tells us that this relationship is a troubled one: "Therefore the world knoweth us not, because it knew him not." On the one hand, the believer shares with Jesus the unspeakable love of the Father, but on the other hand, he shares with Jesus the hostility, estrangement, and even hatred of the world. The reason the world does not know the children of God is because it does not know Jesus.

The world is baffled by what happens to God's people for it cannot understand why they love what they love and hate what they hate. This reaction of the world is evidence of the believer's adoption into God's family, for the world did not know Jesus either; He came unto His own, and His own received Him not. He was in the world, which was created by Him, but the world knew Him not. The world did not recognize Him as the Son of God. Ultimately, it crucified Him.

When a sinner is born again and brought into God's family, he comes to know the great blessings of deliverance in Christ. But the believer also discovers that worldly people no longer understand him. For example, when God converted me at age fourteen, I had to break some of my closest friendships to remain faithful to God. One friend was puzzled. "I thought I knew you, but I do not know what has happened to you," he said. "I cannot understand you. It is as if we are living in two different worlds."

Believers and unbelievers *do* live in different worlds, in different kingdoms, in different families. That cannot help but bring consequences. But adoption into God's family means that we must be willing for Christ's sake to walk in the world even if we are misunderstood, unwanted, despised, even hated, all the while giving no unnecessary offense to the world.

3. *Our relationship to the future.* John goes on to say, "Beloved, now are we the sons of God, and it doth not appear what we shall be: but we know that, when he shall appear, we shall be like him; for we shall see him as he is" (1 John 3:2). The prospects for God's adopted family are great, for His children will receive a glorious inheritance. They cannot even imagine the extent of that inheritance.

Here in this world, we are God's children, even though the world does not understand us. But we have something much greater in store for us—the infinite glory that God the Father is laying up for us in Christ Jesus. God's child is like a poor peasant who has been taken out of the mire and raised to the position of prince of the realm. The adopted prince lives in the palace, has free access to the king, and enjoys the king's favor, love, and protection. The prince tells the king he cannot comprehend the greatness of the king's love. It is unspeakably great to him. The king responds, "You have not begun to see the extent of it. Your inheritance is still coming to you."

If our present privileges as God's adopted children are so great that the world cannot grasp them, our future prospects are so glorious that even we cannot grasp them. As 1 Corinthians 2:9 says, "Eye hath not seen, nor ear heard, neither have entered into the heart of man, the things which God hath prepared for them that love him." Because God is our Father and we are His adopted children, we have a full inheritance awaiting us. The best is yet to be. Today we experience great blessings, despite our infirmities and sins, but one day we shall be in glory, free from sin and in perfect communion with God. Our heavenly Father keeps the best surprises for His children until the end, when He shall turn all their sorrow into joy.

Likewise, today we look at Christ by faith. Though what we see is shadowy and dim, we are being changed from glory to glory by the Spirit of the Lord (2 Cor. 3:18). One day all shadows will be removed. We will see Christ as He is, in all His glory.

Moreover, God is shaping us to share in the glories of our Lord Jesus Christ. As 1 John 3:2 says, "When he shall appear, we shall be like him; for we shall see him as he is." God is changing us now, but then we shall be so changed that we will fully bear His image without spot or wrinkle. Paul tells us in Romans 8:22–23 that the whole creation waits for the day when the inheritance of the children of God will be given to them. What a future!

4. *Our relationship to ourselves.* The children of the heavenly Father know His will and purpose for them. Every adopted child of God also knows that holiness is an important part of God's purpose for his happiness in God's family. As 1 John 3:3 says, "And every man that hath this hope in him purifieth himself, even as he is pure."

In holiness, the child of God identifies himself with His Father's purposes. Sometimes children resent their father's purposes, but the true adopted son of God identifies with His Father's purpose for him. He does not try to find himself apart from his Father in heaven but in his Father's will. Because seeking God's purposes for the believer's life is inseparable from the pursuit of holiness, the believer gives himself to the purpose that his Father has for him.

John tells us, "Every man that hath this hope in him purifieth himself" (3:3). So we are to purify ourselves daily. As Colossians 3 tells us, holiness means putting off everything that is dishonoring to our Father, who has loved us, and the Savior, who died to save us. It means putting on "mercies, kindness, humbleness of mind, meekness, and longsuffering" (3:12). Purifying ourselves involves "the whole man," says John Cotton, "including what we do with our minds, affections, will, thoughts, tongue, eyes, hands, disappointments, injuries, and enemies."[4] Purifying ourselves involves loving all that the Father loves and hating all that the Father hates. From the moment of conversion to the time we take our final breath, we have one pursuit: to purify ourselves before our Father to be more like Christ.

The Greek word for *purify* refers to undivided allegiance, or having one's eyes on one thing. It implies wholeness and singleness of purpose. It means having undivided motives in our living and our service, being wholly dedicated to living to glorify Jesus Christ. The way that Christians become known as sons of God is that they have a new goal for themselves, a new relationship toward themselves. By God's grace, they purify themselves even as Christ is pure.

5. *Our relationship to the family of God.* If we rightly understand that we are adopted into God's family (note the usage of the plural throughout 1 John 3:1–2), our attitude toward our brothers and sisters in the family will be affected (3:14–18). We have not been adopted to live apart from that family but to live within that network of relationships. God's purpose in adopting children is to create a family in which He reflects His gracious purpose that will one day be fulfilled in heaven. He wants the love that exists between the Father and the Son and the Holy Spirit to be extended through the love between brothers and sisters in Christ.

The communion of saints is so essential to the gospel. That is why it is so grievous when people in the church do not show love to one another. If we profess a Savior that laid down His life for us and we are part of His family, we ought to be willing to lay down our lives for other members of the family. We should uphold them, love them, and sacrifice for them. We should not grieve each other, wound each other, or gossip about each other. The way we behave toward other Christians proves whether or not we are adopted children of God (3:14–15).

---

4. John Cotton, *An Exposition of First John* (repr., Evansville, Ind.: Sovereign Grace Publishers, 1962), 331.

If we show little love to other children of God, we prove that we have tasted little of God's love in our life, for those who have experienced much love from Him cannot help but love others. Those who have not tasted the love of God will not love the brethren.

Privileges and Responsibilities

What about you? Have you become a child of God through the triune God's glorious adoption of you into His family? Do you live under God's fatherly grace of love, fellowship, and protection? Do you know experientially the amazing transition from slavery to sonship, so ably expressed by this poet?

> "Abba, Father," we approach Thee
> In our Saviour's precious name;
> We, Thy children, here assembling,
> Now the promised blessing claim.
> From our guilt His blood has washed us,
> 'Tis through Him our souls draw nigh;
> And Thy Spirit too has taught us
> "Abba, Father," thus to cry.
>
> Once as prodigals we wander'd
> In our folly far from Thee;
> But Thy grace, o'er sin abounding,
> Rescued us from misery:
> Clothed in garments of salvation,
> At Thy table is our place;
> We rejoice, and Thou rejoicest,
> In the riches of Thy grace.
>
> Thou the prodigal hast pardon'd,
> "Kiss'd us" with a Father's love;
> "Kill'd the fatted calf," and call'd us
> E'er to dwell with Thee above.
> "It is meet," we hear Thee saying,
> "We should merry be and glad;
> I have found my once lost children,
> Now they live who once were dead."
>
> "Abba, Father!" we adore Thee,
> While the hosts in heaven above

> E'en in us now learn the wonders
> Of Thy wisdom, grace, and love.
> Soon before Thy throne assembled,
> All Thy children shall proclaim
> Abba's love as shown in Jesus,
> And how full is Abba's name![5]

Pray that God will empower us to understand the transforming *blessings and implications* of adoption in relation to the triune God, the world, our future, ourselves, and the family of God. Then we will understand better the greater privileges and benefits of adoption. Privileges like these:

1. Our Father cuts us off from the family to which we naturally belong in Adam as children of wrath and of the devil and ingrafts us into His own family to make us members of the covenant family of God. "Adoption translates us out of a miserable estate, into a happy estate," writes Thomas Cole. "God is in covenant with us, and we in him."[6]

2. Our Father gives us freedom to call on Him by His Father-name and gives us a new name, which serves as our guarantee of admission to the house of God as sons and daughters of God (Rev. 2:17; 3:12).

3. Our Father gifts us with the Spirit of adoption. Believers are, by grace, partakers of the Holy Spirit. This Spirit, Jeremiah Burroughs tells us, enlightens our mind, sanctifies our heart, makes God's wisdom and will known to us, guides us to eternal life, yes, works the entire work of salvation in us and seals it to us unto the day of redemption (Eph. 4:30).[7]

4. Our Father grants us likeness to Himself and His Son. The Father imparts to His children a filial heart and disposition that resemble His own. Roger Drake writes, "All God's adopted children bear their Father's image, as Gideon's brethren did his (Judg. 8:18). They are like

---

5. James G. Deck, "Abba, Father, we approach Thee," in *The Believers' Hymn Book* (Glasgow: Pickering & Inglis, [1900]), 1.

6. Thomas Cole, *A Discourse of Christian Religion, in Sundry Points...Christ the Foundation of our Adoption, from Gal. 4. 5* (London: for Will. Marshall, 1698), 351.

7. Jeremiah Burroughs, *The Saints' Happiness, Delivered in Divers Lectures on the Beatitudes* (repr., Beaver Falls, Penn.: Soli Deo Gloria, 1988), 196.

God, in holiness [and] in dignity (Matt. 5:44–45; Rom. 8:29; Heb. 2:7; 1 John 3:2–3)."[8]

5. Our Father especially strengthens our faith through His gifts of promises and prayer. "If we are adopted," writes Thomas Watson, "then we have an interest in all the promises: the promises are children's bread." They are like a garden, Watson goes on to say, in which some herb is found to cure every ailment.[9]

6. Our Father corrects and chastens us for our sanctification. "He chasteneth and scourgeth every son whom he receiveth" (Heb. 12:6). All chastisement involves discipline that comes from our Father's hand and works together for our best welfare (2 Sam. 7:14; Ps. 89:32–33; Rom. 8:28, 36–37; 2 Cor. 12:7). Our sufferings are "for our education and instruction in his family," writes John Owen.[10]

7. Our Father comforts us with His love and pity and moves us to rejoice in intimate communion with Him and His Son (Rom. 5:5). He does that in several ways, as Samuel Willard notes: "He applies the precious promises to their souls, he gives them cordials of comfort, communicates unto them the sips and foretastes of glory, [and] fills them with inward joys and refreshings."[11]

8. Our Father offers us spiritual, Christian liberty as His sons and daughters (John 8:36). This liberty releases us from bondage (Gal. 4:7). It delivers us from the slavish subjection, the servile pedagogy, the condemning power, the intolerable yoke, and the thundering curses of the law as a covenant of works (Gal. 3:13), though not from the law's regulating power.[12]

---

8. Roger Drake, "The Believer's Dignity and Duty Laid Open, in the High Birth wherewith he is Privileged, and the Honourable Employment to which he is Called," in *Puritan Sermons 1659–1689: Being the Morning Exercises at Cripplegate, St. Giles in the Fields, and in Southwark by Seventy-five Ministers of the Gospel in or near London* (repr., Wheaton, Ill.: Richard Owen Roberts, 1981), 5:333.

9. Watson, *A Body of Practical Divinity*, 160.

10. John Owen, *The Works of John Owen*, ed. William H. Goold (repr., London: Banner of Truth, 1966), 16:257.

11. Samuel Willard, *The Child's Portion* (Boston: Samuel Green, 1684), 22.

12. *The Complete Works of the Late Rev. Thomas Boston, Ettrick*, ed. Samuel M'Millan (repr., Wheaton, Ill.: Richard Owen Roberts, 1980), 1:625; Cole, *Christ the Foundation of our Adoption*, 352–53.

9. Our Father preserves us and keeps us from falling (Ps. 91:11–12; 1 Peter 1:5). He restores us from every backsliding way, recovering and humbling us, always preventing our hypocrisy.[13] Samuel Willard says, "God's sons in this life are like little Children, always tripping, and stumbling, and falling, and so weak that they could never get up again but for him: but by reasons of his hand that is upon them, his everlasting Arm that is under them."[14]

10. Our Father provides everything that we need as His children, both physically and spiritually (Ps. 34:10; Matt. 6:31–33), and will protect us from all harm. He will defend us from our enemies—Satan, the world, and our own flesh—and right our wronged cause. He will assist and strengthen us, always lending us a helping hand to carry us through every difficulty and temptation (2 Tim. 4:17). We may safely leave everything in His fatherly hands, knowing that He will never leave us nor forsake us (Heb. 13:5–6).

Then, too, adoption involves *responsibilities and duties*. The Puritans taught that every privilege of adoption had a corresponding responsibility or duty, each of which transforms the way believers think and live. These may be summarized as follows:

1. Show childlike reverence and love for your Father in everything. Reflect habitually on your Father's great glory and majesty. Stand in awe of Him; render Him praise and thanksgiving in all things. Remember, your holy Father sees everything. Children sometimes commit dreadful acts in the absence of their parents, but your Father is never absent.

2. Submit to your Father in every providence. When He visits you with the rod, don't resist or murmur. Don't immediately respond by saying, "'I am not a child of God, God is not my Father, God deals harshly with me; if He were my Father, He would have compassion on me; He would then deliver me from this grievous and especially this sinful cross—to speak thus does not befit the nature of an upright child," writes Brakel. Rather, "it is fitting for a child to be quiet, to humbly

---

13. Thomas Ridgley, *Commentary on the Larger Catechism* (repr., Edmonton: Still Waters Revival Books, 1993), 2:136.

14. Willard, *The Child's Portion*, 17.

submit, and to say, 'I will bear the indignation of the LORD, because I have sinned against him'" (Mic. 7:9).[15]

3. Obey and imitate your Father, and love His image-bearers. Strive to be like Him, to be holy as He is holy, to be loving as He is loving. We are to be "imitators of God" (Eph. 5:1) to show that we bear the family likeness.

4. Rejoice in being in your Father's presence. Delight in communing with Him. Burgess writes, "A son delights to have letters from his Father, to have discourse about him, especially to enjoy his presence."[16] Resist every hindrance, therefore, that keeps you from relishing your Father's adopting grace.

Concluding Applications

In heaven, this joy will be full; our adoption will then be perfected (Rom. 8:23). Then we will enter into the Father's "presence and palace," where we will be "everlastingly enjoying, delighting, and praising God."[17] Let us wait and long for that as children who eagerly anticipate our full inheritance, where the triune God shall be our all in all.[18]

Meanwhile, let us seek grace to live as children of God in the midst of this fallen world. Then we, too, will often confess with the apostle John, "Behold, what manner of love the Father hath bestowed upon us, that we should be called the sons of God: therefore the world knoweth us not, because it knew him not. Beloved, now are we the sons of God, and it doth not yet appear what we shall be: but we know that, when he shall appear, we shall be like him; for we shall see him as he is. And every man that hath this hope in him purifieth himself, even as he is pure" (1 John 3:1–3).

---

15. Brakel, *Christian's Reasonable Service*, 2:437.

16. Anthony Burgess, *Spiritual Refining: or A Treatise of Grace and Assurance* (London: A Miller for Thomas Underhill, 1652), 240.

17. Thomas Manton, *The Complete Works of Thomas Manton, D.D.* (London: James Nisbet, 1870), 12:125.

18. Drake, *Puritan Sermons*, 5:342; cf. Willard, *The Child's Portion*, 71.

Chapter 4

Gethsemane's King-Lamb:
John 18:7–8, 12–13a

John 18 introduces us to the greatest day in the history of the world: the final twenty-four hours of Jesus's life prior to His crucifixion and death. How packed with action these hours are! We're prone to consider them exclusively as a theological event called the atonement, forgetting that all the events recorded in this chapter happened in real time. We lose the action, the tension, the horror, the pain, the shame, and the bravery of our thirty-three-year-old Savior. Christ did not die a theoretical death. In John 18, Jesus enters the Holy Place as our High Priest where He will tread the winepress of God's wrath. The culmination of His sufferings consists of the events that took place in Gethsemane, the garden of agony; Gabbatha, the judgment hall of Pilate; and Golgotha, the hill of execution.

Our chapter begins with Jesus and the disciples leaving Jerusalem after celebrating the Passover. Christ is about to lay down His life for His disciples, including the ones who were just disputing who was the greatest among them, those who would forsake Him in His darkest hour, and the one who would deny Him that night. To them He said, "With desire I have desired to eat this passover with you before I suffer" (Luke 22:15). Greater love has no man than this!

Jesus and His disciples leave Jerusalem through the gate north of the temple. "He went forth with his disciples over the brook Cedron, where was a garden, into which he entered" (John 18:1). This garden was known as Gethsemane, on the lower slopes of the Mount of Olives, where massive olive trees grew and where the Lord had often gone to pray. But this time He went forth not only to pray but also to suffer betrayal, arrest, and captivity. That is emphasized in verse 4, which says, "Jesus, knowing all things that should come upon him, went forth."

Do the words *He went forth* give you pause? If not, consider that Jesus went forth knowing that His disciples would abandon Him, knowing the bitter suffering that was required to make satisfaction for His people's sins, and knowing the betrayal that Judas, His hand-picked disciple—one of the twelve—had already negotiated with the Jewish authorities. Jesus went forth knowing that He would be whipped and beaten and spat on, knowing that the hairs of His beard would be plucked out, and knowing that great nails would be driven through His hands and feet. Jesus went forth knowing how full and how bitter the cup was that He must drink, down to the dregs, knowing He must be delivered into the hands of wicked men, be crucified, and abide for three dark hours under the wrath of God in the torments of hell itself, until at last He will give Himself up to the power of death itself. Knowing all this, He went forth undaunted and strong in His determination to finish the work He had been given to do in this world.

He knew all that, but He knew you too, and He knew me. He knew His church. He knew that company of people there, which God had told Abraham would be as numerous as the sand on the seashores. He knew us with a loving knowledge, with a sympathetic knowledge, with a forgiving knowledge. He knew that soon we would be with Him forever as His ransomed people and loved ones. What a joy to be surrounded by those we love, without one believer missing! That was the joy and hope set before Him that strengthened Him and enabled Him to endure the shame of the cross.

Jesus went forth not as a martyr or a helpless victim but as the willing Suffering Servant of Jehovah, as the Lion of the tribe of Judah, as the Lamb of God. No one will ever comprehend the magnitude of the sufferings of the King-Lamb in this awesome hour at Gethsemane. In this chapter, I wish to expound the theme of Christ in Gethsemane as the King of Kings and the Lamb of God in John 18, emphasizing verses 7–8 and 12–13: "Then asked he them again, Whom seek ye? And they said, Jesus of Nazareth. Jesus answered, I have told you that I am he: if therefore ye seek me, let these go their way.... Then the band and the captain and officers of the Jews took Jesus, and bound him, and led him away."

I set two major points before you: (1) the King's threefold sovereignty, and (2) the Lamb's threefold submission.

The King's Threefold Sovereignty

Only eleven disciples entered the garden of Gethsemane with Jesus, and only three of those were invited to go with Him still further into the shadows and quiet of the garden. But even those three could not enter all the way into His sufferings. Moving a stone's throw beyond His disciples, Jesus fell to the earth and cried out to God, asking if there be any alternative to drinking this bitter cup of suffering. There are no words strong enough to express His suffering in this garden. Mark says that He was "sore amazed" (Mark 14:33); Luke, that He was "in an agony" (Luke 22:44); and Matthew, that He cried out, "My soul is exceeding sorrowful, even unto death" (Matt. 27:38). In sum, Jesus was overwhelmed, immersed, and burdened down with grief. He knew with perfect clarity, even before they happened, that intense sufferings would descend upon Him. The full weight of sin and the awful curse that His Father placed upon it would be imposed upon Him. Even worse, His Father's comforting presence would be withdrawn from Him in the midst of this horrible suffering.

If the power of His Godhead had not sustained Him, Jesus could not have endured the horrors of Gethsemane, to say nothing of what was to follow. Three times Jesus leaves His disciples to cry out as He writhes in agony of body and soul on the ground. "Father, if thou be willing, remove this cup from me: nevertheless not my will, but thine, be done" (Luke 22:42). Jesus sweats drops of blood as the enemy is approaching to betray Him. He suffers and prays as His choicest friends are sleeping.

After the third session of prayer, Jesus goes forth to meet Judas and a band of soldiers. This is the same disciple who an hour or two before sat with Him at the Last Supper. Judas left the table early to go to the chief priests and Pharisees with an offer to assist them in arresting Jesus. During the time of Passover, hundreds of soldiers, called the Roman *cohort* or *band*, guarded the temple against revolutions or uprisings. They were the most highly trained Roman soldiers in the entire army. They were comparable, I suppose, to Green Berets today.

The chief priests and Pharisees went to the captain of this band to ask for some soldiers to arrest Jesus. They had to convince the captain that the Nazarene named Jesus was about to incite a riot or lead a revolt and needed to be arrested. The captain agreed to send a large part of the band to arrest Jesus. Scripture says a great multitude of people followed Judas to the garden, including Jews and Gentiles, believers and unbelievers. Many of the soldiers in the band came well equipped; they were armed with swords and staves, carrying torches and lamps to light their way in the night and to locate Jesus in case He tried to hide in the foliage of the olive trees. So they approached the garden to surround it and tighten the noose around Jesus. No doubt they expected to find Him cowering under one of the olives trees, hiding behind its foliage like a defeated Saddam Hussein cowering in a pit. Perhaps they feared that He and His followers would offer armed resistance. The only uncertainty was whether they had the right man. That was solved by arranging for Judas to kiss the man they are looking for. Thus the plans are complete. They are certain that this time Jesus will not escape.

The King's Sovereign Question

Suddenly Jesus takes charge as Gethsemane's King. He walks boldly into the moonlight and asks the sovereign question: "Whom seek ye?" Judas is so intent on his devilish plans that he is blind to Jesus's sudden display of His royal glory. Judas boldly greets Jesus with "Hail, master," and kisses Him (Matt. 26:49). The Greek form of the verb implies a repeated action—that is, Judas kisses Jesus repeatedly so that the entire multitude knows this is the dangerous Nazarene. Those kisses burn—they sting and betray. Astonishingly, God permits this; and even more astonishingly, Jesus responds to Judas's audacity with a very mild rebuke, saying, "Judas, betrayest thou the Son of man with a kiss?" (Luke 22:48).

Judas gave every appearance of being a religious, pious man two hours before at the Supper. Now he betrays his Lord with a kiss. What a hypocrite!

Tragically, we by nature are little better than Judas. We, too, have rejected and betrayed Christ with our blatant unbelief and, as believers, with a vain show of religion. We, too, succumbed to the temptation to bargain away our profession of faith in Him for whatever the world offers us. Even after we receive grace, the Holy Spirit must teach us that each new sin is another hypocritical kissing of Jesus. That is particularly true of church leaders who sin far too easily although we know better. How we need to cry out, "O God, preserve me. Keep me from sinning, and from hypocrisy!"

Do we, like Judas, sit with believers one moment and strike up a bargain with God's enemies the next? Are we two-faced in our walk and our talk? Do our spouses and children see us behave differently at home than in church? Would our colleagues in the office recognize the men we try to be at church?

In a loud, clear, kingly voice, Jesus asks, "Whom seek ye?" There is such boldness in these words. The band of soldiers is prepared to surround the garden and lift their lamp-poles high to search for a man in hiding. But now Jesus steps boldly into the light and asks, "Whom seek ye?"

This question also comes to us today: "Whom seek ye?"

We are all seekers, but what or whom do we seek? Jesus, the only Savior? Then what kind of Jesus do we seek? The multitude in the garden also seeks Jesus. They want "Jesus of Nazareth"—literally, "Jesus the Nazarene." Nazareth is considered a place of reproach; you may recall how Nathaniel asked, "Can any good thing come out of Nazareth?" Though the title *Jesus of Nazareth* can be used reverently (see, Acts 2:22), this multitude is implying that Jesus is a false prophet and a wicked man. They want to arrest Jesus so they can ridicule, despise, and trample on Him.

We also do this by nature. We try to ignore the true Savior and His calling. We shrug off Jesus's question by saying, "I can't save myself anyway." But if we refuse to answer His question, "Whom seek ye?" now we will be forced to answer it when everything and everyone we have sought will become public on the day of judgment.

You may argue, "But I am much more religious than that!" Indeed, you may well be. But what kind of Jesus are you seeking? What kind of Jesus are people in your church seeking? Perhaps you are a minister. Do you preach in a searching manner, separating the precious from the vile? Is your preaching discriminatory? Millions of people today say they have received Christ, yet give little or no evidence that they have been spiritually awakened from the dead. They do not need Jesus as living Savior and Lord and remain unresponsive to His spiritual beauty and glory. Unlike Paul, they don't count everything loss for the sake of the excellency and surpassing worth of knowing Christ Jesus as the altogether lovely Bridegroom and Lord (Phil. 3:8).

John Piper describes this problem well:

> When these people say they "receive Christ," they do not receive him as *supremely valuable*. They receive him simply as sin-forgiver (because they love being guilt-free), and as rescuer-from-hell (because they love being pain-free), and as healer (because they love being disease-free), and as protector (because they love being safe), and as prosperity-giver (because they love being wealthy), and as Creator (because they want a personal universe), and as Lord of history (because they want order and purpose); but they don't receive him as supremely and personally valuable for who he is.... They don't receive him as he really is—more glorious, more beautiful, more wonderful, more satisfying, than everything else in the universe. They don't prize *him*, or treasure *him*, or cherish *him*, or delight in *him*. Or to say it another way, they "receive Christ" in a way that requires no change in human nature. You don't have to be born again to love being guilt-free and pain-free and disease-free and safe and wealthy. All natural men without any spiritual life love these things. But to embrace Jesus as your supreme treasure requires a new nature. No one does this naturally. You must be born again (John 3:3). You must be a new creation in Christ (2 Cor. 5:17; Gal. 6:15). You must be made spiritually alive (Eph. 2:1–4).[1]

The King's Sovereign Self-identification

Jesus then responds to the multitude with a second manifestation of His kingship, declaring His sovereign self-identification. He says simply, yet profoundly,

---

1. John Piper, *Think: The Life of the Mind and the Love of God* (Wheaton, Ill.: Crossway, 2010), 71.

"I am he." *Ego eimi*—literally, "I am." As He does in other "I am" statements in the Gospel of John, it appears that here, too, Jesus is proclaiming His deity. In John 8:58, Jesus says, "Before Abraham was, I am." In response, the Jews took up stones to kill Him. Jesus now uses the same language that the Lord used in Exodus 3 and is repeated throughout Isaiah 40–55, in identifying Himself as "I am." Leon Morris writes, "The soldiers had come out secretly to arrest a fleeing peasant. In the gloom they find themselves confronted by a commanding figure, who so far from running away comes out to meet them and speaks to them in the very language of deity."[2]

Jesus's proclamation has such profound effects on the multitude that the people fall backward to the ground (John 18:6). What good are all the torches, lamps, swords, staves, officers, soldiers, and captains against Jesus, who proclaims that He is the great "I am"—the great Jehovah, the unchangeable covenant-keeping God who was, is, and will always be what He is? Even in the state of His humiliation, one word from Jesus's lips is enough to make an entire multitude fall to the ground.

What, then, will be His power when He comes as Judge at the last day? Scripture tells us that every knee will bow—some out of gratitude and love for being saved, and others in fear of everlasting perdition who cry out for the mountains and hills to cover them. Robert Rollock (*c.* 1555–1599) wrote,

> If the bleating of a lamb had such force, what force shall the roaring of a lion have? Where shall the wicked stand? And if the voice of the Lord Jesus, humbly, and like a lamb, standing before them himself alone, and speaking with such gentleness, had such an effect as to throw them down upon the ground, what effect shall that roaring, full of wrath and indignation, at that great day, not out of the mouth of a lamb, nor of an humble man, Jesus of Nazareth, but out of the mouth of a lion, out of the mouth of Jesus Christ the Judge, sitting in his glory and majesty, and saying to the wicked, "Away, ye cursed, to that fire which is prepared for the devil and the angels" (Matt. 25:41), what effect, then, shall that voice have?[3]

What a difference between these two responses to Jesus's sovereign self-identification, "I am"! These words comfort His disciples and terrorize His enemies. Those who were once enemies are now His friends, causing them to fall forward in respect before Him. What must it have been for Peter and the disciples to see not only the multitude but also Judas fall back before Gethsemane's

2. Leon Morris, *The Gospel according to John* (Grand Rapids: Eerdmans, 1995), 658.

3. *Select Works of Robert Rollock*, ed. William M. Gunn (1844–1849; repr., Grand Rapids: Reformation Heritage Books, 2008), 2:24.

Lamb? As they gaze upon a helpless Judas, their former friend, how can they help but think, "There but for the grace of God, go I!"

Has the great "I am" ever made you fall before Him in awe of His powerful justice and merciful grace, crying out, "Have mercy upon me, O Lord, thou Son of David"?

Gethsemane's King lets the confused and frightened band of soldiers get back on their feet. With royal authority, He then repeats the question: "Whom seek ye?" (John 18:7). At this point, don't you want to cry out to the multitude, "Do you not understand that the One you are seeking to arrest is not only Jesus of Nazareth but the very Son of God? Don't you see the danger of challenging this King? Repent! Repent and bow before Him before He destroys you."

But the multitude is still totally blind. Incredibly, they repeat their first answer, "Jesus of Nazareth." We should not be surprised. God is a God of second chances, but unbelievers will continue to cling to their rejection of God's Word if the Holy Spirit does not cause the scales to fall from their eyes.

The King's Sovereign Substitution

To their second rejection of Him, Gethsemane's King not only speaks with a sovereign question and sovereign self-identification but also with sovereign substitution. "I have told you that I am he: if therefore ye seek me, let these go their way" (v. 8). What a staggering expression of kingly love this is! Not a single soldier dares to draw his sword against Jesus or His disciples—not even when Peter lunges at Malchus and cuts off his right ear.

Charles Spurgeon (1834–1892) wrote, "Those words, 'If ye seek me, let these go their way,' were like coats of mail to them.... The disciples walked securely in the midst of the boisterous mob.... The words of Jesus proved to be a right royal word; it was a divine word; and men were constrained to obey it."[4]

Christ's mediatorial grace for His people is expressed in verse 9: "That the saying might be fulfilled, which he spake, Of them which thou gavest me have I lost none." Protecting His disciples was more than just kindness on Christ's part; He was fulfilling the Father's commission to save His sheep. The Father has entrusted His elect to Christ for salvation, and now Christ will walk alone to the cross so that not one will be lost. Christ's royal words will come true (John 6:39; 10:28; 17:2, 12, 19). As Don Carson notes, Christ's care for the

---

4. Charles Spurgeon, "The Captive Savior Freeing His People," Sermon 722 on John 18:8, 9, Nov. 25, 1866, in *Metropolitan Tabernacle Pulpit* (repr., Pasadena, Tex.: Pilgrim Publications, 1973), 12: 650.

physical safety of His disciples offers us an "illustration" of His work for their spiritual salvation.[5]

So Christ tells the soldiers to take Him but to let His disciples go. Those who could not watch with Him even for one hour now hear their glorious King declare that He is willing to be arrested, bound, and led away as a lamb to the slaughter so that they might go free. *He* will be scourged, but not *they*. *He* will be crucified, but not *they*. He will fulfill the words of Isaiah 53:5, "But he was wounded for our transgressions, he was bruised for our iniquities: the chastisement of our peace was upon him; and with his stripes we are healed." Truly, there is nothing more loving than what He says: "Let Me be bound for their sakes." Have you seen Christ standing in the place of His apostles, His people, His church—and you? Have you experienced the power of His substitutionary, royal love?

If Jesus Christ had fled at this moment or simply destroyed His enemies, our salvation would have been impossible. So He stands His ground, saying, "Let these go their way." He stands His ground so that even cowards like us may be caught in His eternal net of love and drawn to safety with His cords of love. But He also stands His ground so that servants of God like us could be given "a royal passport in the way of providence," as Spurgeon called it, then added, "Fear not, servant of Christ, you are immortal till your work is done."[6]

Verse 12 says, "Then [literally, therefore] the multitude took Jesus." So after He clearly showed who was in charge in uttering His sovereign questions, revealing His sovereign self-identification, and declaring His sovereign substitution, Jesus is bound and led away (vv. 12–13a). He turns Himself over to His enemies. The King's amazing sovereignty gives way to the Lamb's equally amazing submission.

The Lamb's Threefold Submission

The Lamb's Willingness to be Arrested

We first see Christ's submission in His willingness to be arrested. Verse 12 says, "Then the band and the captain and officers of the Jews took Jesus." The original word translated "took" is actually the official term for a formal arrest. So the soldiers formally arrest Jesus for the purpose of charging Him. And Christ willingly submits. See how the Good Shepherd is willing to lay down His life for His sheep! Behold the voluntary offering of Christ! See how He lays down His life, and no one takes it from Him (John 10:17–18).

---

5. D. A. Carson, *The Gospel according to John* (Grand Rapids: Eerdmans, 1991), 579.
6. Spurgeon, "The Captive Savior Freeing His People," 12:652.

Spurgeon said, "You are clear that he went willingly, for since a single word made the captors fall to the ground, what could he not have done? Another word and they would have descended into the tomb; another, and they would have been hurled into hell.... There was no power on earth that could possibly have bound the Lord Jesus, had he been unwilling."[7] Instead, the sovereign, speaking King willingly becomes a submissive, silent Lamb.

Jesus wasn't intimidated. He believed the promises of the word of God that He would have God with Him. He believed the prophecies of that word would be fulfilled. Jesus knew that this was His Father's appointed hour of suffering. All history had been moving toward this hour of Jesus's arrest and crucifixion. God had been at work during all the previous centuries from the creation of the world and the fall of man, down to this very night, with this hour ever before Him. God willed it, God planned it, God worked it all out. The incarnate Son of God, Jesus of Nazareth, the Son of man, is publicly arrested and taken. No one can tamper with God's plan—not Judas, Caiaphas, Herod, or Pilate, much less the fearful disciples. God decreed the rise and fall of nations and empires for this end; He decreed that the high priest and his cohorts should conspire to kill Jesus, that Judas should betray Him into their hands, that wicked King Herod and weak Pontius Pilate should fall in with their plans. So Jesus knew what was coming. Satan's hour had arrived, but ultimately it would be Jesus's hour. In dying, He would destroy the devil who had the power of death (Heb. 2:14). He would make the destruction of death itself an absolute certainty.

Jesus knew that His hour had also come—*His* hour! He wasn't afraid because His Father, the God of providence, with His hand of almighty and everywhere present power, was in absolute control. Judas, Caiaphas, Herod, Pilate, the Roman soldiers, and the Jerusalem multitude could not so much as move without His will. That same God is in control of your life also. Nothing happens because of chance. When your worst fears are realized, it isn't that the Son of God has stepped away from the throne of the universe, abdicating responsibility for what is happening and abandoning you to the evil that is in the world. Rather, He is operating among the affairs of men. Do you believe the paraphrase of Psalm 115 in Psalter 308, stanza 1:

> Not unto us, O Lord of heaven,
> But unto Thee be glory given;
> In love and truth Thou dost fulfill
> The counsels of Thy sov'reign will;

---

7. Spurgeon, "The Captive Savior Freeing His People," 650.

> Though nations fail Thy power to own,
> Yet Thou dost reign, and Thou alone!

And with William Cowper:

> Blind unbelief is sure to err
> And scan His work in vain
> God is His own interpreter
> And He will make it plain.

Everything that happens to us is according to a plan and timetable that was fixed before the foundation of the world. No one but the Lamb of God has been found worthy to execute that plan for the salvation of His people. What befalls us in this life is all part of the will of our Father in heaven as executed by our Savior. What a comfort for a Christian!

The Lamb's Willingness to Be Bound
Second, we see Christ's submission in His willingness to be bound. Jesus's hands are chained like those of a murderer or criminal. Tradition claims that when people were arrested to be brought to a Roman judge, the accusers bound the hands of the accused so tightly that blood came out of the ends of their fingers. The goal was to prejudice the judge against the accused and so incline him to find the accused guilty as charged. That is probably what the soldiers do to Jesus. The soldiers bind the hands of One who would gladly have gone with them unfettered. They bind the blessed hands of One who never sinned, healed the lame and the blind, and blessed little children. They bind the hands of One who washed His disciples' feet and broke bread for them in the upper room. They bind the hands that have dripped with bloody sweat in prayer to the Father. Yet Jesus offers His hands to be bound in meekness and humility.

Jesus's bound hands are symbolic of much more. Let me mention four ways this is so.

First, Jesus is bound to set us free from the bands of sin. Proverbs 5:22 says that by nature we are "holden with the cords of [our] sin." By grace, Jesus became sin for us (2 Cor. 5:21). Fettered with our sins, He let Himself be arrested and be held captive to free us from the captivity of sin and Satan and from the bondage of being prisoners of hell. As Rollock observed, Christ's bondage corresponds to and counteracts our being bound as captives to sin, the devil, and death. He is a fit Redeemer for sinners because He was bound as we were.[8] Therefore, when He arose and ascended on high, He led captivity captive—bound by the cords of love—to capture His people in the net of His substitutionary gospel. By His Spirit, He is still drawing sinners with those bands of love today.

Second, Jesus is bound so that His people might be bound to Him by obedience and love to serve Him all their days. When they see Him voluntarily bound for their sake, they become willing to be His servants forever. When they see Him bound for their sake, no persecution becomes too much. When they view His bonds, their afflictions and trials are sweetened and sanctified. They may even rejoice in suffering under His banner of love like Paul and Silas, who sang in prison and counted it joy that they were reckoned worthy to suffer for Christ's sake (Acts 16:25). When the early church father Ignatius was bound and chained for confessing Christ, he regarded his bands as spiritual pearls. Do you know the joy of being bound for Christ's sake as His willing servant? Do you ever feel the sweetness of His bonds in pastoral ministry when you are persecuted for Christ's sake?

Third, Jesus is bound as the last Adam to restore in the garden of Gethsemane what was lost by the first Adam in the garden of Eden: (1) The first Adam sinned in the garden of Eden; the last Adam bore sin in the garden of Gethsemane. (2) The first Adam was surrounded with glory, beauty, and harmony in Eden and refused to obey; the last Adam was surrounded with bitterness and sorrow in Gethsemane and was obedient unto death. (3) The first Adam was tempted by Satan and fell; the last Adam was tempted by all the forces of hell and did not fall. (4) The first Adam's hands reached out to grasp sin; the last Adam's hands were bound to pay for sin. (5) The first Adam was guilty and arrested by God during the cool of the day; the last Adam was innocent and arrested by men in the middle of the night. (6) The first Adam hid himself after fleeing; the last Adam revealed Himself after walking into the moonlight. (7) The first Adam took fruit from Eve's hand; the last Adam took the cup from His Father's hand. (8) The first Adam was conquered by the devil; the last Adam conquered the devil. (9) The first Adam forfeited and lost grace in Eden; the last Adam merited and applied grace in Gethsemane. (10) The first Adam was driven out of Eden; the last Adam was willingly led out of Gethsemane so that room might be made in the heavenly garden of paradise for sinners who trusted in Him. Praise be to God—Christ regained all that was lost in Adam and more; in Eden, the sword was drawn and the conflict

---

8. Rollock, *Select Works*, 2:39.

of the ages began; in Gethsemane the sword was sheathed, and the eternal gospel was displayed.

Finally, Jesus is bound above all by the will of the Father. "He spared not His own Son" that His people might be spared. His being bound is one of the ingredients of the cup that He had to swallow in paying for the sins of His people. He was bound to Himself and to His own work, which He had undertaken from eternity. He was bound to fulfill the eternal covenant of redemption. God bound to God—how wondrous our God of salvation is!

In the Garden of Gethsemane, Christ is the lowly Servant of the Lord. He did not come to earth to do His own will but to do the will of Him who sent Him. As Isaiah 42:1–2 tells us, Jesus was the obedient Servant of the Lord whom God chose, in whom God delights, and upon whom God puts His Spirit. Likewise, it pleases the Lord to bruise Him as the suffering Servant, to put Him to grief, and to make His soul an offering for sin (Isaiah 53). Jesus thus moves ahead with quiet determination to do God's will. As He says in John 10:17–18, "Therefore doth my Father love me, because I lay down my life, that I might take it again. No man taketh it from me, but I lay it down of myself. I have power to lay it down, and I have power to take it again. This commandment have I received of my Father."

The Lamb's Willingness to Be Led Away

Third, we see the Lamb's submission in His being led away. The Leader and Shepherd of God's people is led away as a "lamb to the slaughter." "He was oppressed, and he was afflicted, yet he opened not his mouth: he is brought as a lamb to the slaughter, and as a sheep before her shearers is dumb, so he openeth not his mouth" (Isa. 53:7).

It is remarkable how fully this prophecy was fulfilled. Sheep that were fed in the fields of Cedron were often led through a sheep-gate to be sacrificed. This was a type of the messianic Lamb of God to come, for the Lamb of lambs is now led through that same gate to be sacrificed. He is led from place to place like a wandering sheep so that you and I, who are wandering sheep, might find rest and guidance in Him.

Jesus is led a total distance of seven miles before being crucified. He is led from Annas to Caiaphas to Pilate to Herod, back to Pilate and then to the cross to be crucified. What a wonder that this innocent Lamb not only lets Himself be taken and bound but is willing to be taken from place to place while knowing that His end will be the cross!

Let us ever thank the triune God for our great substitutionary Lamb, who was led away so that we might one day be led into heavenly mansions! Have you ever seen such a complete and willing substitute? Praise God that He was taken for criminals, bound for captives, and led away for wanderers.

In the midst of it all, He was a willing, submissive servant. We are like sponges soaked in salt water: when people press on us, we squirt out bitter words of complaint and resentment. But when Christ is crushed under malice and hatred, not one evil word comes out of His mouth. His gentleness reveals that He is a perfect Savior from sin and a perfect example for us.

We read in 1 Peter 2:21–25, "For even hereunto were ye called: because Christ also suffered for us, leaving us an example, that ye should follow his steps: who did no sin, neither was guile found in his mouth: who, when he was reviled, reviled not again; when he suffered, he threatened not; but committed himself to him that judgeth righteously: who his own self bare our sins in his own body on the tree, that we, being dead to sins, should live unto righteousness: by whose stripes ye were healed. For ye were as sheep going astray; but are now returned unto the Shepherd and Bishop of your souls."

Conclusion

Jesus is the Lord God Almighty, the great *I Am*. His very name and word can bring men and angels to their knees. He is a Savior for the lost, a Redeemer for the guilty, a Physician for the sick, a Friend for the needy, an Intercessor for the sin-accused, an Advocate for the law-condemned, a Surety for the debt-plagued, a Healer for the brokenhearted, a Helper for the self-ruined, and an altogether lovely Bridegroom for an unfaithful bride. He is everything we need.

We cannot imagine a fuller redemption or a deeper love than what is provided by Gethsemane's Lamb. He who is taken and arrested also takes and arrests sinners, causing them to cry out, "What must I do to be saved?" He who is bound binds His people so that they declare death on their self-righteousness and flee to Christ alone. He who is led away leads sinners to see that salvation is exclusively in Him and applies it to them so that they glorify Him for His full and free salvation.

Apart from His great love for us, nothing explains our Lord's willingness to be arrested, bound, and led away; but in so doing He shows Himself to be the perfect Christ for His own. He is *arrested* so that He can arrest us as our Prophet and bring us from darkness into His marvelous light. He is *bound* so that we can be freed from the burden of sin and guilt that threatens to destroy us, when as both Priest and victim He offers an acceptable sacrifice to God on our behalf. He is *led away* so He can govern us as our King by His word and Spirit, leading us back to God, and preserving, guiding, and defending us in the salvation He has purchased for us.

How unspeakably beautiful is our Lord Jesus Christ! Jonathan Edwards (1703–1758) said, "In the person of Christ do meet together infinite majesty, and transcendent meekness."[9] This, Edwards said, is what makes Christ so very excellent. He is the mighty and terrifying King, at whose presence the earth quakes. Yet He exhibits the greatest humility, even under the bitter attacks and injuries of His enemies. May Christ's unique combination of majesty and meekness win your heart to forever adore Him.

What a wonder it is that the great Deliverer delivers Himself up; the divinely appointed Judge is arrested as a common criminal; the great Liberator is bound; the great Leader is led away. Let us praise Gethsemane's Christ, the King of Kings and the Lamb of God, and resolve to trust Him more fully, follow Him more obediently, and look the more expectantly for His return to take us to Himself. Let us take with us five practical ways in which Christ as Gethsemane's King and Lamb should impact our faith and life:

+ Let us honor His authority as King with greater fear and reverence.

+ Let us submit to the trials He imposes on us without complaint—indeed, with cheerfulness and thanksgiving—so that we may drink the cup He places in our hands rather than to plead for another.

+ Let us learn to know when silence is a more powerful testimony in the presence of evil and unbelief than any words we might say.

+ Like Paul, let us cherish the privilege of being admitted to the fellowship of His sufferings.

+ Let us honor His giving up of Himself for us with more complete surrender of ourselves to Him so that we would request to be His willing servant, now and forever.

---

9. *The Works of Jonathan Edwards, Volume 19, Sermons and Discourses, 1734–1738*, ed. M. X. Lesser (New Haven: Yale University Press, 2001), 568.

Chapter 5

The Man of Sin:
2 Thessalonians 2:1–12

Persecution remains a sobering reality for the church of Jesus Christ today. True Christians live under the shadow of the cross. When Paul wrote his second epistle to the believers in Thessalonica, he noted that they suffered "persecutions and tribulations" for being Christians (2 Thess. 1:4) yet they persevered in faith, hope, and love. Therefore, he encouraged them with the promise of Christ to punish the wicked and glorify His saints (2 Thess. 1:6–10). However, Paul had learned that this church was also troubled by false doctrine concerning Christ's return. Thus in 2 Thessalonians 2 he reminds them of the doctrine of "the man of sin," whom we also call the "antichrist."[1]

The man of sin is the embodiment and consummation of satanic evil. He has been the subject of many frightening legends through the centuries and continues to fascinate many today in "end-time" predictions, books, and movies. However, God's purpose in this part of His Word is not to frighten or disturb us but to comfort us (2 Thess. 2:17). Let us, therefore, not approach this topic with a morbid interest in evil. Nor should we come away from this subject dreading the future and desiring to escape from it. The Holy Spirit inspired these words to encourage believers in their faith and to give them the solid hope that cannot be shaken.

The great lesson about the man of sin is that although Satan, "that old serpent called the devil" (Rev. 12:9), will seduce the world with lies and idolatry, Christ will crush this serpent's head (Gen. 3:15). Satan's campaign to establish a kingdom of evil and a cult of false worship on earth will only serve God's purpose to punish those who reject God's truth. All the power of Satan and the wrath of men will only result in glory to God, especially thanksgiving for our salvation through Jesus Christ (Ps. 76:10; 1 Thess. 2:13–14).

---

1. The term *antichrist* comes from John's epistles (1 John 2:18, 22; 4:3; 2 John 7), though the Lord Jesus did speak of "false Christs" (Matt. 24:24; Mark 13:22).

In speaking about the man of sin, we will address three matters in this sermon: (1) God's revelation of the man of sin, (2) God's restraint of the man of sin; and (3) God's reason for the man of sin.

God's Revelation of the Man of Sin

In 2 Thessalonians 2, Paul addresses the problem of false teaching in the church. The devil had brought this false teaching into the minds of these believers, where it stirred up much confusion and distress. They were "shaken in mind" and "troubled" (v. 2).

The Disturbing Effects of False Doctrine

Paul writes in 2 Thessalonians 2:1–2, "Now we beseech you, brethren, by the coming of our Lord Jesus Christ, and by our gathering together unto him, that ye be not soon shaken in mind, or be troubled, neither by spirit, nor by word, nor by letter as from us, as that the day of Christ is at hand." The first words could be translated, "We ask you, brothers, concerning the coming of our Lord."[2] The Thessalonians had been disturbed by misinformation about the second coming. Note that Paul does not rebuke these believers but uses the gentle "we beseech you" or "ask you" to lovingly instruct them in the truth about Christ's return. Let this remind us not to harshly rebuke those who err in the doctrine of the end times, for true Christians can be misinformed and confused on this subject.

Paul also wrote about the return of our Savior in 1 Thessalonians 4 and 5, and Christ addressed the matter in Matthew 24. The key word "coming" (*parousía*, vv. 1, 8) used of Christ's return is also apparent in the teaching of Jesus and Paul (Matt. 24:3, 27, 37, 39; 1 Thess. 4:15). Just as Paul has told believers of the resurrection of the godly dead and the "catching up" of all believers to meet Christ and be with Him forever (1 Thess. 4:16–17), so here Paul writes of "our gathering together unto him."[3] The noun translated "gathering together" (*episunagōgē*) comes from the same root as the verb that appears in Matthew 24:31, "He shall send his angels with a great sound of a trumpet, and they shall *gather together* his elect."[4] Paul, who has written of "the day of the Lord" (1 Thess. 5:2), now writes of "the day of Christ."

---

2. The word "by" (2 Thess. 2:1) translates *hupèr* with the genitive, a construction that generally means "for," "in the place of," "with reference to," or "concerning."

3. F. F. Bruce, *1 & 2 Thessalonians*, Word Biblical Commentary 45 (Waco, Tex.: Word, 1982), 163.

4. Compare *episunagōgē* (1 Thess. 2:1) with *episunágō* (Matt. 24:31).

A serious misunderstanding about Christ's return had arisen in the Thessalonian church. They had heard that "the day of Christ is at hand." They did not think that Christ might come at any moment but that Christ *had come already* (the verb "is at hand" means "is present.")[5] False teachers had probably spiritualized Christ's return and the resurrection of the saints, saying that those were not future, visible, physical events (1 Cor. 15:12) but invisible, spiritual events that had already happened (2 Tim 2:18).[6] Paul did say that in a spiritual sense we are already "raised up with Christ" (Eph. 2:6), but he also said that we still await the coming of Christ in glory to raise His people from the dead (1 Cor. 15:22–23). False teaching collapsed the future into the present and denied a visible, bodily return of Christ to earth, in a manner similar to ancient skeptics who said "there is no resurrection of the dead" (1 Cor. 15:12) and modern skeptics who claim to be Christians even as they "de-mythologize" the Bible.[7] Another similar teaching today is "full preterism," which asserts that all New Testament prophecies of Christ's return were fulfilled in the destruction of Jerusalem in AD 70.

The presence of false teaching in the church is greatly disturbing. Paul did not seem to know whether that happened by a prophecy ("spirit"), a teaching ("word"), or a written communication ("letter"). The point was not how it happened but the effect it had on the church: Christians were "shaken in mind" and "troubled." The word *shaken* can refer to an earthquake that causes buildings to collapse.[8] You can imagine how this false teaching would rock the world of believers, for they had endured all kinds of persecution in hope of Christ's coming again, and now they heard that He had already come and there was no hope of a future coming or resurrection of the dead! The words *shaken* and *troubled* also appear in Matthew 24. Paul thus counseled believers that when they felt like their world was coming to an end they must not allow themselves to be distressed, for the end had not yet come.[9]

False doctrine continues to disturb the church of Jesus Christ today. It throws the church into confusion, discouragement, disorder, and division.

---

5. Perfect *enístēmi*. Cf. Rom. 8:38; 1 Cor. 3:22; 7:26; Gal. 1:4; 2 Tim. 3:1; Heb. 9:9.

6. G. K. Beale, *1–2 Thessalonians*, The IVP New Testament Commentary Series (Downers Grove: InterVarsity, 2003), 200.

7. Rudolf Bultmann, "New Testament and Mythology," in *Kerygma and Myth: A Theological Debate*, ed. Hans Werner Bartsch, trans. Reginald H. Fuller (London: S.P.C.K., 1954), 4–5.

8. Greek *saleúō*. Cf. Luke 6:48; Acts 4:31; 16:26; Heb. 12:26–27.

9. The verb "shaken" (*saleúō*) is used of the eschatological shaking of the cosmos (Matt. 24:29; par. Mark 13:25; par. Luke 21:26; Heb. 12:26–27). The verb "troubled" (*throéō*) appears only here and in Matt. 24:6 (par. Mark 13:7), "And ye shall hear of wars and rumours of wars: see that ye be not troubled."

Ministers and elders must thus guard the church from false doctrine (Acts 20:28–31; Titus 1:9). Christ gave pastors and teachers to the church to build it up "in the unity of the faith…that we henceforth be no more children, tossed to and fro, and carried about with every wind of doctrine, by the sleight of men, and cunning craftiness, whereby they lie in wait to deceive" (Eph. 4:11–14).

When your pastors "contend for the faith which was once delivered unto the saints" (Jude 3) by patiently confronting and correcting those who oppose the truth, do not discourage them. Such pastors are doing their work to protect the flock. They are guarding your hearts, confirming your faith, and securing your future in Christ.

The Prediction of End-Time Apostasy

Paul responded to the Thessalonians' distress by teaching them that certain things must happen before the return of the Lord. He writes in 2 Thessalonians 2:3–4, "Let no man deceive you by any means: for that day shall not come, except there come a falling away first, and that man of sin be revealed, the son of perdition; who opposeth and exalteth himself above all that is called God, or that is worshipped; so that he as God sitteth in the temple of God, shewing himself that he is God."

The apostle reminds Christians to resist Satan's lies, saying, "Let no man deceive you." You cannot be like a piece of driftwood floating wherever human opinion carries you. You must set your course by the Word of God and steadily resist everything that would draw you away from it. The Bible resounds with warnings not to let people deceive you.[10] You cannot just throw up your hands and give up on understanding biblical doctrine but must "hear, read, mark, learn, and inwardly digest" the Holy Scriptures.[11] Think of the "noble Bereans" who "received the word with all readiness of mind, and searched the scriptures daily, whether those things were so" (Acts 17:11). In this passage Paul again echoes Christ's words in Matthew 24:4, "Take heed that no man deceive you." Jesus taught that the last days will be times of great deception (Matt. 24:5, 11, 24), and Paul was already warning people in his day that they could see signs of it all around (2 Tim. 3:1–13).

Paul's response reminds us that Christ's coming is a future historical event, not a private experience. It occurs in the flow of human events and is preceded by certain events. He names two such events that must come before Christ returns: "a falling away" and the revelation of "the man of sin."

---

10. Jer. 29:8; Gal. 6:7; Eph. 5:6; Col. 2:8; James 1:16; 1 John 3:7.
11. "Collect for the Second Sunday in Advent," *Book of Common Prayer* (1662).

"Falling away," or apostasy, refers to abandoning the beliefs, practices, and fellowship once held.[12] The apostate Christian or church ceases to "continue in the apostles' doctrine and fellowship" (Acts 2:42). This apostasy does not refer to the falling away of ethnic Israel, since that apostasy had already occurred. Most Jews at that time did not believe in Jesus Christ so could not fall away from the true faith and the true church (1 Thess. 2:14–16).[13] But Christ warns in Matthew 24:11–13 that in the last days many professing Christians will turn away from the truth and fall into unbelief and ungodliness: "Many false prophets shall rise, and shall deceive many. And because iniquity shall abound, the love of many shall wax cold. But he that shall endure unto the end, the same shall be saved." Paul likewise says in 1 Timothy 4:1, "Now the Spirit speaketh expressly, that in the latter times some shall depart from the faith, giving heed to seducing spirits, and doctrines of devils." This end-time apostasy will cause many professing Christians to forsake the church of Christ.

When we see professing Christians, local congregations, even entire denominations fall away from the truth, we should not be shocked. Our Lord told us that apostasy would be part of the history of His church. Whether we consider the inroads of Gnosticism in early Christianity; the temporary triumph of Arianism in the early church of the Roman Empire; the false doctrine, hierarchy, and sacraments of the Roman Catholic Church in the medieval period; the rejection of biblical authority and inerrancy by many Protestant churches since the nineteenth century; or the unbiblical embrace of homosexuality by various denominations today, the deadly pattern of apostasy is repeated again and again. The question is: Will we remain faithful? While the Bible teaches that true believers can never fully fall away (Jer. 32:40; John 6:39; 10:28), it also warns us that many who respond positively to God's Word at first will later reject it (Luke 8:13). It also says churches may lose their first love, compromise with error, or become morally bankrupt and spiritually dead (Revelation 2–3).

Paul predicted that the end-time falling away would be associated with or led by "the man of sin," or "the man of lawlessness" as some Greek manuscripts read (2 Thess. 2:3).[14] Later in verse 8 this man of sin is called "the lawless one"

---

12. Greek *apostasía*. Cf. Gerhard Kittel, Geoffrey W. Bromiley, and Gerhard Friedrich, eds., *Theological Dictionary of the New Testament* (Grand Rapids: Eerdmans, 1964), 1:512–14. Beale notes that the term can refer to political changes, but in the Greek Old Testament and New Testament, it always refers to religious crises (Josh. 22:22; 2 Chron. 29:19; Jer. 2:19; 1 Macc. 2:15; Acts 21:21). Beale, *1–2 Thessalonians*, 203.

13. Beale, *1–2 Thessalonians*, 207.

14. The Byzantine manuscripts, with A D F G, read "sin" (*hamartías*), but the eclectic text follows other manuscripts (א B etc.) which read "lawlessness" (*anomías*). "For the larger context, the difference is

(*ho ánomos*; "that wicked one"), to whom the law of God means nothing. The expression "man of" is idiomatic for someone characterized by a particular trait or activity, such as a "man of war" or a soldier (1 Sam. 17:33), or "man of God," a minister or servant of God (2 Tim. 3:17). Literally, the text calls him "the man" (*ho ánthrōpos*). Therefore, this person is *the preeminent sinner* in human history. He is "the son of perdition" who is destined for eternal destruction.[15]

"Man of sin" and "son of perdition" refer to two great enemies of Christ and His church.[16] Paul thought it might have been the person who sought to compel the Jews to forsake the faith of their fathers for a more modern or "Hellenized" version. His name was Antiochus IV, surnamed Epiphanes or "God made manifest," of whom Daniel prophesied[17] and whom the Maccabean Jews called "the sinner" and the "man of sin" (1 Macc. 2:48, 62).[18] Paul also relates "the man of sin" to Judas Iscariot, whom Christ called "the son of perdition" (John 17:12).[19] Thus, this person might be a wicked king who corrupts the state and persecutes the godly, or an apostate official in the church who promotes false doctrine and betrays Christ by turning many from the truth and leading many into sin.

Paul identified this evil person as an "antichrist" or counterfeit messiah who has yet to be "revealed" (2 Thess. 2:3, 6, 8). Paul had just written in 2 Thessalonians 1:7, "The Lord Jesus shall be revealed from heaven with his mighty angels."[20] Verse 8 of our text tells about the "coming" of Christ, using the Greek word *parousía*, which is the same word used in verse 9 to announce the "coming" of the man of sin. Paul is saying that in some ways, this person appears like Christ, even though he is the polar opposite of Christ. Just as Christ's "coming" will reveal Him as King of Kings, so the antichrist will appear as a king with supernatural powers.[21]

The man of sin seeks to usurp the place of God as the supreme king and warlord. Verse 4 says that he "opposeth and exalteth himself above all that is called God, or that is worshiped." Paul alludes to Daniel 11:36, "The king shall

---

slight." Rick Brannan and Israel Loken, *The Lexham Textual Notes on the Bible*, Lexham Bible Reference Series (Bellingham, Wash.: Lexham Press, 2014), on 2 Thess. 2:3.

15. The Greek word translated "perdition" (*apōleia*) means destruction or ruin.

16. Thomas Manton, *Eighteen Sermons on the Second Chapter of the Second Epistle to the Thessalonians*, in *The Works of Thomas Manton* (1871; repr., Edinburgh: Banner of Truth, 1993), 3:31–33.

17. See Dan. 8:9–14, 21–25; 11:31–35; 12:11.

18. Compare *ho ánthrōpos tēs hamartías* (2 Thess. 2:3) to *anēr hamartoloũ* (1 Macc. 2:62).

19. In both John 17:12 and 2 Thess. 2:3, the phrase is *ho huiòs tēs apōleías*.

20. Compare *apokalúptō* (2 Thess. 2:3, 6, 8) with *apokálupsis* (2 Thess. 1:7; cf. 1 Cor. 1:7; 1 Peter 1:7, 13; 4:13).

21. Christ spoke three times of "the coming [parousia] of the Son of man" (Matt. 24:27, 37, 39), an allusion to the prophecy of Dan. 7:13–14, in which the Son of man receives a universal kingdom.

do according to his will; and he shall exalt himself, and magnify himself above every god, and shall speak marvellous things against the God of gods, and shall prosper till the indignation be accomplished: for that that is determined shall be done." Daniel described this king as an arrogant person who deifies war, conquers nations, and troubles God's people until the dead are raised (Dan. 11:37–12:3). Though some scholars believe this passage continues the description of Antiochus Epiphanes (Dan. 11:31–35), others believe Daniel was referring to another king who would reign in the last days.[22] Clearly Paul looks ahead to the antichrist as he cites these words from Daniel describing the antichrist as an arrogant man who claims to be the God of all gods. The antichrist embodies the principle of human government as an absolutist, totalitarian ruler who persecutes God's people (Rev. 13:1–7).

Antichrist, however, appears to be not a pagan king so much as a Judas among God's people. We are told he "sitteth in the temple of God." That implies that the man of sin enthrones himself in the priestly office, as if he should receive worship and be a mediator of worship, even though he defiles God's temple.[23] According to Daniel 11:37–38, "he shall magnify himself above all," and "honour the God of forces." He is a god of war, not "the God of his fathers." This false god is the deification of war, just as the antichrist is the deification of fallen man, and both personify the great murderer Satan (Rev. 13:4). Paul did not say the man of sin declares himself to be God or says, "I am God," but that he "shows" or "publicly presents" himself as God by his actions. He does so by "sitting"—a picture of his enthronement.[24] The antichrist acts like the ruler of God's holy worship.[25]

The antichrist seizes a central place in the church and seeks to displace God in public worship. Some Christians have understood the temple to refer to the physical building in Jerusalem,[26] but this use of "temple" (naós) in Paul's writings

---

22. Stephen R. Miller, *Daniel*, The New American Commentary 18 (Nashville: Broadman & Holman, 1994), 304–306.

23. There may be an allusion here to the abomination of desolation in the temple, such as Antiochus's defiling the temple in his wars against the Jews and the Romans' defilement of the temple (Dan. 11:31; Matt. 24:15). However, the abomination texts do not speak of someone sitting in the temple.

24. On sitting as the posture of a ruler, compare Ps. 29:10b, "Yea, the LORD sitteth King for ever."

25. "The idea may be that the antichrist assumes so much influence and religious authority in the worldwide community of faith that he might as well be calling himself God." Beale, *1–2 Thessalonians*, 210.

26. For example, see Irenaeus, *Against Heresies*, 5.30.4, in *The Ante-Nicene Fathers*, ed. Alexander Roberts and James Donaldson (New York: Charles Scribner's Sons), 1:560. Henceforth cited as *ANF*. For his teachings on the antichrist, see *Against Heresies*, 5.25.1–4; 5.28.2; 5.29.2; 5.30.1–4, in *ANF*, 1:553–54, 557–60.

is unusual, for elsewhere Paul says that the temple of God is not a building of stone but is the living members of Christ's body, the church.[27] As noted earlier, Paul envisioned a great apostasy in the visible or professing church. The temple mentioned here is therefore the church. Paul predicted that a large portion of the professing church would fall into apostasy and turn from the Lord to worship the world's greatest sinner. That will be man's greatest insult to God, and it will not go unpunished.

Let us pause for a moment to consider what this prophecy reveals about *our* sin. "The man of sin" embodies the worst form of human evil. If we would see the essence and magnitude of our sin, look at the antichrist. The essence of sin in us is an arrogant attempt to cast God off His throne and take His place so that the world glorifies us, not God. Sin at its core is hatred of God because He is God (Rom. 1:21, 23, 25, 28, 30; 8:7). Just as the first and Great Commandment is to "love the Lord thy God with all thy heart, and with all thy soul, and with all thy mind" (Matt. 22:37), so sin—all sin and every sin—is hatred against God. And yet hatred against God can hide in man's most religious and worshipful activities.

Do not look upon the man of sin as if he were some alien power that invades our world and takes us captive against our will. He is *man*, the embodiment of fallen humanity. Just as Christ is the man of obedience, the last Adam who has begotten a new human race that lives to glorify God and enjoy Him forever, so the man of sin is the man of disobedience, who represents the old human race, to which we all belong by nature in the first Adam. The world and many in the professing church will follow the antichrist because he embodies all that we desire unless God gives us new hearts.

Therefore, the proper application of this doctrine is not to be afraid of the man of sin but to fear and grieve over our own sin. Oh, how wicked and rebellious is the human heart that we hate our Creator and strive to dethrone Him! What are we who have the Bible as our guide that we would rush to follow such a blasphemer against God? How right it is for God to pour out His wrath upon sinners and punish them! If God removed His restraining hand and permitted Satan to do his will, any one of us could become the man of sin and rejoice in it until judgment falls. However, God does restrain sin in this world, and in particular, He restrains or holds back the man of sin.

---

27. 1 Cor. 3:16–17; 6:19; 2 Cor. 6:16; Eph. 2:21; cf. Eph. 3:16–19; 1 Tim. 3:15. In 1 Cor. 9:13, Paul refers to the priestly rituals of the Jewish "temple" (*hierón*); this seems to be his only reference to the physical temple.

God's Restraint of the Man of Sin

Although the fallen world, the apostate church, and the man of sin may rage against God, they "imagine a vain thing," says Psalm 2:1–3. They take counsel together against the Lord and against His Christ, but God remains firmly in control. The Lord will give Satan a limited time of freedom, but the devil cannot do anything without God's permission (Job 1:10, 12).

The Mystery of "Limited Lawlessness"

Paul writes in 2 Thessalonians 2:5–7, "Remember ye not, that, when I was yet with you, I told you these things? And now ye know what withholdeth that he might be revealed in his time. For the mystery of iniquity doth already work: only he who now letteth will let, until he be taken out of the way." "To let" means "to obstruct or hinder." Paul begins these verses by saying, "Remember." Sometimes preachers must remind people of what they already know, and such reminders are profitable for us (2 Tim. 2:14; 2 Peter 1:12). So when you hear something from the Word of God that you heard before, say, "I need to hear this again, for I do not yet believe it and obey it as I should."

Evidently Paul had given believers substantial instruction in the doctrine of the last things (eschatology) while he was in Thessalonica. He is a model for pastors. I fully understand why we might shy away from teaching on these matters, for I have felt the same way at times. But the end of this age and the beginning of the age to come are revealed in the whole counsel of God, which we must preach and teach (Acts 20:27). They are part of God's Word and therefore "profitable for doctrine, for reproof, for correction, for instruction in righteousness" (2 Tim. 3:16).

Some places in Scripture, however, are "hard to be understood" (2 Peter 3:16), and this is one of them. Paul is building on truths he had already taught and does not fully explain what he has in mind. Therefore, let us go as far as the text of Scripture allows us but no farther, lest we get lost in a labyrinth of speculation.

Paul says, "The mystery of iniquity doth already work." The forces personified in the man of sin are already active in our world. A "mystery" is something that we do not know until God reveals it to us (Rom. 16:25; Eph. 3:3–4). There is a mystery about "iniquity" or lawlessness (anomía), for we do not understand the depth of our sinfulness until God reveals it to us in all its ugliness (cf. Rev. 17:5). The power of sin is also in the world, and the principle of antichrist is at work around us. According to the Bible, the last days began with Christ's first coming, death, resurrection, and ascension into heaven.[28] We are living in the last days. Therefore, we are dealing with powers and principles that have raised their ugly heads during the last two thousand years and will one day culminate in a grand apostasy and final manifestation of Satan's power.

First John 2:18 tells us, "Little children, it is the last time: and as ye have heard that antichrist [literally, 'the antichrist'] shall come, even now are there many antichrists; whereby we know that it is the last time." So while one great antichrist is yet to come, many lesser antichrists have already appeared as false teachers who draw people away from the true gospel of Christ and the church (1 John 2:19, 22, 4:3; 2 John 7). Note that John links antichrist to people in the church who are falling away, just as Paul links apostasy with the coming of the man of sin. Though there are many antichrists, the man of sin is *the* antichrist.

What prevents the man of sin from arising out of heretical movements at any point in history? God restrains it. The phrases "what withholdeth" and "he who now letteth" translate the same verb (*katéchō*), which means "to hold firmly" or "to hold back." It may also mean "to hold down" or "to suppress" (Rom. 1:18). So the forces that would bring forth the man of sin are already present with us today but are restrained and suppressed by some power. The word for this power is both neuter and masculine, deepening the mystery. This person or power has restrained and will restrain the man of sin until he is "taken out of the way."

What is this power that restrains? Interpreters have offered various explanations.

+ The restrainer is *the church*, which will be raptured away at the beginning of the tribulation. However, as seen in 1 Thessalonians 4 and 5, the biblical doctrine of rapture is not a secret event separate from the day of the Lord. Christ will rapture the church when He comes in visible glory on the day of the Lord. Furthermore, the church does not fit Paul's words here, for the Greek word for church (*ekklēsía*) is feminine, while this restrainer is described in neuter and masculine terms.

+ The restrainer is *civil government*. Tertullian thought so,[29] and Augustine said that it was a reasonable idea.[30] This interpretation has the strength of recognizing that God has ordained government to restrain moral evil

---

28. Acts 2:17; 1 Cor. 10:11; Heb. 1:2; 9:26; 1 Peter 1:20; 1 John 2:18; cf. Mark 1:15; John 4:21, 23; 5:25; Gal. 4:4.

29. "What obstacle is there but the Roman state, the falling away of which, by being scattered into ten kingdoms, shall introduce Antichrist upon (its own ruins)?" Tertullian, *The Resurrection of the Flesh*, 25, in *ANF*, 3:563. Cf. Rev. 17:12, 16.

30. Augustine, *The City of God*, 20.19, in *A Select Library of Nicene and Post-Nicene Fathers*, Series 1, ed. Philip Schaff (Buffalo, N.Y.: Christian Literature Co., 1887), 2:438. Henceforth cited as *NPNF1*.

(Rom. 13:1–4; 1 Peter 2:13–14).[31] The neuter gender could refer to the institution of government and the masculine to the civil magistrate or king. One problem with this interpretation is that civil government can be easily manipulated by Satan as a tool of the antichrist and false religion, not a power that restrains him (Dan. 3; Rev. 13). However, the collapse of legitimate civil authority can lead to chaos into which a charismatic leader can step to seize power.

- The restrainer is an *angel of God,* for we see angels in the Bible sent to restrain evil in this world (Dan. 10:13, 20–21; Rev. 20:1–3).[32]

- The restrainer is *the Holy Spirit* in His "common" or general operations. The word for Spirit (*pneūma*) in Greek is neuter, but the Spirit is a personal being and is referred to with masculine words (John 14:26; 15:26; 16:13–14). Paul says that Christ will destroy the man of sin "with the spirit of his mouth" (2 Thess. 2:8). John opposed "the spirit of antichrist" with "he that is in you," that is, "the Spirit of God" (1 John 4:2–4). The Holy Spirit cannot be removed from the earth, for as God, He is omnipresent (Ps. 139:7), but He can withdraw or cease from some of His operations. In this context, Paul emphasizes the power of the Holy Spirit to save people through the gospel, in contrast to the delusion of antichrist that ensnares those who reject the truth of the gospel (2 Thess. 2:10, 12–13; cf. 1 Thess. 1:5). Christ says in Matthew 24:14, "This gospel of the kingdom shall be preached in all the world for a witness unto all nations; and then shall the end come." Perhaps the Holy Spirit restrains the emergence of the great apostasy and the man of sin by empowering the gospel mission until that mission is complete. If so, then the man of sin, at least in his final manifestation, will appear only at the end of the age.

Whoever the restrainer may be, it is clear that God has the situation under control and will not permit the man of sin to be revealed until God's appointed time. Though the man of sin will be a horrendous enemy of God, we need not fear him. He is a dog on a leash. He is subject to God's timetable and plan. God will bring him out for God's purposes, then destroy him.

The Man of Satanic Deception and Doom

Paul goes on to write in 2 Thessalonians 2:8–10, "And then shall that Wicked [the Lawless One] be revealed, whom the Lord shall consume with the spirit of his mouth, and shall destroy with the brightness of his coming: even him,

---

31. Bruce, *1 & 2 Thessalonians,* 172, 176.
32. Beale, *1–2 Thessalonians,* 216–17, apparently favors this interpretation.

whose coming is after the working of Satan with all power and signs and lying wonders, and with all deceivableness of unrighteousness in them that perish; because they received not the love of the truth, that they might be saved."

To increase the confidence of believers so they do not fear the antichrist, Paul reminds them that Christ will overcome the man of sin. Paul describes this in two ways.

First, the Lord "shall consume"[33] the man of sin "with the spirit of his mouth." Paul is alluding to Isaiah 11:4, where the prophet describes the work of Messiah: "With righteousness shall he judge the poor, and reprove with equity for the meek of the earth: and he shall smite the earth with the rod of his mouth, and with the breath of his lips shall he slay the wicked." In their context, the words of Isaiah point to the King anointed by the Spirit of God to overcome sinners and reign in peace (Isa. 11:1–9).

Second, the antichrist will be "destroyed" by Christ's "appearing" (*epipháneia*, "brightness") in glory (1 Tim. 6:14; 2 Tim. 4:1, 8; Titus 2:13). His shining majesty in the skies will fill our hearts with joy. However, that same radiance is a holy flame that will consume all the powers and ambitions of the wicked, and the man who enthrones himself in God's temple will be cast into God's hell.

It is not entirely clear whether these descriptions represent two phases of antichrist's overthrow or one event described in two ways. Already Christ is ruling from heaven by the Holy Spirit's operations through the word of God, and it is possible that Paul is referring to Christ subduing antichrist partly during this age through the ministry of the gospel, and fully at Christ's return.[34] However, both clauses may also describe Christ's return, when He destroys His enemies with "the sword of His mouth" (Rev. 19:15, 21). Isaiah's words, "With the breath of his lips shall he slay the wicked," seem to look forward to judgment day.

The man of sin, however, will succeed for a while. Just as Christ will have His "coming" (1 Thess. 2:8), antichrist will also have his "coming" (v. 9), which are both referred to as *parousía*. Antichrist's coming will happen "after the working of Satan with all power and signs and lying wonders." Though he is not God, the man of sin will possess supernatural power from the devil. He is not merely a military or political leader but a miracle worker, just as the Egyptian sorcerers opposed Moses with miracles of their own (Ex. 7:11–12, 22; 8:7, 18–19).

---

33. The KJV follows the Byzantine reading *analṓsei* here, from *analóō* or *analískō*, which means to "use up, spend, waste, consume, kill, destroy," a NT *hapax legomenon*. See Henry George Liddell and Robert Scott, *A Greek-English Lexicon* (Oxford: Clarendon Press, 1996), 111. Other manuscripts read *analeî*, from *anairéō*, which means to "take up," and thus sometimes, "destroy, kill, cancel."

34. Manton, *Eighteen Sermons*, in *Works*, 3:60, 64.

Christ warns us of this in Matthew 24:24, "There shall arise false Christs, and false prophets, and shall shew great signs and wonders; insomuch that, if it were possible, they shall deceive the very elect." People are vulnerable to miracles, as we can see in both the Roman Catholic Church and modern Pentecostalism. Crowds will follow anyone who works wonders.

The miracles of the man of sin are part of Satan's work to deceive the lost (2 Thess. 2:10). Satan is the great deceiver of the world (2 Cor. 11:3; Rev. 12:9). He hooks men, women, and children through the nose with his lies and drags them to destruction. Antichrist will be Satan's greatest instrument of deception. Just as the man of sin is a self-anointed king and an idolatrous priest, so he is a false prophet; in all his usurped offices, he is a tool of the devil to lead sinners to hell.

The Identity of the Antichrist

Can we identify the antichrist based on what we have learned about him? We have sometimes spoken of him in the future tense because that is the perspective of the apostles, but is it possible that the antichrist has already appeared? Who is the man of sin? Rather than speculating about the news or playing number games with 666, we must find our answers by humbly listening to God's Word.[35]

Christian writers through the ages have proposed different identities for the man of sin.[36] We may group them into four major lines of thought: (1) Antichrist is not a church leader but a political or military leader, such as the Roman emperors Nero, Diocletian, or Julian the Apostate; a false Jewish Messiah; a false prophet, such as Mohammed; or a modern dictator, such as Stalin or Hitler. (2) Antichrist is not just one but all church leaders that teach heresy and persecute true believers. (3) Antichrist is the pope of Rome, not an individual pope, so much as the institution of the papacy that exalts itself, promotes heresy, and persecutes God's saints. That is the historic Lutheran and Reformed view. The Puritans embraced this view too, though many Puritans said that bishops in the Church of England who opposed sound doctrine were also antichrist (a version of the second view). (4) Antichrist is an individual who

---

35. Irenaeus noted that 666 can be derived from the numerical values of the letters *lateinos* in Greek, pointing to the Romans, but he also gave other possibilities and stated, "It is therefore more certain, and less hazardous, to await the fulfilment of the prophecy, than to be making surmises, and casting about for any names that may present themselves, inasmuch as many names can be found possessing the number mentioned." He tended to interpret 666 as a symbol for the recapitulation of all evil. Irenaeus, *Against Heresies*, 5.29.2; 5.30.3, in *ANF*, 1:558–59.

36. For a survey of these views with sources, see the appendix.

leads the church in apostasy at the end of the age. This last view is held by a number of Reformed theologians today.

We have already seen that the antichrist has the following characteristics: He is a man, not a demon or spirit. He is characterized by sin and lawlessness and so is the opposite of the incarnate Lord Jesus, the Righteous One. He counterfeits Christ in His offices, for he is a deceiving prophet, an idolatrous priest, and a tyrannical king. He is empowered by Satan to work miracles. He is associated with great apostasy in the church. He disregards the deities worshiped by men and demands the worship of himself, usurping the place of God in His temple. He will be revealed for a season at some time after the writing of this epistle, and then destroyed by the word and Spirit of Christ and the glory of Christ's coming to judge the world.

On the basis of these characteristics, we can eliminate the first line of interpretation. The man of sin cannot be merely a political or military leader but one who also is a leader in the church, for Paul foresees an apostasy within the church (2 Thess. 2:3–4; 1 Tim. 4:1). When John writes of "many antichrists" in distinction from the coming of the antichrist, he clearly refers to false teachers within the church (1 John 2:18, 22; 4:3; 2 John 7).

As for the second line of interpretation, we may legitimately call heretical teachers antichrists, but we should distinguish them from *the* antichrist. As John says, "Little children, it is the last time: and as ye have heard that antichrist [literally, 'the antichrist'] shall come, even now are there many antichrists; whereby we know that it is the last time" (1 John 2:18). It should not surprise us that there have been many false prophets and false Christs, for our Lord told us they would come. Yet these are not preeminently "the man of sin."

What about the third line of interpretation? There are good reasons to consider the pope of Rome to be the man of sin. In the institution of the papacy are concentrated all the characteristics about the man of sin. This is especially true of the papacy as it reached its height in the late medieval and early modern era, when the papacy was experienced by the Reformers and Puritans. Many medieval popes ("the black popes") were notorious sinners.

The papacy usurps the offices of Christ, for it makes a mere man into the supreme prophet whose teachings are infallible even when they add to the Bible, the supreme priest who commands new sacrifices for our sins (the Mass and penance) and grants saving merit to the works of men, and the supreme king who would enthrone himself in the consciences of men and over the secular powers of this world. One of the papacy's great claims is that God has confirmed the authority of its church by miracles. From the decline of the Roman Empire until 1870, the pope was the king over large tracts of land in northern

Italy (the Papal States) and a commander over significant military forces. He has ordered, encouraged, and celebrated the murderous persecution of countless evangelical Christians, down to our own times.

Today the pope's political domain (Vatican City) and armed forces (the Swiss Guards) are a tiny fraction of what they once were. Nevertheless, he claims to be the "sole vicar" of Christ on earth, receives the adoration of more than a billion people, and presides over a worldwide institution that continues to seek salvation through human merit, the mediation of Mary, and the intercession of the saints. Roman Catholics are devoted to Mary as the Mediatrix of grace and sometimes claim to receive visions and miraculous healings from her, whether in the Marian "apparitions" at Lourdes, France (1858), at Fatima, Portugal (1917), or even the supposed image of Mary in the windows of a building in Clearwater, Arizona (1996–2004).[37] We must never treat the Roman Catholic Church as just another branch of Christianity, much less evangelical Christianity. The system of religion asserted by the pope in the name of Christ is a perversion of the gospel. Is the pope the antichrist? At the very least, he is *an* antichrist, one of the greatest false prophets ever known to man. He may very well be the man of sin that Paul foretold.

One problem with seeing the papacy as the man of sin, however, is that the apostasy and man of sin in verses 3–4 seem to appear shortly before Christ's return. Perhaps Paul's language in verse 8 allows for a progressive destruction of the antichrist until his final doom, which would fit the recent decline of the papacy's power. However, both Daniel and Paul link the man of sin with the second coming of Christ. Perhaps shortly before Christ returns we will see a far greater revelation of the man of sin. A future pope, or someone like him, may arise and fulfill the prophecies of antichrist as no one has done before.

However, we should be cautious in identifying any particular person as the ultimate man of sin. The restless evil of apostasy and antichrist raises its head again and again in history, and it may not be clear who is the final antichrist until the end.[38] Thus, in answer to the question, "Who is the antichrist?" I think the best answer is a combination of the third and fourth views: the papacy is

---

37. On the last, see Chris Tisch, "For Mary's Faithful, a Shattering Loss," *St. Petersburg Times*, March 2, 2004, http://www.sptimes.com/2004/03/02/Tampabay/For_Mary_s_faithful__.shtml, accessed July 22, 2016.

38. "Patterns of inaugurated fulfillment may be cyclically escalated throughout history so that believers living in the midst of such events might well think that the final end is here.... The mistake lies in the inability to discern when precisely the apostasy has reached its consummate, universal zenith and when one individual sufficiently incarnates lawlessness to the complete degree Paul has in mind in 2:4." Beale, *1–2 Thessalonians*, 205.

the greatest manifestation of antichrist seen to date, but a future, final man of sin may yet arise at the end of the age.

The Secret of Antichrist's Success

We have seen that the man of sin is a figure of tremendous evil. But how does he gain so much power and influence over men and nations? Notice the words of verse 10: "because they received not the love of the truth, that they might be saved." While fallen mankind resists all truth about God, even what is revealed in the creation (Rom. 1:18–21), Paul refers specifically to the truth of the gospel, for he says in verses 13 and 14 that the Thessalonian believers were chosen by God "from the beginning" to salvation through "sanctification of the Spirit and belief of the truth: whereunto he called you by our gospel." Natural man does not love the truth of the gospel; he rejects it, even opposes it, to his own great loss.

To stand firm against antichrist, overcoming his deceptions and escaping his damnation, believe the gospel of Jesus Christ. Receive this "good news" as the word of God, and it will do its powerful work in you (1 Thess. 2:13). Trust in Christ to save you, sanctify you, and deliver you from evil. Paul says the damned "received not the love of the truth." You must love the gospel, for the gospel reveals the glory of Jesus Christ (2 Cor. 4:6), and you must love Christ. True faith works hand in hand with love (Gal. 5:6). Though our good works can never merit God's salvation or any part of it, for we are justified by faith alone (Gal. 2:16), true faith in Christ always brings with it true love for Jesus Christ. Therefore, the only way to overcome the deceitful spirit of antichrist is to become a lover of the truth as it is in Jesus Christ. Unless you are in Christ, joined to Him by faith, you are an easy target for antichrist and his lies.

Why does God allow evil to prevail so much on earth? To answer that question, let us proceed to the next part of our text in 2 Thessalonians.

God's Reason for the Man of Sin

When we see evil kings and false teachers rise up in the world, we may fear that their presence and activity will destroy the church. When we see many professing Christians turn from the truth to follow a lie, we may tremble. We should grieve over such sin and apostasy, but we need not fear. God is still in control of all His creatures and their acts, including the man of sin and the evil he promotes in the world.

Delusion Sent from the Sovereign God

Paul writes in 2 Thessalonians 2:11, "For this cause God shall send them strong delusion, that they should believe a lie." Ultimately, the explanation for the massive delusion that enables or empowers the antichrist is the righteous judgment of God. Some might say that this delusion comes from Satan. Indeed it does, for Paul writes of "the working of Satan" (v. 8). However, the same word translated "working" appears here, for strong delusion is literally an operation or working of deception.[39] The sovereign God rules over Satan and uses the devil for His own purposes.[40] Do not think when antichrist rises in power that God is losing ground. The Lord reigns in heaven and on earth and is ever accomplishing His will and good pleasure (Ps. 135:6).

Some may say that if God sends this deception He is a liar and sinner. God forbid that we should ever say so! God is light, and in Him is no darkness at all. God cannot lie, for he is not a man (Num. 23:19; Titus 1:2). Satan is the liar and father of lies (John 8:44).

Why, then, would God ordain that Satan successfully lead men into deception? God does not delight in sin, but He does delight in justice, and He gives sinners over to the power of the sin they choose. When Paul writes, "for this cause," he is referring to the end of verse 10, "because they received not the love of the truth, that they might be saved." Fallen mankind despises God's word and rejects God's offer of salvation, and therefore God rightly gives them up to the power of the great deceiver and the father of lies. This is an example of judicial abandonment, in which God gives people over to the power of their sins when they reject Him (Rom. 1:18–32). The enslaving power of the man of sin is not Satan's triumph over God but God's judgment on an unbelieving world.

Damnation from the Righteous God

Paul explains God's holy purpose further in 2 Thessalonians 2:12, "That they all might be damned who believed not the truth, but had pleasure in unrighteousness." God condemns unbelief and unbelievers (John 3:18–19). This is terrible but true. Christ comes to justly damn the wicked. Paul wrote earlier in 2 Thessalonians 1:6–9,

> Seeing it is a righteous thing with God to recompense tribulation to them
> that trouble you; and to you who are troubled rest with us, when the Lord
> Jesus shall be revealed from heaven with his mighty angels, in flaming fire
> taking vengeance on them that know not God, and that obey not the gospel

---

39. The same word "working" (*enérgeian*) is used on both phrases in vv. 9 and 11.
40. See Deut. 13:1–3; Judg. 9:23; 1 Sam. 16:14; 1 Kings 22:21.

of our Lord Jesus Christ: who shall be punished with everlasting destruction from the presence of the Lord, and from the glory of his power.

God is a just judge. The term "damn" literally means to "judge," or in this verse "to condemn as guilty."[41] When God abandons sinners to the power of antichrist, He gives them time to pour out the depth of their wicked hearts so that His power and justice will be magnified in destroying them.

Note the justice of God as described in this text. Those whom God damns are guilty of two great sins. First, they "believed not the truth." They have heard the word of the Lord but refused to place their trust in it.[42] They scorned the Savior who died for sinners. They rejected the Lord who has offered Himself to them in love. Therefore, they will rightly be rejected by the Judge on the last day.

Second, they "had pleasure in unrighteousness." Ultimately, no one rejects God's word on intellectual grounds alone. Sinners delight in sin. Satan offers them pleasure in sin "for a season" (Heb. 11:25). However, the essence of sin is hatred of God. Thus, the sinner loves to hate God. When people reject the light of God's word, they do so because they love the darkness (John 3:19–20). God rightly damns them to hell, for they are enemies of God.

Concluding Application

Are you rejecting the gospel of Jesus Christ? Failing to trust in Christ is choosing the darkness and clinging to your sin. If that is your state, you are an enemy of God and Christ. You are under the deception of Satan and vulnerable to the power of antichrist. Will you follow the man of sin straight into the mouth of hell? What, then, will you do on judgment day when Christ returns with flaming fire to damn you? You will face eternal punishment, eternal torment, and eternal destruction for your sins. Oh, sinner, turn away from darkness and the pleasures of sin, and run to the Lord Jesus Christ before it is too late! Come to Christ as Savior and Lord before He comes to you as your Judge.

You who are believers in the Lord Jesus Christ, fall down and thank God for His mercy. In His love, He has sent Christ into the world to save sinners. In His power, He has sent the Holy Spirit to bring you out of darkness into the light of the gospel. He has drawn you to Christ. He has worked faith in your hearts to believe the truth and be saved. He has renewed your will so that you have forsaken the pleasures of sin and now delight to do the will of your Father in heaven. In His great faithfulness, He promises that you who persevere in

---

41. Greek *krínō*. Cf. John 3:17–18; 16:11; Acts 13:27; Rom. 2:1, 3, 12; 14:3.

42. This is another indication that Paul may have in view an apostasy coming at the end of the age, because only then will the gospel reach the entire world (Matt. 24:14).

faith and holiness will one day behold the face of Christ and dwell in glory with Him (2 Thess. 2:13–14).

Thank God for the glory of Jesus Christ, God's gift to you! In our sins, we were no better than the man of sin and his worshipers. It is entirely by God's grace that we are saved. Therefore, the last and greatest application of the doctrine of the antichrist is to give all glory to the God of our salvation! "Therefore shall my mouth and heart show forth the praise of the Lord from this time forth, for evermore. Amen."[43]

---

43. "Form for the Administration of the Lord's Supper," in *The Psalter*, 140.

APPENDIX:
A Survey of Historical Interpretations of the Antichrist

A bewildering variety of interpretations have been proposed over the centuries to identify the man of sin or antichrist. Entire books have been written to study the history of how Christians handled this subject.[44] Strange legends have sprung up around this theme, mixing folklore with biblical doctrine. Some Christians tend to declare that any prominent heretic or persecutor of the church is the antichrist. The label can also be quite useful when attacking one's ecclesiastical end or political opponents.[45] For the sake of simplicity, we may trace four main lines of thought that appear in historic Christianity.

One line of interpretation sees the man of sin as an outsider to the church who rallies the wicked to persecute God's people. A very early Christian document, *The Ascension of Isaiah*, indicates that the antichrist will be Satan in the form of the revived Emperor Nero.[46] Irenaeus believed the antichrist would be a Jewish leader from the tribe of Dan, and Hippolytus believed he would be a Jew who rebuilds the temple in Jerusalem.[47] Around 1200, Pope Innocent III and many of his contemporaries declared that Mohammed was the antichrist.[48] More recently, people claimed that the antichrist was Napoleon, Mussolini, or Hitler. We find a view of the antichrist as a non-Christian political and military leader in modern Dispensationalism.[49]

A second line of interpretation identifies the antichrist with the triumph of heresy and authoritarianism in the visible church. Athanasius said the Council of Nicea declared the Arian heresy to be "the forerunner of Antichrist."[50] John Wycliffe declared that the marks of antichrist were seduction from biblical doctrine, adding laws not found in the Bible, worldliness, neglect of preaching,

---

44. W. Bousset, *The Antichrist Legend: A Chapter in Christian and Jewish Folklore*, trans. A. H. Keane (London: Hutchinson and Co., 1896); Christopher Hill, *Antichrist in Seventeenth-Century England* (London: Oxford University Press, 1971); Bernard McGinn, *Anti-Christ: Two Thousand Years of the Human Fascination with Evil* (San Francisco: Harper Collins, 1994); Stephen J. Vicchio, *The Legend of the Anti-Christ: A History* (Eugene, Or.: Wipf and Stock, 2009).

45. "The charge of being a forerunner of Antichrist, or Antichrist himself, was part of the normal vocabulary of abuse of medieval politicians, freely used by popes and emperors from the eleventh century onwards." Hill, *Antichrist in Seventeenth-Century England*, 7.

46. Ascension of Isaiah 4.1–3, cited in McGinn, *Anti-Christ*, 48. Cf. Bruce, *1 & 2 Thessalonians*, 182–83.

47. Irenaeus, *Against Heresies*, 5.30.2, in *ANF*, 1:559; Hippolytus, *On Christ and Antichrist*, 6, in *ANF*, 5:206. Irenaeus cited Jer. 8:16; Hippolytus argued on the basis of parallels with Christ.

48. Vicchio, *The Legend of the Anti-Christ*, 143.

49. McGinn, *Anti-Christ*, 252–59.

50. Athanasius, *On the Councils of Ariminum and Seleucia*, sec. 5, in *Nicene and Post Nicene Fathers, Second Series*, ed. Philip Schaff and Henry Wace (New York: Christian Literature Co., 1892), 4:453. Henceforth cited as *NPNF2*.

assertion of civil authority, use of physical force, and lack of humility.[51] Thus any traditionalist, erroneous, and authoritarian religious hierarchy could be called antichrist. Some early Anabaptists believed that not only the Roman Catholics but also the magisterial Protestants who persecuted the radical Reformers were antichrist.[52] Menno Simons said that the church that allows membership and participation in the sacraments without repentance and persecutes true believers is "the church of anti-christ."[53] Those who renounce the pope (that is, Protestants) but retain the substance of ritual externalism and religious persecution have cut off "many branches of the tree of anti-christ," but "the roots and body still remain."[54] The Confession of Faith in the Geneva Bible (1560) returned the favor by referring to "all idolaters and heretics," including "papists" and "Anabaptists" as "limbs of Antichrist."[55] The Church of England was considered anti-Christian by early Separatists, and this same accusation was taken up by radical sectaries against the Presbyterians in the mid-seventeenth century.[56] Many Puritans considered Arminian bishops in the Church of England to be antichrist, as may be seen in Puritan sermons to Parliament in the midst of the civil war years.[57]

A third line of interpretation identifies the man of sin as a universal bishop over the professing Christian church, that is, the pope. Gregory the Great, though significantly consolidating his power as bishop of Rome, nevertheless said in the sixth century that anyone who sought the title of "universal priest" over the church is "the forerunner of antichrist."[58] As early as the twelfth century, some Catholics such as Joachim of Fiore believed that the man of sin would be a great leader in the church, even a pope.[59] In the fourteenth century, Wycliffe, followed by the Lollards, identified the entire institution of the papacy as the antichrist.[60] Jan Hus believed that good popes were servants of Christ but sinful

---

51. Wycliffe, *Opera minor*, 120–24, cited in Gordon Leff, "John Wyclif: The Path to Dissent," *Proceedings of the British Academy* 52 (1967): 169.

52. McGinn, *Anti-Christ*, 213–17.

53. Menno Simons, *Reply to a Publication of Gellius Faber*, in *The Complete Works of Menno Simons* (Elkhart, Ind.: John F. Funk and Brother, 1871), 2:22.

54. Simons, *Reply to a Publication of Gellius Faber*, in *Works*, 2:23.

55. James T. Dennison Jr., comp., *Reformed Confessions of the 16th and 17th Centuries in English Translation: 1523–1693* (Grand Rapids: Reformation Heritage Books, 2008–2014), 2:184. Cf. Hill, *Antichrist in Seventeenth-Century England*, 146.

56. McGinn, *Anti-Christ*, 220–21; Hill, *Antichrist in Seventeenth-Century England*, 90–98.

57. Hill, *Antichrist in Seventeenth-Century England*, 78–88.

58. Gregory, Epistle 7.13, cited in Philip Schaff, *History of the Christian Church* (New York: Charles Scribner's Sons, 1886), 4:220.

59. McGinn, *Anti-Christ*, 141–42. Joachim's followers among the Franciscan Spirituals in the thirteenth and fourteenth centuries attacked popes as antichrists (143, 161, 166).

60. McGinn, *Anti-Christ*, 181–82.

or heretical priests and popes were antichrists because Christ's ministers rely on Christ and His word, but the ministers of antichrist rely on human traditions.[61]

The papal antichrist became a dominant theme in the Reformation of the sixteenth century. Martin Luther initiated his calls for reform in hopes of a favorable response from church authorities, but by 1520 he had become convinced that the papacy was the antichrist.[62] In 1529, Reformed leader William Farel also declared the pope to be antichrist.[63] John Calvin said that the pope is "the leader and standard bearer" of the kingdom of antichrist, though God preserves "a remnant of his people, however woefully dispersed and scattered," in the Roman Catholic Church.[64] The Belgic Confession links "the kingdom of antichrist" with "idolatry and false worship."[65] The identification of the pope with antichrist became a standard interpretation in Reformation Christianity.[66]

The doctrine of the papal antichrist was perpetuated by English Reformed writers, both Puritans and non-Puritans.[67] John Jewel saw the pope of Rome to be the antichrist, for he sits in the church as its supreme, divine ruler, and opposes true doctrine and godliness.[68] William Perkins taught that the papacy best fits Paul's description of the man of sin as claiming absolute supremacy over the church.[69] The Westminster Confession of Faith (25.6) affirmed that the papacy is "that Antichrist, that man of sin," and that identification carried over in the Savoy Declaration (26.4) of the Congregationalists and the 1689 Confession (26.4) of the Particular Baptists.[70] Bunyan deduced from 1 Thessalonians 2

---

61. John Huss, *The Church*, trans. David S. Schaff (New York: Charles Scribner's Sons, 1915), 87, 90, 128, 140, 159.

62. James Estes, introduction to *To the German Nobility*, in *The Annotated Luther, Volume 1, The Roots of Reform*, ed. Timothy J. Wengert (Minneapolis: Fortress, 2015), 370; cf. Luther's statements on pp. 387, 391–94, 409, 415, 441–43.

63. William Farel, *Summary and Brief Declaration*, ch. 27, in *Reformed Confessions*, 1:80.

64. John Calvin, *Institutes of the Christian Religion*, ed. John T. McNeill, trans. Ford Lewis Battles (Philadelphia: Westminster, 1960), 4.3.12. See John Calvin, *Commentaries* (repr., Grand Rapids: Baker, 2003), on 2 Thess. 2:4.

65. *Reformed Confessions*, 2:447–48.

66. Hill, *Antichrist in Seventeenth-Century England*, 9. See Wilhelmus à Brakel, *The Christian's Reasonable Service*, trans. Bartel Elshout, ed. Joel R. Beeke (Grand Rapids: Reformation Heritage Books, 1992–1995), 2:44–53.

67. Hill, *Antichrist in Seventeenth-Century England*, 13–32. A major exposition of 2 Thess. 2:1–12 from the Puritan perspective may be found in Manton, *Eighteen Sermons*, in *Works*, 3:1–102. See Ronald C. Cooke, *Antichrist Exposed: The Reformed and Puritan View of the Antichrist*, 2 vols. (Max Meadows, Va.: Truth International Ministries, 2006).

68. John Jewel, *An Exposition upon the Two Epistles of the Apostle Saint Paul to the Thessalonians*, in *The Works of John Jewel*, ed. Richard William Jelf (Oxford: Oxford University Press, 1848), 7:152–62.

69. William Perkins, *A Reformed Catholike: or, a Declaration Shewing How Neere We May Come to the Present Church of Rome in Sundrie Points of Religion* (London: John Legat, 1598), 292–93.

70. *Reformed Confessions*, 4:264–65, 484, 562.

that the antichrist appeared "in the church of God," and consists of a group of men who animated a "spirit of error" to engage in "masses, prayers for the dead, images, pilgrimages, monkish vows, sinful fasts, and the beastly single life of priests," together with "civil laws that impose and enforce them also...as in the Spanish inquisition."[71] John Owen said "the fundamental principle of the Reformation" is "that the church of Rome is the idolatrous, antichristian state which is foretold in the Scriptures."[72]

A fourth line of interpretation is that the man of sin is indeed a figure who arises within the professing church but who will appear at the end of the age, not the historical papacy. Augustine thought the Nero myth was foolish and was not sure whether the "temple" in Paul's letter to the Thessalonians was the building in Jerusalem or the church of Jesus Christ.[73] However, Augustine did teach that "the kingdom of Antichrist shall fiercely, though for a short time, assail the Church before the last judgment of God shall introduce the eternal reign of the saints."[74] He said antichrists in general are all heretics that arise in the church and depart from it, and "certainly antichrist will first come, and then will come the day of judgment."[75] A futurist, ecclesiastical view of antichrist is popular among Reformed amillennialists today, who understand the "temple" to be the church but the man of sin not to be the historic papacy but a church leader who will preside over a great apostasy in the last day.[76]

In summary, our analysis finds four main lines of interpretation:

(1) Antichrist is not a church leader but a political or military leader.

(2) Antichrist is all church leaders that teach heresy and persecute true believers.

(3) Antichrist is the pope, not an individual so much as a religious institution.

(4) Antichrist is an individual who will lead the church in apostasy at the end of the age.

---

71. John Bunyan, *Of Antichrist, and His Ruin*, in *The Works of John Bunyan* (repr., Edinburgh: Banner of Truth, 1999), 2:46, 49.

72. John Owen, *A Brief and Impartial Account of the Nature of the Protestant Religion; Its Present State in the World; Its Strength and Weakness; with the Ways and Indications of the Ruin or Continuance of Its Public National Profession*, in *The Works of John Owen* (repr., Edinburgh: Banner of Truth, 1965), 14:549.

73. Augustine, *The City of God*, 20.19, in *NPNF1*, 2:437–38.

74. Augustine, *The City of God*, 20.23, in *NPNF1*, 2:443.

75. Augustine, *Homilies on 1 John*, 3.3–4, in *NPNF1*, 7:476.

76. Thus Beale, *1–2 Thessalonians*, 206–210; Anthony A. Hoekema, *The Bible and the Future* (Grand Rapids: Eerdmans, 1994), 162; Kim Riddlebarger, *The Man of Sin: Uncovering the Truth about the Antichrist* (Grand Rapids: Baker, 2006), 127–28, 134.

Chapter 6

Delighting in God:
A Guide to Sabbath-Keeping

If thou turn away thy foot from the sabbath, from doing thy pleasure on my holy day; and call the sabbath a delight, the holy of the LORD, honourable; and shalt honour him, not doing thine own ways, nor finding thine own pleasure, nor speaking thine own words: then shalt thou delight thyself in the LORD; and I will cause thee to ride upon the high places of the earth, and feed thee with the heritage of Jacob thy father: for the mouth of the LORD hath spoken it.

—Isaiah 58:13–14

Keeping the Sabbath holy was once woven into the fabric of our culture. In 1862, this duty was recognized by the president of the United States in his regulations for the armed services, requiring that "Sunday labor in the Army and Navy be reduced to the measure of strict necessity."[1] Alexis de Tocqueville, visiting from France, wrote in 1831 that few people in the United States were allowed to engage in hunting or recreations on Sunday. Yet still in the nineteenth century theological forces were on the move to undermine the Christian Sabbath.[2]

Today, our nation has largely lost any sense that the Sabbath is a holy day. A modern writer wrote in the *New York Times* that in a culture overwhelmed with work and busyness, "the Sabbath, the one day in seven dedicated to rest by divine command, has become the holiday Americans are most likely never to take." The Lord's Day has become "overscheduled" with activities such as sports,

---

1. "The President, commander in chief of the army and navy, desires and enjoins the orderly observance of the Sabbath by the officers and men in the military and naval service. The importance for man and beast of the prescribed weekly rest, the sacred rights of Christian soldiers and sailors, a becoming deference to the best sentiment of a Christian people, and a due regard for the Divine will demand that Sunday labor in the Army and Navy be reduced to the measure of strict necessity." Abraham Lincoln, Nov. 15, 1862, "Order for Sabbath Observance," in *Complete Works*, ed. John G. Nicolay and John Hay (New York: The Century Co., 1920), 2:254.

2. Alexis McCrossen, *Holy Day, Holiday: The American Sunday* (Ithaca: Cornell University Press, 2000), 28.

housework, entertainment, and shopping—with church crammed into the morning for those who take the time.[3]

It is not my present purpose to convince you that you should go to church on the Lord's Day. I will take that for granted, especially in light of the clear command of Hebrews 10:25 that we must not forsake "the assembling of ourselves together." Just as old covenant Israel was commanded to gather on the Sabbath for a "holy convocation" or sacred assembly (Lev. 23:3), so on the Lord's Day we must gather with the local congregation. Nor do I intend to talk about how to listen to sermons for the greatest profit while in church. For that topic, I refer you to my small book, *The Family at Church*.[4]

My purpose in this chapter is to exhort you to keep the whole Lord's Day in a manner that honors God and profits your soul. God calls us to embrace the divine institution of the Sabbath with holy discipline, in order to delight in Christ and deepen our desire for the eternal Sabbath. I will address keeping the entire first day of the week as the Christian Sabbath. There are many helpful books that explore the doctrine of the Sabbath from a Reformed and Puritan perspective, drawing from a wealth of biblical teaching.[5] Here we will focus

3. Judith Shulevitz, "Bring Back the Sabbath," *New York Times* (March 2, 2003), 90. Shulevitz writes from the perspective of Judaism and a concern about over-work, but with respect for the Christian Sabbath.

4. Joel R. Beeke, *The Family at Church: Listening to Sermons and Attending Prayer Meetings* (Grand Rapids: Reformation Heritage Books, 2008).

5. In addition to Reformed treatises on the Ten Commandments and the Westminster Standards, see Nicholas Bownd, *Sabbathum Veteris et Novi Testamenti: Or, The True Doctrine of the Sabbath*, 2nd ed., enlarged (London: by Felix Kyngston, for Thomas Man and John Porter, 1606), recently reprinted as Nicholas Bownd, *Sabbathum Veteris et Novi Testamenti: Or, The True Doctrine of the Sabbath*, ed. Chris Coldwell (Dallas, Tex.: Naphtali Press; Grand Rapids: Reformation Heritage Books, 2015); in this chapter, we cite the 1606 edition; William Gouge, *The Sabbaths Sanctification* (London: by G. M. for Joshua Kirton, 1641); Daniel Cawdrey and Herbert Palmer, *Sabbatum Redivivum: Or, The Christian Sabbath Vindicated* (1652; repr., Grand Rapids: Reformation Heritage Books, 2011); Richard Bernard, *A Threefold Treatise of the Sabbath* (London: by Richard Bishop for Edward Blackmore, 1641); Thomas Shepard, *The Doctrine of the Sabbath* (London, 1655); John Owen, *An Exposition of the Epistle to the Hebrews*, ed. W. H. Goold (London: Johnstone & Hunter, 1855), vols. 3–4 on Hebrews 3–4; George Swinnock, "How to Exercise Ourselves to Godliness on a Lord's Day," and "Brief Directions for the Sanctification of the Lord's Day from Morning to Night," *The Christian Man's Calling* in *The Works of George Swinnock* (1868; repr., Edinburgh: Banner of Truth, 1992), 1:222–60; Jonathan Edwards, "The Perpetuity and Change of the Sabbath," in *The Works of Jonathan Edwards* (1834; repr., Edinburgh: Banner of Truth, 1974), 2:93–103; Robert Dabney, "The Christian Sabbath: Its Nature, Design, and Proper Observance," in *Discussions: Evangelical and Theological* (1890; repr., London: Banner of Truth, 1967), 1:496–550; Matthew Henry, "A Serious Address to Those that Profane the Lord's Day," in *The Complete Works of Matthew Henry* (1855; repr., Grand Rapids: Baker, 1979), 1:118–33; W. B. Whitaker, *Sunday in Tudor and Stuart Times* (London: Houghton, 1933); Daniel Wilson, *The Divine Authority and Perpetual Obligation of the Lord's Day* (1827; repr., London: Lord's Day Observance Society, 1956); John Murray, "The Moral Law and the Fourth Commandment," in *Collected Writings*

on Isaiah 58:13–14, which teaches us that in order to glorify God and edify ourselves, we must keep the Sabbath as a doctrine and divine institution with discipline and delight and with desire for the eternal Sabbath in heaven with Christ. Hence, we want to consider four words in relation to Sabbath-keeping: doctrine, discipline, delight, and desire.

Doctrine: Be Convinced the Sabbath Is God's Sacred Day

Isaiah 58:13 says, "If thou turn away thy foot from the sabbath, from doing thy pleasure on *my holy day*; and call the sabbath a delight, *the holy of the* LORD, *honourable*" (emphasis added). You will not be able to wholeheartedly pursue a profitable Sabbath day until you are convinced that the Lord's Day is truly set apart by God as sacred time devoted to Him. You must be able to say with absolute conviction, "This is God's holy day." If your conscience is gripped with a sense that God commands us to honor the Lord's Day, then you will do what it takes to honor it. And, if you love the Lord, you will do it with pleasure because it is His will.

The Sabbath was instituted by God as His holy day.[6] In the fourth commandment God says, "The seventh day is the sabbath of the LORD thy God" (Ex. 20:10). These words remind us that God commanded us to observe the weekly Sabbath and that He claims the day as His own. As God said through Isaiah, it is "my holy day." Not to devote the day to the purposes and activities commanded for its sanctification robs God of that which belongs to Him.

The Sabbath is a creation ordinance. Genesis 2:1–3 recounts how on the seventh day of the creation week God rested from all His work as Creator. God, who does not need to rest, rested as an example for the man and woman He had created in His image. They were to follow His example, resting from their

---

(Edinburgh: Banner of Truth, 1976), 1:193–228; James I. Packer, "The Puritans and the Lord's Day," in *A Quest for Godliness* (Wheaton: Crossway, 1990), 233–43; Roger T. Beckwith and Wilfrid Stott, *The Christian Sunday: A Biblical and Historical Study* (1978; repr., Grand Rapids: Baker, 1980); Errol Hulse, "Sanctifying the Lord's Day: Reformed and Puritan Attitudes," in *Aspects of Sanctification*, Westminster Conference of 1981 (Hertfordshire, U.K.: Evangelical Press, 1982), 78–102; Walter Chantry, *Call the Sabbath a Delight* (Edinburgh: Banner of Truth, 1991); Joseph A. Pipa, *The Lord's Day* (Ross-shire, U.K.: Christian Focus Publications, 1997); Iain D. Campbell, *On the First Day of the Week: God, the Christian, and the Sabbath* (Leominster, U.K.: DayOne, 2001); James T. Dennison, Jr., *The Market Day of the Soul: The Puritan Doctrine of the Sabbath in England, 1532–1700* (Grand Rapids: Reformation Heritage Books, 2008); Ryan M. McGraw, *The Day of Worship: Reassessing the Christian Life in Light of the Sabbath* (Grand Rapids: Reformation Heritage Books, 2011).

6. Portions of this article are adapted from two of my sermons on Heidelberg Catechism, Q. 103, and Joel R. Beeke and Ray Lanning, "The Didactic Use of the Law," in *Puritan Reformed Spirituality* (Darlington, U.K.: Evangelical Press, 2006), 112–18.

work as He did from His; thus it is a divine institution that God crowned with His blessing, setting it apart for all of time. A common error is to assume that the Sabbath originated with the giving of the law at Sinai. Such a view ignores the fact that Exodus 20 does not introduce the Sabbath as something new but rather acknowledges something ancient and historic that is to be remembered and observed by God's people: "Remember the sabbath day, to keep it holy" (Ex. 20:8).

What, specifically, is to be remembered in the pattern of six days of work punctuated by a day of holy rest? "In six days the LORD made heaven and earth, the sea, and all that in them is, and rested the seventh day: wherefore the LORD blessed the sabbath day, and hallowed it" (Ex. 20:11). Every Sabbath we remember that we are not in this world by chance; we are not products of evolution. Every Sabbath, God declares to us, "Remember that you are accountable to Me. Remember that you are under My authority as your Creator."

Jesus Christ owned the Sabbath. The first three evangelists record that He said, "The Son of man is Lord of the sabbath" (Matt. 12:8; Mark 2:28; Luke 6:5). In one blow, Christ asserted His full deity as the God of Israel and reaffirmed the claim of God on the weekly Sabbath, restating that claim in His own name. The claim left its mark on the apostolic church so that by the end of that era, the Christian Sabbath was known as "the Lord's day" (Rev. 1:10). Are we really to believe that Christ declared Himself Lord of the Sabbath so that in a few years He could abolish it? As Walter Chantry says, such an argument "makes nonsense of Jesus' words."[7]

Therefore, while the ceremonial and civil regulations of the old covenant law no longer bind us in Christ (though they still point us to Him), the Sabbath continues. Our Lord Jesus Christ did not treat the Sabbath the way He treated the ceremonial laws. For example, He taught His disciples that food cannot make a person unclean (Mark 7:18), pointing them beyond the Mosaic distinction between clean and unclean food. However, when it came to the Sabbath, Christ taught His disciples the proper way to keep the Sabbath, implying that He expected His church to continue observing it. Indeed, by saying that He is "Lord of the sabbath," Christ stamped the day with an indelible, Christian character. Henceforth, it was only right to speak of the *Christian* Sabbath.

When Christ died on the cross, He fulfilled the law of God in both its demands for complete obedience and its penalties for sin. His work of redemption was finished (John 19:30). He ratified the promise of the new covenant, by which God's law is written on the hearts of His covenant people, and they desire to do His will. The body of the Lord Jesus rested in the grave on the

---

7. Chantry, *Call the Sabbath a Delight*, 57.

seventh day and His human spirit rested in paradise. Then on the first day of the week, Christ rose from the dead, the Firstborn of the new creation, and met with His disciples, teaching them the meaning of the Word, filling their hearts with understanding, joy, and peace by the Holy Spirit, and giving them their worldwide mission (Luke 24; John 20:19–23). One week later, or on the next first day of the week, Christ appeared to the gathered disciples a second time to renew their faith and peace (John 20:26–29). Again, seven weeks later, on the day of Pentecost, which also falls on the first day of the week (Lev. 23:15–16), Christ poured out the Spirit upon His church (Acts 2).

Since then, the apostles directed the churches of all lands to set apart the first day of the week as the day for sacred assemblies to give their offerings and receive God's Word and sacraments (Acts 20:7; 1 Cor. 16:1–2). By Christ's example and the apostles' direction, the sacred day was changed from the seventh day to the first day, giving it a new name: "the Lord's day" (Rev. 1:10). Thus, while the early church distanced itself from the Jewish Sabbath, it wholeheartedly embraced holy rest on the Lord's Day. Justin Martyr (d. 165) wrote in the mid-second century that on Sunday the church gathers to read Scripture, hear the preaching of the Word, pray, partake of the sacraments, and collect money for the poor because that is the day when Christ our Savior rose from the dead.[8] And around the same time, Dionysius of Corinth wrote, "Today being the Lord's Day, we kept it as a holy day."[9]

Perhaps you question whether God really expects us to keep the first day of the week as His holy day. I encourage you to dig deeper into the Bible. Give careful consideration to God's resting on the seventh day of creation, blessing it, and making it holy. Why would God do that, unless He did it for mankind? Meditate on how our Lord Jesus explained and observed the Sabbath. Why did He spend so much time explaining the true meaning of the Sabbath, unless He intended for His disciples to keep the Sabbath?

To have a firm foundation for keeping the Sabbath in a profitable manner, you must be convinced from the Scriptures that the Sabbath is the sacred day of God. Then you are able to wake up on the first day of the week and say to yourself, "My God has set apart one day in seven for Himself since the beginning of time. Christ declared that He is Lord of the Sabbath. I am Christ's disciple, and because I love Him I will keep His commandments. Today is the Lord's Day, and I will keep it holy."

---

8. Justin Martyr, *First Apology*, ch. 67, in *The Ante-Nicene Fathers*, ed. Alexander Roberts and James Donaldson (New York: Charles Scribner's Sons, 1913), 1:186.

9. Quoted in Eusebius, *The History of the Church from Christ to Constantine*, trans. G. A. Williamson (Middlesex, Eng.: Penguin, 1965), 185 [4.23].

Discipline: Exercise Self-control for the Sake of God's Worship

Isaiah 58:13 says, "If thou turn away thy foot…from doing thy pleasure on my holy day…not doing thine own ways, nor finding thine own pleasure, nor speaking thine own words." The Sabbath is not primarily about "Thou shalt not"; in fact, it is one of only two commandments out of ten that begin with a positive command. However, to say *yes* to God on the Sabbath, we must say *no* to other things that would take up our time. J. Alec Motyer writes, "The Sabbath calls for careful, thoughtful living."[10]

Isaiah's reference to turning away the foot suggests that you are walking in a particular direction but then remember something, stop in your tracks, and go in a different direction. The same metaphor is used in Psalm 119:59, "I thought on my ways, and turned my feet unto thy testimonies." This is what we must do on the Sabbath. During the week we walk in the way of our daily employments and recreations, but as the Lord's Day approaches, we remember the Sabbath, stop what we were doing, and devote ourselves to communion with God and seeking His gracious work in our souls.[11] That takes disciplined self-control.

Sometimes people say that we should live every day for God and, therefore, we have no special obligations on the Lord's Day. Certainly we should live every day for God, but in our human limitations, the Lord knows we need a day set apart to focus on Him. John Calvin said, "If we think we have done all we need to do when we reflect upon God but one day of the week, we are incredibly dense hypocrites, for if our lives come from him, we are not to spend a single minute without considering him…. So why did he sanctify the seventh day? It was to gather us all together so that we might not be distracted."[12]

Isaiah tells us that to say yes to God on the Sabbath we must say no to "doing thy pleasure." "Doing thy pleasure" means doing whatever you choose,[13] doing whatever indulges your pleasure or preference.[14] I have already said that

---

10. J. Alec Motyer, *The Prophecy of Isaiah: An Introduction and Commentary* (Downers Grove, Ill.: InterVarsity Press, 1993), 483.

11. "Oecolampadius thus writeth…. If thou hast appointed to do any of thy work upon the Sabbath, and shalt draw thy foot away from the Sabbath, that is…shalt leave off that work because of the Sabbath, and for the remembrance of the Sabbath; that is, that thou mayest give place and glory unto God, and suffer him to work his will in thee: then thou shalt sanctify the Sabbath, for such a Sabbath is acceptable unto him." Bownd, *True Doctrine of the Sabbath*, 234. The ellipses are Latin quotations from Oecolampadius. For the contrary interpretation that turning the foot "refers to restrictions on travel on the Sabbath (Ex. 16:29)," see John D. W. Watts, *Isaiah 34–66*, Word Biblical Commentary 25, rev. ed. (Nashville: Thomas Nelson, 2005), 845.

12. John Calvin, *Sermons on Genesis, Chapters 1–11*, trans. Rob Roy McGregor (Edinburgh: Banner of Truth, 2009), 127–28.

13. Compare the same Hebrew expression in Isa. 46:10; 48:14.

14. Motyer, *The Prophecy of Isaiah*, 483.

to profit from the Sabbath you must be convinced that it is God's sacred day. You must also translate that conviction into action. Submit your will to God, and determine by His grace to do His will. Say to the Lord, "This is Thy special day, and I willingly dedicate the whole day to Thy worship." We cannot jump into worship for an hour or two and then return to whatever we want to do. We must give the whole day to God. We need this discipline, for it is not as easy to break out of our busy rush through daily life as one might think. Even non-Christians recognize that "interrupting the ceaseless round of striving requires a surprisingly strenuous act of will, one that has to be bolstered by habit as well as social sanction," as one journalist wrote[15]—and, for the Christian Sabbath, we add, a will empowered by divine grace.

Keeping the Sabbath requires the exercise of self-discipline both before and during the Lord's Day. Before the day, we must make all necessary preparations so that we are free to enjoy the Sabbath. We must plan ahead. The day should be blocked off on our calendars from unnecessary work. Homework and school projects due on Monday should be finished on Saturday. Household chores should be planned and performed on the other six days. There are works of necessity, such as nursing the sick and police work, and God blesses such work on the Sabbath. However, even then you should seek a rotation so that you can participate in worship as regularly as possible. The point here is to look ahead and prepare for the Lord's Day.

During the Sabbath Day, you will need to resist the temptation to do tasks that properly belong to the other six days, not just the work of our gainful employment but also such "recreations as are lawful on other days," as the Westminster Shorter Catechism says.[16] Nicholas Bownd, who wrote "the classic presentation of the Puritan view,"[17] said that this is not because we despise recreation or think it ungodly but because we simply cannot devote ourselves to recreation and worship at the same time. Men cannot be "in the great congregation praising God with their brethren, and in the open fields playing with their fellows at one time."[18] Henry Scudder pointed out that "sports and games" make it even more difficult for our minds to engage in worship than our vocational

---

15. Shulevitz, "Bring Back the Sabbath," 90. She notes that this is the rationale behind the restrictions of the Puritan Sunday and the Jewish Orthodox Sabbath.

16. Westminster Shorter Catechism, Q. 60, in *The Reformation Heritage KJV Study Bible*, 2058.

17. Dennison, *The Market Day of the Soul*, 42. Bownd was the stepson of Puritan pioneer Richard Greenham. His book (1st ed. 1595) originated in sermons preached in 1586. It attracted heavy criticism by Thomas Rogers, the chaplain of Archbishop Bancroft, but was still popular and was reprinted in an enlarged second edition in 1606 (see Dennison, *The Market Day of the Soul*, 39–49).

18. Bownd, *True Doctrine of the Sabbath*, 262.

work does.[19] Why is this? Experience teaches us, as Bownd observed, that games and sports move and affect us, captivating all our senses and thoughts so that we cannot occupy ourselves with the Lord's worship as we should.[20] I am not speaking here of small children, who often benefit from a measure of games or physical activity on the Lord's Day so that they can concentrate better when they are in the worship service. I am speaking of the self-discipline of teenagers and adults. This is God's special day. Ryan McGraw writes, "Worldly recreations on the Sabbath are no more appropriate than if a groom paused in the middle of his wedding ceremony to check the scores of a football game."[21]

Turning your feet from doing your own pleasure also means repenting of sinful desires and practices. The expression in Isaiah 58:13, "finding thine own pleasure," also appears in verse 3, where God rebukes people for oppressing others for the sake of gratifying their greed. It is a horrible abuse of the Sabbath to participate in outward worship while your heart is full of wickedness. Amos 8:5 gives a similar rebuke to people who say, "When will the new moon be gone, that we may sell corn? And the sabbath, that we may set forth wheat, making the ephah small, and the shekel great, and falsifying the balances by deceit?" When God considers people in public worship who are secretly full of greed or lust or selfish ambition, He turns away from their worship with hatred, loathing, and disgust (Isa. 1:11–15). We also must repent of sins of omission, particularly our coldness toward God and weariness at prayer and worship, treating God as tedious and thus profaning His holy name (Isa. 43:22; Mal. 1:11–13).

The Sabbath cannot benefit us if we live as hypocrites on the other six days of the week. In the context of Isaiah 58, the Lord severely criticized Israel for hypocrisy in making much of days of fasting while neglecting compassion and justice. Isaiah 58:6–7 says, "Is not this the fast that I have chosen? To loose the bands of wickedness, to undo the heavy burdens, and to let the oppressed go free, and that ye break every yoke? Is it not to deal thy bread to the hungry, and that thou bring the poor that are cast out to thy house? When thou seest the naked, that thou cover him; and that thou hide not thyself from thine own flesh?" It is wrong for anyone to say, "I have given one day to the Lord. Now I will live for myself on the other six days"?

The one to whom the Lord looks with favor is the Sabbath-keeper who is broken and repentant over his sins (Isa. 66:2). David said in Psalm 119:101, "I have refrained my feet from every evil way, that I might keep thy word." The

---

19. Henry Scudder, *The Christian's Daily Walk in Holy Security and Peace* (Harrisonburg, Va.: Sprinkle, 1984), 64.

20. Bownd, *True Doctrine of the Sabbath*, 263.

21. McGraw, *The Day of Worship*, 52.

Heidelberg Catechism reminds us that the Sabbath requires of us "that all the days of my life I cease from my evil works, and yield myself to the Lord, to work by His Holy Spirit in me."[22] Then our sins are covered by Christ's blood, our worship pleases God, and He is quick to bless us.

Turning your feet from doing your own pleasure also means making the Sabbath a day of quiet. We need to turn down the volume of chatter that normally fills our mouths and ears and minds so that we can concentrate on worshiping God. Notice that Isaiah wrote of not "speaking thine own words," literally, not "speaking a word."[23] Ecclesiastes 5:1–2 says, "Keep thy foot when thou goest to the house of God, and be more ready to hear, than to give the sacrifice of fools: for they consider not that they do evil. Be not rash with thy mouth, and let not thine heart be hasty to utter any thing before God: for God is in heaven, and thou upon earth: therefore let thy words be few."

This does not mean that we may not talk on the Lord's Day but that we should focus our talk on matters that promote the knowledge of God with faith, love, fear, obedience, and gratitude. There are many things that are quite legitimate to talk about on other days, but such talk distracts us from God on the Sabbath. Bownd wrote, "Much talk about worldly matters doth as well hinder the sanctification of the day as much work...for our minds cannot be wholly set upon the worship of God as they should, and at the same time be speaking of and listening unto the affairs of this life."[24]

The purpose is not to focus on the negative of what we should not do but to release us to focus on the positive duty of seeking God on the Sabbath. Jeremiah Burroughs said that we must prepare ourselves for worship because we are drawing near to "a great and glorious God."[25] Burroughs pointed out that, in the Bible, seeking God especially requires the preparation of the heart (1 Sam. 7:3; 2 Chron. 12:14; 19:3). We must believe in our hearts "the majesty of that God whom we are going to worship," especially by meditating on who God is and how we must worship Him. We must pull our hearts away from sin and untangle them from earthly business and concerns. We must be spiritually

---

22. Heidelberg Catechism, LD 38, Q. 103, in *The Reformation Heritage KJV Study Bible*, ed. Joel R. Beeke, Michael P. V. Barrett, and Gerald M. Bilkes (Grand Rapids: Reformation Heritage Books, 2014), 2002.

23. "'Talking talk' is found elsewhere only in Deuteronomy 18:20, where it is used of a word without divine authorization, a mere human word, hence here, 'chit-chat'" (Motyer, *The Prophecy of Isaiah*, 483).

24. Bownd, *True Doctrine of the Sabbath*, 273.

25. Jeremiah Burroughs, *Gospel Worship*, ed. Don Kistler (Orlando: Soli Deo Gloria, 1990), 52.

alert and praying, lifting up our hearts in love and adoration to God.[26] This requires disciplined effort and focus.

The key to making the disciplines of the Sabbath an act of love is to remember that this is the Lord's Day and we do all these things in order to meet with our Lord. Thomas Watson writes, "If a prince were to come to your house, what preparation would you make for his entertainment!… On the blessed Sabbath, God intends to have sweet communion with you…. Now, what preparation should you make for entertaining this King of glory?"[27]

Delight: Use the Sabbath to Glorify and Enjoy God

Isaiah 58:13–14 says, "Call the sabbath a delight…then shalt thou delight thyself in the LORD." The Sabbath is to be a day of joy. We are to count it not a burden but a delight, literally "an exquisite delight." Motyer explains, "It is a day, therefore, for reverential, thoughtful use coupled with sweet joy."[28] God is our example in this. Exodus 31:17 says that God was "refreshed" by His resting on the seventh day of the creation week. This does not mean that the Almighty was tired and needed to renew His strength, for He does not grow weary (Isa. 40:28); rather God was refreshed by rejoicing in the good work that He had done. He teaches us by example that we must regularly rest in order to enjoy the glory of God's work, including His work in and through us. Ray Ortlund says,

> The Sabbath is meant to structure our weekly schedules around glorifying and enjoying God together. The Sabbath is God's appointed release for us from our self-worshiping addiction to work and productivity and efficiency and organization and busyness. The Sabbath is God's way of saying, "No, your highest values will not be professional and commercial. They will only end up destroying you and others through you. Your highest values will be worship and freedom and delight, enriching you and all around you."[29]

Thus the Sabbath is not just a doctrine and a discipline but also a delight. After creating the world in six days, Genesis 2:3 says, "God blessed the seventh day, and sanctified it." Thomas Watson observed, "It is not only a day of honour to God, but a day of blessing to us; it is not only a day wherein we give God worship, but a day wherein he gives us grace."[30] We must not go to church and for the rest of the day mope about our homes and say, "Well, I can't do this and

---

26. Burroughs, *Gospel Worship*, 56–61.

27. Thomas Watson, *The Ten Commandments* (Edinburgh: Banner of Truth, 1965), 100–101.

28. Motyer, *The Prophecy of Isaiah*, 483.

29. Raymond C. Ortlund, Jr., *Isaiah: God Saves Sinners*, Preaching the Word, ed. R. Kent Hughes (Wheaton, Ill.: Crossway Books, 2005), 391.

30. Watson, *The Ten Commandments*, 94.

I can't do that." The Sabbath is not an idle day. It is a day of activity. It is not a legalistic, negative day; it is a positive, glorious gift, a day of joy, a day of worship for the child of God, because for one day a week he may be relieved from his worldly responsibilities and dedicate himself wholly to his first love, to worship the living God.

So the Christian idea of Sabbath is not the pharisaical idea. The Pharisees, perhaps you know, made dozens of rules about what one may and may not do on the Sabbath. They made the Sabbath a day of burdens, a day of prohibitions. There are prohibitions, but the Sabbath is primarily about the positive acts of adoration and devotion. It is the delight of surrendering our will to God's will and worshiping Him. The Westminster Larger Catechism makes this point well when it says, "The sabbath or Lord's day is to be sanctified by an holy resting all the day…and making it our delight to spend the whole time (except so much as is to be taken up in works of necessity and mercy) in the public and private exercises of God's worship."[31]

I ask you in love, and I ask myself, What does our Sabbath-keeping look like? Do you look forward to it? Do you awake on Sunday morning with the first thought in your mind, "What joy, because it is the Sabbath today. I get to go up to God's house. We get to worship Him"? My friend, do you call the Sabbath a delight, or do you merely go through the rituals expected of you? Is it only an outward shell of habit? If you find no delight in giving a whole day to seeking and serving God, then you need to seriously consider if you are even saved. The mark of a true believer is to hunger and thirst for God's presence (Ps. 63:1–2).

There are people who call the Sabbath a delight. They rejoice to set aside their own wills and to worship God on His holy day as their earthly concerns fall away and God becomes their focus. They are the people who have learned that true rest is found only in Jesus Christ, who said, "Come unto me, all ye that labour and are heavy laden, and I will give you rest" (Matt. 11:28). You cannot keep the Sabbath without trusting in the Lord of the Sabbath to save you from your sins.

The Sabbath is a picture of the wonderful grace of God. God Himself painted this picture, saying in effect, "Israel, you work hard for six days. But then I give you a day of worship, and instead of requiring you to climb up to Me to get salvation on this day of worship, I come down to you by dwelling in My holy of holies, dwelling in My tabernacle. In My Word, I come to speak to you and to save your soul. This is not a day for you to work, for your works do not bring you close to Me. This is a day for you to rest, while My priests work for you through their sacrifices and prayers." Do you see? The Sabbath taught

---

31. Westminster Larger Catechism, Q. 117, in *The Reformation Heritage KJV Study Bible*, 2078.

Israel to rest in the work of Jesus Christ, the coming Priest and Sacrifice, as their only way to draw near to God. So now when God says to us, "Remember the sabbath day," He is saying, "Remember that I am a gracious God who will save you through faith in the blood of My Son."

Just as the old covenant Sabbath was a memorial of Israel's redemption from slavery in Egypt (Deut. 5:15), so the new covenant Sabbath is a memorial of our redemption from slavery to sin and misery. The old covenant ceremonial law expanded the Sabbath principle to include Sabbath years, one year in every seven, and then after seven Sabbath years, the year of Jubilee, the great Sabbath of Sabbaths in the ceremonial law. The Jubilee was the "acceptable year of the Lord" (Isa. 61:2), a year of liberation and restoration. Indentured Hebrew servants were set free and alienated family property was restored to its rightful owners (Lev. 25:8–16, 28–33, 39–41, 54). Jesus is our Jubilee!

What then should we do on the Lord's Day when we are not in public worship? If we are to rest from much of our ordinary activity, how can we be active in seeking the Lord? Bownd gives us eight excellent directions for keeping the whole day as a spiritual Jubilee. We should engage in:

1. *Self-examination* to confess our sins and give thanks for our graces.[32]

2. *Prayer* for ourselves, others, and especially the Spirit's empowerment of the ministry of God's Word, that the Holy Spirit would illuminate our minds with the truth, and furthermore that our affections would be shaped by our knowledge, recognizing that our affections—the strong motives of our hearts—have more direct influence on what we do than our understanding has.[33]

3. *Private reading of the Scriptures*, both reading widely in the Scriptures and reading specific texts and passages on which the sermons of the day are based.[34]

4. *Meditation* on God's truth, "which is the very life and strength" of reading the Bible, so that "by God's Holy Spirit, using earnest and diligent meditation in the Scripture, we shall most easily perceive how to apply that to our own practice, which hath been publicly taught."[35] Use meditation to feed prayer. George Swinnock wrote, "Meditation is the best beginning of prayer, and prayer is the best conclusion of meditation."[36]

---

32. Bownd, *True Doctrine of the Sabbath*, 379.
33. Bownd, *True Doctrine of the Sabbath*, 379–81.
34. Bownd, *True Doctrine of the Sabbath*, 382–83.
35. Bownd, *True Doctrine of the Sabbath*, 383–91.
36. George Swinnock, *The Christian Man's Calling*, in *The Works of George Swinnock* (1868; repr., Edinburgh: Banner of Truth, 1992), 1:112.

5. *Holy conversation* with others about what we have read in the Word or heard in the preaching of the Word, which is a duty in the Christian family (Deut. 6:6; 11:19).[37] You might ask a friend, "What have you read in the Word that has been of special help or benefit to you?"

6. *Meditation and conversation on God's works in creation and providence*, as commended to us in Psalm 92, "A Psalm or Song for the Sabbath day."[38] How can you "show forth" God's lovingkindness and faithfulness? What works of God make you glad? What do you learn from His judgments in the earth? Give thanks to God and sing praises to His name.

7. *Singing the Psalms*, many of which are well suited to be sung privately at home, enabling Christians to rejoice in the Lord, and to serve Him with gladness (Ps. 100:2). Singing God's praises, Bownd points out, is especially appropriate for the Sabbath because it is "the time of joy" more than any other day, and "therefore as the Lord then offereth himself wholly unto us, and his Son Christ Jesus to be made ours, with all his merits in the Word, the sacraments, and prayer, thereby doth fill our hearts with the joy of the Holy Ghost, even that joy that is unspeakable and most glorious [1 Peter 1:8]; so then especially we ought to sing for joy of the Lord."[39] The Lord's Day is to be a day not just to fill our minds but also to fire our hearts. Bownd wrote, "For even as all knowledge is increased especially by hearing, reading, and conferring about the Scripture; so all affections are most of all stirred up by meditation, prayer, and singing of Psalms."[40]

8. *Serving people in mercy and love*, especially the poor, the sick, the widows, the fatherless, and the foreigner, which includes making peace with those with whom we have a quarrel and speaking the gospel of peace to sinners.[41]

The Sabbath, then, is a day for seeking God in His Word and works. John Calvin said, "We have one definite day of the week which is to be completely spent in hearing God's word, in prayers and petitions, and in meditating upon his works so that we may rejoice in him."[42] And again, the key to delighting in

---

37. Bownd, *True Doctrine of the Sabbath*, 391–403.
38. Bownd, *True Doctrine of the Sabbath*, 403–17.
39. Bownd, *True Doctrine of the Sabbath*, 418–33.
40. Bownd, *True Doctrine of the Sabbath*, 423.
41. Bownd, *True Doctrine of the Sabbath*, 433–48.
42. Calvin, *Sermons on Genesis, Chapters 1–11*, 130.

the Sabbath is doing it all out of love for God. Watson wrote, "On the Sabbath the soul fixes its love on God; and where love is, there is delight."[43]

We see that the Sabbath is not a time for idleness and boredom but time to lay aside our earthly vocations so that we can devote ourselves to spiritual life and work. It is a time to feed and exercise your soul. Watson said, "The Sabbath is the market-day of the soul."[44] Similarly, Henry Scudder said, "For this is God's great [market], or fair-day for the soul, on which you may buy of Christ, wine, milk, bread, marrow, and fatness (Isa. 55:1–4), gold, white raiment, eye-salve (Rev. 3:18), even all things which are necessary, and which will satisfy, and cause the soul to live."[45] This day of rest is your opportunity to stock up for the coming week! Use it well.

Desire: Keep the Lord's Day in Hopeful Anticipation of the Day of the Lord
If we keep the Sabbath with delight, then the Lord promises us that He "will cause thee to ride upon the high places of the earth, and feed thee with the heritage of Jacob thy father: for the mouth of the LORD hath spoken it" (Isa. 58:14). To "ride upon the high places of the earth" refers to the way God provided for all of Israel's needs in the wilderness on their way to the promised land (Deut. 32:13).[46] The "heritage" or inheritance of Jacob is more than the land of Canaan; according to Isaiah 54, it is the spiritual and eternal riches promised in the new covenant.[47] This is not, then, just a promise of provision for our daily needs but a promise of inheritance in the eternal kingdom of God.

The Sabbath is a sign of the ultimate glory of the church's future.[48] The prophecy of Isaiah closes with the announcement of the promise of the new heavens and the new earth for God's people: "For, behold, I create new heavens and a new earth: and the former shall not be remembered, nor come into mind" (Isa. 65:17). In this new creation, the labor of God's people shall be wholly redeemed from the curse that has mingled pain and death with all our work:

---

43. Watson, *The Ten Commandments*, 118.

44. Watson, *The Ten Commandments*, 97.

45. Scudder, *The Christian's Daily Walk*, 93. The text reads "mart" for "market."

46. "He found him in a desert land, and in the waste howling wilderness; he led him about, he instructed him, he kept him as the apple of his eye. As an eagle stirreth up her nest, fluttereth over her young, spreadeth abroad her wings, taketh them, beareth them on her wings: so the LORD alone did lead him, and there was no strange god with him. He *made him ride on the high places of the earth*, that he might eat the increase of the fields; and he made him to suck honey out of the rock, and oil out of the flinty rock" (Deut. 32:10–13, emphasis added). The phrase is the same Hebrew words as those used in Isa. 58:14.

47. Isa. 54 ends with the statement, "This is the heritage of the servants of the LORD, and their righteousness is of me, saith the LORD" (Isa. 54:17b).

48. The following is adapted from Beeke, *Puritan Reformed Spirituality*, 114–15.

"They shall not labour in vain, nor bring forth trouble; for they are the seed of the blessed of the LORD, and their offspring with them" (v. 23).

This new (or renewed) order of creation will abide as the consummation of the promise of redemption. Not only is the labor of God's people to be wholly redeemed from the curse; the Sabbath also will at last come into its own as the universal day for the worship of Jehovah. Such is the promise of God: "For as the new heavens and the new earth, which I will make, shall remain before me, saith the LORD, so shall your seed and your name remain. And it shall come to pass, that from one new moon to another, and from one sabbath to another, shall all flesh come to worship before me, saith the LORD" (Isa. 66:22–23).

Therefore, to keep the Sabbath profitably today is to cultivate hope in the coming of our Lord, or "to begin in this life the eternal sabbath," as the Heidelberg Catechism says.[49] The Lord's Day is Resurrection Day, recalling Christ's resurrection and looking forward to the resurrection of all who are in Christ.[50] "Remember the sabbath" means there is a rest coming for the people of God. A perfect world is about to dawn. There will be a new order at the end of life's journey, and all those who know God by faith in Jesus will enter into eternal glory, the eternal Sabbath with their eternal Lord. And oh, what an eternal Sabbath this will be, friends—to be eternally with God! To be eternally resting in the very finished work in which God Himself rested and continues to rest, even the work of His only-begotten Son! Happy eternal Sabbath, when with perfected soul and resurrected body you shall glory in the King of Kings forever. "Remember the sabbath day" means "Remember eternity."

Robert Murray M'Cheyne said, "This is the reason why we love the Lord's day. This is the reason why we 'call the Sabbath a delight.'" When a believer steps away from his office cubicle or his station in the factory, sets aside his work clothes and worldly cares, and comes to the house of God, it is like the dawn of the resurrection. When he sits under the preaching of God's Word and hears the voice of the Shepherd leading and feeding his soul, it reminds him of the day when "the Lamb which is in the midst of the throne shall feed them, and shall lead them unto living fountains of waters: and God shall wipe away all tears from their eyes" (Rev. 7:17). When he joins in singing psalms of praise, it reminds him that one day he will join the voices of myriads of angels and redeemed men to worship God and the Lamb. Thus M'Cheyne wrote, "A well-spent Sabbath we feel to be a day of heaven upon earth."[51]

---

49. Heidelberg Catechism, LD 38, Q. 103, in *The Reformation Heritage KJV Study Bible*, 2002.
50. Campbell, *On the First Day of the Week*, 216.
51. Robert Murray M'Cheyne, "I Love the Lord's Day," in *Memoirs and Remains of Robert*

All our earthly Sabbaths should be kept with a desire to join in the worship of the angels and saints in glory. Every Lord's Day, look forward to the Day of the Lord. Make heaven a special focus of your meditations. The Sabbath gives unparalleled opportunities to "seek those things which are above, where Christ sitteth on the right hand of God" (Col. 3:1). We need the Sabbath so that the weeds of worldly cares and concerns do not choke the Word and smother the hope that is ours in Christ. Richard Sibbes said, "For whose good hath God appointed the Lord's day? Is it not for our own? Should we not grow base and earthly-minded, if one day in seven we should not be heavenly-minded, and think upon our everlasting condition in another world?"[52]

Conclusion

We have followed the Lord's teaching in Isaiah 58:13–14 to discover four steps toward profitable Sabbath-keeping. First, we must be convinced in our minds that the doctrine of the Sabbath is God's revealed truth. Second, we must exercise personal self-discipline and say *no* to other things so we can say *yes* to seeking God on the Sabbath. Third, in order that our Sabbath-keeping not become a hollow shell or proud legalism, God calls us to make the Sabbath a day of spiritual delight. Fourth, the best Sabbath on earth is only a foretaste of the feast of heaven, and that must be our ultimate hope and desire.

When we bring these four principles together, we see more clearly what the Lord is communicating through Isaiah's words: He is calling us to embrace the biblical doctrine of the Sabbath with holy discipline in order to delight in Christ and foster desire for the eternal Sabbath. *Remember the Sabbath day, to keep it holy.* It is God's day with His people and your day with God. If you had the opportunity to spend a whole day with someone very dear to you, wouldn't you be glad for it? Imagine a day to be with a kind father or mother, a loving spouse, or a dear friend. Would you resent putting aside your work to be with this loved one? Wouldn't you avoid anything that would distract or interrupt your time together? Let that be your attitude toward the Sabbath. Make it a day of love for God and love for Christ as Lord of the Sabbath day.

Murray M'Cheyne, ed. Andrew Bonar (1892; repr., Edinburgh: Banner of Truth, 1995), 596–97. The sentences between the quotes are slightly paraphrased from M'Cheyne's own words.

52. *The Works of Richard Sibbes*, 6:557, cited in Campbell, *On the First Day of the Week*, 219.

SYSTEMATIC AND
HISTORICAL THEOLOGY

Chapter 7

God-Centered Theology in the Ministry of the Word

The What, the Why, and the How of Proclaiming God-Centered Theology in Our Sermons

The ministry that centers on preaching the Word of God should be God-centered.[1] However, ever since the time of Simon the Sorcerer (Acts 8), men have been drawn to the work of the ministry and have done that work in ways that are more man-centered and man-pleasing than those commended to us in Scripture.

To be truly God-centered, ministry must also be Christ-centered. We confess that in Jesus Christ, "God was manifest in the flesh" (1 Tim. 3:16) and that "this is the work of God, that ye believe on him whom he hath sent" (John 6:29). If our work is centered on the Christ of Scripture, we cannot help but be centered on the God of Scripture. True Christianity does not offer a generalized theism.

To determine what a God-centered preaching ministry should look like, we should review the most important sources and models of Christian ministry: the work of the apostles. In particular, we shall look at ministry as described by the apostle Paul in 1 Corinthians 1:1–2:5. We shall consider the preacher, the hearers, the message, the method, the resources, and the goal of God-centered preaching of the Word.

The Preacher

How do we view ourselves as ministers of the Word? Why are we in the ministry? What does our work consist of?

THE WORD

"An apostle of Jesus Christ through the will of God" (1:1)

As an apostle, Paul was called to serve Jesus Christ as His authorized representative or "ambassador" (2 Cor. 5:20) to unbelievers. He was sent in the name of Christ and given the authority of Christ to do the work of Christ. He

---

1. This article is an expanded version of an address given at Ligonier's Pastor's Conference in 2007. I wish to thank Ray Lanning for his assistance.

was called to lay the foundation of the Christian church by preaching the gospel, gathering churches, and building them on the foundation of Christ Jesus. The work of an apostle was God-centered and Christ-centered. As Paul said in 2 Corinthians 4:5, "We preach not ourselves, but Christ Jesus the Lord; and ourselves your servants for Jesus' sake."

Ministers of the Word are not apostles and should not claim to be so. Even so, we are to follow the example of the apostles who gave themselves "continually to prayer, and to the ministry of the word" (Acts 6:4). The apostles laid the foundation of the ministry of the Word, then they entrusted the work to others. These others are described as "they who labor in the word and doctrine" (1 Tim. 5:17), "pastors and teachers" (Eph. 4:11), "ministers of God" (1 Thess. 3:2), and "ministers of Jesus Christ" (1 Tim. 4:6). Their charge is to "preach the word; be instant in season, out of season; reprove, rebuke, exhort with all longsuffering and doctrine" (2 Tim. 4:2).

Do we, as ministers of the Word, take this view of our office? Is our view of the ministry rooted in what Christ has ordained through the ministry and writings of His apostles?

Paul goes on to say that he holds his office "through the will of God," that is, as a calling and commission from God. God sent Christ into the world to redeem and reconcile man to God. God raised Christ from the dead and received Him into heaven. God gave Christ gifts that He then gave to His church—first, apostles, prophets, and evangelists of the New Testament period and, subsequently, the ministers of the Word, ruling elders, and deacons who followed them. These leaders were appointed according to a principle as old as the Old Testament: that "no man taketh this honour unto himself, but he that is called of God" (Heb. 5:4).

In addition to a saving knowledge of Christ and personal experience of the truth of the gospel, the first requirement for ordination to the ministry of the Word is a clearly perceived, well-articulated, and well-attested call from God to preach, so that we can say with Paul, "Woe is unto me, if I preach not the gospel!" (1 Cor. 9:16). Indeed, the difficulties, heartaches, and frustrations of the ministry are so great that only a person who is convicted that he is a minister through the will of God will have the fortitude to persevere to the end in the work of the ministry.

So fellow ministers of the Word, I urge you to go back to first things. How did you come to hold this office? Have you been ordained by the laying on of unseen hands? How were you called to this work? What does that imply for the way you go about doing it? And to whom are you accountable for the faithfulness with which you do it?

To keep God central to our theology as preachers of the Word, we must not only have a sense of our God-ordained calling as ministers of the Word but we must also have a right understanding of our hearers.

The Hearers

To whom are the ministers of the Word sent? On whom are they to bestow their labors?

THE WORD
"The church of God which is at Corinth" (1:2)

As ministers of the Word, we are to preach the gospel to all mankind, according to the command of Jesus Christ. However, we are called in particular to serve local assemblies of the church of Christ. So let us examine what the church is as a divine institution and what that implies for our ministry.

Paul describes those to whom he addresses his epistle as "the church of God which is at Corinth." The church at Corinth had a distinct human history in its origins, its growth and development, and its descent into division, disorder, and immorality. No one knew that history better than Paul; yet, the first aspect of the church that he mentions here is the awesome truth that the church at Corinth is "the church of God."

Paul addresses his epistle to "the assembly" or "congregation" of God. These terms suggest a body of people called together as a permanent society to deal with matters of common interest. The members of this assembly are human beings with never-dying souls, and so are the messengers who report good news to them, the teachers who inform and instruct them, the governors who preside over them, and the stewards who serve them. Even so, the One who gathers, nurtures, governs, protects, and sustains this congregation is God, not man. To this the Scriptures bear witness.

Human agents are only the instruments of God's will and good pleasure; Christ is the One who builds the church. The human agents who "plant" and "water" the church are nothing in themselves, Paul says. It is "God that giveth the increase" (1 Cor. 3:6–7). Human efforts will come to naught unless God uses them to accomplish His purposes for His church.

This God-centered view of the church is the foundation of the apostle's hopes as he writes to a church in disarray. Paul's conviction that God had established His church at Corinth fortifies all Paul's efforts to recover this church from its fallen state. The apostle views the members of this church as set apart or "sanctified in Christ" and "called to be saints." That is the basis of every appeal, entreaty, and command in his epistle. So long as Corinthian Christians "call upon the name of Jesus Christ our Lord," there is hope for the recovery and reformation of this church, no matter how badly disordered its conduct, how erroneous its doctrine, or how chaotic its worship.

So let us preach to our congregations with hope in God and the gospel message. Let us preach, as François Fenelon says, "with the zeal of a friend, the generous energy of a father, and the exuberant affection of a mother."[2] Let us preach the full message of God with such conviction that we can say with Martin Luther, "I preach as though Christ were crucified yesterday, rose from the dead today, and is coming back to earth again tomorrow."[3]

The Message
What should be the content of a God-centered ministry of the Word?

THE WORD
"Grace be unto you, and peace from God" (1:3);
nothing "among you, save Jesus Christ, and him crucified" (2:2).

The apostle Paul greeted the church at Corinth as he customarily greeted all of his churches: "Grace be unto you, and peace from God our Father, and from the Lord Jesus Christ" (1:3). Still, we might pass over the importance of this greeting to the Corinthians unless we recognized that Paul would not say such words if he did not mean them.

The grace of God bestowed on us in Christ and the peace of God that we enjoy through Christ are the fruits of being justified by faith (Rom. 5:1). They are a summary of all that Paul has to say to the churches in his care. They assure believers how their salvation is the work of God's grace, whether it be the electing grace of the Father, the redeeming grace of the Son, or the sealing and sanctifying grace of the Holy Spirit (Eph. 1:3–14). They also express the apostle's longing for believers to know the fullest measure of God's grace and love, which is "the peace of God, which passeth all understanding" (Phil. 4:7).

Sadly, it is possible to preach grace with little or no reference to the love of God or the work of Jesus Christ. But such grace is merely a general kind of benevolence or good cheer. It is something human and ordinary, something we more or less deserve and practice as good citizens and kindly neighbors. Such grace is mere graciousness. Preaching about this type of grace is like a

---

2. Cited in J. J. S. Bird, ed., *The Preacher's Analyst* (London: Elliot Stock, 1884), 8:286.
3. Cited in Steven J. Lawson, *The Kind of Preaching God Blesses* (Eugene, Ore.: Harvest House, 2013), 61.

mild-mannered man addressing a company of mild-mannered people, advising them to become more mild-mannered.

Likewise, it is possible to reduce peace to mere peace of mind, an emotional or psychological state of well-being or calm. The preacher of this type of peace becomes a counselor or therapist who massages away knots of unhappiness that may intrude upon our psyches. Grace loses its meaning when it is divorced from the gospel revelation of the wrath of God against sin and the sufferings of Christ on the cross to atone for sin. Peace loses its meaning when it is no longer seen as a precious gift purchased for us at great cost, enjoyed only in communion with the Father and the Son, and possible only because the blood of Christ cleanses from all sin (1 John 1:7).

Because of the Spirit's blessing on Paul's God-centered preaching of the gospel, the Corinthians knew much intellectually and spiritually of God's grace. So they understood what Paul meant when he said, "I thank my God always on your behalf, for the grace of God which was given you by Christ Jesus" (1 Cor. 1:4). They also understood that the reason they lacked true peace was because of divisions among themselves as a church and various ways they were sinning against Christ, but especially against the Holy Spirit.

They also knew that Paul's mission as a God-called apostle was to preach the truth about God's only begotten Son, Jesus Christ. So he wrote in 1 Corinthians 2:2: "For I determined not to know anything among you, save Jesus Christ, and him crucified." Nothing else was as important to ministry as to know Christ. Paul wasn't just referring here to his preaching but to his entire ministry. His driving conviction was to know Christ. He deliberately renounced every consideration but Christ crucified. Paul lived in a society ripe with issues to address. There was much to be said to philosophers who demanded a hearing, to civic and political leaders who had problems and vices. But Paul's message first and foremost was to preach Christ crucified.

Paul's words here have puzzled some. But understanding its meaning is crucial because this statement of Paul is the defining statement of Christian ministry. Paul is not saying here that he preached only the scenes of the cross. He did tell the Galatians that before their eyes, he publicly portrayed Christ as crucified (Gal. 3:1). No doubt he did that everywhere to help believers gain a greater appreciation of the cost of their redemption and to help bring the lost to Christ.

Paul also preached Christ crucified to impress listeners with the seriousness of God's wrath against sin. He preached Christ to proclaim Him as the One who absorbed the full weight of divine wrath against sin so that God might receive sinners back into His presence. Paul preached Christ to stress the significance of Christ's death and that He who knew no sin was made sin for us "that we might be made the righteousness of God in him" (2 Cor. 5:21). Paul preached Christ to show that His vicarious curse-bearing and His innocent suffering for the guilty offered just grounds for imputed righteousness.

But Paul preached the whole counsel of God. So in saying he preached nothing but Christ crucified, Paul was speaking in comprehensive terms. *The gospel* (1:17), *the preaching of the cross* (1:18), *Christ crucified* (1:23), and *Jesus Christ and Him crucified* (2:2) are all synecdochic yet comprehensive phrases that relate to the same subject. Paul was saying that he preached a complete message about the person and work of Jesus Christ. He preached the message of Jesus's saviorhood and lordship. The Lord Jesus was the center of Paul's preaching because God the Father says Jesus Christ deserves to be that center. Christ is the Lord from heaven in whom the world is reconciled to God. He is Savior, and He is Lord.

Likewise, Charles Spurgeon said to his theological students after preaching for fifteen years at the Metropolitan Tabernacle, "I have been preaching nothing but this name of Jesus Christ. That, brethren, is the magnet; He will draw His own to Himself. If we cry out to see conversion, this must be our preaching—more constant preaching of Christ. He must be in every sermon; He must be the top and bottom of all the theology that we preach."[4]

We as ministers must be like Paul in setting Jesus Christ in all His glory and grandeur before men and women, not only for the sake of evangelism but also for the sake of the spiritual growth and maturity of those who are under our pastoral care. Theologically that is critical, for the central means by which God works out His salvation is by uniting believers with Jesus Christ. We grow in the Christian life by growing in the knowledge of Christ and His work. Moreover, every spiritual blessing that God has provided for His people in their journey through this world to glory is found in Jesus Christ.

But still the question remains: Why does Paul speak here in such exclusive terms? How can he say that his message was nothing but the person and work of Christ?

The most obvious answer is that Jesus Christ was the *central focus* of Paul's preaching. This is certainly part of what Paul is saying. When men and women came to hear Paul preach, they came expecting to hear about Jesus. And they did. But this statement also offers us a glimpse into Paul's hermeneutic, or interpretation of the gospel. This apostle who claimed to preach all the counsel of God claimed also to preach only Christ. That is to say, *to preach the whole counsel*

---

4. C. H. Spurgeon, *Lectures to My Students* (Peabody, Mass.: Hendrickson, 2017), 82.

of God is to preach Christ. Christ is the central theme throughout God's Word. Christ is the centerpiece of Scripture. The Bible is a Christocentric book. And so Paul preached the message of God about Jesus Christ.

But let us take this one step further. Paul does not merely say here that Christ is his primary focus; he says that Christ, ultimately, is his *only subject.* Everything he says goes back to Christ. Apart from Christ crucified, there is nothing to say.

Today, we tend to divide theological studies into categories: pneumatology, ecclesiology, soteriology, eschatology, and so on. That has its place for theological study, to be sure. But for Paul, Christology was the overarching head of every kind of theology. Take away Christ and we have no theology at all, he seems to say. "Christ is all" was *the* apostolic theme. Everything we believe and are and have is in relation to Christ. He is our only theme, our only theology.

Knowing this, we can begin to understand why Paul confronted every problem by referring back to Christ. If the problem was divisions in the assembly, Paul ran back to Christ, asking, "Is Christ divided? Was Paul crucified for you, or were ye baptized in the name of Paul?" (1:13). If the problem was immorality, he ran back to Christ, saying, "Purge out therefore the old leaven, that ye may be a new lump.... For even Christ our passover is sacrificed for us" (1 Cor. 5:7). If the problem was temptation, Paul ran back to Christ, saying, "And such were some of you: but ye are washed, but ye are sanctified, but ye are justified in the name of the Lord Jesus, and by the Spirit of our God" (1 Cor. 6:11). If instruction on home life was needed, he ran back to Christ, saying, "Wives, submit yourselves unto your own husbands, as unto the Lord" (Eph. 5:22); "Husbands, love your wives, even as Christ also loved the church, and gave himself for it" (5:25); and "Children, obey your parents in the Lord" (Eph. 6:1).

In all aspects of Christian life, Paul focused on Christ. When he tells us to forgive one another, Paul reminds us of Christ, who forgave us (Col. 3:13; Eph. 4:32). When he teaches us to be generous in our giving, he refers to Christ, who gave so much for us (2 Cor. 8:9). When he tells us about humility, he teaches us to put on the mind of Christ (Phil. 2:5–8). When he preaches on everyday holiness, it is on the ground that we are crucified and risen with Christ to new life in Him (Rom. 6:1–14).

Christ is the answer to every problem in life. To the lost and to the saved, Christ is the answer. So Paul says, "He is all I preach. He is the whole sum and substance of my theology and my ministry. He is our only hope, yes, but He is more. He is our highest incentive to holiness."

Let us resolve to preach God-centered theology by preaching Christ. As Charles Bridges says, "Let Him be the diamond in the bosom of your every sermon."[5] Preach Christ with theological articulation, with divine grandeur, and with human passion. By working out the implications of "Jesus Christ and him crucified," we provide people with all the material the Holy Spirit uses to bring them from glory to glory (2 Cor. 3:18). This is Paul's objective in all his preaching: Jesus Christ, "whom we preach, warning every man, and teaching every man in all wisdom; that we may present every man perfect in Christ Jesus" (Col 1:28). That must also be our comprehensive theme in ministry.

Some speak of balance in preaching today, meaning we should be careful to spread out the topics we cover across Scripture. However, Paul tells us that if Christ is not the sum and substance of our message, then we are not balanced at all. So do not relegate Christ to certain aspects of the Bible or to certain aspects of life. Rather, let Him be your exclusive theme. This, according to Paul, is the only message that works. If we do not preach Christ alone, we are no better than secular moralists.

"Jesus Christ and Him crucified" is the distinctive message of the gospel. Jesus is our only theme, yes, and the whole of it. As Richard Baxter says, "If we can but teach *Christ* to our people, we teach them all."[6] Or as Spurgeon says: "A sermon without Christ as its beginning, middle, and end is a mistake in conception and a crime in execution.... When we preach Jesus Christ, then we are not putting out the plates, and the knives, and the forks, for the feast, but we are handing out the bread itself.... [Let us] preach Christ to sinners if we cannot preach sinners to Christ.... I wish that our ministry—and mine especially— might be tied and tethered to the cross."[7]

Are you known first as a preacher of Christ? Can you say with Samuel Rutherford, "Next to Christ I have one joy, to preach Christ my Lord"?[8] William Perkins, often called the father of Puritanism, closed his classic homiletics book, *The Art of Prophesying*, by declaring that all he had said could be summarized in this: "Preach one Christ by Christ to the praise of Christ."[9] Let Christ be our God-centered message, our God-centered theology, and our God-centered calling.

The Method
How can we keep God the center of our preaching?

---

5. Charles Bridges, *The Christian Ministry* (London: Seeleys, 1849), 258.

6. *The Practical Works of...Mr. Richard Baxter* (London: Thomas Parkhurst, 1707), 4:358.

7. *The Complete Works of C. H. Spurgeon*, vol. 33 (n.p.: Delmarva, 2013), Sermon no. 1940, p. 1.

8. Cited by Scott Brown, ncfic.org/blogs/643; accessed May 7, 2020

9. *The Works of William Perkins*, ed. Joseph A. Pipa and J. Stephen Yuille (Grand Rapids: Reformation Heritage Books, 2020), 10:356.

THE WORD

"The power of God, the wisdom of God,
the deep things of God" (1:24; 2:10)

Paul kept God central in his preaching by determining not to know anything "save Jesus Christ and him crucified" (1 Cor. 2:2). He might have taken other approaches, such as entertaining the troubled Corinthians with a display of "excellency of speech" or impressing them with his knowledge of Greco-Roman philosophy or overwhelming them with his wisdom. He might have used those approaches to resolve their difficulties and assure them of prosperity and happiness in the world (2:1).

Instead, Paul came to the troubled Corinthians with a very specific message: "the testimony of God" (2:1). Some assume this meant Paul advocated preaching "the simple gospel," devoid of any deep theology, abstracting Christ's atoning death from its biblical context and presenting it as a simple remedy for all life's problems. "Christ is the answer," they say, resenting it when someone with better sense asks, "But what was the question?"

Paul's summary of his message goes beyond being a "simple gospel." Rather, it addresses the "deep things of God" as it asks: Who is Jesus of Nazareth? What did He say and do? Why is He proclaimed as the Christ, and what does that mean? In a day when the Romans were crucifying many people, what was unique about Christ's death on the cross? What could it possibly mean for the people of Corinth, or anyone else in the whole world?

Paul's summary addresses such deep things as God's wrath against sin, the love of God for sinners and His eternal decree or plan to save them, the promises God made to the fathers long ago, the distinct persons in the Godhead, the incarnation of the eternal Son of God as Jesus of Nazareth, the law of atonement, the efficacy of Christ's death as an offering for sin, and God's divine attestation in the resurrection of Christ and His ascension into heaven. No wonder that Paul calls it "the testimony of God." Paul's sermons in the book of Acts show that he covered all these themes in his preaching.

For Paul, preaching Christ includes the kind of preaching Vance Havner describes as declaring "sin black, hell hot, judgment certain, eternity long, and salvation free."[10] Such preaching aims to give young and old a sense of God and His presence. As Martyn Lloyd-Jones once said, "I can forgive the preacher almost anything if he gives me a sense of God."[11]

---

10. Vance Havner, *It Is Time* (New York: Fleming H. Revell, 1943), 1.
11. Martyn Lloyd-Jones, *Preaching and Preachers* (Grand Rapids: Zondervan, 1972), 98.

In 1 Corinthians 1 and 2, Paul says that even though preaching "Christ and him crucified" was discounted by the Greeks as nonsense or "foolishness" and opposed by the Jews as something scandalous or offensive and a "stumbling block," it is nonetheless "the power of God, and the wisdom of God" (1:24). If the Greeks could not perceive the wisdom of God in the gospel in preaching, it was because of their natural blindness, Paul said. If the Jews were offended by the spectacle of a crucified Messiah, it was because of the unbelief and hardness of their hearts.

Paul could take this view because he knew that the elect understood the power of God in the gospel, when in due time they were called to faith by the preaching of the Word and the work of the Spirit (1:24). The wisdom of God revealed in the gospel was hidden from those who, as "natural men," were strangers to the illuminating work of the Spirit (2:14).

In election and reprobation, Paul sees the fulfillment of God's great purpose to glorify Himself in the sight of the whole world. By sovereignly choosing, calling, and making use of "the foolish, the weak, the base, and the despised, yea, and things which are not" (1:27–28), God displays His supreme wisdom, power, glory, honor, and being. He shows that He has no need of the world's wisdom or the help of man or the wealth and power of the rich and famous of this world, "that no flesh should glory in his presence" (1:29).

In sum, Paul focused his preaching on "the deep things of God" (2:10) and "the things that are freely given us of God" (2:12). He focused on the grace of God, the peace of God, the power of God, and the wisdom of God revealed in the death of Christ on the cross, which pardons God's chosen ones who believe on "Jesus Christ and him crucified."

Paul did not preach the great things of God as theological abstractions or intellectual puzzles. Rather, he spoke in plain words with the conviction of true faith and ablaze with love for God and man because he disdained empty rhetoric and cheap theatrics in the pulpit (2:4). Paul goes on to explain that the God of the Bible is at the center of it all, "for of him, and through him, and to him, are all things" (Rom. 11:36).

One cannot be a true minister of the New Testament without a thorough knowledge of the great doctrines of the Bible, an understanding of how they relate to each other and to Christ, and a clear conception of "what man is to believe concerning God, and what duty God requires of man" (Shorter Catechism, Q. 3). The minister of the Word has nothing to gain from ignorance, error, simplistic thinking, or intellectual laziness.

A God-centered ministry focuses on Scripture, the gospel, and the way of salvation. The minister of the Word must battle the human tendency to be self-centered and man-centered in his thinking by applying himself wholly to the Scriptures, and the Scriptures wholly to himself. We find help in this battle by searching the Scriptures daily and by reading the best of Reformed and Puritan theology and preaching.

The Resources

What does a God-centered ministry depend on for effectiveness?

THE WORD

*"That your faith should not stand in the wisdom
of men, but in the power of God" (2:5)*

The God-centered ministry of the apostle Paul was effective, both in his day and today. His teaching continues to bear abundant fruit in the church, for every Christian who is "a Gentile by nature" (cf. Gal. 2:15) is indebted to the unwavering, faithful work of the apostle Paul as a minister of the Word.

It is tempting to view Paul as one of the wonders of his time in being brilliant, cultured, charismatic, good-looking—a true, strong, natural leader that pulpit committees are forever hoping to discover. Yet here is Paul's own account of himself at Corinth: "I was with you in weakness, and in fear, and in much trembling. And my speech was not with enticing words of man's wisdom, but in demonstration of the Spirit and of power" (1 Cor. 2:3–4). The writer of these words offers no impression of tanned, sleek, "muscular" Christianity, no jaunty self-confidence and ability to master a bad case of nerves. Instead, he confesses he has no winning way with words, no salesman's ability to close a deal, no clever responses to his detractors and opponents.

Paul was not resorting here to false modesty. He was a strong advocate of sober thinking about oneself and one's abilities (Rom. 12:3). That said, 1 Corinthians 2 does indicate that Paul knew the tricks of public speaking, and that, had he wished to, he could have used them to make a name for himself as a preacher. The point is that Paul, indeed, did approach the church at Corinth with fear and trembling. Corinth was a wicked city, and the task of dealing with a fractious bunch of believers was daunting. Indeed, it was a situation impossible for Paul, who had a profound sense of inadequacy, to correct. He did not come to Corinth bounding with confidence, convinced of success. He did not believe he carried "revival in his briefcase," as certain modern-day evangelists have claimed. Rather, he felt the work was too great for him, the calling too high. Paul was a brilliant man, and he surely could have influenced many to make human decisions for Christ. But he knew he could not in himself do lasting good in his listeners.

And yet, Paul did enjoy success in Corinth. But that success was due to the Spirit of God. As Paul writes, "My speech and my preaching was not with enticing words of man's wisdom, but in demonstration of the Spirit and of power" (1 Cor. 2:4). As Paul preached, God's Spirit was at work. The Spirit powerfully demonstrated the truth of Paul's message to those who heard him. His gospel was made effective, not by external means but by the inward, efficacious call of God (cf. 1:18–31).

Despite Paul's fear and weakness, he felt confident, not in himself but in God. One of the strange, mysterious, yet holy things about preaching is that we can often feel unequal to the task, perhaps even to the point of physical weakness and sickness. At the same time we are bold in preaching the message of God because we are dependent on the Holy Spirit. When we rely fully on that power, we believe that God will work through His preached Word in the lives of sinners. We preach, believing that God will, by the power and grace of His Spirit, not return our words to Him void. The Spirit of God will work through the proclamation of the God-centered Word. That fills us with holy expectation as we ascend the pulpit in personal weakness and inadequacy.

Paul made a deliberate choice to depend on other resources for the effectiveness and fruitfulness of his ministry of the Word. He relied on the truth of God's Word and the power of the Holy Spirit to carry the day with his hearers. He did not try to gather a following around himself or his abilities. He wanted the faith of every Christian to stand not "in the wisdom of men but in the power of God" (2:5).

Are we failing to preach the unsearchable riches of Christ by resorting to storytelling, trendy topics, or foolish humor to win popularity and entertain our hearers? It is clear from Paul's epistle that such preaching offers no confidence in the power of truth, the powerful truth of God's Word.

Paul took his stand with the inspired psalmist who declared, "I believed, and therefore have I spoken" (Ps. 116:10; 2 Cor. 4:13), believing that faith in God and in His Word were essential for a God-centered ministry. Paul was well aware that in any faithful ministry of the Word, much seed falls on unproductive soil (Matt. 13:3–23). But he also knew that to produce lasting effects the preached Word must be accompanied by the sovereign, life-giving, life-changing operation of the Holy Spirit. Almost any well-trained speaker can thrill an audience, but only the Holy Spirit can use those words to move sinners to repentance and kindle the light of faith in darkened, unbelieving hearts.

So Paul took pains to prune away anything that savored of man and to preach the gospel message of "Jesus Christ, and him crucified" so that "the Holy Ghost sent down from heaven" (1 Peter 1:12) might open a way for that message in the minds and hearts of the hearers. He was careful in his preaching to direct people to trust in God's power alone. To run to Paul for help would not do; they must run to God.

Paul was never so arrogant as to assume the Spirit's role. He was very concerned that no one believe something simply because he said so. Rather, he trusted God to work in listeners through the plain preaching of the gospel.

Though Paul was not eloquent or mighty in the Scriptures, like Apollos of Alexandria, who had a following at Corinth (1:12), that preacher soon discovered that eloquence is no substitute for a thorough knowledge of the doctrines of grace (Acts 18:25–26). Apollos only became helpful to others when his eloquence served God's Word, through the grace of God.

Clearly Paul agonized over the problematic Corinthian church, asking himself such questions as, *What will become of these Corinthian Christians when I am gone?* If their faith depends on Paul and his words, what will happen when he leaves? They should regard him as only a messenger, a mere earthen vessel, and merely the servant of Christ. The message was the important thing, not the messenger. These Corinthian Christians would persevere in believing that message only by the power of God, not because of the wisdom of men.

Simply put, Paul staked his ministry on the faithfulness of God. Because God is faithful, a minister of the Word may look to God to honor His Word, to bless the faithful proclamation of "Jesus Christ and him crucified" to bring to glorious perfection the illumining, quickening, sanctifying, and sustaining work of His Spirit in the lives of His people (Ps. 138:8; Phil. 1:6).

The Goal

What is the aim of God-centered ministry? How can that be achieved? How should it be measured?

THE WORD
"He that glorieth, let him glory in the Lord" (1:31)

The aim of a God-centered ministry is to glorify God. It is to extol God to the highest, in the splendor of all His attributes. Faithful ministers aim to give God the same place in their own hearts and in the hearts of their people as He holds in the universe. Every other consideration, whether it be building the church or extending Christ's kingdom or contributing to the happiness of people, must be subordinate to this one all-controlling motive. What is not done to God's glory is sin.

Likewise, what is done to God's glory must be done according to God's revealed will. We sometimes speak of God's "prescriptive" will. The revelation of God's will in His written Word is a word of command. It is not descriptive but prescriptive in ordaining how ministers are to go about doing the work He has put into their hands.

Some people believe the authority of Scripture extends only to the truths that Scripture teaches but not to its specific commands. For example, we view the matter of Christian worship as "open-ended," finding in the Bible only a few basic ideas that we are free to develop as we please. Not surprisingly, Christians who learn in church to pay little regard to the biblical regulation of worship go home with little concern for observing the biblical regulation of their life and conduct.

Truth begins with the ministry of the Word. As ministers, we must strive to bring listeners into subjection to God and to Christ. We must model that subjection in everything we say and do, in and out of the pulpit. We must make the Word of God the sole rule of our faith, our preaching, our worship, and the way we live. We must aim to be as holy out of the pulpit as we appear to be in it. Our lives must be transcripts of our sermons. We must die to ourselves, to the world, and to the praise and criticism of men. Like John the Baptist, who pointed his own disciples away from himself to Christ (John 3:30), our motive must be "Not I, but Christ!" In this way, we glorify God and do the greatest good to others.

Success in the ministry may be measured in various ways. Too often we measure it in terms of numbers and recognition. We ask, Who preaches to the most people? Who raises the most money? Who sells the most books? Whose radio broadcast is on the most stations? Who is invited to appear at public meetings and political rallies or to endorse candidates for office? Whose opinions are cited in the periodicals and newspapers? Whose website garners the most hits? Whose church is growing in numbers? We may deny it, but we are impressed by such things.

Those measurements hardly apply to Paul's goals in ministry. The living God at the center of Paul's theology and ministry makes use of things that appear to men to be foolish, weak, base, and despised, or even nothing at all. We must remember that "the world by wisdom knew not God" (1:21). A God-centered ministry cannot be achieved by consulting the wisdom of the world, by courting the favor of men, or by forsaking the ways of the Word of God. True success in the ministry should be measured by depth of true faith, consistency of life, faithfulness in doing the will of God, and persevering to the end. The ministry that glorifies God in these ways is truly a success.

That is the kind of ministry we need. All the attention must be Godward (cf. 1:31). Our faith and the faith of our people must be in the triune God. Our faith and the faith of our people must stand firm in God's power and serve His glory. Let us resolve to conduct our ministry accordingly. That is what Paul is saying to you today. Do not pretend that you can have success and take the credit. To have real success, God alone must have the glory.

The apostolic model for Christian ministry is thus a God-centered ministry based on sound theology that is in keeping with the gospel. There is no room for personal glory in the ministry, much less divisions over the popularity of ministers (1:11–13). Stay humble and dependent on the One who calls you to ministry. Focus on the glory of God and on the white fields of harvest rather than on yourself. Let your comfort in life and death be your faithful Savior and Sender, Jesus Christ. To every preacher of the Word, Paul says: Preach the message of God about Jesus Christ, relying on the Holy Spirit to do what He alone can do. And do all of this to the glory of God, who alone is worthy. As Philip Doddridge writes, "Perish each thought of human pride, / Let God alone be magnified; / His glory let the heavens resound, / Shouted from earth's remotest bound."[12]

Luther once said that Paul's pen could not stop writing about God in Christ because Paul could not get God in Christ out of his mind and heart. From 1 Corinthians 1:1 to 2:5 alone, Paul references the various names of God more than sixty times. God was central to the apostle's theology, his preaching, his life. Christ was all in all for Paul. That is why he could say, "For me to live is Christ, and to die is gain" (Phil. 1:21).

Paul was on fire for God. Let us not rest until we, too, are consumed with God. Think of Lloyd-Jones's remarkable definition of preaching: "Preaching is theology come through a man who is on fire."[13] Let us storm the mercy seat to ask God to revive our hearts with God-centered lives and theological depth and preaching, for then we would surely see better days in the church of Jesus Christ.

---

12. *The Works of Philip Doddridge* (London: W. J. and S. Richardson, 1803), 5:31.
13. Lloyd Jones, *Preaching and Preachers*, 97.

Chapter 8

Reading the Puritans

A medieval Talmudic scholar, R. Isaiah Di Trani (*c.* 1200–1260), once asked, "Who can see farther, a giant or a dwarf?"

The answer was, "Surely the giant, because his eyes are higher than those of the dwarf."

"But if the giant carries the dwarf on his shoulders, who can see farther?" Di Trani persisted.

"Surely the dwarf, whose eyes are now above the eyes of the giant," was the answer.

Di Trani then said, "We too are dwarfs riding on the shoulders of giants.... It is by virtue of the power of their wisdom that we have learned all that we say, and not because we are greater than they were."[1]

The point is: a dwarf must realize his place among giants. This is true of all human achievement. When we survey church history, we discover giants of the faith, such as Aurelius Augustine (354–430), Martin Luther (1483–1546), John Calvin (1509–1564), John Owen (1616–1683), and Jonathan Edwards (1703–1758). Amid those giants the Puritans also rise as giants of exegetical ability, intellectual achievement, and profound piety.

Upon this mountain our Reformed "city" is built. We are where we are because of our history, though we are dwarves on the shoulders of giants. Who would George Whitefield (1714–1770), Charles Hodge (1797–1878), Charles Spurgeon (1834–1892), Herman Bavinck (1854–1921), J. Gresham Machen (1881–1937), or D. Martyn Lloyd-Jones (1899–1981) be if not for their predecessors? Despite this, Puritan studies were sorely neglected until the resurgence

---

1. Cited in Hanina Ben-Menahem and Neil S. Hecht, eds., *Authority, Process and Method: Studies in Jewish Law* (Amsterdam: Hardwood Academic Publishers, 1998), 119. For a shorter version of this article, see *Southern Baptist Journal of Theology* 14, 4 (Winter 2010): 20–37. Several parts of this article have been adapted from other writings by the author who wishes to thank Kyle Borg for his research assistance on its first sections.

of Puritan literature in the late 1950s. In many evangelical circles today, Puritan theology is still marginalized. While the Puritans built palaces, we are comfortable building shacks; where they planted fields, we plant but a few flowers; while they turned over every stone in theological reflection, we content ourselves with pebbles; where they aimed for comprehensive depth, we aim for catchy sound bites.

The Latin phrase *tolle lege*, meaning "pick up and read," offers a remedy for this apathy toward spiritual truth. Our ancestors have left us a rich theological and cultural heritage. We can say of the Puritans what Niccolò Machiavelli (1469–1527) said of his evening routine of reading the ancients, "I enter the ancient courts of rulers who have long since died. There I am warmly welcomed, and I feed on the only food I find nourishing."[2]

Returning to Puritan writings will also reward a diligent reader. Whitefield said, "Though dead, by their writings they yet speak: a peculiar unction attends them to this very hour."[3] Whitefield predicted that Puritan writings would be read until the end of time due to their scriptural truth. Spurgeon agreed, saying, "In these [writings] they do live forever. Modern interpreters have not superseded them, nor will they altogether be superseded to the end of time."[4] Today we are witnessing a revival of sorts in reading the Puritans. Initiated largely by the Banner of Truth Trust, which has been systematically and carefully publishing Puritan literature since the late 1950s,[5] Puritan reprints in the last sixty years now include two hundred Puritan authors and nine hundred Puritan titles printed by more than eighty publishers. Reformation Heritage Books (RHB) alone—of which the Puritan line of Soli Deo Gloria is an imprint—carries approximately two hundred Puritan titles and also sells at discount prices close to six hundred Puritan titles that are currently in print.

We are grateful for this resurgence of interest in Puritan writings. However, this resurgence faces some challenges and poses some questions, which I will address in this chapter. I wish to address six points. First, I will offer a brief overview of Puritan emphases, and then, second, point out several ways of how to benefit by reading the Puritans. Third, I will consider some ideas on

---

2. Cited in *Modern Political Thought: Readings from Machiavelli to Nietzsche*, ed. David Wootton (Indianapolis: Hackett Publishing Company, 1996), 7.

3. George Whitefield, *The Works of the Reverend George Whitefield, M.A....: containing all his sermons and tracts which have been already published: with a select collection of letters* (London: printed for Edward and Charles Dilly, 1771–72), 4:307.

4. Cited in Steven C. Kettler, *Biblical Counsel: Resources for Renewal* (Newark, Del.: Letterman Associates, 1993), 311.

5. Cf. Ligon Duncan, in *Calvin for Today*, ed. Joel R. Beeke (Grand Rapids: Reformation Heritage Books, 2010), 231.

how to begin reading the Puritans then, fourth, look at a reading plan for the writings of an individual Puritan, Thomas Goodwin. Fifth, I will look at some of my favorite Puritans, and finally, I will consider some ideas for printing more Puritan books in the future.

Definition and Emphases of Puritanism

Much ink has been spilled in defining who the Puritans were. The difficulty is that Puritanism, which dates from the 1560s to the early 1700s, was never identified with a particular denomination or group. As Edward Hindson noted, Puritanism included "those preachers and laymen who held certain spiritual convictions that transcended confessional boundaries. It was more a religious term than an ecclesiastical label."[6]

In this brief study, our use of the word *Puritan* includes not only those people who were ejected from the Church of England by the Act of Uniformity in 1662 but also those in Britain and North America who, for several generations after the Reformation, worked to reform and purify the church and to lead people toward biblical, godly living consistent with the Reformed doctrines of grace.[7] Puritanism grew out of at least three needs: (1) the need for biblical preaching and the teaching of sound, Reformed doctrine; (2) the need for biblical, personal piety that stresses the work of the Holy Spirit in the faith and life of the believer; and (3) the need for a restoration of biblical simplicity in liturgy, vestments, and church government so that a well-ordered church life would promote the worship of the triune God as prescribed in His Word.[8]

---

6. Edward Hindson, *Introduction to Puritan Theology: A Reader* (Grand Rapids: Baker Books, 1976), 17.

7. Richard Mitchell Hawkes, "The Logic of Assurance in English Puritan Theology," *Westminster Theological Journal* 52 (1990): 247. For the difficulties in, and attempts at, defining Puritanism, see Ralph Bronkema, *The Essence of Puritanism* (Goes: Oosterbaan and LeCointre, 1929); Leonard J. Trinterud, "The Origins of Puritanism," *Church History* 20 (1951):37–57; Jerald C. Brauer, "Reflections on the Nature of English Puritanism," *Church History* 23 (1954):98–109; Basil Hall, "Puritanism: The Problem of Definition," in G. J. Cumming, ed., *Studies in Church History* (London: Nelson, 1965), 2:283–96; Charles H. George, "Puritanism as History and Historiography," *Past and Present* 41 (1968):77–104; William Lamont, "Puritanism as History and Historiography: Some Further Thoughts," *Past and Present* 42 (1969):133–46; Richard Greaves, "The Nature of the Puritan Tradition," in R. Buick Knox, ed., *Reformation, Conformity and Dissent: Essays in Honour of Geoffrey Nuttall* (London: Epworth Press, 1977), 255–73; D. M. Lloyd-Jones, "Puritanism and Its Origins," *The Puritans: Their Origins and Successors* (Edinburgh: Banner of Truth, 1987), 237–59; J. I. Packer, "Why We Need the Puritans," in *A Quest for Godliness: The Puritan Vision of the Christian Life* (Wheaton, Ill.: Crossway, 1990), 21–36; Joel R. Beeke, *The Quest for Full Assurance: The Legacy of Calvin and His Successors* (Edinburgh: Banner of Truth, 1999), 82–84; Randall J. Pederson, "Puritan Studies in the Twenty-First Century: Preambles and Projections," *Puritan Reformed Journal* 2, 2 (July 2010):108–122.

8. Peter Lewis, *The Genius of Puritanism* (Grand Rapids: Reformation Heritage Books, 2008), 11–16.

Tom Webster suggests three elements of being a Puritan. First, Puritans had a dynamic fellowship with God that shaped their minds, affected their emotions, and penetrated their souls. They were grounded in someone outside of themselves, namely, the triune God of the Scriptures. Second, Puritans embraced a shared system of beliefs grounded in the Scriptures. This system is today referred to as Reformed orthodoxy. Third, out of this spiritually dynamic worldview, the Puritans established a network of relationships among believers and ministers.[9]

Puritans were committed to search the Scriptures, organize their findings, and then apply those to all areas of life. This created a confessional, theological, and Trinitarian movement. It sought personal conversion and communion with God, and the spiritual well-being of the family, the church, and national life.[10]

Today it is almost an insult to be called a Puritan. That is because people have such a misguided opinion of the Puritans. Perry Miller and Thomas Johnson said, "Confusion becomes more confounded if we attempt to correlate modern usages with anything that can be proved pertinent to the original Puritans themselves."[11] Today a Puritan is often viewed through the lens of Nathaniel Hawthorne's (1804–1864) *The Scarlet Letter* (1850) or the Salem witch trials; he is seen as a stoic killjoy more bent on fire, brimstone, and damnation than the joys of salvation. However, this is a gross misrepresentation; with rare exceptions, the Puritans were none of these.

Rather than defending the Puritan against false ideas, we will take note of a former saying that "[Puritanism] is more easily described than defined."[12] Scott Clark says Reformed theology has always had its own particular theology, piety,

---

9. "It has proved possible to trace a network of godly divines in early Stuart England, similar to William Haller's 'spiritual brotherhood,' but going far beyond the great names of Sibbes, Gouge, Preston, and Dod to draw in the humblest of the painful preachers and the most junior of the aspirant ministers coming out of Oxford and Cambridge…. It was rooted in what Peter Lake called a 'certain evangelical protestant world-view' predicated upon the 'potentially transforming effects of the gospel on both individuals and on the social order as a whole.' It is Lake's contention that if Puritanism is to be defined at all it must be in terms of this 'spiritual dynamic'…the nature of that spiritual dynamic [being] a sense of communion with God, scripturally informed, deeply emotional, and yet aspiring to something beyond the subjective" (Tom Webster, *Godly Clergy in Early Stuart England: The Caroline Puritan Movement, c. 1620–1643* [Cambridge: Cambridge University Press, 1997], 333. Webster cites William Haller, *The Rise of Puritanism* (New York: Columbia University Press, 1938), chap. 1, and Peter Lake, *Moderate Puritans and the Elizabethan Church* (Cambridge: Cambridge University Press, 1982), 279, 282–83.

10. Beeke and Pederson, *Meet the Puritans*, xvii.

11. Perry Miller and Thomas H. Johnson, eds., *The Puritans*, revised ed. (New York: Harper Torchbooks, 1963), 1:1–2.

12. Miller and Johnson, *The Puritans*, 1:1.

and practice.[13] This is also true of Puritanism. So let us turn to a brief overview of the theology, piety, and practice of this movement.

Theology

In doctrine, the Puritans were thoroughly Calvinistic. Miller and Johnson wrote of the Puritans, "They approved this doctrine not because he [Calvin] taught it, but because it seemed inescapably indicated when they studied scripture or observed the actions of men."[14] Calvinism, as the Puritans understood it, was an entire worldview. That is quite different from the way contemporary people think of Calvinism. Often Calvinism is viewed merely as a soteriological doctrine that emphasizes the sovereignty of God. Many people define Calvinism simply as the doctrines of grace summarized in the acronym TULIP.

But Calvinism is much more than that. Being rooted in the sixteenth-century religious renewal in Europe that we refer to as the Protestant Reformation, Calvinism was not exclusively soteriological but was an entire system of theology developed by Protestant Reformers. Calvinistic theology includes all the essential evangelical doctrines, such as the deity of Christ, objective atonement, and the person and work of the Holy Spirit. This system of theology has been clarified in various confessions of the Reformed and Presbyterian churches, such as the Belgic Confession of Faith (1561), Heidelberg Catechism (1563), Second Helvetic Confession (1566), Canons of Dort (1618–1619), and the Westminster Standards (1640s).[15]

Puritan theology "was not a mere reduplication of the dogmas of the *Institutes*," however.[16] Puritanism developed several Calvinistic doctrines more thoroughly, such as covenant theology, spiritual adoption, assurance of faith, and sanctification. Puritanism also sought further reform in the Church of England.[17] As Miller and Johnson noted, "Puritan theorists worked out a substantial addition to the theology of Calvinism."[18]

---

13. R. Scott Clark, *Recovering the Reformed Confession* (Phillipsburg, N.J.: P&R, 2008), 3. Peter Lewis emphasizes a similar structure in *Genius of Puritanism*, 11–20.

14. Miller and Johnson, *The Puritans*, 1:56.

15. For an overview and parallel harmony of these seven confessions, see Joel R. Beeke and Sinclair B. Ferguson, eds., *Reformed Confessions Harmonized* (Grand Rapids: Baker, 1999). See also James Dennison, *Reformed Confessions of the 16th and 17th Centuries*, 4 vols. (Grand Rapids: Reformation Heritage Books, 2009–2014).

16. Miller and Johnson, *The Puritans*, 1:57.

17. Miller and Johnson, *The Puritans*, 1:5–6.

18. Miller and Johnson, *The Puritans*, 1:57.

Piety

While the Puritans were great exegetes, their intellectual rigor was matched or even surpassed by their piety.[19] The cultivation of spirituality or piety has been addressed in various ways by Christian traditions. Reformed Christianity advocates a spiritual life shaped by Scripture's teachings and directives. It derives from the conviction that "all scripture is given by inspiration of God, and is profitable for doctrine, for reproof, for correction, for instruction in righteousness" (2 Tim. 3:16). Hindson wrote, "Their view of life was theocentric, direct and controlled by God's Word."[20]

No movement promoted Reformed piety and spirituality more than the Puritans. This Word-centered piety involved every facet of life. The all-consuming passion of the Puritan was to live *coram Deo*—before the face of God. This belief grew out of the conviction that God has sovereignly saved us so, in response, we live out of gratitude in visible piety. As Kelly Kapic writes, "For the Puritan, intellectual assent to Christian doctrine had to be balanced with the practical outworking of God's grace in life experiences."[21]

This emphasis is evident in William Ames's (1576–1633) definition of theology as "the doctrine of living to God."[22] It demonstrates the common theme in Puritan piety of *experimental* or *experiential* Christianity. The Puritans were convinced that theology must be brought into the daily experience of the believer. Richard Sibbes (1566–1635) wrote, "Experience is the life [of] a Christian. What is all knowledge of Christ without experience, but a bare knowledge.... It is the experimental knowledge of Christ, and of the life of Christ, that doth us good."[23] Thomas Manton (1620–1677) noted that it is by experience the Holy Spirit establishes the Word in our hearts.[24]

The Puritans' experiential faith is not the same as experientialism, which makes experience the end-all, thereby losing its biblical moorings. This is common in contemporary Pentecostalism. Rather, experiential Reformed Christianity addresses how the Holy Spirit brings the truth of God's Word into the experience of the Christian, both in terms of what he ought to be *idealistically* as a believer in Christ (e.g., Rom. 6:10–23 and chap. 8) and what he finds himself

---

19. For a discussion on Puritan piety, see Joel R. Beeke, *Puritan Reformed Spirituality* (Darlington, U.K.: Evangelical Press, 2006).

20. Hindson, *Puritan Theology*, 24.

21. Kelly Kapic and Randall Gleason, *The Devoted Life: An Invitation to the Puritan Classics* (Downers Grove, Ill.: IVP, 2004), 25.

22. William Ames, *The Marrow of Theology* (Grand Rapids: Baker, 1968), 77.

23. Richard Sibbes, *The Works of Richard Sibbes* (Edinburgh: Banner of Truth, 1983), 4:412.

24. Thomas Manton, *The Works of Thomas Manton* (Birmingham, Ala.: Solid Ground, 2008), 6:403.

to be *realistically* in his holy war against sin (e.g., Rom. 7:14–25). All this is meant to be God-centered and not experience-centered—that is to say, the goal of the believer's examination of his own experience is to trace the Spirit's work in his own soul so as to give glory to God. William Guthrie (1620–1655) rightly said, "The Spirit speaking in the Scripture is judge of all."[25] This includes the full scope of our individual experiences in communion with God. Such experience is necessary for a true and vital religion. William Gurnall (1616–1679) said, "If gospel truths work not effectually on thee for thy renovation and sanctification, thou art a lost man; they will undoubtedly be 'a savor of death' to thee. O how can you then rest till you find them transforming your hearts and assimilating your lives to their heavenly nature!"[26] This experiential emphasis was the heartbeat of Puritan piety, for the Puritans believed that Christianity is a Spirit-worked, vital, heartfelt faith that produces a genuine Christian walk.

Practice

The Puritans also practiced piety. Richard Steele (1629–1692) wrote, "There are thousands of beams and rays, yet they all meet and center in the sun. So an upright man, though…he has many subordinate ends—to procure a livelihood, to preserve his credit, to provide for his children—but he has no supreme end but God alone."[27] Within the relationships a Puritan had with himself, others, and the world, he was to practice godliness. Thomas Shepard (1605–1649), who said, "God hath not lined the way to Christ with velvet," spoke of four narrow gates that are essential for a believer to pass through in daily practice: humiliation, faith, repentance, and opposition to the world, devils, and self.[28] Consequently, the Puritans taught that believers were to live circumspectly and moderately, understanding that their pleasures and emotions "must not be liked for themselves, but so far as God is enjoyed with them and in them."[29]

The practice of Puritan piety was not limited to one's personal life. The Puritans also maintained a rigorous and devout ecclesiastical life. Sabbath worship was the high point of the Puritan week, for in the congregated assembly God works by the Spirit in the hearts of His people. Puritan worship services were governed by the ordinances God has explicitly laid down in Scripture,

---

25. William Guthrie, *The Christian's Great Interest* (Edinburgh: Banner of Truth, 2002), 25.

26. William Gurnall, *The Christian in Complete Armour* (Edinburgh: Banner of Truth, 2002), 2:569.

27. Richard Steele, *The Character of an Upright Man* (Morgan, Pa.: Soli Deo Gloria, 2004), 13.

28. Thomas Shepard, *The Sincere Convert* (Morgan, Pa.: Soli Deo Gloria, 1999), 64–65.

29. Nathanael Vincent, *Attending Upon God Without Distraction* (Grand Rapids: Reformation Heritage Books, 2010), 14–15.

which are preaching the Word, the sacraments, and prayer. These ordinances, wrote Thomas Vincent, are the "ordinary means whereby Christ communicateth to us the benefits of redemption."[30]

The Puritans did not seek approval from the world but diligently fought the fight of faith to win their Master's approbation. In their pursuit of living *soli Deo gloria* (to the glory of God), they were true-hearted, single-hearted, and wholehearted.

In short, Puritanism was a kind of vigorous Calvinism. Experientially, it was warm and contagious; evangelistically, it was aggressive yet tender; ecclesiastically, it was theocentric and worshipful; and politically, it advocated right relations between king, Parliament, and subjects. Puritan doctrine embraced all personal, domestic, ecclesiastical, societal, and national life.[31]

How to Profit from Reading the Puritans

Here are nine ways you can grow spiritually by reading Puritan literature today:

1. *Puritan writings help shape life by Scripture.* The Puritans loved, lived, and breathed Holy Scripture. They also relished the power of the Spirit that accompanied the Word. Rarely can you open a Puritan book and not find its pages filled with Scripture references; their books are all Word-centered. More than 90 percent of their writings are repackaged sermons rich with scriptural exposition. The Puritan writers truly believed in the sufficiency of Scripture for life and godliness.

If you read the Puritans regularly, their Bible-centeredness will become contagious. These writings will teach you to yield wholehearted allegiance to the Bible's message. Like the Puritans, you will become a believer of the Living Book, echoing John Flavel (1628–1691), who said, "The Scriptures teach us the best way of living, the noblest way of suffering, and the most comfortable way of dying."[32]

2. *Puritan writings show how to integrate biblical doctrine into daily life.* Cornelis Pronk wrote, "The Puritan's concern...was primarily ethical or moral rather than abstractly doctrinal."[33] The Puritan writings express this emphasis in three ways.

---

30. Thomas Vincent, *The Shorter Catechism Explained from Scripture* (Edinburgh: Banner of Truth, 2004), 234.

31. Sidney H. Rooy, *The Theology of Missions in the Puritan Tradition* (Grand Rapids: Eerdmans, 1965), 310–28.

32. Cited in John Blanchard, *The Complete Gathered Gold* (Darlington, U.K.: Evangelical Press, 2006), 49.

33. Cornelis Pronk, "Puritan Christianity," *The Messenger* (March 1997): 5.

First, they *address your mind*. In keeping with the Reformed tradition, the Puritans refused to set mind and heart against each other but viewed the mind as the palace of faith. William Greenhill (1591–1671) stated, "Ignorance is the mother of all errors."[34] The Puritans understood that a mindless Christianity fosters a spineless Christianity. An anti-intellectual gospel quickly becomes an empty, formless gospel that never gets beyond catering to felt needs. Puritan literature is a great help for understanding the vital connection between what we believe and how that affects the way we live.

Second, Puritan writings *confront your conscience*. Today many preachers are masterful at avoiding convicting people of sin, whereas the Puritans were masters at convicting us about the heinous nature of our sin against an infinite God. This is amply displayed in Ralph Venning's (*c*. 1622–1674) *The Sinfulness of Sin*. For example, Venning wrote, "Sin is the dare of God's justice, the rape of his mercy, the jeer of his patience, the slight of his power, the contempt of his love."[35]

The Puritans excelled at exposing specific sins, then asked questions to press home conviction of those sins. As one Puritan wrote, "We must go with the stick of divine truth and beat every bush behind which a sinner hides, until like Adam who hid, he stands before God in his nakedness."

Devotional reading should be confrontational as well as comforting. We grow little if our consciences are not pricked daily and directed to Christ. Since we are prone to run for the bushes when we feel threatened, we need daily help to come before the living God, "naked and opened unto the eyes of him with whom we have to do" (Heb. 4:13). In this, the Puritans excelled. Owen wrote: "Christ by his death destroying the works of the devil, procuring the Spirit for us, hath so killed sin, as to its reign in believers, that it shall not obtain its end and dominion…. Look on him under the weight of your sins, praying, bleeding, dying; bring him in that condition into thy heart of faith."[36]

Third, Puritan writers *engage your heart*. They feed the mind with solid biblical substance, and they move the heart with affectionate warmth. They wrote out of love for God's Word, love for the glory of God, and love for the souls of readers. They did this because their hearts were touched by God and they, in turn, longed for others to feel and experience salvation. As John Bunyan (1628–1688) exclaimed, "O that they who have heard me speak this day did

---

34. William Greenhill, *Exposition on the Prophet of Ezekiel* (London: Samuel Holdsworth, 1839), 110.

35. Ralph Venning, *The Sinfulness of Sin* (Edinburgh: Banner of Truth, 2001), 32. Venning adapts this statement from John Bunyan.

36. John Owen, *The Works of John Owen* (Edinburgh: Banner of Truth, 2000), 6:85.

but see as I do what sin, death, hell, and the curse of God is; and also what the grace, and love, and mercy of God is, through Jesus Christ."[37]

3. *Puritan writings show how to exalt Christ and see His beauty.* The Puritan Thomas Adams (1583–1652) wrote, "Christ is the sum of the whole Bible, prophesied, typified, prefigured, exhibited, demonstrated, to be found in every leaf, almost in every line, the Scriptures being but as it were the swaddling bands of the child Jesus."[38]

The Puritans loved Christ and relished His beauty. The best example of this is probably Samuel Rutherford's (1600–1661) *Letters*, which sing the sweetest canticles of the Savior. To an elder, Rutherford wrote, "Christ, Christ, nothing but Christ, can cool our love's burning languor. O thirsty love! Wilt thou set Christ, the well of life, to thy head, and drink thy fill? Drink, and spare not; drink love, and be drunken with Christ!"[39] To another friend, he wrote, "I have a lover Christ, and yet I want love for Him! I have a lovely and desirable Lord, who is love-worthy, and who beggeth my love and heart, and I have nothing to give Him! Dear brother, come further in on Christ, and see a new wonder, and heaven and earth's wonder of love, sweetness, majesty, and excellency in Him."[40] If you would know Christ better and love Him more fully, immerse yourself in Puritan literature.

4. *Puritan writings highlight the Trinitarian character.* The Puritans were driven by a deep sense of the infinite glory of a Triune God. Edmund Calamy (1600–1666) noted this doctrine should "be allowed to be of as great importance in itself and its consequences, as any of our most distinguishing Christian principles."[41] When the Puritans said in the Shorter Catechism that man's chief end was to glorify God, they meant the triune God: Father, Son, and Holy Spirit. They took Calvin's glorious understanding of the unity of the Trinity in the Godhead and showed how that worked out in electing, redeeming, and sanctifying love and grace in the lives of believers.

Owen wrote an entire book on the Christian believer's distinct communion with each person in the Godhead—with God as Father, Jesus as Savior, and the Holy Spirit as Comforter. Samuel Rutherford echoed the conviction of many

---

37. John Bunyan, *The Works of John Bunyan* (Edinburgh: Banner of Truth, 1991), 1:42.
38. Thomas Adams, *The Works of Thomas Adams* (Edinburgh: James Nichol, 1862), 3:224.
39. Samuel Rutherford, *The Letters of Samuel Rutherford* (Edinburgh: Banner of Truth, 2006), 173.
40. Rutherford, *Letters*, 426.
41. Edmund Calamy, *Sermons Concerning the Doctrine of the Trinity* (London, 1722), 6.

Puritans when he said that he did not know which divine person he loved the most, but he knew that he needed each of them and loved them all. The Puritans teach us how to remain God-centered while being vitally concerned about Christian experience so that we don't fall into the trap of glorifying experience for its own sake.

5. *Puritan writings show how to handle trials.* Puritanism grew out of a great struggle between the truth of God's Word and its enemies. Reformed Christianity was under attack in England at the time of the Puritans, even more than Reformed Christianity is under attack today. The Puritans were good soldiers in the conflict; they endured great hardships and suffered much. Their lives and writings arm us for battle and encourage us in suffering. The Puritans teach us how affliction is necessary to humble us (Deut. 8:2), to teach us what sin is (Zeph. 1:12), and to bring us back to God (Hos. 5:15).

Much of the comfort the Puritans offer grows out of the very nature of God. Henry Scougal (1650–1678) said of afflicted believers that it comforts them "to remember that an unerring providence doth overrule all their seeming disorders, and makes them all serve to great and glorious designs."[42] And Thomas Watson (*c.* 1620–1686) declared, "Afflictions work for good, as they conform us to Christ. God's rod is a pencil to draw Christ's image more lively upon us."[43]

6. *Puritan writings describe true spirituality.* The Puritans stressed the spirituality of the law, the spiritual warfare against indwelling sin, the childlike fear of God, the wonder of grace, the art of meditation, the dreadfulness of hell, and the glories of heaven. If you want to live deeply as a Christian, read Oliver Heywood's *Heart Treasure.* Read the Puritans devotionally, then pray to be like them. Ask questions such as: Am I, like the Puritans, thirsting to glorify the triune God? Am I motivated by biblical truth and biblical fire? Do I share their view of the vital necessity of conversion and of being clothed with the righteousness of Christ? Do I follow the Puritans as they followed Christ? Does my life savor of true spirituality?

7. *Puritan writings show how to live by holistic faith.* The Puritans applied every subject they discussed to practical "uses," which propel a believer into passionate, effective action for Christ's kingdom. In their daily lives they integrated

---

42. Henry Scougal, *The Works of Henry Scougal* (New York: Robert Carter, 1846), 169.
43. Thomas Watson, *All Things for Good* (Edinburgh: Banner of Truth, 2001), 28.

Christian truth with covenant vision; they knew no dichotomy between the sacred and the secular. Their writings can help you live in a way that centers on God. They will help you appreciate God's gifts and declare everything "holiness to the Lord."

The Puritans excelled as covenant theologians. They lived that theology, covenanting themselves, their families, their churches, and their nations to God. Yet they did not fall into the error of "hyper-covenantalism," in which the covenant of grace became a substitute for personal conversion. They promoted a comprehensive worldview that brought the whole gospel to bear on all of life, striving to bring every action in conformity with Christ so that believers would mature and grow in faith. The Puritans wrote on practical subjects such as how to pray, how to develop genuine piety, how to conduct family worship, and how to raise children for Christ. In short, as J. I. Packer noted, they taught how to develop a "rational, resolute, passionate piety [that is] conscientious without becoming obsessive, law-oriented without lapsing into legalism, and expressive of Christian liberty without any shameful lurches into license."[44]

8. *Puritan writings teach the primacy of preaching.* William Perkins (1558–1602) explained why preaching is so critical: "Through preaching those who hear are called into the state of grace, and preserved in it."[45] To the Puritans, preaching was the high point of public worship. "It is no small matter to stand up in the face of a congregation, and deliver a message of salvation or damnation, as from the living God, in the name of our Redeemer," wrote Richard Baxter (1615–1691).[46]

The Puritans taught that preaching must be expository and didactic, evangelistic and convicting, experiential and applicatory, powerful and plain in its presentation, ever respecting the sovereignty of the Holy Spirit. For the Puritans, what transpired on Sabbath mornings and evenings was not merely a pep talk but an encounter with God by the Spirit through the Word.

9. *Puritan writings show how to live in two worlds.* The Puritans said we should have heaven in our eye throughout our earthly pilgrimage. They took seriously the New Testament passages that say we must keep the hope of glory before our minds to guide and shape our lives here on earth. They viewed this life as

---

44. J. I. Packer, *A Quest for Godliness: The Puritan Vision of the Christian Life* (Wheaton, Ill.: Crossway, 1990), 24.

45. William Perkins, *The Art of Prophesying* (Edinburgh: Banner of Truth, 2002), 7.

46. Richard Baxter, *The Practical Works of Richard Baxter* (Morgan, Pa.: Soli Deo Gloria, 2001), 4:383.

"the gymnasium and dressing room where we are prepared for heaven," teaching us that preparation for death is the first step in learning to truly live.[47]

These nine points are reason enough to demonstrate the benefit of reading the Puritans. We live in dark days where it seems the visible church in many areas around the globe, and particularly in the West, is floundering. Waning interest in doctrinal fidelity and a disinterest in holiness prevails in many Christians. The church's ministry has been marginalized or ignored. The Puritans were in many ways ahead of their times. Their books address the problems of our day with a scriptural clarity and zeal that the church desperately needs.

Where to Begin Reading the Puritans

The sheer amount of Puritan literature being reprinted today and offered online can be intimidating. Furthermore, the number of books written about the Puritans is nearly as vast as the collection of Puritan titles. Our Puritan Research Center alone contains three thousand books of primary and secondary sources plus thousands of articles about the Puritans.[48]

The Puritans were people of their time, and even while much of what they wrote is timeless, we must understand them within their context. They battled the spirit of their age and waged doctrinal debates pertinent to their day and which, at times, seem quite removed from issues of today. Secondary sources help us understand their historical milieu. The goal of this section is to offer bibliographic information that can help you read the Puritans.

The best overall introduction to the worldview of the Puritans is Leland Ryken's *Worldly Saints: The Puritans as They Really Were*.[49] Other somewhat shorter yet helpful introductions include Peter Lewis, *The Genius of Puritanism*; Erroll Hulse, *Who Are the Puritans? And What Do They Teach?*[50]; and *Following God Fully: An Introduction to the Puritans* by Michael Reeves and me. For basic biographies of the 150 Puritans that have been reprinted in the last fifty years, together with brief reviews of 700 reprinted Puritan titles, see *Meet the Puritans, with a Guide to Modern Reprints* by Randall J. Pederson

---

47. Packer, *A Quest for Godliness*, 13. For a more in-depth look at various ways reading the Puritans profit us, see Joel R. Beeke and Brian G. Hedges, *Thriving in Grace: Twelve Ways the Puritans Fuel Spiritual Growth* (Grand Rapids: Reformation Heritage Books, 2020).

48. www.puritanseminary.org

49. Leland Ryken, *Worldly Saints* (Grand Rapids: Zondervan, 1990).

50. Peter Lewis, *The Genius of Puritanism* (Grand Rapids: Reformation Heritage Books, 2008); Erroll Hulse, *Who Are the Puritans?* (Darlington, England: Evangelical Press, 2000); Joel R. Beeke and Michael Reeves, *Following God Fully: An Introduction to the Puritans* (Grand Rapids: Reformation Heritage Books, 2019).

and me.[51] We suggest the best way to use *Meet the Puritans* is to read one biography and reviews of that Puritan writer per day, thus using the book as a kind of daily biographical devotional. For short biographies of more obscure Puritans who have not been reprinted in the last fifty years, see Benjamin Brook (1776–1848), *The Lives of the Puritans*.[52] For brief biographies of most of the Puritans at the Westminster Assembly, see William S. Barker's *Puritan Profiles*.[53] For individual studies of various Puritan divines and aspects of their theology, begin with J. I. Packer's *A Quest for Godliness: The Puritan Vision of the Christian Life* and my *Puritan Reformed Spirituality*.[54]

The Puritans can be difficult to read. Their wording, grammatical structure, and detail can be hard for the modern mind to grasp. It is best to read short books from some popular Puritan writers before attempting to read Puritans of more theological profundity, such as Owen and Thomas Goodwin (1600–1679). I recommend beginning with Puritan divines like Thomas Watson (*c.* 1620–1686), John Flavel (1628–1691), and George Swinnock (*c.* 1627–1673). Watson wrote succinctly, clearly, and simply. His *Art of Divine Contentment, Heaven Taken by Storm* and *The Doctrine of Repentance* are good places to begin.[55]

Flavel, who was pastor at the seaport of Dartmouth, became known as a seaman's preacher. He is one of the simplest Puritans to read. His *Mystery of Providence* is filled with pastoral and comforting counsel.[56] Swinnock showed a special sensitivity to the Scriptures and could explain doctrines with great wisdom and clarity. You might try his *The Fading of the Flesh and the Flourishing of Faith*, recently edited by Stephen Yuille and printed in a contemporary style.[57] Both Flavel and Swinnock have had their entire works published in multivolume sets.[58]

---

51. Joel R. Beeke and Randall J. Pederson, *Meet the Puritans, with a Guide to Modern Reprints* (Grand Rapids: Reformation Heritage Books, 2006).

52. Benjamin Brook, *The Lives of the Puritans*, 3 vols. (Pittsburgh: Soli Deo Gloria, 1994).

53. William S. Barker, *Puritan Profiles* (Fearn: Mentor, 1999).

54. J. I. Packer, *A Quest for Godliness: The Puritan Vision of the Christian Life* (Wheaton, Ill.: Crossway, 1990); Joel R. Beeke, *Puritan Reformed Spirituality* (Darlington, England: Evangelical Press, 2006).

55. Thomas Watson, *The Art of Divine Contentment* (Morgan, Pa.: Soli Deo Gloria, 2001); idem, *Heaven Taken by Storm* (Orlando: Northampton Press, 2008); Thomas Watson, *The Doctrine of Repentance* (Edinburgh: Banner of Truth, 1988).

56. John Flavel, *The Mystery of Providence* (Edinburgh: Banner of Truth, 1963).

57. George Swinnock, *The Fading of the Flesh and the Flourishing of Faith*, ed. Stephen Yuille (Grand Rapids: Reformation Heritage Books, 2009). Other easy-to-read Puritan titles in this new series include William Greenhill, *Stop Loving the World* (Grand Rapids: Reformation Heritage Books, 2010) and John Flavel, *Triumphing Over Sinful Fear* (Grand Rapids: Reformation Heritage Books, 2011).

58. *The Works of John Flavel*, 6 vols. (repr., London: Banner of Truth, 1968); *The Works of George Swinnock*, 5 vols. (repr., Edinburgh: Banner of Truth, 2002).

The books of Richard Sibbes and Thomas Brooks (1608–1680) are also a good place to start, especially Sibbes's *The Bruised Reed* and Brooks's *Precious Remedies Against Satan's Devices*.[59] You may also benefit from that master of allegory, John Bunyan, though some of his treatises reflect an unexpected intellectual depth for a tinker from Bedford.[60] Then, too, you could move your way through the Banner of Truth's line of Puritan Paperbacks (which is how I began reading the Puritans at age fourteen) or the more recent Pocket Puritans series. Some Puritan titles written by Owen have been abridged by R. J. K. Law and made easier to read. These are good places to start reading the experiential writings of the Puritans.

How to proceed next depends on your particular interest. After becoming acquainted with various styles of Puritan literature, you have a broad spectrum of possibilities to consider. What joys you might have wrestling with Owen's weighty treatments of the glory of Christ, his soul-searching treatise on sin, and his exegetical masterpiece on Hebrews. Or how thrilling it would be to ascend the heights of the intellectual and spiritual atmosphere with Jonathan Edwards or to plumb the depths of divine attributes with Stephen Charnock (1628–1680). You may probe the redemptive glories of the covenant with John Ball (1585–1640) and Samuel Petto (*c*. 1624–1711) or be allured by the redemptive doctrines of justification and sanctification with Walter Marshall (1628–1680), Peter van Mastricht (1630–1706), or Robert Traill (1642–1716). You could entrust yourself to a competent guide like Edward Fisher (d. 1655) to bring you safely through the law/gospel distinction or be impressed with the profound but simple writings of Hugh Binning (1627–1653). Prepare to be challenged by the soul-penetrating works of Thomas Shepard (1605–1649) and Matthew Mead (1629–1699) or be instructed by the plain reason of Jeremiah Burroughs (*c*. 1600–1646), Richard Baxter (1615–1691), and George Hammond (*c*. 1620–1705).

Whatever topic you select, you may be sure that the Puritans have addressed it with scriptural precision, vivid illumination, practical benefit, experiential warmth, and an eye to the glory of God. The reader who diligently probes Puritan writings with the willingness to gaze under every rock they overturn and prayerfully consider what they say will be drawn ever more deeply into the revealed mysteries of God. When you follow the writings of these faithful men, you will find that it will be for the betterment of your soul.

---

59. Richard Sibbes, *The Bruised Reed* (Edinburgh: Banner of Truth, 1998), Thomas Brooks, *Precious Remedies Against Satan's Devices* (Edinburgh: Banner of Truth, 1968).

60. *The Works of John Bunyan*, 3 vols. (repr., Edinburgh: Banner of Truth, 2004).

How to Read an Individual Puritan

There are no rules for reading individual Puritans, but here are some suggestions. Generally speaking, Puritans are best read slowly and meditatively. Don't rush through their books. Look up the texts they cite to prove their points. Intersperse your reading with prayer.

Here are some guidelines for reading Thomas Goodwin, who was, for twenty years, my favorite Puritan writer. The first collection of Goodwin's works was published in five folio volumes in London from 1681 to 1704, under the editorship of Thankful Owen, Thomas Baron, and Thomas Goodwin Jr. An abridged version of those works was later printed in four volumes (London, 1847–50). James Nichol printed a more reliable collection of Goodwin's works in twelve volumes (Edinburgh, 1861–66) in the Nichol's Series of Standard Divines. It is far superior to the original five folio volumes and was reprinted in 2006 by Reformation Heritage Books.

Goodwin's exegesis is massive; he leaves no stone unturned. His first editors (1681) said of his work, "He had a genius to dive into the bottom of points, to 'study them down,' as he used to express it, not contenting himself with superficial knowledge, without wading into the depths of things."[61] Calamy said, "It is evident from his writings [that] he studied not words, but things. His style is plain and familiar; but very diffuse, homely and tedious."[62]

Here is a plan for reading Goodwin's works:

1. Begin by reading some of the shorter, more practical writings of Goodwin, such as *Patience and Its Perfect Work*, which includes four sermons on James 1:1–5. This book was written after much of Goodwin's personal library was destroyed by fire (*Works*, 2:429–67). It contains much practical instruction on the spirit of submission.

2. Read *Certain Select Cases Resolved*, which offers three experiential treatises that reveal Goodwin's pastoral heart for afflicted Christians. Each deals with specific struggles in the believer's soul: (a) "A Child of Light Walking in Darkness" encourages the spiritually depressed based on Isaiah 50:10–11 (3:241–350). The subtitle summarizes its contents: "A Treatise Shewing The Causes by which, The Cases wherein, and the Ends for which, God Leaves His Children to Distress of Conscience, Together with Directions How to Walk so as to Come Forth of Such a Condition." (b) "The Return of Prayers," based on

---

61. For the reprinting of the original preface, see *The Works of Thomas Goodwin* (Grand Rapids: Reformation Heritage Books, 2006), 1:xxix–xxxii.

62. Edmund Calamy, *The Nonconformist's Memorial*, ed. Samuel Palmer (London: Alex. Hogg, 1778), 1:186.

Psalm 85:8, is a uniquely practical work. It offers help in ascertaining "God's answers to our prayers" (3:353–429). (c) "The Trial of a Christian's Growth" (3:433–506), based on John 15:1–2, centers on sanctification, specifically mortification and vivification. This is a mini-classic on spiritual growth.

You might also read *The Vanity of Thoughts*, based on Jeremiah 4:14 (3:509–528). This work, often republished in paperback, stresses the need to bring every thought captive to Christ. It also describes ways to foster that obedience.

3. Read some of Goodwin's great sermons. They are strong, biblical, Christological, and experiential (2:359–425; 4:151–224; 5:439–548; 7:473–576; 9:499–514; 12:1–127).

4. Delve into Goodwin's works that explain major doctrines, such as:

(a) *An Unregenerate Man's Guiltiness Before God in Respect of Sin and Punishment* (10:1–567). This is a weighty treatise on human guilt, corruption, and the imputation and punishment of sin. In exposing the total depravity of the natural man's heart, this book aims to produce a heartfelt need for saving faith in Christ.

(b) *The Object and Acts of Justifying Faith* (8:1–593). This is a frequently reprinted classic on faith. Part 1, on the *objects of faith*, focuses on God's nature, Christ, and the free grace of God revealed in His absolute promises. Part 2 deals with the *acts of faith*: what it means to believe in Christ, to obtain assurance, to find joy in the Holy Spirit, and to make use of God's electing love. One section beautifully explains the "actings of faith in prayer." Part 3 addresses the *properties of faith*: their excellence in giving all honor to God and Christ, their difficulty in reaching beyond the natural abilities of man, their necessity in requiring us to believe in the strength of God. The conclusion provides "directions to guide us in our endeavours to believe."

(c) *Christ the Mediator* (2 Cor. 5:18–19), *Christ Set Forth* (Rom. 8:34), and *The Heart of Christ in Heaven Towards Sinners on Earth* are great works on Christology (5:1–438; 4:1–92; 4:93–150). *Christ the Mediator* presents Jesus in His substitutionary work of humiliation. It is a classic. *Christ Set Forth* proclaims Christ in His exaltation, and *The Heart of Christ* explores the tenderness of Christ's glorified human nature shown on earth. Goodwin is more mystical in this work than anywhere else in his writings, but as Paul Cook has ably shown, his mysticism is kept within the bounds of Scripture. Cook says Goodwin is unparalleled "in his combination of intellectual and theological power with evangelical and homiletical comfort."[63]

(d) *Gospel Holiness in Heart and Life* (7:129–336) is based on Philippians 1:9–11. It explains the doctrine of sanctification in every sphere of life.

(e) *The Knowledge of God the Father, and His Son Jesus Christ* (4:347–569) combined with *The Work of the Holy Spirit* (6:1–522) explore the profound work in the believer's soul of the three divine persons. *The Work of the Spirit* is particularly helpful for understanding the doctrines of regeneration and conversion. It carefully distinguishes the work of "the natural conscience" from the Spirit's saving work.

(f) *The Glory of the Gospel* (4:227–346) consists of two sermons and a treatise based on Colossians 1:26–27. It should be read along with *The Blessed State of Glory Which the Saints Possess After Death* (7:339–472), based on Revelation 14:13.

(g) *A Discourse of Election* (9:1–498) delves into issues such as the supralapsarian-infralapsarian debate, which wrestles with the moral or rational order of God's decrees. It also deals with the fruits of election (e.g., see Book IV on 1 Peter 5:10 and Book V on how God fulfills His covenant of grace in the generations of believers).

(h) *The Creatures and the Condition of Their State by Creation* (7:1–128) is Goodwin's most philosophical work.

5. Prayerfully and slowly digest Goodwin's nine-hundred-plus page exposition of Ephesians 1:1 to 2:11 (1:1–564; 2:1–355). Alexander Whyte wrote of this work, "Not even Luther on the Galatians is such an expositor of Paul's mind and heart as is Goodwin on the Ephesians."[64]

6. Save for last Goodwin's exposition of Revelation (3:1–226) and his only polemical work, *The Constitution, Right Order, and Government of the Churches of Christ* (11:1–546). Independents would highly value this polemic, while Presbyterians probably would not, saying Goodwin is trustworthy on nearly every subject except church government. Goodwin's work does not degrade Presbyterians, however. A contemporary who argued against Goodwin's view on church government confessed

---

63. Paul Cook, "Thomas Goodwin—Mystic?" in *Diversities of Gifts* (London: Westminster Conference, 1981), 45–56.

64. Alexander Whyte, *Thirteen Appreciations* (Edinburgh: Oliphant, Anderson & Ferrier, 1913), 162.

that Goodwin conveyed "a truly great and noble spirit" throughout the work.

Whichever Puritan you choose, familiarize yourself with his various writings. With major and voluminous works, be sure to note earlier writings from later writings. This is particularly important with Puritans such as Owen. The young Owen did not agree completely with the later Owen in certain areas, such as the necessity of the atonement. Familiarity with these matters will help you grasp the particular nuances of individual Puritans.

Some of My Favorite Puritans

My favorite Puritan-minded theologian from the English tradition is Anthony Burgess; from the Dutch tradition, Wilhelmus á Brakel; and from the Scottish tradition, Samuel Rutherford. Let me explain why.

Anthony Burgess (d. 1664)

In my opinion, Anthony Burgess, vicar of Sutton Coldfield, Warwickshire, from 1635 to 1662, is the most underrated Puritan of all time. I once asked Iain Murray why Burgess was not included in the nineteenth-century sets of the works of the best Puritans. He responded that Burgess was the greatest glaring omission from those reprints.

In fifteen years (1646–1661), Burgess wrote at least a dozen books based largely on his sermons and lectures. His writings reveal a scholarly acquaintance with Aristotle, Seneca, Augustine, Aquinas, Luther, and Calvin. He made judicious use of Greek and Latin quotations while reasoning in the plain style of Puritan preaching. Burgess was a cultured scholar and experimental preacher who produced astute, warm, devotional writings.

Burgess wrote about the mysteries of God and was also an experimental writer. He masterfully separated the precious from the vile in *The Godly Man's Choice*, based on thirteen sermons on Psalm 4:6–8. His detailed exegesis in his 145-sermon work on John 17, his 300-page commentary on 1 Corinthians 3, and his 700-page commentary on 2 Corinthians 1 are heart-warming. They fulfilled Burgess's goal to "endeavour the true and sound Exposition...so as to reduce all Doctrinals and controversials to practicals and experimentals, which is the life and soul of all."[65]

Several of Burgess's major works are polemical. His first major treatise, *Vindiciae Legis* (1646), based on twenty-nine lectures given at Lawrence-Jewry,

---

65. Anthony Burgess, *Second Corinthians 1*, intro.

vindicated the Puritan view of the moral law and the covenants of works and grace in opposition to Roman Catholics, Arminians, Socinians, and Antinomians. Two years later, Burgess wrote against the same opponents, plus Baxter, in his first volume on justification. He refuted Baxter's work for its Arminian tendencies in arguing for a process of justification that involves the cooperation of divine grace with human works. His second volume on justification, which appeared six years later (1654), discusses the natural righteousness of God and the imputed righteousness of Christ. Those two volumes contain seventy-five sermons. His 555-page *Doctrine of Original Sin* (1659) drew Anabaptists into the fray.

Burgess's best and largest work, *Spiritual Refining: The Anatomy of True and False Conversion* (1652–54)—two volumes of 1,100 pages—has been called an "unequaled anatomy of experimental religion." The first volume, subtitled *A Treatise of Grace and Assurance*, contains 120 sermons; the second, subtitled *A Treatise of Sin, with its Causes, Differences, Mitigations and Aggravations*, contains 42 sermons.[66]

In the first section of the first volume, Burgess refutes the antinomian error that internal marks of grace in a believer are no evidence of his justification. In my opinion, the first sixty pages of the facsimile edition include the best short treatment on assurance in all Puritan literature. Here is one choice quotation in which Burgess shows the need to give priority to Christ and His promises rather than to the marks of grace in ascertaining one's assurance:

> We must take heed that we do not so gaze upon ourselves to find graces in our own hearts as thereby we forget those Acts of Faith, whereby we close with Christ immediately, and rely upon him only for our Justification.... The fear of this hath made some cry down totally the use of signs, to evidence our Justification. And the truth is, it cannot be denied but many of the children of God, while they are studying and examining, whether grace be in their souls, that upon the discovery thereof, they may have comfortable persuasions of their Justification, are very much neglective of those choice and principal Acts of Faith, whereby we have an acquiescency or recumbency upon Christ for our Acceptation with God. This is as if old Jacob should so rejoice in the Chariot Joseph sent, whereby he knew that he was alive, that he should not desire to see Joseph himself. Thus while

---

66. International Outreach has recently done two two-volume editions of Burgess's *Spiritual Refining* (Ames, Iowa: International Outreach, 1986–96). Only one hundred copies were printed of the first edition, a facsimile, which contains the complete unabridged text of 1658. The second edition of *Spiritual Refining*, an abridged edition, is worth the investment for those who have difficulty reading facsimile print, though many sections are not included.

thou art so full of joy, to perceive grace in thee, thou forgettest to joy in Christ himself, who is more excellent than all thy graces.[67]

Sections two and three describe numerous signs of grace. The remaining nine sections of this volume discuss grace in terms of regeneration, the new creature, God's workmanship, grace in the heart, washing or sanctifying grace, conversion, softening the stony heart, God's Spirit within us, and vocation or calling. Throughout, Burgess distinguishes saving grace from its counterfeits.

In the second volume of *Spiritual Refining*, Burgess focuses on sin. He addresses the deceitfulness of the human heart, presumptuous and reigning sins, hypocrisy and formality in religion, a misguided conscience, and secret sins that often go unrecognized. Positively, he explains the tenderness of a gracious heart, showing "that a strict scrutiny into a man's heart and ways, with a holy fear of sinning, doth consist with a Gospel-life of faith and joy in the Holy Ghost." His goal, as stated on the title page, is to "unmask counterfeit Christians, terrify the ungodly, comfort and direct the doubting saint, humble man, [and] exalt the grace of God."

I discovered Burgess's *Spiritual Refining* a few days before completing my doctoral dissertation on assurance of faith in the mid-1980s. When I read the first sixty pages of this masterpiece, I was overwhelmed at Burgess's scriptural clarity, insightful exegesis, balance, thoroughness, and depth. I spent two days incorporating some of Burgess's key thoughts into my dissertation. Later, when called on to speak on Burgess's life and his views on assurance for the Westminster Conference (1997), I acquired a nearly complete collection of his writings and immersed myself in them. That fall Burgess surpassed Goodwin as my favorite Puritan author and has remained so ever since. One of my goals is to bring several of Burgess's works back into print—or better yet, do a complete edition of his works.

• *Recommended reading*: Burgess's *Spiritual Refining*.

Wilhelmus á Brakel (1635–1711)

Wilhelmus á Brakel was a prominent preacher and writer of the *Nadere Reformatie* (Dutch Further Reformation). This movement of the seventeenth and early eighteenth centuries paralleled English Puritanism.[68] Like English Puritanism, the *Nadere Reformatie* stressed the necessity of vital Christian piety, was true to

---

67. *Spiritual Refining*, 1:41.
68. For summaries of the *Nadere Reformatie* in English, see Joel R. Beeke, *Assurance of Faith: Calvin, English Puritanism, and the Dutch Second Reformation* (New York: Peter Lang, 1991), 383–413; Fred A. van Lieburg, "From Pure Church to Pious Culture: The Further Reformation in the

the teachings of Scripture and the Reformed confessions, and consistently high-lighted how faith and godliness work in all aspects of daily life. Consequently, I feel justified in including Dutch "puritans" in a selection of favorite authors.

I was once asked what book I would take with me if I were stranded on a desert island. My choice was Wilhelmus à Brakel's *The Christian's Reason-able Service.*[69] In my opinion, this is the most valuable set of books available in English today because of the rich doctrinal, experiential, practical, pastoral, and ethical content this classic conveys. For centuries this set of books was as popular in the Netherlands as John Bunyan's *Pilgrim's Progress* was in English-speaking countries. In the eighteenth and nineteenth centuries, most Dutch farmers of Reformed persuasion would read a few pages of "Father Brakel," as he was fondly called, every evening during family worship. When they completed the entire work, they would start over!

This massive work is arranged in three parts. The first volume and most of the second consist of a traditional Reformed systematic theology that is packed with clear thinking, thorough presentation, and helpful application. The concluding applications at the end of each chapter applying the particular doctrines are the highlight of this section. I believe à Brakel's practical casuistry in these applications supersedes any other systematic theologian in his day and ever since. They represent Reformed, Puritan, experiential theology at its best.

The second part expounds Christian ethics and Christian living. This largest section of à Brakel's work is packed with salient applications on topics pertinent to living as a Christian in this world. In addition to a masterful treatment of the Ten Commandments (chaps. 45–55) and the Lord's Prayer (chaps. 68–74), this part addresses topics such as living by faith out of God's promises (chap. 42); how to exercise love toward God and His Son (chaps. 56–57); how to fear, obey, and hope in God (chaps. 59–61); how to profess Christ and His truth (chap. 63); and how to exercise spiritual graces, such as courage, content-ment, self-denial, patience, uprightness, watchfulness, neighborly love, humility, meekness, peace, diligence, compassion, and prudence (chaps. 62, 64–67, 76, 82–88). Other topics include fasting (chap. 75), solitude (chap. 77), spiritual meditation (chap. 78), singing (chap. 79), vows (chap. 80), spiritual experience (chap. 81), spiritual growth (chap. 89), backsliding (chap. 90), spiritual deser-tion (chap. 91), temptations (chaps. 92–95), indwelling corruption (chap. 96), and spiritual darkness and deadness (chaps. 97–98).

Seventeenth-Century Dutch Republic," in *Later Calvinism: International Perspectives*, ed. W. Fred Graham (Kirksville, Mo.: Sixteenth Century Journal Publishers, 1994), 409–430.

69. Wilhelmus à Brakel, *The Christian's Reasonable Service*, 4 vols., trans. Bartel Elshout, ed. Joel R. Beeke (Grand Rapids: Reformation Heritage Books, 2001).

The third part (4:373–538) includes a history of God's redemptive, covenantal work in the world. It is reminiscent of Jonathan Edwards's *History of Redemption*, though not as detailed; à Brakel's work confines itself more to Scripture and has a greater covenantal emphasis. It concludes with a detailed study of the future conversion of the Jews (4:511–38).

The Christian's Reasonable Service is the heartbeat of the Dutch Further Reformation. Here systematic theology and vital, experiential Christianity are scripturally and practically woven within a covenantal framework. The entire work bears the mark of a pastor-theologian richly taught by the Spirit. Nearly every subject treasured by Christians is treated in a helpful way, always aiming for the promotion of godliness.

In my opinion, this pastoral set of books is an essential tool for every pastor but is also valuable for lay people. The book has been freshly translated into contemporary English. Buy and read this great classic. You won't be sorry.

+ *Recommended reading:* Brakel's *The Christian's Reasonable Service.*

Samuel Rutherford (1600–1661)
While divided by history, nationality, and race, and to some extent, language, England's Puritans and Scotland's Presbyterians were united by close spiritual bonds of doctrine, worship, and church order. For this reason, I include a Scotsman on my short list of favorite Puritans.

Actually, three Scottish divines have influenced me greatly: Thomas Boston (1676–1732) led me to the depths of my original sin and the beauty and symmetry of covenant theology;[70] Thomas Halyburton (1674–1712) taught me the power of bringing every personal experience to the touchstone of Scripture;[71] and Samuel Rutherford taught me much about loving Christ and being submissive in affliction. For twenty years, I kept a copy of Rutherford's *Letters* (unabridged) on my nightstand, and turned to it countless times when I felt discouraged, challenged, or afflicted. On many occasions, I read until I found my bearings once more in Prince Immanuel. No writer in all of history can so make you fall in love with Christ and embrace your afflictions as Samuel Rutherford can. I agree with Charles Spurgeon who said, "When we are dead and gone let the world know that Spurgeon held Rutherford's *Letters* to be

---

70. Thomas Boston, *The Complete Works of the Late Rev. Thomas Boston, Ettrick*, 12 vols., ed. Samuel M'Millan (repr., Wheaton, Ill.: Richard Owen Roberts, 1980).

71. Thomas Halyburton, *The Works of Thomas Halyburton*, 4 vols. (Aberdeen: James Begg Society, 2000–2005).

the nearest thing to inspiration which can be found in all the writings of mere man."[72] I thank God for this great man of God.

Though Boston and Halyburton rate a close second, my favorite Scottish divine is Rutherford, who first pastored in Anwoth, then was exiled to Aberdeen, and later became professor at St. Andrews. Rutherford's heart was a vast treasure chest filled with unspeakable love for God. Rutherford wrote as one whose heart transcended this world and lighted upon eternal shores. In the midst of trial and affliction, he wrote, "Christ hath so handsomely fitted for my shoulders, this rough tree of the cross, as that it hurteth me no ways."[73] Even on his deathbed, Rutherford focused on Christ. To those gathered around him, he said, "This night will close the door, and fasten my anchor within the veil.... Glory, glory dwelleth in Immanuel's land!"[74] In life and in death, he found his Savior "altogether lovely" (Song 4:16). "No pen, no words, no image can express to you the loveliness of my only, only Lord Jesus," he wrote.[75] This is what makes him so devotional, so beneficial, so engaging to read.

Most of Rutherford's letters (220 of 365) were written while he was in exile. The letters beautifully harmonize Reformed doctrine and the spiritual experiences of a believer. They basically cover six topics: (1) Rutherford's love and desire for Christ, (2) his deep sense of the heinousness of sin, (3) his devotion for the cause of Christ, (4) his profound sympathy for burdened and troubled souls, (5) his profound love for his flock, and (6) his ardent longings for heaven.[76]

Although he did not write his letters for publication, the compilation of them is Rutherford's most popular work. It has been reprinted more than eighty times in English, fifteen times in Dutch, and several times in German and French and Gaelic.

Several of Rutherford's diversified writings have also been republished. His *Communion Sermons* (1870s), a compilation of fourteen sacramental sermons, was recently published by Westminster Publishing House. *The Covenant of Life Opened* (1655), an exegetical defense of covenant theology, was edited and republished by Puritan Publications. In this, Rutherford reveals himself as an apt apologist and polemicist in defending the bi-covenantal structure of Scripture. His work *Lex Rex* has become a standard in law curriculum; nearly every

---

72. Charles Spurgeon, *The Sword and the Trowel*, 189. http://en.wikipedia.org/wiki/Samuel _Rutherford (accessed August 31, 2010).

73. Samuel Rutherford, *The Letters of Samuel Rutherford* (Edinburgh: Banner of Truth, 1984), 144.

74. Rutherford, *Letters*, 21–22.

75. Samuel Rutherford, *The Loveliness of Christ* (Edinburgh: Banner of Truth, 2007), 88.

76. Adapted from Beeke and Pederson, *Meet the Puritans*, 729–30.

member of the Westminster Assembly owned a copy. This book helped instigate the Covenanters' resistance to King Charles I and was later used to justify
the French and American revolutions. History has generally regarded this work
as one of the greatest contributions to political science.

In addition, Soli Deo Gloria has republished *Quaint Sermons of Samuel
Rutherford* (1885), composed from compiled shorthand notes taken by a listener. The warmth of Rutherford's preaching is particularly evident in "The
Spouse's Longing for Christ." Like many divines in his day, Rutherford drafted
his own catechism, *Rutherford's Catechism: or, The Sum of Christian Religion*
(1886), recently reprinted by Blue Banner Publications. This was most likely
written during the Westminster Assembly and is filled with many quaint sayings. *The Trial and Triumph of Faith* (1645) contains twenty-seven sermons
on Christ's saving work in the Canaanite woman (Matt. 15:21–28). In nearly
every sermon, Rutherford shows the overflowing grace of Christ to Gentiles.
He explores the nature of genuine prayer and addresses practical aspects of the
trial of faith. Most recently, Banner of Truth published *The Loveliness of Christ*
(2007), a little book that contains Christ-centered quotes from Rutherford.

Rutherford's *Letters*, however, remain the author's masterpiece. They are
filled with pastoral advice, comfort, rebuke, and encouragement.

✦ *Recommended reading*: Rutherford's *Letters*.

More Puritan Favorites
It is difficult to conclude this section, for I would love to include so many more
Puritan authors. But, to keep this list concise, I will conclude with a list of fif-
teen favorite Puritans followed by five favorite Scottish divines, then five favorite
Dutch divines, adding up to a list of twenty-five favorite Puritan writers:

1. *Anthony Burgess* (see above)

2. *Thomas Goodwin* (see above)

3. *John Owen* (1616–1683): This author's sixteen volumes of works, seven
volumes on Hebrews, and a book titled *Biblical Theology*, make up a learned
library.[77] The sixteen-volume set, which is a reprint of the 1850–55 Goold edition, includes the following:

---

77. John Owen, *The Works of John Owen*, 16 vols. (repr. Edinburgh: Banner of Truth, 1996);
idem, *An Exposition of the Epistle to the Hebrews*, 7 vols. (London: Banner of Truth, 1985); idem,
Biblical Theology, trans. Stephen Westcott (Morgan, Penn.: Soli Deo Gloria, 1994).

Doctrinal (vols. 1–5). The most noteworthy works in these volumes are: *On the Person and Glory of Christ* (vol. 1); *Communion with God* (vol. 2); *Discourse on the Holy Spirit* (vol. 3); and *Justification by Faith* (vol. 5). Mastery of these works, Spurgeon wrote, "is to be a profound theologian."

Practical (vols. 6–9). Especially worthy here are *Mortification of Sin, Temptation, Exposition of Psalm 130* (vol. 6); and *Spiritual-Mindedness* (vol. 7). Volumes 8 and 9 comprise sermons. These books are suitable for the educated layperson and have immense practical applications.

Controversial (vols. 10–16). Noteworthy are *The Death of Death in the Death of Christ* and *Divine Justice* (vol. 10); *The Doctrine of the Saints' Perseverance* (vol. 11); *True Nature of a Gospel Church* and *The Divine Original of the Scriptures* (vol. 16). Several works in this section have historical significance (particularly those written against Arminianism and Socinianism) but tend to be tedious for a non-theologian.

Owen's wide range of subjects, insightful writing, exhaustive doctrinal studies, profound theology, and warm devotional approach explain why so many people regard his work with such high esteem. Owen may be wordy on occasion, but he is never dry. His works are invaluable for all who wish to explore the rich legacy left by one who is often called "Prince of the Puritans."

Dozens of Owen's works have been published individually in the past half century, but I advise serious readers of Puritan literature to purchase the sixteen-volume set of Owen's works. For those who have difficulty reading Owen, I recommend R. J. K. Law's abridged and simplified editions of *Communion with God* (1991), *Apostasy from the Gospel* (1992), *The Glory of Christ* (1994), and *The Holy Spirit* (1998), all published by the Banner of Truth Trust.

I was most influenced by Owen when I spent the summer of 1985 studying his views on assurance. The two books that influenced me most were Owen's treatment of Psalm 130, particularly verse 4, and his amazing *Communion with God*, which focuses on experiential communion between a believer and individual persons of the Trinity.

4. *Jonathan Edwards* (1703–1758): A class at Westminster Theological Seminary, taught by Sam Logan, motivated me to read most of Edwards's two-volume works in 1983.[78] His sermons convicted and comforted me beyond words. What a master wordsmith Edwards was!

---

78. Jonathan Edwards, *The Works of Jonathan Edwards* (London: Banner of Truth, 1974). Cf. *The Works of Jonathan Edwards*, 26 vols. (New Haven: Yale, 1957–2008). Each volume in the Yale series has been thoroughly edited by scholars, and includes, on average, 35 to 150 pages of introduction. This

More than sixty volumes of Edwards's writings have been published in the last fifty years.[79] The two books that influenced me most were *Religious Affections*, which is often regarded as the leading classic in American history on spiritual life, and Edwards's sermons on justification by faith.[80] Earlier, I was greatly influenced by *The Life and Diary of David Brainerd*.[81]

I was touched by Edwards's concept of "fittedness" throughout his writings and have often found that concept a great tool for leadership and decision-making. Edwards grounded this concept in God; a God who is always fitting will guide His people to want to do what is fitting in each life situation to bring Him the most glory. Hence, we must ask of every decision we face: What is most fitting in God's sight according to His Word? What will bring God the most honor?

5. *William Perkins* (1558–1602): Perkins's vision of reform for the church combined with his intellect, piety, writing, spiritual counseling, and communication skills helped set the tone for the seventeenth-century Puritan accent on Reformed, experiential truth and self-examination, and Puritan arguments against Roman Catholicism and Arminianism. Perkins as rhetorician, expositor, theologian, and pastor became the principal architect of the Puritan movement. By the time of his death, Perkins's writings in England were outselling those of John Calvin, Theodore Beza, and Henry Bullinger combined. He "moulded the piety of a whole nation," H. C. Porter said.[82] Little wonder, then, that Perkins is often called the father of Puritanism.

Perkins first influenced me while I was studying assurance of faith for my doctoral dissertation. Ten years later, his *Art of Prophesying*, a short homiletic textbook for Puritan seminarians, helped me understand how to address listeners according to their various cases of conscience.[83] My appreciation for Perkins has increased over the years. In the last seven years, I have had the privilege of

---

series is essential for aspiring scholars of Edwards. Those interested in reading Edwards for devotional benefit could better purchase the two-volume edition of his *Works*, since the Yale volumes are expensive. The Puritan Reformed Theological Seminary library collection contains the complete unpublished works of Jonathan Edwards in 48 volumes additional to the 26-volume Yale set.

79. Beeke and Pederson, *Meet the Puritans*, 193–233.

80. Jonathan Edwards, *The Religious Affections* (Edinburgh: Banner of Truth, 2001); idem, *Justification by Faith Alone* (Morgan, Pa.: Soli Deo Gloria, 2000).

81. Jonathan Edwards, *The Life and Diary of David Brainerd* (Grand Rapids: Baker, 1989).

82. H. C. Porter, *Reformation and Reaction in Tudor Cambridge* (London: Cambridge University Press, 1958), 260.

83. William Perkins, *The Art of Prophesying*, ed. Sinclair B. Ferguson (Edinburgh: Banner of Truth, 1996).

reading and editing Perkins's complete works, now published in ten volumes.[84] What a feast this has been!

6. *Thomas Watson* (c. 1620–1686): Watson was my favorite Puritan after I was converted in my mid-teens. I read his *Body of Divinity* as a daily devotional. His *All Things for Good* was a wonderful balm for my troubled soul in a period of intense affliction in the early 1980s. His winsome writing includes deep doctrine, clear expression, warm spirituality, appropriate applications, and colorful illustrations. I love his pithy, quotable style of writing.[85]

7. *Thomas Brooks* (1608–1680): Brooks became my favorite Puritan writer in my late teens. His *Precious Remedies Against Satan's Devices, The Mute Christian Under the Smarting Rod, Heaven on Earth: A Treatise on Assurance*, "The Unsearchable Riches of Christ" (vol. 3), "The Crown and Glory of Christianity" (vol. 4)—a classic on holiness consisting of 58 sermons on Hebrews 12:14—all ministered to me. Brooks's books are real page-turners. He often brought me to tears of joy over Christ and tears of sorrow over sin. His writings exude spiritual life and power.[86]

8. *John Flavel* (1628–1691): With the exception of Jonathan Edwards, no Puritan divine was more helpful to me in sermon preparation as a young minister than Flavel. His sermons on Christ's suffering also greatly blessed my soul. What lover of Puritan literature has not been blessed by Flavel's classics: *The Mystery of Providence, Keeping the Heart, The Fountain of Life, Christ Knocking at the Door of the Heart*, and *The Method of Grace?*[87]

9. *John Bunyan* (1628–1688): When I was nine years old and first experienced a period of conviction of sin, I read Bunyan's *The Life and Death of Mr. Badman*. When I saw the book in my father's bookcase, I figured that since I had such a bad heart, that book must be for me!

More importantly, my father read Bunyan's *Pilgrim's Progress* to us every Sunday evening after church. When he finished, he started over. I must have listened

---

84. Joel R. Beeke and Derek W. H. Thomas, *The Works of William Perkins*, 10 vols. (Grand Rapids: Reformation Heritage Books, 2014–2020).

85. Seventeen of Watson's titles have been reprinted in recent decades, though to date no complete works set has ever been printed (Beeke and Pederson, *Meet the Puritans*, 606–613).

86. Thomas Brooks, *The Works of Thomas Brooks*, 6 vols. (repr., Edinburgh: Banner of Truth, 2001).

87. John Flavel, *The Works of John Flavel*, 6 vols. (repr., London: Banner of Truth, 1968).

to that book fifteen times. From the age of fourteen on, I would ask questions about how the Holy Spirit works in the soul and about Mr. Talkative, the Man in the Iron Cage, the House of the Interpreter, and scores of other characters and matters. My father often wept as he answered my questions. When I became a minister, I realized what a rare gift those sessions were. Forty years later, illustrations from Bunyan's great classic still come to mind while I'm preaching.[88]

10. *Thomas Vincent* (1634–1678): When we find ourselves cold and listless, Vincent can help kindle the fire of Christian love. Just try reading *The True Christian's Love to the Unseen Christ* (1677) without having your affections raised to heavenly places and yearning to love Christ more. Let it be your frequent companion.

Only a handful of Vincent's writings were ever published, and of those, only six have been reprinted in the past fifty years. In addition to *The True Christian's Love to the Unseen Christ*, Vincent wrote *The Shorter Catechism Explained from Scripture* (1673), a very helpful book for young people and children; and *The Good Work Begun* (1673), an evangelistic book for young people, explaining how God saves sinners and preserves them for Himself. Three additional books by Vincent are more solemn treatises. They include *God's Terrible Voice in the City* (1667), an eyewitness account of London's Great Fire and Great Plague and an analysis of how God judges wickedness in a city; *Christ's Certain and Sudden Appearance to Judgment* (1667), which was also written after the Great Fire of London and was designed to prepare sinners for the great and terrible day of the Lord; and *Fire and Brimstone* (1670) was written to warn sinners to flee the wrath to come. All these titles, minus *The Shorter Catechism*, were reprinted by Soli Deo Gloria Publications from 1991 to 2001.[89]

Vincent's works are uniquely refreshing. He used the English language in a captivating way to glorify God and strike at the heart of Christians. It is no wonder that Vincent's works were bestsellers in the eighteenth century.[90]

---

88. John Bunyan, *The Works of John Bunyan*, 3 vols. (Edinburgh: Banner of Truth, 1999).

89. Thomas Vincent, *The True Christian's Love to the Unseen Christ* (Morgan, Pa.: Soli Deo Gloria, 1994); idem, *The Shorter Catechism Explained from Scripture* (Edinburgh: Banner of Truth, 1991); idem, *The Good Work Begun: A Puritan Pastor Speaks to Teenagers* (Morgan, Pa.: Soli Deo Gloria, 1999); idem, *God's Terrible Voice in the City* (Morgan, Pa.: Soli Deo Gloria, 1997); idem, *Christ's Certain and Sudden Appearance to Judgment* (Morgan, Pa.: Soli Deo Gloria, 2001); idem, *Fire and Brimstone* (Morgan, Pa.: Soli Deo Gloria, 1999).

90. Andrew R. Holmes, *The Shaping of Ulster Presbyterian Belief and Practice, 1770–1840* (England: Oxford University Press, 2006), 277.

11. *Matthew Henry* (1662–1714), the great British commentator, has added spice to many preachers' sermons, including my own. I am also indebted to Henry for his practical books on spiritual disciplines, particularly family worship, private prayer, and preparation for Communion. For many years, I read portions of Henry's *How to Prepare for Communion* during preparatory weeks.[91]

12. *Richard Sibbes* (1577–1635) was a lifelong bachelor with a huge network of friends. He wrote tenderly about the heavenly Bridegroom and the Spirit's sealing work in the soul. I became enamored with Sibbes after reading his comment that the believer ought to "entertain" the Holy Spirit in the courtroom of his soul, much as we entertain guests in our living rooms. Later, I gave a conference address titled "Sibbes on the Entertainment of the Spirit."[92]

13. *Matthew Poole* (1624–1679) left his mark on me with his careful exegesis of Scripture. Many times I wanted to interpret a text a certain way, but Poole reigned me in. In nearly every case, those who say the Puritans were not good exegetes have not read Poole.[93]

14. *Walter Marshall* (1628–1680) helped me understand justification and sanctification from a Christ-centered perspective through his *Gospel Mystery of Sanctification* classic.[94]

15. William Spurstowe (*c.* 1605–1666) wrote an amazing book on gospel promises, *The Wells of Salvation Opened*, which served as a tonic for my ailing soul.[95] James La Belle and I have summarized its contents in contemporary language in our recent book, *Living by God's Promises*.[96]

91. Matthew Henry, *Commentary on the Whole Bible*, 6 vols. (repr., Peabody, Mass.: Hendrickson Publishers, 1991); idem, *Family Religion: Principles for Raising a Godly Family* (Ross-shire, U.K.: Christian Focus, 1998); idem, *A Method for Prayer* (Greenville, S.C.: Reformed Academic Press, 1994); idem, *How to Prepare for Communion* (Lafayette, Ind.: Sovereign Grace Trust Fund, 2001).

92. Richard Sibbes, *The Complete Works of Richard Sibbes*, ed. A. B. Grosart, 7 vols. (repr., Edinburgh: Banner of Truth, 1973–82).

93. Matthew Poole, *A Commentary on the Whole Bible*, 3 vols. (repr., London: Banner of Truth, 1983).

94. Walter Marshall, *The Gospel Mystery of Sanctification* (Grand Rapids: Reformation Heritage Books, 1999).

95. William Spurstowe, *The Wells of Salvation Opened: Or, A Treatise Discovering the nature, preciousness, usefulness of Gospel-Promises, and Rules for the right application of them* (London: T. R. & E. M. for Ralph Smith, 1655).

96. Joel R. Beeke and James A. La Belle, *Living by Gospel Promises* (Grand Rapids: Reformation Heritage Books, 2010).

Favorite Scottish Divines
1. *Samuel Rutherford* (see above)

2. *Thomas Boston* (see above)

3. *Thomas Halyburton* (see above)

4. *Andrew Gray* (1633–1656): Several of the short treatises in *The Works of Andrew Gray*, particularly *The Mystery of Faith Opened, Great and Precious Promises, Directions and Instigations to the Duty of Prayer*, and *The Spiritual Warfare* have influenced me for good, as has his rare volume of fifty sermons (*Loving Christ and Fleeing Temptation*), which was edited and published in 2007.[97]

5. *Ebenezer* (1680–1754) and *Ralph Erskine* (1685–1752): The Erskine brothers have impressed me with their lives, their emphasis and insights into God's promises, and their passionate offering of the gospel.[98]

Favorite Dutch Further Reformation Divines[99]
1. *Wilhelmus à Brakel* (see above)

2. *Willem Teellinck* (1579–1629): *The Path of True Godliness* is the best Puritan-style manual on sanctification that I have ever read.[100]

3. *Herman Witsius* (1636–1708): The masterful trilogy of *The Economy of the Covenants* (2 vols.), *The Apostles' Creed* (2 vols.), and *The Lord's Prayer* is generations ahead of its time.[101]

---

97. Andrew Gray, *The Works of Andrew Gray* (Morgan, Pa.: Soli Deo Gloria, 1992); idem, *Loving Christ and Fleeing Temptation*, ed. Joel R. Beeke and Kelly Van Wyck (Grand Rapids: Reformation Heritage Books, 2007).

98. Ebenezer Erskine, *The Works of Ebenezer Erskine*, 3 vols. (Glasgow: Free Presbyterian Publications, 2001); Ralph Erskine, *The Works of Ralph Erskine*, 6 vols. (Glasgow: Free Presbyterian Publications, 1991).

99. I limit myself here to selecting those who have at least one volume in English.

100. Willem Teellinck, *The Path of True Godliness*, trans. Annemie Godbehere, ed. Joel R. Beeke (repr., Grand Rapids: Reformation Heritage Books, 2008).

101. Herman Witsius, *The Economy of the Covenants between God and Man, Comprehending a Complete Body of Divinity*, trans. William Crookshank, 2 vols. (repr., Grand Rapids: Reformation Heritage Books, 2010); idem, *Sacred Dissertations on the Apostles' Creed*, trans. Donald Fraser, 2 vols. (repr., Grand Rapids: Reformation Heritage Books, 2010); idem, *Sacred Dissertations on the Lord's Prayer*, trans. William Pringle (repr., Grand Rapids: Reformation Heritage Books, 2010).

4. *Johannes VanderKemp* (1664–1718): His Heidelberg Catechism sermons, reprinted by Reformation Heritage Books, are rich in pointed, heartfelt, and diverse applications and are remarkably readable today.[102]

5. *Alexander Comrie* (1706–1774): His *The ABC of Faith*, a popular treatment of various biblical terms that describe faith, was a great help to me in my twenties for understanding that terms such as *coming to Christ, resting in Christ*, and *clinging to Christ* focus on various aspects of faith and ultimately are nearly synonymous with faith.[103]

Ideas for Printing the Puritans

If you are skeptical about reading Puritan authors, thinking them outdated and no longer applicable for today, think again. Puritans have much to offer to spiritually hungry young people and older folk today. Though some Puritan titles are not worthy of reprinting, there still are hundreds of great Puritan titles that have not been reprinted since the seventeenth century. At Reformation Heritage Books, we envision bringing many of these back into print by using a five-tier approach:

+ First, a radical purist approach (that is, no changes in punctuation or word choice, though spelling may or may not be updated), which is reserved mostly for scholars and libraries. This is the approach of Chad Van Dixhoorn and Reformation Heritage Books in printing definitive volumes related to Westminster Assembly materials, including the reprinting in facsimile form of all the books written by Westminster Assembly divines. This will offer an expanding library of English Puritan literature to a new generation of scholars. Such books are not intended for most laypeople.

+ Second, Reformation Heritage Books will continue to print several Puritan titles per year using the purist approach, which means changing a minimal number of words and punctuation. With this approach, we will print titles under our Soli Deo Gloria imprint. Thousands of people continue to buy such material, but the readership is shrinking as people move away from the Authorized Version of the Bible

---

102. Johannes VanderKemp, *The Christian Entirely the Property of Christ, in Life and Death, Exhibited in Fifty-three Sermons on the Heidelberg Catechism*, trans. John M. Van Harlingen, 2 vols. (Grand Rapids: Reformation Heritage Books, 1997).

103. Alexander Comrie, *The ABC of Faith*, trans. J. Marcus Banfield (Ossett, U.K.: Zoar Publications, 1978).

and eventually can no longer grasp old fashioned language without hard work.

+ Third, more substantial editing will be done on other Puritan titles. Examples of this include Sinclair Ferguson's substantial editing of William Perkins's *The Art of Prophesying*, published by Banner of Truth Trust, and to a somewhat lesser degree, my editing on Soli Deo Gloria's first printing of Thomas Watson's *Heaven Taken by Storm*. This approach would retain the Authorized Version of the Bible for scriptural quotations and the Thee/Thou usage for Deity, with accompanying verb forms, so that it does not read like it is altogether removed from its historical milieu, but would use contemporary pronouns and verb forms for others. Obsolete illustrations would be contemporized or deleted. The advantage of this approach is that it will enhance readability and sales. It is not a coincidence that the top-selling Soli Deo Gloria book for many years was the one edited most thoroughly.

+ A fourth level is to rewrite Puritan books using the author's main thoughts. This is the approach Ernest Kevan used with *Moral Law* a few decades ago to summarize Anthony Burgess's work, reducing it from several hundred pages to about one hundred pages. More recently, Stephen Yuille used this approach to rewrite George Swinnock's *The Fading of the Flesh and the Flourishing of Faith*. Reformation Heritage Books used this book as its inaugural volume in a new series titled Puritan Treasures for Today. Presently, we have published a dozen of these volumes. Kris Lundgaard also used this approach in rewriting John Owen's *The Enemy Within*. To date, this book has sold more than sixty thousand copies. This type of editing may become the preferred way to print Puritan titles to appeal to more contemporary readers.

+ A fifth level is combining several authors' thoughts under a theme. James La Belle and I are experimenting with this approach as we launch the first volume of a series titled Deepen Your Christian Life. In the first volume, *Living by God's Promises*, we draw heavily from three Puritan treatises on God's promises, written by Edward Leigh, William Spurstowe, and Andrew Gray. The next two volumes are *Living Zealously* and *Living in a Godly Marriage*. In each case, we use extracts from a number of Puritan works, collate their thoughts, then write a book on the subject for the average layperson.

When levels three through five are used, it is critical that the editor and/or author is very familiar with how Puritans think, so as to avoid misrepresentation.

Concluding Advice

Where our culture is lacking, the Puritans abounded. J. I. Packer says, "Today, Christians in the West are found to be on the whole passionless, passive, and one fears, prayerless."[104] The Puritans were passionate, zealous, and prayerful. Let us be as the author of Hebrews says, "followers of them who through faith and patience inherit the promises" (6:12). The Puritans demanded a hearing in their own day, and they deserve one today as well. They are spiritual giants upon whose shoulders we should stand.

Their books still praise the Puritans in the gates. Reading the Puritans will keep you on the right path theologically, experientially, and practically. As Packer writes, "The Puritans were strongest just where Protestants today are weakest, and their writings can give us more real help than those of any other body of Christian teachers, past or present, since the days of the apostles."[105] I have been reading Christian literature for nearly sixty years and can freely say that I know of no group of writers in church history that can benefit the mind and soul more than the Puritans. God used their books for my spiritual formation and to help me grow in understanding. They are still teaching me what John the Baptist said, "Christ must increase and I must decrease" (John 3:30)—which is, I believe, a core definition of sanctification.

Read Puritan writings. With the Spirit's blessing, they will enrich your life as they open the Scriptures to you, probe your conscience, bare yours sins, lead you to repentance, and conform your life to Christ. By the Spirit's grace, let the Puritans bring you to full assurance of salvation and a lifestyle of gratitude to the triune God for His great salvation.

Finally, consider giving Puritan books to your friends. There is no better gift than a good book. I sometimes wonder what would happen if Christians spent fifteen minutes a day reading Puritan writings. Over a year that would add up to about twenty books, and fifteen hundred books over a lifetime. Who knows how the Holy Spirit might use such a spiritual diet of reading! Would it usher in a worldwide revival? Would it fill the earth with the knowledge of the Lord from sea to sea? That is my prayer. *Tolle Lege*—take up and read!

---

104. Ryken, *Worldly Saints*, xiii.
105. Cited in Hulse, *Reformation & Revival*, 44.

Chapter 9

Godefridus Udemans:
Life, Influence, and Writings

Godefridus Cornelis Udemans (*c.* 1581–1649) was one of the most influential Dutch Further Reformation divines of his generation. With the exception of Willem Teellinck (1579–1629), no seventeenth-century theologian from the Zeeland province exerted greater influence upon his contemporaries than Udemans, the preacher from Zierikzee. Through his preaching and writing, Udemans promoted Reformed piety in Zeeland and neighboring provinces for nearly half a century.[1]

Life

Godefridus Udemans was born at Bergen op Zoom in 1581 or 1582 into a Reformed family. His father played a significant role in helping found the Reformed church at Bergen op Zoom. Godefridus was converted in his youth and may have studied theology under his spiritual father, Marcus Zuerius, a seasoned minister of good reputation at Bergen op Zoom. Zuerius was also the grandfather of Marcus Zuerius Boxhorn (1612–1653), who became a professor of theology at Leiden. Udemans retained a close friendship with his teacher until Zuerius's death.

Udemans sustained his classical examinations for ministerial candidacy on April 19, 1599. Seven months later, he accepted a pastoral call from Haamstede.

---

1. This article is primarily drawn from the introduction of Godefridus Udemans, *The Practice of Faith, Hope, and Love*, trans. Annemie Godbehere, ed. Joel R. Beeke (Grand Rapids: Reformation Heritage Books, 2013). It is a compilation drawn from the following Dutch sources: W. Fieret, *Udemans: Facetten uit zijn leven en werk* (Houten: Den Hertog, 1985); P. J. Meertens, "Godefridus Cornelisz. Udemans," *Nederlandsch Archief voor Kerkgeschiedenis* 28 (1935):65–106; W. J. op 't Hof, "Godefridus Udemans," in *Het blijvende Woord*, ed. J. van der Haar, A. Bergsma, L. M. P. Scholten (Dordrecht: Gereformeerde Bijbelstichting, 1985), 222–25; B. W. Steenbeek, "Udemans, Godefridus," in *Biografisch Lexicon voor de Geschiedenis van het Nederlandse Protestantisme*, ed. D. Nauta, et al. (Kampen: Kok, 1978), 1:385–86; A. Vergunst, *Godefridus Cornelisz Udemans en zijn 't Geestelijk Roer van 't Coopmans Schip* (Utrecht: Theol. Instituut, 1970). Thanks to Adam Slingerland for his translation assistance. See also F. Ernest Stoeffler, *The Rise of Evangelical Pietism* (Leiden: Brill, 1965), 124–26.

A week later, on November 23, Classis Schouwen examined and admitted him into the ministry of the Reformed churches. He was ordained on December 12, succeeding Jan Cornelis Kempe, who had died early in that year. Initially, the young minister received some opposition, but when he received a pastoral call to the Reformed church in Zierikzee in 1602, the congregation opposed his departure. Ultimately, the civil authorities of the Zeeland province intervened. On April 11, 1604, nearly two years after being called, he was finally installed in Zierikzee, where he served the church faithfully for forty-five years. On January 29, 1613, he married Magdalena Stoutenburg (*c.* 1582–1662), daughter of the mayor of Brouwershaven. In 1620, the Udemans family was blessed with twins.

Udemans died at Zierikzee on January 20, 1649, still active in the ministry though in his late sixties. He was buried in the St. Lievensmonster church of Zierikzee.

Influence

Appointments

Udemans was a major influence on the Dutch Reformed church in his day in a variety of ways. Due to his diversity of gifts, both ecclesiastical and civil authorities called upon him to serve on various committees and in other capacities.

Udemans became involved in the Remonstrant (Arminian) debate early on. In 1616, Udemans and Herman Faukelius (1560–1625), author of *The Compendium* (a shortened version of the Heidelberg Catechism), were delegated by the Zeeland churches to go to Amsterdam to meet with deputies from other districts for the purpose of organizing the contours of a national synod. The following year, at the request of Prince Maurice, Udemans, together with Antonius Walaeus (1573–1639) and Jacobus Trigland (1583–1654), served the congregation of 's-Gravenhage as ministers on loan. In 1618, Udemans received a similar appointment to serve the Dome Church at Utrecht for two months. There, together with three other ministers, he wrote the Utrecht Church Order of 1619, the same year in which the Church Order of Dort was written.

In 1618, the Provincial Synod of Zeeland chose Udemans as one of its delegates for the National Synod of Dort. Though he was still in his thirties, respect for him and his gifts were so extensive, he was chosen as vice president of that august body. Additionally, the synod assigned him several tasks:

+ to organize the sessions of the commission that were assigned to develop a doctrinal statement regarding the five points of doctrinal difference between the Reformed and the Remonstrants;

- to serve on the committee appointed to compare the Latin, French, and Dutch texts of the Belgic Confession of Faith; and

- to serve on the committee mandated to compose two small catechism booklets.

After the famed international synod was over, the Reformed church at Dordrecht called Udemans in 1620 to be its pastor. He declined this call, as well as several calls from 's-Hertogenbosch, a city to which he felt very attached. When that city was conquered by Dutch troops in 1629, Udemans was sent, with Gisbertus Voetius (1589–1676) and several other ministers, to introduce Reformed doctrine in the capital city of Brabant, a task to which Udemans devoted several months.

Writings

Udemans wrote approximately twenty books in his lifetime; additionally, he translated four books that he saw through the press. Over the centuries, his books have been reprinted in Dutch about one hundred times. These reprints continue until the present day. Five of his books have been translated into German. *The Practice of Faith, Hope, and Love* is his first book in English. Hopefully, more will follow.

Udemans's writings may be divided into two categories: experientially edifying books and polemical books.

Experientially Edificatory Works

Most of Udemans's books were written to promote godly piety, revealing him to be an authentic Dutch Further Reformation divine. He generally focused on themes that touched the ordinary believer's inner, experiential life. That is true already of his first book, "Christian Meditations, Which the Believer Ought to Engage in Each Day, Provided for Each Day of the Week" (1608)[2]; Udemans asserts that believers should meditate on matters that concern our salvation on a daily basis. Meditation provides spiritual nutrition for the soul. It strengthens our faith, increases our knowledge, arouses zealous prayer, and kindles fruits of godliness. Beginning with Monday, Udemans provides meditations for each day of the week, using this weekly sequence of subject matter: "about our misery," "about the blessings of God toward us," "about our obligation to gratitude," "about the course of nature," "about the course of this world," and, finally, "about

---

2. The Dutch book titles are translated into English. They are placed within quotation marks in non-italic print to show that they have not been published in English.

the church triumphant." Cases of conscience and experiential themes are interwoven throughout, and each chapter concludes with a prayer.

Udemans's experiential and edifying emphases are also transparent in the only commentary he wrote, "A Short and Clear Explanation about the Song of Solomon" (1616). For Udemans, the Song of Songs is a metaphorical presentation of the covenant of grace that unveils the amazing spiritual marriage that God the Father, in Christ, made with the elect. In this Old Testament book, the Holy Spirit has, as Udemans writes in his preface, "intended to portray for us not only the true description of the Lord Christ and His church, but also the wonderful union of everlasting love and faithfulness which exists between these two parties."

Consequently, Udemans expounds the Song phrase by phrase and text by text, focusing on the Christ-church, Bridegroom-bride relationship. In this book, he leans on Bernard of Clairvaux (1090–1153) and Joseph Hall (1574–1656), an English pietist who showed mystical streaks at times. Unlike some of the later Dutch Further Reformation divine writers, however, Udemans does not fall into any kind of experientialism that becomes overly, subjectively mystical. In his exposition of the Song of Solomon, he retains an objective ecclesiastical dimension while not denying the experiential fellowship between the Bridegroom, Jesus Christ, and His adored bride, the church.

Udemans's "The Ladder of Jacob" (1628) is an experiential and allegorical exposition of Jacob's vision at Bethel (Gen. 28:10) that focuses on the steps of grace in the Christian life. The ladder Jacob saw, which stretched from earth to heaven, depicts Christ Jesus as mediator and intercessor, for He said of Himself, "I am the way." Udemans then presents eight rungs on this spiritual ladder that enable a babe in grace to reach spiritual adulthood in Christ: authentic humility and repentance, knowing Christ, sincere faith, true confession of faith, a godly walk of life, Christian patience, spiritual joy in Christ, and perseverance of the saints. These rungs of grace comprise the straight way to heaven, and it is the task of every Christian, while proceeding from virtue to virtue, to not rest before arriving at the heavenly Zion.

Additionally, Udemans wrote a small book, "Preparation for the Lord's Supper in the Form of a Dialogue," in which Urbanus and Theophilus carry on a discourse regarding the Lord's Supper. It was added to the "Christian Catechism of the Netherlands' Reformed Churches" by Gellius de Bouma and was added to "The Right Use of the Holy Supper of the Lord." Both these titles were edifying works that were reprinted several times in the seventeenth century.

Another experiential work of edification is Udemans's "The Last Trumpet" (1653), a 750-page, four-volume exposition of Jesus's last discourse in Matthew

25, which includes the parable of the wise and foolish virgins, the parable of the talents, and a description of some events on the final day of judgment. The major theme of this work is that the Christian's entire life must be a preparation for eternity. Since Christ, the Bridegroom of His church, will appear as a thief in the night, everyone who wishes to enter into the marriage feast of the Lamb must approach Him fully prepared. Whoever is not prepared will not be admitted into the wedding chamber, and after this life there is no more time of grace (Matt. 25:1–13). Moreover, Christ, like the master in the parable of the talents, will require from us an account of the gifts He has entrusted to us before we may enter His kingdom (vv. 14–30). This will occur at the final judgment, when the Son of man will separate the sheep from the goats and the righteous will enter into everlasting life as the unrighteous will enter into everlasting pain.

In 1640, Udemans published "A Blessed New Year," a sermon that he had preached the previous year on January 1 based on 2 Corinthians 5:17: "Therefore if any man be in Christ, he is a new creature: old things are passed away; behold, all things are become new." Being a new creature means having a renewed mind—a mind that has spiritual understanding and discernment—and striving to live a sanctified life through a pure conscience, a sanctified will, and sanctified affections. It also means having a renewed tongue and being renewed in our visible conduct. And it means constantly strengthening all these marks and graces by using the spiritual armor Paul speaks of in Ephesians 6:10–20 and through watchfulness and prayer, humility and meekness, and simplicity and caution.

Udemans had a large heart for common laborers, especially seafaring people. Since his church at Zierikzee consisted mostly of fishermen and personnel of merchant ships, Udemans wrote three books as practical Christian guides for the life and work of these seafaring men. In these books, he provided a practical and ethical manual for their trades as well as a justification for the commercial and nautical life of the republic in regard to the East and West India companies (e.g., see "The Spiritual Rudder of the Merchant's Ship"). He also spiritualized their trades and developed the ideals of the Further Reformation in a particularly helpful way for all those involved with seafaring occupations.

First among these books was "The Spiritual Compass" (1617), which was greatly expanded in its fourth edition thirty years after its first publication. In the preface to this expanded edition, Udemans provides his reasons for writing this book. To avoid sandbars and hidden rocks, no seafarer, skipper, or fisherman will dare to sail the oceans without a good compass. Nevertheless, many people sail on the sea of life without regard to the perils of their own souls, which arise from the devil, the world, and their own flesh. There are complaints that the catch at sea is decreasing daily; the boat owners invest heavily but see little in return. Everyone assigns his own reasons for this disappointment. But the true cause, which is that God is angry with man's sin, is overlooked. Then, too, few take to heart God's remedies for this chastisement: faith and repentance. Most people forget that the God who made the sea and the dry land is and remains the sole Lord and Master of both and without His will neither sea nor land will supply anything fruitful. Udemans writes, "For this reason, if we wish to sail the sea profitably, to our spiritual and temporal prosperity, then the Lord Christ must be our Admiral, the Holy Spirit must be our Pilot, God's Word must be our compass, faith must be our ship, hope must be our anchor, and prayer must be our convoy. If we are so equipped, we need have no fear, even if the sea fumed and tossed so much that the mountains would collapse due to her tumult, and even if the world perished and the hills tumbled into the sea, since God is on board with us" (cf. Ps. 46).

After carefully treating this subject of seafaring with spiritual and practical applications, Udemans discusses the specific tasks of the godly seafarer. He explains how he must conduct himself while on a journey and how he must live after he returns home. He then explains the history of Paul's shipwrecks and provides numerous prayers for various aspects of seafaring. The book concludes with Jonah's song of praise from the fish's belly (see Jonah 2).

Twenty years later, Udemans provided a second seafaring volume, "Merchant's Ship" (1637), which is an allegorical explanation of Moses's blessing on Zebulon and Issachar (Deut. 33:18–19). Like all of Udemans's treatises, this book is carefully subdivided. Much of "Merchant's Ship" stresses the need for contentment and joy in pursuing one's daily calling. After emphasizing in typical Puritan style that everyone should be satisfied in his calling, Udemans details the responsibilities of four callings: magistrates, ministers, merchants, and seafarers. He then writes extensively about the sea, describing it as an overflowing treasure house in which numerous temporal blessings lie hidden. Though land-based occupations are useful, earning a living from the sea, generally speaking, exceeds living on the land, for it brings blessings from the harvests of many lands rather than just one. Ships also bring in double income, for they are sent away loaded with goods and return loaded with goods. After extolling living from the sea, Udemans adds a detailed recommendation for unrestricted maritime activity, offering twelve reasons why the idea of the free passage of ships should be promoted and honored.

Udemans intended his "Merchant's Ship" as an introduction to the "Spiritual Rudder of the Merchant's Vessel" (1638), printed a year later. This considerably larger work is, according to the title page, a "faithful testimony of how the merchant and the mariner must each conduct himself in his dealings" under all circumstances, in war and in peace, before God and man, on the water and on land, but especially among the heathen in the East and West Indies. In seven hundred pages, Udemans explains how people in these callings are always to aim at honoring God, edifying the church, saving souls, caring for family members, and supporting the fatherland. He then details the seafaring worker's responsibilities toward God, family members, colleagues and employees, the state, authorities, and the heathen. In sum, "Spiritual Rudder" is a handbook on living the Christian life in the church, at home, and in society.

"Spiritual Rudder" is historically significant for its groundbreaking work on the ethics of economics among the Dutch Further Reformation divines. Udemans wrote positively of the Calvinist merchant's goal of acquiring and increasing capital without contradicting his faith. He was less ascetic in his economic views than Willem Teellinck, the father of the Dutch Further Reformation. Udemans put less stress on being a stranger in the world and more stress on moving faith from the inner chamber out into the world's marketplace. He emphasized that the believing merchant is not a believer on one hand and a merchant on the other, but he must always be a believer, both in public Sabbath worship and as a merchant, since he is always called, no matter the circumstances in which he finds himself, to think, speak, and act like a Christian. According to Udemans, Christianity always has profound and broad ramifications for the believer's relationship with his neighbors and colleagues.

Some of the books that Udemans translated also reveal his Reformed, experiential, and edificatory emphases, of which two are worthy of mention here. First, Udemans translated Pierre de la Place's (1520–1572) "An Appealing Tract Regarding the Excellence of the Christian" (1611), in which this erudite Huguenot delineates his orthodox Calvinistic concepts regarding election and predestination. Second, that same year he translated Jean Taffin's (1529–1602) "A Clear Exposition of the Apocalypse."

In most of these books, Udemans strongly opposed nominal Christians who spoke freely about Christ's grace but whose lives showed no fruits of having been born again. Most of all, however, Udemans delighted to comfort God's people and promote their sanctification. He focused with precision on the practice of piety (*praxis pietatis*) in both its practical and experiential dimensions. Inner piety as evidenced through various cases of conscience, as well as inward spiritual joyfulness, receives a good portion of his attention. It is no coincidence that the only book of the Bible on which he wrote in full was the Song of Solomon. Like other Dutch Further Reformation divines, he grapples with questions related to assurance of faith, such as the internal evidences of the

Holy Spirit, the practical syllogism, and the marks of saving grace. Yet, even as he deals with such matters, Udemans does not lose an objective-subjective balance. Justification and sanctification continue to function harmoniously in his theology, much like in John Calvin's.

The experiential, edificatory emphasis in Udemans's writings reflected his personal library, which was recorded at Zierikzee in 1653. His library provides evidence that he was well versed both in ancient and medieval theology as well as the works of theologians in his own day. His love for experiential piety is evident from the large number of English and Scottish experiential works in his library. He had a thorough collection also of his fellow writers in the Dutch Further Reformation, including numerous books by Willem Teellinck and Eewoud Teellinck.

Polemical Works

First, Udemans did not hesitate to write polemically on practical and ethical issues of his day. For example, in 1643, he entered into a debate about whether it was wrong for men to have long hair by writing his last book, "Absalom's Hair," a robust treatise against men having long hair. Udemans chose to publish this book under a pseudonym (Iranaeus Poimenander), probably because he wrote the book in a rather strong and fiery manner. In this debate, he chose to support the side of Gisbertus Voetius, Carolus de Maets (1597–1651), and Jacobus Borstius (1612–1680), all of whom, based on 1 Corinthians 11:14, had strongly opposed the then-current fashion of men wearing long hair.

Second, Udemans, like most other notable, conservative Reformed writers of his day, wrote against the Roman Catholic Church. He coauthored two books (one with Voetius) exposing Roman Catholic error and translated the substantial book of Andreas Rivetus (1572–1651) against Roman Catholic theology. Udemans also translated a little work of Andreas Hyperius (1511–1564), a professor of Marburg, titled "Tract of the Bacchus-feasts" (1610), in which Hyperius opposed the celebration of fast evenings, circuses, and various Roman Catholic amusements that the Reformation had not yet managed to eradicate.

Third, three of Udemans's books were written against the Anabaptists. In Zierikzee in 1609, Udemans took an active role in a three-day Reformed/Baptist debate, primarily revolving around the nature of Christ's incarnation. The debaters included the three Reformed ministers of Zierikzee and three prominent Anabaptist representatives. In 1613, Udemans published the minutes of the discussions of the debate, showing the validity of the Reformed viewpoint that Jesus grew in the womb of Mary as a real baby rather than merely passing through Mary as water passes through a trough, as the Anabaptists claimed.

Later, in 1620, Udemans wrote "Necessary Improvement," a detailed rebuttal against Francois de Knuyt, one of the Anabaptist representatives in the 1609 debate, who had written "A Short Acknowledgment of Faith." In his response, Udemans effectively refuted erroneous Anabaptist views concerning God's attributes, the creation of man, the fall of man, the incarnation of Christ, baptism, the role of the magistrates, the taking of oaths, and prayer.

Udemans's "The Peace of Jerusalem" (1627) was a response to the polemical book written by the Anabaptist Anthony Jacobsz (c. 1594–1624; often called Roscius after the friend and teacher of Cicero), titled "Babel: The Confusion of the Paedo-baptists among Themselves about the Subject of Baptism and Its Adherence, To Be a Mirror for Hermanno Faukelio." Roscius's book, in turn, was written against Herman Faukelius's "Babel, that is, the Confusions of the Anabaptists Among Themselves Regarding Virtually All the Components of Christian Doctrine." In "The Peace of Jerusalem," Udemans responded to Jacobsz's book point by point. In sum, he attempted to show how much the Reformed church agreed on issues related to baptism with the convictions of the oldest apostolic church of Jerusalem. His polemical skills, though a bit tedious at times, were intellectually astute, sharp, and devastating.

Throughout these writings, Udemans not only answered traditional Anabaptist arguments related to the baptism of infants but also responded at length to the Anabaptist charge that Reformed doctrine promotes careless living.

The Practice of Faith, Hope, and Love
Udemans's first major work, originally titled "Practice: The Actual Exercises of the Primary Christian Virtues—Faith, Hope, and Love," was published in 1612. In this book, Udemans, as a Reformed pietist, presents faith, hope, and love as experientially active Christian virtues. Justification, which establishes the believer's union with Christ, is presented as the experiential commencement of sanctification, and therefore faith itself cannot but produce good works. This is really the burden of the book, as Udemans acknowledges in the preface.

The book commences with a portrayal of the essence and distinctions of the Christian's three primary virtues:

+ True faith is a fruit of the Spirit, planted in our hearts by the hearing of the Word and confirmed by the use of the sacraments.

+ Hope is the fruit of the Spirit whereby we look forward with patience and endurance to the fulfillment of God's promises.

+ Love is a fruit of the Holy Spirit by which we love God for His sake and our neighbors (meaning everyone, including our enemies) for God's sake.

Udemans then explains all that affects the experience of these three virtues. When he discusses the practice of faith, he blends into it an exegesis of the Twelve Articles of Faith. When discussing the experience of hope, he incorporates an exposition of the Lord's Prayer. When discussing love, he thoroughly expounds the Ten Commandments. In this way, *The Practice of Faith, Hope, and Love* serves as a comprehensive doctrinal work of faith and ethics.

In expounding the Apostles' Creed and the Lord's Prayer, Udemans follows an effective pattern of first providing a basic explanation and proofs of each phrase being expounded then offering comforts for believers that flow from that phrase.

In keeping with the Reformed practice of catechizing, the Ten Commandments receive the most lengthy treatment, taking up two-thirds of the book. Udemans unveils a remarkable array of sins and virtues with regard to each commandment. In our day, when our consciences are so desensitized, we are naturally prone to think at certain points that Udemans yielded to legalism—especially when he deals with the Sabbath and various issues often relegated to the category of asceticism, such as fasting. If Udemans went too far in promoting rules that flow out of the Ten Commandments, however, our generation surely doesn't go far enough. And let us not forget that his treatment of the commandments shows how serious the Dutch Further Reformation divines were about living all of life to God's glory by following His will fully in all that we are called to do and not to do. They would not have viewed Udemans's treatment as legalistic but as a sincere effort to bring all of life to the touchstone of Scripture and into submission to the will of our Father, which ought to be our meat and drink to do.

The Practice of Faith, Hope, and Love resonated well with the God-fearing people of the seventeenth-century Netherlands. It was reprinted at least four times in that century (Dordrecht: 1621, 1632, 1640; Amsterdam: 1658) and became one of Udemans's most important books. When the third edition was printed, Udemans added an article on meditation, titled "Divine Contemplation: That Is, Spiritual Means of Warfare by Which to Attain Heaven with Such Violence as Is Pleasing to God." This tract, based on Christ's words spoken to His disciples—"and from the days of John the Baptist until now the kingdom of heaven suffereth violence, and the violent take it by force" (Matt. 11:12)—was well placed, as it was very similar to *The Practice of Faith, Hope, and Love* in its goal of stirring up lukewarm Christians to become active in promoting the kingdom of God.

Conclusion

What William Perkins (1558–1602) did for England, Godefridus Udemans strove to do for the Netherlands—to point people to their divine calling in Christ. Udemans's work was deeply appreciated by many of his contemporaries. Eewoud Teellinck said that he was a faithful prophet to the Netherlands. Cornelius Boy said that Udemans's preaching was blessed to the conversion of thousands.

Udemans is one of the most significant, typical, and influential ministers in the early period of the Dutch Further Reformation during the first half of the seventeenth century. This is to be largely attributed to his many-faceted gifts and interests. He was a godly Christian with a heart that was sensitive to the needs of the poor, a great exegete and biblical scholar, a well-known and able Reformed preacher who stressed the practice of piety (*praxis pietatis*), a faithful and beloved shepherd of souls, a gifted historical theologian, an influential writer in the mainstream of the Dutch Further Reformation, and a capable guide in church affairs in Zeeland. He enjoyed great respect at classes and synods and became particularly well known after his important role as vice president of the Synod of Dort. He was a great help for the Dutch Reformed Church in battling Arminianism before, during, and after the Remonstrant controversy.

Udemans had a great vision for the spiritual renewal of the Netherlands. He did not live to see that vision fulfilled as he wished, but he was given God's grace to strive after it, and in the process, he made a huge positive and spiritual impact on the lives of thousands.

Chapter 10

John Bunyan on Justification

John Bunyan (1628–1688), author of *The Pilgrim's Progress*, is one of the best-known Puritans. While much of his work is eclipsed by *The Pilgrim's Progress*, the famous "tinker" from Bedford possessed remarkable theological prowess. His ability to "earnestly contend for the faith which was once delivered unto the saints" (Jude 1:3) is aptly demonstrated in such works as *Questions about the Nature and Perpetuity of the Seventh-Day Sabbath* and his *Exposition of the First Ten Chapters of Genesis*.[1] He had no university degree, yet he clearly grasped the central tenets of the Christian faith and masterfully applied them to his readers. Bunyan was also "very distinctly and consistently a teacher,"[2] whose schoolbook was the Bible. As J. H. Gosden says, "Other authority he seldom adduces.... His appeal constantly is: 'What saith the Scripture?'"[3] Bunyan's ability to wed orthodoxy and orthopraxy made him dangerous to his critics, beloved to his friends, and invaluable to future generations.

Of particular interest to us here is Bunyan's concern for vindicating the doctrine of justification. Bunyan readily acknowledges that the term *justification* is used in various ways in the Scriptures; he is primarily concerned with the justification by which "a man stand[s] clear, quit, free, or in a saved condition before [God] in the approbation of his holy law."[4] Justification is the act

---

1. *The Works of John Bunyan*, ed. George Offor, 3 vols. (Edinburgh: Banner of Truth, 1991), 2:361–85, 413–501 (henceforth cited by the title of the individual writing as well as *Works* volume and page number). References to *The Miscellaneous Works of John Bunyan*, gen. ed. Roger Sharrock, 13 vols. (Oxford: Oxford University Press, 1976–1994) will be cited as *MW* volume and page number. Many thanks to Paul Smalley for his assistance on this article, which is revised from what was printed in *Midwestern Journal of Theology* 10, no. 1 (2011): 166–89.

2. A. R. Buckland, *John Bunyan* (London: Religious Tract Society, 1857), 97.

3. J. H. Gosden, *Bunyan: His Doctrine* (London: Sovereign Grace Union, 1929), 2.

4. *Justification by an Imputed Righteousness*, in *Works*, 1:301. In addition to this, Bunyan speaks of justification of actions and a justification before men. However, these two concerned Bunyan very little compared to our justification before God.

whereby a person may stand before God's law and be declared "not guilty" or, positively, be declared righteous.

Though Bunyan is not unique in his defense of the Protestant doctrine of justification by faith alone, he shows greater clarity and pastoral concern in expounding this doctrine than most of his contemporaries. For this reason alone, Bunyan's doctrine of justification is a worthwhile study. Let us look at how:

+ Bunyan's own spiritual experience helped shape his views on justification,

+ Bunyan's writings respond to his historical-polemical situation,

+ Bunyan's doctrine of justification answers a variety of important questions, and

+ Bunyan's pastoral concern applies the comforts flowing from justification.

Bunyan's Personal Experience

Though Bunyan experienced sporadic convictions of sin in his youth that helped restrain rebellion, he confessed that he was "filled with all unrighteousness" and had "few equals, both for cursing, swearing, lying, and blaspheming the holy name of God."[5] God began to deal with Bunyan's soul in an abiding way in his early twenties, when he realized that, in his own words, "I was lost if I had not Christ, because I had been a sinner; I saw that I wanted a perfect righteousness to present me without fault before God, and this righteousness was nowhere to be found but in the person of Jesus Christ."[6]

About that same time, God greatly blessed to Bunyan's soul the reading of Martin Luther's commentary on Galatians, which strongly emphasized the necessity of basing the whole of one's salvation on the imputed righteousness of Christ. Bunyan later wrote: "I do prefer this book of Martin Luther upon the Galatians (excepting the Holy Bible) before all the books that ever I have seen, as most fit for a wounded conscience."[7]

Luther's book, together with the preaching and pastoral ministry of John Gifford, pastor of the Bedford Independent Church, brought Bunyan to see the necessity and beauty of the doctrine of justification by faith alone. Bunyan was particularly influenced by a sermon Gifford preached on Song of Solomon 4:1, "Behold thou art fair, my love, behold thou art fair." Nevertheless, Bunyan was greatly assaulted by the devil's wiles before being able to reach a comfortable degree of assurance that he was personally justified before God in Christ's

---

5. *Grace Abounding to the Chief of Sinners*, in *Works*, 1:6.
6. *Grace Abounding to the Chief of Sinners*, in *Works*, 1:16.
7. *Grace Abounding to the Chief of Sinners*, in *Works*, 1:22.

righteousness alone. Happily, the day finally came when this great doctrine of imputed righteousness brought Bunyan into spiritual liberty. Bunyan writes of that unforgettable experience:

> But one day, as I was passing in the field…this sentence fell upon my soul: Thy righteousness is in heaven; and methought withal I saw, with the eyes of my soul, Jesus Christ, at God's right hand; there, I say, as my righteousness; so that wherever I was, or whatever I was a-doing, God could not say of me, He wants my righteousness, for that was just before him. I also saw, moreover, that it was not my good frame of heart that made my righteousness better, nor yet my bad frame that made my righteousness worse; for my righteousness was Jesus Christ himself, the same yesterday, today, and forever. Now did my chains fall off my legs indeed, I was loosed from my afflictions and irons; my temptations also fled away…now I went home rejoicing, for the grace and love of God…. I lived for some time, very sweetly at peace with God through Christ; oh, methought, Christ! Christ! there was nothing but Christ that was before my eyes, I was not now only looking upon this and the other benefits of Christ apart, as of his blood, burial, and resurrection, but considered him as a whole Christ!… It was glorious to me to see his exaltation, and the worth and prevalency of all his benefits, and that because of this: now I could look from myself to him, and would reckon that all those graces of God that now were green in me, were yet but like those cracked groats and fourpence-halfpennies that rich men carry in their purses, when their gold is in their trunk at home! Oh, I saw that my gold was in my trunk at home! In Christ my Lord and Saviour! Now Christ was all.[8]

Michael Davies comments, "Bunyan's language, at the moment of saving faith in Christ, seems to approach something intensely mystical…. [But] we should not let his rhapsodic, ecstatic prose cloud our understanding of the doctrinal point here. In clear, covenant terms Bunyan's conversion has been effected as a shift to grace from the law."[9] Bunyan saw with the eyes of his heart that the living Christ was his righteousness, not his own works, and his heart rested upon Christ and found peace.

No wonder, then, that the doctrine of Christ's imputed righteousness lay at the center of Bunyan's teaching and preaching all his life. As Robert Oliver notes, this doctrine was

---

8. *Grace Abounding to the Chief of Sinners*, in *Works*, 1:35–36.
9. Michael Davies, *Graceful Reading: Theology and Narrative in the Works of John Bunyan* (Oxford: Oxford University Press, 2002), 101.

fundamental to the thinking of a man who took seriously the demands of the Law of God. He knew by painful experience that he had no hope of meeting those demands for 'there is none righteous, no not one.' Only as the Law's demands were met by Jesus Christ and imputed to him could he stand before God. The sufferings of Christ were endured for his sins and Christ's active obedience imputed to him ensured that the Law's demands were met. Only as he grasped these truths for himself could he see that there was 'Grace abounding to the chief of sinners.'[10]

Bunyan's Historical-Polemical Context

Bearing in mind, then, Bunyan's personal experience, let us consider the polemical context in which he found himself—a context that moved him to defend justification by faith alone in three of his books. Bunyan wrote on justification against both the Quakers and the Latitudinarian Anglicans.[11]

The Quaker controversy with Bunyan was led by Edward Burrough (1634–1663) in his *The True Faith of the Gospel of Peace* (1656). Burrough was educated in the Church of England, then joined the Presbyterians, only to be converted to Quakerism by the preaching of George Fox in 1652. He was responding to Bunyan's first book, *Some Gospel-Truths Opened According to the Scriptures* (1656), written after Bunyan had participated in public debates with Quakers. Bunyan also published *A Vindication of the Book Called, Some Gospel-Truths Opened* (1657). Burrough then responded with *Truth (the Strongest of All) Witnessed Forth in the Spirit of Truth, Against All Deceit* (1657).[12]

Burrough accused Bunyan of approaching popish legalism by denying "the Christ within."[13] He castigated Bunyan for denying that the light of conscience is a saving grace of Christ's Spirit given to all men. The Quakers asserted that Christ works His light and law in all people who are then saved by the choice of their own wills. By not resisting the inner light, men become holy and so are justified.[14] Bunyan rebuked Burrough for confusing "justification wrought by the man Christ without, and sanctification wrought by the Spirit of Christ, within." Their debate was marred by heated and uncharitable language. Bunyan

---

10. Robert Oliver, "'Grace Abounding': Imputed Righteousness in the Life and Work of John Bunyan," *The Churchman* 107, no. 1 (1993): 79.

11. Davies, *Graceful Reading*, 53–54, 75–77. Cf. I. M. Green, "Bunyan in Context: The Changing Face of Protestantism in Seventeenth-Century England, in *Bunyan in England and Abroad*, ed. M. Os and G. J. Schutte (Amsterdam: Vrije Universiteit, 1990), 1–27.

12. Richard L. Greaves, *Glimpses of Glory: John Bunyan and English Dissent* (Stanford: Stanford University Press, 2002), 75–78; Oliver, "Grace Abounding," 73–77.

13. Davies, *Graceful Reading*, 17.

14. Oliver, "Grace Abounding," 77.

called the Quakers "painted hypocrites," and Burrough called Bunyan's teaching "wonderful trash, and muddy stuff."[15]

Bunyan's controversy with Latitudinarian Anglicanism was no less rancorous. *A Defence of the Doctrine of Justification by Faith in Jesus Christ* (1672)[16] is a polemical work that Bunyan wrote particularly against Edward Fowler (1632–1714), vicar of Norhill near Bedford at that time, though ten years earlier he had been a Presbyterian, ejected from the Church of England as a result of the Act of Uniformity (1662). In the mid-1660s, Fowler conformed and was reinstated in the Church of England. Later, he would be appointed Bishop of Gloucester. Fowler wrote two books that deeply troubled Bunyan. In 1670, he published *The Principles and Practices of Certain Moderate Divines of the Church of England* as a defense of the growing Latitudinarian school of theology that promoted religious rationalism at the expense of the doctrines of predestination and Christ's imputed righteousness. Moreover, in this book Fowler denigrated Puritan experiential theology—as did most Latitudinarians—as mere "enthusiasm." Several months later, Fowler published *The Design of Christianity*, which taught, among other errors, that genuine Christianity only aims to purify men's natures and reform their lives so that they could be restored to the Adamic pre-fall state. Attacking the doctrine of justification directly, Fowler wrote, "The free grace of God is infinitely more magnified, in renewing our natures, than it could be in the bare justification of our persons."[17] Fowler said that the gospel teaches us "to perform good Actions," as exemplified in Jesus whose life was "one Continued Lecture of the most Excellent Morals.... He was a Person of the Greatest Freedom, Affability, and Courtesie."[18] He said it was "stupid folly" to think that Christ's righteousness is our own.[19] In a word, Fowler preached a gospel of gentlemanly good manners rather than Christ's imputed righteousness.

In *A Defence of the Doctrine of Justification by Faith*, Bunyan strongly condemned Fowler for abusing Scripture and the doctrines of his own church— particularly articles 10, 11, and 13 of The Thirty-Nine Articles of the Church of England.[20] If our holiness must derive partly from us and from the purity of our nature, then Fowler was really offering little else than "the religion of the

---

15. Greaves, *Glimpses of Glory*, 82–85.

16. *A Defence of Justification*, in *Works*, 2:281–34.

17. Quoted in Richard L. Greaves, *John Bunyan* (Grand Rapids: Eerdmans, 1969), 83. Cf. Oliver, "Grace Abounding," 74.

18. Quoted in Davies, *Graceful Reading*, 75.

19. Quoted in Greaves, *Glimpses of Glory*, 282.

20. *A Defence of Justification*, in *Works*, 2:232.

Socinians, Quakers, etc., and not the religion of Jesus Christ."[21] Bunyan earnestly warned Fowler that his writing in such a vilifying manner of true religion, if not repented of, would bring the blood of the damned upon his own head.[22]

Fowler responded to Bunyan caustically. Instead of refuting Bunyan's arguments, he called Bunyan a problematic schismatic whose book was ill-conceived, and goes on to suggest that someone else must have written the bulk of it for him, since this lowly tinker used all kinds of vocabulary and phrases beyond his capacity of understanding. Fowler even provides a list of these terms and phrases. He carries on for seventy pages replying to Bunyan, of whom he said at the beginning that he was not even worth replying to.[23] That is one way to do polemics!

Later, Bunyan wrote a shorter treatise, *Justification by an Imputed Righteousness*, which was found among his papers after his death in 1688 and was first published in 1692.[24] This book addresses the doctrines of justification and imputation more directly, in greater detail, and more pastorally than polemically, as we shall see. Throughout, Bunyan decries all self-righteousness and calls upon unbelievers to flee to Christ alone for justifying righteousness. He writes, "In the matter of thy justification thou must know nothing, see nothing, hear nothing, but thine own sins and Christ's righteousness."[25]

Many of Bunyan's other writings—such as *The Pharisee and the Publican, Doctrine of Law and Grace Unfolded, Light for Them that Sit in Darkness, Saved by Grace, A Vindication of Gospel Truths, The Work of Jesus Christ as Advocate, The Intercession of Christ*, and *Come and Welcome to Jesus Christ*—are sprinkled with references to the doctrine of justification by faith alone. Not surprisingly, therefore, Bunyan considers justification essential for every believer, stating, "It is absolutely necessary that this be known of us; for if the understanding be muddy as to this, it is impossible that such should be sound in the faith."[26]

Bunyan's Doctrine of Justification

Let us now turn to consider his doctrinal treatment of justification by faith alone. For Bunyan, that means answering six questions.

---

21. *A Defence of Justification*, in *Works*, 2:292.

22. *A Defence of Justification*, in *Works*, 2:313–14.

23. John Brown, *John Bunyan (1628–1688): His Life, Times, and Work* (London: Hulbert Publishing, 1928), 218–19.

24. *Justification by an Imputed Righteousness*, in *Works*, 1:301–334. It may have been written in 1676 but hidden due to increasing government persecution (Greaves, *Glimpses of Glory*, 339, 341–42).

25. *Justification by an Imputed Righteousness*, in *Works*, 1:327.

26. *Justification by an Imputed Righteousness*, in *Works*, 1:303.

1. What is the function of the moral law?

From the time of the Reformation, not to mention the days of the apostles, a central question in the debate on justification has been this: Can a sinner be justified by doing the works of the law? The answer to this question depends on how we view the gospel of grace. In Bunyan's day, as in our own, many have proposed views that do not direct people to Christ and His accomplished work but to themselves and their own works. George Offor says Bunyan offers "powerful arguments [to] counteract these errors."[27]

The need for justification arises from the nature of the law. Bunyan saw the law in the context of the two covenants between God and man: the covenant of works and the covenant of grace. The covenant of works laid upon Adam in the garden of Eden the requirement for perfect obedience to God's moral law, later expressed in the Ten Commandments.[28] To be right with God, a person must be perfectly righteous, meaning he or she is fully obedient to the law of God. Bunyan cites Moses in his *Exposition on Genesis*, saying, "It shall be our righteousness, if we observe to do all these commandments before the Lord our God, as he hath commanded us."[29] Our obedience is our righteousness, and this righteousness involves *negative* as well as *positive* holiness. Negative holiness means a person must cease from sin, or the transgression of the law;[30] positive holiness means a person must also perform the duties commanded in the law, or the practice of holiness: "For it is not what a man is not, but what a man does, that declares him a righteous man."[31] The requirement of the law is perfect righteousness.[32]

The law demands obedience but also threatens to punish disobedience. Bunyan asserts, "The law is itself so perfectly holy and good as not to admit of the least failure."[33] Anything less than perfect obedience to this law brings upon the sinner the curse and condemnation of the law (Gal. 3:10). In his *The Doctrine of Law and Grace Unfolded*, Bunyan says this law "doth not onely condemn words and actions...but it hath authority to condemn the most secret thoughts of the heart, being evil; so that if thou do not speak any word that is evil...yet if there should chance to passe but one vain thought...the Law taketh hold

---

27. *Justification by an Imputed Righteousness*, in *Works*, 1:300.
28. Davies, *Graceful Reading*, 22–23.
29. *Exposition of Genesis*, in *Works*, 2:425–26, citing Deuteronomy 6:25.
30. *Pharisee and the Publican*, in *Works*, 2:222–23; 2 Timothy 2:22; 1 Corinthians 10:14.
31. *Pharisee and the Publican*, in *Works*, 2:223; cf. 1 Timothy 6:11.
32. *Justification by an Imputed Righteousness*, in *Works*, 1:302.
33. *Justification by an Imputed Righteousness*, in *Works*, 1:316.

of it, accuseth, and also will condemn thee for it."[34] Wherever this law shines, it exposes wrongdoing, even in the smallest measure, and pronounces a death sentence on the wrongdoer, for, as Bunyan says, "Sin and death is forever its language."[35] In the vivid imagery of *Pilgrim's Progress*, Moses cannot show mercy to a pilgrim but can only destroy his fancied righteousness.[36]

In the light of the law, can anyone declare himself exempt from its curse and condemnation? Bunyan says, "If thou findest thy self guilty, as I am sure thou canst not otherwise choose but do, unless thou shut thy eyes against thy every dayes practice; then I say conclude thyself guilty of the breach of the first Covenant."[37] The law daily exacerbates a person's guilt: "Strike a steel against a flint, and the fire flies about you; strike the law against a carnal heart, and sin appears, sin multiplies, sin rageth, sin is strengthened!"[38] Davies writes, "To believe that one can attain righteousness by works is supreme folly for Bunyan, as the ability to fulfill the law was forfeited for everyone by Adam (mankind's representative, or 'publick person') in his act of disobedience in the Garden of Eden."[39] Pieter de Vries observes, "The doctrine of the justification of a sinner has its significance in the light of man's total depravity.... As long as we are strangers to the depravity of our hearts, we shall not esteem Christ."[40]

Since everyone has broken the law and lacks both negative and positive holiness, "therefore now for ever, by the law, no man can stand just before God."[41] Even works that might, at face value, seem ethically good are defiled because they are tainted by sin.[42] Those who seek to come to God on the basis of their own righteousness are like the Pharisee who stood on a street corner thanking God that he was not a publican. Bunyan comments, "Indeed, thou mayest cover thy dirt, and paint thy sepulcher.... But Pharisee, God can see through the white of this wall, even to the dirt that is within... nor can any of thy most holy duties, nor all, when put together, blind the eye of the all-seeing majesty from

---

34. *Doctrine of Law and Grace Unfolded*, in *MW*, 2:33.

35. *Justification by an Imputed Righteousness*, in *Works*, 1:317.

36. *Pilgrim's Progress*, in *Works*, 3:118–19.

37. *Doctrine of Law and Grace Unfolded*, in *MW*, 2:35. Bunyan, agreeing partly with the Federal Theology of his day, affirms that man was created in a covenant of works, which operated under the strict nature of law: "do this and live." Therefore, to break that covenant is to break the law (*Exposition of Genesis*, in *Works*, 2:426–27).

38. *Justification by an Imputed Righteousness*, in *Works*, 1:317.

39. Davies, *Graceful Reading*, 23.

40. Pieter de Vries, *John Bunyan on the Order of Salvation*, trans. C. van Haaften (New York: Peter Lang, 1994), 149.

41. *Exposition of Genesis*, in *Works*, 2:426.

42. *Justification by an Imputed Righteousness*, in *Works*, 1:315.

beholding all the uncleanness of thy soul."[43] God thus rightfully rejects "man's righteousness, for the weakness and unprofitableness thereof."[44]

The law requires that a person be justified by perfect obedience, yet no one is capable of such perfection. The law thus demands the condemnation of all. As Bunyan says, "No, saith the Law, thou hast sinned, therefore I must curse thee; for it is my nature to curse, even, and nothing else but curse every one that doth in any point transgress against me, Gal. 3.10."[45] In his autobiography, *Grace Abounding to the Chief of Sinners*, Bunyan expresses how many people feel when the law penetrates their conscience: "I had no sooner thus conceived in my mind, but suddenly this conclusion was fastened on my spirit…that I had been a great and grievous sinner, and that it was now too late for me to look after heaven."[46] How then can a sinner find acceptance by a righteous and holy God? He cannot do it by his own merit, for his sins leave him void of any righteousness, and God thus rejects his obedience altogether.

2. How can a person be made right with God?

In this quagmire of sin, hopelessness, and helplessness, we find hope, Bunyan says, by looking to the righteousness of another. Bunyan directs his readers to the incarnate Mediator of the covenant of grace, who alone can justify. This is the gospel promise already offered to our first parents by God in the *proto-evangelium* of Genesis 3:15. Bunyan impersonates God as saying, "Now because I have grace and mercy, I will therefore design thy recovery."[47] Sinners stand before the indictment of the law in need of supernatural help; they can by no means recover themselves from their fallen state. So God promises this recovery through the work of Jesus Christ, His beloved Son. Bunyan again uses impersonation: God promises that His Son will save sinners by "fulfilling my law, and by answering the penalties thereof. He shall bring in a righteousness which shall be 'everlasting,' by which I will justify you from sin, and the curse of God due thereto."[48] Because the law has been transgressed, its demands have

---

43. *Pharisee and Publican*, in *Works*, 2:229.

44. *Pharisee and Publican*, in *Works*, 2:229. This will remind us of Christian's journey in *The Pilgrim's Progress* when he came upon By-path Meadow. Having ventured onto tough terrain he sought a different path to lead them to the Celestial Gate. They took the easier road and as they did it began thundering and lightning, reminding us of Sinai and not Zion. It was here that they stumbled upon Vain-confidence and later Doubting Castle and Giant Despair (see *Pilgrim's Progress*, in *Works*, 3:138ff.).

45. *Doctrine of Law and Grace Unfolded*, in *MW*, 2:36.

46. *Grace Abounding to the Chief of Sinners*, in *Works*, 1:8.

47. *Exposition of Genesis*, in *Works*, 2:437.

48. *Exposition of Genesis*, in *Works*, 2:438.

strengthened. For the Son to satisfy God's justice, He must both pay the penalty for sin and fulfill the righteous requirements of the law. His obedience must be both active and passive, positive and negative: "For the accomplishing of righteousness, there was both doing and suffering; doing, to fulfill all the commands of the law; suffering, to answer to its penalty for sin."[49]

Within the economy of salvation, this promised Savior is considered "a *public* person, or one that presents the body of mankind in himself."[50] Christ did not do what He did for Himself; rather, He was a representative—not for all mankind, but for His promised seed. Bunyan writes, "Christ stood as a common person, presenting in himself the whole lump of the promised seed, or the children of the promise; wherefore, he comes under the law for them, takes upon him to do what the law required of them, takes upon him to do it for them."[51] As the representative of His chosen seed, Christ always works on their behalf. While affirming this doctrine, Bunyan also asserts the mystery of it, saying, "That one particular man should represent all the elect in himself, and that the most righteous should die as a sinner, yea, as a sinner by the hand of a just and holy God, is a mystery of the greatest depth!"[52]

3. Why are Christ's active and passive obedience both essential for justification?

As a public person, Christ's vicarious obedience applies to both His life and His death. The Savior fulfilled the law both actively and passively, by works He performed and the things that He suffered, which are tasks delegated to Him from eternity. In Christ's passive obedience, the penalty of sin is paid; as Bunyan says, "Thou hast sinned; the law now calls for passive...obedience."[53] Suffering is necessary for justification because "the threatening of death and the curse of the law lay in the way between heaven's gates and the souls of the children, for their sins; wherefore he that will save them must answer Divine justice, or God must lie, in saving them without inflicting the punishment threatened."[54]

The law, which is a reflection of God's perfect justice, demands that all transgressions must be punished. Christ submitted to the punishment decreed by the law, dying for sin, in order to purge its guilt through the shedding of His blood. Citing Hebrews 1:3, Bunyan says Christ has "purged our sins...by his

---

49. *Justification by an Imputed Righteousness*, in *Works*, 1:323.

50. *Justification by an Imputed Righteousness*, in *Works*, 1:303.

51. *Light for Them that Sit in Darkness*, in *Works*, 1:406; for more on Bunyan's view of particular redemption, see *Come and Welcome to Jesus Christ*, in *Works*, 1:242–43.

52. *Justification by an Imputed Righteousness*, in *Works*, 1:303.

53. *Justification by an Imputed Righteousness*, in *Works*, 1:317.

54. *Light for Them that Sit in Darkness*, in *Works*, 1:405.

precious blood; for that alone can purge our sins."[55] Christ's death was designed to meet the demands of God's justice. "Christ, when he died, died not to satisfie Satan, but his Father; not to appease the Devil, but to answer the Demands of the Justice of God…. He redeemed us, therefore, from the Curse of the Law, by his Blood."[56] Therefore, if Christ is to justify sinners, He "must…have suffered; the manner of the work laid a necessity upon him to take our flesh upon him, he must die, he must die for us, he must die for our sins."[57]

Likewise, Christ's active obedience is necessary, for paying the penalty is only half of the equation. Had Christ only suffered punishment, obedience to the commands of the law would still be necessary, for the whole law, every jot and tittle of it, must be fulfilled to establish righteousness. So Bunyan writes, "That at the very time when Jesus Christ did hang on the cross on Mount Calvary, was buried, rose again from the dead, and ascended above the clouds from his disciples, at that very time was all the law fulfilled for righteousness. He is the end of the law, mark; he is the end of the law for righteousness."[58] As a righteous man, Christ obeyed the law perfectly, fulfilling *all* the demands of the law, both in His passive obedience of paying for sin through His suffering and death and in His active obedience by doing the things commanded, loving God above all, and loving His neighbor as Himself.

4. How are we justified by faith?

In speaking of the first covenant God made with man in the garden of Eden, Bunyan says that if man kept the law both positively and negatively, his obedience would be his righteousness. This is precisely what Christ has done, for in Him there was no transgression and in all that He did He lived a holy life. Therefore, we can say that Christ *is* righteous: He has done what man, weakened by flesh, could not do.

As a public man, Christ represented the promised seed; all that He did was done for them, on their behalf. His people are made righteous, not by their own righteousness but by *His*. Bunyan writes, "For if he hath undertaken to bring in a justifying righteousness, and that by works and merits of his own, then that righteousness must of necessity be inherent in him alone, and ours only by imputation."[59] Just as Adam's sin was imputed to his physical posterity, so

55. *Justification by an Imputed Righteousness*, in *Works*, 1:323.
56. *The Advocateship of Jesus Christ*, in *MW*, 11:127. The second issue of the first edition of this work was retitled *The Work of Jesus Christ as an Advocate* (cf. *Works*, 1:151–54).
57. *Light for Them that Sit in Darkness*, in *Works*, 1:405.
58. *A Vindication of Gospel Truths*, in *Works*, 2:189.
59. *Justification by an Imputed Righteousness*, in *Works*, 1:324.

the righteousness of Christ is imputed to His spiritual posterity, or those who believe in Him. Of this Bunyan says, "It is improper to say, Adam's eating of the forbidden fruit was personally and inherently an act of mine. It was personally his, and imputatively mine; personally his, because he did it; imputatively mine, because I was then in him."[60] It follows that "the righteousness of the other [Christ] is reckoned the righteousness of those that are his."[61] Hence, "saving comes to us by what Christ did for us."[62]

Bunyan, therefore, is an avid promoter of the forensic character of justification. He believed that Christ's righteousness is personally imputed to each and every elect as sinners. By that imputation of righteousness, they are justified individually and corporately before God. The believing sinner, led by the Spirit and Word of God, gives up the vain attempt to produce his own righteousness and takes refuge in Christ's righteousness.

Like John Owen (1616–1683) and Thomas Goodwin (1600–1679), Bunyan distinguished justification from the forgiveness of sin. As de Vries writes, "In his opinion the forgiveness of sin is the fruit of someone's being covered with the righteousness of Christ. Quite consciously Bunyan refrained from equating justification and forgiveness, making a logical distinction between them in order to point out that Christ's imputed righteousness is the sole legal ground for the forgiveness of sins. In doing this he sought to exclude any possibility for a Socinian interpretation of justification," as they defined justification exclusively in terms of forgiveness.[63]

Bunyan taught that the imputed righteousness of Christ is received by us through *faith*, which is defined as "receiving, embracing, accepting, or trusting."[64] Above all, faith appropriates Christ's righteousness, which is readily available in and from Christ Himself. Faith does not justify us by its own virtue but by virtue of its object, Christ and His righteousness; hence, it always bears a

---

60. *Justification by an Imputed Righteousness*, in *Works*, 1:324.

61. *Justification by an Imputed Righteousness*, in *Works*, 1:324.

62. *Christ a Complete Saviour*, in *Works*, 1:207.

63. De Vries, *John Bunyan on the Order of Salvation*, 148.

64. *Justification by an Imputed Righteousness*, in *Works*, 1:328. Bunyan taught that the imputation of Christ's righteousness immediately precedes faith, which then apprehends Christ's righteousness consciously. He argued that God must justify before He can bless the sinner with the grace of faith, for an unjustified sinner is under His curse, not His blessing. Faith was a sign of justification, not its cause (*The Pharisee and the Publican*, in *Works*, 2:250–51; cf. de Vries, *John Bunyan on the Order of Salvation*, 151–54; Davies, *Graceful Reading*, 30–31). However, Bunyan's view is not the same as the later British Baptist John Gill (1697–1771), for Bunyan taught a justification logically prior to but temporally simultaneous with faith, not an eternal justification innate in God. Bunyan did teach that the elect were saved in one sense before the creation of the world but in another sense saved when drawn to Jesus Christ to trust in Him (*Saved by Grace*, in *Works*, 1:338–39).

relational character. Faith justifies us only because through it we rest on Christ's work. This is the only way for Christ and His righteousness to become a personal, experiential reality for us. Bunyan thus says, "To be saved is to be brought to, and helped to lay hold on, Jesus Christ by faith."[65] To trust in anything other than Christ, whether the merit of the law or the merit of faith, is to undermine the glorious doctrine of justification. Bunyan asks, "What, then, must [faith] rely upon or trust in? Not in itself; that is, without Scripture; not in its works, they are inferior to itself.... Therefore it must trust in Christ."[66] Because of what Christ suffered for us, He alone became the "meritorious cause of our justification.... Thou art, therefore, as I have said, to make Christ Jesus the object of thy faith for justification."[67]

Bunyan emphasizes the relationship between faith and Christ, saying, "Faith, then, as separate from Christ, doth nothing; nothing, neither with God nor man; because what it wants is relative; but let it go to the Lord Jesus—let it behold him as dying, and it fetches righteousness, and life, and peace, out of the virtue of his blood."[68] Faith is nothing more than trusting Jesus Christ and His righteousness to be *our* righteousness. Here we come full circle, for Bunyan defines justification as that act whereby man stands free and clear before God in the approbation of His law. This cannot be accomplished by any inherent righteousness in man, who by nature is a lawbreaker, but only by faith in Jesus Christ and His meritorious work.

Behind Christ's meritorious work stands the irrevocable love of God to His elect. That love moves the Father to give Christ as heaven's Savior for sinners. Thus, for Bunyan, the love of God is the first and ultimate cause of justification, the merits of Christ are the second, and then, Spirit-worked faith, which is only the instrumental cause—not the meritorious cause—of justification. Without the Spirit's work, there is no possibility of our believing.[69] This faith, which is the gift of God, is not parceled out indiscriminately but given to the elect alone. Faith has to be worked in our heart by the Spirit, or as Bunyan also puts it, we have to be "implanted into the faith of Christ."[70] Only when understood this way can the Calvinist avoid falling into the Arminian and Socinian error of making faith itself the savior, instead of Christ.

---

65. *Saved by Grace*, in *Works*, 1:339.
66. *Justification by an Imputed Righteousness*, in *Works*, 1:326.
67. *Saved by Grace*, in *Works*, 1:339.
68. *Justification by an Imputed Righteousness*, in *Works*, 1:310.
69. Greaves, *John Bunyan*, 71.
70. Quoted in Greaves, *John Bunyan*, 70.

5. How does justifying faith relate to obedience to the law?
Clearly Bunyan held that justifying faith does not look to one's own good works in the least. However, Bunyan taught that justifying faith produces good works. Faith is "a principle of life by which a Christian lives,…a principle of motion by which [the soul] walks towards heaven in the way of holiness…. It is also a principle of strength, by which the soul opposeth its lust, the devil and this world, and overcomes them." Spirit-worked faith is an active grace; it fuels the believer's engine all his lifetime. Greaves comments that Bunyan's view of faith is "an all-embracing principle or source of the Christian life from its inception to its consummation."[71]

Faith in Christ alone justifies a sinner before God. But since faith is invisible, good works justify us before men. Visible obedience to the law plays a crucial role in demonstrating our new spiritual state to our fellow men. Bunyan wrote,

> When I think of justification before God from the dreadful curse of the law; then I must speak of nothing but grace, Christ, the promise, and faith. But when I speak of our justification before men, then I must join to these good works. For grace, Christ, and faith, are things invisible…. He that would shew to his neighbors that he hath truly received this mercy of God, must do it by good works; for all things else to them is but talk.[72]

Faith initiates the believer into the enjoyment of the covenant of grace without abolishing the law from the believer's life. Bunyan believed that the moral law has a place in both the covenant of works and the covenant of grace. He noted that the Lord gave the law to Moses twice, once with thunder and fire in Exodus 19–20 and again with a revelation of grace in Exodus 34. He wrote,

> I think the first doth more principally intend its force as a covenant of works, not at all respecting the Lord Jesus Christ; but this second time not, at least in the manner of its being given, respecting such a covenant, but rather as a rule, or directory [set of directives], to those who already are found in the cleft of the rock, Christ: for the saint himself, though he be without law to God, yet even he is not without law to him as considered under grace, not without law to God, but under the law to Christ. 1 Co. ix. 21.[73]

Bunyan was so convinced that "good works must flow from faith" that he wrote, "The best way both to provoke ourselves and others to good works, it

---

71. Quoted in Greaves, *John Bunyan*, 71–73.
72. *A Holy Life the Beauty of Christianity*, in *Works*, 2:507.
73. *The Law and a Christian*, in *Works*, 2:388.

is to be often affirming to others the doctrine of justification by grace, and to believe it ourselves."[74]

6. In the order of salvation, which has priority, justification or sanctification?
Bunyan emphasized the necessity of imputed righteousness, personal righteousness, and practical righteousness in the true Christian. Anjov Ahenakaa observed that Bunyan "confirms the Reformed position of taking justification and sanctification together, not one at the expense of the other as the Antinomians and Arminians were rightly accused of doing—Antinomians emphasizing free justification at the expense of sanctification, and the Arminians emphasizing sanctification at the expense of justification."[75] Bunyan wrote,

> Thus, therefore, we have described the righteous man. First. He is one whom God makes righteous, by reckoning or imputation. Second. He is one that God makes righteous by possessing of him with [or putting him in possession of] a principle of righteousness. Third. He is one that is practically righteous.... I dare not give a narrower description of a righteous man than this, because whoever pretends to justification, if he be not sanctified, pretends to what he is not; and whoever pretends to sanctification, if he shows not the fruits thereof by a holy life, he deceiveth his own heart, and professeth but in vain.[76]

But Bunyan insisted that the righteousness of imputation must be kept distinct from the righteousness of personal transformation and that imputation must come first: "Righteousness by imputation must be first, that justification may not be of debt, but of mercy and grace."[77] This is further necessary so "the sinner may stand just in God's sight from the curse, and that God might deal with him both in a way of justice as well as mercy, and yet do the sinner no harm."[78] Only after a person is counted righteous in Christ can he begin to live in holiness. Bunyan says, "Wherefore our holy actions are the fruits of righteousness, that is by Jesus Christ, not by our human nature, or the purity of it in us; yea, they are the fruits of the Spirit of God."[79] For Bunyan, righteousness by imputation always and necessarily precedes holy works.

---

74. *Christian Behavior*, in *Works*, 2:570.

75. Anjov Ahenakaa, "Justification and the Christian Life in John Bunyan: A Vindication of Bunyan from the Charge of Antinomianism" (PhD diss., Westminster Theological Seminary, 1997), 126.

76. *The Desire of the Righteous Granted*, in *Works*, 1:750–51.

77. *Pharisee and Publican*, in *Works*, 2:254.

78. *Pharisee and Publican*, in *Works*, 2:255.

79. *A Defence of Justification*, in *Works*, 2:285.

Consequently, sanctification may never precede justification (as in Roman Catholicism), and justification and sanctification may never be commingled (as in Baxterian neonomianism). No one may build his case for salvation on his own sanctification in even the smallest degree. In fact, building salvation on self-righteousness or on anything else in us is our greatest hindrance in exercising faith in Christ's imputed righteousness.[80]

Excursus: Contemporary Justification Issues

It is obvious from what has been laid out above that Bunyan's view of justification is at odds with views about justification often being published today. One increasingly influential view is known as the New Perspective on Paul (NPP). Essentially it argues that the Reformers misunderstood Paul on two levels and that this misunderstanding has dominated later discussions of Paul's view of justification down to the late twentieth century, which would include Bunyan. First, the NPP maintains that when Paul discussed justification, he was not talking about how a sinner can find peace with a holy God. That perspective, NPP advocates maintain, is rooted in the guilty conscience of a Martin Luther or, one could say, the guilt-laden conscience of a John Bunyan. Besides, the argument continues, such a position is typical of a Western mind-set beset with legal notions of sin and justice and beginning to be afflicted by the individualism that is so much a part of occidental *mentalité*. Rather, the NPP asserts, when Paul talks about justification, he is not so much thinking about how one is saved from the wrath and judgment of God but of the evidence that one is already saved. To be justified by faith means that the marks of true conversion are evident, namely, faith in the Lord Jesus and the good works of the Christian life. Justification is not about entry into the Christian life but about what that life looks like. Thus, Paul's polemic against "the works of the law" is not against the attempt to win God's favor by good works—which was very much the mind-set of medieval Roman Catholic piety. Rather, the NPP tells us, "the works of the law" are the marks of Judaism that indicate membership in God's covenant people: circumcision, the keeping of the food laws, etc.[81]

In the NPP, then, Paul is attacking the idea that to belong to the corporate people of God one must keep the distinctive aspects of Judaism. It is faith in

---

80. De Vries, *John Bunyan on the Order of Salvation*, 149.

81. N. T. Wright, *What Saint Paul Really Said: Was Paul of Tarsus the Real Founder of Christianity?* (Grand Rapids: Eerdmans, 1997), 119–22; James D. G. Dunn, *Romans 1–8*, Word Biblical Commentary, Volume 38A (Nashville: Thomas Nelson, 1988), lxiii–lxxii, 192; Mark M. Mattison, "A Summary of the New Perspective on Paul," http://www.thepaulpage.com/a-summary-of-the-new-perspective-on-paul/ (accessed April 27, 2011).

Christ that typifies the truly saved. Most advocates of the NPP also go further and make a second assertion, namely, that Paul says nothing about imputed righteousness. The NPP is rooted in the idea that first-century Judaism was just as grace-oriented as early Christianity, that the final judgment is based on one's works, and that the Greek word for faith means faithfulness, the equivalent of obedience.

But close examination of Paul's writings (for example, Ephesians 2 and Titus 3) reveal a theologian quite conscious that the onset of our salvation is always entirely a matter of grace, which runs against the human tendency to seek self-justification by works before a holy God. The Epistle to the Hebrews sets forth the weight of sin and clearly argues that nothing human beings can do by way of good works or obedient faithfulness can make us holy enough to stand before the majestic purity of the living God. Only Jesus's death and one's faith in that death lead to salvation. Bunyan has rightly understood Paul and Hebrews at this point. First-century Judaism was no more grace-oriented than much of seventeenth-century Anglicanism that Bunyan contended with or the early twenty-first-century secular confidence in the essential goodness of men and women that we must contend with today. Moreover, the doctrine of Christ's imputed righteousness is obviously central to Bunyan's understanding of justification and was the key to his conversion, in which he saw that the flawless righteousness he needed to stand before a holy God was to be found only in the Lord Jesus at the right hand of the Father. Books like Brian Vickers's *Jesus' Blood and Righteousness: Paul's Theology of Imputation*, a close study of the Pauline writings that bear on this issue of Christ's imputed righteousness, show that Bunyan, not to mention the Reformers, rightly understood Paul.[82]

Bunyan's Pastoral Applications

We would be remiss if we ended the discussion of Bunyan on justification here, for Bunyan's trademark is his pastoral concern. This experimental emphasis is evident in most of his writings, in which he applies the truth of a doctrine to

---

82. For helpful short articles on the New Perspective, see J. Ligon Duncan, "The Attractions of the New Perspective(s) on Paul," http://www.alliancenet.org/partner/Article_Display_Page /0,,PTID307086_CHID560462_CIID1660662,00.html (accessed April 27, 2011); Paul F. M. Zahl, "Mistakes of the New Perspective on Paul," *Themelios* 27, no. 1 (2001): 5–11. For books on the topic, see Cornelis P. Venema, *The Gospel of Free Acceptance in Christ: An Assessment of the Reformation and New Perspective on Paul* (Edinburgh: Banner of Truth, 2006); Guy Prentice Waters, *Justification and the New Perspectives on Paul: A Review and Response* (Phillipsburg: P&R, 2004). For investigations related to the New Perspective by New Testament scholars, see D. A. Carson, Peter T. O'Brien, and Mark A. Seifrid, eds., *Justification and Variegated Nomism*, 2 vols. (Grand Rapids: Baker Academic, 2001, 2004); Brian Vickers, *Jesus' Blood and Righteousness: Paul's Theology of Imputation* (Wheaton, Ill.: Crossway, 2006).

a believer's life. Bunyan was well acquainted with the weaknesses and temptations of the human heart, so his explanation of the doctrine of justification takes on a consoling and comforting tone.

In all that can be said regarding justification by faith, Bunyan notes many things that have "great power with the heart to bend it to seek life before God by the law."[83] In sinning, Adam and his heirs take on a new relationship to the law, which no longer promises them life but rather "shakes Mount Sinai, and writeth death upon all faces, and makes the church itself cry out, A mediator! else we die."[84] We need to stop turning to the law as if it might justify us before God, for in turning to it, "the law...doth veil the heart from Christ, and holds the man so down to doing and working for the kingdom of heaven, that he quite forgets the forgiveness of sins by mercy through Christ."[85]

We must, rather, look to Christ as the end of the law. As Bunyan says, "He has done that in his own person, and justified me thereby, and for my part, I will not labour now to fulfill the law for justification, least I should undervalue the merits of the Man Christ Jesus, and what he hath done without me."[86] Justifying righteousness is found only in the person of Christ apart from the law,[87] and we must thus warn ourselves not to seek righteousness in anything we do. For those who cling to Christ by faith, His righteousness *becomes* their righteousness. Bunyan quips, "Wherefore, in this sense, we are said to *do* what only was done by him."[88] Therefore, a justified man owes no more penalty or obedience to the law for his justification—indeed, he is in a better state than Adam since his state of acquittal before God is irrevocable in Christ! Fittingly then, Bunyan always points us back to Christ, the ground of our justification. He writes, "Look, then, upon Christ as the man, the mediator, the undertaker, and accomplisher of that righteousness in himself, wherein thou must stand just before God; and that he is the covenant or conditions of the people to God-ward, always having in himself the righteousness that the law is well pleased with, and always presenting himself before God as our only righteousness."[89]

In Bunyan's allegory of the pilgrim, Christian encounters two men who tumble over the wall into the narrow way instead of entering by the gate. One

---

83. *Justification by an Imputed Righteousness*, in *Works*, 1:320. Bunyan reasoned extensively that believers are no longer under the law as a covenant of works, but are under grace (see *The Doctrine of Law and Grace Unfolded*, in *MW*, 2:83ff.).

84. *Justification by an Imputed Righteousness*, in *Works*, 1:317.

85. *Justification by an Imputed Righteousness*, in *Works*, 1:321.

86. *A Vindication of Gospel Truths*, in *Works*, 2:194.

87. *A Defence of Justification*, in *Works*, 2:286–87.

88. *Justification by an Imputed Righteousness*, in *Works*, 1:304.

89. *Justification by an Imputed Righteousness*, in *Works*, 1:327.

was named Formalist; the other, Hypocrisy. Christian questions them, and they tell him they are confident that they can perform "laws and ordinances" as well as he and say the only thing he has that they do not is his coat, which no doubt his neighbors gave him out of pity to cover his nakedness. In fact, Christian received that coat when he stood at the foot of the cross of Jesus Christ. Bunyan has Christian reply to these vain men:

> By laws and ordinances you will not be saved, since you came not in by the door. And as for this coat that is on my back, it was given me by the Lord of the place whither I go; and that, as you say, to cover my nakedness with. And I take it as a token of his kindness to me; for I had nothing but rags before. And, besides, thus I comfort myself as I go: Surely, think I, when I come to the gate of the city, the Lord thereof will know me for good, since I have his coat on my back—a coat he gave me freely in the day that he stripped me of my rags.[90]

Another benefit of justification by faith is that it serves as the ground for Christ's advocacy before the Father. Whatever charge may be leveled against us, Christ takes upon Himself. Bunyan says, "He taketh the whole Charge upon himself, acknowledging the Crimes to be his own. 'O God,' says he, 'thou knowest my foolishness, and my Sins; my Guiltiness is not hid from thee, Psal. 69.5.'"[91] Christ then becomes our advocate before the throne of justice, for "all, then, that we, in this matter, have to do, is, to stand at the Bar by Faith among the Angels, and see how the business goes."[92] At the bar of God, Christ pleads the goodness of God, and "God is never weary of being delighted with Jesus Christ; his blood is always precious with God; his merits being those in which justice hath everlasting rest."[93] God is pacified by the accomplished work of Christ so that no believer, whatever his sins, can be found guilty before the throne of God.

In the same way, Christ argues against Satan, our accuser. Illustrating this point from Zechariah 3, where Joshua the high priest stands before the Angel of the Lord and is confronted by Satan as his adversary, Bunyan writes, "Come, then, says the Lord Jesus, the Contention is not now against my People, but myself, and about the Sufficiency of the Amends that I have made for the Transgressions of my People; but he is near that justifieth me, that approveth and accepteth of my Doings.... Who is mine Adversary? let him come near

---

90. *Pilgrim's Progress*, in *Works*, 3:104.
91. *The Advocateship of Jesus Christ*, in *MW*, 11:124.
92. *The Advocateship of Jesus Christ*, in *MW*, 11:125.
93. *Justification by an Imputed Righteousness*, in *Works*, 1:329.

me."[94] This challenge shuts the mouth of Satan, and he no longer can lay any-thing to the charge of the justified people of God. This should move us to praise God. Bunyan says, "Let us therefore by him offer praise for the gift of his Son, and for that we stand quit through him in his sight, and that in despite of all inward weakness, and that in despite of all outward enemies."[95]

Finally, justification by faith enables us to live in gospel obedience. While obedience is not the ground of our justification, it is a proper fruit of justifica-tion. Only after we receive the imputed righteousness of Jesus Christ can we begin to live in a way that pleases the heavenly Father. Once, we were nothing but lawbreakers, but through Christ and the continuing operation of the Holy Spirit, we are enabled more and more to live in holiness. Faith alone saves, but the faith that saves is never alone.[96]

In all of these applications, Bunyan is concerned that Christians never seek to move beyond Christ. They must not say, "I see not that in Christ now, that I have seen in him in former days. Besides, I find the Spirit leadeth me forth to study other things."[97] Bunyan's response is that the fault for this apathy toward Christ does not lie in Christ but in those who are no longer delighted with Him.[98] How we need to replay that same note today, stressing with professing Christians everywhere that there is nothing to be had beyond the doctrine of justification by faith alone, in Christ alone. To look anywhere beyond Christ is to look beyond where God looks.

Conclusion

The doctrine of justification is critically important in Bunyan's writing. In his own confession, he places justification before calling and election.[99] Bunyan was a staunch defender of the forensic nature of justification. Salvation in Christ, by His righteousness alone, without the works of the law, is foundational in all his preaching.

Bunyan believed that the doctrine of justification by faith alone offers believers much practical comfort. His words offer guidance to us as we find ourselves engaged in a life-and-death struggle to maintain the truth of the

---

94. *The Advocateship of Jesus Christ,* in *MW,* 11:128.

95. *Light for Them that Sit in Darkness,* in *Works,* 1:427.

96. Cf. Richard L. Greaves, "Amid the Holy War: Bunyan and the Ethic of Suffering," in *John Bunyan and His England, 1628–1688,* eds. Anne Laurence, W. R. Owens, and Stuart Sim (London: The Hambledon Press, 1990), 63–75.

97. Bunyan wrote this against the Quaker claim to immediate inspiration and Anglican appeals to reason, over against Scripture.

98. *A Defence of Justification,* in *Works,* 2:327.

99. *A Confession of My Faith,* in *Works,* 2:597–99.

gospel. The doctrines of the profound sinfulness of sin, the need for personal union with Christ, and the glorious truth of justification are being undermined today within and without the church. To rid ourselves of the truths that were so foundational in Bunyan's writings is to rid ourselves of biblical Christianity. Bunyan says, "No man that buildeth forsakes the good foundation; that is the ground of his encouragement to work, for upon that is laid the stress of all; and without it nothing that is framed can be supported, but must inevitably fall to the ground."[100]

Christians must never abandon the doctrine of justification by imputed righteousness. They must build their confession, confidence, and life upon the glorious truth that Christ has become their righteousness. Bunyan writes, "Never think to live always on Christ for justification is a low and beggarly thing, and as it were a staying at the foundation; for let me tell you, depart from a sense of the meritorious means of your justification with God, and you quickly grow light, and frothy, and vain."[101] May we never "grow light, frothy and vain" but take warning and encouragement from those who by faith have inherited the promises and daily live in obedience to their Lord and Savior, Jesus Christ.

To the unbeliever, the doctrine of justification by faith in Christ's righteousness alone contains both a note of warning and a note of invitation. Bunyan writes:

> Ah how many thousands that can now glory that they were never troubled for sin against God, I say, how many be there that God will trouble worse than he troubled cursed Achan, because their peace, though false, and of the devil, was rather chosen by them than peace by Jesus Christ, than "peace with God by the blood of his cross." Awake, careless sinners, awake! And rise from the dead and Christ shall give you light. Content not yourselves with either sin or righteousness, if you be destitute of Jesus Christ, but cry, O cry to God for light to see your condition by; cry for light in the Word of God, for therein is the righteousness of God revealed. Cry therefore for light to see this righteousness by; it is a righteousness of Christ's finishing, of God's accepting and that which alone can save the soul from the stroke of eternal justice.[102]

---

100. *Justification by an Imputed Righteousness*, in *Works*, 1:328.
101. *Justification by an Imputed Righteousness*, in *Works*, 1:328.
102. *Justification by an Imputed Righteousness*, in *Works*, 1:333.

Chapter 11

Reformed Orthodoxy
in North America

I write the Wonders of the Christian Religion, flying from the deprava-
tions of Europe, to the American Strand; and, assisted by the Holy Author
of that Religion, I do with all conscience of Truth, required therein by
Him, who is the Truth itself, report the wonderful displays of His infinite Power, Wisdom, Goodness, and Faithfulness, wherewith His Divine
Providence hath irradiated an Indian Wilderness.[1]

So wrote Cotton Mather (1663–1728) in the introduction to *The Great
Works of Christ in America* (1702). Cotton Mather wrote as the grandson of
Richard Mather (1596–1669) and John Cotton (1584–1652), both of whom
were founding ministers of New England.[2] In the seventeenth and eighteenth
centuries, a host of immigrants trusting in Divine Providence came to the
"American Strand," among whom were many considering themselves Reformed.
John Bratt writes, "As a consequence of this extensive immigration and internal
growth it is estimated that of the total population of three million in this country in 1776, two-thirds of them were at least nominally Calvinistic."[3] North
American theology before the Revolutionary War was dominated by Reformed
perspectives about the veracity, reasonableness, meaning, and application of
Reformed doctrines.[4]

---

1. Cotton Mather, *Magnalia Christi Americana; or The Ecclesiastical History of New-England,*
(repr. Edinburgh: Banner of Truth, 1979), 1:25. I wish to thank Paul Smalley for his assistance on this
chapter. A shorter form of this article is printed in Herman Selderhuis, ed., *A Companion to Reformed
Orthodoxy* (Leiden: Brill, 2013), 323–49. To retain space constraints, the sampling of lists of books in
each section of this chapter has not been updated beyond 2013 when this was first written.

2. Portions of this chapter are abridged from Joel R. Beeke and Randall J. Pederson, *Meet the
Puritans* (Grand Rapids: Reformation Heritage Books, 2006).

3. John H. Bratt, "The History and Development of Calvinism in America," *The Rise and
Development of Calvinism,* ed. idem (Grand Rapids: Eerdmans, 1959), 122.

4. E. Brooks Holifield, *Theology in America: Christian Thought from the Age of the Puritans to the
Civil War* (New Haven: Yale University Press, 2003), 10–12.

America was born during the flourishing of Reformed Orthodoxy. Protestant Europeans began to immigrate to the New World in the first half of the seventeenth century. Reformed Orthodoxy flowed from the Old World to the New in six major streams: the English Puritan Reformed coming to New England, the Scot-Irish Presbyterians to the middle and southern colonies, the English Anglicans to Virginia and later other colonies, the Huguenot French Reformed to New France and various British colonies, the German Reformed to the middle colonies, and the Dutch Reformed to New Netherlands (New York).[5] This chapter will survey these streams, giving special attention to significant leaders (together with selected bibliographies of them), and conclude with a brief consideration of the Great Awakening, which bridged Reformed Orthodoxy and modern Evangelicalism.

Puritan New England

The Puritans of New England occupy a singular place in the North American self-consciousness, but often through popular caricatures of fanatical men in black on a mission to stamp out all pleasure in life. In reality Puritanism was a vibrant expression of English Reformed Orthodoxy seeking to glorify God and enjoy Him in every area of practical life.[6]

The story of New England began when about a hundred people arrived at Plymouth on the Mayflower in 1620, as recorded by Governor William Bradford (1589–1657). Plymouth grew slowly to about three hundred in 1630 and remained less than a thousand in 1650.[7] They were Separatists, Englishmen seeking to start a new church pure of the corruptions of the Church of England. By contrast, the Massachusetts Bay Colony was founded in 1630 upon non-separating principles, expressed in 1648 in the Cambridge Platform. They sought to plant a purified Congregational form of the Church of England on American soil. They hoped that the daughter would reform the mother across the Atlantic. As Governor John Winthop (1588–1649) said in his sermon "A Model of Christian Charity" aboard the ship *Arbella* in 1630, their love and justice practiced in their various social stations would be as "a city on a hill" for all to observe.[8] Massachusetts outnumbered its Pilgrim predecessors threefold from

---

5. See Bratt, "The History and Development of Calvinism in America," 114–22.

6. For a helpful study of the primary sources seeking to correct misconceptions of Puritan views of marriage, money, and many other topics, see Leland Ryken, *Worldly Saints: The Puritans As They Really Were* (Grand Rapids: Zondervan, 1986).

7. William Bradford, *Of Plymouth Plantation, 1620–1647*, ed. Samuel E. Morison (New York: Modern Library, 1952), xi.

8. Francis J. Bremer, *John Winthrop: America's Forgotten Founding Father* (Oxford: Oxford University Press, 2003), 173–84.

its start and swelled to twenty thousand in ten years, absorbing Plymouth by the end of the seventeenth century. Together with the other New England colonies it produced a theological literature that dwarfed that of any other North American Reformed movement in the seventeenth and eighteenth centuries.

Since the 1930s an immense amount of scholarly attention has been given to the New England Puritans. Of the 940 American, British, Canadian, and German doctoral dissertations on the American Puritans written from 1882 to 1981, nearly 90 percent are from 1931 to 1981 and more than half from the last fifteen years of that period.[9] The interest continues today. This revival of Puritan studies arose in part from the writings of Perry Miller.[10] Puritan studies today range from psychology to folk religion to poetry to family life to politics.[11] But the center of Puritan studies is theology, following their own God-centered, doctrinally-defined approach to life.

Puritan theology in New England was biblical and Reformed. It recognized only one source and inerrant authority for teaching: the Holy Scriptures. The Puritans interpreted and applied the Bible by comparing one place in Scripture with another and by the use of Ramist logic. Petrus Ramus (1515–1572) was a French Protestant philosopher who aimed to make logic simpler and more practical than the Aristotelian methods of the medieval scholastics.[12] Puritan preachers and writers consciously functioned as heirs of a great tradition of biblical reflection, rooted in the church of all ages and especially the Reformed tradition. They drew from the theological wells of Continentals such as John Calvin, Henry Bullinger, and Theodore Beza and British divines such as William Perkins and especially William Ames (1576–1633), a theologian who never came to the New World but whose writings profoundly influenced New England ministers for generations.[13]

---

9. Michael Montgomery, *American Puritan Studies: An Annotated Bibliography of Dissertations, 1882–1981* (Westport: Greenwood, 1984), ix. For other bibliographies see *Early Puritan Writers: A Reference Guide: William Bradford, John Cotton, Thomas Hooker, Edward Johnson, Richard Mather, Thomas Shepard*, eds. Edward J. Gallagher and Thomas Werge (Boston: G. K. Hall & Co., 1976); Beeke and Pederson, *Meet the Puritans*, 861–88.

10. Perry Miller, *Orthodoxy In Massachusetts* (Gloucester: Peter Smith, 1933, 1965); idem, *The New England Mind: The Seventeenth Century* (Cambridge: Harvard University Press, 1939); idem, *The New England Mind: From Colony to Province* (Cambridge: Harvard University Press, 1953); idem, *Errand into the Wilderness* (Cambridge: Harvard University Press, 1956, 1984). See also *The Puritans: A Sourcebook of Their Writings*, eds. Perry Miller and Thomas H. Johnson (Mineola: Dover, 1938, 2001).

11. See the sources listed at the end of this section.

12. Holifield, *Theology in America*, 32–33. See *The Logicke of the Most Excellent Philosopher P. Ramus Martyr* (London: Thomas Vantroullier, 1574).

13. William Ames, *The Marrow of Theology*, ed. John D. Eusden (Grand Rapids: Baker Books, 1968), 10–11 in Eusden's introduction.

The grand theme of Puritan Reformed theology was the covenant of grace wherein the triune God gives Himself to unworthy sinners whom He chose.[14] The Father appointed their redemption, the Son purchased it, and the Spirit applies it. All the blessings of this covenant are in Christ alone, for Christ gave Himself to redeem God's elect from God's wrath against their sins. His self-sacrifice was infinite in value yet effective only for the elect because He died as their surety in the covenant.[15] Christ alone could perform the offices needed to bring His sinful people back to God. Christ is the Prophet for their ignorance, the Priest for their guilt, the King for their powerlessness.[16] The Puritans held together doctrines that other Christians have sometimes seen as polar opposites or even contradictions: unconditional election and the gospel covenant, conviction of sin and joyful assurance, justification by faith alone and the necessity of keeping the law, being heavenly minded and doing much earthly good.

Puritanism distinguished itself from broader English Protestantism by founding church worship on Scripture alone with no human invention.[17] The New England Puritans also applied this principle to church government. Their interpretation of Scripture led them to reject Episcopacy and embrace Congregationalism, though sometimes with a Presbyterian flavor. Puritanism in one respect was a quest to purify the church of unbiblical forms. More broadly it was a quest to reform all of life by the Word of God. Yet in seeking purity, the Puritans did not expect perfection on earth. They were a pilgrim people. This is so, not merely in immigrating to America, but the Puritans saw all of life as a challenging journey to heaven under the shepherding hand of God.

To expound, defend, and apply the heavenly themes of Scripture, the Puritans demanded a learned and godly ministry. They highly valued education, authorizing the founding of their first college (Harvard) in 1636, only six years after landing in the wilderness and fifty-seven years before the first college in Virginia.[18] From Harvard and later Yale arose a well-educated clergy in the Reformed scholastic tradition of late sixteenth- and early seventeenth-century Oxford and Cambridge. While Puritan pastor-theologians wrote many theological and devotional treatises, their primary means of discourse was the

---

14. John Cotton, *The New Covenant* (London: Francis Eglesfield & John Allen, 1654), 8–10.

15. Thomas Hooker, *The Application of Redemption…the first eight Books* (London: Peter Cole, 1657), 5–7, 11–23, 57–66, 73.

16. Ames, *The Marrow of Theology* 1.19.10–11, 132.

17. William Ames, *A Sketch of the Christian's Catechism* (Grand Rapids: Reformation Heritage Books, 2008), 161–62.

18. Mark A. Noll, *A History of Christianity in the United States and Canada* (Grand Rapids: Eerdmans, 1992), 44.

sermon. In fact, many Puritan treatises were sermon series edited for publica-tion. Pious New Englanders listened to three sermons a week, seven thousand in a lifetime, each an hour or more in length. The Puritan sermon was not an exercise in entertainment or art for its own sake but a closely argued Bible teaching aimed at personal application. Timothy Edwards (1669–1758), father of Jonathan Edwards, could have over fifty numbered headings in a sermon, each giving a distinct point of biblical interpretation, doctrine, or application.[19] The sermon was the sword of the Spirit by which God warred with Satan over the souls of men. It was the sowing of the seed of eternal life seeking the hearts of God's elect. New England was never a theocracy. Church leaders did not hold political office. But the Puritan pastor exercised tremendous power by his office as a preacher of the Word of the Lord, combined with the New England consciousness of being a society in covenant with the Lord. New England was shaped by the preaching of Puritan pastors.

For further sources on Puritan New England, see:
James F. Cooper Jr., *Tenacious of Their Liberties: The Congregationalists in Colonial Massachusetts* (Oxford: Oxford University Press, 1999); Timothy George, *John Robinson and the English Separatist Tradition* (Macon: Mercer University Press, 1982); David D. Hall, *Worlds of Wonder, Days of Judgment: Popular Religious Belief in Early New England* (New York: Knopf, 1989); George D. Langdon Jr., *Pilgrim Colony: A History of New Plymouth, 1620–1691* (New Haven: Yale University Press, 1966); Edmund S. Morgan, *The Puritan Dilemma: The Story of John Winthrop* (Boston: Little, Brown, and Co., 1958); B. R. White, *The English Separatist Tradition: From the Marian Martyrs to the Pilgrim Fathers* (Oxford: Oxford University Press, 1971).

On Puritan New England sermons, see:
The Puritan Pulpit: The American Puritans: Solomon Stoddard, 1643–1729, ed. Don Kistler (Orlando: Soli Deo Gloria, 2005); *The Puritan Pulpit: The American Puritans: Ebenezer Pemberton, 1704–1777*, ed. Don Kistler (Orlando: Soli Deo Gloria, 2006); Ronald A. Bosco, *The Puritan Sermon in America, 1630–1750*, 4 vols. (Delmar: Scholars' Facsimiles & Reprints, 1978).

---

19. Wilson H. Kimnach, "Edwards as Preacher," *The Cambridge Companion to Jonathan Edwards*, ed. Stephen J. Stein (Cambridge: Cambridge University Press, 2007), 104.

On Puritan theology, see:

J. I. Packer, *A Quest for Godliness: The Puritan Vision of the Christian Life* (Wheaton: Crossway, 1990) and the papers presented at the Westminster Conference (indexed at http://www.westminsterconference.org.uk/past papers/, accessed 10-21-10), which are published in annual volumes. The early papers (1956–1967) are collected in *Puritan Papers*, 5 vols., eds. D. Martin Lloyd-Jones and J. I. Packer (Phillipsburg: P&R Publishing, 2000–2005). See also Joel R. Beeke, *Heirs with Christ: The Puritans on Adoption* (Grand Rapids: Reformation Heritage Books, 2008); idem, *Puritan Reformed Spirituality* (Darlington: Evangelical Press, 2006); Joel R. Beeke and Mark Jones, *A Puritan Theology: Doctrine for Life* (Grand Rapids: Reformation Heritage Books, 2012); George N. Boardman, *A History of New England Theology* (New York: A. D. F. Randolph, 1899); Frank H. Foster, *A Genetic History of the New England Theology* (Chicago: University of Chicago, 1907); Norman Fiering, *Moral Philosophy at Seventeenth-Century Harvard: A Discipline in Transition* (Chapel Hill: University of North Carolina Press, 1981); Lisa M. Gordis, *Opening Scripture: Bible Reading and Interpretive Authority in Puritan New England* (Chicago: University of Chicago Press, 2003); Janice Knight, *Orthodoxies in Massachusetts: Rereading American Puritanism* (Cambridge: Harvard University Press, 1994); Donald K. McKim, "Ramism in William Perkins" (PhD diss., University of Pittsburg, 1980).

On Puritan worship, see:

Horton Davies, *The Worship of the American Puritans, 1629–1730* (New York: Peter Lang, 1990); E. Brooks Holifield, *The Covenant Sealed: The Development of Puritan Sacramental Theology in Old and New England, 1570–1720* (New Haven: Yale University Press, 1974).

On Puritan political thought, see:

David W. Hall, *Calvin in the Public Square: Liberal Democracies, Rights, and Civil Liberties* (Phillipsburg: P&R Publishing, 2009); John Witte, Jr., *The Reformation of Rights: Law, Religion, and Human Rights in Early Modern Calvinism* (Cambridge: Cambridge University Press, 2007).

On psychological studies of the Puritans, see:

Charles L. Cohen, *God's Caress: The Psychology of Puritan Religious Experience* (Oxford: Oxford University Press, 1986); Emory Elliott, *Power and the Pulpit in Puritan New England* (Princeton: Princeton University Press, 1975); David Leverenz, *The Language of Puritan Feeling: An Exploration in Literature, Psychology, and Social History* (New Brunswick: Rutgers University Press, 1980).

On Puritan family life, see:

Edmund S. Morgan, *The Puritan Family: Religion and Domestic Relations in Seventeenth-Century New England*, rev. ed. (New York: Harper & Row, 1966); Levin L. Schucking, *The Puritan Family: A Social Study from the Literary Sources*, trans. Brian Battershaw (New York: Schocken Books, 1970); Laurel T. Ulrich, "Good Wives: A Study in Role Definition in Northern New England, 1650–1750" (PhD diss., University of New Hampshire, 1980).

On Puritan poetry, see:

Mark A. Noll, "The Poetry of Anne Bradstreet (1612–1672) and Edward Taylor (1642–1729)," in *The Devoted Life: An Invitation to the Puritan Classics*, eds. Kelly M. Kapic and Randall C. Gleason (Downers Grove: InterVarsity, 2004), 251–69; *Studies in Puritan American Spirituality: A Journal of Puritanism and the Arts in America*, ed. Michael Schuldinger (Lewiston, N.Y.: Edwin Mellen Press, 1990–2004).

John Cotton (1584–1652)

John Cotton is remembered as one of the patriarchs of New England. He was educated at Cambridge where he served for six years as head lecturer, dean, catechist, and a tutor to many pupils. Initially he viewed the Puritanism of William Perkins with hostility, even rejoicing at Perkins's death. But the preaching of Richard Sibbes convinced Cotton he had been building his salvation on intellectual prowess rather than on Christ alone. Cotton's conversion also led him to reject the popular elegant pulpit style in favor of plain preaching of Christ. Henceforth, he called his listeners to "finde Christ, and finde life."[20]

Cotton served as the vicar (resident pastor) in Boston, Lincolnshire, England, for twenty-one years. His preaching, correspondence, and counsel established his reputation for Reformed, experiential ministry. John Preston (1587–1628), William Ames, and Dutch minister Willem Teellinck (1579–1629) sent ministerial students to sit under him. After a year of disability suffering from malaria (which killed his wife), Cotton looked into moving to New England. He had already preached a farewell sermon for John Winthrop. In 1632 Cotton was summoned to appear before William Laud's Court of High Commission. He hid in London and then escaped the country, arriving in Massachusetts in September 1633 with his colleague Thomas Hooker.

Cotton was joyfully received in New England and quickly given the most important position in the largest church of the colony, First Church of Boston.

---

20. John Cotton, *Christ the Fountaine of Life* (London: Robert Ibbitson, 1651), 1.

His influence, both in ecclesiastical and in civil affairs, was probably greater than that of any other minister in New England at the time. Yet Cotton was known for his Christlike humility, responding to criticism by acknowledging his fallibility and asking his critics to pray for him. He served First Church until his death in 1652.

Cotton is most often remembered for his participation in the controversies surrounding Anne Hutchinson and Roger Williams. These will be discussed later. However, his most significant contributions to Reformed Orthodoxy may lie in his children's catechism and his Congregationalism. His catechism, *Milk for Babes* (1646), bound with the New England Primer, became standard fare for New England children down to the late nineteenth century.

Cotton advocated congregational church polity in *The Way of the Churches of Christ in New England* (1641) and *The Keys of the Kingdom of Heaven, and the Power Thereof* (1644). These books, which went through several printings, were used extensively by the Independents at the Westminster Assembly. After being attacked by Robert Baillie, a Scottish Presbyterian, Cotton responded in 1648 with his *The Way of Congregational Churches Cleared*, in which he presented New England Congregationalism as steering between strict independency and Presbyterianism. All these writings were followed up with a final call to accommodation in Cotton's *Certain Queries Tending to Accommodation* (1655). No New England minister was as influential as Cotton in promoting congregational church practice.

For further sources on John Cotton, see:
Wayne H. Christy, "John Cotton: Covenant Theologian" (Master's thesis, Duke University, 1942); Michael J. Colacurcio, "Primitive Comfort: the Spiritual Witness of John Cotton," *English Literary History* 67 (2000): 655–95; Donald R. Come, "John Cotton, Guide of the Chosen People" (PhD diss., Princeton University, 1949); Everett H. Emerson, *John Cotton* (New York: Twayne, 1965); James W. Jones III, "The Beginnings of American Theology: John Cotton, Thomas Hooker, Thomas Shepard and Peter Bulkeley" (PhD diss., Brown University, 1970); John Norton, *Abel, Being Dead, Yet Speaketh* (1658) (Delmar: Scholars' Facsimiles & Reprints, 1978); Harry A. Poole, "The Unsettled Mr. Cotton" (PhD diss., University of Illinois, 1956); Larzer Ziff, *The Career of John Cotton: Puritanism and the American Experience* (Princeton: Princeton University Press, 1962).

Thomas Hooker (1586–1647)

While studying at Emmanuel College, Cambridge, Thomas Hooker became acutely afflicted by "the spirit of bondage" (Rom. 8:15). He was distressed by thoughts of the just wrath of God. Hooker clung to the promises of Scripture until he was soundly converted. With a certainty born of experience, he would later say to others, "The promise of the gospel was the boat which was to carry a perishing sinner over into the Lord Jesus Christ." He graduated with a master's thesis in 1611 and served as lecturer and catechist until 1618 at Emmanuel. There many of England's spiritual leaders (including Stephen Marshall, Anthony Burgess, Jeremiah Burroughs, and William Bridge) listened to him preach. Beginning in 1619 Hooker served parish churches in England with visible reformation among his hearers. His listeners compared him to John the Baptist. In 1629, however, Hooker's preaching against some Anglican rituals brought him into conflict with Archbishop William Laud of Canterbury. After several disputes, Hooker barely escaped imprisonment by boarding a ship to the Netherlands while government agents scoured the pier looking for him.

Thomas Hooker served English and Scottish believers in the Netherlands, ministering for a time alongside William Ames. Hooker deeply respected Ames, saying, "If a scholar was but well studied in Dr. Ames's *Marrow of Theology* and *Cases of Conscience*, so as to understand them thoroughly, he would make a good divine, though he had no more books in the world." Hooker wrote a complimentary preface for Ames's *A Fresh Suit against Human Ceremonies in God's Worship*. Ames, in turn, wrote of Hooker that though he had been "acquainted with many scholars of diverse nations, yet he never met with Mr. Hooker's equal, either for preaching or for disputing."

In 1633 Hooker sailed for Massachusetts on the *Griffin* along with his friend Samuel Stone (1602–1663), John Cotton, and two hundred others. People quipped that they now had "Cotton for their clothing, Hooker for their fishing, and Stone for their building." Later Hooker and thirty-five families—the majority of his congregation—left the colony and settled in the Connecticut valley at Hartford. They sold their homes to the latest arrivals from England, who were led by Thomas Shepard. In 1637, he visited Boston to serve as one of the moderators of the synod that condemned the teachings of Anne Hutchinson and her followers. When the General Court of Connecticut began drafting a constitution, Hooker preached a sermon on Deuteronomy 1:13, which advocated democratic principles. In 1647 when Hooker was dying, a close friend said to him, "You are going to receive the reward of all your labors." Hooker responded, "Brother, I am going to receive mercy."

Hooker preached that a sinner's heart must be prepared with conviction of sin before it can receive Christ. This view is called *preparatory grace*. Hooker wrote, "The Heart must be broken and humbled, before the Lord will own it as His, take up His abode with it, and rule in it." But this humbling lay not in the power of man's free will. Hooker said,

> The effectual operation of the Word, the breaking and so converting the heart of a sinner depends not upon any preparation a man can work in himself, or any thing he can do in his corrupt estate for the attaining of life and Salvation…. Yet now the Lord presseth in upon them, by the prevailing power of his spirit and word and doth good to them, when they set themselves by all the policy and rage they could to oppose the work of the Lord and their own everlasting welfare.[21]

Though Hooker sometimes dwelt on the evils of sin so long that he may have bruised tender souls, his overall ministry was framed by a Reformed theology of sovereign grace calling poor, doubting sinners to Christ as their all-in-all. Cotton Mather wrote of Hooker, "The very spirit of his ministry lay in the points of the most practical religion, and the grand concerns of a sinner's preparation for, implantation in, and salvation by, the glorious Lord Jesus Christ."[22]

For further sources on Thomas Hooker, see:
John H. Ball III, *Chronicling the Soul's Windings: Thomas Hooker and His Morphology of Conversion* (Lanham: University Press of America, 1992); Sargent Bush Jr., *The Writings of Thomas Hooker: Spiritual Adventure in Two Worlds* (Madison: University of Wisconsin Press, 1980); Robert H. Horn, "Thomas Hooker—The Soul's Preparation for Christ," *The Puritan Experiment in the New World* (London: Westminster Conference, 1976), 19–37; Hubert R. Pellman, "Thomas Hooker: A Study in Puritan Ideals" (PhD diss., University of Pennsylvania, 1958); Frank Shuffleton, *Thomas Hooker, 1586–1647* (Princeton: Princeton University Press, 1977).

On Hooker and Preparationism, see:
Iain H. Murray, "Thomas Hooker and the Doctrine of Conversion," *Banner of Truth* 195 (1979): 19–29; 196 (1980): 22–32; 197 (1980): 12–18; 199 (1980): 10–21; 206 (1980): 9–21; David L. Parker, "The Application of Humiliation: Ramist Logic and the Rise of Preparationism in New England" (PhD diss.,

---

21. Thomas Hooker, *The Application of Redemption… The Ninth and Tenth Books* (London: Peter Cole, 1657), 5, 297–98.
22. Cited in Miller, *Errand into the Wilderness*, 28.

University of Pennsylvania, 1972); Norman Pettit, *The Heart Prepared: Grace and Conversion in Puritan Spiritual Life* (New Haven: Yale University Press, 1966).

Thomas Shepard (1605–1649)

Thomas Shepard was born in Towcester, Northamptonshire. Both his parents died during his childhood, and he was largely raised by his older brother, John. His days at Emmanuel College, Cambridge, were initially marked by spiritual neglect and immorality. But the preaching of John Preston opened Shepard's mind first to his own sins and then to the sweetness and fullness of Christ the Savior. From 1627 to 1635 he ministered within the Church of England with increasing difficulty as William Laud persecuted Nonconformists.

The Shepards finally reached New England on October 3, 1635. His wife became ill from tuberculosis and died four months later. Shepard settled in Newtown (now Cambridge), Massachusetts, where he became pastor of the newly established Congregational church. He acquired a reputation for effectiveness as an evangelist. In line with the Congregational way, he asked all who applied for church membership to confess their personal experience of conversion to Christ. He also helped to establish Harvard College in Cambridge and to support the mission to the Native Americans by John Eliot. He served in Cambridge until his death.

Thomas Shepard was unswerving in opposing the Antinomians and was one of the leaders in the synod at Cambridge that condemned them for separating the revelations of the Holy Spirit from the Holy Scriptures and from a holy life. His sermons on the parable of the ten virgins, published after his death, argued that the saving work of Christ must conquer sinful lusts. Shepard wrote, "There is a kind of resurrection of a man's soul when it is brought home to Christ.... Do you think, brethren, that Christ's blood was shed to work no more in his people than in hypocrites? Was it only shed to take away the guilt of sin from God's sight, and then let a man wallow in the sins of his own heart?"[23] Jonathan Edwards quoted Shepard's book frequently in his *Religious Affections*.

For further sources on Thomas Shepard, see:
God's Plot: Puritan Spirituality in Thomas Shepard's Cambridge, ed. Michael McGiffert, rev. ed. (Amherst: University of Massachusetts Press, 1972, 1994); Richard A. Hasler, "Thomas Shepard: Pastor-Evangelist (1605–1649): A Study

---

23. Thomas Shepard, *The Works of Thomas Shepard*, 3 vols. (repr. New York: AMS Press, 1967), 2:208.

in the New England Puritan Ministry" (PhD diss., Hartford Seminary, 1964); Richard A. Humphrey, "The Concept of Conversion in the Theology of Thomas Shepard (1605–1649)," (PhD diss., Drew University, 1967); Doris G. Marquit, "Thomas Shepard: The Formation of a Puritan Identity" (PhD diss., University of Minnesota, 1978); George J. Selement, "The Means to Grace: A Study of Conversion in Early New England" (PhD diss., University of New Hampshire, 1974); Thomas Werge, *Thomas Shepard* (Boston: G. K. Hall, 1987); Alexander Whyte, *Thomas Shepard: Pilgrim Father and Founder of Harvard* (Grand Rapids: Reformation Heritage Books, 2007).

Anne Hutchinson and the Antinomian Controversy

Anne Hutchinson and the Antinomian Controversy

Out of the Puritan concern for true conversion arose a controversy over the role of good works in personal assurance of salvation. Some Puritans reacted against what they perceived as antinomianism, the teaching that the grace of God releases believers from obedience to the law. So they emphasized the necessity of conviction of sin and submission to the commandments in order to ground assurance in true conversion. Other Puritans reacted against the danger of falling into a "covenant of works," making one's obedience the condition of acceptance with God as it was with Adam in the garden. So they emphasized justification by faith alone based on the merits of Christ alone.

Both the necessity of good works and justification by faith alone were part of the same theological system shared by the Puritans in New England.[24] But different emphases could lead to controversy as different sides saw the others in danger of heading down the slippery slope into error. In this way John Cotton debated with Thomas Hooker and Thomas Shepard. Hooker and Shepard emphasized conviction and obedience in conversion while also teaching justification by faith alone. Cotton emphasized faith and Christ while also teaching the necessity of Christlike living.[25]

Anne Hutchinson (1591–1643), an admirer of John Cotton, took this debate to a new level and ignited a firestorm of controversy. Highly intelligent, knowledgeable in the Bible, and gifted as a nurse and midwife, Anne began hosting popular meetings in her home to discuss Cotton's sermons. She accused all the ministers of New England except Cotton and her brother-in-law, John Wheelwright, of embracing a covenant of works. Hutchinson denied that good works were important evidences of true conversion. A nimble debater, she could not be pinned down by the theologians in any particular error. But then Anne

---

24. See chapters 11 and 16 in the *Savoy Declaration* and the *Westminster Confession of Faith*.
25. John Cotton, *Christ the Fountaine of Life*, 59–65.

boldly declared that the Holy Spirit spoke to her directly—immediate revelation from God. The church condemned her as a heretic, and the government banished her from the colony. In 1638 Anne and her husband moved to the colony of Rhode Island. There she preached anarchy, that is, the doctrine that there should be no civil government. Five years later she and almost her entire family were murdered by Native Americans after moving to a remote portion of New Netherlands. Anne Hutchinson has been variously understood as an early champion of feminism, a sufferer of mental illness, or a mystic in line with English radicals known as Familists seeking to dissolve her soul into God. Certainly her life ended in tragedy.

Some of the followers of Hutchinson joined with the Quaker movement. The Quakers, or "Friends" (as they called themselves) followed the inner light they believed Christ gave to all men, sometimes to the denigration of Scripture as a dead letter. This occasionally led to bizarre and provocative behavior. Persecuted by the Massachusetts establishment, the Quakers found more congenial resting places in Rhode Island and Pennsylvania.[26]

For further sources on Anne Hutchinson and the Antinomian Controversy, see: *The Antinomian Controversy, 1636–1638: A Documentary History*, Second Edition, ed. David D. Hall (Durham: Duke University Press, 1990); *Early Quaker Writings, 1650–1700*, eds. Hugh Barbour and Arthur O. Roberts (Grand Rapids: Eerdmans, 1973); Emery Battis, *Saints and Sectaries: Anne Hutchinson and the Antinomian Controversy in the Massachusetts Bay Colony* (Chapel Hill: University of North Carolina Press, 1962); Philip F. Gura, *A Glimpse of Sion's Glory: Puritan Radicalism in New England, 1620–1660* (Middletown: Wesleyan University Press, 1984); Amanda Porterfield, *Female Piety in Puritan New England: The Emergence of Religious Humanism* (Oxford: Oxford University Press, 1992), 95–106; Selma R. Williams, *Divine Rebel: The Life of Anne Marbury Hutchinson* (New York: Holt, Rinehart, and Winston, 1981).

Reformed Orthodoxy, Soul Freedom, and the Baptists

Religious liberty in the New World is strongly associated with the name of Roger Williams (1603–1683). Williams was not an Enlightenment free thinker but a radical Puritan Reformed Separatist. He was educated at Cambridge, ordained by the Church of England, Reformed in doctrine and holy in life, and a friend of Oliver Cromwell. Williams came to Massachusetts in 1631. To the astonishment of the Boston authorities, he called for the state to grant religious

---

26. Holifield, *Theology in America*, 320–23.

liberty to its citizens because, he stated, civil power has no authority over the conscience. He insisted that the Congregational churches formally separate from the Church of England because the latter did not limit its membership to visible saints. He also declared that the English crown had no right to grant land to the colonists as it belonged first to the Native Americans.

Banished in 1635 from the Massachusetts Bay Colony, Williams formed a new settlement named Providence on land purchased from the Native Americans. There in 1639 he helped to form the first Baptist church in America but withdrew after a few months to become a "seeker" still looking for the true church. In 1644 he obtained a charter from the English Parliament to organize towns in the region into the colony of Rhode Island. At that time he also published his most famous writing, *The Bloudy Tenent of Persecution*, a biblical argument for religious liberty or "soul freedom."

Roger Williams and John Cotton carried on an extensive debate over the rights of civil government to regulate worship. Against Cotton, Williams argued that the New Testament abolishes the judicial laws of Israel, for the physical kingdom of Israel was a type fulfilled in the spiritual kingdom of Christ. The sovereignty of God in creating faith excludes human coercion in matters of conscience, for only God can save. The history of the church displays the perils of religious oppression in the name of orthodoxy. On the basis of these principles, he befriended the Native Americans and evangelized them; he welcomed the Quakers to Rhode Island yet preached against their teachings. Williams is remembered as a pioneer theologian of religious liberty, yet he should also be remembered as a Puritan Reformed minister with radical leanings.[27]

Though Williams did not remain in the Baptist church, the Baptist church remained in Rhode Island. Other Baptists soon followed. John Clarke (1609–1676) started a second Baptist church in Newport in 1639. In 1648 they were joined by Mark Lucar, a Particular Baptist from John Spilsbury's congregation in England, then by Obadiah Holmes, who had been harassed by the Plymouth Court for holding Baptist meetings in private homes. In 1651 Clarke, Holmes, and John Crandall visited the Massachusetts town of Lynn to fellowship with blind, old William Witter. In the midst of Clarke's sermon, constables arrived and arrested the three Rhode Islanders. Clarke and Crandall paid fines, but Holmes refused, receiving instead thirty lashes with a whip. John Clarke published an account of this event, *Ill Newes from New-England*. In it he argued

---

27. Leighton H. James, "Roger Williams: The Earliest Legislator for a Full and Absolute Liberty of Conscience," *The Puritan Experiment in the New World*, 51–72; Tom Nettles, *The Baptists: Key People Involved in Forming a Baptist Identity, Volume 2: Beginnings in America* (Ross-Shire: Christian Focus, 2005), 41–44.

that no servant of Christ has the authority to use physical force to restrain the worship of another. He based this argument on the supremacy of Christ alone as Prophet, Priest, and King to rule His church by His Word and His Spirit. Clarke and Holmes left confessions of faith indicating their belief in the Reformed Orthodox doctrines of God's decree of all that comes to pass, unconditional election, substitutionary atonement for the elect, and perseverance of the saints.[28]

Particular Baptists formed the Philadelphia Association in 1707, and in 1742 this association affirmed a version of the Second London Confession (1677/1689), a Baptist revision of the Congregationalist Savoy Declaration (1658), itself a revision of the Westminster Confession (1646).[29] In so doing they desired to indicate that this stream of Baptists in America stood in substantial continuity with the Reformed Orthodoxy of seventeenth-century Puritan England.[30] Of course, there were other streams of Baptists that did not.

For further sources on Roger Williams and early American Baptists, see: William H. Brackney, *A Genetic History of Baptist Thought* (Macon: Mercer University Press, 2004); Edwin S. Gaustad, *Liberty of Conscience: Roger Williams in America* (Grand Rapids: Eerdmans, 1991); Stanley Grenz, *Isaac Backus—Puritan and Baptist* (Macon: Mercer University Press, 1983); William G. McLoughlin, *New England Dissent, 1630–1833: The Baptists and the Separation of Church and State* (Cambridge: Harvard University Press, 1971); Edmund S. Morgan, *Roger Williams: The Church and the State* (New York: Harcourt, Brace & World, 1967); Hugh Spurgin, *Roger Williams and Puritan Radicalism in the English Separatist Tradition*, Studies in American Religion, 34 (Lewiston: Edwin Mellen, 1989); Ola E. Winslow, *Master Roger Williams: A Biography* (New York: Macmillan, 1957).

A Theological Dynasty: Richard, Increase, and Cotton Mather
Richard Mather (1596–1669) was born in Lowtown, near Liverpool, England. From age fifteen to eighteen, he experienced an intense, lengthy conversion as a result of reading and hearing Puritan sermons. In 1619, Mather was ordained

---

28. Their confession is quoted in Isaac Backus, *A History of New England with Particular Reference to the Denomination of Christians Called Baptists*, 2nd ed. (Newton: Backus Historical Society, 1871; repr. Paris: Baptist Standard Bearer, n.d.), 1:206–9.

29. A tabular, color-coded comparison of these confessions may be viewed at http://www.proginosko.com/docs/wcf_sdfo_lbcf.html, accessed 10-19-10.

30. Nettles, *The Baptists, Volume 2*, 44–49; *Baptist Piety: The Last Will and Testimony of Obadiah Holmes*, ed. Edwin S. Gaustad (Grand Rapids: Christian University Press, 1978), 17–29.

in the Church of England by Thomas Morton, bishop of Chester. He preached at Toxteth for fifteen years with growing success. After being twice suspended from ministry for denigrating the Church of England's ceremonies, Richard Mather sailed for America in 1635. The next year he helped found the church of Dorchester, Massachusetts, on the basis of a congregational covenant in God's presence, "promising first and above all to cleave unto him as our chiefe and onely good, and to our Lord Jesus Christ as our onely spirituall husband and Lord, and our onely high priest and Prophet and King."[31] There he ministered until his death in 1669. He wrote ten works, mostly on issues of ecclesiology. Mather was a powerful preacher, known for shooting his arrows not over the heads but into the hearts of his hearers.

Richard Mather helped produce *The Bay Psalm Book* (1637), but he was best known for his defense of "the Congregational Way" of church government in the 1640s during debates with Samuel Rutherford, a staunch Scottish Presbyterian. Mather drafted a form of church government for the Massachusetts Bay Colony, which after modification by the Cambridge Synod emerged as "The Cambridge Platform of Church Government" (1648). A close friend of John Cotton, Mather nevertheless opposed Cotton's tendency to open the doors of church membership to those unable to testify to God's saving grace in their lives. In the late 1650s, Mather became deeply involved in the baptismal controversy that engulfed the New England churches. He participated in the "Half-Way Covenant" Synod of 1662 and wrote a tract defending its conclusions. This arrangement allowed baptized people who could not attest to their own experience of saving grace to nevertheless present their children for baptism. Solomon Stoddard (1643–1729) took this a step further in 1677 to allow baptized persons of moral life to take the Lord's Supper without a confession of personal conversion. Mather saw this as a violation of Congregationalism, launching a controversy lasting well into the eighteenth century.

Increase Mather (1639–1723) was born in Dorchester, Massachusetts. He was raised according to the strict Puritanism of his father, Richard Mather. He studied under John Norton in Boston, entered Harvard College at the age of twelve, and graduated with a Bachelor of Arts degree in 1656. He earned a master's degree in 1658, then preached in England and the British island of Guernsey until the Restoration.

Increase Mather returned to Boston, Massachusetts, in 1661. In March of 1662, Mather married Maria, daughter of John Cotton, bringing two influential

---

31. The full text of the church covenant may be found in David A. Weir, *Early New England: A Covenanted Society* (Grand Rapids: Eerdmans, 2005), 153–54.

Puritan families closer together. That same year he opposed his father and other ministers by arguing against the Half-Way Covenant, which he thought weakened Congregationalism by lowering standards for church membership. After serving alongside his father, in 1664 Increase Mather was called to pastor Second Church ("Old North") in Boston, a large congregation of fifteen hundred members. He served there for nearly sixty years until his death. For decades, he had a leading role in various synods that sought to reform the church. He presided at the Boston Synod of 1680 and wrote the preface to the Confession of Faith agreed upon at that synod which was their version of the Savoy Declaration. He wrote 175 books and pamphlets. He also served as president of Harvard College from 1685 until 1701.

In the early days of his ministry, Increase Mather believed that New England had a crucial role in the anticipated growth of God's kingdom and inspiration to the Reformed churches throughout the world. So when things did not go right in New England and churches began to decline spiritually, Mather was deeply distressed. He preached jeremiads, that is, sermons of warning and calls to repentance, to the colony as a covenanted people.[32] By 1675 he changed his mind regarding the Half-Way Covenant, publishing two books in its defense as a means to strengthen the church's influence in New England.

Increase Mather's son Cotton joined his father in pastoral ministry in 1683. Cotton Mather (1663–1728) was destined to become the most renowned member of the Mather family. He was the eldest son of Increase Mather and grandson of Richard Mather and John Cotton, after whom he was named. Cotton had mastered Hebrew, Greek, and Latin as a child, then entered Harvard at the unprecedentedly early age of eleven, where he exhibited seriousness, a keen mind, and a capacity for strict self-examination. Upon his father's death in 1723, Cotton Mather became the primary pastor at North Church, Boston, a position he held until his own death five years later.

Cotton Mather shared his father Increase's commitment to promote orthodox and evangelical Calvinism and to oppose its detractors. Yet father and son were very different. Increase Mather focused on preaching and corporate worship. Cotton Mather focused on outreach, going door to door in Boston, evangelizing the unchurched. He also organized small group lay societies for Bible study and spiritual fellowship. Then, too, Cotton Mather, unlike his father, dabbled with mysticism. For example, he wrote that he had meetings with angels.

---

32. *Departing Glory: Eight Jeremiads by Increase Mather*, ed. Lee Schweninger (Delmar: Scholars' Facsimiles & Reprints, 1986).

It was his indefatigable writing that made Cotton Mather one of the most celebrated New England ministers. He wrote 469 published works on biblical subjects, theology, church history, biography, science, and philosophy. His theological writings, now largely forgotten, were greatly influential in his time. They abounded with quotations from patristic and Reformation scholarship as well as from Greek and Roman literature. Cotton Mather wrote the first American commentary on the entire Bible.[33]

Today Cotton Mather is generally regarded as the archetype of the narrow, intolerant, severe Puritan who took part in the Salem witch trials of 1692. Although he did not approve of all the trials, he did help stir up the wave of hysteria with his *Memorable Providences Relating to Witchcraft and Possessions* (1689). Cotton's father, Increase Mather, played a key role in ending the witch trials. He published *Cases of Conscience Concerning Evil Spirits* (1692), in which he argued that courts not allow people's testimony about seeing ghosts to be used as evidence. The Mathers and other ministers did believe in the possibility and criminality of witchcraft and were willing to see people tried as witches. But they believed that hysteria was perverting justice and endangering the innocent.

Cotton Mather was remarkably broadminded. For example, in 1718 he participated in the ordination of a Baptist minister. For most Congregationalists, that was scandalous; for Mather, it was an act that signified unity in Christ beyond church differences. He thought it was unethical that Puritans had persecuted Quakers. Cotton Mather also simplified the requirements for church membership. He said that, ultimately, the three things that were necessary for a Christian are fearing God, accepting the righteousness of Christ to justify sinners by faith, and honoring God by loving one's fellow man. By expressing briefly and simply what was essential, he tried to encourage ways of showing Christian unity.

Cotton Mather was an advocate of caring for orphans and the homeless. He promoted education, medicine, and science, and was the first native-born American to be a fellow of the Royal Society. On February 13, 1728, aged sixty-five, he died peacefully at home from asthma and a fever, surrounded by family and friends, survived by two children.

Three generations of Mathers were strong Puritan leaders in Massachusetts. From Richard Mather's arrival in 1635 until Cotton Mather's death in 1728, the Mathers formed a spiritual dynasty laboring for the spirituality, faithfulness, and purity of the church. Cotton Mather earnestly prayed throughout

---

33. Cotton Mather, *Biblia Americana* is now being published for the first time in a projected 10-volume set (Grand Rapids: Baker Academic and Tübingen: Mohr Siebeck, 2010–).

his life that God would do a great and reviving work in New England that would have worldwide ramifications. Only twelve years after his death, revival did come to New England in the Great Awakening.

For further sources on the Mathers and their controversies, see:
James A. Goulding, "The Controversy between Solomon Stoddard and the Mathers: Western versus Eastern Massachusetts Congregationalism" (PhD diss., Claremont Graduate School, 1971); Holifield, *The Covenant Sealed,* 169–196; Thomas J. Holmes, *Cotton Mather: A Bibliography of His Works,* 3 vols. (Newton: Crofton, 1940, 1968); idem, *Increase Mather: A Bibliography of His Works,* 2 vols. in one (Mansfield Centre: Martino, 1931, 2003); Robert Middlekauff, *The Mathers: Three Generations of Puritan Intellectuals, 1596–1728* (Berkeley: University of California Press, 1999); Robert G. Pope, *The Half-Way Covenant: Church Membership in Puritan New England* (Princeton: Princeton University Press, 1969).

John Eliot (1604–1690) and Native American Missions
John Eliot was born in England, growing up in Hertfordshire and later in Essex. His parents died while he studied at Jesus College, Cambridge. Eliot was ordained in the Anglican Church, but he soon became dissatisfied with its rules and policies. Instead of searching for a parish, he chose to teach at the grammar school in Little Baddow, Essex, where Thomas Hooker was master.

Eliot lived for some time with Hooker and was strongly influenced by him. He later explained how this teaching experience brought him to conversion: "To this place I was called, through the infinite riches of God's mercy in Christ Jesus to my poor soul: for here the Lord said unto my dead soul, live; and through the grace of Christ, I do live, and I shall live for ever! When I came to this blessed [Hooker] family I then saw, and never before, the power of godliness in its lively vigour and efficacy." Soon after his conversion, Eliot devoted himself to the ministry.

In 1630 John Eliot left England, where nonconformist pastors were being persecuted, and went to the Netherlands, then to Massachusetts, arriving in Boston on November 3, 1631. He settled in Roxbury with his godly wife, Hannah. Eliot served the Roxbury church as teacher and later as pastor for more than fifty years. The first fifteen years he devoted himself wholly to the work of the church and the next thirty-five to pastoring the congregation and working among Native Americans. When once challenged by a Native American sagamore (great chief) with a knife, Eliot said, "I am about the work of the great God, and He is with me, so that I fear not all the sachems of the country. I'll go on, and do you touch me if you dare." All three of the Eliots' adult sons served as missionaries to the Native Americans.

Eliot was gifted in languages, and he used his gifts for God's kingdom. His fluency in Hebrew earned him a position on the translation team of the Bay Psalm Book (1640). Three years later, he began studying the Algonquian language. He began preaching to the natives in their own language in 1646. In 1661 and 1663 the New Testament and Old Testament were translated and published. He also translated other works, ranging from simple primers and catechisms to works of Puritan piety. To fund these efforts, Eliot and others wrote what became known as the Eliot Indian Tracts, published in London, to win supporters.

Eliot began to set up towns of "praying Indians." Natick was the first (1651). By 1674, there were fourteen praying towns, with an estimated population of 3,600; approximately 1,100 had been converted. In each town, the natives made a solemn covenant to give themselves and their children "to God to be His people" as the basis of the new civil government. These towns were almost entirely self-governing, though major issues could be referred to the Massachusetts General Court. For the most part, the natives were expected to adopt the Puritan lifestyle along with the Christian faith. After organizing the civil government, Eliot started establishing churches with the Congregationalist form of government. After overcoming numerous difficulties in a fifteen-year period, the first native church was officially established in 1660 at Natick, and other churches in praying towns soon followed.

Eliot's work prospered until the onset of King Philip's War in 1675. Fearing for their lives, numerous native converts moved to an island in the Boston harbor. Many died there. That pattern was repeated in other towns, where praying Indians were destroyed by either warring tribesmen or angry colonists. Unfortunately, the praying Indians were considered enemies of both the English and native Indians; only Eliot and a few others stood by them during the war. In the end, the fourteen praying towns were wiped out. After the war, the surviving Native Americans returned to Natick. Eliot attempted to start over, rebuilding Natick and three other towns despite the distrust of the English. It seemed at first that Eliot's experiment in the New World might still be successful, but that effort never recovered.

In the last days of his life, Eliot was in much physical pain. However, all he could think about was Christ and his beloved Native Americans. "There is a cloud, a dark cloud among the poor Indians," he said. "The Lord revive and prosper that work, and grant it may live when I am dead. It is a work, which I have been doing much and long about. But what was the word I spoke last?

I recall that word, 'my doings.' Alas, they have been poor and small and lean doings, and I'll be the man that shall throw the first stone at them all." Eliot died May 20, 1690, at the age of eighty-six. His last words were "Welcome joy!"

For further sources on John Eliot, see:
John Eliot's Indian Dialogues: A Study in Cultural Interaction, eds. Henry W. Bowden and James P. Ronda (Westport: Greenwood Press, 1980); Richard W. Cogley, *John Eliot's Mission to the Indians before King Philip's War* (Cambridge: Harvard University, 1999); Frederick F. Harling, "A Biography of John Eliot, 1604–1690" (PhD diss., Boston University, 1965); Sidney H. Rooy, *The Theology of Missions in the Puritan Tradition: A Study of Representative Puritans: Richard Sibbes, Richard Baxter, John Eliot, Cotton Mather, and Jonathan Edwards* (Grand Rapids: Eerdmans, 1965); Ola E. Winslow, *John Eliot: "Apostle to the Indians"* (Boston: Houghton Mifflin, 1968).

Puritan New England is illustrated in many ways by Eliot's life. It was a world of deep theological convictions, fervent gospel preaching, warm human compassion, violent bloodshed, complex intercultural relationships, frontier hardship, bitter disappointments, and persevering ideals. Despite the voluminous river of publications analyzing and debating its nature and legacy, Puritan New England continues to invite further study.

Scotch Presbyterianism in the New World

Unlike the Puritans established in New England, Scotch Presbyterianism in America was just getting started in the late seventeenth century, and its beginnings were fragile. In the early 1680s the Scotch Presbyterians of Ireland sent Francis Makemie (1658–1708) as their first missionary to the New World. He served his countrymen for a time in Barbados, then in Somerset County, Maryland, before marrying and settling in Accomack County, Virginia. He also itinerated in New York. Makemie often had to appear in court to defend his right to preach in lands ruled by Anglican authorities, and spent some time in jail. He corresponded with Increase Mather in Boston, who considered him "a Reverend and judicious minister." His ministry was broad and powerful, and some consider him the father of American Presbyterianism. In 1706 the first American presbytery was formed in Philadelphia by the ministers Francis Makemie, George McNish, John Hampton, Samuel Davis, John Wilson, Nathaniel Taylor, and Jedediah Andrews.[34]

---

34. William B. Sprague, *Annals of the American Presbyterian Pulpit*, 3 vols. (repr. Birmingham: Solid Ground Christian Books, 2005), 1:xi, 1–4.

In 1717 the presbytery gained a new member in the New Englander Jonathan Dickinson (1688–1747). Dickinson, a gifted theologian and practicing physician, later proved a cautious but supportive friend of the revivals. He wrote a highly esteemed defense of Reformed soteriology. In it he said,

> Whoever are chosen to eternal salvation, will be brought to see their undone state and inability to help themselves; to despair of salvation by anything they can do; to receive the Lord Jesus Christ by faith; and to depend upon him as their wisdom, righteousness, sanctification, and redemption. Until they thus lead the life that they live here in the flesh, by faith in the Son of God, they can have no evidence at all of their election.[35]

William Tennent (1673–1746), just having arrived from Ireland, also joined the Synod of Philadelphia in 1718. He established the "Log College" in Pennsylvania to train ministers and later became a friend of George Whitefield. One of Tennent's sons, Gilbert, would play a large role in fanning the flames of the Great Awakening. In 1729 the American Presbyterians passed the adopting act requiring all its ministers to subscribe to the Westminster Confession, Larger Catechism, and Shorter Catechism—the products of British Reformed Orthodoxy at its pinnacle.[36]

For further sources on early Presbyterianism in America, see:
Sermons of the Log College: Being Sermons and Essays by the Tennents and their Contemporaries, ed. Archibald Alexander (repr. Ligonier: Soli Deo Gloria, 1995); *The Presbyterian Enterprise: Sources of American Presbyterian History*, eds. Maurice W. Armstrong, Lefferts A. Loetscher, and Charles A. Anderson (Philadelphia: Westminster Press, 1956); Archibald Alexander, *The Log College: Biographical Sketches of William Tennent & his students together with an account of the revivals made under their ministries* (London: Banner of Truth, 1968); J. G. Craighead, *Scotch and Irish Seeds in American Soil: The Early History of the Scotch and Irish Churches and Their Relations to the Presbyterian Church of America* (Philadelphia: Presbyterian Board of Publication, 1878); William H. Foote, *Sketches of Virginia: Historical and Biographical* (Richmond: John Knox, 1850, 1966); D. G. Hart and John R. Muether, *Seeking a Better Country: 300 Years of American Presbyterianism* (Phillipsburg, N.J.: P&R Publishing, 2007); Bryan F.

---

35. Jonathan Dickinson, *The True Scripture Doctrine Concerning Some Important Points of the Christian Faith: Particularly Eternal Election, Original Sin, Grace in Conversion, Justification by Faith, and the Saints' Perseverance* (Philadelphia: Presbyterian Board of Publication, 1841), 50–51.

36. Sprague, *Annals of the American Presbyterian Pulpit*, 1:14–18, 23–27; Charles Hodge, *The Constitutional History of the Presbyterian Church in the United States of America* (Philadelphia: Presbyterian Board of Publication, 1851), 1:127, 146.

Le Beau, *Jonathan Dickinson and the Formative Years of American Presbyterianism* (Lexington: University Press of Kentucky, 1997); Robert E. Thompson, *A History of the Presbyterian Churches in the United States*, 3rd ed. (repr. Eugene: Wipf & Stock, 2003).

Anglicanism and Reformed Orthodoxy in England's Colonies

Whereas Massachusetts began as a city on a hill for English Puritans, New York as a Dutch Reformed trading post, and Maryland as a refuge for English Catholics, the colony of Virginia was a company of Anglicans. The issue of Reformed Orthodoxy in Virginia and other colonies dominated by the Church of England is a complex matter. The "Reformed Church of England" affirmed Reformed doctrines in its 39 Articles (1562) and later in the Lambeth Articles (1595). The Lambeth Articles never received formal creedal status but were endorsed by the archbishop of Canterbury and the archbishop of York.[37] Though the church was polarized by debates over worship and authority, most leaders of the church under Elizabeth I and James I were essentially Reformed in their views of God, Scripture, salvation, and obedience to the law of God.[38] Therefore, many Anglicans in Virginia would have held to elements of Reformed Orthodoxy.[39] Black slave Jupiter Hammon (1711–1806) was a New York Anglican who preached particular election, spiritual regeneration, and holy living. He was influenced by the writings of Solomon Stoddard, a New England Puritan.[40] The Virginia Anglican and first president of the United States, George Washington (1732–1799), cherished his faith in the God of sovereign providence, an almighty heavenly Father who decreed and orders all things according to His wisdom and goodness—even in the tumults of war.[41]

Nevertheless, Reformed Orthodoxy never fully prevailed in the Church of England and came under a dark cloud during the ascendancy of Archbishop Laud in the 1630s and later after the Restoration of the Monarchy in the 1660s. Anglican leaders such as Herbert Thorndike (1598–1672) and George

---

37. Philip Schaff, *The Creeds of Christendom* (repr. Grand Rapids: Baker Books, 1998), 3:486, 521.

38. Nigel Yoak, *Richard Hooker and Reformed Theology* (Oxford: Oxford University Press, 2003), 3. Mark A. Noll, *A History of Christianity in the United States and Canada* (Grand Rapids: Eerdmans, 1992), 37. Yoak's book argues that Hooker (1554–1600), often viewed as the classic advocate of the Anglican "middle-way" between Reformed and Roman Christendom, began in the Reformed tradition but shifted away from it over time.

39. Robert W. Pritchard, *A History of the Episcopal Church* (Harrisburg: Morehouse, 1991), 4.

40. Holifield, *Theology in America*, 308–309.

41. Peter Lillback, *George Washington's Sacred Fire* (Bryn Mawr: Providence Forum Press, 2006), 573–87, 592–93.

Bull (1634–1710) viewed the Reformed doctrine of justification by faith alone in Christ alone as a threat to Christian morality. Thomas Bray (1656–1730) was organizer of the Society for Promoting Christian Knowledge and the first Anglican missionary to Maryland. Bray advocated a neonomian theology where God's covenant of grace accepted man's imperfect obedience as the fulfillment of God's conditions of righteousness. Similarly, Samuel Johnson (1696–1772), at one time a teacher at the Reformed citadel of Yale University, defected to Anglicanism, rejected predestination and limited atonement, and embraced high-church sacramentalism and salvation for the righteous of any religion. When Anglicans such as Devereux Jarratt and George Whitefield preached Reformed doctrines of grace on American soil in the mid-eighteenth century, their greatest opponents were their fellows in the Church of England.[42] Theological diversity has long characterized Anglicanism.

For further sources on early American Anglicanism, see:
John K. Nelson, *A Blessed Company: Parishes, Parsons, and Parishioners in Anglican Virginia, 1690–1776* (Chapel Hill: University of North Carolina Press, 2001); Samuel Wilberforce, *A History of the Protestant Episcopal Church in America*, 2nd ed. (London: Rivington, 1846).

The Huguenot Dispersion in America

From the mid-sixteenth century onward, the Reformed church in France was bathed in its own blood. Early in the religious wars and persecution of the so-called "Huguenots,"[43] the Reformed explored possibilities of a new home in the New World. Attempts to colonize Brazil (1555), South Carolina (1562), and Florida (1564) met with failure, indeed disaster.[44] The Edict of Nantes (1598) provided a temporary peace in France. But even before the Edict of Nantes was repealed in 1685, Reformed families were fleeing persecution in France for asylum around the world. Protestants participated in the colonization of New France (Canada). But in 1627 Cardinal Richelieu barred the Huguenots from settling or trading in the French colony, closing the door for the Reformed to immigrate there.

Many Huguenots came to the American Colonies under English rule, including New York, Massachusetts, Pennsylvania, Maryland, Virginia, and

---

42. Holifield, *Theology in America*, 57, 84–88.
43. The term *Huguenot* is of uncertain derivation, being variously connected to meeting at night, or meeting in homes, or swearing an oath of allegiance, or the proper name Hugh or Hugo.
44. Arthur H. Hirsch, *The Huguenots of Colonial South Carolina* (Hamden: Archon Books, 1962), 6–7.

the Carolinas. It may well be that some brought with them the French Confession of Faith (1559), drafted by John Calvin, which was often bound with French Bibles. Peter Minuits, the governor of New Amsterdam in the early 1620s, was not Dutch but French Reformed. Many Huguenot families settled on Staten Island. In what would later become New York, the French Protestants were known for their purity of worship and life.[45] Pastors such as Elias Prioleau of Charleston and Claude Philippe de Richebourg of Virginia served with distinction in their purity of doctrine and fervent piety. Prioleau had witnessed the demolition of his church building by hostile forces in France in 1687 before coming to Charleston.[46] Richebourg served from 1700–1710 in a parish granted the French by the government of Virginia on condition that they would use the Anglican liturgy.[47]

The French Reformed lost their distinctiveness over time in America, often assimilating into Puritan Reformed in New England, the Dutch Reformed in New Netherlands, and the Church of England in New York, Virginia, and South Carolina. Unlike the English and Dutch Reformed, the French lacked a strong supporting church in their homeland. But the Huguenot dispersion enriched the English and Dutch Reformed with their faith and talents.

For further sources on the Huguenot dispersion in America, see:
Timothy Bergsma, "In Search of Canada's Reformed Heritage: The Protestants of New France" (master's thesis, Puritan Reformed Theological Seminary, 2010); Jon Butler, *The Huguenots in America: A Refugee People in New World Society* (Cambridge: Harvard University Press, 1983); Otto Zoff, *The Huguenots: Fighters for God and Human Freedom*, trans. E. B. Ashton and Jo Mayo (New York: L. B. Fischer, 1942). See also the bibliography offered by the National Huguenot Society, http://www.huguenot.netnation.com/general/histread.htm (accessed 10-12-10).

The German Reformed in the American Colonies
Few Germans immigrated to the New World until the last quarter of the seventeenth century, releasing a flood that flowed for a hundred years. Among them

---

45. William H. Foote, *The Huguenots; or, Reformed French Church* (repr. Harrisonburg: Sprinkle, 2002), 504, 509.

46. Hirsch, *The Huguenots of Colonial South Carolina*, 9–13, 51–53. M. Charles Weiss, *History of the French Protestant Refugees*, trans. Henry W. Herbert (New York: Stringer & Townsend, 1854), 331–32, 377.

47. George M. Brydon, *Virginia's Mother Church* (Richmond: Virginia Historical Society, 1947), 263.

came the German Reformed, first to New York and then later to Pennsylvania. They were driven by devastating wars with France, bitterly cold winters, and religious persecution in Germany. They brought with them the Heidelberg Catechism, that Reformed experiential book of comfort. John Frederick Hager preached among the Germans in New York, arriving there in 1709. The first German Reformed minister in Pennsylvania was Samuel Guildin from Berne (Switzerland), a Pietist who arrived in America in 1710 and devoted himself to evangelism.[48] In 1727 George Michael Weiss arrived in Pennsylvania from the Palatinate. He ministered in the Philadelphia area and also near Albany, New York. John Philip Boehm had already come to the New World and served initially as a lay minister in the Philadelphia area from 1725 until he was able to continue serving under formal ordination through the Dutch Reformed church in New York (1729). In a controversy with the Moravians, Boehm defended the doctrines of election and reprobation. His gospel labors extended to many settlements, preparing the way for new churches founded on the Heidelberg Catechism and the Canons of the Synod of Dort.[49] In 1747 the German Reformed churches organized the *coetus* (association) of Pennsylvania. Later they united as the Reformed Church in the United States (1893).

For further sources on German Reformed Christians in America, see:
Joseph H. Dubbs, "History of the Reformed Church, German," in *American Church History*, ed. Philip Schaff, et al., 2nd ed., 13 vols. (New York: Charles Scribner's Sons, 1894), 8:213–423; David Dunn, et al., *A History of the Evangelical and Reformed Church* (New York: The Pilgrim Press, 1990).

The Dutch Reformed in New Netherlands
New York and northeastern New Jersey were originally settled by Dutch immigrants after Henry Hudson's exploratory journey in 1609. Dutch culture strongly influenced the region as late as the eighteenth and early nineteenth centuries.[50]

Early attempts by the Dutch West India Company to turn its small settlements on the Hudson River into a profitable endeavor made little progress. Similarly, the first two Dutch Reformed ministers, Jonas Michaelis and Everardus Bogardus, struggled to organize or edify the local population in the

---

48. James I. Good, *History of the Reformed Church in the United States, 1725–1792* (Reading: Daniel Miller, 1899), 68–88.

49. H. Harbaugh, *The Fathers of the German Reformed Church in Europe and America* (Lancaster: Sprenger & Westhaeffer, 1857), 1:265–91.

50. Gerald F. DeJong, *The Dutch in America, 1609–1974* (Boston: G. K. Hall, 1975), 10, 67.

faith. Johannes Megapolensis served the colony from 1643 to 1673 with better results. He also labored among the Mohawk tribe of the Native Americans, studying their language and customs in order to spread the gospel among them. Similarly, Samuel Drisius, who could preach in Dutch, French, and English, served the mixed community well. Henricus Selyns ministered in New York City from 1682 to 1701. One of his Latin poems was published with the works of Cotton Mather, with whom Selyns corresponded. These ministers taught the people the Reformed doctrines of the Heidelberg Catechism and the Synod of Dort, and led them in worship consisting of Scripture reading, prayer, and the singing of psalms.[51]

Reformed ministers like Megapolensis were supported by the political leadership of Peter Stuyvesant, who led the colony into order and success from 1647 until he surrendered to British warships in 1664. Stuyvesant initially attempted to impose Reformed conformity upon the population, barring a Lutheran minister and expelling Quakers. But the Dutch West India Company reversed his policy of conformity to attract English Dissenters to settle in the area. The English also generally practiced a limited tolerance when they took power, except for occasional attempts to impose Anglican ministers on Reformed churches. The Dutch found it hard to persuade ministers to come and serve in the New World, often relying on lay ministers, some of whom were poorly prepared for the ministry. Others served with distinction and zeal, such as William Bartholf, who ministered in New Jersey. Influenced by Dutch Pietist Jacobus Koelman, Bartholf labored tirelessly to preach against formalism and to declare the necessity of personal regeneration. He eventually returned to the Netherlands for ordination in 1694 and came back to America to evangelize and establish new churches. For the next fifteen years he was the only Dutch Reformed minister in New Jersey. Even his enemies came to respect him as an honorable and pious man.[52]

For further sources on the Dutch Reformed in America, see:
E. T. Corwin, "History of the Reformed Church, Dutch," in *American Church History*, ed. Philip Schaff, et al., 2nd ed., 13 vols. (New York: Charles Scribner's Sons, 1894), 8:xi–212; Randall H. Balmer, *A Perfect Babel of Confusion: Dutch*

---

51. DeJong, *The Dutch in America*, 79, 89. W. A. Speck and L. Billington, "Calvinism in Colonial North America, 1630–1715," *International Calvinism, 1541–1715*, ed. Menna Prestwich (Oxford: Clarendon Press, 1985), 272–76.

52. Speck and Billington, "Calvinism in Colonial North America," 276–78; W. R. Ward, *The Protestant Evangelical Awakening* (Cambridge: Cambridge University Press, 2002), 243–44.

Religion and English Culture in the Middle Colonies (Oxford: Oxford University Press, 1989).

Theodorus Frelinghuysen (1691–1747)

Theodorus Jacobus Frelinghuysen, raised and educated in the Netherlands in the teachings of Voetius, became another flaming torch among the American Dutch. Frelinghuysen arrived in New Jersey in 1720. His preaching focused on the Voetian themes of the narrow way of salvation and the priority of internal motives that effect external observance. He spoke out forcefully against sin and stressed the Spirit's work of convicting sinners of their sin and the solemn judgment of God against sin. He invited sinners to come to Christ, stressing that only those who have experienced conversion in Christ as needy sinners would be saved.

While some were offended by Frelinghuysen's preaching, most of his congregants rallied behind him. At least three hundred people were converted under his ministry. Several small revivals under Frelinghuysen's ministry paved the way for the Great Awakening. His preaching and friendship influenced Gilbert Tennent (1703–1764), a Scotch Presbyterian minister who came to New Jersey to work among English-speaking colonists. The revival that began under Frelinghuysen in the Dutch community spread to English-speaking settlers under Tennent's ministry, later blossoming into the Great Awakening under George Whitefield, who called Frelinghuysen "the beginner of the great work."

Frelinghuysen applied the evidences of conversion—repentance, faith, and holiness—as tests for admission to the Lord's Supper. This divided the Dutch Reformed community, leading to a prolonged controversy that undermined Frelinghuysen's health. He also advocated and ultimately prevailed in securing for the American Dutch Reformed church the right to preach in English and train and ordain its own ministers. His untiring work, zeal, and piety triumphed as many of his former enemies came to respect him.

For further sources on Theodorus Frelinghuysen, see:
Forerunner of the Great Awakening: Sermons by Theodorus Jacobus Frelinghuysen, ed. Joel R. Beeke (Grand Rapids: Eerdmans, 2000); James Tanis, *Dutch Calvinistic Pietism in the Middle Colonies: A Study in the Life and Theology of Theodorus Jacobus Frelinghuysen* (The Hague: Martinus Nijhoff, 1967).

Reformed Orthodox Roots of the Great Awakening

By the end of the seventeenth century, English Reformed Orthodoxy was in decline. The decades of persecution following the 1662 ejection of Puritan Reformed ministers from the Church of England had taken their toll. Popular Anglican preacher John Tillotson (1630–1694) sought to supplant Reformed teachings with what he deemed a more rational religion. In the early eighteenth century many of the rich in England lived in open immorality, while the poor drowned their sorrows in gin. Ministers lamented a withdrawal of the influences of the Spirit of God. The Age of the Enlightenment had begun, when men looked increasingly to the light of human reason instead of the Scriptures. Meanwhile, human misery and social injustices abounded.

In New England, rationalism and Arminianism made inroads into the Puritan Reformed establishment. In 1702 Increase Mather published a sermon in which he warned that the glory of God stood on the threshold of the temple (Ezek. 9:3)—about to leave New England.[53] Concern over the theological drift at Harvard led to the founding of Yale College. Yet even Yale was not immune to change, as illustrated by the 1722 resignation and "great apostasy" to Anglicanism of its entire faculty, led by Timothy Cutler. Yale recovered, but the Puritan concerns continued.

Ironically American Reformed spirituality was revived not through a Puritan but an Anglican. George Whitefield (1714–1770), an ordained priest in the Church of England, visited the American colonies seven times from 1738–1770 to preach to crowds of thousands. With him spread a series of revivals now known as the Great Awakening. In reality, the revival began through the ministries of Theodorus Frelinghuysen and Gilbert Tennent. But Whitefield played a key role in broadening the scope of the revival throughout the American colonies. What is sometimes overlooked is that Whitefield's preaching was firmly rooted in the Reformed Orthodoxy of England and Scotland. Next to the Bible, his favorite books were those of the Puritans. His conversion came through reading Henry Scougal (1650–1678), and throughout his life he read from Reformed experiential writers such as Joseph Alleine (1634–1668), Thomas Boston (1676–1732), and especially the Bible commentaries of the English Puritan Matthew Henry (1662–1714).[54] Whitefield openly confessed and preached the Reformed doctrines of salvation and commended "the Puritans

---

53. Increase Mather, "Ichabod...the Glory of the Lord is Departing from New-England," in *Departing Glory: Eight Jeremiads by Increase Mather*, 46.

54. Arnold A. Dallimore, *George Whitefield: The Life and Times of the Great Evangelist of the Eighteenth-Century Revival* (Edinburgh: Banner of Truth, 1970 and 1980), 1:82, 404–405.

of the last century" as "burning and shining lights."[55] In 1829 selections of his works were published with the title *The Revived Puritan*, a description that J. I. Packer called "uncannily apt."[56] After Whitefield's death he was eulogized in Boston by Ebenezer Pemberton as a man who preached "those great Doctrines of the Gospel which our venerable Ancestors brought with them from their Native Country."[57]

For further sources on the Great Awakening, see:
The Great Awakening: Documents Illustrating the Crisis and Its Consequences, eds. Alan Heimart and Perry Miller (Indianapolis: Bobbs-Merrill Educational Publishing, 1967); Thomas S. Kidd, *The Great Awakening: The Roots of Evangelical Christianity in Colonial America* (New Haven: Yale University Press, 2007); Joseph Tracy, *The Great Awakening: A History of the Revival of Religion in the time of Edwards & Whitefield* (reprint ed., Edinburgh: Banner of Truth, 1976).

Jonathan Edwards (1703–1758)
Jonathan Edwards is often called America's greatest theologian and philosopher and the last Puritan. He was a powerful participant in the Great Awakening as well as a champion of Christian zeal and spirituality. Both Christian and secular scholarship concur on his importance in American history. Edwards was a biblical exegete, theologian, philosopher, preacher, advocate of revival, and missionary to the Native Americans. As the huge body of his writings shows, Edwards was intellectually brilliant, multifaceted in his interests, and abundantly creative. The literature on Edwards is immense, a scholarly field unto itself.

Jonathan Edwards was born October 5, 1703, in East Windsor, Connecticut. His father, Timothy Edwards, and maternal grandfather, Solomon Stoddard, were Puritan ministers who had experienced revivals in their ministry. Edwards studied at Yale College, graduating valedictorian with his BA in 1720, then with his MA in 1723 after giving a Latin oration on justification by faith alone. While working on his MA, he experienced a life-changing sense of God's loveliness and sweetness while meditating on 1 Timothy 1:17, "Now unto the King eternal, immortal, invisible, the only wise God, be honour and

---

55. George Whitefield, *The Works of the Reverend George Whitefield* (London: Dilly, 1771), 4:306.

56. J. I. Packer, "The Spirit with the Word: The Reformational Revivalism of George Whitefield," in *The Bible, the Reformation, and the Church: Essays in Honour of James Atkinson*, ed. W. P. Stephens (Sheffield, U.K.: Sheffield Academic Press, 1995), 176.

57. Harry S. Stout, *The Divine Dramatist: George Whitefield and the Rise of Modern Evangelism* (Grand Rapids: Eerdmans, 1991), 282.

glory for ever and ever, Amen." In 1726 he moved to Northampton, Massachusetts, to assist at his grandfather's church. When Stoddard died in 1729, Edwards became their sole pastor. In 1734–1735 and 1740–1742, Edwards saw remarkable awakenings among his people, the latter during the broader Great Awakening. Edwards's attempt to limit the Lord's Supper to those confessing a personal experience of saving grace—contrary to his grandfather's long-established position—helped lead to his dismissal by the church in 1750. From 1751–1757 Edwards served the English and Native American population in Stockbridge, Massachusetts. In 1758 he became the president of the College of New Jersey at Princeton, but he developed an infection after receiving a smallpox inoculation and died on March 22, 1758.

Jonathan Edwards received the Reformed doctrines he inherited from the Savoy Declaration, the Congregationalist revision of the Westminster Confession of Faith. Edwards defended these doctrines against rising Enlightenment rationalism and explored them deeply regarding the distinguishing marks of true godliness and the progress of history toward its God-ordained goals. Best known for his sermon, "Sinners in the Hands of an Angry God," Edwards also preached a famous sermon titled "Heaven Is a World of Love."

Some of Jonathan Edwards's publications are:

+ *Discourses on Various Important Subjects* (1738), the publication of sermons on conversion, justification by faith alone, and damnation.

+ *Religious Affections* (1746), the culmination of a decade of reflecting on revival in order to distinguish between true conversion and hypocrisy.

+ *Life of David Brainerd* (1749), a biography of a missionary to the Native Americans that inspired many in later generations to sacrificial missions.

+ *Freedom of the Will* (1754), a philosophical assault upon the notion that man can exercise self-determination independent of the sovereign will of God.

+ *Original Sin* (1754), a defense of the Reformed doctrine of the universal corruption and total depravity of human nature since the fall of man.

+ *History of the Work of Redemption* (1774), a series of sermons preached in 1739 on God's program to establish the worldwide kingdom of His Son.

Though Theodorus Frelinghuysen, George Whitefield, and Jonathan Edwards stood in distinct church traditions, they shared a common heritage in Reformed thought concerning the doctrines of salvation and vital piety. The North American experience of the Great Awakening was profoundly shaped by these men and others like them. From this revival sprang forces that continue to propel and shape the North American evangelical movement today. American evangelicalism is grounded in the Great Awakening, but its roots ultimately lie in Reformed Orthodoxy.[58] Thus, Reformed Orthodoxy has had a more profound impact on North American Christianity than is generally acknowledged.

For further sources on Jonathan Edwards, see:

The Cambridge Companion to Jonathan Edwards, ed. Stephen J. Stein (Cambridge: Cambridge University Press, 2007); John Carrick, *The Preaching of Jonathan Edwards* (Edinburgh: Banner of Truth, 2008); William J. Danaher Jr., *The Trinitarian Ethics of Jonathan Edwards* (Louisville: Westminster John Knox Press, 2004); John H. Gerstner, *The Rational Biblical Theology of Jonathan Edwards*, 3 vols. (Orlando: Ligionier, 1991); M. X. Lesser, *Reading Jonathan Edwards: An Annotated Bibliography in Three Parts, 1729–2005* (Grand Rapids: Eerdmans, 2008); George M. Marsden, *Jonathan Edwards: A Life* (New Haven: Yale University, 2003); Iain H. Murray, *Jonathan Edwards: A New Biography* (Edinburgh: Banner of Truth, 1987). All 26 volumes of the Yale edition of *The Works of Jonathan Edwards* plus many other unpublished sources with scholarly introductions are available online at http://edwards.yale.edu/.

---

58. See *The Advent of Evangelicalism: Exploring Historical Continuities*, eds. Michael A. G. Haykin and Kenneth J. Stewart (Nashville: B&H Academic, 2008).

Chapter 12

The Perspicuity of Scripture

The perspicuity of Scripture was a key issue debated by Protestants and Roman Catholics during the sixteenth-century Reformation. They wrestled with this question: Is Scripture so difficult to understand that it can only be interpreted by the educated clergy, or is Scripture essentially clear, that is, perspicuous, and hence understandable by untrained laity?

Although the Roman Catholic Church did not prohibit uneducated parishioners from reading Scripture, its leaders discouraged such reading by teaching that the clergy were the sole authoritative interpreters of Scripture. Protestants, on the other hand, affirmed that even the most uneducated Christian believers could understand Scripture. The practical result of this approach was the translation of the Bible into the common language of the people, the printing and distribution of the Bible for the laity, and the promotion of Scripture reading and study by all.

Robert Preus and Rudolph Hermann treated the doctrine of perspicuity from a Lutheran perspective in the 1950s; Richard Muller's *magnum opus* devotes eighteen pages to its exposition by post-Reformers such as Edward Leigh, Petrus van Mastricht, Benedict Pictet, and Robert Rollock; and Gregg Allison's 1995 dissertation attempts to reformulate the doctrine based on biblical teaching.[1] But few theologians besides Moisés Silva, James Callahan, and T. D. F. Maddox have written helpful articles in the last twenty years[2] on the subject once held so dear by Protestants.

---

1. Robert Preus, *The Inspiration of Scripture: A Study of the Theology of the Seventeenth Century Lutheran Dogmaticians* (Mankato, Minn.: Lutheran Synod Book Co., 1955); Richard Muller, *Post-Reformation Reformed Dogmatics, Volume Two: Holy Scripture, The Cognitive Foundation of Theology*, 2nd ed. (Grand Rapids: Baker, 2003), 322–40; Gregg R. Allison, "The Protestant Doctrine of the Perspicuity of Scripture: A Reformulation on the Basis of Biblical Teaching" (PhD diss., Trinity Evangelical Divinity School, 1995). Much of this paper relies heavily on these excellent treatments. This chapter was first delivered as a conference address for Sola Scriptura in Ontario.

2. Happily, a few systematics treat perspicuity at some length, such as Herman Bavinck, *Reformed*

In this chapter, I will examine the subject primarily from a historical and theological perspective, considering the views of Luther and Calvin and post-Reformation writers. I will then conclude with some scriptural, theological, and practical ways in which the doctrine of perspicuity is relevant for us today.

Historical Development

The Latin verb *perspicio* means "to see through," that is, "to penetrate by a look." A book that is perspicuous, therefore, is one that may be "penetrated by a look." Its meaning or message can be discerned and understood by the reader. There are various levels of perspicuity; some books are less clear than others, but all can be understood.

In English, *perspicuity* has a slightly different meaning. It means that some effort may be needed to "penetrate" the true meaning of a work. The term nonetheless implies that the meaning can be discerned and understood by a reader.

The doctrine of perspicuity has its origins in the writings of the major Reformers and was further developed in the seventeenth century by post-Reformation theologians. Lutheran and Reformed theologians of this latter period, often called the age of Protestant Scholasticism, refined the doctrine of perspicuity through their debates with Roman Catholics.

Martin Luther

First let us examine the doctrine of perspicuity in the context of the Reformation. Noting that the printing press and the rise of literacy in the Renaissance gave impetus to the Reformation, T. D. F. Maddox goes on to say, "Luther was swept up in the Renaissance impact of Erasmian humanism that rejected the institutional control of Scripture, a force that insisted that the individual take up the tool of reading and encounter the potency of Scripture for oneself." This, in turn, led to various hermeneutic methods of interpreting the Bible in a direct and literal way so that the Bible became an open book for every believer to read and interpret with clarity.[3]

Martin Luther addressed the doctrine of the clarity of Scripture at some length in four of his writings, the first being *To the Christian Nobility of the*

Dogmatics (Grand Rapids: Baker, 2003); Wayne Grudem, *Systematic Theology* (Grand Rapids: Zondervan, 1994), 105–113. For older works, see Heinrich Heppe, *Reformed Dogmatics*, trans. G. T. Thomson (reprint London: Wakeman Trust, 2002), 33–41; Francis Turretin, *Institutes of Elenctic Theology*, ed. James T. Dennison Jr., trans. George M. Giger (Phillipsburg: P&R, 1992), 1:143–47; William Whitaker, *A Disputation on Holy Scripture*, trans. and ed. William Fitzgerald (reprint Orlando: Soli Deo Gloria, 2005).

3. Maddox, "Scripture, Perspicuity, and Postmodernity," 558–59.

German Nation (1520).[4] In response to the Roman Catholic Church's claim that the proper interpretation of the Scriptures ultimately rested with the pope, Luther argued that proper interpretation depends more on the character of the interpreter than upon one's ecclesiastical position. Luther particularly exalted the qualities of being a believer who is "taught by God" and "pious in heart," that is, a "good Christian" who has "the true faith, spirit, understanding, word, and mind of Christ," and especially "has the Holy Spirit."[5] Luther minced no words in comparing such a Christian with the pope, saying, "Why, then, should we reject the word and understanding of good Christians and follow the pope, who has neither faith nor the Spirit?"[6]

Luther's second defense of perspicuity was based on his understanding of the priesthood of believers in 1 Corinthians 2:15 and 2 Corinthians 4:13. According to Luther, each Christian should "test and judge what is right and wrong in matters of faith" to "ascertain what is consistent with faith and what is not." This discernment is exercised on the basis of one's "believing understanding of the Scriptures."[7] Key to Luther's thinking, here, was his conviction that Scripture itself is clear and understandable.

Jerome Emser (1477–1527), a former professor of Luther's, responded angrily to Luther's arguments with *Against the Unchristian Book of the Augustinian Martin Luther, Addressed to the German Nobility*. That motivated Luther to produce four more writings, the most substantial of which was *Answer to the Hyperchristian, Hyperspiritual, and Hyperlearned Book by Goat Emser in Leipzig*. (Luther called his opponent "the goat in Leipzig" because Emser's coat of arms—a shield and helmet adorned with a goat—was displayed on the title page of his writings.)

Emser said there are three weapons to be used in theological sword-fighting: the "sword" of Scripture, the "long spear" of tradition, and the "short dagger" of interpretation by church fathers. The church fathers and tradition help illumine the obscure Scriptures, Emser concluded. Luther responded by saying that since the human words of the church fathers and of tradition are more obscure than the clear testimony of Scripture, one cannot argue that the fathers and tradition illumine Scripture. That would be like saying that the stars illumine the sun. Luther said that the way we evaluate tradition and

---

4. Helmut T. Lehmann, gen. ed., *Luther's Works, Volume 44: The Christian in Society* (Philadelphia: Fortress Press, 1966), 115–217.

5. *Luther's Works*, 44:134–45.

6. *Luther's Works*, 44:135.

7. *Luther's Works*, 44:135.

the church fathers' teachings is by comparing them to the Scripture, not by comparing Scripture to them.[8]

Luther went on to reject the twofold or fourfold interpretation of Scripture supported by Emser. Actually, the twofold and fourfold interpretation are synonymous in intent, since twofold refers to the distinction between a literal and a spiritual meaning. A fourfold interpretation breaks it down to literal, allegorical, anagogical, and topological senses, but the last three are simply three divisions of the spiritual meaning used in the twofold classification.

Luther felt that Scripture would lose its content if stripped of its literal meaning, which is its natural meaning. He said the literal understanding of the Bible is "the highest, best, strongest, in short, the whole substance, nature and foundation of Scripture. If one abandons it, the whole Scripture would be nothing." Other spiritual interpretations—particularly the allegorical—only wreak havoc with Scripture. The literal sense of Scripture is so important, Luther said, because it is in line with the Holy Spirit's inspiration of Scripture, and "the Holy Spirit is the simplest writer and adviser in heaven and on earth. That is why his words could have no more than the one simplest meaning which we call the written one, or the literal meaning of the tongue." Moreover, the very nature of effective communication necessitates a simple, literal meaning, if words and language are not to be stripped of meaning itself.[9]

Luther did not deny the distinction between figurative language and the figurative interpretation of Scripture. Figurative language is a common method of communication in Scripture, which, Luther said, even schoolboys readily understood. But figurative interpretation is something else. Hermeneutically, there is only one sense, the literal meaning, which Luther commonly calls the "grammatical, historical meaning"[10] of Scripture. So Luther argued against the scholastic system of multiple senses for interpreting Scripture.[11]

That same year (1521), Luther once more argued for perspicuity in his reponse to Latomus, a professor of theology at the University of Louvain. In a work published in 1521, Latomus defended the university's position against Luther's in his *Articulorum doctrinae fratris M. Lutheri*. Luther responded with *Confutatio rationis Latomianae*, which covers several major doctrines, including the perspicuity of Scripture. At one point Luther admonished Latomus for favoring the church fathers over the apostle Paul, then added that allegiance

---

8. *Luther's Works*, 44:164–66; Allison, "The Protestant Doctrine of the Perspicuity of Scripture, 5–6.

9. *Luther's Works*, 44:177–78.

10. *Luther's Works*, 44:180–81.

11. Allison, "The Protestant Doctrine of the Perspicuity of Scripture," 9–12.

to Paul was critical because the church fathers "speak more obscurely and less forcefully than he [Paul] does. Paul's words are too clear to need any gloss; indeed, interpretation rather obscures them."[12] Commenting on Luther, Allison concludes, "Luther maintains the perspicuity of Scripture over the obscurity of human words since the One who communicates through the Scriptures understands Himself better than man does and thus is able to communicate clearly those things which He reveals about Himself."[13]

Luther's primary development of the doctrine of perspicuity, however, was in his 1524–1525 encounter with Erasmus. Luther wrote *The Bondage of the Will* in response to Erasmus's *Diatribe seu collation delibero arbitrio*. Luther began his discussion of perspicuity by disagreeing with Erasmus's division of Christian doctrines into the categories of recondite (not easily understood) and plain. Erasmus asserted that only plain doctrines, not the recondite, needed to be known. After showing Erasmus's exegetical errors in trying to find biblical support for this view from Isaiah 40:13 and Romans 11:33, Luther argued that the distinction between the recondite and the plain are not in the doctrines of Scripture but in our understanding of God. "Nobody questions that there is a great deal hid in God of which we know nothing," Luther said.[14] Who can understand the Trinity and the Incarnation, for example? Yet, the *facts* of the mysteries of faith are abundantly clear in Scripture. Hence, according to Luther, Erasmus's assertion that obscurity exists in Scripture is "a godless and unproven contention."[15]

The problem, Luther argued, is not the obscurity of Scripture, or even the exaltedness of God, so much as the darkness of man's fallen heart, which obscures his understanding. According to Luther, Erasmus projected the interpreter's inability to understand Scripture back upon Scripture itself rather than upon the interpreter's darkened understanding.[16] Luther concluded, "Let miserable men, therefore, stop imputing with blasphemous perversity the darkness and obscurity of their own hearts to the wholly clear Scriptures of God."[17]

Luther argued quite successfully that the end results of Erasmus's perversity was the undermining of Scripture and the bolstering of the pope's authority, for everyone was dependent on papal interpretation for their understanding

---

12. Helmut T. Lehmann, gen. ed., *Luther's Works, Volume 32: Career of the Reformer II* (Philadelphia: Muhlenberg, 1958), 214–17.

13. Allison, "The Protestant Doctrine of the Perspicuity of Scripture," 16.

14. Martin Luther, *The Bondage of the Will*, trans. J. I. Packer and O. R. Johnston (Old Tappan, N.J.: Revell, 1957), 71.

15. Allison, "The Protestant Doctrine of the Perspicuity of Scripture," 21.

16. Callahan, "Perspicuity in Protestant Hermeneutics," 354.

17. Luther, *Bondage of the Will*, 111.

of Scripture. Erasmus's view frightened people from reading Scripture for themselves.[18]

Luther went on to explain that there is a marked difference between the *text* of Scripture, which may be obscure, and its *subject matter*, which is fully knowable: "I certainly grant that many *passages* in the Scriptures are obscure and hard to elucidate, that is due, not to the exalted nature of their subject, but to our own linguistic and grammatical ignorance; and it does not in any way prevent our knowing all the *contents* of Scripture."[19] He said the content of Scripture is clear because of Jesus Christ, who has broken all seals, bringing all Scriptures to light in and through Himself.[20] As our resurrected Lord, Jesus opens our understanding of Scripture by means of His Spirit so that all things are written for our instruction (Rom. 15:4). Moreover, those difficulties of obscurity that remain due to linguistic and grammatical complexities are few in number. And they very seldom produce insurmountable problems because one can learn to interpret these texts correctly by using the principle of the analogy of faith (*analogia fidei*). "If words are obscure in one place, they are clear in another," Luther concluded. That means following "the lead and light of the clearer passages" in addressing issues being discussed in more obscure passages.[21] In short, Scripture is perspicuous because even though some portions of Scripture seem obscure to us, they can be rightly understood when other portions of Scripture shine their light upon them to remove their obscurity.[22]

Luther then argued for another kind of twofold perspicuity of Scripture. He said that, first, there is an external perspicuity that relates to Scripture as it is read, preached, proclaimed, and taught. When done rightly, this exposition will be clear because Scripture itself is clear. Scripture itself is thus the judge between conflicting positions on doctrinal and spiritual matters. Luther concluded: "It should be settled as fundamental, and most firmly fixed in the minds of Christians, that the Holy Scriptures are a spiritual light far brighter even than the sun, especially in what relates to salvation and all essential matters."[23]

Second, there is an internal perspicuity in the "knowledge of the heart," which, because of our innate darkness, demands the enlightening work of the Holy Spirit. Luther stated firmly: "If you speak of internal perspicuity, the

---

18. Luther, *Bondage of the Will*, 168.
19. Luther, *Bondage of the Will*, 71.
20. Luther, *Bondage of the Will*, 71.
21. Henri Blocher, "The 'Analogy of Faith' in the Study of Scripture," *The Scottish Bulletin of Evangelical Theology* 5 (1987): 20.
22. Allison, "The Protestant Doctrine of the Perspicuity of Scripture," 22–23.
23. Luther, *Bondage of the Will*, 125.

truth is that nobody who has not the Spirit of God sees a jot of what is in the Scriptures.... The Spirit is needed for the understanding of all Scripture and every part of Scripture."[24]

Most of the texts Luther selected to support his doctrine of perspicuity— Deuteronomy 17:8; Psalms 19:8 and 119:105, 130; Isaiah 8:20; Malachi 2:7; John 5:35, 39, 8:12, and 9:15; Acts 17:11, Romans 1:2 and 3:21; 2 Corinthians 3 and 4; Philippians 2:15–16; and 2 Peter 1:19—use the metaphor of light or speak of enlightenment. If these Scriptures do not support perspicuity, and the Scriptures are really obscure after all, Luther then concluded that such passages as Luke 21:15, 2 Timothy 3:16, and Titus 1:9 should be revoked. Resting his case, Luther asked Erasmus, "And why do you, Erasmus, draw up an outline of Christianity for us, if the Scriptures are obscure to you?"[25]

Finally, two things must be noted to balance Luther's views on perspicuity. First, Luther's strong views on perspicuity do not argue against the need for good scholarship or for the limitations of an interpreter's knowledge. Luther acknowledged that Christians had different levels of interpretive maturity and that the church benefited from specialists. As Silva notes, "Luther himself was a man of broad erudition and of fine philological skills," who felt that knowledge of the original languages of the Scriptures was essential for pastors and teachers. On one occasion, he and two helpers spent four days translating three lines in the book of Job.[26]

Second, Luther and other Reformers did not deny the church's traditional interpretation of Scripture when that tradition bowed to the authority of Scripture. As Jaroslav Pelikan writes, "Luther could not have been the exegete he was without the help of the church's tradition. The tradition gave him a footing on which he could and did move and shift, but which he never lost. But under this footing was the foundation of the Scriptures themselves, which he, as an expositor of the Scriptures and also as a son of the church was to receive gratefully."[27] Perhaps Silva puts it best: "The Reformers opposed the authority of tradition and of the church, but *only insofar as this authority usurped the*

---

24. Luther, *Bondage of the Will*, 73–74.

25. Luther, *Bondage of the Will*, 128; Allison, "The Protestant Doctrine of the Perspicuity of Scripture," 28–30.

26. Silva, "Clear or Obscure?," 66; A. Skevington Wood, *Luther's Principles of Biblical Interpretation* (London: Tyndale, 1960), 29.

27. Jaroslav Pelikan, *Luther the Expositor: Introduction to the Reformer's Exegetical Writings* (companion volume to *Luther's Works* [St. Louis: Concordia, 1959], 88).

authority of Scripture. They never rejected the value of the church's exegetical tradition when it was used in submission to the Scriptures."[28]

John Calvin

Unlike Luther, Calvin's view on perspicuity cannot be developed from a few sustained treatments of the subject. Nowhere does Calvin address the subject at length; yet, throughout his *Institutes,* commentaries, and sermons, a plethora of statements he made enable us to construct Calvin's views on perspicuity.[29]

Calvin argued for scriptural perspicuity on at least four grounds. First, Scripture itself affirms its perspicuity. Those who deny perspicuity are wicked and blasphemous, Calvin said, "because the mere doctrine of the word exposes and refutes their errors. We reply with David, 'Thy word, O Lord, is a lamp to our feet, and a light to our paths' (Ps. 119:105). We reply with Isaiah and the rest of the prophets, that the Lord has taught nothing that is obscure, or ambiguous, or false. We reply also with Peter, that 'the prophetic word is more sure, and you do well if you take heed to it, as to a lamp burning in a dark place, till the day dawn, and the morning-star arise in our hearts' (2 Peter 1:19)."[30]

Second, the clarity of Scripture is essential to make us feel our need for God and to lead us to Him. Natural revelation is insufficient for this because of our depravity and spiritual blindness. The Scriptures are our spectacles to make things clear for us. Calvin wrote, "Just as old or bleary-eyed men and those with weak vision, if you thrust before them a most beautiful volume, even if they recognize it to be some sort of writing, yet can scarcely construe two words, but with the aid of spectacles will begin to read distinctly; so Scripture, gathering up the otherwise confused knowledge of God in our minds, having dispersed our dullness, clearly shows us the true God."[31] Of what use would Scripture be to us if we found it unintelligible? Our need to know God as Creator, Provider, and Redeemer as well as Scripture's provision to meet that need emphasizes the perspicuity of Scripture.

Third, Scripture is clear to the believer because it illuminates truth for us. Like Luther, Calvin often used the metaphor of light to describe the clarity of Scripture. He wrote, "Whosoever, then, will open his eyes through the obedience of faith, shall by experience know that the Scripture has not been in vain

---

28. Silva, "Clear or Obscure?," 73.

29. Cf. Richard Gamble, "*Brevitas et Facilitas*: Toward an Understanding of Calvin's Hermeneutic," *Westminster Theological Journal* 47 (1985).

30. John Calvin, *Commentary on Isaiah* (Grand Rapids: Eerdmans, 1948), 420.

31. John Calvin, *Institutes of the Christian Religion*, ed. John T. McNeill, trans. Ford Lewis Battles (Philadelphia: Westminster Press, 1960), 1.6.1 (hereafter: *Inst.*).

called a light. It is indeed obscure to the unbelieving; but they who are given up to destruction are willfully blind. Execrable, therefore, is the blasphemy of the Papists, who pretend that the light of Scripture does nothing but dazzle the eyes, in order to keep the simple from reading it."[32]

Finally, Scripture is clear because God accommodates Himself to our level in it. God adapts His speech to the level of fallen man, the object of His revelation. "For who, even of slight intelligence," Calvin asked, "does not understand that, as nurses commonly do with infants, God is wont in a measure to 'lisp' in speaking to us?"[33] Quoting Augustine, Calvin compared God to a "mother stooping to her child...so as not to leave us behind in our weakness."[34] Since God speaks so clearly throughout Scripture and performs the ultimate act of accommodation in the incarnation and at the cross, how can Scripture not be perspicuous? Would that not contradict the very purpose of His special revelation?[35]

Because of God's accommodation to us in matters glorious and sublime, Scripture has a simple style and uses simple words. Though its "heavenly mysteries [are] above human capacity," Scripture presents its material in "lowly words" and in a "humble and lowly style," fit for the most simple and untrained people.[36]

From these grounds, Calvin concluded that Scripture is clear and everything outside of it tends to be obscure because of sin. God Himself warns us in Deuteronomy 29:29 not to investigate matters beyond the boundaries of Scripture, for the secret things belong to God, while the revealed belong to us and our children. Consequently, Calvin urged this "rule of modesty and sobriety: not to speak, or guess, or even to seek to know, concerning obscure matters anything except what has been imparted to us by God's Word."[37] This caution enabled Calvin to rein in his discussions of such profound mysteries as "Whence evil?" or causation in decretal election or God's immeasurable judgments. He warned us not to attempt to penetrate "the sacred precincts of divine wisdom" beyond what Scripture reveals.[38]

Calvin recognized that not all of Scripture is equally perspicuous. He affirmed that Old Testament revelation is more obscure than the New Testament, since God, all along, veiled the Old Testament Scriptures to prepare the

---

32. John Calvin, *Commentaries on the Catholic Epistles* (Grand Rapids: Eerdmans, 1948), 388–89.

33. Inst. 1.13.1.

34. Inst. 1.14.3.

35. Cf. T. H. L. Parker, *Calvin's New Testament Commentaries* (Grand Rapids: Eerdmans, 1971), 57–58; Ford Lewis Battles, "God was Accommodating Himself to Human Capacity," *Interpretation* 31 (1977):33.

36. Inst. 1.8.2, 11; 1.11.1; 3.10.1.

37. Inst. 1.14.4.

38. Inst. 3.21.1–2; cf. Allison, "The Protestant Doctrine of the Perspicuity of Scripture," 89–99.

Jews for the revelation of His Son in the New Testament age. Calvin wrote, "Now, the Lord allows nothing to be added or taken away from the ministry of Moses—obscure, so to speak, because of its very many wrappings—until he shall administer a clearer doctrine through his servants, the prophets, and at last through his beloved Son."[39] Thus, though the gospel was revealed under the old covenant, "the clarity of the gospel was obscured by those Jewish shadows,"[40] Calvin said. With the coming of Christ, these shadows dissipated, and the light of the gospel began to shine brightly and clearly.[41]

Second, in their ignorance, the apostles could not fully understand the teachings of Jesus until the Holy Spirit was poured out upon them at Pentecost. They had difficulty understanding why Christ had to suffer and why He would not usher in an earthly kingdom. Once illumined by the Spirit, however, they were led into a much clearer understanding of the Old Testament Scriptures, the gospel of atonement, and the spirituality of Christ's kingdom.[42]

Third, Calvin, like Luther, argued that Scripture is a closed and obscure book for unbelievers. Though sinners cannot use their failure to understand Scripture as an excuse for unbelief, since they are willfully blind,[43] yet "we cannot gainsay the fact that, to those whom he pleases not to illumine, God transmits his doctrine wrapped in enigmas in order that they may not profit by it except to be cast into greater stupidity."[44]

Fourth, Calvin went beyond Luther in admitting that certain passages are difficult even for believers. When preaching from 1 Timothy 3:8–10, Calvin said, "When we come to hear the sermon or to take up the Bible, we must not have the foolish arrogance of thinking that we shall easily understand everything we read or hear."[45] Such obscurity is because of our ignorance rather than the obscurity of Scripture, however. That is why apparently obscure passages do not always remain obscure. If believers search the Scriptures, patiently wait on God for more light, and are willing to obey Him, what is obscure may become clear in due time. Calvin said, "If we be not wearied with reading, it shall at length come to pass that the Scripture shall be made more familiar by continual use."[46]

---

39. Inst. 4.10.17.
40. Inst. 3.19.3.
41. Inst. 3.2.6; 4.8.7.
42. Inst. 4.8.9.
43. John Calvin, *Commentaries on the Catholic Epistles*, 388–89.
44. Inst. 3.24.13.
45. Cited by Klaas Runia, "The Hermeneutics of the Reformers," *Calvin Theological Journal* 19 (1984):152.
46. John Calvin, *Commentary on Acts* (Grand Rapids: Eerdmans, 1948), 1:354.

Finally, Calvin said that in a sense all Scripture is obscure—even to a believer—compared to how clear its meaning will become to us in the life to come. Commenting on 1 Corinthians 13:12, Calvin wrote, "The knowledge of God, which we now derive from His Word, is undoubtedly reliable and true, and there is nothing muddled, or unintelligible or dark about it; but when it is called 'obscure' (*aenigmaticam*) it is in a relative way, because it falls a long way short of that clear revelation to which we look forward when we shall see face to face." Nevertheless, Calvin said that neither 1 Corinthians 13:12 nor any other biblical text denies the perspicuity of Scripture itself: "So this verse is not in conflict in any way with others, which speak of the clarity, sometimes of the law, sometimes of the whole of Scripture, and most of all of the Gospel. For there is an open and naked revelation of God in the Word (enough to meet our needs), and there is nothing recondite (*involutum*) about it, as unbelievers imagine, to keep us in a state of uncertainty."[47]

In working out his interpretation of the clarity of Scripture, Calvin used several hermeneutical principles:

+ The interpreter must be a believer and must strive to grow in such qualities as humble wisdom, attentive listening, sound judgment, reverential piety, obedient teachableness, and mature perseverance.[48]

+ The interpreter must be theologically informed and Christologically oriented, for the more one understands doctrine, loves Christ, and searches the Scripture, the more clear Scripture, generally speaking, will become.[49]

+ The interpreter must seek to grasp the author's intent of the passage in terms of the literal rather than a fanciful allegorical meaning.[50]

+ The interpreter must engage in serious word studies, which includes a consideration of its various contexts, such as designated recipients, historical circumstances, and syntagmatic relationships.[51]

+ The interpreter must allow clearer passages of Scripture to illumine those that are less clear.[52]

---

47. John Calvin, *Commentary on the Epistles of Paul the Apostle to the Corinthians* (Grand Rapids: Eerdmans, 1948), 429–30; cf. Allison, "The Protestant Doctrine of the Perspicuity of Scripture," 99–109.

48. Inst. 2.8.50; 3.4.29, 37; 3.21.1; *Commentary on Acts*, 1:354, 360.

49. Allison, "The Protestant Doctrine of the Perspicuity of Scripture," 113–15.

50. John Calvin, *Commentary on the Epistle of Paul to the Romans* (Grand Rapids: Eerdmans, 1948), xxiii; *Commentary on the Epistles of Paul to the Galatians and Ephesians* (Grand Rapids: Eerdmans, 1948), 135–36; Inst. 2.5.19; 3.4.4–5.

51. Inst. 3.2.9; 4.16.31; 4.17.26.

52. Inst. 2.7.17; 3.16.3–4.

+ The interpreter should focus on showing the simple meaning of the text that naturally presses itself out of the text and, as much as possible, should avoid complex interpretations that "stretch the truth" of the text.[53]

+ The interpreter should lean on the teaching ministry of the church and should ask often for the divine inward guidance of the Holy Spirit, who enlightens the mind and applies Scripture to the heart.[54] Private interpretation must be balanced "by a recognition that no Christian is an island but is part of the body of Christ."[55]

Post-Reformers

Post-Reformers differed from the Reformers in their methodological approach to the perspicuity of Scripture, but in terms of content, they showed continuity. Protestant orthodoxy provided a meticulous argument for Scripture's clarity, due in part to its reaction to a revived Roman Catholicism (which stated in the decrees of Trent that "holy mother church...[is] judge of the true sense and interpretation of the holy Scriptures")[56] and to Socinianism, but, as Bob Godfrey and Richard Muller have shown, there was no change in "fundamental theological direction."[57] Like the Reformers, the post-Reformers "were fond of echoing Gregory's adage that Scripture is a river in which the lamb may ford and the elephant may swim."[58]

The major change in the post-Reformers' understanding of perspicuity was its issue with Luther's assertion that all Scripture is equally perspicuous by all. As James Callahan notes, "The Westminster Confession affirms that not only are 'all things in Scripture not alike plain in themselves' but neither are all things 'clear unto all.' Both Scripture and the reader are, in some sense, obscure or obscured. One should not stray too far into an either/or choice between whether Scripture is clear or the reader is obscured in her understanding. Such a dichotomy does not account for the complex relationship between reader and text."[59]

---

53. Inst. 3.2.3; 3.11.8

54. Inst. 4.1.5; 4.14.11; Allison, "The Protestant Doctrine of the Perspicuity of Scripture," 112–31.

55. Silva, "Clear or Obscure?," 63.

56. *Canons and Decrees of the Council of Trent* (fourth session, April 8, 1546); cf. Philip Schaff, *The Creeds of Christendom* (reprint Grand Rapids: Baker, 1983), 2:83.

57. W. Robert Godfrey, "Biblical Authority in the Sixteenth and Seventeenth Centuries: A Question of Transition," in *Scripture and Truth*, eds. Don A. Carson and John D. Woodbridge (Grand Rapids: Zondervan, 1983), 225; Muller, 2:324–40.

58. F. W. Farrar, *History of Interpretation* (Grand Rapids: Baker, 1961), 329.

59. James Callahan, "Perspicuity in Protestant Hermeneutics," 361.

The post-Reformers emphasized three things about the perspicuity of Scripture. First, all things necessary to salvation are clear in Scripture. For example, Abraham Calov (1612–1686), professor of theology at the universities of Koenigsberg and Wittenberg, wrote, "In those things which are necessary to be known for salvation, the Scriptures are abundantly and admirably explicit, both by the intention of God their author, and by the natural signification of the words, so that they need no external and adventitious light."[60]

Francis Turretin (1623–1687), renowned professor of theology in Geneva, enlarged that definition, saying, "The question then comes to this—whether the Scriptures are so plain in things essential to salvation (not as to the things delivered, but as to the mode of delivery; not as to the subject, but the object) that without the external aid of tradition or the infallible judgment of the church, they may be read and understood profitably by believers. The papists deny this; we affirm this."[61]

Second, many post-Reformers further stated that all elements of faith and fundamental doctrines are also clear in Scripture. Thus, John William Baier wrote:

> Those things which are necessary to be believed and done by man in seek-
> ing to be saved, are taught in Scripture in words and phrases so clear and
> conformed to the usage of speech, that any man acquainted with the lan-
> guage, possessed of a common judgment, and paying due attention to the
> words, may learn the true sense of the words, so far as those things are
> concerned which must be known, and may embrace these fundamental
> doctrines by the simple grasp of his mind; according as the mind of man
> is led, by the Scriptures themselves and their supernatural light, or the
> divine energy conjoined with them, to yield the assent of faith to the word
> understood and the things signified.[62]

Finally, some post-Reformers stressed the clarity of Scripture in teaching moral precepts. For example, Quenstedt wrote:

> The articles of faith and the moral precepts are taught in Scripture in their
> proper places, not in obscure and ambiguous words, but perspicuously
> in such as are fitted to them, and free from all ambiguity, so that every

---

60. Abraham Calov, *Systema Locorum Theologicorum* (Wittenberg, 1653), 1:467.

61. Francis Turretin, *Institutes of Elenctic Theology*, ed. James T. Dennison Jr., trans. George M. Giger (Phillipsburg: P&R, 1992), 1:144.

62. John William Baier, *Compendium Theologiae Positivae*, 178, cited in Heinrich Schmid, *Doctrinal Theology of the Evangelical Lutheran Church*, trans. Charles Hay and Henry Jacobs (Minneapolis: Augsburg, 1899), 70.

diligent reader of Scripture, who reads it devoutly and piously can understand them.[63]

Quenstedt hastened to add, however, that even those genres of Scripture that are most difficult to understand—such as the allegorical, typological, and prophetic passages—seldom constitute major problems if the believing interpreter uses the analogy of faith as a basic hermeneutic.[64]

Like Luther and Calvin, the post-Reformers offered many texts to support their view of perspicuity—many of them identical to those already mentioned. Like the Reformers, they emphasized that perspicuity applies to the Spirit-illumined believer, not to the unbeliever, whose understanding remains obscure, though the unbeliever can grasp some sense of what Scripture is saying. Francis Turretin said, "We do not deny that the Scriptures are obscure to unbelievers and the unrenewed, to whom Paul says his gospel is hid (2 Cor. 4:3). Also we hold that the Spirit of illumination is necessary to make them intelligible to believers."[65]

New emphases by the post-Reformers regarding scriptural clarity have emerged, however. For example, Calov emphasized Christ, arguing that Scripture could not be obscure or ambiguous since it is the fruit of "the Light of the world," and, in particular, of Christ's prophetic office. If Christ's reasoning with the Jews was so clear that He convinced them of the truth, how could His own inspired Word be obscure? Calov went on to stress the clarity of Christ's preaching in Matthew 22:16, John 3:2, and John 7:46.[66] The post-Reformers put more stress than the Reformers on the diligent study of the Bible and continual teaching and writing by theologians and the church. Perspicuity should never promote laxity in studying the Word.[67]

In addition, post-Reformers argued for perspicuity, stating: (1) Scripture itself attests that it is written for all people, which means it must be clear to them (1 Cor. 1:2; Phil. 1:1; Col. 4:16; 1 Thess. 1:4); (2) since Scripture is inspired by God, who reveals Himself in it to man, a lack of clarity would indicate that God missed His purpose for Scripture, the very thought of which is blasphemous; and (3) literary considerations support perspicuity. As Turretin noted: "The perspicuity of Scripture is further proved...by the matter (viz., the law

---

63. Schmid, *Doctrinal Theology*, 71.

64. Schmid, *Doctrinal Theology*, 72.

65. Turretin, *Elenctic Theology*, 1:143. Turretin goes on to say that even the unbeliever can understand some of the Bible's teaching.

66. Cf. Robert Preus, *The Inspiration of Scripture: A Study of the Theology of the Seventeenth Century Lutheran Dogmaticians* (Mankato: Minn.: Lutheran Synod Book Co., 1955), 162–63.

67. Cf. Turretin, *Elenctic Theology*, 1:144, 149; Schmid, *Doctrinal Theology*, 72–74.

and the gospel, which anyone can easily apprehend); [and] the form (because they are to us in place of a testament, contract of a covenant or edict of a king, which ought to be perspicuous and not obscure)."[68]

Finally, the post-Reformers wrestled with why God allowed any obscurity in interpreting the Scriptures. They concurred that if it does occur, it is because God wills it for our profit. Turretin suggested that God allows obscurity "to excite the study of believers and increase their diligence, to humble the pride of man, and to remove from them the contempt which might arise from too great plainness."[69]

Quenstedt said God allowed some obscurity in His Word "to remind us of our congenital blindness, to encourage us to approach Scripture with reverence and with prayer for growth in sanctification, and to stimulate us to more zealously strive for a deeper knowledge of Scripture."[70] This relative obscurity of Scripture, however, should not dampen our hopes in this life but should make us hanker more for eternal glory when we shall grasp more than we presently do.[71]

Scriptural and Theological Conclusions

From a scriptural context, the following conclusions can be drawn about the perspicuity of Scripture:

+ Although some portions of Scripture are more difficult to grasp than others, all Scripture is understandable in and of itself. Luther's assertion of this is supported by several texts in Scripture, most notably Deuteronomy 29:29 ("the revealed things belong to us and to our children"), which make clear that whatever God has revealed to His people is intelligible, understandable, and accessible. In revelation, God makes Himself knowable. That is true of divine revelation in general and of special revelation in particular. God reveals Himself in all parts of Scripture; therefore, all parts of Scripture are inherently perspicuous. That is true even of those portions of Paul's epistles that Peter says are difficult to understand (2 Peter 3:14–16), for Peter does not say that they are *impossible* to understand. Perspicuity does not mean that every part of Scripture is easily understandable, but it does mean that every part—even the difficult—is inherently intelligible to the believer. By claiming clarity for all Scripture, we do not mean that the believer is always certain of his interpretation of

---

68. Turretin, *Elenctic Theology*, 1:145.

69. Turretin, *Elenctic Theology*, 1:143.

70. Allison, "The Protestant Doctrine of the Perspicuity of Scripture," 154; cf. Preus, *The Inspiration of Scripture*, 163.

71. Turretin, *Elenctic Theology*, 1:146; Allison, "The Protestant Doctrine of the Perspicuity of Scripture," 132–56.

every text, for our hermeneutics and exegesis and knowledge will always contain blind spots and errors due to our human fallibility, but that the language and matters of Scripture are, in themselves, intelligible.

• Scripture can be understood by all believers, regardless of their educational and cultural background. Just as the covenant in Deuteronomy had to be understood and absorbed by believing parents, then communicated to their children in understandable terms (Deut. 6:4–9), so the New Testament leads believers to understanding by letting the Word of Christ dwell richly in us and spreading it abroad (Col. 3:16). Paul's command in 1 Timothy 4:13 to read Scripture publicly in the congregation presupposes the intelligibility of the Word for the church of God. The New Testament epistles are addressed to the entire church—not just to pastors and elders and mature saints—and are thus meant to be read to the entire church. Even "newborn babes" can grasp the Word, Peter says (1 Peter 1:22–2:3). Scripture is a lamp to all believers (2 Peter 1:19), from the smallest child in grace to the most mature saint, though the mature will understand it more fully. The babes, young men, and fathers in grace will comprehend Scripture according to how they are led by the Spirit (1 John 2:12–14; cf. Romans 8).

As a general rule, male and female, young and old, educated and uneducated, rich and poor, Jew and Gentile, enslaved and free, may understand Scripture. Traits that normally divide people dissipate among believers when it comes to comprehending Scripture. The only exception would be, of course, people who lack the ability to understand what is read or heard, such as babies or the mentally impaired. Such conditions are particularly highlighted in Nehemiah; "all who were able to understand" (Neh. 8:2) could participate in the reading of God's Law in the congregational assembly.

• Perspicuity is affirmed in the context of the believing church and calls for a response. First Corinthians 2:6–3:3 traces the role of the Spirit from His knowledge of the deep things of God through His revelation of the appropriate matters to His work in fostering the communication of that divine wisdom to the believers. Second Corinthians 3:12–4:6 says that the meaning of Scripture is grasped by individual believers only in dependency on the Holy Spirit. Isaiah 8:19–22 says we must be obedient to the law and testimony of God's Word. We must not only know and understand Scripture, we must also obey what it says. John 5:31–47 reveals the tragic results of failing to obey the Word.[72] We must read Scripture to know God's will and be willing to follow it.

---

72. Allison, "The Protestant Doctrine of the Perspicuity of Scripture," 514–34.

Practical Conclusions

I leave you with four practical conclusions. First, we need to reemphasize the classic Protestant doctrine of perspicuity. Our current lack of concern about this doctrine compared to the concern shown by the Reformers and post-Reformers begs the question: Do we still believe in the clarity of Scripture for all believers?

Second, the perspicuity of Scripture ought to move us to encourage ourselves and all believers to study the Word—individually, in small groups, and in the church—invoking the Holy Spirit with confident and hopeful expectation, knowing that He will help us understand what we are studying. We should also make good use of other members of the community of faith, including biblical scholars and commentators, pastors, teachers, and seasoned saints. And we should teach others to trust, embrace, and obey what we learn from the Scriptures.

Third, the doctrine of perspicuity should remind preachers and teachers how awesome our task is. We are called to teach Scripture clearly, to explore new areas of understanding, to defend the Scriptures against errors and heresies, and to relate the teachings of Scripture to every branch of theology.[73] We need to encourage the laity to understand the value of reading, studying, and growing in the Scriptures. How critical it is that we help people study the Scriptures while avoiding any suggestion that we alone can understand and interpret God's Word. We need to steer people between Roman Catholicism's dependence on hierarchical interpretation and modern evangelicalism's radical strong sense of individualism, which often rejects confessionalism and often does not appreciate submitting one's "understanding of Scripture to the judgment of the established church."[74]

Finally, the doctrine of perspicuity encourages us to grow together as a body of believers in understanding the Scriptures. We should not be discouraged by Scripture's more difficult portions but, rather, be encouraged to dig more deeply in the Word, as Richard Greenham says, like digging for hid treasure, being confident that our labor is not in vain and that studying God's Word together may strengthen the bonds of unity and communion among believers.[75] In cases of disagreement, we need to openly and prayerfully examine whether "we are seeking to make affirmations where Scripture itself is silent" or whether "we

---

73. Grudem, *Systematic Theology*, 110–11.

74. Silva, "Clear or Obscure?," 63–64.

75. Richard Greenham, "A Profitable Treatise Containing a Direction for the Reading and Understanding of the Holy Scriptures," in *Works* (London: Felix Kingston, 1599), 390–91; Allison, "The Protestant Doctrine of the Perspicuity of Scripture," 571–73.

have made mistakes in our interpretation of Scripture" through "some personal inadequacy on our part, whether it be, for example, personal pride, or greed, or lack of faith, or selfishness, or even failure to devote enough time to prayerfully reading and studying Scripture."[76]

In every case, we should pray that we will cultivate the kind of respect, love, and obedience to the Scriptures that the psalmist shows in Psalm 119 so that we might hide God's Word in our heart (v. 11), find it sweet in its gift of understanding and light (vv. 103–105), and make haste to obey all its commandments (v. 32).

---

76. Grudem, *Systematic Theology*, 109.

Chapter 13

Laurence Chaderton:
His Life and Ecclesiology

Laurence Chaderton (*c.* 1536–1640) was the spiritual patriarch of the Puritan movement that emanated from Cambridge University and ushered in renewal to the church in Britain, the Continent, and the New World. Combining rigorous academic discipline, a fifty-plus-year career in teaching and educational administration, warm spirituality, and endearing love, Chaderton influenced a rising generation of both ministers and magistrates. Yet he remains a largely unknown figure, standing in the backdrop of the very leaders he mentored. While his published works are few,[1] some very significant unpublished notes remain[2] as well as a small but meaty body of secondary literature on his life.[3]

---

1. Laurence Chaderton, *An Excellent and Godly Sermon…Preached at Paul's Cross the XXVI Daye of October, An. 1578* (London: Christopher Barker, [1578]); *A Fruitfull Sermon, Vpon the 3. 4. 5. 6. 7. & 8. verses of the 12. Chapiter of the Epistle of S. Paul to the Romanes* (London: Robert Walde-graue, 1584); *De justificatione coram Deo et fidei perseverantia non intercisa,* published in a bundle of treatises by Matthew Hutton, George Estey, Robert Some, and others, edited by Anthony Thysius under the title *Brevis et dilucida explicatio…de electione, praedestinatione ac reprobatione* (Hardrovici [Harderwijk], 1613). The authorship of the anonymous *Fruitfull Sermon* will be discussed below. Many thanks to Paul Smalley for his research assistance on this article; a shorter version of it is published as "Laurence Chaderton: An Early Puritan Vision for Church and School," in *Church and School in Early Modern Protestantism: Studies in Honor of Richard A. Muller on the Maturation of a Theological Tradition,* ed. Jordan J. Ballor, David S. Sytsma, and Jason Zuidema (Leiden: Brill, 2013), 321–37.

2. For example, there are Chaderton's papers in Pembroke College Library, Cambridge, MSS LC. II. 2. 164, and Lambeth Palace Library, MS 2550. There are also his handwritten marginal notes in a number of extant books.

3. William Dillingham, *Vita Laurentii Chadertoni…Una Cum Vita Jacobi Usserii* (London, 1700); translated into English in William Dillingham, *Laurence Chaderton (First Master of Emmanuel),* trans. and ed. E. S. Shuckburgh (Cambridge: Macmillan and Bowes, 1884); John G. Mager, "The Life of Laurence Chaderton, Puritan, 1536–1640" (MA Thesis, Washington University, 1949); H. C. Porter, *Reformation and Reaction in Tudor Cambridge* (Cambridge: Cambridge University Press, 1958), 235–42; Everett H. Emerson, *English Puritanism from John Hooper to John Milton* (Durham, N.C.: Duke University Press, 1968), 102–108; Patrick Collinson, *The Religion of Protestants: The Church in English Society 1559–1625* (Oxford: Clarendon Press, 1982), 151–52; Rebecca S. Rolph, "Emmanuel College, Cambridge, and the Puritan Movements of Old and New England" (PhD diss., University of Southern California, 1979), 23–31, 42–140; Peter Lake, *Moderate Puritans and the Elizabethan Church*

This chapter will first summarize Chaderton's life; second, examine Chaderton's work at Cambridge; and third, explore his view of church offices as expressed in his *Fruitfull Sermon* on Romans 12:3–8 (1584).

The Life of Laurence Chaderton

Laurence Chaderton was probably born in 1536, in Oldham, near Manchester. His father was of an ancient and honored lineage with considerable wealth[4] and was devoted to the pre-Reformation faith. It was only in 1534 that the Act of Supremacy declared the English monarch to be the church's head instead of the pope. During Chaderton's childhood, he saw both Edward VI reign briefly as a reforming king and Queen Mary drive many Protestants into exile.

Initially a poor student more interested in hunting and hawking, Laurence's interest in reading revived under a skillful tutor. He entered Christ's College in 1562, four years after Elizabeth was crowned Queen. He engaged in archery and wrestled against Richard Bancroft (1544–1610), saving him from harm during a violent "town and gown" brawl, which won him a valuable ally for later days when Bancroft became archbishop of Canterbury.

Chaderton also came into the sphere of influence of the developing Puritan movement. In the 1560s, men such as Thomas Cartwright and Edward Dering taught in Cambridge, while studying alongside Chaderton were future Puritan pastors like Richard Greenham, Richard Rogers, and Walter Travers. Queen Elizabeth was consolidating her hold on the church by insisting on uniformity of practice among the clergy, enforced by Matthew Parker, archbishop of Canterbury.[5]

Chaderton was thrust into this bubbling pot of controversy as a young undergraduate. Through study and struggle of soul, Chaderton became convinced of the Reformed faith. His father, dismayed by the change, sought to move him from the university to the Inns of Court to study law, with a promise of thirty pounds a year. When he declined the offer, he was sent a shilling, a

---

(Cambridge: Cambridge University Press, 1982), 25–54, 116–68, 243–61; Arnold Hunt, "Laurence Chaderton and the Hampton Court Conference," in *Belief and Practice in Reformation England: A Tribute to Patrick Collinson from His Students*, ed. Susan Wabuda and Caroline Litzenberger (Aldershot, UK: Ashgate, 1998), 207–228; Sarah Bendall, Christopher Brooke, and Patrick Collinson, *A History of Emmanuel College, Cambridge* (Woodbridge, Eng.: Boydell Press, 1999), 30–42, 177–86. Rolph, Lake, and Hunt are especially valuable for quotations of Chaderton's unpublished notes.

4. Various sources identify his father as Thomas Chaderton or Edmund Chaderton. For "Thomas" see Dillingham, *Laurence Chaderton*, 28; Emerson, *English Puritanism*, 102. For "Edmund" see F. R. Raines in Dillingham, *Laurence Chaderton*, 31; Bendall, Brooke, and Collinson, *A History of Emmanuel College*, 31.

5. Emerson, *English Puritanism*, 8–15.

wallet, and the advice to beg for a living.[6] But Chaderton persevered in his newfound faith, graduating with a BA in 1567, becoming a fellow of the college the next year, and graduating with an MA in 1571. He served as lecturer (or preacher) at St. Clement's Church, Cambridge, for fifty years, preaching the Bible with zeal for conversion and personal piety.[7] Gabriel Harvey summed up Chaderton's preaching with the word "methodical"—a very Puritan term.[8]

Chaderton married Cecelia Culverwell in 1576 after establishing himself financially.[9] The story is told that the minister accidentally used the name of the bride's sister in the ceremony, to which Chaderton exclaimed, "No, no; it is Cecelia I want!"[10] His wife was "a very pious, modest, and sensible woman, with whom he lived in the closest affection for about fifty years."[11] She died in 1631. They had one child, Elizabeth, who married Abraham Johnson.[12]

Collinson says that Chaderton became "the pope of Cambridge puritanism."[13] Rebecca Rolph writes, "His great influence resulted from his erudition, character, high ideals, political tact, teaching ability, and probably not least, his remarkable longevity."[14] In the 1570s and 1580s, Chaderton busied himself at Christ's College in various posts. In 1578, he completed his BD degree. In 1581, he engaged in a controversy with Peter Baro (1534–1599), a French professor of theology at Cambridge, over the nature of justifying faith.[15]

Sir Walter Mildmay (d. 1589), the Chancellor of the Exchequer and Privy Councilor under Queen Elizabeth, was zealously seeking a way to raise up Reformed preachers of the gospel. He drafted Chaderton in 1584 to be the first master of Emmanuel College.[16] When Chaderton had an offer for a position with ten times the financial remuneration, Mildmay told him that if he would not be the master, there would be no college; Chaderton took the plunge.

---

6. Dillingham, *Laurence Chaderton*, 4.

7. Dillingham, *Laurence Chaderton*, 12–13.

8. G. Gregory Smith, ed., *Elizabethan Critical Essays* (Oxford: Oxford University Press, 1904), 2:281.

9. Dillingham, *Laurence Chaderton*, 35.

10. Dillingham, *Laurence Chaderton*, 9.

11. Dillingham, *Laurence Chaderton*, 8.

12. On Chaderton's Culverwell relations, see Porter, *Reformation and Reaction*, 231–35.

13. Patrick Collinson, *The Elizabethan Puritan Movement* (Berkeley: University of California Press, 1967), 125.

14. Rolph, "Emmanuel College," 42.

15. Dillingham, *Laurence Chaderton*, 6.

16. "Sir Walter Mildmay's deed of foundation was dated May 25th 1584, his statutes for the college, October 1st 1585.... By December 1587, it was possible to clear away the builders' rubble and to hold a ceremony of dedication" (Bendall, Brooke, and Collinson, *A History of Emmanuel College*, 42).

When John Whitgift (*c.* 1530–1604) became archbishop of Canterbury in 1583, he led a systematic suppression of nonconformity in the church, including attempts to reform the church along the lines of Presbyterianism.[17] It was in this context that the anonymous *Fruitfull Sermon* (1584) was published. Chaderton was "an active Presbyterian" who helped organize an elder-based discipline in the 1580s and tended to avoid wearing the surplice and kneeling at Communion.[18] As Peter Lake has written, Puritan concerns about church order were driven by the "intensely evangelical impulse" of shaping the church for the sake of "edification."[19] The classis movement fell apart in the 1590s through the pressure of Archbishop Whitgift and the offensiveness of the Marprelate tracts (1588–1589) against the bishops.[20]

In 1595–1596, Cambridge was engulfed in a controversy over the sovereignty of divine grace. William Barrett publicly opposed the Reformed doctrines of predestination, assurance, and perseverance of the saints; under fire, he left Cambridge and converted to Roman Catholicism.[21] The Lambeth Articles (1595), which Chaderton signed along with seven other college heads, sought to safeguard the Reformed orthodoxy of Cambridge.[22] Though never incorporated into the Anglican Articles of Religion, the Lambeth Articles did influence the Irish Articles of Religion (1615), which in turn were a major source for the Westminster Confession of Faith (1647). Baro became embroiled in this controversy, which forced him to leave Cambridge.

After Elizabeth died and James ascended to the throne, Chaderton attended the Hampton Court Conference (January 1604) as one of four representatives of Puritan concerns about the doctrine and liturgy of the church.[23] The king

---

17. Emerson, *Early Puritanism*, 22–24.

18. Emerson, *English Puritanism*, 103. See Lake, *Moderate Puritans*, 46; Bendall, Brooke, and Collinson, *A History of Emmanuel College*, 179.

19. Lake, *Moderate Puritans*, 2–3.

20. Emerson, *English Puritanism*, 25–26. See Queen Elizabeth I, *A Proclamation against Certain Seditious and Schismatical Bookes and Libels* (London: Christopher Barker, 1588 [1589]).

21. Bendall, Brooke, and Collinson, *A History of Emmanuel College*, 40–41; Rolph, "Emmanuel College," 102.

22. Rolph, "Emmanuel College," 100.

23. On the Hampton Court Conference and its context, see Roland G. Usher, *Reconstruction of the English Church* (New York: D. Appleton, 1910), 1:285–333; 2:331–65. M. H. Curtis, "Hampton Court Conference and Its Aftermath," *History* 46 (1961): 1–16; Stuart B. Babbage, *Puritanism and Richard Bancroft* (London: SPCK, 1962), 43–73; Frederick Shriver, "Hampton Court Re-visited: James I and the Puritans," *Journal of Ecclesiastical History* 33, no. 1 (Jan. 1982):48–71; Patrick Collinson, "The Jacobean Religious Settlement: The Hampton Court Conference," in *Before the English Civil War: Essays on Early Stuart Politics and Government*, ed. Howard Tomlinson (New York: St. Martin's Press, 1983), 27–51; K. C. Fincham, "Ramifications of the Hampton Court Conference in the Dioceses, 1603–1609," *Journal of Ecclesiastical History* 36, no. 2 (Apr. 1985): 208–27; Peter White, *Predestination*,

called the conference in response to the Millenary Petition for reformation in the church's ministry, discipline, and prayer book. The classic (but biased) record of the Hampton Court Conference is William Barlow's *The Sum and Substance of the Conference*.[24] Barlow reports that Chaderton requested of the king not to compel godly ministers to use the surplice and the sign of the cross in baptism; the king is said to have replied that "men quiet of disposition, honest of life, and diligent in their callings" could request exemptions from the bishop, but men "of a turbulent and opposite spirit" would be forced to conform.[25] However, Chaderton was rebuked for the practice of "sitting communions in Emmanuel College" (instead of kneeling to receive the Lord's Supper).[26]

After the Hampton Court Conference, the Puritan cause suffered. By November 1604, Richard Bancroft had replaced Whitgift as archbishop of Canterbury. He was zealous and severe in demanding strict conformity. Chaderton's friendship with Bancroft, having once saved the Archbishop's skin in their undergraduate days, shielded him from some of the political liabilities of his own Puritanism. Chaderton himself did not wear the surplice until ten months after the Hampton Court Conference, when the king gave an order to "remove him if he continue[d] obstinate."[27]

In the midst of the negative fallout for the Puritans, the Hampton Court Conference did implement one of their requests: the production of a new revision of the Bishops Bible, based upon the Hebrew and Greek texts with comparison being made to the Tyndale, Matthew, Coverdale, Great, and Geneva Bibles. In 1611, this translation was published and became known as the Authorized Version or the King James Version. Chaderton, a good Hebrew scholar, was one of seven men who worked on the section from Chronicles to Song of Solomon.[28] All the men on the team would work independently on a text and then meet together to choose the best translation.[29] Chaderton's

---

Policy, and Polemic: Conflict and Consensus in the English Church from the Reformation to the Civil War (Cambridge: Cambridge University Press, 1992), 140–52; Hunt, "Laurence Chaderton and the Hampton Court Conference," 207–28.

24. William Barlow, *The Svmme and Svbstance of the Conference, which, it pleased his Excellent Maiestie to have with the Lords, Bishops, and other of his Clergie…at Hampton Court, Ianuary 14, 1603* (London: by Iohn Windet, for Mathew Law, 1604).

25. Barlow, *Svmme and Svbstance*, 99–100, sig. O2r–v.

26. Barlow, *Svmme and Svbstance*, 102–103, sig. O3v–O4r.

27. Hunt, "Laurence Chaderton and the Hampton Court Conference," 219.

28. Gordon Campbell, *Bible: The Story of the King James Version* (Oxford: Oxford University Press, 2010), 35, 39, 49–50.

29. Rolph, "Emmanuel College," 125.

handwritten notes were still visible years later in a Hebrew Bible with Rabbinic commentaries published by Daniel Bomberg.[30]

In 1613, Prince Charles came to the school with Frederick, Prince Elector Palatine,[31] and virtually forced the venerable professor to accept the honor of Doctor of Divinity. It is said they almost had to break down the door of his library to get Chaderton to come out.[32] Around 1618, he let go of his lectureship at St. Clement's Church, being about eighty-two years old and having preached there for almost fifty years. Forty ministers signed a letter pleading with him not to resign, attesting to God's saving blessing upon his preaching. Dillingham said that his preaching was marked by "diligence" and "consistency"; he preached on nearly the entire New Testament.[33] Sadly, his sermons were not preserved for future generations.

Chaderton resigned his mastership of Emmanuel College on October 26, 1622, exhorting the fellows to mutual peace, humility, and dependence on the grace of God.[34] The resignation was skillfully managed so as to guarantee passing the baton to John Preston and thus continue the Puritan succession. He gave himself to a quiet, disciplined life of private study in Cambridge. In his old age, he could still read his Greek New Testament in small print without glasses, and "in his Hebrew Bible the smallest point did not escape his sight."[35]

Chaderton lived to see three grandsons and one step-grandson graduate with an MA from Emmanuel College.[36] He died on November 13, 1640, over one hundred years old; thus Everett Emerson dubs him "the Puritan Methuselah."[37] His moderate Puritan stance led him to teach Reformed and Presbyterian doctrine, though not to openly resist the powers that be but, instead, as he wrote, "to pray for the change."[38]

Chaderton's Work at Cambridge
The Church of England faced a dire lack of ministerial competence in the latter half of the sixteenth century. In 1551, John Hooper examined 311 clergy

---

30. Dillingham, *Laurence Chaderton*, 5.

31. Dillingham, *Laurence Chaderton*, 11. From late 1612 to early 1613, Frederick V (1596–1632) visited England to marry Elizabeth, daughter of King James I.

32. Dillingham, *Laurence Chaderton*, 11.

33. Dillingham, *Laurence Chaderton*, 12.

34. Thomas Ball claimed that the fellows and others pressured Chaderton to resign, but Dillingham rejected that as "invention or imagination." See Thomas Ball, *The Life of the Renowned Doctor Preston*, ed. E. W. Harcourt (Oxford: Parker, 1885), 79–86; Dillingham, *Laurence Chaderton*, 15–16.

35. Dillingham, *Laurence Chaderton*, 22.

36. Porter, *Reformation and Reaction*, 235.

37. Emerson, *English Puritanism*, 102.

38. Hunt, "Laurence Chaderton and the Hampton Court Conference," 218.

and found that 168 could not repeat the Ten Commandments and 31 did not know the author of the Lord's Prayer.[39] Edward Dering remarked decades later that "scarce one parish of an hundred" had a godly minister capable of rightly fulfilling his office.[40] Chaderton inherited Dering's concerns and gave his life to raising up gospel preachers. Lake wrote, "In many ways he can be regarded as Dering's successor."[41]

Chaderton lamented that the church suffered everywhere from "swarms of idle, ignorant, and ungodly curates and readers, who neither can, nor will, go before the dear flock of Christ in soundness of doctrine, and integrity of life."[42] To meet this need, he trained great Puritan leaders at Christ's College such as Arthur Dent, William Perkins, and Arthur Hildersham. He also promoted the Ramist method for theology and preaching, which influenced Perkins and his student, William Ames, whose *Marrow of Theology* exemplifies Ramist analysis.[43]

Chaderton believed that the preaching of the Bible was a special means of grace blessed by God, even more useful than the printed page. He wrote that the reading of a sermon is not half as profitable as hearing it preached, for written material lacks "the zeal of the speaker, the attention of the hearer,…[and] the mighty and inward working of his Holy Spirit," which God promises to the preaching of the Word.[44] Therefore the greatest work of the college was the training of ministers, which is precisely what the statutes of Emmanuel College said.[45]

The breadth of Chaderton's influence is illustrated by the students under his mastership. In its first two decades of operation (1584–1604), Emmanuel College trained 832 men. In 1621, a year before Chaderton's retirement, the college had 260 members. That is not to say that all these men became ministers; in fact, only a third entered ordained ministry, and a substantial number

---

39. *Later Writings of Bishop Hooper*, ed. Charles Nevinson (Cambridge: Parker Society, 1852), 130, 151.

40. Edward Dering, epistle to the reader of *A Briefe and Necessarie Catechisme or Instruction*, in *Workes, More Large than Ever* (London: I. R. for Paule Linley, and Iohn Flasket, 1597), sig. A3v.

41. Lake, *Moderate Puritans*, 25. On Edward Dering see Patrick Collinson, "A Mirror of Elizabethan Puritanism: The Life and Letters of 'Godly Master Dering,'" in *Godly People: Essays on English Protestantism and Puritanism* (London: Hambledon Press, 1983), 288–323.

42. Chaderton, *Excellent and Godly Sermon*, C3r. See Mal. 2:7.

43. Wilbur S. Howell, *Logic and Rhetoric in England, 1500–1700* (New York: Russell & Russel, 1961), 179, 206–7, 222, 210.

44. Laurence Chaderton, "To the Christian Reader," in *An Excellent and Godly Sermon*, A3v.

45. Statute 21, in *The Statutes of Sir Walter Mildmay Kt Chancellor of the Exchequer and One of Her Majesty's Privy Councillors; Authorized by Him for the Government of Emmanuel College*, trans. and intro. Frank Stubbings (Cambridge: Cambridge University Press, 1983), 60.

became lawyers and magistrates. The college was thus a culture-shaping force in producing and positioning Puritan leaders in callings sacred and secular.[46]

Emmanuel's influence reached across the Atlantic. Of the approximately one hundred Cambridge men who immigrated to New England from 1629 to 1640, thirty-three were of Emmanuel College, including Thomas Hooker, John Cotton, Isaac Johnson, Nathaniel Ward, John Ward, Nathaniel Rogers, Samuel Stone, Thomas Shepard, Richard Saltonstall, Simon Bradstreet (husband of the poet Anne), and John Harvard, namesake of Harvard College.[47] Thus it was that this oak scattered acorns of gospel ministry across England and the New World.

Training a minister of the gospel was no small task. Chaderton felt that every minister must be able "to teach sound doctrine by the true interpretation of the word and to confute all contrary errors by unanswerable arguments and reasons."[48] For a minister to be competent in this high calling, he must be well qualified in Hebrew and Greek, rhetoric, logic, the whole Bible to compare Scripture with Scripture, scholarly commentaries, ancient church councils, and secular history.[49] They must hold disputations on "all the principal questions in controversy between us and the papists and other heretics."[50] Such requirements highlight what Lake calls "the central role to be played by the university in the propagation of true religion."[51]

Chaderton not only connected young men with godly tutors at Cambridge but also used his network of friendships in the Puritan brotherhood to find pulpits for graduates and (as much as in his power) defend them from anti-Puritan authorities.[52] Furthermore, he organized "prophesyings" where ministers would gather, several would preach, and then all would discuss the doctrine and its manner of application so as to sharpen each other's preaching skills.[53] He himself had participated in a study group with John Carter, Lancelot Andrewes, Ezekiel Culverwell, John Knewstub, and others, where after prayer one man would comment on the Greek or Hebrew terms, another on the grammar, another the logic, another the sense and meaning, and another the doctrine

---

46. Bendall, Brooke, and Collinson, *A History of Emmanuel College*, 45, 47–48.

47. Porter, *Reformation and Reaction*, 241–42.

48. Lake, *Moderate Puritans*, 36.

49. Lake, *Moderate Puritans*, 36–37.

50. Lake, *Moderate Puritans*, 37.

51. Lake, *Moderate Puritans*, 38.

52. Lake, *Moderate Puritans*, 39–40.

53. Lake, *Moderate Puritans*, 43; Collinson, *The Elizabethan Puritan Movement*, 126–27. See also Paul S. Seaver, *The Puritan Lectureships: The Politics of Religious Dissent, 1560–1662* (Stanford: Stanford University Press, 1970).

of a Scripture text.[54] Chaderton brought this practice of conference into the academy for the training of new preachers and theologians.[55]

Yet religion was not simply a matter of knowledge, skill, and organization. Chaderton said that faith is "not the bare naked knowledge" of God's revealed truth but "a sure and certain persuasion of the heart grounded upon the promises of God and wrought in me by the Holy Ghost whereby I am persuaded that whatsoever Christ hath done for man's salvation he hath done it not only for others but also for me."[56] This is nearly an exact quotation of the Heidelberg Catechism (Q. 21), showing the linkage between the Puritans and the continental Reformed.[57]

The ministry is a spiritual work—not merely a form of education but a means of supernatural experience that Chaderton said changes "our affections" by "the power of the Spirit whereby all the faculties of his mind are moved."[58] The college statutes indicated that fellows should select preachers for churches based on who was "best endowed with those gifts which the Holy Spirit bestows upon the true pastor."[59] Chaderton said, "They shall hear his [Christ's] voice by his ministers.... Therefore he will send his ministers to gather and call his sheep." Preaching is nothing less than "the voice of Christ" by which "we shall be brought to Christ."[60]

Yet Chaderton did not place the power of salvation in the hands (or voice) of the minister. He made a distinction between "the calling of the minister of God" and "of God himself": "The second calling is the voice of God himself which is applied to the inward ear of the inward man." This is the office of "God himself and of his Spirit"[61]; salvation belongs to the electing God. Lake writes that Chaderton held the "orthodox" position on predestination unto salvation by grace alone.[62] Chaderton said that while men have wills, "yet the changing of our will, and making it unto good...do proceed only from the Spirit of

---

54. Samuel Clarke, "The Life and Death of Master John Carter," in *The Lives of Thirty-two English Divines Famous in Their Generations for Learning and Piety* (London: William Birch, 1677), 133.

55. Bendall, Brooke, and Collinson, *A History of Emmanuel College*, 50–51.

56. Chaderton, lectures on John, cited in Lake, *Moderate Puritans*, 127.

57. Chaderton's Presbyterian contemporaries Thomas Cartwright, Samuel Culverwell, and Robert Wright were students in Heidelberg in the early 1570s (Bendall, Brooke, and Collinson, *A History of Emmanuel College*, 35).

58. Chaderton, lectures on John, cited in Lake, *Moderate Puritans*, 128.

59. Statute 38, in *The Statutes of Sir Walter Mildmay*, 82; Bendall, Brooke, and Collinson, *A History of Emmanuel College*, 26.

60. Chaderton, lectures on John, cited in Lake, *Moderate Puritans*, 130.

61. Chaderton, lectures on John, cited in Lake, *Moderate Puritans*, 156–57.

62. Lake, *Moderate Puritans*, 150.

regeneration."[63] Christ purchased all good thoughts and desires by His death, and the Spirit gives them.[64]

Chaderton said that ministers of the sovereign Savior must preach "true doctrine" in "plain evidence of the Spirit, and power."[65] Many men "stuff their sermons" with unnecessary technicalities or showmanship,[66] when instead they should preach heavenly doctrine "after a heavenly and spiritual manner."[67] God rejects preaching that entertains rather than convicts and converts men to God.[68] Ministers must serve with "contempt of all earthly praise" and "zeal of God's glory."[69] And they must do all this in tender love for the flock, with gentleness like nursing mothers and pleading fathers.[70]

This was Chaderton's vision for the ministry of the Word. This was the "product" that his school aimed to construct. He knew that such a ministry would bear the reproach of the world; but if the Lord Jesus was hated by men for His preaching, in the same way His servants will be slandered—"hence," Chaderton said, "cometh these slanderous names of puritan and precisian."[71]

William Bedell (1571–1642) remembered Chaderton in a more positive way. Writing in 1628 to James Ussher, he recalled how, in his days as a student at Emmanuel College, "that good father Dr. Chaderton" taught him "the arts of dutiful obedience, and just ruling."[72] Chaderton taught men by precept and example to be servants faithful in their stewardship.

Chaderton's View of Church Offices

In this final section of the chapter, I wish to give focused attention to the sermon in which Chaderton gave strong expression to his Presbyterian views. In the classis movement in the late sixteenth century, English ministers sought to set up a system of Presbyterian collegiality among pastors under the umbrella of the official (and still episcopal) church. From their perspective, they were trying to form the wings of a biblical church inside the chrysalis of unbiblical traditions.

---

63. Chaderton, *Excellent and Godly Sermon*, C8v [no pagination].
64. Chaderton, *Excellent and Godly Sermon*, C7v–C8v [no pagination].
65. Chaderton, *Excellent and Godly Sermon*, F4r [no pagination].
66. Chaderton, *Excellent and Godly Sermon*, F6v–7r [no pagination].
67. Chaderton, *Excellent and Godly Sermon*, F5v [no pagination].
68. Chaderton, *Excellent and Godly Sermon*, F6r [no pagination].
69. Chaderton, *Excellent and Godly Sermon*, F8r–v [no pagination].
70. Chaderton, *Excellent and Godly Sermon*, G2r [no pagination].
71. Chaderon, lectures on John, cited by Lake, *Moderate Puritans*, 132.
72. William Bedell, letter of April 15, 1628, in *The Whole Works of the Most Rev. James Ussher* (Dublin: Hodges, Smith, and Co., 1864), 15:398.

Chaderton operated within this episcopal system. William Sancroft went so far as to claim that Chaderton "often professed that they who dislike the government by bishops would bring in a far worse both for church and state."[73] However, as the biographical sketch above has indicated, Chaderton's private writings strongly favored Presbyterianism versus episcopacy. He regularly attended Presbyterian synods; indeed, he sometimes led them as moderator. The participants regarded him as an expert regarding questions of Presbyterian church order.[74] We find this ecclesiological order expressed firmly in the sermon we now consider.

The *Fruitfull Sermon* on Romans 12:3–8 was published anonymously in 1584. It consists of eighty pages, octavo, and would have taken approximately two hours to preach as written. The preacher said "my time is almost spent"— on page 69![75] It was evidently a popular tract. A sermon preached in 1590 to confute it noted that there had already been "diverse impressions of the *Fruteful Sermon*," that is, more than one printing.[76] Emerson writes that the sermon went through four editions and was regarded as "an authoritative statement of Puritan principles," being cited by Dudley Fenner in 1587 and John Udall in 1588.[77]

While acknowledging that Chaderton had Presbyterian beliefs, Rolph finds the sermon too harsh in its criticism of the Anglican hierarchy for the moderate Cambridge academic, and hypothesizes that it might instead originate from daring Edward Dering.[78] However, it was widely believed at the time that Chaderton was the author. Lake and Collinson offer the testimony of four Separatists in the 1590s and 1600s that attributed the sermon to Chaderton,[79] and separatists were not the only ones to say so. George Cranmer (1563–1600), grand-nephew of Archbishop Thomas Cranmer and student of Richard Hooker, made critical remarks on "Mr. Chatterton in the fruitful sermon."[80]

---

73. Bendall, Brooke, and Collinson, *A History of Emmanuel College*, 36.

74. Lake, *Moderate Puritans*, 26.

75. Chaderton, *A Fruitfull Sermon*, 69.

76. Thomas Rogers, *A Sermon vpon the 6. 7. and 8. Verses of the 12. Chapter of S. Pauls Epistle vnto the Romanes; Made to the Confutation of So Much Another Sermon, Entituled, A Frutful Sermon* (n.p.: Iohn Windet, 1590), A1v.

77. Emerson, *English Puritanism*, 103. Neither Fenner nor Udall identified the author.

78. Rolph, "Emmanuel College," 91.

79. Lake, *Moderate Puritans*, 26–27; Collinson, *The Religion of Protestants*, 151n36.

80. George Cranmer, "Notes on the Sixth Book of the Laws of Ecclesiastical Polity," in *The Works of that Learned and Judicious Divine, Mr. Richard Hooker* (New York: D. Appleton, 1844), 2:125. Cranmer disputed Chaderton's interpretation of "him that teacheth to be a doctor, him that exhorteth to be pastor, him that distributeth to be a deacon, him that ruleth a lay elder, him that showeth mercy a widow." He was plainly referring to this sermon.

Lake writes, "The actual text of the sermon corresponds almost exactly with Chaderton's other known attitudes and in fact provides a beautiful example of the moderate, respectable puritan attitude to presbyterianism."[81] We do well, however, to bear in mind the caution that Chaderton may not have authorized its publication nor had opportunity to revise what may be the notes of an auditor. Nor do we know when he preached it prior to its publication in 1584. Part of the severity of its language linking episcopacy to the antichrist and whore of Babylon could perhaps be attributed to his more youthful days (he would not be the only person whose basic beliefs endure unchanged but whose manner of expression mellows with age). But the following observations may be made about the doctrine of the *Fruitfull Sermon*.

First, it teaches *absolute truth on the basis of the divine authority of Scripture.* The sermon opens with an assertion that Romans 12:3–8 "contain a perpetual law, touching the government of Christ's church," and a warning that while keeping this law is "the safety of the body," the breaking of it is "the destruction thereof."[82] The apostle Paul was only the scribe writing the Lord's words, "the penman of the Lord's inditement," just as Moses was the writer of God's commands.[83] Of its principles this sermon said that Christ "himself is the author and no man."[84] If we add to the doctrine of the Scriptures, then we dishonor Christ "as perfect governor of his church."[85]

Thus Chaderton had a high view of Scripture, regarding it as the word of God. The apostle had the "authority" to give a law in the "name" of Christ, which binds the church "even to the coming of Christ." For his teaching did "not proceed from himself, or any other mortal man, but only from the Lord of hosts, whose apostle he was."[86] The teaching of the apostles was the law of Christ and, hence, not a matter of changing customs or culture but perpetual and sufficient.[87] These biblical teachings of the apostles are "the eternal decrees of Christ."[88] The church must not dam up the life-giving waters of divine grace or muddy them with "man's inventions, and popish traditions."[89] Like the noble Bereans (Acts 17:11), the hearers of a teacher must "search diligently" to confirm

---

81. Lake, *Moderate Puritans*, 27.

82. Chaderton, *A Fruitfull Sermon*, 1.

83. Chaderton, *A Fruitfull Sermon*, 2. To "indite" is to compose, write, or dictate what is to be written.

84. Chaderton, *A Fruitfull Sermon*, 77.

85. Chaderton, *A Fruitfull Sermon*, 78.

86. Chaderton, *A Fruitfull Sermon*, 3.

87. Chaderton, *A Fruitfull Sermon*, 77–79.

88. Chaderton, *A Fruitfull Sermon*, 72.

89. Chaderton, *A Fruitfull Sermon*, 7. The streams of water here are biblical church officers.

that the doctrine they receive is true and "soundly and purely gathered out of the Word."[90] Chaderton said, "Faith leaneth only upon the Word."[91]

Second, the sermon teaches *faithfulness in our callings and submission to proper human authorities for the public good.* Each person has a place in the structure of society where he must serve with contentment, using the gifts God provides.[92] Like soldiers in an army, each one should keep his place in the ranks lest disorder and sorrow result.[93] Lake writes, "Chaderton outlined the doctrine of callings, which saw society as an interdependent whole with each person given a finite social role to which he ought assiduously to keep. For both the role and the gifts necessary to fulfill it come directly from God."[94]

This is no social or political radicalism but a vision for a carefully ordered and hierarchical society where all live in the wisdom of "discreet moderation."[95] The wise man of a low position will no more attempt to pluck the crown from the king's head than a heavy stone flies up into the sky.[96] Collinson wrote of Chaderton's view of society, "Order should be preserved by each member respecting his proper place."[97] Yet he was no utopian; he realized that from the twin fountains of "self-love and ambition" a corrupt stream poisoned all fallen mankind with envy toward those above us, strife with our peers, and contempt for those below our social status.[98] The proper posture of all men "from the highest to the lowest" is to bow down "before the majesty of God" and seek the humble graces of the Holy Spirit.[99] Let each one use his gift for the public good and not try "to stretch it farther" beyond his calling.[100]

As Paul wrote in Romans 12:4–5, the church is a body with many different members and different offices.[101] Each member must have his office and only one office.[102] The Lord gives to each one his vocation "to be as it were his standing place, out of which he should not step one foot."[103] Every member belongs

---

90. Chaderton, *A Fruitfull Sermon*, 60.
91. Chaderton, *A Fruitfull Sermon*, 61.
92. Chaderton, *A Fruitfull Sermon*, 11.
93. Chaderton, *A Fruitfull Sermon*, 16.
94. Lake, *Moderate Puritans*, 28.
95. Chaderton, *A Fruitfull Sermon*, 10.
96. Chaderton, *A Fruitfull Sermon*, 24.
97. Collinson, *The Religion of Protestants*, 151.
98. Chaderton, *A Fruitfull Sermon*, 20.
99. Chaderton, *A Fruitfull Sermon*, 24.
100. Chaderton, *A Fruitfull Sermon*, 28.
101. Chaderton, *A Fruitfull Sermon*, 32–34.
102. Chaderton, *A Fruitfull Sermon*, 38–41.
103. Chaderton, *A Fruitfull Sermon*, 13.

to the others and must serve for the benefit of all.[104] Collinson wrote, "In the view of this presbyterian, the disorder of society was due to a profound and structural disorder in the Church."[105] Chaderton therefore made an extended appeal to the queen and her councilors to implement what he believed to be biblical church principles.[106]

Third, the sermon teaches *the distinct offices of pastors, teachers (or doctors), rulers, deacons, and attenders upon the poor.* Chaderton derives these public offices from Romans 12:6–8. These are gifts of God that the people of God must receive.[107] The sermon compares each office to part of the body. "God hath given us in great mercy pastors and doctors to be our eyes, to lead and direct us in the ways of truth and holiness: elders, and deacons to be our hands, to keep us and hold us in the way, and also to reach unto us those things we want: attenders upon us, to be our feet when we are not able otherwise to do."[108]

Therefore the Church of England is maimed in its lack of biblical officers and is monstrous in the multiplications of unnatural members, like a body with only one leg but two heads. Chaderton boldly declared, "Archbishops, bishops, deans, archdeacons, deacons, chancellors, commissaries, officials, and all such as be rather members and parts of the whore and strumpet [prostitute] of Rome."[109]

This Puritan and Presbyterian viewpoint appears in Chaderton's handwritten marginal notes in various books. In margins of the 1559 Ordinal (book of liturgical rites for ordaining church officers), he wrote that "the work and ministry of a bishop" is "all one ministry with the priest," and episcopacy is "no ministry ordained by Christ." The ministers should be chosen by the people, not appointed merely by the bishop.[110] In the margins of one of William Barlow's sermons (published in 1606), Chaderton wrote regarding presbyters and bishops, "Yes, the names are distinct, not their office, or function."[111] Where Barlow had written of bishops being "ordained," Chaderton wrote "elected."[112] Thus his views on church government remained fundamentally the same from the reigns of Queen Elizabeth I to King James I.

---

104. Chaderton, *A Fruitfull Sermon*, 46–50.
105. Collinson, *The Religion of Protestants*, 151. See Chaderton, *A Fruitfull Sermon*, 17, 72–73.
106. Chaderton, *A Fruitfull Sermon*, 73–77.
107. Chaderton, *A Fruitfull Sermon*, 51–53.
108. Chaderton, *A Fruitfull Sermon*, 48.
109. Chaderton, *A Fruitfull Sermon*, 36–37.
110. Hunt, "Laurence Chaderton and the Hampton Court Conference," 215; Rolph, "Emmanuel College," 77–78.
111. Hunt, "Laurence Chaderton and the Hampton Court Conference," 210.
112. Hunt, "Laurence Chaderton and the Hampton Court Conference," 216.

The *Fruitfull Sermon* explains the function of the true offices: A "prophet" is a "minister of the Word of God, which abideth in the true and sincere interpretation thereof, to the edification of his own peculiar flock."[113] There are two kinds of prophets: doctors and pastors. The doctor is a teacher who expounds the canonical Scriptures in true doctrine.[114] The pastor applies that doctrine by exhortation and administers the sacraments.[115] In these two offices, Chaderton observed "the wisdom and mercy of God" who has provided us with ministers to address the two parts of the soul: the mind in its "darkness and ignorance" and the heart in its "rebellion and enmity" against God.[116]

It is interesting to note that, in 1588, the society of Emmanuel College assigned two of its senior fellows to focus on exhortation and application of doctrine to the students and administering the sacraments, and two senior fellows to give themselves to teaching sound doctrine and confuting error. This reflects the division of labor between pastors and teachers. Chaderton was directed to focus on preaching to reflect his great gifts.[117]

The pastor must apply his exhortations with discernment and discrimination, giving milk to some and meat to others, exhorting rich and poor, slave and free, educated and uneducated. He must lead the sheep to wholesome food, heal the sick, bring home the straying, and strengthen the weak. He must rightly divide the Word (2 Tim. 2:15). To the weak he brings promises of divine mercy, the godly he exhorts to make progress, and the wicked he exhorts to repentance by the everlasting judgments of God. In all things, he seeks to "feed, feed, feed" the flock of God with the Word of God.[118] Lake says, "There could be no clearer statement of the evangelical core of the puritan impulse than that."[119]

Next we pass from "the ministers of the Word" to "other officers." There is the deacon, who distributes the shared generosity of the church to the poor.[120] There are ruling elders, who include the pastors and doctors and assist them in "admonishing the unruly, and encouraging the good."[121] There are also widows appointed to help the poor and immigrants.[122]

---

113. Chaderton, *A Fruitfull Sermon*, 56.
114. Chaderton, *A Fruitfull Sermon*, 57.
115. Chaderton, *A Fruitfull Sermon*, 61.
116. Chaderton, *A Fruitfull Sermon*, 64.
117. Lake, *Moderate Puritans*, 45.
118. Chaderton, *A Fruitfull Sermon*, 62–63.
119. Lake, *Moderate Puritans*, 33.
120. Chaderton, *A Fruitfull Sermon*, 65.
121. Chaderton, *A Fruitfull Sermon*, 67–68.
122. Chaderton, *A Fruitfull Sermon*, 70.

Fourth and lastly, this sermon teaches that *proper church government glorifies God in Christ*. Chaderton said, "Christ the king and governor of his church, must rule it till the coming of himself by his own offices and laws."[123] All the members of the body should have one head, Jesus Christ—not a pope or bishop.[124]

The author realized that his point will cause him to be "slandered of the papists and others, with the devilish sect of Puritans: we are thought to bear scarce good will unto her Majesty." He declared "my love and affection towards my sovereign," indeed his willingness to die to preserve the queen's life.[125] But Christ is "the king of kings, and prince of princes," and gave the offices of the church "in the day of his coronation, when he led his enemies in triumph, to show the glory of his kingdom, and his princely power," and therefore we dare not lightly regard His order for His church.[126]

Chaderton ends with a prayer that "only the glory and victory of Christ, our only king, prophet and priest, may be established, to whom with the Father and the Holy Ghost, three persons and one eternal God, be all praise, glory and honor, now and forever. Amen."[127]

Conclusion

In Laurence Chaderton we find a man of radical convictions regarding the proper structure of the Church of England, yet also a man of remarkable moderation in his willingness to operate within the existing episcopal system. What motivated him to do so? In the end it appears that his abiding passion was the vision of training men who would proclaim the Scriptures to his nation. Making the gospel of Christ his great priority and believing that preaching was the great means of applying the gospel to sinners, he poured out his long life into a university education that prepared ministers to serve Christ in England. Though many passing through the halls of Emmanuel College ended up in legal professions, this too satisfied his purpose, for the magistrates were "nursing fathers" and "nursing mothers" to the gospel ministry (Isa. 49:23).

Chaderton carried out this vision with remarkable academic and administrative gifts, aided by his network of relationships with both family and friends.

---

123. Chaderton, *A Fruitfull Sermon*, 78. Cf. p. 12.

124. Chaderton, *A Fruitfull Sermon*, 41–45.

125. Chaderton, *A Fruitfull Sermon*, 45. "The devilish sect of Puritans" probably refers to the heretical Cathari, an ascetic, Docetic sect, for Puritan is an English rendering of the Greek *katharoi* or "pure ones."

126. Chaderton, *A Fruitfull Sermon*, 65.

127. Chaderton, *A Fruitfull Sermon*, 80.

His legacy was over a thousand men trained and sent out—and all the lives they have affected even to this day. In 1899, J. B. Peace wrote in the *Emmanuel College Magazine*, "We must recognize in the personal influence of Chaderton perhaps the finest endowment any college ever enjoyed."[128]

128. Cited in Rolph, "Emmanuel College," 31.

Chapter 14

Natural Theology:
Some Historical Perspective

God reveals Himself in a limited manner through His visible creation (Rom. 1:19–20) and in man's conscience (Rom. 2:14–16), resulting in a universally available knowledge that God exists, has a distinct nature as God, is transcendent over this world, will hold human beings accountable for their obedience or disobedience to His moral law, and is angry with all the sins of mankind. "The heavens declare the glory of God; and the firmament showeth his handiwork," says Psalm 19:1. Stephen Charnock said, "Every plant, every atom, as well as every star, at the first meeting, whispers this in our ears, 'I have a Creator; I am witness to a Deity.'"[1]

Fallen mankind responds to this revelation by resisting the truth about God, refusing to honor Him, worshiping idols, and clinging to sin without repentance (Rom. 1:21–32). However, those who are saved by God's Word and Spirit have their hearts open to acknowledge the revelation of God's glory in creation. The church may therefore appeal to general revelation as testimony to the guilt of sinners against God and their need for the salvation revealed in the gospel of Christ (Acts 14:15–17; 17:24–29). The church may also use general revelation as a guide in worship to the Creator, Redeemer, and Sanctifier (Psalms 8, 19, etc.).

May the church use rational arguments based on general revelation to prove that God exists? That would be one task of building a natural theology. General revelation is sometimes called natural revelation because it operates through the ordinary workings of God's creation in divine government and providence and we can appropriate it through the ordinary workings of our minds and hearts.[2] We must speak not only of natural revelation but also of natural theology, a

---

1. Stephen Charnock, *The Existence and Attributes of God* (1853; repr., Grand Rapids: Baker, 1996), 1:43.

2. Douglas F. Kelly, *Systematic Theology: Grounded in Holy Scripture and Understood in the Light of the Church, Volume 1, The God Who Is: The Holy Trinity* (Ross-shire, Scotland: Christian Focus, 2008), 153; cf. Benjamin B. Warfield, "The Biblical Idea of Revelation," in *The Inspiration and Authority of the Bible* (Phillipsburg, N.J.: Presbyterian and Reformed, 1948), 73–74.

system of doctrine about God derived by rational reflection upon observable reality. Natural revelation is a work of God; natural theology is a work of man.

In the modern era, natural theology has taken different directions. Some people have attempted to derive a natural religion common to all humanity instead of a religion founded on special revelation. For example, Lord Herbert of Cherbury (1583–1648) proposed that all religions teach the basic truth that God exists, that we must worship Him, that true worship consists of moral virtue and piety, that sinners must repent, and that God will reward righteousness and punish sin both in this world and the next. This approach formed the basis of the seventeenth- and eighteenth-century belief system known as deism.[3]

Apologists for Christianity attempted to formulate rational, empirical arguments to defeat deism and establish the Christian religion. Most notably, Bishop Joseph Butler (1692–1752) published *An Analogy of Religion, Natural and Revealed, to the Constitution and Course of Nature* (1736),[4] and Canon William Paley produced *Natural Theology* (1802).

Others, however, attacked the fundamental assumptions of natural theology. Skeptic David Hume (1711–1776) denied that we can reason from effect to cause, for causation is only a construct of our minds.[5] Transcendentalist philosopher Immanuel Kant (1724–1804) argued that it is impossible for us to know any ultimate reality beyond what is immediately present to our minds and senses.

Christian apologists to this day seek to present counter-arguments, both rational and empirical, to demonstrate the reasonableness and truth of Christian theism. For them, natural theology is a rational tool for apologetic and polemical theology. However, some Christians, including theologians in the Reformed tradition, have severely criticized the use of natural theology. In this chapter, we will consider these criticisms, provide some historical perspective, and offer a response.

Various Rejections of Natural Theology and Theistic Proofs

While the twentieth century was a period of much apologetic activity using arguments from natural theology, it was also when strong reactions against natural theology erupted from two very different perspectives. We will examine these reactions by focusing on two key theologians: Karl Barth and Cornelius Van Til.

---

3. Herbert of Cherbury, "Common Notions Concerning Religion," in *Christianity and Plurality: Classic and Contemporary Readings*, ed. Richard J. Plantinga (Oxford: Blackwell, 1999), 169–81.

4. John M. Frame, *A History of Western Philosophy and Theology* (Phillipsburg, N.J.: P&R, 2015), 231–35.

5. Kelly, *Systematic Theology*, 1:87–90; for a response to Hume from Thomas Reid, see 1:119–27.

Karl Barth's Nein to Natural Theology

Controversy broke out in the 1930s between Karl Barth (1886–1968) and Emil Brunner (1889–1966), who before had stood together as "neo-orthodox" critics of modernist theological liberalism. Brunner distanced himself from Barth's teaching that sin had obliterated the image of God in every respect and that creation and conscience held no general revelation; there was only special revelation in Christ.[6] Barth responded to Brunner's affirmation of general revelation with an angry *Nein*. He rejected every "formulation of a system" that is not an exposition of "the revelation of God in Jesus Christ." For Barth, "natural theology" is a contradiction in terms, a non-entity.[7] He said, "There is no room for revelation in the Christian sense in any human inquiry or any human faculty of reason."[8] Apart from the special revelation of Christ, fallen man is totally blind to God, and man's contemplation of the creation only reveals demons and idols.[9] There is no "point of contact" between the natural wisdom of men and the revelation of the Holy Spirit.[10] Barth initially said Romans 1 and Acts 17 describe only "the possibility of the knowledge of revelation" but not the reality, for apart from the Word, the Creator remains "the unknown God."[11] Later, Barth argued that Romans 1:18–32 must refer to man's response to God's revelation through the gospel (Rom. 1:16–17), not through the cosmos.[12] As his theology developed, Barth became willing to speak of created things as "lights" that show God's glory, but was never comfortable speaking of "revelation" through creation.[13]

To affirm general revelation and natural theology in any sense, Barth said, is to return to the scholasticism of Thomas Aquinas.[14] According to Barth, Calvin renounced this approach in principle even if not in explicit words,[15] for "against

---

6. Emil Brunner, "Nature and Grace," in *Natural Theology*, intro. John Baillie (London: Geoffrey Bles, 1946), 20. For Brunner's view of general revelation, see Emil Brunner, *Revelation and Reason: The Christian Doctrine of Faith and Knowledge*, trans. Olive Wyon (Philadelphia: Westminster Press, 1946), 58–80.

7. Karl Barth, "No!" in *Natural Theology*, 74–75.

8. Karl Barth, "The Christian Understanding of Revelation," in *Against the Stream: Shorter Post-War Writings, 1946–52*, ed. Ronald Gregor Smith (New York: Philosophical Library 1954), 211.

9. Karl Barth, "No!" in *Natural Theology*, 81–82.

10. Karl Barth, "No!" in *Natural Theology*, 92.

11. Karl Barth, *The Göttingen Dogmatics: Instruction in the Christian Religion*, ed. Hannelotte Reiffen, trans. Geoffrey W. Bromiley (Grand Rapids: Eerdmans, 1991), 15.4 (1:341–42).

12. Karl Barth, *Church Dogmatics*, ed. G. W. Bromiley, T. F. Torrance (Edinburgh: T & T Clark, 1936), II/1, sec. 26.1 (119–21).

13. Barth, *Church Dogmatics*, IV/3, 140–43, cited and discussed in Demarest, *General Revelation*, 126.

14. Karl Barth, "No!" in *Natural Theology*, 90, 95–99.

15. Karl Barth, "No!" in *Natural Theology*, 102–109.

the philosophers he sets the teaching of Scripture and nothing else."[16] He said the Reformed and Lutheran orthodox divines erred in embracing a medieval distinction of two forms of knowledge, resulting during the eighteenth century in a conflict between the two in which special revelation lost and human reason and nature triumphed.[17]

Barth identified "the core of natural theology" as the so-called proofs for the existence of a divinity.[18] He recognized that the orthodox theologians of the later sixteenth and seventeenth centuries did not regard the proofs as providing the basis for faith in God's Word; instead, the value of the proofs lies in their demonstration that God is "a necessary element in human thought."[19] However, Barth objected to the proofs because we do not meet God by satisfying our intellectual demands for understanding but by disturbing our complacency through an encounter with the Mystery that we cannot understand.[20]

It is notable that Brunner, for all his differences with Barth on general revelation, also regarded the proofs as unnecessary, saying they were fraught with assumptions derived from Scripture, vague in their conclusions about the Supreme Being, and overly rationalistic.[21] "We do not begin our inquiry with reason and then work up to revelation, but, as a believing Church, we begin our inquiry with revelation and then work outwards to reason."[22]

Barth taught that the Scriptures bear witness to Jesus Christ, who is the Word of God, and that He alone is the Christian revelation of God.[23] Barth wrote, "Because it [the revelation of God in Christ] is the Word of God, the revelation of God cannot be recommended and defended; it has no advocates and no propagandists," but "can only be presupposed in our thinking and our speaking, and in our Christian theology."[24] Seeing an inherent contradiction in natural theology, he wrote, "As a 'Christian' natural theology, it must really represent and affirm the standpoint of faith.... But as a 'natural' theology, its initial

---

16. Karl Barth, "No!" in *Natural Theology*, 106.
17. Barth, *The Göttingen Dogmatics*, 15.4 (1:345).
18. Barth, *The Göttingen Dogmatics*, 15.4 (1:346).
19. Barth, *The Göttingen Dogmatics*, 15.4 (1:347). Barth saw not only Reformed orthodox theologians but also the medieval theologian Anselm of Canterbury as using reason in the context of the presupposed doctrines of the faith. See *Church Dogmatics*, II/1, sec. 26.1 (92–93).
20. Barth, *The Göttingen Dogmatics*, 15.4 (1:349–50).
21. Brunner, *Revelation and Reason*, 340–48.
22. Brunner, *Revelation and Reason*, ix. Hence the order of the title.
23. Barth, "The Christian Understanding of Revelation," in *Against the Stream*, 214.
24. Barth, "The Christian Understanding of Revelation," in *Against the Stream*, 215.

aim is to disguise this and therefore to pretend to share in the life-endeavor of natural man," that is, the endeavor to reject God and be one's own master.[25]

Some aspects of Barth's rejection of natural theology have appealed to orthodox Reformed Christians. We affirm the biblical doctrine of man's total depravity, inward darkness, and complete inability to turn to God apart from saving grace (Eph. 2:1–10; 4:17–19). We exult in Christ as the only Mediator between God and man (1 Tim. 2:5). We recognize that the Word of Christ is foundational for our beliefs (1 Cor. 3:11). We also agree that modernist theological liberalism has turned away from the divine Word to consult mere man and nature (Gal. 1:12). We bow before the unfathomable depths of the wisdom and knowledge of God and of His judgments and ways (Rom. 11:33–34).

However, Barth's absolute rejection of general revelation does not fit with biblical teachings about creation and conscience, such as Romans 1:19–20: sinful human beings are without excuse "because that which may be known of God is manifest in them; for God hath showed it unto them. For the invisible things of him from the creation of the world are clearly seen, being understood by the things that are made, even his eternal power and Godhead; so that they are without excuse." Barth failed to appreciate the positive use that the apostle Paul made of natural revelation in Romans 1 and the particular ideas of a Greek philosophical poet in his evangelistic "Mars' Hill sermon," as reported in Acts 17.

Van Til's Rejection of Theistic Arguments

Cornelius Van Til (1895–1987) was a strong critic of Barth's theology and considered it an assault on Christian orthodoxy on a number of points.[26] However, Van Til had his own reasons to reject natural theology. He wrote, "No one truly understands the revelation of God in nature unless he first understands the revelation of God in Scripture."[27] Since nature was created by God, "we cannot know nature truly, and man truly, unless we know God truly."[28] Van Til's approach came to be known as "presuppositionalism" and "presuppositional apologetics."

Van Til did not deny the reality of general revelation but insisted on the inability of fallen man to know God apart from special revelation (the outward witness of Scripture) coupled with the inner witness (illumination of saving

---

25. *Church Dogmatics*, II/1, sec. 26.1 (94).

26. Cornelius Van Til, *Christianity and Barthianism* (Philadelphia: Presbyterian and Reformed, 1962). Note the title's play on Machen, *Christianity and Liberalism*, by which Machen implicitly called Liberalism another religion than Christianity.

27. Van Til, *An Introduction to Systematic Theology*, 112.

28. Van Til, *An Introduction to Systematic Theology*, 176.

grace). God reveals not only His existence but also His nature in the works of His hands (Rom. 1:20).[29] Van Til said, "In Paradise…man would be able to reason correctly from nature to nature's God." Adam did not reason his way from a state of ignorance of God to knowledge of God but was aware of God from the first moment of his existence (cf. Gen. 2:7–17). Even in Paradise, man's knowledge of God was not independent of God's presence with him.[30]

However, since the fall of man and God's curse upon the earth, "nature has a veil cast over it," and "the mind of man has been corrupted by sin." Consequently, man's attempts to reason from nature to God can only produce "a distorted notion of God."[31] Instead of functioning rightly as God's image-bearers and seeing creation in reference to God, unsaved sinners try to reason about the world only in reference to themselves. As a result, they strive to stand in God's place, and fail. Indeed, they refuse to recognize the transcendent Lord over all things. The only way for sinners to reason about creation under God's Lordship is to step down from their thrones, acknowledge their sin in making themselves ultimate, and submit to God's authority, which they are unwilling and unable to do (Rom. 8:7).[32]

At this point, Van Til made a startling move. He admitted the validity of the proofs or arguments for the existence God in terms of what man *ought* to do. He said,

+ "Men ought to realize that nature could not exist as something independent."

+ "Men ought to reason that the order of nature is due to the providence of God."

+ "Men ought to reason that the disorder that is found in nature is unnatural…. Nature must be suffering under the wrath of God."

+ "Men ought to conclude that it is by the grace of God that they live at all, and that nature is not fallen into complete disorder."[33]

In other words, the theistic proofs demonstrate that our thought and the world around us are rational and intelligible based only on the presupposition that the true God exists.

---

29. Van Til, *An Introduction to Systematic Theology*, 176–77.

30. Van Til, *An Introduction to Systematic Theology*, 133.

31. Van Til, *An Introduction to Systematic Theology*, 133.

32. Van Til, *An Introduction to Systematic Theology*, 178–79. He used the terms "univocal" for reasoning that takes man as the ultimate reference point and "analogical" that takes God as the ultimate reference point.

33. Van Til, *An Introduction to Systematic Theology*, 179–81.

However, the proofs fail when presented on the basis that human reason is independent from God and competent to be the absolute judge of reality. This autonomy is precisely what fallen man insists upon pursuing, and therefore, Van Til said, man's reasoning has produced at best only a divinity immanent in the world, for it will not acknowledge the transcendent One who is truly Lord over man.[34] Van Til explained that an unbeliever may "give a formal assent to the intellectual argument for the existence of God," but his mind-set and life will be "a continual falsification" of what he is compelled to admit. Such assent may go hand-in-hand with behavior that conforms outwardly to the requirements of the divine law as the product of "God's restraining grace." However, Van Til said, such an unbeliever lives like a Pharisee, engages in "the most diabolical falsification of the truth," and at the end of the day accepts nothing more than "a finite god," not the infinite Lord who rules over every aspect of knowledge and reality.[35] Such an approach, which is inevitable for the non-Christian, makes theistic arguments "invalid," for they result in a false god or gods. However, Van Til said, "We would distinguish between a Christian and a non-Christian use of the proofs." Christians may take up the proofs when they stand on the ground of God's revelation and use them to "argue that it is the only reasonable thing to do for a human being to accept this revelation."[36]

Van Til believed that the theistic proofs have some value in the context of a Christian system of thought grounded in the Bible. He denied that they can be rightly developed or used by unbelievers, yet he placed them in a role of showing to unbelievers that Christianity is reasonable. This position is both complex and nuanced. It can also be confusing, as Van Til's students have acknowledged.[37]

The apologist, said Van Til, cannot make a "direct" argument from brute "facts" or "laws," only an "indirect" argument that shows the irrationality of the unbeliever's position.[38] John Frame summarizes this approach as follows: "Nothing is intelligible unless God exists, and God must be nothing less than the Trinitarian, sovereign, transcendent, and immanent absolute personality of the Scriptures."[39] According to Frame, Van Til restricted the Christian apologist to negative arguments that show other positions than Christianity to be

---

34. Van Til, *An Introduction to Systematic Theology*, 178.
35. Van Til, *An Introduction to Systematic Theology*, 315–16.
36. Van Til, *An Introduction to Systematic Theology*, 317.
37. Brian K. Morley, *Mapping Apologetics: Comparing Contemporary Approaches* (Downers Grove, Ill.: IVP Academic, 2015), 59–61.
38. Cornelius Van Til, *Christian Apologetics*, ed. William Edgar, 2nd ed. (Phillipsburg, N.J.: P&R, 2003), 129.
39. John M. Frame, *Apologetics: A Justification of Christian Belief*, ed. Joseph E. Torres, 2nd ed. (Phillipsburg, N.J.: P&R, 2015), 95.

irrational and absurd (such as by a *reductio ad absurdum* argument). However, Frame pointed out that a negative argument can be rearranged as a positive argument. The problem of human autonomy is not solved by avoiding positive methods of reasoning but by spiritual humility and watchfulness.[40] Other critics have argued that refuting one non-Christian viewpoint does not prove that Christianity is true, for there are many other non-Christian alternatives.[41] Others have criticized Van Til for failing to recognize rational points of contact with unbelievers. R. C. Sproul, John Gerstner, and Arthur Lindsley write, "The triad of the law of noncontradiction, the law of causality, and the basic reliability of sense perception is integral to all knowledge."[42] These three laws, it is said, form a basis on which theistic arguments can be built.

The rejection of natural theology by some Reformed theologians raises serious questions about its use in apologetics and theology. It also shows the complexity of the issues involved. The debate over this matter often revolves around the teachings of major theologians in church history, such as Thomas Aquinas and John Calvin. To provide some perspective on the matter, we will offer a historical survey of natural theology through the period of Reformed orthodoxy (i.e., the end of the seventeenth century). Then we will draw some conclusions and attempt to sketch a way forward.

Ancient Roots of Natural Theology

Questions regarding natural theology have a history that reaches back centuries. Sometimes the tale of natural theology starts with Thomas Aquinas, leaps to John Calvin, and ends with Karl Barth, but the story is much older and more complex. Therefore, we begin with ancient pagan philosophers and early Christian theologians.

Ancient Pagan Philosophy and Natural Theology
The term *natural theology* appeared first in the literature of pagan philosophy. According to Augustine, the Roman writer Marcus Varro (116–27 BC) said there were three types of theology: (1) mythical theology, consisting of fictitious stories about the gods as if they were wicked men; (2) natural theology, which the philosophers used to answer academic questions about the properties of divinity; and (3) civil theology, which priests administered through the rites

---

40. Frame, *Apologetics*, 83.
41. Morley, *Mapping Apologetics*, 84.
42. R. C. Sproul, John Gerstner, and Arthur Lindsley, *Classical Apologetics: A Rational Defense of the Christian Faith and a Critique of Presuppositional Apologetics* (Grand Rapids: Zondervan, 1984), 90.

and sacrifices of temples.[43] Greek mythic theology is exemplified in the epic poems of Homer and Hesiod, which are not based on reasoning so much as creative inspiration and informative revelation attributed to divine spirits called the Muses.[44] This theology claimed special revelation from the gods about the gods. Civil theology was closely associated with the myths but gave the myths practical, religious value in the ritual worship of idols.[45]

Pagan natural theology, though formulated in the cultural context of mythical polytheism, sought to transcend it by rational reflection on the nature of divinity. In so doing, the philosophers abstracted certain principles about the being and activity of the deity. Plato (427–347 BC), following Socrates (c. 470–399 BC), theorized about the one, supreme Good; Aristotle (384–322 BC), about the first unmoved Mover of all things; and Zeno (c. 334–c. 262 BC), the founder of Stoicism, about the divinity that permeates the universe and provides its rational, regular order.[46]

Plato urged people to ascend from the beauty of a particular object of the senses to the beauty held in common by all beautiful things to the beauty of wisdom expressed in laws and sciences and ultimately to "divine beauty" itself. The pinnacle of contemplation is "beauty absolute, separate, simple, and everlasting, which without diminution and without increase, or any change, is imparted to the ever-growing and perishing beauties of all other things." By beholding and communing with this beauty, Plato said, a person increases in virtue, becomes "the friend of God," and strains toward immortality.[47]

Frederick Copleston (1907–1994) summarizes the reasoning of Aristotle about God as follows:

> Every motion, every transit from potentiality to act, requires some principle in act, but if every becoming, every object in movement, requires an actual moving cause, then the world in general, the universe, requires a First Mover.... The First Mover is the eternal source of eternal motion. Moreover, the First Mover is not a Creator-God: the world existed from all eternity....

---

43. Augustine, *The City of God*, 6.5, in *NPNF1*, 2:112–13. Much of Varro's work is no longer extant.

44. William Smith, ed., *Dictionary of Greek and Roman Biography and Mythology* (Boston: Little, Brown, and Co., 1870), 2:1125. On the interface between human craft and spiritual inspiration claimed by the Greek poets, see P. Murray, "Poetic Inspiration in Early Greece," in *Homer: Critical Assessments*, ed. Irene J. E. De Jong (London: Routledge: 1999), 4:21–41.

45. See Augustine, *The City of God*, 6.6–7; 8.5, in *NPNF1*, 2:113–16, 147.

46. Frame, *A History of Western Philosophy and Theology*, 65, 73–74, 77.

47. Plato, *Symposium*, 210–11, in *The Dialogues of Plato*, trans. B. Jowett (New York: Random House, 1937), 1:334–35.

Aristotle shows that his moving Principle must be of such a kind that it is pure act, *energeia*, without potentiality…and if it is pure act, then it must be immaterial, for materiality involves the possibility of being acted upon and changed….

The First Mover, being immaterial, cannot perform any bodily action: His activity must be purely spiritual, and so intellectual…. The knowledge enjoyed by God cannot be knowledge that involves change…. Aristotle, then, defines God as "Thought of Thought," *noēsis noēseōs*. God is subsistent thought, which eternally thinks itself. Moreover, God cannot have any object of thought outside Himself, for that would mean He had an end outside Himself. God, therefore, knows only Himself….

There is no indication that Aristotle ever thought of the First Mover as an object of worship, still less as a Being to Whom prayers might profitably be addressed…. Aristotle says expressly that those are wrong who think that there can be a friendship towards God.[48]

It is obvious that Aristotle reasoned his way to a Supreme Being, but the picture of that Being that Aristotle deduced is very different from the God of the Bible.

By building a ladder of intellectual concepts and logical thinking, the philosophers sought to ascend to the highest reality and say something about God. However, we cannot draw a sharp line between reason and special revelation in pagan thought, for some philosophers such as Parmenides of Elea, Socrates, and Plotinus claimed to be inspired by personal, supernatural revelation.[49] The blurring of the distinction between general revelation and special revelation reflects the pantheism inherent in paganism.[50] Even the use of human reason, according to ancient Greek thought, engages the divinity that supposedly dwells to some extent in us all. Such deification of human reason reflected their commitment to "rational autonomy," which is John Frame's phrase for "their insistence on the supremacy of human reason."[51]

---

48. Frederick Copleston, *A History of Philosophy, Volume 1: Greece and Rome* (New York: Doubleday, 1993), 314–17. He cites Aristotle, *Metaphysics*, Delta; Lambda, 6–9; *Physics*, Theta, 6, 258 b 10–11; *Magna Moralia*, 1208 b, 26–32.

49. On Parmenides and Plotinus, see Stephen R. L. Clark, "The Classical Origins of Natural Theology," in *The Oxford Handbooks of Natural Theology*, ed. Russell Re Manning (Oxford: Oxford University Press, 2013), 11, 20. Socrates's claims to revelation from a god or spirit (*daimonion*) appear in Plato's *Apology* and other dialogs.

50. It may be more precise to categorize some ancient philosophies as *panentheism* (literally, "all in God"), which does not say that all things are God (*pantheism*) but that God pervades the universe in a manner closely linked to it as a soul is to the body. Panentheism often identifies all minds or spirits as part of the divine being.

51. Frame, *A History of Western Philosophy and Theology*, 51.

Early Christian Apologists: Aristides, Justin Martyr, and Tertullian

In the centuries following the apostolic age, Christian apologists rose up to defend the faith against the intellectual attacks of the cultural paganism in the Roman Empire. The apologists believed there was a measure of common ground to which they could appeal in the best insights of the philosophers. In the second century, Aristides addressed his *Christian Apology* to the emperor Hadrian. After he "had considered the heaven and the earth and the seas," Aristides concluded that God caused them all, particularly the God who is not made, eternal, immortal, perfect, incomprehensible, without bodily parts, emotional disturbances, limitation, ignorance, or need.[52] Gerald Bray writes, "This, let it be said at once, was the common ground between Christians and their philosophically educated opponents."[53]

However, these Christian writers did not regard religious and philosophical viewpoints outside of Christianity to be alternative paths to God or to be approximations of the truth. Bray argues that "the Apologists were not nearly as well disposed toward Greek intellectual culture as has often been supposed, and that their writings, far from being a polite attempt to enter into dialogue with non-Christians, were in fact an aggressive attack on all forms of paganism." Bray says further, "They were evangelists rather than diplomats, and their primary objective was to win converts to the Christian faith, not to find ways in which that faith could be integrated into the prevailing culture of the time."[54] They would assert that the very first article of the church's creed, "I believe in God, the Father, Almighty, Maker of heaven and earth," is a frontal assault on Greco-Roman paganism and philosophy.

Justin Martyr, a Christian apologist of the second century, had been well schooled in philosophy, especially in Platonism, before his conversion.[55] Justin wrote, "For whatever either lawgivers or philosophers uttered well, they elaborated by finding and contemplating some part of the Word. But since they did not know the whole of the Word, which is Christ, they often contradicted themselves."[56] Though the term *Word* (Greek *logos*) would have resonated with the concept of universal reason in Greek philosophy, Justin's references to the

---

52. Aristides, *Apology*, ch. 1, in *ANF*, 9:263–64.

53. Gerald Bray, "Explaining Christianity to Pagans," in *The Trinity in a Pluralistic Age: Theological Essays on Culture and Religion*, ed. Kevin J. Vanhoozer (Grand Rapids: Eerdmans, 1997), 18.

54. Bray, "Explaining Christianity to Pagans," in *The Trinity in a Pluralistic Age*, 11.

55. A. Craig Troxel, "'All Things to All People': Justin Martyr's Apologetical Method," *Fides et historia* 27, no. 2 (Summer 1995): 29 (full article, pp. 23–43).

56. Justin Martyr, *Second Apology*, ch. 10, in *ANF*, 1:191.

Word consistently look to Jesus Christ, not to a philosophical concept.[57] Thus Justin believed that the Son of God had granted some truth to ancient peoples outside of Israel, either by general revelation accessible to the human mind or by the broader dissemination of the Holy Scriptures, which Justin believed that Plato had read.[58] Indeed, many had read (and admired) the Hebrew Scriptures in their Greek translation, the Septuagint. Justin even called a few Greek philosophers such as Socrates "Christians,"[59] though some scholars argue that he did so only because those philosophers opposed idolatry and suffered for it just as Christians did.[60] Justin did not think ancient philosophy developed an accurate view of God but recognized that there were true insights about God scattered across various philosophical systems[61] as well as a universal recognition of basic principles of justice.[62] However, Justin believed that pagan religion was demonic,[63] and though its myths contained some echoes of the truth, they did not acknowledge the gospel of Christ crucified.[64] On the one hand, Justin affirmed that "whatever things are rightly said among all men are the property of us Christians." On the other hand, Justin said that non-Christian philosophy was dark and self-contradictory and its adherents lacked a real, personal "participation" in Christ by "grace."[65] This second-century Christian apologist did not believe in a natural theology that could develop apart from the Bible but only affirmed that fragments of knowledge and rationality remain in corrupt mankind.

Tertullian also spoke out against a blend of philosophy and theology. He asked, "What indeed has Athens to do with Jerusalem? What concord is there between the Academy [pagan philosophy] and the Church? What between

---

57. Troxel, "All Things to All People," 30–40.

58. Justin Martyr, *First Apology*, ch. 44, in *ANF*, 1:177.

59. Justin Martyr, *First Apology*, ch. 46, in *ANF*, 1:178.

60. Adam Sparks, "Was Justin Martyr a Proto-Inclusivist?" *Journal of Ecumenical Studies* 43, no. 4 (Fall 2008): 500–502 (full article pp. 495–510); Shawn C. Smith, "Was Justin Martyr an Inclusivist?" *Stone-Campbell Journal* 10 (Fall 2007): 199–205 (full article pp. 193–211). Tertullian gave examples of non-Christian attacks on idols and said, "Here, then, you have amongst your own forefathers, if not the name, at all events the procedure, of the Christians, which despises the gods." Tertullian, *Ad Nationes*, ch. 10, in *ANF*, 3:119. Thus when a non-Christian instinctively acknowledged that God is his Judge, Tertullian exclaimed, "O noble testimony of the soul by nature Christian!" Tertullian, *Apology*, ch. 17, in *ANF*, 3:32. Smith also notes that Socrates did participate in some idolatry, making it unlikely that Justin would count him a true Christian (201–202).

61. Justin Martyr, *First Apology*, ch. 20, in *ANF*, 1:169–70.

62. Justin Martyr, *Dialogue with Trypho*, ch. 93, in *ANF*, 1:246.

63. Justin Martyr, *First Apology*, ch. 5, in *ANF*, 1:164.

64. Justin Martyr, *First Apology*, ch. 55, in *ANF*, 1:181.

65. Justin Martyr, *Second Apology*, ch. 13, in *ANF*, 1:193; cf. Graham Keith, "Justin Martyr and Religious Exclusivism," *Tyndale Bulletin* 43, no. 1 (1992): 67–68 (full article pp. 57–80).

heretics and Christians?"[66] However, he also said that God presents Himself to the minds of men so that "this is the crowning guilt of men, that they will not recognize One of whom they cannot possibly be ignorant." God's works provide great and numerous proofs, and the testimony of our souls moves men, sometimes unwittingly, to acknowledge that God is Ruler and Judge of all.[67] But Tertullian also acknowledged some common ground with ancient philosophy:

> We have already asserted that God made the world, and all which it contains, by His Word, and Reason, and Power. It is abundantly plain that your philosophers, too, regard the Logos—that is, the Word and Reason—as the Creator of the universe. For Zeno lays it down that he is the creator, having made all things according to a determinate plan; that his name is Fate, and God, and the soul of Jupiter, and the necessity of all things. Cleanthes ascribes all this to spirit, which he maintains pervades the universe.[68]

Tertullian made use of Stoic ideas to demonstrate the reasonableness of Christianity to pagans.[69] However, he did not argue for the existence of a generic deity that Christians and non-Christians alike could acknowledge—the Greek schools of philosophy could not agree about God even among themselves[70]—but for God the Father, the Son, and the Holy Spirit, who has manifested Himself in the incarnate work of Jesus Christ, whom the gospel proclaims.[71] Tertullian called people to faith, which he viewed not as a perpetual search for truth by human reasoning but as submission to God's authoritative Word. "My first principle is this. Christ laid down one definite system of truth, which the world must believe without qualification, and which we must seek precisely in order to believe it when we find it."[72]

Early Greek Fathers: Athanasius, Gregory Nazianzen, and John of Damascus
In the fourth century, Athanasius wrote a polemical tract titled Contra Gentes ("Against the Gentiles"), in which he argued against Greek polytheism and nature worship and attempted to reason out a proof of the truth of Christianity.

---

66. Tertullian, *Prescription against Heretics*, ch. 7, in *ANF*, 3:246.

67. Tertullian, *Apology*, ch. 17, in *ANF*, 3:32.

68. Tertullian, *Apology*, ch. 21, in *ANF*, 3:34.

69. For an assessment of Tertullian's critical use of Stoicism to defend Christianity and attack other philosophies, see Marcia L. Colish, *The Stoic Tradition from Antiquity to the Early Middle Ages, Volume II: Stoicism in Christian Latin Thought through the Sixth Century* (Leiden: Brill, 1990), 9–29.

70. Colish, *The Stoic Tradition from Antiquity to the Early Middle Ages*, 15.

71. Tertullian, *Apology*, ch. 21, in *ANF*, 3:34–35.

72. Tertullian, *Prescription against Heretics*, ch. 9, in *Early Latin Theology*, trans. and ed. S. L. Greenslade, Library of Christian Classics, Ichthus Edition (Louisville: Westminster Press, 1956), 37.

"Creation almost raises its voice against [these pagans], and points to God as its Maker and Artificer, who reigns over creation and over all things, even the Father of our Lord Jesus Christ," and that "the proof of this is not obscure, but is clear enough in all conscience to those the eyes of whose understanding are not wholly disabled."[73] He assumed a common notion of deity shared with the pagans as "an admitted truth about God that He stands in need of nothing, but is self-sufficient and self-contained, and that in Him all things have their being, and that He ministers to all rather than they to Him" (cf. Acts 17:24–29).[74] He argued that the attribution of divinity to nature (i.e., the physical creation) must be mistaken because God is without a body, invisible, and almighty.[75] Athanasius even said that "the road to Him" is "in us," reasoning that our awareness of our own rational soul demonstrates that God must be invisible, spiritual, and immortal.[76] He also argued that that order and harmony of the universe, despite all its contrary forces, proves it was made and is ruled by one God through His rational Word, that is, the Father through His Son.[77] Peter Leithart comments, "In contrast to some versions of neo-orthodoxy, Athanasius clearly teaches that the world manifests God's character and power, but in contrast to most modern natural theology, Athanasius insists that the creation reveals not some generic 'deity' but specifically the Son."[78]

While the Cappadocian theologians[79] of the fourth century made significant use of philosophical arguments, they also warned that heresy arises from teaching the alien wisdom of pagan philosophers instead of the doctrines of the Holy Scriptures. Not only does overreliance on philosophy lead to error but it also builds the Christian faith on the sandy ground of human reasoning instead of the rock of divine revelation. Then, as Gregory of Nazianzus said, the weakness of our human arguments makes God's truth appear to be weak, though the source of that weakness is the limitation of our own minds, not God's Word and Spirit.[80]

---

73. Athanasius, *Contra Gentes*, 27.3, 5, in *NPNF2*, 4:18.

74. Athanasius, *Contra Gentes*, 28.1, in *NPNF2*, 4:18.

75. Athanasius, *Contra Gentes*, 29.1–2, in *NPNF2*, 4:19.

76. Athanasius, *Contra Gentes*, 30.1; 34.1–2, in *NPNF2*, 4:20, 22.

77. Athanasius, *Contra Gentes*, 35–40, in *NPNF2*, 4:23–25.

78. Peter J. Leithart, *Athanasius*, Foundations of Theological Exegesis and Christian Spirituality (Grand Rapids: Baker Academic, 2011), 99.

79. "The Cappadocian fathers" refers to Basil the Great, Gregory of Nyssa (brothers), and Gregory of Nazianzus. A fourth Cappadocian is sometimes added: Macrina, the older sister and teacher of Basil and Gregory.

80. Jaroslav Pelikan, *Christianity and Classical Culture: The Metamorphosis of Natural Theology in the Christian Encounter with Hellenism*, Gifford Lectures at Aberdeen 1992–1993 (New Haven: Yale University Press, 1993), 18–19.

John of Damascus, writing in the eighth century, affirmed God's self-revelation in created nature[81] and presented a form of the cosmological argument:

> All things, that exist, are either created or uncreated. If, then, things are created, it follows that they are also wholly mutable.... But things that are created must be the work of some maker, and the maker cannot have been created. For if he had been created, he also must surely have been created by someone, and so on till we arrive at something uncreated. The Creator, then, being uncreated, is also wholly immutable. And what could this be other than Deity?...
>
> What is it that gave order to things of heaven and things of earth, and all those things that move in the air and in the water, or rather to what was in existence before these, viz., to heaven and earth and air and the elements of fire and water? What was it that mingled and distributed these? What was it that set these in motion and keeps them in their unceasing and unhindered course?[82]

Alluding to Aristotle, the Damascene said, "The first mover is motionless, and that is the Deity."[83] He regarded such arguments unnecessary for those who believed the Bible, or even for "most of the Greeks," for God had implanted a knowledge of His existence into us "by nature." However, Satan has led some men into the utter foolishness of denying God.[84] So John of Damascus writes, "With those that do not believe in the Holy Scriptures we will reason thus," and proceeds to philosophical arguments.[85] The *Exposition of the Orthodox Faith* greatly influenced Greek theology and, after its translation into Latin (circa 1150 AD),[86] the Western church as well.

Latin Christianity and Pagan Natural Theology: Augustine

Augustine initially rejected the Christianity of his mother, studied pagan philosophies in a quest for truth, and finally returned to Christ as the one Truth who brings both wholeness and holiness. In hindsight, Augustine considered Platonism to come closest to Christianity in its philosophical view of God; Platonism held an idea of God as the cause of all existence, the basis of true rationality, and the blessed goal of life. As the best of Greek philosophy, it posits a God who is the unchangeable, simple, living spirit who made all things, and

---

81. John of Damascus, *An Exact Exposition of the Orthodox Faith*, 1.1, in NPNF2, 9.2:1.
82. John of Damascus, *An Exact Exposition of the Orthodox Faith*, 1.3, in NPNF2, 9.2:2–3.
83. John of Damascus, *An Exact Exposition of the Orthodox Faith*, 1.4, in NPNF2, 9.2:4.
84. John of Damascus, *An Exact Exposition of the Orthodox Faith*, 1.3, in NPNF2, 9.2:2.
85. John of Damascus, *An Exact Exposition of the Orthodox Faith*, 1.5, in NPNF2, 9.2:5.
86. Prologue to John of Damascus, *An Exact Exposition of the Orthodox Faith*, in NPNF2, 9.2:vii.

asserts that ultimate happiness is found only in knowing and imitating this God.[87] In this, Augustine said, the philosophers confirm Paul's teaching that God's invisible things are seen by what He created (Rom. 1:20).[88] Augustine said that the beauty of heaven and earth and humanity is like a voice saying, "We are not God, but He made us," but apart from God's sovereign grace, men have "deaf ears."[89]

Therefore, Augustine wrote, "If those who are called philosophers, and especially the Platonists, have said aught that is true and in harmony with our faith, we are not only not to shrink from it, but to claim it for our own use from those who have unlawful possession of it." Just as Israel rightly plundered the Egyptians of silver and gold, so Christian theologians may use the truths recognized by non-Christian philosophers as "their gold and silver, which they did not create themselves, but dug out of the mines of God's providence which are everywhere scattered abroad, perversely and unlawfully prostituting to the worship of devils."[90] We may plunder the gold of Egypt, but we must not set our hearts on the idols of Egypt, which they served with God's gold (cf. Hos. 2:8).[91] The Christian may use the truths of philosophy, though he must be "on his guard" against the errors of philosophy (Col. 2:8), for the Romans, Greeks, and Egyptians "gloried in the name of wisdom" but foolishly turned from God to worship idols (Rom. 1:21–23).[92] They despised the message of Christ born as a child of a woman, crucified on a cross (1 Cor. 1:19–25), and resurrected from the dead (Acts 17:30–31).[93]

True, saving knowledge of God, according to Augustine, "starts from faith."[94] Demarest writes, "Augustine is insistent that saving wisdom (*sapientia*) is not possible without faith, understood both as intellectual assent to truths mediated in Scripture and personal commitment to Christ. It is in this sense that Augustine writes of the priority of faith: 'If you will not believe, you will not understand.'"[95] Augustine said, "Understanding is the reward of faith.

---

87. Augustine, *The City of God*, 8.4, 6, 8–9, in *NPNF1*, 2:147–50.
88. Augustine, *The City of God*, 8.6, in *NPNF1*, 2:149. Augustine also considered the possibility that Plato had learned elements of the Old Testament Scriptures in his travels (*The City of God*, 8.11, in *NPNF1*, 2:151–52).
89. Augustine, *Confessions*, 10.6, in *NPNF1*, 1:144.
90. Augustine, *On Christian Doctrine*, 2.40, in *NPNF1*, 2:554.
91. Augustine, *Confessions*, 7.9, in *NPNF1*, 1:109.
92. Augustine, *The City of God*, 8.10, 12, in *NPNF1*, 2:150–52.
93. Augustine, *The City of God*, 10.28, in *NPNF1*, 2:198.
94. Augustine, *On the Trinity*, 9.1, in *NPNF1*, 3:125.
95. Cited in Demarest, *General Revelation*, 29. The quotation comes from the Septuagint's rendering of Isa. 7:9 (*kai mē pisteusēte, oude mē sunēte*).

Therefore, do not seek to understand in order to believe, but believe that thou mayest understand."[96] Faith does not set aside the mind but engages the mind to receive God's authoritative Word and thus to know and love Him. Augustine himself had attempted to pursue understanding apart from faith, and it led him to skepticism and despair.[97] Demarest says, "Augustine was convinced that Christianity's special revelation represents the fulfillment and perfection of what was lacking in the Platonic tradition. Augustine held out little hope for the salvation of the heathen apart from the gospel of God's grace."[98] Non-Christian philosophers see God as men with poor eyesight view another land "at a distance" without knowing the way there.[99]

Assessment of Ancient and Early Christian Natural Theology

The interaction of early Christian theologians with ancient philosophies illustrates some basic principles about a Christian approach to non-Christian philosophy.[100] This requires balance and a healthy tension. However, from Aristides to Augustine, we find Christians willing to acknowledge that non-Christian philosophers offered some good and useful truths, such as the dependence of our world on a higher power for its existence, goodness, and order. But because these truths were embedded in and distorted by systems of thought antithetical to the gospel, early Christian apologists and divines did not hold an optimistic assessment of pagan philosophy. As Augustine said, true wisdom must begin with faith in God's Word, generated by a supernatural grace of the Spirit to overcome man's deeply-rooted rebellion against God. Darkness envelops the nations, and only Christ can dispel it.

These early Christian thinkers sought to expose the idolatrous and foolish philosophies of man by radical, biblical critique. They quoted the Scriptures and employed legitimate methods of reasoning shared by Christian and non-Christian alike. Greek fathers such as Athanasius and John of Damascus tried to prove some Christian doctrines to non-Christians through human reasoning. Although Augustine saw some signs of doctrines such as the Trinity in the natural world, he focused on using reasoning to critique non-Christian

---

96. Augustine, *On the Gospel of St. John*, in *NPNF1*, 7:184.

97. See Etienne Gilson, *The Christian Philosophy of Saint Augustine*, trans. L. E. M. Lynch (London: Victor Gollancz, 1961), 27–31, 38.

98. Demarest, *General Revelation*, 26.

99. Augustine, *The City of God*, 10.29, in *NPNF1*, 2:199.

100. For a biblical development of these thoughts, see Joel R. Beeke and Paul M. Smalley, "General Revelation: Philosophy and Science," in *Reformed Systematic Theology* (Wheaton: Crossway, 2019), 214–30.

perspectives and reveal the superiority of the Christian religion. Apart from Christ, man's best reasoning leaves him shortsighted: he has blurry glimpses of the heavenly country but is stranded far from it.

Medieval Development of Natural Theology

The study of Greek philosophy declined in the Western, Latin-speaking church until many ancient Greek texts, such as the metaphysical and ethical writings of Aristotle, were translated into Latin in the twelfth century. However, Aristotelian studies had flourished in Arabic culture from the ninth century on through the efforts of scholars such as Al-Kindi (801–873). In the centuries that followed, several Muslim and Jewish scholars carefully studied ancient Greek philosophy with a view toward integrating its insights into the analysis and defense of their own religious beliefs. Their writings influenced Christians in Europe.

Islam, Judaism, and Aristotelian Natural Theology

As early as Philo of Alexandria in the first century AD, Jewish philosophers were appropriating elements of Aristotle's argument for a Supreme Being as the cause of all things.[101] The philosophy of Aristotle penetrated non-Christian monotheistic thinking in a significant way through the writings of Muslim scholars such as Al-Farabi (c. 872–c. 951), Ibn Sina (Avicenna) (c. 980–1037), and Ibn Rushd (Averroes) (1126–1198) and the Jewish scholars Saadia Gaon (882–942) and Moses Maimonides (1135–1204). They pursued the systematic harmonization and philosophical defense of their religious beliefs.[102] Particularly relevant is their development of what is sometimes called the "kalam" or cosmological argument to prove the existence of God.[103] Though written from a non-Christian perspective, the translated works of Averroes and Maimonides would profoundly affect late medieval Christian theologians such as Thomas Aquinas.[104]

A significant project undertaken by these scholars was the development of natural theology. Averroes said, "We maintain that the business of philosophy is nothing other than to look into creation and to ponder over it in order to be guided to the Creator.... For the knowledge of creation leads to the cognizance

---

101. Wayne Hankey, "Natural Theology in the Patristic Period," in *The Oxford Handbook of Natural Theology*, 40.

102. Daniel H. Frank, "Jewish Perspectives on Natural Theology," in *The Oxford Handbook of Natural Theology*, 143.

103. William L. Craig, *The Kalām Cosmological Argument* (Eugene: Ore.: Wipf and Stock, 1979), 3–41.

104. Brian Davies, *The Thought of Thomas Aquinas* (Oxford: Oxford University Press, 1992), 26.

of the Creator, through the knowledge of the created."[105] Maimonides used Aristotelian arguments in an attempt to prove that there must be a First Mover from whom all motion or change comes and that this First Mover is one, without body, unchangeable, and eternal.[106]

Though Judaism and Islam share with Christianity some elements of monotheism, the former two religions lack the Bible's emphasis on sin's darkening of the human mind, man's perverse inclination toward idolatry, and salvation through Christ alone by the grace of the Spirit. That has significant implications for full-blown natural theology, which depends on human ability and willingness to acknowledge God as He reveals Himself in His works.

Christian Medieval Scholasticism: Anselm and Thomas Aquinas
In the latter half of the eleventh century, Anselm of Canterbury sought in his *Monologion* to prove, without appealing to the Bible, the existence of one, supreme, simple Good from which all other good things receive their goodness,[107] a line of thought reminiscent of ancient Platonism. He claimed to prove God's attributes, the Trinity, and divine creation, all by rational thinking.[108] Anselm also argued in his book *Proslogion* that when we consider that God is "a being than which none greater can be thought," we realize that this being must necessarily exist, for a being which necessarily exists is greater than one which might not exist.[109] This so-called ontological argument for the existence of God has proven controversial and difficult to accept even among Christians, but some philosophers still defend it—including the Westminster Divines (Westminster Confession, 1.1, 21.1).[110]

In the early twelfth century, Peter Lombard continued the Augustinian legacy of recognizing that non-Christian philosophy potentially deduced some truths about God, such as His eternity, omnipotence, wisdom, immutability,

---

105. *The Philosophy and Theology of Averroes*, trans. Mohammad Jamil-Ur-Rehman (Baroda: A. G. Widgery, 1921), 14, accessed October 14, 2016, http://oll.libertyfund.org/titles/rushd-the-philosophy-and-theology-of-averroes.

106. Moses Maimonides, *The Guide for the Perplexed*, trans. M. Friedländer, 2nd ed. (New York: Dover, 1956), 2.1 (145–54).

107. Anselm, *Monologion*, in *Saint Anselm: Basic Writings*, trans. S. N. Deane, intro. Charles Hartshorne, 2nd ed. (La Salle, Ill.: Open Court, 1962), 35–144. See Kelly, *Systematic Theology*, 1:66; Alexander W. Hall, "Natural Theology in the Middle Ages," in *The Oxford Handbook of Natural Theology*, 60.

108. Demarest, *General Revelation*, 33.

109. Anselm, *Proslogion*, ch. 2, in *A Scholastic Miscellany*, 73–74.

110. See the discussion in Kelly, *Systematic Theology*, 1:68–72.

simplicity, and goodness.[111] Bonaventure, writing in the thirteenth century, said that the study of the natural world is like the first rung on Jacob's ladder by which "we can step up to God, the supreme Craftsman"; we discern His "power, wisdom, and goodness" in "the origin, vastness, multitude, beauty, fullness, operation, and order of all things."[112] Only the blind, deaf, dumb fool will fail to "discover the First Principle through all these signs" and give Him praise.[113] Bonaventure may have assumed that climbing this ladder was an exercise performed by those who already had faith in God.[114] He also offered a form of the ontological argument based on our awareness that the good, true, and beautiful must exist: "If God is God, God is."[115]

The theologian most closely associated with natural theology is Thomas Aquinas, a contemporary of Bonaventure. Aquinas rejected Anselm's argument for the necessary existence of "something than which nothing greater can be thought."[116] However, based on Paul's teaching (Rom. 1:20), Aquinas asserted that God's existence can be demonstrated through what He has created.[117] Aquinas opposed forms of Aristotelianism that contradicted divine revelation, such as the philosophies that arose in Europe through the study of Averroes, but he welcomed the use of Aristotelian reasoning that complemented divine revelation.[118] He located the demonstration of God's existence according to his distinction between nature and grace, saying: "The existence of God and other like truths about God, which can be known by natural reason, are not articles of faith, but are preambles to the articles; for faith presupposes natural knowledge, even as grace presupposes nature, and perfection supposes something that can be perfected."[119]

Thus the doctrine of God's existence belongs to the natural realm of human reasoning. It is not an exercise in theology so much as in philosophy, specifically metaphysics.[120] Aquinas wrote, "The existence of God can be proved in five ways," then argued from visible effects to their divine source, as follows:

---

111. Peter Lombard, *The Sentences*, trans. Giulio Silano (Toronto: Pontifical Institutes of Mediaeval Studies, 2007), 1.3 (1:18–20).

112. Bonaventure, *The Journey of the Mind to God*, 1.9, 14, in *The Works of Bonaventure*, trans. Jose de Vinck (Paterson, N.J.: St. Anthony Guild Press, 1960), 1:13, 15.

113. Bonaventure, *The Journey of the Mind to God*, 1.15, in *Works*, 1:16.

114. Leo J. Elders, *The Philosophical Theology of St. Thomas Aquinas* (Leiden: Brill, 1990), 73.

115. Cited in Kelly, *Systematic Theology*, 1:72.

116. Thomas Aquinas, *Summa Theologica*, Pt. 1, Q. 2, Art. 1, Reply Obj. 2.

117. Thomas Aquinas, *Summa Theologica*, Pt. 1, Q. 2, Art. 2, Answer.

118. Hall, "Natural Theology in the Middle Ages," in *The Oxford Handbook on Natural Theology*, 64–65.

119. Thomas Aquinas, *Summa Theologica*, Pt. 1, Q. 2, Art. 2, Reply Obj. 1.

120. Elders, *The Philosophical Theology of St. Thomas Aquinas*, 83–84.

1) *Argument from Change.* All change must be put in motion by something else, and "this cannot go on to infinity," for then the process would never start; therefore, "it is necessary to arrive at a first mover, put in motion by no other; and this everyone understands to be God."

2) *Argument from Causation.* Everything in this world must have an "efficient cause" prior to itself, and an infinite series of causes is impossible, so there must be a "first efficient cause."

3) *Argument from Contingency.* Natural things have the possibility of being or not being, so it is possible that "at one time there could have been nothing in existence." However, nothing would ever exist since nothing can come from nothing. Therefore, something must exist whose being is not merely possible but necessary. If its necessity is caused by another necessary being, then at some point we must have a necessary being that exists of itself and not of another. God is this necessary being.

4) *Argument from Perfection.* We see degrees of goodness in everything. One degree of goodness is always caused by something that has a higher degree of goodness or other perfections. "Therefore, there must also be something which is to all beings the cause of their being, goodness, and every other perfection; and this we call God."

5) *Argument from Design.* Many things in nature lack intelligence, yet they often act with evident design to produce good results. An arrow shot to its mark requires an archer. "Therefore some intelligent being exists by whom all natural things are directed to their end; and this being we call God."[121]

These proofs all follow the same basic formula in arguing from God's works to God's existence: "The greater does not arise from the less; only the higher explains the lower."[122] Aquinas then argued that if God is the First Mover and pure act, He must be spirit, not a material body, a being of absolute simplicity without composition or parts.[123] However, he soon turned to the Scriptures, catholic Christian tradition, and other arguments to develop a fuller picture of God's attributes. Thus the "five ways" are not a comprehensive proof for Christian theism but only a starting point to introduce the reality of God.[124]

In the five proofs of Aquinas, we sense echoes of non-Christian natural theology, such as Aristotle's First Mover (proof #1), his argument against an

---

121. Thomas Aquinas, *Summa Theologica*, Pt. 1, Q. 2, Art. 3, Answer.
122. R. Garrigou-Lagrange, cited in Kelly, *Systematic Theology*, 1:83.
123. Thomas Aquinas, *Summa Theologica*, Pt. 1, Q. 3.
124. Davies, *The Thought of Thomas Aquinas*, 26.

infinite regress of natural causes (#2), and his view of natural teleology (#5) as well as Plato's distinction between the necessary being of the Forms and this transitory world (#3) and his concept of the supreme Good (#4)—ideas that resonated with Averroes, Avicenna, and Maimonides, whose writings Aquinas had studied.[125] At the same time, we should recognize that medieval theologians such as Aquinas could also look to the precedent set by Athanasius and John of Damascus who argued confidently from natural revelation to fundamental truths about God.

Aquinas believed that people can know God in this life by natural reason (citing Rom. 1:19) by reasoning from sensible things to God as from effects to their cause: "We can be led from them so far as to know of God whether He exists, and to know of Him what must necessarily belong to Him, as the first cause of all things, exceeding all things caused by Him."[126] Aquinas wrote, however, "We can have a more perfect knowledge of God by grace than by natural reason" (citing 1 Cor. 2:10). Divine revelation reveals some things "to which natural reason cannot reach, as, for instance, that God is Three and One."[127] Knowledge of God by natural reason is not sufficient for salvation but must be supplemented by supernatural knowledge obtained by faith.[128] Furthermore, the things that natural reason teaches us about God are better accepted by faith in God's Word, for "human reason is very deficient in things concerning God." The philosophers "have fallen into many errors," and certainty is only attained by trusting in "God Himself who cannot lie."[129] Therefore, Aquinas did not see the five ways to prove God's existence as necessary or superior to simple faith in the gospel. He said, "There is nothing to prevent a man, who cannot grasp a proof, accepting, as a matter of faith, something which in itself is capable of being scientifically [philosophically] known and demonstrated."[130]

Assessment of Thomist Natural Theology

Aquinas has had a major impact on Christian thought both before and since the Reformation. Though some of Aquinas's teachings were condemned in 1277 by church authorities, in 1323 Pope John XXII canonized him as a saint, and in 1567 Pope Pius V declared him to be a *doctor* (authoritative teacher)

---

125. Elders, *The Philosophical Theology of St. Thomas Aquinas*, 71, 89–127; cf. Davies, *The Thought of Thomas Aquinas*, 28–30.

126. Thomas Aquinas, *Summa Theologica*, Pt. 1, Q. 12, Art. 12, Answer.

127. Thomas Aquinas, *Summa Theologica*, Pt. 1, Q. 12, Art. 13, Answer and Reply Obj. 1.

128. Thomas Aquinas, *Summa Theologica*, Pt. 2.2, Q. 2, Art. 3.

129. Thomas Aquinas, *Summa Theologica*, Pt. 2.2, Q. 2, Art. 4, Answer.

130. Thomas Aquinas, *Summa Theologica*, Pt. 1, Q. 2, Art. 2, Reply Obj. 1.

of the Roman Catholic Church. Though Aquinas's influence waned somewhat in the centuries that followed, in 1879 Pope Leo XIII declared that Aquinas's systematics was a solid Roman Catholic remedy to false teaching, and directed educational institutions to use his writings extensively.[131] The Thomist proofs for God's existence remain a significant part of Roman Catholic theology, as evidenced in the church's catechism issued in the late twentieth century.[132]

Aquinas worked out his rational proofs with confidence in their persuasive power of "natural reason, to which all men are forced to give their assent."[133] The effectiveness of those proofs is debatable. Some find them convincing; we think that they have an intuitive appeal that resonates with general revelation, yet they fail to provide absolute and independent rational proof. Others think that they only confirm what Christians already know and believe. As one scholar quips, "The proofs are only efficacious for those who do not need them."[134] They also have an underlying circularity, for Aquinas assumed a certain view of God and then deduced that this God exists. Even so, the conclusions of the arguments prove at best that a Supreme Being exists, but this Being is a philosophical abstraction far from being the personal God revealed in the Bible.[135]

Demarest writes, "Thomas Aquinas must be commended for stressing the rationality of the Christian faith,…the indisputable connection between the divine Reality 'out there' and empirical data 'down here.'"[136] Aquinas spoke out against the tendency of some medieval writers, following Averroes, to build a solid wall of separation between philosophy and theology and thus split the Christian worldview into two contradictory compartments. Kelly comments, "It was St. Thomas's massive achievement convincingly to affirm the unity of truth within the intellectual turmoil of medieval Christian Europe."[137]

However, Aquinas leaned too much on human reasoning and, ironically, not enough on God's general revelation as sufficient in itself to make God known and to render man without excuse. Demarest says,

> Our chief criticism of Thomas is that he broke with the Platonic-Augustinian intuitive approach and promoted the Aristotelian method that seeks knowledge of ultimate Reality on the basis of a purely empirical analysis of natural phenomena…. By denying man's possession of first principles,

---

131. Brian Davies, *Aquinas*, Outstanding Christian Thinkers (London: Continuum, 2002), 6–7.
132. *Catechism of the Catholic Church* (New York: Doubleday, 1994), sec. 32, 34.
133. Thomas Aquinas, *Summa contra Gentiles*, 1.2.3, cited in Demarest, *General Revelation*, 35.
134. Gabriel Marcel, paraphrased in Elders, *The Philosophical Theology of St. Thomas Aquinas*, 89.
135. Demarest, *General Revelation*, 38.
136. Demarest, *General Revelation*, 41.
137. Kelly, *Systematic Theology*, 1:166.

including intuitive apprehension of the Creator, Thomas in his quest to demonstrate the existence and infinite perfections of God was crippled from the start. Whereas the apostle Paul teaches in Romans 1:19–21 that God is known from His created effects, Aquinas made the much more ambitious claim that the existence and infinite perfections of God can be demonstrably proved.[138]

The reliance of medieval theologians on human reason presupposed a clear and inward light by which all men can accurately see and understand the truth. This assumption fails to take account of the "noetic effects" of the fall and the corruption of all human faculties by sin, darkening the mind and making its reasoning futile (Rom. 1:21–22; Eph. 4:17–18). Perhaps this assumption was unwittingly imported from the philosophers of Islam and Judaism. While medieval scholastics such as Anselm and Aquinas put confidence in human reasoning in tension with the necessity of supernatural grace and special revelation in Christ, their theology granted a place for human rational autonomy apart from God. In so doing, they may have opened the door for the development of a philosophical approach to God that supplements or contradicts the Bible. Kelly writes, "In general, what they said was orthodox…. However, insofar as they attempted to demonstrate that God is and more particularly who He is apart from the Trinitarian witness of Holy Scripture, they unwittingly began a bifurcation between the God of nature and the God of Scripture that would eventually lead to a God of nature who was different from the one of Scripture."[139]

The medieval theologians may also have sought to accommodate the man-centered demand that God prove His existence to those who are inclined to be skeptical and rebellious. However, God's Word does not attempt to prove anything before the judgment seat of men; rather, man is summoned before the judgment seat of God. Man has no right to judge God but must hope in His mercy.

General revelation cannot be co-opted by fallen man's quest for rational autonomy and demand for proof. As one scholar wrote, "The insufficiency of the proofs for the existence of God is explained by the fundamental fact that God alone is the criterion of His truth, God alone is the argument for His being. God can never be subject to logical demonstrations nor enclosed in the causal chain."[140] Instead, the existence of God is the foundation for all rational thinking. Kelly thinks this is Anselm's insight: "Unless we presuppose God as

---

138. Demarest, *General Revelation*, 41–42, emphasis original.
139. Kelly, *Systematic Theology*, 1:163.
140. Paul Evdokimov, quoted in Kelly, *Systematic Theology*, 1:65.

the one [than] whom no greater can be conceived, then we cannot make sense of anything else.... Some kind of 'ontological' presupposition seems necessary for any and every comprehensive system of reasoning.... Systems of thought that reject the Holy Trinity need some other ultimate reference point to make their system work; some necessary thing." Thus God's existence is not something proven by a string of logic so much as is the great "given" that undergirds and enables all human thinking.[141]

The Reformation's Critical Assessment of Natural Theology

The Renaissance and Reformation profoundly affected Christian theology. With the rise of modern science, man's confidence in the power of human reasoning mushroomed and spawned a multiplication of heretical theistic and atheistic philosophies. It is impossible in the scope of this article to survey all the major Reformed thinkers of the modern era and their views of natural theology. Rather, we will highlight some emphases of major Reformers Martin Luther and John Calvin, then examine developments in the work of theologians of later Reformed orthodoxy.

Critique of Natural Theology: Luther and Calvin

Luther taught that there are two kinds of knowledge of God: a general knowledge of God's existence and justice that all men possess but which remains futile, and a particular knowledge of God as Savior through Jesus Christ.[142] Natural reason recognizes that the motions of celestial bodies (sun, moon, and stars) follow an order ordained by a Ruler who will judge all men. This is a knowledge of God according to the law, but only the Word of God reveals the knowledge of God according to the gospel.[143] Thus human reason speaks of God as "a blind man discusses color."[144] Though men cannot escape the knowledge that God exists, reason gropes in the dark and "plays blind man's bluff with God."[145]

While human reason created by God helps man to serve God, it is infected by pride and is a spiritual prostitute to the devil. Philosophical speculation about God, according to Luther, is powerless to bring men to God.[146] Thus

---

141. Kelly, *Systematic Theology*, 1:74–75.

142. Martin Luther, *Lectures on Galatians, Chapters 1–4*, trans. Jaroslav Pelikan, in *Luther's Works*, 26:399–400.

143. Martin Luther, *Sermons on the Gospel of St. John, Chapters 1–4*, trans. Martin H. Bertram, in *Luther's Works*, 22:149–52.

144. Luther, *Sermons on the Gospel of St. John, Chapters 1–4*, in *Luther's Works*, 22:153.

145. Martin Luther, *Lectures on Jonah, The German Text, 1526*, trans. Martin H. Bertram, in *Luther's Works*, 19:53–55.

146. Demarest, *General Revelation*, 43–49.

Luther said Aristotle's reasoning is almost entirely useless.[147] Luther wrote, "Philosophers argue and ask speculative questions about God and arrive at some kind of knowledge"; however, such knowledge is "merely objective" and does not draw men to God as Savior.[148]

Early Lutheran acceptance of general revelation while rejecting medieval Aristotelian arguments for God's existence appears in Melanchthon's comment in 1521: "God has declared his majesty to all men by the creation and governance of the whole universe. But arguing how God's existence can be deduced with a human syllogism is characteristic more of curiosity than piety, especially since it is not safe for human reason to blather about such things."[149] Luther regarded the "Aristotelian or philosophical god" as the deity of false religion and said, "He is of no concern to us," for "our God is He whom the Holy Scriptures show."[150] However, in 1535, Melanchthon included proofs for God's existence in his *Loci*, apparently with Luther's approval, indicating that Lutheran theology found them useful as it developed systematically.[151]

Calvin had a magnificent view of God's self-revelation in creation and the seed of religion in all mankind.[152] On this basis, Calvin said that the philosophers attained to some truth. Plato "taught that the highest good of the soul is likeness to God."[153] Philosophers recognized that man is a "microcosm" of the world, containing in himself miraculous reflections of the Creator's glory.[154] They had also made helpful distinctions in logic with regard to causation, which Calvin himself used.[155] However, he warned that though men can grasp some concept of the divine, they immediately slip into foolish and corrupt imaginations about God, demonstrating the "stupidity and silliness" of "the whole tribe of philosophers," including "Plato, the most religious of all."[156] They "conceive that all parts of the universe are quickened by God's secret inspiration," but "they

---

147. Martin Luther, *Disputation against Scholastic Theology*, trans. Harold J. Grimm, in *Luther's Works*, 31:12, #44, 50.

148. Martin Luther, *Lectures on Genesis, Chapters 45–50*, trans. Paul D. Pahl, in *Luther's Works*, 8:17.

149. Philip Melanchthon, *Commonplaces: Loci Communes 1521*, trans. and ed. Christian Preus (St. Louis: Concordia, 2014), 63. Curiosity refers not merely to the desire for knowledge, but a wicked delight in it.

150. Martin Luther, *Lectures on Genesis, Chapters 21–25*, trans. George V. Schick, in *Luther's Works*, 4:145.

151. Muller, *Post-Reformation Reformed Dogmatics*, 3:172.

152. Calvin, *Inst.*, 1.3 and 1.5.

153. Calvin, *Inst.*, 1.3.3.

154. Calvin, *Inst.*, 1.5.3.

155. Calvin, *Inst.*, 1.16.9; 3.14.17, 21.

156. Calvin, *Inst.*, 1.5.11.

are far from that earnest feeling of grace which he [Paul] commends, because they do not at all taste God's special care, by which alone his fatherly favor is known."[157] Comfort is found not in the concept of God as a "first agent" who causes all motion but in the sovereign providence of the God of the Psalms.[158]

Calvin's grasp of the doctrine of human depravity kept him from embracing a too-high view of non-Christian philosophy. Man's mind is a "labyrinth" of confusion and a "vast, full spring" pouring out false gods, he wrote. The philosophers "tried with reason and learning to penetrate the heavens," their great minds producing a diversity of "fleeting unrealities" that contradicted each other.[159] Though Plato, Aristotle, and other philosophers might enthrall the reader with their rhetoric, the Bible penetrates the heart with such power that man's words vanish away.[160] Calvin concluded that "the truth of God has been corrupted by them all."[161]

One of the great errors of the philosophers, Calvin said, is that they view human reason as "suffused with divine light," and thus, "the best ruling principle for the leading of a good and blessed life."[162] However, the Bible depicts the mind and thought of fallen men as darkness (John 1:5). Man's reason, while not "completely wiped out," lies in "misshapen ruins" so that though "some sparks still gleam," they are "choked with dense ignorance."[163] Calvin said, "We conceive that there is a Deity; and then we conclude, that whoever he may be, he ought to be worshipped: but our reason here fails, because it cannot ascertain who or what sort of being God is."[164] He went on to say that the Creator has given the philosophers enough of a sense of His divinity to remove all excuse of their ungodliness, but "they are like a traveler passing through a field at night who in a momentary lightning flash sees far and wide, but the sight vanishes so swiftly that he is plunged again into the darkness of the night before he can take even a step—let alone be directed on his way by its help."[165]

Although Calvin rejected all non-Christian natural theologies, he did not reject God's general revelation or the possibility of Christians using natural theology for apologetics and edification. He compared our situation to an old man with poor vision who cannot read a book until putting on spectacles: We

---

157. Calvin, *Inst.*, 1.16.1.
158. Calvin, *Inst.*, 1.16.3.
159. Calvin, *Inst.*, 1.5.12.
160. Calvin, *Inst.*, 1.8.1.
161. Calvin, *Inst.*, 1.10.3.
162. Calvin, *Inst.*, 2.2.2.
163. Calvin, *Inst.*, 2.2.12.
164. Calvin, *Commentaries*, on Rom. 1:20.
165. Calvin, *Inst.*, 2.2.18.

cannot perceive God's glory in the created world without the Holy Spirit's guidance in the Scriptures.[166] Calvin himself did not construct a natural theology.[167] However, he said the apostle Paul modeled an evangelistic method according to which pagans are first shown there is one God, not many, before being taught of Christ.[168] "God was showed by natural arguments," though Paul did not present complex reasoning "after the manner of the philosophers" but spoke "plainly" to ordinary people "that in the order of nature there is a certain and evident manifestation of God."[169] When Paul addressed the philosophers in Athens, Calvin noted, the apostle "showeth by natural arguments [or 'proofs,' *probationes*] who and what God is, and how he is rightly worshiped."[170]

Calvin did not discount the use of reasoning in theology. He believed there are three kinds of human reasoning:

> There is a reason naturally implanted which cannot be condemned without insult to God, but it has limits which it cannot overstep without being immediately lost. Of this we have a sad proof in the fall of Adam. There is another kind of reason which is vicious, especially in a corrupt nature, and is manifested when mortal man, instead of receiving divine things with reverence, would subject them to his own judgment.... But there is a third kind of reason, which both the Spirit of God and Scripture sanction.

The last type of reason is "derived from the word of God and founded on it." It accepts God's Word even when it seems contrary to our wisdom and philosophy. In context, Calvin is arguing against what he deems illogical views and absurd arguments regarding the Lord's Supper.[171]

Calvin did not completely reject the use of rational arguments to demonstrate the existence of God. He even offered an example of the argument from design: "There is some God; for the world does not by chance exist, nor could it have proceeded from itself."[172] He also presented similar arguments for God from the "innumerable and yet distinct and well-ordered variety of the heavenly host," "the structure of the human body," and the "great excellence" of human

---

166. Calvin, *Inst.*, 1.6.1; cf. 1.14.1.
167. Muller, *Post-Reformation Reformed Dogmatics*, 1:271.
168. Calvin, *Commentaries*, on Acts 14:15.
169. Calvin, *Commentaries*, on Acts 14:17.
170. Calvin, *Commentaries*, on Acts 17:22. The rendering "proofs" (*probationes*) is from Muller, *Post-Reformation Reformed Dogmatics*, 1:274.
171. John Calvin, *The True Partaking of the Flesh and Blood of Christ in the Holy Supper*, in *Tracts Containing Treatises on the Sacraments, Catechism of the Church of Geneva, Forms of Prayer, and Confessions of Faith*, trans. Henry Beveridge (Edinburgh: Calvin Translation Society, 1849), 2:512–13.
172. Calvin, *Commentaries*, on Rom. 1:21.

nature.[173] Though these are not rigorous and extended philosophical proofs, they are rational inferences based on observations of the natural order.[174] Though Calvin did not develop anything comparable to Aquinas's five ways to prove God's existence, he did use simple arguments to convict men that they are without excuse for not worshiping the Creator.

Critical Appropriation of Theistic Arguments: Vermigli, Junius, and Turretin
The Reformation preserved a stream of Christian thought sympathetic to the scholastic use of philosophical arguments. Another early Reformer, Peter Martyr Vermigli, wrote,

> When natural philosophers studied them [the visible signs of God in creation], they were led to the knowledge of God on account of the wonderful properties and qualities of nature. Knowing the series of causes and their relation to effects, and clearly understanding that it is not proper to posit an infinite progression, they reasoned that they must arrive at some highest being, and so concluded that there is a God. Plato, Aristotle, and Galen have set forth these matters exceedingly well.[175]

Peter Martyr said that the Holy Scriptures "have described the same path to us"[176]: Christ points us to birds and flowers, Solomon to the ant, David to the heavens, and the book of Job to the animals and weather to learn of God and His ways. It is notable that many, if not all, of these examples take place in the context of faith nurtured by God's Word.

After the mid-sixteenth century, Reformed orthodox theologians labored to systematize their insights and dig deeper into the Word. In his seminal text on the nature of theology, Franciscus Junius (1545–1602) distinguished between natural and supernatural theology, both authored by God, but one granted by nature and the other by grace.[177] Junius said that "natural theology" proceeds "by the natural light of human understanding, in proportion to the method of human reason."[178] Though he might consider it a kind of knowledge, he could not call it "wisdom." Alluding to the ancient philosophers, Junius said natural

---

173. Calvin, *Inst.*, 1.5.2–3.

174. Michael Sudduth, *The Reformed Objection to Natural Theology*, Ashgate Philosophy of Religion Series (Farnham, England: Ashgate, 2009), 61.

175. Peter Martyr, *Loci Communes*, in *The Peter Martyr Library*, 4:21.

176. Peter Martyr, *Loci Communes*, in *The Peter Martyr Library*, 4:21.

177. Junius, *A Treatise of True Theology*, 141–42 (thesis 14). Cf. Belgic Confession of Faith (1561), art. 2.

178. Junius, *A Treatise of True Theology*, 145 (thesis 15).

theology draws conclusions from natural things and their motions, based on the relationship between cause and effect.[179]

Junius said natural theology suffers from a number of limitations. Human reason can make mistakes about human and natural phenomena and therefore is limited in deductions about supernatural realities. Beginning with the foundation of what we intuitively know, reason must argue from the general to the specific, penetrate into matters that are somewhat veiled in nature, and overcome its imperfect knowledge. Thus, though by nature we know that "God is to be worshiped," we do not know who the true God is. We cannot see Him directly, and what we can learn about God by reasoning is incomplete (Acts 14:15–17; 17:23–27; Rom. 1:18–20).[180] Even in Adam, before the fall, natural theology had to be nurtured by reasoning and could reach perfection only by supernatural grace.[181] Junius's emphasis on the limitations of Adam's prelapsarian reason is a departure from the theology of Aquinas, which has a more optimistic view of man's original ability to reason his way to God.[182]

Junius further taught that after the fall human nature was so depraved that "the natural gifts have been corrupted and the supernatural ones lost."[183] In this he agreed with Calvin and Augustine.[184] He wrote that man's mind is like a beautiful house struck down by force and is now "broken and ruined" and "buried in piles of broken pieces."[185] Nature teaches all humanity that "there is a God," but shrouded in spiritual darkness, "we see something of the truth as though distantly through the gloom."[186] Natural theology cannot bring us to a true knowledge of God or even prepare us effectively for it; such knowledge of God is a gift of saving grace. Though in some ways the conclusions of natural theology overlap with those of supernatural theology granted through the Word of God, they are as distinct as "music and arithmetic."[187] The illustration suggests that natural theology contains some of the basic principles of the true knowledge of God (just as arithmetic contains some principles that form the basis of music theory) but utterly fails to express its beauty or to move men's hearts (as actual music does).

---

179. Junius, *A Treatise of True Theology*, 145–46.

180. Junius, *A Treatise of True Theology*, 147–50.

181. Junius, *A Treatise of True Theology*, 151–54 (thesis 17).

182. John Platt, *Reformed Thought and Scholasticism: The Arguments for the Existence of God in Dutch Theology, 1575–1650* (Leiden: Brill, 1982), 135.

183. Junius, *A Treatise of True Theology*, 154–55 (thesis 18).

184. Calvin, *Inst.*, 2.2.12.

185. Junius, *A Treatise of True Theology*, 156.

186. Junius, *A Treatise of True Theology*, 94.

187. Junius, *A Treatise of True Theology*, 157–58 (thesis 19).

The result of natural theology in fallen, idolatrous mankind is "false theology," whether the "common" kind popular among men or the "philosophical" kind that reasons carefully but mistakenly to erroneous conclusions.[188] Philosophical knowledge of God, attained by "damaged reasoning" in sinners, is accessible only to a few intellectuals and takes time to work out; its relatively few true insights are mixed with many errors.[189] Junius did not reject philosophy completely. He continued to use Aristotelian categories to classify academic disciplines and kinds of causation,[190] and he referred extensively to ancient non-Christian writers such as Aristotle and Cicero.[191] Furthermore, Junius reproduced Aquinas's five proofs, albeit in a different order and with his own nuances.[192] Junius carefully restated the Thomist arguments in the light of Reformed doctrines of the supernatural character of faith and Calvin's reduction of man's natural knowledge of God to "bare and corrupt seeds."[193] How then could Junius produce a natural theology to argue for God's existence? What fallen nature cannot accomplish, renewed nature can trace out when guided by God's Word, he said. "God has tempered these same principles of nature corrupt in us, restored and renewed in the word of grace by the heavenly and supernatural means which we call the grace of God or the Spirit from the use of Scripture."[194] In other words, he appears to have believed that non-Christians cannot find the true God through reasoning, but a Christian theologian, guided by the Spirit through the Word, can formulate proper arguments that press non-Christians to recognize the witness of God's general revelation. These arguments, then, have apologetic value to cast down intellectual obstacles to the gospel but are without the power to save.[195]

Similarly, Johann Alsted (1588–1638) developed a natural theology upon a triple foundation: reason, universal experience, and the Holy Scriptures.[196]

---

188. Junius, *A Treatise of True Theology*, 95–96 (thesis 4).

189. Junius, *A Treatise of True Theology*, 151.

190. Willem J. Van Asselt, introduction to Junius, *A Treatise of True Theology*, xxix, xxxv.

191. Junius, *A Treatise of True Theology*, index and the translator's preface by David C. Noe.

192. Junius, *Theses Theologicae Heidelbergenses*, theses 21–25; *Summa Aliquot Locorum Communium SS. Theologia*, 1.3–4, quoted in Platt, *Reformed Thought and Scholasticism*, 139–42.

193. Junius, *Theses Theologicae Heidelbergenses*, theses 7, 9, 14–15; cf. *Summa Aliquot Locorum*, 1.5, cited in Platt, *Reformed Thought and Scholasticism*, 138, 141–42.

194. Junius, *Summa Aliquot Locorum*, 1.5, cited in Platt, *Reformed Thought and Scholasticism*, 142.

195. It seems to us that this last statement quoted by Junius answers Platt's charge that Junius is a "strange hybrid" (143), for he is not contradicting his previous assertions of natural man's inability to produce a true natural theology but asserting that regenerate man can produce one that vindicates Christianity against its accusers and convicts them of their refusal to honor God.

196. "Fundamentum Theologiae naturalis est triplex, Ratio, Experientia universalis, et Scriptura Sacra." Johann Alsted, *Theologia Naturalis* ([Frankfurt]: Antonium Hummium, 1615), 1.6 (5); cf. Muller, *Post-Reformation Reformed Dogmatics*, 3:167.

Stephen Charnock (1628–1680) presented several arguments for God's existence with a mixture of Scripture and reasoning.[197] He believed that the apostolic
example in Acts 17 showed that the truth of God's existence is not just "probable"
but "demonstrable by natural reason."[198] This Reformed use of the Thomistic
arguments for God is not a purely natural theology but a biblically informed
natural theology. It is seeing the world through the spectacles of Scripture.

Francis Turretin (1623–1687) viewed the existence of God as "an indubi-
table first principle of religion" that should "be taken for granted rather than
proved," and yet the "madness of modern atheists" requires that the question be
addressed. Turretin claimed that "the existence of God can be demonstrated by
unanswerable arguments, not only from the Scriptures, but also from nature
herself."[199] He proposed several arguments, including: (1) the universe must
have a cause, and an infinite series of causes is impossible; (2) the universe cannot be eternal but must have a beginning in time, and its beginning must arise
from someone; (3) the "wonderful beauty and order of the universe...requires
wisdom and intelligence" to bring it about; (4) all things tend to act toward
some end, which requires the direction of a designer.[200] These arguments are
similar to the approach of Aquinas. Turretin also argued for God's existence
from (5) the excellence of man in body and mind, which is an image of his
Creator; (6) the testimony of conscience against the crimes of men; and (7) the
universal consent of all nations through history that "there is some deity who
ought to be religiously worshipped."[201]

There is some tension between Turretin's statements that God's existence is
a "first principle" that should be presupposed, and this may be "demonstrated by
unanswerable arguments." However, Turretin sought to resolve that tension or
at least maintain it in proper balance. He said that the conclusions that biblical
doctrine has in common with "natural theology and sound reason" are "presupposed"—that is, they operate at a presuppositional level.[202] By using reason
as a means of argument, the Reformed do not elevate human reasoning to the
level of a judge, rule, foundation, or master to biblical religion but only employ
it as its instrument and servant.[203] Turretin said that rational, philosophical
arguments are limited in what they can demonstrate because the articles of the

197. Charnock, *The Existence and Attributes of God*, 1:23–77.
198. Charnock, *The Existence and Attributes of God*, 1:29.
199. Turretin, *Institutes*, 3.1.3–4 (1:169).
200. Turretin, *Institutes*, 3.1.6–12 (1:170–72).
201. Turretin, *Institutes*, 3.1.13–18 (1:173–75).
202. Turretin, *Institutes*, 1.8.1 (1:24).
203. Turretin, *Institutes*, 1.8.3, 5, 6 (1:24–25), cf. 1.13 (1:44–47).

Christian faith cannot be deduced by human reason but must be revealed by God's Word, though sound reason will not contradict them.[204] Sound reason is not "that which is blind and corrupted by sin, but that which is restored and enlightened by the Holy Spirit."[205] As God restores His image in men by His Word through His Spirit, He progressively heals their power of reason to serve in its proper, subordinate role to revelation. Stephen Grabill comments, "Turretin's stricture here not only indicates a positive use of regenerate natural theology but also simultaneously acknowledges the noetic effects of the fall."[206] Turretin said, "Although human understanding is very dark, yet there still remain in it some rays of natural light and certain first principles.... Faith, so far from destroying, on the contrary borrows them from reason and uses them to strengthen its own doctrines."[207]

How does reason function in the arguments against atheists for the existence of God? Turretin said atheists can be dealt with either by "arguments founded on Scripture" or by "philosophical" arguments, "that by principles of reason the prejudices against the Christian religion drawn from corrupt reason may be removed."[208] Therefore, he did not reject rational arguments for God's existence, but neither did he see them as foundational for faith. They were only helpful instruments to dismantle man's foolish objections against the testimony God gives to all men.

Turretin criticized some church fathers (including Justin Martyr) and medieval scholastics (possibly including Aquinas) because they "endeavored to bring Gentiles over to Christianity by a mixture of philosophical and theological doctrines" in a manner that "depends more upon the reasonings of Aristotle and other philosophers than upon the testimonies of the prophets and apostles."[209] Somewhat like the rationalists of Turretin's own day (such as the Socinians), these apologists made human reasoning the (partial) foundation of the faith.

Turretin's approach to natural theology is complex and nuanced, but we can summarize it in the following points: (1) The existence of God is rightly presupposed (inferred) by men because of the testimony of creation and conscience. (2) Most wicked men corrupt this sense of deity or the divine (*sensus deitatis*)

---

204. Turretin, *Institutes*, 1.9.6, 10 (1:30).

205. Turretin, *Institutes*, 1.10.1 (1:32).

206. Stephen J. Grabill, "Natural Law and the Noetic Effects of Sin: The Faculty of Reason in Francis Turretin's Theological Anthropology," *Westminster Theological Journal* 67 (2005):268 (full article, pp. 261–79).

207. Turretin, *Institutes*, 1.9.5 (1:29–30).

208. Turretin, *Institutes*, 1.8.23 (1:28).

209. Turretin, *Institutes*, 1.13.1 (1:44).

into idolatry. (3) Some wicked men reject this testimony entirely and deny that God exists. (4) Rational and philosophical arguments can demonstrate that such a denial of God is foolish, thereby snatching away the shield of atheists. (5) Such rational arguments cannot be constructed in a reliable way by human reason until they are renewed by the Holy Spirit through the Word. (6) Philosophical arguments are no basis for faith and therefore cannot bridge the gap between unbelief and belief, much less provide the foundation for Christianity. Rather, they prepare men intellectually for the gospel by removing a rational justification for atheism. They also help believers to dismantle the rational facade that covers their doubts. (7) To bring men to Christ, we must lay the foundation of God's written revelation upon which to build faith. Therefore, the arguments of natural theology provide negative weapons to demolish foolish and irrational prejudices, but they do not provide positive bridges to bring sinners to Christianity. As the apostle wrote, God's general revelation leaves men "without excuse," but the gospel alone reveals God's salvation (Rom. 1:20; 10:17).[210]

While some Reformed theologians of the sixteenth and seventeenth century gave arguments for the existence of God, they did not do so as a foundation upon which to build the structure of faith and, thus, the rest of theology. Instead, they valued them only for apologetic and polemical use. Richard Muller explains, "Their discussions of the proofs recognize that believers fundamentally and ultimately need no proof.... but also that believers do need, mediately, as it were, tools and weapons for their spiritual arsenals. The proofs fill a need in a world where doubts arise and atheists abound."[211]

Assessment of Early Reformed Views of Natural Theology
The Reformers and later Reformed orthodox theologians had a pessimistic view of natural human ability to reason its way to the true God. They said the minds of fallen sinners are shrouded in darkness. Even the light of God's self-revelation in nature is largely resisted or rejected. What divinity man perceives is corrupted into idolatry. Thus, the best of the pagan philosophers were like men with poor vision peering at God from a great distance, and their conclusions were blurred by sin and stained with errors.

However, Luther, Melanchthon, Calvin, Vermigli, Junius, and Turretin all affirmed the reality of general revelation through creation. Furthermore, the Reformed divines taught that Christians, with minds renewed by the Holy

---

210. Turretin, *Institutes*, 1.4.4–5 (1:10).
211. Muller, *Post-Reformation Reformed Dogmatics*, 3:170.

Spirit through the Word of God, can reason rightly from God's works to God. They used these arguments in the context of faith. In other words, they avoided the rationalism of a purely natural theology and sought to build a biblically informed theology of nature. They placed no confidence in such arguments to convert sinners but did believe that they could confront unbelievers with the irrationality of their unbelief, thereby removing excuses and laying bare their rebellion against the Creator.

As heirs of the great traditions of the Christian church, the early Reformed writers affirmed a limited use of arguments for God's existence and divine nature. This affirmation was rooted not primarily in philosophy but in the Bible's appeals to God's self-revelation in nature. As Bavinck noted, "Scripture contains germinally all that was later elaborated and dialectically unfolded in the proofs.... Scripture gives us a beginning and analogy of the etiological proof in Romans 1:20, of the teleological proof in Psalm 8 and Acts 14:17, of the moral proof in Romans 2:14," and "reasons from the being of humans to the being of God" in Psalm 94:9 and Acts 17:29.[212]

For Calvin, theistic arguments took the form of simple, rational inferences from causation or order. In this, he followed the path of the Holy Scriptures. Junius and Turretin developed more philosophical arguments, perhaps running the risk of putting undue confidence in human reason. The danger of highly developed philosophical arguments for the existence of God is that Christian theologians "became convinced that the truths of natural religion were demonstrable in the same way as those of mathematics or logic."[213] This we must avoid, for it shifts a fundamental article of religious faith out of the realm of submission to God into the realm of independent human inquiry. It also rests the truth of God's existence on the weak and fallible ground of fallen human reasoning, so that if the arguments stumble, God seems to fall. On the contrary, though men stumble in the darkness, God's light remains undimmed in creation and His Word.

Though we must guard against rationalism, it has also become clear in our study of historical theology that Barth's absolute rejection of general revelation and arguments for God's existence put him at odds not just with scholasticism but also with the mainstream of the Christian tradition, including Augustine and Calvin. Furthermore, while Van Til's warnings against the corruption of human autonomous reason resonate with the anthropology of the early Reformed divines, their writings show us that we need not fear all forms of

---

212. Bavinck, *Reformed Dogmatics*, 2:76.
213. Bavinck, *Reformed Dogmatics*, 2:77.

argumentation for God's existence. There is an approach to such arguments that is biblical and Reformed.

Toward a Biblical, Reformed Approach to Theistic Arguments

Having surveyed the history of natural theology from ancient times to Reformed orthodoxy, we may now offer some perspective on the rejection of natural theology and theistic proofs. We believe that the best approach to these matters is to affirm general revelation but reject natural theology[214]—at least, in the classic sense of a system of beliefs about God built entirely by human observation of the natural world and logical reasoning.[215]

For the church, general revelation is part of the infrastructure by which our faith in Christ addresses all of life, indeed, the meaning of the entire universe. Without an acknowledgement of general revelation, Christianity becomes unnatural and otherworldly instead of the means of a gracious God to heal fallen nature and restore His creation.[216] To avoid such a distorted and fragmented worldview, Christians have confessed through the ages, "I believe in God the Father, Almighty, Maker of heaven and earth."[217] The Creator makes Himself known through His creation, and the Redeemer does not destroy His creation but supernaturally regenerates and restores it.

Our historical investigation has underlined the complexity of the question and the need for balance. On the one hand, theologians have recognized the debilitating effects of man's depravity upon his mind and the need for special revelation and inward grace. Human philosophy is corrupted by our proud rebellion; its very attempts to reason about God are impaired by its assertion of independence from God. On the other hand, Christian theologians have taught that general revelation continues to transmit some knowledge of God to all men and that Christians may appeal to this knowledge as they declare the gospel of Jesus Christ to the nations.

We conclude with the following points:

1. *God testifies to Himself through the natural world* that He created, sustains, and rules (Acts 14:17; Rom. 1:20) and through human conscience (Rom. 2:14–16). In natural revelation, the initiative belongs to God. Bavinck said, "Natural theology presupposes, first of all, that God reveals himself in his handiwork.

---

214. Erickson, *Christian Theology*, 136.
215. Some Reformed theologians, like Junius, spoke of natural theology, but not in this sense.
216. Bavinck, *Reformed Dogmatics*, 1:322.
217. Apostles' Creed (art. 1), in *Doctrinal Standards*, 1.

It is not humans who seek God but God who seeks humans."[218] Therefore, knowledge of God, even through nature, is an effect of divine revelation, not an independent deduction of men.

2. *Belief in God is a valid presupposition for human thought*, without which life is irrational. God has manifested Himself to mankind (Rom. 1:19). When men hold back the truth from attaining its proper ends of worship and thankfulness in their hearts and lives, their minds darken and they become fools (Rom. 1:18, 21).

3. *The proper posture of human reason is to fear God as His servant*, not to view itself as wise and the judge of all things. Proverbs 1:7 says, "The fear of the LORD is the beginning of knowledge: but fools despise wisdom and instruction." God gave us our minds, like all other faculties, to acknowledge Him and honor Him as God. Considering yourself to be wise and depending on your intelligence to reason through life's questions is a mark of rebellion against God. Proverbs 3:5–7 says, "Trust in the LORD with all thine heart; and lean not unto thine own understanding. In all thy ways acknowledge him, and he shall direct thy paths. Be not wise in thine own eyes: fear the Lord, and depart from evil."

4. *The sinner's mind is alienated from God and cannot reason its way to its Creator* without wandering into foolishness and futility (Eph. 4:17). The Canons of Dort say that "glimmerings of natural light" remain in fallen man, but though "he retains some knowledge of God" and "virtue," this knowledge cannot bring men to salvation, and they are "incapable of using it aright even in things natural and civil" but defile it with sin and are thus "inexcusable before God."[219]

5. *The philosophy of non-Christians is distorted by Satan*, who "deceiveth the whole world" (Rev. 12:9). Non-Christians at times seek wisdom through pagan spirituality, as was admitted by some philosophers. Even atheistic philosophers may speak in terms of spirituality or seek a sense of transcendence—generally by a form of pantheism that divinizes the material world and treats men as gods. Therefore, unregenerate reason is far from neutral but is dominated and directed by God's greatest enemy.

6. *A right use of reason depends on the Spirit-illuminated Word* to acknowledge the glory of the Creator in His creation. Apart from the Word, "there is no light in

---

218. Bavinck, *Reformed Dogmatics*, 2:74.
219. Canons of Dort (3/4.4), in *The Three Forms of Unity*, 141.

them" (Isa. 8:20), but by union with Christ we are "light in the Lord" and have the capacity to be discerning and wise (Eph. 5:8, 10, 15). Scott Swain writes, "In the state of grace, natural theology is healed under the tutelage of Holy Scripture and through the Holy Spirit's work of regeneration and renewal."[220]

Bavinck says, "Accordingly, Christians follow a completely mistaken method when, in treating natural theology, they, as it were, divest themselves of God's special revelation in Scripture and the illumination of the Holy Spirit, discuss it apart from any Christian presumptions, and then move on to special revelation."[221] We reject as unbiblical and semi-Pelagian the stance on natural theology taken by the Roman Catholic First Vatican Council (1870) that divides knowledge into two categories, one "by natural reason" and the other "by divine faith." Vatican I asserts that natural reason may achieve a "certain" (*certus*) or sure knowledge of God apart from God's Word, and "right reason demonstrates the foundations of faith."[222] Classic Roman Catholicism is mere rationalism. On the contrary, a sure knowledge of God eludes the wicked, idolatrous man, and human reason does not operate in a separate compartment from believing knowledge, much less as its foundation, but operates in conjunction with one's faith commitments. Therefore, a true theology of nature, including apologetic theology, must be biblically sanctified, informed and directed.

7. *Christians may make rational inferences from creation to God.* Paul argues that men should not worship men "of like passions," but "the living God" (Acts 14:15). We should not view God as anything like an idol in a temple because "he giveth to all life, breath, and all things" (Acts 17:24), a concept acknowledged by Greek philosophers.[223] Insofar as we have records of Paul's messages, he did not use demonstrative, logical proofs but called upon unbelievers to draw logical inferences from the natural world, and he affirmed the logical inferences they made. We can and should do the same.

---

220. Scott Swain, "Theses on Natural Theology," Thesis IV.3, http://www.reformation21.org /blog/2015/07/theses-on-natural-theology.php, July 10, 2015, accessed October 21, 2016. Dr. Swain is Professor of Systematic Theology at Reformed Theological Seminary and Academic Dean at their Orlando campus.

221. Bavinck, *Reformed Dogmatics*, 2:74.

222. Dogmatic Constitution of the Catholic Faith (April 24, 1870), chs. 2, 4, in *The Creeds of Christendom*, ed. Philip Schaff, rev. David S. Schaff (1931; repr., Grand Rapids: Baker, 1983), 2:240, 247, 249.

223. David G. Peterson, *The Acts of the Apostles*, The Pillar New Testament Commentary (Grand Rapids: Eerdmans, 2009), 495.

8. *Christians may use arguments to show the foolishness of those who deny God* intellectually or practically, applying general revelation to show them that they are without excuse (Rom. 1:20). For example, when men denied that an omniscient God knew their sins and would call them to account, the psalmist rebuked them for foolishness and reasoned that our knowledge of the world around us must come from a Creator who knows far more (Ps. 94:6–10). When a natural argument "refutes unbelievers by exposing their willful suppression of the truth that God has made manifest through creation and providence," it also fortifies believers against doubts and, "with natural law," to bring a measure of order and restraint to society, though it cannot elevate men to saving wisdom and holiness.[224]

9. *The wise use of theistic arguments will vary with culture and education.* When addressing Jews and Gentile proselytes who knew and respected the Holy Scriptures, Paul appealed to biblical history and made no reference to the witness of creation (Acts 13:16–41). When exhorting a crowd of pagans ready to worship anyone who worked a miracle, the apostle appealed to simple facts about human nature and everyday experience (Acts 14:11–18). When addressing the intellectual elite of Athens, he made a reasoned argument that included reference to their own practice and quotations from pagan writers (Acts 17:22–31).

10. *Christians should beware of glorying in human wisdom* or attempting to convert people through artful human rhetoric or argumentation. Paul knew "the Greeks seek after wisdom" (1 Cor. 1:22). They loved the kind of reasoning that their culture deemed wise. However, Paul also knew that "in the wisdom of God the world by wisdom knew not God" (v. 21). God had designed salvation so that "no flesh should glory in his presence," but "glory in the Lord (vv. 29, 31). Therefore, Paul refused to speak "with excellency of speech or of wisdom" (1 Cor. 2:1). This declaration is not a renunciation of reason but a sanction for the use of plain and direct speech in our evangelism and avoiding anything that smacks of intellectual pride.

One example of foolish pride is the demand for rational and empirical proof for all knowledge. Brian Morley writes, "We cannot expect to have 100-percent proof, in the normal sense of the term *proof*, for most of what we believe. As non-omniscient beings, we do not have absolute, airtight proof for real-world

---

224. Swain, "Theses on Natural Theology," Thesis VIII.1–3. Swain lists these as three "ends of natural theology," but does not make the latter two dependent on the first as we have.

things."[225] We must not flatter ourselves or our hearers by claiming to offer an infallible logical demonstration of God's existence. Absolute, infallible certainty in these matters belongs only to the Word of the One who is omniscient, true, and worthy of all trust.

11. *Theistic arguments are appeals to God's own witness in creation:* "He left not himself without witness," says Acts 14:17. Christ's "witnesses" are prominent in Acts in the Spirit-empowered preaching of the apostolic church (Luke 24:48; Acts 1:8, etc.); what is surprising is the application of the idea of "witness" to creation. The legal terminology of *witness* and *testimony* in the Bible is covenantal in orientation. In the Mosaic covenant, the Lord invoked heaven and earth as witnesses to His covenant with Israel.[226] Isaiah wrote that Israel was God's witness to declare to the nations that He is the only God, not their idols (Isa. 43:9–13; 44:8–9), in a legal case in which God asserts His rights as the Creator of heaven and earth.[227] In a similar fashion, God uses creation as His witness to the sons and daughters of Adam that their failure to worship Him demonstrates that they are cursed covenant-breakers (cf. Isa. 24:4–6).

Bavinck noted, "Scripture makes no attempt to prove the existence of God." The Bible speaks of natural revelation "in the language of witness, not appealing to the reasoning intellect" to judge whether the argument is compelling but speaking "with authority" to "the human heart and conscience."[228] We must not attempt to formulate a natural theology that sets up human reason as the authority. Rather, we must declare God as the supreme Judge and bring sinners into the courtroom where God's natural witnesses testify of His glory and of their ungodliness. Bavinck says of these witnesses: "Though weak as proofs, they are strong as testimonies"[229] when they are used properly. Unbelievers may always find some counter-argument to resist the truth, but God's revelation in creation reaches their hearts nonetheless.

12. *Theistic arguments are at best like the law that convicts but cannot save.* They cannot lead anyone to salvation apart from the gospel of Christ (Rom. 10:13–17). The Canons of Dort link the "light of nature" with "the law,"[230] and then state, "What therefore neither the light of nature, nor the law could do,

---

225. Morely, *Mapping Apologetics*, 351.
226. Deut. 4:26; 30:19; 31:28; 32:1; Ps. 50:4; Isa. 1:2.
227. Isa. 40:25–28; 41:20–24; 42:5; 43:1, 7, 15; 45:7–8, 12, 18.
228. Bavinck, *Reformed Dogmatics*, 2:75–76.
229. Bavinck, *Reformed Dogmatics*, 2:91.
230. Canons of Dort (3/4.4–5), in *The Three Forms of Unity*, 141–42.

that God performs by the operation of the Holy Spirit through the Word or ministry of reconciliation, which is the glad tidings concerning the Messiah, by means whereof it hath pleased God to save such as believe, as well under the Old, as under the New Testament."[231] John Frame says, "There are arguments for God's existence…that are of some value. Even the unregenerate sometimes confess the existence of God on the basis of argument, experience, or feeling. But they do not live for him. Such tentative beliefs are not sufficient to produce a God-centered life."[232] Such "tentative beliefs" cannot overcome the power of sin and unbelief in the heart.

Conclusion

Thus, we conclude with Augustine, who said, "That God is a certain life eternal, unchangeable, intelligent, wise, making wise, some philosophers even of this world have seen. The principles of all things created, they saw indeed, but afar off…. They saw (as far as can be seen by man) the Creator by means of the creature, the Worker by His work." Yet, as the apostle Paul said, they held (or held down) the truth in unrighteousness, and became as fools (Rom. 1:18–22). Augustine said, "What by curious search they found, by pride they lost." What then is the truth? How shall we find the way back to God? How shall we live and not die? Augustine directs us to the words of Christ: "I am the way, the truth, and the life: no man cometh unto the Father, but by me" (John 14:6).[233]

---

231. Canons of Dort (3/4.6), in *The Three Forms of Unity*, 142.
232. John M. Frame, *The Doctrine of God* (Phillipsburg, N.J.: P&R, 2002), 740.
233. Augustine, *Sermons on New Testament Lessons*, Sermon 91, in *NPNF1*, 6:531–32.

EXPERIENTIAL THEOLOGY

Chapter 15

Calvin as an Experiential Preacher

John Calvin embraced a high view of preaching. He called the preaching office "the most excellent of all things," commended by God that it might be held in the highest esteem. "There is nothing more notable or glorious in the church than the ministry of the gospel," he concluded.[1] In commenting on Isaiah 55:11, he said, "The Word goeth out of the mouth of God in such a manner that it likewise goeth out of the mouth of men; for God does not speak openly from heaven but employs men as his instruments."[2]

Calvin viewed preaching as God's normal means of salvation and benediction. He said that the Holy Spirit is the "internal minister" who uses the "external minister" in preaching the Word. The external minister "holds forth the vocal word and it is received by the ears," but the internal minister "truly communicates the thing proclaimed, [which] is Christ."[3] Thus, God Himself speaks through the mouth of His servants by His Spirit. "Wherever the gospel is preached, it is as if God himself came into the midst of us," Calvin wrote.[4] Preaching is the instrument and the authority that the Spirit uses in His saving work of illuminating, converting, and sealing sinners. "There is...an inward efficacy of the Holy Spirit when he sheds forth his power upon hearers, that they may embrace a discourse [sermon] by faith."[5]

Calvin taught that the preached Word and the inner testimony of the Spirit should be distinguished but cannot be separated. Word and Spirit are joined

---

1. John Calvin, *Institutes of the Christian Religion*, ed. John T. McNeill and trans. Ford Lewis Battles (Philadelphia: Westminster Press, 1960), 4.3.3 [hereafter: Inst.]. This chapter draws at some points from "Calvin and Preaching: The Power of the Word," in *Calvin: Theologian and Reformer*, ed. Joel R. Beeke and Garry Williams (Grand Rapids: Reformation Heritage Books, 2010), 137–167.

2. Calvin, *Commentary on Isaiah*, 4:172.

3. Calvin, *Tracts and Treatises*, trans. Henry Beveridge (Grand Rapids: Eerdmans, 1958), 1:173.

4. Calvin, *Commentary on Synoptic Gospels*, 3:129.

5. Calvin, *Commentary on Ezekiel*, 1:61.

together organically; without the Spirit, the preached Word only adds to the condemnation of unbelievers. On the other hand, Calvin admonished the radicals who accented the Spirit at the expense of the Word, saying that only the spirit of Satan separates itself from the Word.[6]

This stress on preaching moved Calvin to be active on several fronts in Geneva. First, he showed his convictions through his own example. Calvin preached from the New Testament on Sunday mornings, the Psalms on Sunday afternoons, and the Old Testament at 6:00 a.m. on one or two weekdays. Following this schedule during his last stay in Geneva from 1541 to 1564, Calvin preached nearly 4,000 sermons, more than 170 sermons a year. On his deathbed, he spoke of his preaching as more significant than his writings.[7]

Second, Calvin often preached to his congregation about their responsibility to hear the Word of God aright. He taught his members in what spirit they should come to the sermon, what to listen for in preaching, and what was expected of those who hear. Since, for Calvin, all true preaching is biblical preaching and ministers are to preach only what God commands by opening His Word, people were to test sermons by this criterion. Unscriptural sermons were to be rejected; scriptural sermons were to be accepted and obeyed. Calvin's goal was that the people would grasp the importance of preaching, learn to desire preaching as a supreme blessing, and participate as actively in the sermon as the preacher himself. Their basic attitude should be one of "willingness to obey God completely and with no reserve," Calvin said.[8]

Calvin was motivated to stress profitable hearing of the Word because he believed that few people hear well. Here is a typical assessment of Calvin: "If the same sermon is preached, say, to a hundred people, twenty receive it with the ready obedience of faith, while the rest hold it valueless, or laugh, or hiss, or loathe it."[9] I found more than forty similar comments in Calvin's sermons (especially on Deuteronomy), commentaries (e.g., on Psalm 119:101 and Acts 11:23), and the *Institutes* (especially 3.21 to 3.24). If profitable hearing was a problem in Calvin's day, how much more so today, when ministers have to compete for their congregation's attention with all the mass media that bombard us on a daily basis?

Third, the Genevan system Calvin established emphasized preaching. The Genevan *Ordinances* stipulated that on Sundays, sermons be preached in each

---

6. Willem Balke, "Het Pietisme in Oostfriesland," *Theologia Reformata* 21 (1978):320–27.

7. William Bouwsma, *John Calvin: A Sixteenth-Century Portrait* (New York: Oxford University Press, 1988), 29.

8. Leroy Nixon, *John Calvin: Expository Preacher* (Grand Rapids: Eerdmans, 1950), 65.

9. Inst. 3.24.12.

of the three churches at daybreak and again at 9:00 a.m. After the children were catechized at noon, a third sermon was preached in each church at 3:00 p.m. Weekday sermons were also scheduled in the churches on Mondays, Wednesdays, and Fridays at varying hours so that they could be heard one after the other. That way people could take in three sermons in one day, if they so desired. By the time Calvin died, there was at least one sermon preached in every church every day of the week.

Calvin's gifts and high view of preaching both theologically and in practice motivates us to study his sermons. In this chapter, I want to first briefly define experiential preaching, then step back to look in broad overview at how Calvin preached before focusing more narrowly on the question of how he preached experientially and how such preaching interfaced with corollary doctrines such as assurance of faith, election, and self-examination.

Experiential Preaching Defined

Experiential or experimental preaching addresses the vital matter of how a Christian experiences the truth of Christian doctrine in his life. The term *experimental* comes from the Latin *experimentum*, meaning trial. It is derived from the verb *experior*, meaning to try, prove, or put to the test. That same verb can also mean to find or know by experience, thus leading to the word *experientia*, meaning knowledge gained by experiment. Calvin used *experiential* and *experimental* interchangeably, since both words in biblical preaching indicate the need for measuring experienced knowledge against the touchstone of Scripture.

Experimental preaching stresses the need to know the great truths of the Word of God by Spirit-worked experience. A working definition of experimental preaching might be thus: Experimental preaching seeks to explain the Holy Spirit's saving work in believers in terms of biblical truth as to how spiritual matters ought to go, how they do go, and what the goal is of the Christian life. It aims to apply divine truth to the whole range of the believer's personal experience as well as to his relationships with family, the church, and the world around him.

Experimental preaching is discriminatory preaching. It clearly defines the difference between a Christian and non-Christian, opening the kingdom of heaven to one and shutting it from the other. Discriminatory preaching offers the forgiveness of sins and eternal life to all who embrace Christ as Savior and Lord by true faith, but it also proclaims the wrath of God and His eternal condemnation upon those who are unbelieving, unrepentant, and unconverted. Such preaching teaches that unless our religion is experiential, we will perish— not because experience itself saves but because the Christ who saves sinners must be experienced personally as the foundation upon which the house of our eternal hope is built (Matt. 7:22–27; 1 Cor. 1:30; 2:2).

Experimental preaching is applicatory. It applies the text to every aspect of a listener's life, promoting a religion that is truly a power and not mere form (2 Tim. 3:5). Robert Burns defined such religion as "Christianity brought home to men's business and bosoms" and said the principle on which it rests is "that Christianity should not only be known, and understood, and believed, but also felt, and enjoyed, and practically applied."[10]

Experiential preaching, then, teaches that the Christian faith must be experienced, tasted, and lived through the saving power of the Holy Spirit. It stresses the knowledge of scriptural truth, "which is able to make us wise unto salvation through faith in Christ Jesus" (2 Tim. 3:15). Specifically, such preaching teaches that Christ, who is the living Word (John. 1:1) and the very embodiment of the truth, must be experientially known and embraced. It proclaims the need for sinners to experience who God is in His Son. As John 17:3 says, "And this is life eternal, that they might know thee the only true God, and Jesus Christ, whom thou hast sent." The word *know* in this text, as well as other biblical usages, does not indicate a casual acquaintance but a deep, abiding relationship. For example, Genesis 4:1 uses the word *know* to suggest marital intimacy: "And Adam knew Eve his wife; and she conceived, and bare Cain." Experiential preaching stresses the intimate, personal knowledge of God in Christ.

Such knowledge is never divorced from Scripture. According to Isaiah 8:20, all our beliefs, including our experiences, must be tested against Holy Scripture. "If I can't find my experiences back in the Bible, they are not from the Lord but from the devil," Martin Luther once said. That is really what the word *experimental* intends to convey. Just as scientific experiment tests a hypothesis against a body of evidence, so experimental preaching involves examining Christian experience in the light of the teaching of the Word of God.

Calvin's Preaching

Calvin preached serially from various Bible books, striving to clearly show the meaning of a passage and how it should impact the lives of his hearers. Much like a homily in style, his sermons have no divisions or points other than what the text dictates. As Paul Fuhrman writes, "They are properly homilies as in

---

10. Robert Burns, introduction to *Works of Thomas Halyburton* (London: Thomas Tegg, 1835), xiv–xv.

the ancient church: expositions of Bible passages [in] the light of grammar and history, [providing] application to the hearers' life situations."[11]

Calvin was a careful exegete, an able expositor, and a faithful applier of the Word. His goals in preaching were to glorify God, to cause believers to grow in the grace and knowledge of Christ Jesus, and to unite sinners with Christ so "that men be reconciled to God by the free remission of sins."[12] This aim of saving sinners blended seamlessly with his emphasis on scriptural doctrines. He wrote that ministers are "keepers of the truth of God; that is to say, of His precious image, of that which concerneth the majesty of the doctrine of our salvation, and the life of the world."[13] Calvin frequently admonished ministers to keep this treasure safe by handling the Word of God carefully, always striving for pure, biblical teaching. That did not exclude bringing contemporary events to bear on people's lives, however. As current events related to the passage being expounded, Calvin felt free to apply his sermon to those events in practical, experiential, and moralistic ways.[14]

The image of the preacher as a teacher moved Calvin to emphasize the importance of careful sermon preparation. How he accomplished that himself with his frequency of preaching and heavy workload remains a mystery, but he obviously studied the text to be expounded with great care and read widely what others had said about it. He preached extemporaneously, relying heavily on his remarkable memory. He often declared that the power of God could best be exhibited in extemporaneous delivery.

That's why there are no manuscripts of Calvin's sermons extant. As far as we know, he never wrote out any sermons. The only reason that we have more than two thousand of Calvin's sermons is that a certain Denis Raguenier took them down in shorthand from 1549 until the scribe's death in 1560. Apparently, Calvin never intended for them to be published.

The average length of texts covered in each of Calvin's sermons was four or five verses in the Old Testament and two or three verses in the New Testament. His sermons were fairly short for his day (perhaps due in part to his asthmatic condition), probably averaging thirty-five to forty minutes. He is reported to have spoken "deliberately, often with long pauses to allow people to think," though others say that he must have spoken rapidly to complete his sermon on time.[15]

---

11. Paul T. Fuhrmann, "Calvin, Expositor of Scripture," *Interpretation* 6, 2 (Apr 1952):191.

12. *Commentary* (on John 20:23).

13. *The Mystery of Godliness* (Grand Rapids: Eerdmans, 1950), 122.

14. A. Mitchell Hunter, "Calvin as a Preacher," *Expository Times* 30, 12 (Sept 1919):563.

15. Philip Vollmer, *John Calvin: Theologian, Preacher, Educator, Statesman* (Richmond: Presbyterian

Calvin's style of preaching was plain and clear. In a sermon titled "Pure Preaching of the Word," Calvin states, "we must shun all unprofitable babbling, and stay ourselves upon plain teaching, which is forcible."[16] Rhetoric for its own sake or vain babbling must be shunned, though true eloquence, when subjected to the simplicity of the gospel, is to be coveted. When Joachim Westphal charged Calvin with "babbling" in his sermons, Calvin replied that he stuck to the main point of the text and practiced "cautious brevity."[17]

Calvin's sermons abound with application throughout. In some cases, application consumes more time than exposition. Short, pungent applications, sprinkled throughout his sermons, constantly urge, exhort, and invite sinners to act in obedience to God's Word. "We have not come to the preaching merely to hear what we do not know, but to be incited to do our duty," Calvin said to his flock.

T. H. L. Parker suggests that Calvin's sermons follow a certain pattern:

1. Prayer.

2. Recapitulation of previous sermon.

3a. Exegesis and exposition of the first point.

3b. Application of the first point and exhortation to obedience of duty.

4a. Exegesis and exposition of the second point.

4b. Application of the second point and exhortation to obedience of duty.

5. Closing prayer, which contains a brief, implicit summary of the sermon.

John Gerstner points out that though this was the structural order that Calvin often did follow and probably intended to follow, he frequently departed from it because "he was so eager to get at the application that he often introduced it in the midst of the exposition. In other words, application was the dominant element in the preaching of John Calvin to which all else was subordinated."[18]

Calvin's Stress on Piety in Preaching

Calvin understood true religion as fellowship between God and man. The part of the fellowship that moves from God to man Calvin called *revelation*; the part of the fellowship that moves from man to God, which involves man's obedient response, he called *piety*. Such piety functions through God's grace by faith and involves such devout acts as childlike trust, humble adoration, godly fear, and

---

Committee of Publication, 1909), 124; George Johnson, "Calvinism and Preaching," *Evangelical Quarterly* 4, 3 (July 1932):249.

　16. *Mystery of Godliness*, 55.

　17. John C. Bowman, "Calvin as a Preacher," *Reformed Church Review* 56 (1909):251–52.

　18. John H. Gerstner, "Calvin's Two-Voice Theory of Preaching," *Reformed Review* 13, 2 (1959): 22.

undying love. Calvin's applications in preaching often aimed for exciting these kinds of graces.

For Calvin, the goal of the preacher is to promote such piety, even as the preacher himself must remain acutely aware that the listener cannot produce this piety himself. He is only a recipient of such piety by the grace of the Holy Spirit and not the author of it. Nevertheless, the Spirit accompanies the Word with this divine gift of pious graces.

Calvin's piety, like his theology, is inseparable from the knowledge of God. The true knowledge of God results in pious activity that stretches its goal beyond personal salvation to embrace the glory of God. Where God's glory is not served, piety cannot exist. This compels discipline, obedience, and love in every sphere of the believer's life. For Calvin, the law gives love its mandate and content to act, to obey God out of discipline, and so to live to His glory. Indeed, love is the fulfilling of the law. Thus, for Calvin, true piety is both a vertical (God-ward) and horizontal (man-ward) relationship of love and law.

Grace and law, therefore, are both prominent in Calvin's theology and preaching. Keeping the law is especially important because of its supreme purpose to lead us to consecrate our entire lives to God. Lionel Greve writes, "Grace has priority in such a way that Calvin's piety may be considered as a quality of life and response to God's grace that transcended law but at the same time included it." Greve goes on to conclude, "Calvin's piety may be termed 'transcendent piety.' It transcends the creature because it is founded in grace but yet includes the creature as he is the subject of faithfulness. He is the subject in such a way that his piety is never primarily for his welfare.... The general movement of Calvin's piety is always Godward. The benefits of God's goodness are merely byproducts of the main purpose—glorifying God."[19]

Calvin's combined emphases on God's glory and the believer's Spirit-worked piety led him to a theology of experience. Experience was a theological and spiritual necessity for him. That is quite understandable, given his accent on the Spirit's work in the life of the believer—an accent that earned him the title of "the theologian of the Holy Spirit." So we ought not be surprised that his pneumatological, experiential emphasis of piety also spilled over into his sermons. The question is not whether Calvin was an experiential preacher—that is obvious from his sermons, commentaries, and even in his *Institutes*; the question is, What role does experience (*experientia*) play in his theology and preaching?

---

19. Lionel Greve, "Freedom and Discipline in the Theology of John Calvin, William Perkins, and John Wesley: An Examination of the Origin and Nature of Pietism" (PhD diss., Hartford Seminary Foundation, 1976), 149.

Calvin and Experience

Calvin values experience so long as it is rooted in Scripture and springs out of the living reality of faith. He repeatedly defines the experience of believers as beyond verbal expression. For example, he writes, "Such, then, is a conviction that requires no reasons, such a knowledge with which the best reason agrees—in which the mind truly reposes, more securely and constantly than in any reasons: such finally, a feeling that can be born only of heavenly revelation. I speak of nothing other than what each believer experiences within himself—though my words fall far beneath a just explanation of the matter."[20] Calvin goes on to say that believers' recognition of God "consists more in living experience than in vain and high-flown speculations." But then he hastens to add: "Indeed, with experience as our teacher, we find God just as he declares himself in his Word."[21]

False experience fabricates a god that does not square with the Scriptures, but true experience always flows out of the truths of Scripture and underscores them. Holy Scripture is consistent with sacred, Spirit-worked experience, since Calvin understands that the Bible is not a book of abstract or scholastic doctrines but a book of doctrines that is rooted in real, experiential, daily living. Thus, experience plays an important role in Calvin's exegesis. Willem Balke writes, "Experience can serve as a hermeneutical key in the explanation of the Scriptures. The Bible places us in the center of the struggle of faith, *coram Deo*, and therefore Calvin can recommend himself as exegete as he does in the introduction to the Commentary on the Psalms (1557) since he has experienced what the Bible testifies."[22]

Calvin views his multifaceted experiences as a Reformer as an important qualification for exegeting and preaching God's Word. Though he relates his experiential qualification particularly to the Psalms since the Psalms relate best to the suffering people of God and are, as he calls them, "an anatomy of all parts of the soul," all his sermons and commentaries reveal that he believes no book of Scripture can be reduced to mere doctrine.

Though Calvin ascribes a large place to experience in his exegesis and preaching, he understands that experience has significant limitations. When divorced from the Word, experience is altogether unreliable. And it is always

---

20. Inst. 1.7.5.

21. Inst. 1.10.2.

22. Willem Balke, "The Word of God and *Experientia* according to Calvin," in *Calvinus Ecclesiae Doctor*, ed. W. H. Neuser (Kampen: Kok, 1978), 22. Much of this and the following subheading is a summary and fine-tuning of Balke's helpful effort to grapple with Calvin's understanding of experience in the life of the believer.

incomplete. Calvin concludes that the depths of the human heart, which always remain a focal point for the mystic, is not the way to God. Rather, he agrees with Luther that the only way to God is by Word-centered faith. The believer does not learn to know God's will from *"nuda experientia,"* Calvin says, but only through the testimony of Scripture.[23]

If Scripture is not the foundation of our experience of faith, Calvin says we will only be left with vague feelings that have no anchor. True faith, however, anchors itself in the Word. We ought not measure the presence of God in our lives by our experience, for that would soon bring us to despair. "If we should measure out the help of God according to our feelings," Calvin writes, "our faith would soon waver and we would have no courage or hope."[24]

Thus, Calvin is careful not to be an experientialist—that is, one who frequently calls attention to his own experiences in a rather mystical manner. He well understands that experience is to be defined by the testimony of the written Word.

Calvin avoids both experientialism and dry scholasticism. He does not see the Bible as a collection of doctrines but, rather, views biblical doctrines as "embedded in the life and faith of the church and of the individual, in the natural habitat of the verification of faith in Christian and ecclesiastical existence."[25]

Experientia Fidei or *Sensus Fidei*

The experience or sense of faith (*experientia fidei* or *sensus fidei*), according to Calvin, is also inseparable from the ministry of the Holy Spirit. The Spirit renews the very core of man. That work involves illumination and sealing; the Spirit's illumination of the mind and His efficacious work in the heart coalesce. The Spirit's sealing work certifies the authority of the Word and the reality of the Spirit's saving work. It promotes confidence in God's promises of mercy and experience of them. This doctrine, Calvin says, is "not of the tongue, but of life. It is not apprehended by the understanding and memory alone, as other disciplines are, but it is received only when it possesses the whole soul, and finds a seat and resting place in the inmost affection of the heart."[26]

Such *experientia fidei* is thus not a part of the believer's own ability, but it is the creative effect of the Spirit who uses the Word. It contains both objective

---

23. *Opera quae supersunt omnia*, ed. Guilielmus Baum, Eduardus Cunitz, and Eduardus Reuss, vols. 29–87 in Corpus Reformatorum (Brunsvigae: C. A. Schwetschke, 1863–1900), 31, 424 [hereafter, CO].

24. CO, 31, 103.

25. Balke, "The Word of God and *Experientia* according to Calvin," 22.

26. Inst. 3.6.4.

and subjective truth. The Spirit testifies both in the Word of God and in the heart of the believer, and the believer hears and experiences its reality. Through the Spirit's objective and subjective testimony, the believer is persuaded experientially of the absolute truth of God and of His Word. Being made willing by the powerful operations of the Spirit, the heart, will, and emotions all respond in faith and obedience to the Triune God. Since the Spirit is the Spirit of the Son whose great task it is to lead the believer to Christ and through Him to the Father, the center of faith's experience is, as John called it, having "fellowship with the Father and the Son" (1 John 1:3). True experience always leads, then, to true communion and to *praxis pietatis*.

This is not to say that true experience is always that easily dissected and understood. The experience of faith contains numerous paradoxes. For example, a paradox exists in the life of faith when we are called to believe that God is still with us when we feel that He has deserted us. Or, how can we believe that God is favorably inclined to us when He strips us at times of all consciousness of that favor and seems to providentially postpone fulfilling His merciful promises?[27]

The believer can experience such apparent contradictions on a daily basis, Calvin says. He can feel forsaken of God, even when he knows deep within that he is not (Isa. 49:14–16). These conflicting experiences transpire within one heart and seem, like hope and fear, to cancel each other out. If fear gets the upper hand, Calvin writes, we ought to simply throw ourselves wholly on the promises of God.[28] Those promises will give us courage to go on in spite of temptations to doubt. Moreover, it is especially when we acknowledge God as present by faith though we cannot see or feel His goodness and power that we truly honor His lordship and His Word.[29] To believe in God when experience seems to annul His promises takes great faith, but it is precisely this experience of faith that enables believers to remain undisturbed when their entire world seems to be shaken.[30]

Experience and Assurance of Faith

Calvin's doctrine of assurance reaffirmed the basic tenets of Martin Luther and Ulrich Zwingli and disclosed emphases of his own. Like Luther and Zwingli, Calvin says faith is never merely assent (*assensus*) but involves both knowledge (*cognitio*) and trust (*fiducia*). Faith rests firmly on God's Word; faith always

---

27. CO, 31, 344.
28. CO, 31, 548.
29. CO, 31, 525.
30. CO, 31, 703; 32:194. This section is largely a revision of my *Quest for Full Assurance of Faith: The Legacy of Calvin and His Successors* (Edinburgh: Banner of Truth, 1999), 37–65.

says amen to the Scriptures.[31] Hence, assurance must be sought *in* the Word and flows *out of* the Word.[32] Assurance is as inseparable from the Word as sunbeams are from the sun.

Faith and assurance are also inseparable from *Christ and the promise of Christ*, for the totality of the written Word is the living Word, Jesus Christ, in whom all God's promises are "yea and amen."[33] Calvin makes much of the promises of God as the ground of assurance, for these promises are based on the very nature of God, who cannot lie. The promises are fulfilled by Christ; therefore Calvin directs sinners to Christ and to the promises as if they were synonyms.[34] Since faith takes its character from the promise on which it rests, faith takes on the infallible stamp of God's own Word. Consequently, faith possesses assurance in its own nature. Assurance, certainty, trust: such is the essence of faith.

More specifically, Calvin argues that faith involves something more than objectively believing the promise of God; it involves personal, subjective assurance. In believing God's promise to sinners, the true believer recognizes and celebrates that God is gracious and benevolent to him in particular. Faith is an assured knowledge "of God's benevolence toward *us*…revealed to *our* minds… sealed upon *our* hearts."[35] Calvin writes, "Here, indeed, is the hinge on which faith turns: that we do not regard the promises of mercy that God offers as true only outside ourselves, but not at all in us; rather that we make them ours by inwardly embracing them."[36]

Thus, as Robert Kendall notes, Calvin repeatedly describes faith as "certainty (*certitudino*), a firm conviction (*solida persuasio*), assurance (*securitas*), firm assurance (*solida securitas*), and full assurance (*plena securitas*)."[37] While faith consists of knowledge, it is also marked by heartfelt assurance that is "a sure and secure possession of those things which God has promised us."[38]

---

31. *Commentary* (on John 3:33; Ps. 43:3). Cf. K. Exalto, *De Zekerheid des Geloofs bij Calvijn* (Apeldoorn: Willem de Zwijgerstichting, 1978), 24. Edward Dowey mistakenly dichotomizes the Scriptures and assurance when he asserts that the center of Calvin's doctrine of faith is assurance rather than the authority of the Scriptures. For Calvin, the separation of the Word of God from assurance is unthinkable (*The Knowledge of God in Calvin's Theology* [New York: Columbia University Press, 1965], 182).

32. *Commentary* (on Matt. 8:13; John 4:22).

33. *Commentary* (on Gen. 15:6; Luke 2:21).

34. Inst. 3.2.32; *Commentary* (on Rom. 4:3, 18; Heb. 11:7, 11).

35. Inst. 3.2.7, emphasis mine.

36. Inst. 3.2.16; cf. 3.2.42.

37. Robert T. Kendall, *Calvin and English Calvinism to 1649* (New York: Oxford University Press, 1979), 19; cf. Inst. 3.2.6, 3.2.16, 3.2.22.

38. Inst. 3.2.41; 3.2.14.

Calvin also emphasizes throughout his commentaries that assurance is integral to faith.[39] In expounding 2 Corinthians 13:5, Calvin even states that those who doubt their union to Christ are reprobates: "[Paul] declares, that all are *reprobates*, who doubt whether they profess Christ and are a part of His body. Let us, therefore, reckon *that* alone to be right faith, which leads us to repose in safety in the favour of God, with no wavering opinion, but with a firm and steadfast assurance."

Throughout his lofty doctrine of faith, however, Calvin repeats these themes: unbelief dies hard; assurance is often contested by doubt; severe temptations, wrestlings, and strife are normative; Satan and the flesh assault faith; trust in God is hedged with fear.[40] Freely Calvin acknowledges that faith is not retained without a severe struggle against unbelief, nor is it left untainted by doubt and anxiety. He writes: "Unbelief is, in all men, always mixed with faith.... For unbelief is so deeply rooted in our hearts, and we are so inclined to it, that not without hard struggle is each one able to persuade himself of what all confess with the mouth, namely, that God is faithful. Especially when it comes to reality itself, every man's wavering uncovers hidden weakness."[41]

In expounding John 20:3, Calvin seems to contradict his assertion that true believers know themselves to be such when he testifies that the disciples had faith without awareness of it as they approached the empty tomb: "There being so little faith, or rather almost no faith, both in the disciples and in the women, it is astonishing that they had so great zeal; and, indeed, it is not possible that religious feelings led them to seek Christ. *Some seed of faith, therefore, remained in their hearts, but quenched for a time, so that they were not aware of having what they had.* Thus the Spirit of God often works in the elect in a secret manner."[42]

This prompts us to ask how Calvin can say that faith is characterized by full assurance, yet still allows for the kind of faith that lacks assurance? The two statements appear antithetical. Assurance is free from doubt, yet not free. It does not hesitate, yet can hesitate. It contains security, but may be beset with anxiety. The faithful have assurance, yet waver and tremble.

Calvin uses at least four principles to address this complex issue. Each helps make sense of his apparent contradictions.

First, consider Calvin's need to distinguish between *the definition of faith* and *the reality of the believer's experience*. After explaining faith in the *Institutes* as embracing "great assurance," Calvin writes:

---

39. *Commentary* (on Acts 2:29 and 1 Cor. 2:12).
40. Inst. 3.2.7; *Commentary* (on Matt. 8:25; Luke 2:40).
41. Inst. 3.2.4, 3.2.15.
42. Cf. Inst. 3.2.12, emphasis mine.

Still, someone will say: "Believers *experience* something far different: In recognizing the grace of God toward themselves they are not only tried by disquiet, which often comes upon them, but they are repeatedly shaken by gravest terrors. For so violent are the temptations that trouble their minds as not to seem quite compatible with that certainty of faith." Accordingly, we shall have to solve this difficulty if we wish the above-stated doctrine to stand. Surely, while we teach that faith *ought* to be certain and assured, we cannot imagine any certainty that is not tinged with doubt, or any assurance that is not assailed.[43]

In short, Calvin distinguishes between the *ought to* of faith and the *is* of faith in daily life. His definition of faith serves as a recommendation about how believers ought "habitually and properly to think of faith."[44] Faith should always aim at full assurance, even if it cannot reach perfect assurance in experience. In principle, faith gains the victory (1 John 5:4); in practice, it recognizes that it has not yet fully apprehended (Phil. 3:12–13).

Nevertheless, the practice of faith validates faith that trusts in the Word. Calvin is not as interested in experiences as he is in validating Word-grounded faith. Experience confirms faith, Calvin says. Faith "requires full and fixed certainty, such as men are wont to have from things experienced and proved."[45]

Thus, bare experience (*nuda experientia*) is not Calvin's goal but experience grounded in the Word, flowing out of the fulfillment of the Word. Experimental knowledge of the Word is essential.[46] For Calvin, two kinds of knowledge are needed: knowledge by faith (*scientia fidei*) that is received from the Word, "though it is not yet fully revealed," and the knowledge of experience (*scientia experientiae*) "springing from the fulfilling of the Word."[47] The Word of God is primary to the former and to the latter, for experience teaches us to know God as He declares Himself to be in His Word.[48] Experience not consonant with Scripture is never an experience of true faith. In short, though the believer's experience of true faith is far weaker than he desires, there is an essential unity in the Word between faith's perception (the *ought-to* dimension of faith) and experience (the *is* dimension of faith).

The second principle that helps us understand Calvin's tension in assurance of faith is the principle of *flesh versus spirit*. Calvin writes:

---

43. Cf. Inst. 3.2.16–17, emphasis mine.

44. Paul Helm, *Calvin and the Calvinists* (Edinburgh: Banner of Truth, 1982), 26.

45. Inst. 3.2.15.

46. Inst. 1.7.5.

47. Cf. Charles Partee, "Calvin and Experience," *Scottish Journal of Theology* 26 (1973):169–81; W. Balke, "The Word of God and *Experientia* according to Calvin," 23–29.

48. Inst. 1.10.2.

It is necessary to return to that division of flesh and spirit which we have mentioned elsewhere. It most clearly reveals itself at this point. Therefore the godly heart feels in itself a division because it is partly imbued with sweetness from its recognition of the divine goodness, partly grieves in bitterness from an awareness of its calamity; partly rests upon the promise of the gospel, partly trembles at the evidence of its own iniquity; partly rejoices at the expectation of life, partly shudders at death. This variation arises from imperfection of faith, since in the course of the present life it never goes so well with us that we are wholly cured of the disease of unbelief and entirely filled and possessed by faith. Hence arise those conflicts, when unbelief, which reposes in the remains of the flesh, rises up to attack the faith that has been inwardly conceived.[49]

Like Luther, Calvin sets the "ought to/is" dichotomy against the backdrop of spirit/flesh warfare.[50] Christians experience this spirit/flesh tension acutely because it is instigated by the Holy Spirit.[51] The paradoxes that permeate experiential faith (e.g., Romans 7:14–25 in the classical Reformed interpretation) find resolution in this tension: "So then with the mind [spirit] I myself serve the law of God; but with the flesh the law of sin" (v. 25).

Calvin sets the sure consolation of the spirit side by side with the imperfection of the flesh, for these are what the believer finds within himself. Since the final victory of the spirit over the flesh will only be fulfilled in Christ, the Christian will perpetually struggle in this life. His spirit fills him "with delight in recognizing the divine goodness" even as his flesh activates his natural proneness to unbelief.[52] He is beset with "daily struggles of conscience" as long as the vestiges of the flesh remain.[53] The believer's "present state is far short of the glory of God's children," Calvin writes. "Physically, we are dust and shadow, and death is always before our eyes. We are exposed to a thousand miseries...so that we always find a hell within us."[54] While still in the flesh, the believer may even be tempted to doubt the whole gospel.

Even as he is tormented with fleshly doubts, the believer's spirit trusts God's mercy by invoking Him in prayer and by resting upon Him through the sacraments. By these means, faith gains the upper hand over unbelief. "Faith ultimately

---

49. Inst. 3.2.18.

50. Cf. C. A. Hall, *With the Spirit's Sword: The Drama of Spiritual Warfare in the Theology of John Calvin* (Richmond: John Knox Press, 1970).

51. Cf. Victor A. Shepherd, *The Nature and Function of Saving Faith in the Theology of John Calvin* (Macon, Ga.: Mercer University Press, 1983), 24–28.

52. Inst. 3.2.18, 3.2.20.

53. *Commentary* (on John 13:9).

54. *Commentary* (on 1 John 3:2).

triumphs over those difficulties which besiege and…imperil it. [Faith is like] a palm tree [that] strives against every burden and raises itself upward."[55]

In short, Calvin teaches that from *the spirit* of the believer rise hope, joy, assurance; from *the flesh*, fear, doubt, disillusionment. Though spirit and flesh operate simultaneously, imperfection and doubt are integral only to the flesh, not to faith; the works of the flesh often *attend* faith but do not *mix* with it. The believer may lose spiritual battles along the pathway of life, but he will not lose the ultimate war against the flesh.

Third, despite the tensions between definition and experience, spirit and flesh, Calvin maintains that faith and assurance are not so mixed with unbelief that the believer is left with *probability* rather than *certainty*.[56] The smallest germ of faith contains assurance in its very essence, even when the believer is not always able to grasp this assurance due to weakness. The Christian may be tossed about with doubt and perplexity, but the seed of faith, implanted by the Spirit, cannot perish. Precisely because it is the Spirit's seed, faith retains assurance. This assurance increases and decreases in proportion to the rise and decline of faith's exercises, but the seed of faith can never be destroyed. Calvin says: "The root of faith can never be torn from the godly breast, but clings so fast to the inmost parts that, however faith seems to be shaken or to bend this way or that, its light is never so extinguished or snuffed out that it does not at least lurk as it were beneath the ashes."[57]

Calvin thus explains "weak assurance in terms of weak faith without thereby weakening the link between faith and assurance."[58] Assurance is normative but varies in degree and constancy in the believer's consciousness of it. So, in responding to weak assurance, a pastor should not deny the organic tie between faith and assurance but should urge the pursuit of stronger faith through the use of the means of grace in dependence on the Spirit.

Experience, the Trinity, and Election

Through a fourth sweeping principle, namely, *a Trinitarian framework* for the doctrine of faith and assurance, Calvin spurs the doubt-prone believer onward. As surely as the election of the Father must prevail over the works of Satan, the righteousness of the Son over the sinfulness of the believer, and the assuring

---

55. Inst. 3.2.17.

56. Cf. Cornelis Graafland, *De Zekerheid van het geloof: Een onderzoek naar de geloof-beschouwing van enige vertegenwoordigers van reformatie en nadere reformatie* (Wageningen: H. Veenman & Zonen, 1961), 31n.

57. Inst. 3.2.21.

58. A. N. S. Lane, "The Quest for the Historical Calvin," *Evangelical Quarterly* 55 (1983):103.

witness of the Spirit over the soul's infirmities—so certainly assured faith shall and must conquer unbelief.

Calvin's arrangement of Book III of the *Institutes* reveals the movement of the grace of faith from God to man and man to God. The grace of faith is from the Father, in the Son, and through the Spirit, by which, in turn, the believer is brought into fellowship with the Son by the Spirit and, consequently, is reconciled to and walks in fellowship with the Father.

For Calvin, a complex set of factors establishes assurance, not the least of which is the Father's election and preservation in Christ. Hence he writes that "predestination duly considered does not shake faith, but rather affords the best confirmation of it,"[59] especially when viewed in the context of calling: "The firmness of our election is joined to our calling [and] is another means of establishing our assurance. For all whom [Christ] receives, the Father is said to have entrusted and committed to Him to keep to eternal life."[60]

Decretal election is a sure foundation for preservation and assurance; it is not coldly causal. Gordon Keddie writes, "Election is never seen, in Calvin, in a purely deterministic light, in which God…is viewed as 'a frightening idol' of 'mechanistic deterministic causality' and Christian experience is reduced to either cowering passivity or frantic activism, while waiting some 'revelation' of God's hidden decree for one's self. For Calvin, as indeed in Scripture, election does not threaten, but rather undergirds, the certainty of salvation."[61]

Such a foundation is possible only in a Christ-centered context; hence Calvin's constant accent on Christ as the mirror of election "wherein we must, and without self-deception may, contemplate our own election."[62] Election turns the believer's eyes from the hopelessness of his inability to meet any conditions of salvation to focus on the hope of Jesus Christ as God's pledge of undeserved love and mercy.[63]

Through union with Christ, "the assurance of salvation becomes real and effective as the assurance of election."[64] Christ becomes ours in fulfillment of

---

59. Inst. 3.24.9.

60. Inst. 3.24.6.

61. Gordon J. Keddie, "'Unfallible Certenty of the Pardon of Sinne and Life Everlasting': The Doctrine of Assurance in the Theology of William Perkins," *Evangelical Quarterly* 48 (1976):231; cf. G. C. Berkouwer, *Divine Election*, trans. Hugo Bekker (Grand Rapids: Eerdmans, 1960), 10–17.

62. Inst. 3.24.5; cf. John Calvin, *Sermons on the Epistle to the Ephesians* (repr. Edinburgh: Banner of Truth, 1973), 47; idem, *Sermons from Job* (Grand Rapids: Eerdmans, 1952), 41–44; CO 8:318–21; 9:757.

63. Inst. 3.24.6; William H. Chalker, "Calvin and Some Seventeenth Century English Calvinists" (PhD diss., Duke, 1961), 66.

64. Wilhelm Niesel, *The Theology of Calvin*, trans. Harold Knight (Grand Rapids: Baker, 1980), 196. Cf. Inst. 3.1.1; Shepherd, *Faith in the Theology of John Calvin*, 51.

God's determination to redeem and resurrect us. Consequently, we ought not to think of Christ as "standing afar off, and not dwelling in us."[65] Since Christ is for us, to contemplate Him truly is to see Him forming in us what He desires to give us, Himself above all. God has made Himself "little in Christ," Calvin states, so that we might comprehend and flee to Christ alone who can pacify our consciences.[66] Faith must begin, rest, and end in Christ. "True faith is so contained in Christ, that it neither knows, nor desires to know, anything beyond Him," Calvin says.[67] Therefore, "we ought not to separate Christ from ourselves or ourselves from Him."[68]

In this Christological manner, Calvin reduces the distance between God's objective decree of election from the believer's subjective lack of assurance that he is elect. For Calvin, election answers, rather than raises, the question of assurance. In Christ, the believer sees his election; in the gospel, he hears of his election.

The question remains, however: How do the elect enjoy communion with Christ, and how does that produce assurance? Calvin's answer is pneumatological: the Holy Spirit applies Christ and His benefits to the hearts and lives of guilty, elect sinners, through which they are assured by saving faith that Christ belongs to them and they to Him. The Holy Spirit especially confirms within them the reliability of God's promises in Christ. Thus, personal assurance is never divorced from the election of the Father, the redemption of the Son, the application of the Spirit, and the instrumental means of saving faith.

The Holy Spirit has an enormous role in the application of redemption, Calvin says. As personal comforter and seal, the Holy Spirit assures the believer of his gracious adoption: "The Spirit of God gives us such a testimony, that when he is our guide and teacher our spirit is made sure of the adoption of God; for our mind of itself, without the preceding testimony of the Spirit, could not convey to us this assurance."[69] The Holy Spirit's work underlies all assurance of salvation without detracting from the role of Christ, for the Spirit is the Spirit *of Christ* who assures the believer by leading him to Christ and His benefits and by working out those benefits within him.[70]

---

65. Inst. 3.2.24.

66. *Commentary* (on 1 Peter 1:20).

67. *Commentary* (on Eph. 4:13).

68. Inst. 3.2.24.

69. *Commentary* (on Rom. 8:16). Cf. *Commentary* (on 2 Cor. 1:21–22). Cf. Inst. 3.2.11, 34, 41; *Commentary* (on John 7:37–39; Acts 2:4; 3:8; 5:32; 13:48; 16:14; 23:11; Rom. 8:15–17; 1 Cor. 2:10–13; Gal. 3:2, 4:6; Eph. 1:13–14, 4:30); *Tracts and Treatises*, 3:253–60; J. K. Parratt, "The Witness of the Holy Spirit: Calvin, the Puritans and St. Paul," *Evangelical Quarterly* 41 (1969):161–68.

70. Inst. 3.2.34.

Experience and Self-Examination

Nevertheless, Calvin is acutely aware that a person may think that the Father has entrusted him to Christ when such is not the case. It is one thing to underscore Christ's task in the Trinitarian, salvific economy as the recipient and guardian of the elect; the center, author, and foundation of election; the guarantee, promise, and mirror of the believer's election and salvation. But it is quite another to know how to inquire about whether a person has been joined to Christ by a true faith. Many appear to be Christ's who are estranged from Him. Says Calvin: "It daily happens that those who seemed to be Christ's fall away from him again.... Such persons never cleaved to Christ with the heartfelt trust in which certainty of salvation has, I say, been established for us."[71]

Calvin never preached to console his flock into false assurance of salvation.[72] Many scholars minimize Calvin's emphasis on the need for a subjective, experiential realization of faith and election by referring to Calvin's practice of approaching his congregation as saved hearers. They misunderstand. Though Calvin practiced what he called "a judgment of charity" (i.e., addressing as saved those church members who maintain a commendable, external lifestyle), we saw that he also frequently asserted that only a minority receive the preached Word with saving faith. He says, "For though all, without exception, to whom God's Word is preached, are taught, yet scarce one in ten so much as tastes it; yea, scarce one in a hundred profits to the extent of being enabled, thereby, to proceed in a right course to the end."[73]

For Calvin, much that resembles faith lacks a saving character. He thus speaks of faith that is unformed, implicit, temporary, illusionary, false, a shadow-type, transitory, and under a cloak of hypocrisy.[74] Self-deception is a real possibility, Calvin says. Because the reprobate often feel something much like the faith of the elect,[75] self-examination is essential. He writes, "Let us learn to examine ourselves, and to search whether those interior marks by which God distinguishes his children from strangers belong to us, viz., the living root

---

71. Inst. 3.24.7.

72. Cf. Cornelis Graafland, "'Waarheid in het Binnenste': Geloofszekerheid bij Calvijn en de Nadere Reformatie," in *Een Vaste Burcht*, ed. K. Exalto (Kampen: Kok, 1989), 65–67.

73. *Commentary* (on Ps. 119:101). More than thirty times in his *Commentary* (e.g., Acts 11:23 and Ps. 15:1) and nine times within the scope of Inst. 3.21–24, Calvin refers to the fewness of those who possess vital faith.

74. Inst. 3.2.3, 5, 10–11. For Calvin on temporary faith, see David Foxgrover, "'Temporary Faith' and the Certainty of Salvation," *Calvin Theological Journal* 15 (1980):220–32; A. N. S. Lane, "Calvin's Doctrine of Assurance," *Vox Evangelica* 11 (1979):45–46; Exalto, *De Zekerheid des Geloofs bij Calvijn*, 15–20, 27–30.

75. Inst. 3.2.11.

of piety and faith."[76] Happily, the truly saved are delivered from self-deception through proper examination directed by the Holy Spirit. Calvin says, "In the meantime, the faithful are taught to examine themselves with solicitude and humility, lest carnal security insinuate itself, instead of the assurance of faith."[77]

Even in self-examination, Calvin emphasizes Christ. He says we must examine ourselves to see if we are placing our trust in *Christ alone*, for this is the fruit of biblical experience. Anthony Lane says that for Calvin self-examination is not so much "Am I *trusting* in Christ?" as it is "Am I trusting in *Christ*?"[78] Self-examination must always direct us to Christ and His promise. It must never be done apart from the help of the Holy Spirit, who alone can shed light upon Christ's saving work in the believer's soul. Apart from Christ, the Word, and the Spirit, Calvin says, "if you contemplate yourself, that is sure damnation."[79]

Conclusion

Calvin was an experiential theologian and preacher who strove to balance how spiritual matters should go in the Christian life, how they do go, and what their end goal is. He hedged himself in from excesses by confining himself to the limits of Scripture and by always tying the Spirit's experiential work to Scripture. At the same time, he used experiential preaching as a way to minister to the needs of believers and as a discriminatory tool for unbelievers. Above all, all his experiential emphases strove to lead the believer to end in glorifying the Trinity through Jesus Christ.

---

76. *Commentary* (on Ezek. 13:9). David Foxgrover shows that Calvin relates the need for self-examination to a great variety of topics: knowledge of God and ourselves, judgment, repentance, confession, affliction, the Lord's Supper, providence, duty, and the kingdom of God, etc. ("John Calvin's Understanding of Conscience," [PhD diss., Claremont, 1978], 312ff.). Cf. J. P. Pelkonen, "The Teaching of John Calvin on the Nature and Function of the Conscience," *Lutheran Quarterly* 21 (1969):24–88.

77. Inst. 3.2.7.

78. Lane, "Calvin's Doctrine of Assurance," 47.

79. Inst. 3.2.24.

Chapter 16

The Puritans on Conscience and Casuistry

When Martin Luther (1483–1546) was asked to recant the views he had expressed in his books, he is said to have replied, "My conscience is captive to the Word of God. I cannot and will not recant anything, for to go against conscience is neither right nor safe."[1] Ever since Luther, the Reformation faith has revolved around questions of having a good conscience in the presence of God.[2] Since conscience speaks directly in the soul as God's representative, the Puritans also recognized that understanding and forming the conscience was central to serving the Lord with gladness. "Conscience, it is either the greatest friend or the greatest enemy in the world," Richard Sibbes (1577–1635) said.[3] The Puritans took up this concept and fleshed it out more fully than the Reformers had done, developing both the doctrine of conscience and considering specific questions of conscience. The Puritan preacher's most momentous task was awakening and guiding the human conscience.

In this chapter, I will first discuss Puritan theology of the *conscience* and, second, the development of the Puritan practice of *casuistry* of conscience.

The Puritans on the Conscience

Several Puritans wrote books on conscience. William Perkins (1558–1602) wrote *A Discourse of Conscience Wherein is Set Down the Nature, Properties, and Differences thereof: as also the Way to Get and Keep a Good Conscience;*[4] William

---

1. Roland H. Bainton, *Here I Stand: A Life of Martin Luther* (New York: Abingdon-Cokesbury Press, 1950), 185. This paper was read at the Sixteenth Century Studies Conference in Dallas, Texas, on October 29, 2011. This article is expanded in Joel R. Beeke and Mark Jones, *A Puritan Theology: Doctrine for Life* (Grand Rapids: Reformation Heritage Books, 2012).

2. For Calvin on conscience, see John Calvin, *Institutes of the Christian Religion*, ed. John T. McNeill, trans. Ford Lewis Battles (Philadelphia: Westminster Press, 1960), 3.19.15. Cf. David Foxgrover, "John Calvin's Understanding of Conscience" (PhD diss., Claremont, 1978).

3. *The Complete Works of Richard Sibbes*, ed. Alexander B. Grosart (1862–1864; reprint, Edinburgh: Banner of Truth, 2001), 7:490.

4. William Perkins, *A Discourse of Conscience* (London, 1596).

Ames (1576–1633) wrote *Conscience, with the Power and Cases Thereof*;[5] William Fenner (1600–1640) wrote *The Souls Looking-Glasse, lively representing its Estate before God: With a Treatise of Conscience; Wherein the definitions and distinctions thereof are unfolded, and severall Cases resolved*;[6] and Nathanael Vincent (1638–1697) wrote *Heaven upon Earth: or, a Discourse Concerning Conscience*.[7]

Under the theme of Puritan theology of the conscience, I will first look at the nature of the conscience as created by God; second, the corrupt state of the conscience due to man's sin; and third, the restoration of conscience by the Word and Spirit of Christ.

The Nature of the Conscience

According to the Puritans, the conscience is a universal aspect of human nature by which God has established His authority in the soul for men to judge themselves rationally. Norman Clifford writes, "The witness of conscience in man's soul was the means by which all natural knowledge of God was sustained. The presence of conscience meant the presence of God's witness and ambassador in the soul of man ever reminding him of his responsibility towards God."[8]

The Puritans stressed:

1. *Everyone has a conscience.* The Puritan authors began their works on conscience by stressing, first, that Scripture, experience, and "the light of nature" affirm that every person has a conscience.[9] For example, Nathanael Vincent wrote, "This thing, called conscience, is in everyone; there is no man without it. You may as well suppose a man without an understanding as without a conscience."[10] Vincent went on to say, "Conscience is not to be escaped; we can no more fly from conscience than we can run away from ourselves."[11]

2. *Conscience empowers self-knowledge and self-judgment.* Samuel Ward (1577–1640), following the medieval theologians Hugo of St. Victor (c. 1096–1141) and Bernard of Clairvaux (1090–1153), wrote of conscience as the soul's

---

5. William Ames, *Conscience, with the Power and Cases Thereof* (London, 1639).

6. William Fenner, *The Souls Looking-Glasse* (Cambridge: Roger Daniel, for John Rothwell, 1643).

7. Nathanael Vincent, *Heaven upon Earth* (London: for Thomas Parkhurst, 1676).

8. Norman Keith Clifford, "Casuistical Divinity in English Puritanism During the Seventeenth Century: Its Origins, Development and Significance" (PhD diss., University of London, 1957), 149.

9. Vincent, *Heaven upon Earth*, 5–17.

10. Vincent, *Heaven upon Earth*, 17–18.

11. Vincent, *Heaven upon Earth*, 21. See also Fenner, *The Souls Looking-Glasse*, 23.

God-given ability to reflect upon itself.[12] Ames defined conscience as "a man's judgment of himself according to the judgment of God on him."[13] The Puritans followed Thomas Aquinas (1225–1274) in viewing conscience as a part of practical reason, that is, an exercise of the mind of man passing moral judgments.[14]

3. *Conscience reasons syllogistically.* The Puritans depicted the reasoning of conscience as a syllogistic form, much as Aquinas did.[15] This form of reasoning includes a major premise stating a general principle, then a minor premise stating an observation or fact, then a conclusion that results from putting these premises together. In his treatise on conscience, Ames illustrated the reasoning of conscience with two syllogisms. The major premise of the first syllogism is: *He that lives in sin shall die.* The minor premise is: *I live in sin.* The conclusion is: *Therefore I shall die.*[16] Ames also offered a syllogism of conscience that arrives at a happier conclusion. The major premise is: *Whoever believes in Christ shall not die but live.* The minor premise is: *I believe in Christ.* If this is established

---

12. Samuel Ward, "Balm from Gilead to Recover Conscience," in *Sermons and Treatises* (1636; reprint, Edinburgh: Banner of Truth, 1996), 97. See Gary Brady, "A Study of Ideas of the Conscience in Puritan Writings, 1590–1640" (ThM thesis, Westminster Theological Seminary, 2006), 46. See also Sibbes, *Works*, 3:208; Samuel Rutherford, *A Free Disputation Against Pretended Liberty of Conscience: Tending to Resolve Doubts* (London: R. I. for Andrew Crook, 1649), 1–22.

13. Ames, *Conscience*, 1. See James I. Packer, *A Quest for Godliness: The Puritan Vision of the Christian Life* (Wheaton, Ill.: Crossway, 1990), 111.

14. Packer says that Ames's definition comes from Aquinas (*Quest for Godliness*, 109). Ames had a copy of the works of Thomas Aquinas in his library (Keith L. Sprunger, "The Learned Doctor Ames" [PhD diss., University of Illinois, 1963], 206). Vincent quoted Aquinas's definition of conscience as the application of our knowledge to our actions to testify regarding our past actions, to judge and bind regarding possible future actions (Vincent, *Heaven on Earth*, 30; citing Thomas Aquinas, *Summa Theologica*, Part I, Q. 79, Art. 13). Most Puritans taught that the seat of the conscience is rooted in the reasonable soul or the understanding, in harmony with the Dominican and Thomistic tradition; a minority placed the seat of the conscience in the will, in accord with the Franciscan tradition. A few, such as Richard Baxter, refused to take sides (*The Practical Works of the Rev. Richard Baxter*, ed. William Orme [London: James Duncan, 1830], 6:96–97). Practically speaking, this variance of views made no substantial difference (Clifford, "Casuistical Divinity," 149–56; cf. Thomas Wood, *English Casuistical Divinity During the Seventeenth Century, With Special Reference to Jeremy Taylor* [London: S.P.C.K., 1952], 67–69).

15. Brian Davies, *The Thought of Thomas Aquinas* (Oxford: Clarendon Press, 1992), 235–37. Syllogistic reasoning as a method dates back to Aristotle (384–322 BC). "A syllogism is a discourse in which, certain things being stated, something other than what is stated follows of necessity from their being so. I mean by the last phrase that they produce the consequence, and by this, that no further term is required from without in order to make the consequence necessary." Aristotle, *Analytica Priora*, trans. A. J. Jenkinson, 1.1, quoted by Brady, 64, and available online at: http://ebooks.adelaide.edu.au/a/aristotle/ (accessed October 17, 2011).

16. Ames, *Conscience*, 3.

as true, the believer is free to draw the conclusion: *Therefore I shall not die but live.*[17] The Puritans say all the acts of conscience have this syllogistic form, even if they take place unconsciously in a moment.

4. *Conscience represents God in our soul.* The Puritans illustrated the divinely authorized role of conscience in the soul with a number of lively pictures and personifications, such as "God's deputy," "the most powerful preacher that can be," "a register, to witness what is done," "God's sergeant he employs to arrest the sinners," and "the soul's glass" or mirror to see itself.[18]

In summary, the Puritans taught that human nature universally includes a conscience, that is, the representation of the voice of God, authoritatively leading us to judge ourselves by rational deductions from our knowledge of God's will and knowledge of ourselves.

The Corruption of Conscience

For the Puritans, sin was not merely a choice but a corruption of the soul resulting from the fall.[19] The Puritans viewed the conscience as profoundly affected by man's fall into sin and misery. They wrote a great deal about various types of evil consciences. Here is a summary of six kinds of evil consciences that they described, moving from the least to the most evil.

---

17. Ames, *Conscience*, 3.

18. *The Works of David Clarkson* (1864; reprint, Edinburgh: Banner of Truth, 1988), 2:475; *The Works of George Swinnock* (1868; reprint, Edinburgh: Banner of Truth, 1992), 5:64; Fenner, *The Souls Looking-Glasse*, 33; Immanuel Bourne, *The Anatomie of Conscience* (London, 1623), 9; William Gurnall, *The Christian in Complete Armour*, 2 vols. in one (1864; reprint, Edinburgh: Banner of Truth, 2002), 1:522; *The Works of Robert Harris* (London: James Flesher for John Bartlet, 1654), 2:18.

19. Daniel Webber, "The Puritan Pastor as Counsellor," in *The Office and Work of the Minister*, Westminster Conference 1986 (London: Westminster Conference, 1987), 84. For the Puritans on sin, see Jeremiah Burroughs, *The Evil of Evils* (1654; reprint, Morgan, Pa.: Soli Deo Gloria, 1995); Ralph Venning, *The Plague of Plagues* (1669; reprint, London: Banner of Truth, 1965); Thomas Watson, *The Mischief of Sin* (1671; reprint, Morgan, Pa.: Soli Deo Gloria, 1994); Samuel Bolton, "Sin: the Greatest Evil," in *Puritans on Conversion* (Pittsburgh: Soli Deo Gloria, 1990), 1–69. The most powerful Puritan work on the dread condition of original sin is Thomas Goodwin, "An Unregenerate Man's Guiltiness Before God in Respect of Sin and Punishment," vol. 10 of *The Works of Thomas Goodwin* (1865; reprint, Eureka, Calif.: Tanski, 1996). The classic doctrinal Puritan work on the subject is Jonathan Edwards, *Original Sin*, vol. 3 of *The Works of Jonathan Edwards* (1758; New Haven: Yale, 1970). The best secondary source on the Edwardsean view is C. Samuel Storms, *Tragedy in Eden: Original Sin in the Theology of Jonathan Edwards* (Lanham, Md.: University Press of America, 1985). Thomas Boston's classic, *Human Nature in Its Fourfold State* (1720; reprint, London: Banner of Truth, 1964), focuses on the four states of innocence, depravity, grace, and glory, but his section on imputed and inherited depravity is especially poignant. He details how Adam's original sin broke man's relationship with God as well as each of the Ten Commandments.

1. *The Trembling Conscience.* The trembling conscience accuses the soul of sin and threatens the soul with God's wrath. Fenner said a guilty conscience is like "a hell to men here on earth,"[20] a pointer to the reality of the hell coming on sinners.[21] John Trapp said, "One small drop [of guilt] troubles the whole sea of outward comforts."[22]

2. *The Moralist Conscience.* This conscience has some good elements, for it is grounded on God's law, and thus, wrote Richard Bernard (1568–1641), it "produceth much good for the exercise of moral virtues in men's living together in societies, to preserve justice, equity, to do good works, and to uphold a common peace among them."[23] But civil virtue cannot save. Bernard said, "A moralist may lift up himself, as the young rich man in the Gospel did, yet can it not give him assurance of eternal life."[24]

3. *The Scrupulous Conscience.* The scrupulous conscience makes too much out of religious duties and moral trifles. It is scrupulously religious but does not look to Christ alone for salvation nor find peace in Christ. The scrupulous conscience "determines a thing to be lawful, yet scarcely to be done, lest it should be unlawful," as Samuel Annesley (ca. 1620–1696) said.[25] It engages in the kind of self-examination that produces aimless introspection and inner gloom. The Puritans would agree with Calvin who said that if you contemplate yourself apart from Christ, the Word, and the Spirit, "that is sure damnation."[26]

4. *The Erring Conscience.* Annesley wrote, "Conscience is sometimes deceived through ignorance of what is right, by apprehending a false rule for a true, an error for the will of God: sometimes, through ignorance of the fact, by

---

20. Fenner, *The Souls Looking-Glasse*, 124.

21. Fenner, *The Souls Looking-Glasse*, 125–26. See also Thomas Fuller, *The Holy and Profane States* (Boston: Little, Brown, and Co., 1865), 102; Thomas Fuller, *The Cause and Cvre of a VVovnded Conscience* (London: G. D. for John Williams, 1649), 28; *The Works of John Flavel* (1820; reprint, Edinburgh: Banner of Truth, 1997), 5:455.

22. John Trapp, *A Commentary on the Old and New Testaments*, ed. Hugh Martin (London: Richard D. Dickinson, 1868), 3:39 [on Prov. 10:22].

23. Richard Bernard, *Christian See to Thy Conscience* (London: Felix Kyngston, 1631), 246. See also Vincent, *Heaven Upon Earth*, 63.

24. Bernard, *Christian See to Thy Conscience*, 246. See Clifford, "Casuistical Divinity," 163–67.

25. Samuel Annesley, "How May We Be Universally and Exactly Conscientious?" in *Puritan Sermons, 1659–1689* (1661; reprint, Wheaton: Richard Owen Roberts, 1981), 1:14.

26. Calvin, *Institutes*, 3.2.24. Cf. Foxgrover, "Calvin's Understanding of Conscience"; Joel R. Beeke, *The Quest for Full Assurance: The Legacy of Calvin and His Successors* (Edinburgh: Banner of Truth, 1999), 59–63, 84–87.

misapplying a right rule to a wrong action. Conscience, evil informed, takes human traditions and false doctrines, proposed under the show of Divine authority to be the will of God."[27]

5. *The Drowsy Conscience.* Annesley wrote of people with such a conscience, "One of the worst kinds of conscience in the world, is the sleepy conscience. Such is the conscience of every unconverted person, that is not yet in horror. Their spirit, that is, their conscience, is asleep (Rom. 11:8)…and therefore, in conversion, Christ doth awaken the conscience."[28] A drowsy conscience produces a silent conscience, making it like a "sleepy careless coachman who giveth the horses the reins and letteth them run whither they will," Fenner said.[29]

6. *The Seared Conscience.* Perkins wrote, "Now the heart of man being exceedingly obstinate and perverse, carrieth him to commit sins even against the light of nature and common sense: by practice of such sins the light of nature is extinguished: and then cometh the reprobate mind, which judges evil good, and good evil: after this follows the seared conscience in which there is no feeling or remorse; and after this comes an exceeding greediness to all manner of sin (Eph. 4:18; Rom. 1:28)."[30] Fenner says that a seared conscience can "swallow down sin like drink and without any remorse."

The Restoration of Conscience

In God's restoration of His image in the soul, He also restores the conscience. This takes place in awakening the conscience by preaching, informing the conscience by Scripture, healing the conscience by the gospel, and exercising the conscience in self-examination.

1. *Conscience must be awakened by preaching.* One mark of a powerful preacher, according to the Puritans, was the way he would "rip up" men's consciences to show them what was at the bottom of their hearts.[31] The *Westminster Directory for Public Worship* says application is difficult for the preacher, for it requires

---

27. Annesley, "How May We Be Universally and Exactly Conscientious?" in *Puritan Sermons*, 1:13.

28. Annesley, "How May We Be Universally and Exactly Conscientious?" in *Puritan Sermons*, 1:8–9.

29. Fenner, *The Souls Looking-Glasse*, 70.

30. *The Workes of that Famous and VVorthy Minister of Christ in the Vniuersitie of Cambridge, Mr. William Perkins* (London: John Legatt, 1612), 1:550.

31. Packer, *Quest for Godliness*, 48.

"much prudence, zeal, and meditation, and to the natural and corrupt man will be very unpleasant." Yet application is necessary so that a preacher's listeners "may feel the Word of God to be quick and powerful, and a discerner of the thoughts and intents of the heart; and that, if any unbeliever or ignorant person be present, he may have the secrets of his heart made manifest and give glory to God."[32]

2. *Conscience must be informed by Scripture.* If conscience is not guided by Scripture, it will still function, but according to inadequate standards. It will fail to condemn when it should, it will justify things that ought not be justified. *The Westminster Confession* (20.2) said that God alone is Lord of the conscience. Richard Baxter (1615–1691) explained, "Make not your own judgments or consciences your law, or the maker of your duty; which is but the discerner of the law of God, and of the duty which he maketh you, and of your own obedience or disobedience to him.... It is not ourselves, but God that is our lawgiver."[33] The purpose of conscience is to make us continually aware of the presence of the holy God. Vincent wrote, "A good conscience will make men set themselves as before God continually."[34]

3. *Conscience must be healed by the Spirit applying the gospel.* William Gurnall (1616–1679) said, "Peace of conscience is nothing but the echo of pardoning mercy."[35] The gospel announces peace and forgiveness for all who trust in Christ, who was crucified for sinners. It is by the Holy Spirit that the conscience lays hold of the gospel by faith in Christ's blood, finds peace with God, and has growing assurance of salvation. Perkins said, "The principal agent and beginner thereof is the Holy Ghost, enlightening the mind and conscience with spiritual and divine light: and the instrument in this action is the ministry of the gospel whereby the word of life is applied in the name of God to the person of every hearer and this certainty is by little and little conceived in a form of reasoning or practical syllogism framed in the mind by the Holy Ghost."[36]

4. *Conscience must be exercised by regular self-examination.* Thomas Watson (c. 1620–1686) wrote, "Self-examination is the setting up a court in conscience

---

32. *Westminster Confession of Faith* (Glasgow: Free Presbyterian Publications, 1994), 380.
33. Baxter, *Works*, 2:336. See Swinnock, *Works*, 5:64.
34. Vincent, *Heaven on Earth*, 277.
35. Gurnall, *The Christian in Complete Armour*, 1:534.
36. Perkins, *Works*, 1:547. See Gurnall, *The Christian in Complete Armour*, 1:525; Fenner, *The Souls Looking-Glasse*, 134; and also Beeke, *The Quest for Full Assurance*, 131–42, 259–62.

and keeping a register there, that by strict scrutiny a man may know how things stand between God and his own soul.... A good Christian begins as it were the day of judgment here in his own soul."[37] Self-examination is especially important, Watson said, in preparation for the Lord's Supper.[38]

Contrary to some caricatures, the Puritans did not glory in guilt. They gloried in Christ. An awakened conscience served to drive men to Christ. A good conscience enabled men to walk with Christ. Therefore they accepted the conscience as a gift of the Creator, diagnosed the conscience in its disorders from the fall of man into sin, and worked to restore the conscience to its healthy functioning through the Word of Christ. This treasuring of a good conscience before God led the Puritans into a quest to answer specific cases of conscience, or the science of casuistry, which is my second main topic in this chapter.

The Puritans on Casuistry

In giving attention to the awakening and shaping of the human conscience, many Puritans also wrote books on various cases of conscience, which came to be called the casuistry of conscience.[39] Casuistry has been defined as "a technique evolved by the Jesuits for finding excuses for not doing what you ought to do."[40] The Puritans would abhor such an idea. For them, casuistry was the art of biblical theology applied with moral integrity to various situations. Thomas Merrill says casuistry "may best be understood as a method of blazing trails through the ethical wilderness that too often separates theory from practice, code from conduct, and religion from morality."[41] The Puritans, as heirs of the Reformers, were deeply concerned to shepherd the flock of God with practical guidance related to what God expected of His covenant people.[42]

---

37. Thomas Watson, *Heaven Taken by Storm*, ed. Joel R. Beeke (Soli Deo Gloria, 1992), 30.

38. Thomas Watson, *The Ten Commandments* (1692; reprint, Edinburgh: Banner of Truth, 2000), 230–36.

39. The word *casuistry* is pronounced with the accent on the first syllable like "casual," thus KA-zhoo-iss-tree.

40. Elliott Rose, *Cases of Conscience: Alternatives Open to Recusants and Puritans Under Elizabeth I and James I* (Cambridge: Cambridge University Press, 1975), 71.

41. Thomas C. Merrill, ed., *William Perkins, 1558–1602: English Puritanist—His Pioneer Works on Casuistry: "A Discourse of Conscience" and "The Whole Treatise of Cases of Conscience"* (Nieuwkoop: B. De Graaf, 1966), x.

42. On the Reformation roots of Puritan practical divinity, see Norman Keith Clifford, "Casuistical Divinity in English Puritanism During the Seventeenth Century: Its Origins, Development and Significance" (PhD diss., University of London, 1957), 1–3, 41–98, 314–18; Ian Breward, "The Life and Thought of William Perkins" (PhD diss., University of Manchester, 1963), 236–77; Martin Bucer, *Concerning the True Care of Souls*, trans. Peter Beale (German 1538; English trans. Edinburgh: Banner of Truth, 2009); John Calvin, *Institutes of the Christian Religion*, ed. John T. McNeill, trans. Ford Lewis Battles (Philadelphia: Westminster Press, 1960), 2.4.12; Jules Bonnet, ed., *Letters of John Calvin*, 4 vols.

This section of my paper will trace the development of Puritan casuistry chronologically from its seminal beginnings to its systematic development in the hands of William Perkins, the father of Puritan casuistry, to its flowering in the early seventeenth century, its fullness in the 1640s through the 1670s, and then in its fading at the end of the Puritan era.[43]

(Philadelphia: Presbyterian Board of Publication, 1858); *John Calvin: Writings on Pastoral Piety*, ed. Elsie A. McKee (New York: Paulist Press, 2001), 291–332.

43. Secondary-source studies on Puritan casuistry include William Whewell, *Lectures on the History of Moral Philosophy in England* (Cambridge: Cambridge University Press, 1852); H. Hensley Henson, *Studies in English Religion in the Seventeenth Century* (New York: E. P. Dutton, 1903); Kenneth E. Kirk, *Conscience and Its Problems: An Introduction to Casuistry* (1927; reprint, Louisville: Westminster John Knox Press, 1999); Louis B. Wright, "William Perkins: Elizabethan Apostle of Practical Divinity," *Huntington Library Quarterly* 3 (1940):171–96; John T. McNeill, "Casuistry in the Puritan Age," *Religion in Life* 12, 1 (Winter, 1942–43):76–89; H. R. McAdoo, *The Structure of Caroline Moral Theology* (London: Longman's Green and Co., 1949); Thomas Wood, *English Casuistical Divinity During the Seventeenth Century, With Special Reference to Jeremy Taylor* (London: S.P.C.K., 1952); George L. Mosse, "Puritan Political Thought and the 'Cases of Conscience,'" *Church History* 23 (1954):109–18; idem, "The Assimilation of Machiavelli in English Thought: The Casuistry of William Perkins and William Ames," *Huntington Library Quarterly* 17, no. 4 (1954):315–26; Clifford, "Casuistical Divinity in English Puritanism During the Seventeenth Century"); George L. Mosse, *The Holy Pretence* (Oxford: Basil Blackwell, 1957); Breward, "The Life and Thought of William Perkins"; Rose, *Cases of Conscience*; P. H. Lewis, "The Puritan Casuistry of Prayer—Some Cases of Conscience Resolved," in *The Good Fight of Faith*, Westminster Conference papers, 1971 (London: Evangelical Press, 1972), 5–22; Peter Lewis, *The Genius of Puritanism* (1975; reprint, Grand Rapids: Soli Deo Gloria, 2009), 63–136; Daniel Webber, "The Puritan Pastor as Counsellor," in *The Office and Work of the Minister*, Westminster Conference papers, 1986 (London: Westminster Conference, 1987), 77–95; Timothy Keller, "Puritan Resources for Biblical Counseling," *Journal of Pastoral Practice* 9, no. 3 (1988):11–44, http://www.ccef.org/puritan-resources-biblical-counseling (accessed June 25, 2011); Margaret Sampson, "Laxity and Liberty in seventeenth-Century English Political Thought," in Edmund Leites, ed., *Conscience and Casuistry in Early Modern Europe* (Cambridge: University Press, 1988), 159–84; James I. Packer, "The Puritan Conscience," in *A Quest for Godliness: The Puritan Vision of the Christian Life* (Wheaton, Ill.: Crossway, 1990), 107–122; Michael Schuldiner, *Gifts and Works: The Post-Conversion Paradigm and Spiritual Controversy in Seventeenth-Century Massachusetts* (Macon, Ga.: Mercer University Press, 1991); Keith Thomas, "Cases of Conscience in Seventeenth-Century England," in John Morrill, Paul Slack, and Daniel Woolf, eds., *Public Duty and Private Conscience in Seventeenth-Century England: Essays Presented to G. E. Aylmer* (Oxford: Clarendon Press, 1993), 29–56; Ken Sarles, "The English Puritans: A Historical Paradigm of Biblical Counseling," in *Introduction to Biblical Counseling: A Basic Guide to the Principles and Practice of Counseling*, John F. MacArthur, Jr., Wayne A. Mack, et al. (Dallas: Word, 1994), 21–43; Edward G. Andrew, *Conscience and Its Critics: Protestant Conscience, Enlightenment Reason, and Modern Subjectivity* (Toronto: University of Toronto Press, 2001); Theodore Dwight Bozeman, *The Precisianist Strain: Disciplinary Religion & Antinomian Backlash in Puritanism to 1638* (Chapel Hill, N.C.: University of North Carolina Press, 2004), 121–44; Gary Brady, "A Study of Ideas of the Conscience in Puritan Writings, 1590–1640" (ThM thesis, Westminster Theological Seminary, 2006). Of these sources, I am most indebted to Breward's and Clifford's dissertations and Packer's article, upon which I have leaned heavily.

The Firstfruits of Puritan Casuistry

The Puritans concurred with Calvin that communicant members of the church should be held accountable to biblical standards for their conduct. Since not all cases were clear, however, Puritan ministers often sought the advice of their colleagues at classis gatherings. These cases became known as *cases of conscience*.[44] When the classis could not come to a clear resolution on a particular case, they customarily referred such matters to Cambridge University, which Norman Clifford says, "undoubtedly foreshadowed the fact that this University was to produce many of the most outstanding Puritan casuists of the period."[45]

One of the most active ministers in those early meetings in Cambridge was Richard Greenham (*c.* 1542–1594), from Dry Drayton, five miles northwest of Cambridge. Thomas Fuller (1608–1661) said that many "who came to him with weeping eyes…went from him with cheerful souls."[46] Scholars today commonly acknowledge Greenham as a pioneer of Puritan casuistry. His pastoral letters and notes recorded by students were later published as "tabletalk" writings.[47] His counsel was incisive. When John Dod (*c.* 1549–1645) came to him in self-pity, Greenham responded, "Son, son, when affliction lies heavy, sin lies light."[48]

Richard Rogers (1550–1618), vicar of Wethersfield and member of Braintree Classis, wrote the book *Seven Treatises* (1604) as a practical manual for Christians with various cases of conscience.[49] Rogers wrote both to offer relief to troubled souls and to counteract the Jesuits who were deriding the Reformed for their lack of moral writings.[50] The book counsels the Christian to rule his life by exercising watchfulness, practicing meditation, using the Christian armor of Ephesians 6, engaging in prayer, reading Scripture and godly authors, offering thanksgiving, and practicing fasting.[51] William Haller writes, "*Seven Treatises*

---

44. For examples of cases of conscience, see Clifford, "Casuistical Divinity," 4–7.

45. Clifford, "Casuistical Divinity," 7.

46. Thomas Fuller, *Church History of Britain*, ed. J. S. Brewer, 3rd ed. (1648; reprint, London: William Tegg, 1845), 5:192–93.

47. Rylands English Manuscript 524, republished in '*Practical Divinity*': *The Works and Life of Revd Richard Greenham*, ed. Kenneth L. Parker and Eric J. Carlson (Brookfield, Vermont: Ashgate, 1998), 129–259. (Originally published in 1599, five years after Greenham's death, in his *Works*.) Cf. Bozeman, *The Precisianist Strain*, 71.

48. Clifford, "Casuistical Divinity," 9.

49. The full title is *Seven Treatises, Containing Such Direction as Is Gathered Out of Holie Scripture, Leading and Guiding to True Happiness, Both in this Life, and in the Life to Come: and May Be Called the Practise of Christianitie: Profitable for Such as Desire the Same: in which more Particularly True Christians Learne How to Lead a Godly and Comfortable Life Every Day* (London: Felix Kyngston for Thomas Man, 1604). This book was reprinted five times in the seventeenth century, but never since.

50. Stephen Egerton, unpaginated preface to *Seven Treatises*.

51. Rogers, *Seven Treatises, passim.*

was the first important exposition of the code of behavior which expressed the English Calvinist, or, more broadly speaking, the Puritan conception of the spiritual and moral life. As such it inaugurated a literature the extent and influence of which in all departments of life can hardly be exaggerated."[52]

The Father of Puritan Casuistry

William Perkins (1558–1602), the renowned preacher at Great St. Andrew's Church, Cambridge, often called "the father of Puritanism," was the first to bring Puritan casuistry to "some form of method and art." Thomas Merrill notes that Perkins's casuistry is important "because it set a pattern for all later work in Protestant moral divinity."[53] Though a theologian, Perkins ministered to common people effectively, including prisoners on death row.[54]

Perkins wrote two treatises on "cases of conscience," titled *A Discourse of Conscience* (1596) and *The Whole Treatise of Cases of Conscience* (1606).[55] The first treatise is more theoretical in its description of conscience.[56] Ian Breward summarizes, "A good conscience was a jewel beyond price, because it gave men the assurance of election which enabled them to rejoice in affliction, and to be bold before God and men whatever the outward circumstances. A bad conscience, on the other hand, was an insupportable burden which brought gnawing terror about Judgment which could only be assuaged by the blood of Christ."[57]

The second treatise provides Bible-based guidance for areas of ethical uncertainty, called cases of conscience. These included personal questions such as how you can know whether you are saved.[58] Or, as Merrill notes, they could be social questions like "the right use of money, truth and falsehood, the right use of leisure, the Christian attitude toward war, vows and promises, proper dress, the lawfulness of recreation, policy and prudence."[59]

---

52. William Haller, *The Rise of Puritanism* (New York: Columbia University Press, 1938), 36. Two other pioneers in Puritan practical divinity were Arthur Dent (1553–1607), rector of South Shoebury, Essex, and author of *The Plain Man's Pathway to Heaven*, and Henry Smith (1560–1591), who was called the "silver-tongued preacher" of his generation.

53. Merrill, ed., *William Perkins, 1558–1602: English Puritanist—His Pioneer Works on Casuistry*, xx.

54. Samuel Clarke, *The Marrow of Ecclesiastical History*, 3rd ed. (London, 1675), 416–17.

55. Republished in Merrill, ed., *William Perkins, 1558–1602: English Puritanist—His Pioneer Works on Casuistry*.

56. Mosse, *The Holy Pretence*, 49.

57. Breward, "Life and Theology of Perkins," 235.

58. Merrill, ed., *William Perkins, 1558–1602: English Puritanist—His Pioneer Works on Casuistry*, 101.

59. Merrill, ed., *William Perkins, 1558–1602*, xx.

By the time of his death, Perkins had become the principle architect of the Puritan movement. In the decades immediately after his death, Perkins's writings in England outsold those of Calvin, Heinrich Bullinger (1504–1575), and Theodore Beza (1519–1605) combined. He "moulded the piety of a whole nation," H. C. Porter says.[60]

The Flowering of Puritan Casuistry

The disciples of Perkins published numerous books on Puritan casuistry. William Gouge (1575–1653) wrote *The Whole Armour of God* (1616), *Of Domestical Duties* (1622), and many other titles winning him the title of being "a sweet comforter of troubled consciences."[61] William Whately (1583–1639), another beneficiary of Perkins's pulpit ministry, wrote several books on practical divinity.[62] Baxter highly recommended Whately's *Ten Commandments* (1622).[63]

Robert Bolton (1572–1631) wrote *Instructions for Comforting Afflicted Consciences* (1626), one of the best Puritan works on consoling the afflicted believer in every aspect of the inner life—mind, heart, conscience, memory, and will.[64] Bolton also published *General Directions for a Comfortable Walking with God* (1626), which he first wrote as a guide for himself.[65] J. I. Packer says of these two books by Bolton, "Richard Baxter went over all this ground a generation later in much greater detail, and with a greater power of thought, but Bolton yields nothing to Baxter in experimental warmth and depth, and sometimes surpasses him."[66]

---

60. H. C. Porter, *Reformation and Reaction in Tudor Cambridge* (London: Cambridge University Press, 1958), 260. Cf. Ian Breward, "William Perkins and the Origins of Puritan Casuistry," in *Faith and a Good Conscience*, Puritan conference papers, 1962 (1963; Stoke-on-Trent, U.K.: Tentmaker, n.d.), 14–17. For the views of Perkins and Ames on liberty of conscience, see L. John Van Til, *Liberty of Conscience, The History of a Puritan Idea* (Nutley, N.J.: Craig Press, 1972), 11–25, 43–51. For a negative assessment of Perkins's treatises on conscience, see Rose, *Cases of Conscience*, 187–94.

61. Samuel Clarke, *A Collection of the Lives of Ten Eminent Divines* (London, 1662), 114.

62. Thomas Fuller, *Abel Redevivus* (1651; reprint, London: William Tegg, 1867), 593.

63. Richard Baxter, *The Practical Works of Richard Baxter* (London: James Duncan, 1830), 5:587.

64. Robert Bolton, *Instructions for Comforting Afflicted Consciences* (1626; reprint, Morgan, Pa.: Soli Deo Gloria, 1991). On Bolton's effectiveness as a pastor and evangelist, see Edward Bagshawe, *The Life and Death of Mr. Bolton* (London, 1635), 19–20.

65. Robert Bolton, *General Directions for a Comfortable Walking with God* (1626; reprint, Morgan, Pa.: Soli Deo Gloria, 1995).

66. J. I. Packer, "Robert Bolton," in *The Encyclopedia of Christianity*, ed. Gary Cohen (Marshallton, Del.: The National Foundation for Christian Education, 1968), 2:131.

Perkins's most famous disciple was William Ames, who wrote *Conscience, with the Power and Cases Thereof* (first published in Latin, 1630; in English, 1639).[67] Samuel Morison, a Harvard historian, describes this important manual of Puritan casuistry as "one of the most valuable sources of Puritan morality."[68] It went through nearly twenty printings in less than thirty years. Ames's *Conscience, with the Power and Cases Thereof* is an expanded commentary of sorts on Book 2 of his most famous work, *The Marrow of Theology*.[69] Baxter said Perkins did valuable service in promoting Reformed casuistry, but "Ames hath exceeded all."[70]

A book that helped popularize the Puritan understanding of conscience for the layperson was William Fenner's (1600–1640) *The Souls Looking-Glasse, lively representing its Estate before God: With a Treatise of Conscience* (1643). "The bond of conscience is the law of God," he said. God's law binds our consciences to Himself and His Word even more than we are bound to governmental leaders and other kinds of human authority.[71] The Scriptures and sacraments form the primary bond of conscience.[72] Human authorities such as a husband, a father, a school teacher, a parent, a magistrate, or an employer form a secondary bond of conscience only insofar as they are authorized by God and His law.[73]

The Fullness of Puritan Casuistry

By the late 1640s, Puritan casuistry was considered such an integral part of ministry that the Westminster Assembly of Divines required a ministerial candidate to be examined in his "skill in the sense and meaning of such places of the Scripture as shall be proposed unto him in cases of conscience."[74] In the mid-seventeenth

---

67. William Ames, *Conscience With the Power and Cases Thereof* (1639; reprint, Norwood, N.J.: Walter J. Johnson, 1975), 1.1. For a basic introduction to Ames and his most famous work, see Joel R. Beeke and Jan Van Vliet, "*The Marrow of Theology* by William Ames (1576–1633)," in *The Devoted Life: An Invitation to the Puritan Classics*, ed. Kelly M. Kapic and Randall C. Gleason (Downers Grove, Ill.: InterVarsity, 2004), 52–65. For more on Ames as a Puritan casuist, see Mosse, *The Holy Pretence*, 68–87.

68. Samuel Eliot Morison, "Those Misunderstood Puritans," http://www.revisionisthistory.org /puritan1.html (accessed August 4, 2011).

69. William Ames, *The Marrow of Theology*, trans. John D. Eusden (Grand Rapids: Baker Books, 1968), 70.

70. Baxter, *Works*, 2:viii.

71. Fenner, *The Souls Looking-Glasse*, 175–206.

72. Fenner, *The Souls Looking-Glasse*, 209, 210.

73. Fenner, *The Souls Looking-Glasse*, 196–99.

74. *A Directory for the Publique Worship of God* (London, 1651), 76. For an example of such an examination, see M. H. Lee, *The Diaries and Letters of Philip Henry* (London: Kegan Paul, Trench & Co., 1887), 36.

century, volumes of casuistry poured off the press, ranging from disputes over Episcopal church government[75] to questions about regeneration.[76]

One of the most significant Puritan casuistry writers in the 1650s was Thomas Brooks (1608–1680), rector of St. Margaret's, New Fish Street Hill, London, the first church that burned to the ground in the Great Fire of London (1666). Tim Keller provides this helpful summary of Brooks's treatise, *Precious Remedies Against Satan's Devices* (1653):

> Brooks discusses twelve types of temptation, eight varieties of discouragement, eight kinds of depression, and four classes of spiritual pride! Brooks' "temptation" sections are addressed to anyone struggling with besetting patterns of sin, particularly to those fighting addictions…. The "discouragement" section applies to persons who suffer from 'burnout' as well as anxiety, grief, and disappointment…. The "depression" section largely deals with persons whose despair arises from guilt and from a "low self-image." The Puritans called this condition "accusation," in which the conscience and the devil attack the person over his failures and sins…. Finally, the section on "pride" deals with several forms of this great sin. It brings out cases of materialism, of power-lust, of intellectual arrogance, of love of ignorance and crudeness, of bitterness, and of jealousy.[77]

In 1659, Samuel Clarke, a Puritan minister and writer, produced three treatises titled *The Medulla Theologiae*, *Golden Apples*, and *Several cases of Conscience Concerning Astrologie*. The first book was one of the largest collections of cases of conscience at that time, yet was only a fraction of what Clarke intended to write before he died.[78] The Cripplegate Morning Exercises also began in 1659. These were early morning sermons delivered by well-known Puritan preachers on various cases of conscience, with titles such as: "How May We Experience

---

75. Clifford, "Casuistical Divinity," 28.

76. David Dickson's *Therapeutica Sacra* was first published in English in 1664 and last reprinted in *Select Practical Writings of David Dickson*, vol. 1 (Edinburgh: Printed for the Assembly's Committee, 1845). The English subtitle was *The Method of Healing the Diseases of the Conscience Concerning Regeneration*. On Dickson's use of the covenant as a scheme for casuistry, see Clifford, "Casuistical Divinity," 27–28. Other relevant works of this period include William Twisse, *Doubting Conscience Resolved* (1652), John Dury, *A Case of Conscience: whether it be lawful to admit Jews into a Christian commonwealth* (1654); Samuel Hartlib, *The Earnest Breathings of Foreign Protestants, Divines, and others* (1658). On Dury and Hartlib's efforts to build an international unity among Reformed divines through practical divinity, see Gunnar Westin, *Negotiations about Church Unity, 1628–1634* (Uppsala: A.-B. Lundequistska, 1932); Karl Brauer, *Die Unionstätigkeit John Duries unter dem Protektorat Cromwells* (Marburg, 1907).

77. Keller, "Puritan Resources for Biblical Counseling," 3.

78. Clifford, "Casuistical Divinity," 33–34; Samuel Clarke, "Autobiography," in his *Lives of Sundry Eminent Persons in this Later Age* (London, 1683), 3–11.

in Ourselves, and Evidence to Others, that Serious Godliness is more than a Fancy?" and "What Are the Best Preservatives Against Melancholy and Over-much Sorrow?" These sermons have recently been republished as the first four volumes in *Puritan Sermons, 1659–1689*.[79]

In 1664, when Richard Baxter was in forced retirement by the Act of Uniformity, he began writing his *Christian Directory*. In this comprehensive survey of practical divinity, Baxter gives directions for ordering one's life before God, performing duties in family relationships, fulfilling responsibilities within the life of the church, and living uprightly with neighbors and public officials. No Puritan work on applied theology has surpassed this treatise; it is one of the most practical and helpful biblical counseling manuals ever written. Though this volume of one million words was too large to become a popular work, it towered over every other work of its kind for the remainder of the century and, in many ways, is still very useful today.

This is but a sampling of the many Puritan works of casuistry from the 1640s to the 1670s.[80]

The Fading of Puritan Casuistry

Puritan casuistry faded during the last two decades of the seventeenth century. Though occasional divines such as Isaac Watts (1674–1748) and Jonathan Edwards (1703–1758) continued to write on casuistry into the eighteenth century, they were the exceptions that prove the rule.[81] Interestingly, Watts titled his 1731 book, *An Humble Attempt toward the Revival of Practical Religion among Christians*, indicating the widespread loss of casuistical divinity.[82] Clifford attributes this loss, at least in part, to "the rise of Deism, the struggle with Socinianism and Arminianism and the attacks of Hobbes and Locke on the validity of the idea of conscience, [which] all worked together to create an intellectual and religious atmosphere that was uncongenial to [its] cultivation

---

79. *Puritan Sermons, 1659–1689* (Wheaton, Ill.: Richard Owen Roberts, 1981). This is a six-volume reprint, but volume 5 is a compilation of Puritan systematic theology, and volume 6 is a polemical volume countering Roman Catholicism (see Beeke and Pederson, *Meet the Puritans*, 637–39).

80. There are scores of additional Puritan books of casuistry that we don't have space to enlarge upon here. For example, there are Thomas Fuller, *The Cause and Cvre of a VVovnded Conscience* (London: G. D. for John Williams, 1649); James Durham, *Heaven upon Earth in the Sure Tranquility and Quiet Composure of a Good Conscience; Sprinkled with the Blood of Jesus*, ed. John Carstairs (Edinburgh: A. Anderson, 1685). Consider also Joseph Alleine's (1634–1668) *Cases Satisfactorily Resolved* (1672) and Nathanael Vincent's *Heaven upon Earth: or, a Discourse Concerning Conscience* (1676).

81. See especially the application sections in Edwards's sermons.

82. Isaac Watts, *An Humble Attempt toward the Revival of Practical Religion among Christians* (London, 1731).

and further development."[83] During the Great Awakening of the early 1740s, there was a major revival of practical divinity, particularly through men such as Theodore Frelinghuysen (1691–1747) and George Whitefield (1714–1770), but that too faded away. The form and method of Puritan casuistry was never fully revived. However, the principles of counseling the soul based on biblical directives continue to be practiced by pastors and biblical counselors today, who find the casuistic writings of the Puritans to be rich sources of guidance even in the twenty-first century.

Conclusion: The Courage of a Good Conscience

By its very nature, conscience must be active. The Puritans aimed to understand the proper role of the conscience and to cultivate it through biblical instruction. They believed that a good conscience does not promote legalism or carelessness about sin. Rather, peace of conscience strengthens a man's moral backbone and makes him as bold as a lion. Richard Sibbes said, "We can do nothing well without joy, and a good conscience, which is the ground of joy."[84] A good conscience was "heaven on earth" because it assured them of eternal bliss.

Another reason why they so cherished their consciences is the power conscience has over present happiness and motivation. As a people often under persecution from the authorities, the Puritans found in conscience a power to stand for the convictions they received from the Bible in the face of harassment, banishment, and death. A sense of divine approval gave them joy in their trials. In the words of Vincent,

> A good conscience steels a man's heart with courage, and makes him fearless before his enemies. Paul earnestly beheld the council. He was not afraid to face them, because his conscience was clear. Nay, we read that Felix the judge trembled, while Paul the prisoner was confident. The reason was, because the judge had a bad conscience…but the prisoner being acquitted by a good conscience, did not tremble but rejoiced at the thoughts of judgment to come.[85]

---

83. Clifford, "Casuistical Divinity," 40.
84. Sibbes, *Works*, 3:223.
85. Vincent, *Heaven on Earth*, 306.

Chapter 17

Assurance of Salvation:
The Insights of Anthony Burgess

Anthony Burgess (d. 1664) served as a fellow (instructor) at Emmanuel College, Cambridge, before becoming the vicar at Sutton Coldfield, Warwickshire, in 1635. During the Civil War, he took refuge in Coventry and then was summoned to serve in the Westminster Assembly. After the war, in 1647, he returned to Sutton Coldfield where he served until being expelled in 1662 by the Act of Uniformity. A gifted and godly scholar, he wrote major treatises on Christ's prayer in John 17,[1] original sin, justification by faith alone, and the goodness and functions of the law of God.[2] Burgess's books were not reprinted in the nineteenth century, thus, he is not as well known today as other Puritans such as John Owen. The following chapter is adapted from his masterpiece on assurance and conversion, *Spiritual Refining*.[3]

* * * * *

Paul commands us, "Examine yourselves, whether ye be in the faith; prove your own selves. Know ye not your own selves, how that Jesus Christ is in you, except ye be reprobates?" (2 Cor. 13:5).

It is a responsibility of great importance for the people of God to be assured that there is a true and saving work of grace in them, so as to distinguish them from hypocrites. There are certain signs of grace by which a man may discern what he is.

---

1. See Joel R. Beeke, "Anthony Burgess on Christ's Prayer for Us," in *Taking Hold of God: Reformed and Puritan Perspectives on Prayer*, ed. Joel R. Beeke and Brian G. Najapfour (Grand Rapids: Reformation Heritage Books, 2011), 83–108.

2. The last of these was recently reprinted as Anthony Burgess, *Vindiciae Legis*, Westminster Assembly Facsimile Series (Grand Rapids: Reformation Heritage Books, 2011).

3. Anthony Burgess, *Spiritual Refining: Or a Treatise of Grace and Assurance* (London: by A. Miller for Thomas Underhill, 1652), 1–59. A second edition of the book was published in 1658 with an additional section on sin. International Outreach reprinted it in the 1990s.

This involves a practical and experiential knowledge, which is much more than mere head knowledge. There is a great difference between hearing that honey is sweet, and tasting it. This is what the Bible often means by "knowing" something—experiential knowledge, not mere knowledge in the brain.

We need a practical, experiential, and well-tested knowledge of our spiritual condition. That is clear for several reasons. First, Christ our Savior pressed this point upon those who heard His sermons. Consider His parables on the sower and the soils (Matt. 13:1–9, 18–23), the ten virgins (Matt. 25:1–13), and the two builders (Matt. 7:24–27). Second, it is easy to make a mistake on this matter, given our tendency to deceive ourselves and have false confidence (Rom. 2:17). Third, it is very dangerous to make a mistake here. Unless you go beyond mere outward morality and religion, you can never enter the kingdom of heaven. Fourth, it is difficult to see the difference between true grace and its counterfeits.

Furthermore, there are many advantages that experiential knowledge brings. It gives us an inward feeling and sense of holiness in our hearts. It's the difference between seeing a place on a map and going there to see it yourself. It makes our hearts a copy of the Bible so that all God's promises and warnings have their echo there. This knowledge of holiness makes us dead to all human greatness and worldly delights. It makes the Word and worship sweet to our souls and helps us to leave behind empty controversies about religion. It gives us the kind of knowledge that produces godly action. It establishes the truth to us in a way that we will endure persecution rather than let it go.

However, this experiential testing of ourselves faces real obstacles. First, we might approach this question with sinful self-love and self-confidence. "He that trusteth in his own heart is a fool" (Prov. 28:26). Second, we might look at good actions but ignore the motives. Real godliness is inward, not outward (Rom. 2:28). Third, we might test ourselves by false standards. Instead of the Word of God, the Bible, we might take up what is old or popular or traditional for our guide. Fourth, we might confuse morality or good manners for godliness.

In general, there are three kinds of people who take the name of Christians. Some have only the name but no power so that they deny Christ by their works. Others have some influences and operations of the Spirit of God upon them. But they are like embryos that miscarry before the new birth. Their affections are somewhat moved by the truth (Matt. 13:20–22), but the Holy Spirit does not dwell in them as members of the body of Christ. However, some are part of Christ's body and receive a life-giving influence from Him, as branches do from the vine (John 15:5). The least of believers is far above the best of hypocrites because he is born again into a true experiential knowledge of Christ's sufferings and resurrection. Someone may have experienced something of the power of spiritual gifts for ministry, the bitterness of sin, a desire for spiritual benefits, an enjoyment of the Word, and a change in their lifestyle—but still be unsaved. The true believer has a different heart (Luke 8:15), for spiritual light dwells in him permanently to make him holier and more dependent on the Lord.

The Bible presents such clear signs of the state of grace that a godly man who faithfully applies them to himself may by the guidance and help of the Spirit of God become assured that he is in that state. There are two main matters to be discussed here: seeking certainty or assurance and using the signs of grace.

Assurance or Certainty about Salvation

Assurance or certainty about a truth in general may come in various ways, such as seeing or hearing something with your eyes and ears, knowing a first principle and making logical deductions from it, or receiving a witness that has authority. No authority is higher than God's revelation. What kind of certainty can the people of God have about their being in Christ? It is a mixed kind of certainty, partly based on faith in God's Word and partly by a spiritual sense and experience worked by the Holy Spirit.

A man who lives in the habit of serious sins should be assured that he is presently in a damnable condition and will be so as long as he lives that way. The works of the flesh are manifest or plainly visible, and those who live that way have no inheritance in God's kingdom (Gal. 5:19–21). If this is your life, do not flatter yourself but wake up. However, no one has warrant to be assured that he is eternally rejected by God, for the Bible does not tell the names of the reprobate and God does not reveal such things directly to anyone.

Paul's command to examine ourselves is not merely a call to test whether your particular church is a true, visible church. It is easier for a particular church to know it is a true church than for a particular Christian to know he is a true believer, for a true church is any congregation where the Word is preached in its purity and there is an external submission to it, but a true Christian has the secret and powerful operation of God's Spirit in his heart.

No one by his natural powers of understanding can come to an assurance of saving grace in his soul. No one can see the sun except by the light of the sun; no one can see Christ in his soul except by the Spirit of Christ. He is the Spirit of adoption who assures the believer. This is why God's people have spiritual combat not only between sin and holiness but also between doubt and faith.

A Christian may be assured in this life of four special mercies: election by God, forgiveness of sins, sanctification of his nature, and perseverance in holiness unto future glory. However, the foundation of all the others is assurance of our sanctification. There can be no certainty that God predestined us, justified us, and will glorify us unless there is certainty that God has made us new within and we see the fruit of sanctifying grace.

It is a very sad delusion when an ungodly man is persuaded that he is in a state of grace, when in fact he is in a state of sin and death. This is worse than being possessed by demons. It is like the condition of the church in Laodicea, who thought they were rich and full, when they were naked and empty (Rev. 3:17). It is like the condition of an insane man who thinks he is a prince with a large estate but in fact is locked in chains in a dungeon. Therefore beware lest your self-love blind your eyes and harden your heart, and pray for God to make you know yourself.

The soul of man has two kinds of acts. One kind is direct acts, as when I take Christ and cling to Him by faith. The other kind is reflexive acts where a man perceives his own direct acts, as when I perceive that I cling to Christ and love God. Certainty or assurance is a reflexive act, a feeling or perceiving of one's own faith.

The assurance of a believer is within his own heart and cannot be made known to another person. Just as only those who have been a father or mother understand what it is like to have such a relationship, so this certainty is only for those who have experienced it. It is compared to a white stone that no one knows except the person who has it (Rev. 2:17). We can have a judgment of certainty toward ourselves but only a judgment of charity toward others. As sweet as fellowship among brothers may be, many whom the godly admired like stars later have fallen out of the skies, and others of questionable hope have remained faithful.

The certainty of all acts of faith, whether direct or reflex, depends more on the work of God's Spirit than the evidence. Christians can have a firm faith in the Scriptures by the power of the Spirit even when they cannot answer all the arguments of their persecutors. In the same way, a believer's confidence that he has real, saving grace depends more on God's Spirit releasing him from fear and bondage than it does on the greatness and beauty of grace within him.

A human being in his natural life knows his natural motions to see, hear, touch, feel, taste, and think. In the same way, a Christian in his spiritual life knows his spiritual motions to love his brothers and God (1 John 3:14). However, natural motions are not opposed by temptations, but spiritual motions are and thus are more difficult.

The Bible speaks of this certainty with words such as persuaded (*peithō*), know (*ginōskō*), faith (*pistis*), confidence (*pepoithēsis*), boldness (*parrēsia*), and assurance (*plērophoria*). We must be careful, however, not to confuse faith, confidence, and assurance—as some theologians have done. One may have justifying faith without assurance. Ephesians 3:12 teaches us that faith has three effects: confidence, boldness or assurance, and freedom to draw near to God in prayer as one welcomed by Him. Some say that faith, confidence, and assurance are the same thing in three different levels of maturity. Others say they are distinct graces. I will not argue about it. This is certain, that faith must apply Christ to us or it cannot justify us.

So do not let your heart despair if you have not attained to assurance. The God who has made you desire Christ and who has supported you in your doubts and fears can bring you to assurance one step at a time. In the end your doubts may produce a much stronger faith, as trees shaken by the wind will have stronger roots. In fact, the Christian's assurance is not so high and full that it excludes all doubting. Nothing in this life is perfect, whether it be our obedience or comfort. Our certainty will be painfully assaulted by Satan and our own unbelief. We may even say that he who never doubted, never believed. There is some bitterness in all our honey.

The Possibility, Necessity, Difficulty, and Excellency of Assurance

It is possible for a Christian to have an assurance of his salvation. We see in Scripture that God's people have enjoyed it. David called God his God and his portion and thanked Him for forgiving his sins. Paul showed his assurance and based it not on a special revelation from God but on grounds that belong to all the people of God (Romans 8). If a man can confess that he believes in God and in other divine truths of the Word, surely he can also know he believes. God gave the sacraments of baptism and the Lord's Supper as signs and seals of His covenant. To throw away the possibility of assurance is to throw away God's seals. If assurance is not possible, then there must be some problem with its object or the means by which we get it. But the object of assurance is the promises of God, which are yes and amen in Christ (2 Cor. 1:20), and the means of assurance is the Spirit of God, who renews the heart to sincerity and effectively works assurance.

We need assurance. The nature of faith is to establish and settle us. It is a pillar and anchor to the soul. Though one can have faith without assurance, doubting and fear are the opposite of believing. Trusting in God is compared in the Bible to rolling ourselves on Him (Ps. 37:5), staying the mind on Him (Isa. 26:3), and resting the heart on Him (Ps. 37:7). Strong and regular exercises of faith in Christ will, over time, bring us to assurance. It is also needed so that we can praise God for His mercies, have more joy and peace in our hearts, and be stirred up to serve Him with greater holiness. Hope leads a Christian to purify himself (1 John 3:3), promises move him to cleanse himself (2 Cor. 7:1), belief motivates him to speak (2 Cor. 4:13), and knowledge of the Father's love makes the child willing and ready to obey (Eph. 5:1; Col. 3:12).

The attaining of assurance faces many difficulties. When a person feels the guilt of his sins, he is quick to look upon God as an enemy and an avenger. Our hearts are deceitful. We are prone to neglect our walk with God and be spiritually careless, but assurance is preserved by a continual exercise of grace (2 Peter 1:10). Satan attacks us with his fiery darts, and if he cannot hurt us in our obedience, he will attack us in our comforts. Pirates wait for the ships most full of gold, and Satan leaves the wicked in peace while tempting the godly with many fears. Even God sometimes hides Himself so that we will not take assurance for granted and grow lazy.

How excellent though is this privilege! It keeps Christians in close fellowship with God so that they can say, "I am my beloved's, and my beloved is mine" (Song 6:3). The Spirit of adoption puts in their hearts the attitude of a humble child motivated to serve the Father with pure motivation (Rom. 8:14–15). Assurance will support them when everything else in life is misery and trouble, so that they triumph over all difficulties (Rom. 8:37). It inflames them in prayer with burning desires, strong hopes, and boldness with God. It makes them walk with great sensitivity to sin, lest they lose their experience of heaven on earth. It makes them sincerely long for Christ's coming so that they can be with Him (Phil. 1:23). Finding full rest and peace in God and Christ makes them content no matter what they lack, for He is sufficient (Ps. 73:25–26). Therefore, how blessed is he who has God for his God and Christ for his Christ!

Assurance versus Presumption

We must carefully distinguish between assurance and presumption. A false assurance is the worst delusion and insanity, but too many people bless themselves even while they are outside the door of the kingdom. Assurance and presumption come from different root causes. Assurance comes from the Spirit of God enlightening the heart and working childlike affections. Presumption comes from a lack of experiential knowledge of the depth and danger of one's sin and the clinging presence of self-love and self-flattery (Prov. 16:2).

Assurance and presumption also differ in their motives and basis. Assurance comes from the Spirit of God working through the Word of God to produce spiritual comfort (Rom. 15:4). Presumption comes from a natural understanding of regeneration, which cannot be spiritually understood without the Spirit's work (John 3:10). Presumption leans at least in part on one's own merits and worthiness, but assurance looks only for sincerity of grace mingled with many faults that Christ's blood must wash away. People often presume that God loves them in a saving way because they have outward prosperity in riches, children, or honors—but they stand in slippery places and may be horribly surprised (Luke 16:25).

God generally works assurance in a manner quite differently than presumption springs up. Though the Spirit is free to save as He pleases (John 3:8), God's ordinary way is to bring a person to sincere humiliation under the burden of his sins (Matt. 11:28). Assurance is often attained after a conflict with doubts and unbelief, for it is the work of the Spirit, and the flesh wars against the Spirit (Gal. 5:17). Assurance with never a doubt is too much like the man who said, "All these have I kept from my youth" (Luke 18:21). It is a good sign when a sense of God's grace in us comes with a feeling of our imperfections, so that we cry, "Lord, I believe, help thou my unbelief" (Mark 9:24).

Assurance also produces effects that go far beyond anything presumption can do. Godly assurance makes a person diligent to use the means of grace and careful to obey God's commands, but the neglect of them weakens assurance (2 Peter 1:10). Sinful self-confidence swells all the bigger even while neglecting prayer and living in sin. Godly assurance ignites the heart with love to God, like a magnifying glass focuses the light of the sun to start a fire. Presumption works more lust for this created world and a proud abuse of God. Assurance has the power to support the heart when discouragements and disruptions abound and sinful confidence fails. True metal proves itself on the anvil.

We may also see the difference in the spiritual companions and enemies of assurance and presumption. Assurance comes with holy fear and trembling (Phil. 2:12) and humility and low self-appraisal (Luke 1:46–48). Presumption keeps out godly fear and comes with a flattering self-comparison to other sinners (Luke 18:11). The only enemies of assurance are sin and coolness of zeal, for it is produced by God's Spirit and sin grieves the Spirit (Eph. 4:30). Presumption may be shaken by outward troubles or psychological depression but not by sin's offense against God.

God has powerful weapons to destroy the fortresses of sinful self-confidence. This is a mercy, for no one has higher obstacles against coming to Christ than the falsely assured Christian. God can, however, destroy these strongholds by a powerful, soul-searching preacher (2 Cor. 10:4–5). Another weapon is an explanation and application of God's laws to the motives of the soul, as Christ did in the Sermon on the Mount (Matthew 5). God might also show people from the Bible how complete and necessary a Savior Jesus Christ is, for if He is everything, then we have nothing in ourselves. God may also accompany the thunder of the Word with the afflictions of earthly grief to awaken sinners. He can use the frightening examples of people who seemed so spiritual (and thought so highly of themselves) but then fell horribly. Indeed, God can use stupid decisions people make in other areas of life to show them that they may be fooling themselves about their spiritual state too.

The Lack of Assurance

What should a person do if he has true saving grace in him but lacks assurance? This is agonizing, more painful than broken bones. Let him consider whether he is living in some sin that he knows is sin yet has not repented (Ps. 32:3–5; 51:8; Eph. 4:30). Let him also ask whether he is neglecting the means of grace. Assurance comes through diligent pursuit of godliness (2 Peter 1:5–10) and prayer (Phil. 4:6–7).

If he still lacks assurance, let him remember that it is a gift of God's sovereign grace, not a natural consequence of what we do (Rom. 8:15–16; 2 Cor. 1:3–4). Even if you lack assurance, keep exercising love, faith, and obedience toward God. Though God often gives new converts a sense of His love because they need it most, solid assurance generally belongs to those who know God over a long time and endure in His ways.

Someone might ask, "Why doesn't God always give us assurance when He works saving grace in our souls?" A prophet told David that his sins were forgiven (2 Sam. 12:18), but David still prayed earnestly for forgiveness and joy (Psalm 51). This implies that God caused the promise to be declared to him outwardly, but He had not yet by His almighty power persuaded his heart.

God has reasons why He may not speak peace to our consciences even after He puts grace in our hearts. This causes us to taste how bitter sin is. It keeps us low and humble. It makes us prize assurance and take more care not to lose it. It gives the Christian the opportunity to show his obedience to God and honor Him by faith even when lacking joy and peace. Lastly, it produces a mature Christian who can use his experience to comfort others in their distresses.

Using Signs of Saving Grace

There are signs of grace by which a man may know whether he is in a state of grace. I need to discuss this more because many today criticize ministers that preach signs of grace. Furthermore, this subject takes wisdom to handle so as to avoid doing yourself spiritual harm.

God's sanctifying grace produces a supernatural life within us. It is the infused principle of a holy life, a new creation produced by regeneration (2 Peter 1:4; 2 Cor. 5:17). Our essence does not change, but the Spirit of God works gracious habits and qualities in us. It is a spiritual resurrection from the dead. We do not have God's essence, but we do have God's image. This supernatural, permanent principle becomes part of the Christian's inner constitution and produces effects and signs that people can see. We are not talking about the gifts of miracles such as those performed by the apostles. Nor are we talking about the common graces of God's Spirit that produce bare belief in the historical facts of the gospel and an outward change of religion and lifestyle. We are talking about holiness in the heart that produces holy actions.

The Bible speaks of some marks of grace that others may see and know that we belong to God and some marks that we may see in our own hearts. For an example of the first, consider John 13:35, "By this shall all men know that ye are my disciples, if ye have love one to another." Thus the work of the Spirit in Christians is said to make them into "an epistle of Christ" (2 Cor. 3:3), for people around them can see evidences that they are saved. But the reality of salvation is in the hidden things of the heart that a man may know only about himself.

The signs of grace given in Scripture belong only to the godly. It is not that the godly have more of them than the wicked but that hypocrites do not have them at all. There are positive signs and negative signs, and the positive signs are more important. It is deceitful and futile to argue that you are saved just because of what you do *not* do (Luke 18:11). The positive signs appear in the Bible's descriptions of the properties of true believers (Gal. 5:25). For them to function as signs, a Christian must see them and see past them to their causes in God's election, justification, adoption, and regeneration. In other words, the signs point beyond themselves to Christ and the Spirit in the soul. The presence of these signs in a person's life does not automatically give him assurance. The Spirit of God must remove his darkness.

Signs of grace must not be abused.

- We must be careful that when we look into ourselves to find graces in our hearts we do not forget to keep relying on Christ alone for our justification. This is one reason why some people oppose using the signs of grace. Christ is better than all the graces within us.

- The Bible attributes salvation to several signs, and if a godly man sees any one of these signs in himself, he may conclude that he is saved and justified. Temptation may hinder us from seeing all the signs in ourselves.

- Do not let the dreams of hypocrites discourage you from using the signs. The fact that they have a false confidence does not mean that we cannot have a true confidence based on the Scriptures.

- Do not demand perfection in the signs. The graces of a truly saved Christian are not perfect, and neither are the signs of grace perfect. Do not doubt your salvation just because you find some hypocrisy, wrong motives, or coolness of zeal in the signs of your graces. Comfort comes from seeing that grace is real in your soul, not from trying to make it the cause or merit of your justification before God.

It is right to seek evidence of our justification by signs of our sanctification. Indeed, it is our duty as Christians. The question is not whether a Christian in his first act of faith, by which he comes to Christ and is engrafted into Him, should see signs of his sanctification. This is the order laid down in 1 John 2:5, "But whoso keepeth his word, in him verily is the love of God perfected: hereby know we that we are in him." We must first be in Christ before we can see fruits of being in Christ. We grasp hold of Christ out of a sense of our guilt and unworthiness. No preacher should say, "You may not rely on Christ for justification until you have evidence of grace in your heart." Scripture calls people to Christ who are burdened, not those who are assured (Matt. 11:28). Nor should a Christian in great temptations, doubts, and darkness search for grace in his soul. It is hard to find treasure in muddy water. In such cases the godly man must throw himself upon the promises and invitations of God.

This is not legalism. The duty of Christians to look for evidence of their salvation in the signs of their sanctification should never be an attempt to live up to the perfect standard of the law. Nor should it be done apart from God's Spirit, for the Spirit seals the believer (Eph. 1:13). Nor should it be a quest after finding the cause or merit of our justification in ourselves. It is, rather, finding certainty about our regeneration by the fruits of holiness flowing from it.

The Bible commends this method of seeking assurance when it gives us descriptions of the characteristics of true saving grace in distinction from counterfeits. For example, Christ does this in the parable of the soils (Matt. 13:1–9, 18–23) and the parable of the sheep (John 10:4–5). Other Scriptures command us to examine ourselves and our works (2 Cor. 13:5; Gal. 6:4) and to make our calling and election sure (2 Peter 1:10). We have examples of godly believers who used their graces as comforting signs of God's love to them (2 Kings 20:3; Neh. 13:14, 22; 2 Cor. 1:12; 2 Tim. 4:7–8).

Our Savior lays down this principle, "the tree is known by his fruit" (Matt. 12:33). If this is true of knowing each other, how much more can a man's spirit know himself (1 Cor. 2:11)? So also the Bible contains many promises to those who have particular graces (Matt. 5:3–10), which would be for nothing if a man could not recognize those graces in himself and by logical deduction apply the promises to himself by the help of the Holy Spirit.

John's first epistle is full of this method of assurance, saying, for example:

+ And hereby we do know that we know him, if we keep his commandments. He that saith, I know him, and keepeth not his commandments,
  is a liar, and the truth is not in him. But whoso keepeth his word, in him
  verily is the love of God perfected: hereby know we that we are in him
  (1 John 2:3–5).

+ In this the children of God are manifest, and the children of the devil:
  whosoever doeth not righteousness is not of God, neither he that loveth
  not his brother (1 John 3:10).

+ We know that we have passed from death unto life, because we love the
  brethren. He that loveth not his brother abideth in death (1 John 3:14).

Therefore let us test ourselves by the biblical marks of grace. In a time when
so many find their confidence in their opinions, disputing about doctrine, or
special revelations from God, the true power of putting sin to death and living
for God is completely neglected. Our Savior did not describe the branches in
Him by their leaves or blossoms but by their fruit (John 15:1–8). Let us not
rest in head knowledge; let us look for holiness.

The Holy Spirit bears witness with the spirit of the children of God so
that they may know they are children of God (Rom. 8:16). God seals them
with His Spirit (Eph. 1:13), impressing upon them His image to show they are
His, just as a seal impresses its image upon the wax to ratify a document. Thus,
the Spirit witnesses to believers even now on earth (1 John 5:8). His testimony
through the graces within believers does not replace faith in God's promises but
assists them in their weakness to believe those promises. This is not hearing an
immediate voice from God's Spirit. Just as the Spirit convinces people that the
Bible is God's Word by enabling to see its divine qualities, so the Spirit assures
Christians that they are saved by enabling them to see the fruits of grace in
themselves.

Cautions about Signs of Grace
Let me close with some cautions about using signs of grace to gain assurance.

First, be careful how you define the marks of grace. On the one hand, do
not require such signs of yourself as no Christian has in this life. A true Christian keeps God's commandments (1 John 3:24), but no Christian ever comes
to the point where he may say he has no sin (1 John 1:8). Although he does
not hunger and thirst for God as much as he should, he does sincerely hunger and thirst for God. On the other hand, do not make signs of saving grace
out of qualities that unbelievers can have. Taking the sacraments, having right

doctrinal beliefs, and exercising great ability in Christian service may all appear in a person who is not born again.

Second, only test your graces by the true standard, the Word of God. Scripture alone is the light to guide our feet (Ps. 119:105), God's wisdom to make us wise for salvation (2 Tim. 3:15).

Third, never use the signs in a way that hinders you from receiving and applying Christ for your souls. Rest on Christ alone for reconciliation with God and atonement of your sins. Your graces are but signs of Christ; they are not Christ Himself.

Fourth, do not make signs of salvation into grounds and causes of salvation. We wrong our souls when we take pride in the evidences of God's grace in our lives and place sinful confidence in the signs. Find comfort in signs but rest in Christ.

Fifth, test yourself with signs only while simultaneously casting out your self-love and self-flattery. Many lie to themselves like the ancient Jews who cried, "The temple of the Lord!" We can only know ourselves by the supernatural teaching of the Holy Spirit. At the same time, however, you must cast out your unbelief that refuses to acknowledge the work of God in your heart. How can you thank God for His grace to you if you will not acknowledge it?

Sixth, do not examine yourself for signs of grace when your soul is full of darkness, doubts, and temptations. You cannot see clearly then.

Seventh, do not think that no sign will be sufficient unless you first persevere to the end. Arminians insist that no one can be sure of his election by God until he has persevered in faith and obedience. Thus no man can be happy until he dies. Perseverance is a promise to the godly (Phil. 1:6), but it is not the only distinctive sign of true godliness.

Eighth, when you examine yourself, pray to God for His Spirit to enlighten your eyes. The Spirit of God is the effective cause of assurance. Just as only the Spirit can bring biblical truth home to the soul, so you can have all kinds of evidence of grace, but your heart will not be persuaded until the Spirit establishes you in certainty.

Ninth, never think that a person may not take hold of Christ until he has this certainty by signs of grace within himself. Do not look for spiritual qualifications before trusting Christ for your justification. Though it is popular to say that faith is a strong persuasion that my sins are forgiven, in reality, justifying faith is not assurance. Assurance is a fruit of faith.

Lastly, do not resist God's Spirit with unbelief when He comes to assure you with evidences of your salvation. It is a great sin to rebel against the Spirit when He convinces a person of sin, but it is a greater sin to rebel against Him when He moves us to claim God as our Father, for His greatest glory lies in being the Spirit of adoption (Rom. 8:15; Gal. 4:6).

Conclusion

Therefore, test yourself by the signs of grace laid in Scripture: obedience to God's commandments (1 John 2:3), sincerity before God (2 Cor. 1:12), turning from sin (1 John 3:9), willingness to be searched by God (Ps. 26:2), growth in grace (John 15:2), serving God out of inner motives of Spirit-worked faith and love (1 John 4:13), and love for other Christians (1 John 3:18). And where such things are present, may the Spirit of adoption work assurance.

Chapter 18

Wilhelmus à Brakel's
Biblical Ethics of Spirituality

In the United States and Canada, when people speak of mighty waterfalls, we naturally think of Niagara Falls. It truly is a beautiful place to visit. However, Niagara is dwarfed by Victoria Falls, known in Zambia as "the smoke that thunders" (*Mosi-oa-Tunya*). This mammoth sheet of water spans 5,604 feet and falls an average of 328 feet before crashing onto the rocks below and casting up a tower of mist visible more than eighteen miles away. As the Zambezi River drops into deep rock gorges, its spray produces a life-giving environment for animals and birds as well as a gorgeous and awe-inspiring place for people to visit.[1]

The Bible speaks of a waterfall far greater than Victoria Falls, a spiritual waterfall that reaches from the highest heaven down to earth. It is the waterfall of God's Spirit poured out through God's Son upon God's people, and it spans all the nations of the world. The Lord said in Isaiah 44:3, "For I will pour water upon him that is thirsty, and floods upon the dry ground: I will pour my spirit upon thy seed, and my blessing upon thine offspring." The result is life and beauty where before there was only death and barrenness. Men, women, and children spring up and say, "I am the LORD's" (v. 5). Where God pours out His Spirit, the wilderness becomes a fruitful field, producing a harvest of justice, righteousness, and peace (Isa. 32:15–18).

Where do we find this waterfall of spiritual life and power so that we may bathe in its life-giving waters? Where can we go to find God's "smoke that thunders"? God has hidden it in a place where few look: the teachings of God's Book. He says in Isaiah 59:21, "As for me, this is my covenant with them, saith the LORD; My spirit that is upon thee, and my words which I have put in thy mouth." In the same way, our Lord Jesus said, "The words that I speak unto

---

1. "Mosi-oa-Tunya/Victoria Falls," *UNESCO: World Heritage List*, accessed July 15, 2015, http://whc.unesco.org/en/list/509. The basic substance of this article was first given as an address at a ministers' conference in Lusaka, Zambia in August, 2015.

you, they are spirit, and they are life" (John 6:63). We find the Spirit of God by listening to the Word of God.

One of the great teachings of the Reformers and Puritans is that we must never separate the power of God's Spirit from the truth of God's Word and we must never isolate doctrine from life. For this reason, Wilhelmus à Brakel (1635–1711), a premier representative and popularizer of the Dutch Further Reformation, opened his great four-volume work of theology, *The Christian's Reasonable Service,* by calling each person "to live unto God at all times and in all things with all that he is and is capable of performing."[2] In a word, the point of theology is that the Christian be so soaked in the thunderous downpour of God's grace and Holy Spirit that he may testify, "I am the LORD's" in every aspect of life. In this chapter, we show that one of the most important aspects of Brakel's *magnum opus* is the way he joins theology and doctrine with practice and spirituality so that people may know the truth and the truth may set them free.

A Practical Theology and Doctrinal Spirituality

The Dutch Further Reformation preachers, like the Puritans, excelled in linking biblical truth with personal experience and practical application. They did not separate Christian theology from Christian living, as if the soul and body could live in different houses; instead, their spirituality was doctrinally derived and their theology was practically applied.

The divines of the Dutch Further Reformation shaped their theology according to Paul's exhortation in 2 Timothy 1:13–14, "Hold fast the form of sound words, which thou hast heard of me, in faith and love which is in Christ Jesus. That good thing which was committed unto thee keep by the Holy Ghost which dwelleth in us." The treasure of sound doctrine must be guarded, not merely intellectually but with the faith and love that the Holy Spirit generates in Christian experience by union with Jesus Christ. As the Dutch *Statenbijbel* noted on this text, "faith and love" are the "two principle heads" of sound doctrine—things to be believed and things to be done. Both require the "work and gift of the Holy Spirit."[3] Thus these divines joined head, heart, and hands in a way that is rarely done in modern theology.

---

2. Wilhelmus à Brakel, *The Christian's Reasonable Service,* trans. Bartel Elshout, ed. Joel R. Beeke, 4 vols. (Grand Rapids: Reformation Heritage Books, 1992–1995), 1:4. Brakel cites Isaiah 44:5 shortly after this statement.

3. *The Dutch Annotations upon the Whole Bible,* trans. Theodore Haak (1657; facsimile repr., Leerdam, The Netherlands: Gereformeerde Bijbelstichting, 2002), on 2 Tim. 1:13–14. This is a translation of the Dutch Staten Bible (*Statenbijbel*), a translation with marginal notes requested by the Synod of Dordt and commissioned by the States-General of the Netherlands.

Classic Theology for the Whole Person: Head, Heart, and Hands

When you buy a book on systematic theology today, you expect to see the major topics or *loci* of theology: the doctrines of the Word, God, man, Christ, salvation by the Spirit's gracious work, sanctification by the Holy Spirit, the church, and things that belong to the end of the age. However, you do not expect to see a section dealing with the meaning and application of God's commandments and various aspects of Christian life and practice. Scan the pages of systematic theologies from the late nineteenth century through today, and you find that though they discuss the doctrine of sanctification, they give little consideration to biblical, practical, and ethical directions for the Christian life.[4] With a few exceptions,[5] theology has been separated from ethics and spirituality and placed in a different category.

That has not always been the case; early Reformed theology went hand in hand with practical directions for the Christian life. For example, in the *Institutes of the Christian Religion*, the sixteenth-century Reformer John Calvin offered substantial treatments of the Ten Commandments (56 pages), Christian self-denial in the hope of heaven (37 pages), and prayer (70 pages).[6] Calvin gave more space to discussing prayer than he did to election! This approach fit Calvin's premise that people do not truly know God except when they love and fear Him. Reformed theology is applied theology.[7]

---

4. This phenomenon is not limited to a single tradition, as is evident from the systematic theologies or dogmatics of Herman Bavinck, Louis Berkhof, Michael Bird, James M. Boice, James P. Boyce, Robert Culver, Millard Erickson, John Frame, James Garrett, Norman Geisler, Wayne Grudem, A. A. Hodge, Michael Horton, Thomas Oden, Wolfhart Pannenberg, Robert Reymond, and William G. T. Shedd—none of which give much attention to God's commands or instructions for Christian spirituality. Charles Hodge addresses each of the Ten Commandments and has an extensive discussion of the means of grace, but he does not include many of the practical, ethical subjects that Brakel discusses. This is not a criticism of these authors—many if not all of whom seek to wed theology and practice in the Christian life—but simply an observation about how the categories of modernity shape our methodology.

5. Examples of modern theologies attending to God's law, all from the Presbyterian tradition, are John Dick, *Lectures on Theology* (Edinburgh: William Oliphant & Son, 1834), 4:404–79; Charles Hodge, *Systematic Theology* (1871–1873; repr., Peabody, Mass.: Hendrickson, 1999), 3:259–465; Robert L. Dabney, *Systematic Theology* (1878; repr., Edinburgh: Banner of Truth, 1985), 110–19, 351–429; Morton H. Smith, *Systematic Theology* (Greenville, S.C.: Greenville Seminary Press, 1994), 617–53.

6. John Calvin, *Institutes of the Christian Religion*, trans. Ford Lewis Battles, ed. John T. McNeill (Philadelphia: Westminster Press, 1960), 2.8 (pp. 367–423), 3.7–10 (pp. 689–725), 3.20 (pp. 850–920).

7. Calvin, *Institutes*, 1.2.1.

In the early seventeenth century, William Ames's *The Marrow of Theology* (1623) defined "theology" as the doctrine of "living to God."[8] He said, "The two parts of theology are faith and observance,"[9] and devoted over a hundred pages to "observance," that is, instructions on godliness and keeping God's commandments.[10] Later in that same century, Francis Turretin in *Institutes* (1679–1685) spent 167 pages discussing the Ten Commandments.[11] In the eighteenth century, similar explanations of godliness and the commandments of God are evident in John Gill's *Body of Divinity* (1769–1770)[12] and John Brown of Haddington's *Systematic Theology* (1782).[13] When we add to these teachings many Reformed expositions of the Westminster Shorter Catechism,[14] we can see that Reformed writers devoted a significant amount of attention to the laws of God and the practice of biblical spirituality.

The combination of theology, faith, and obedience was one of the defining marks of the Dutch Further Reformation in the seventeenth and eighteenth centuries. The father of the movement, Willem Teellinck, said, "The true Christian faith is knowledge that leads to godliness."[15] This requires that we "heartily wish and sincerely desire to understand as much as we can of the revealed will of God concerning us," and so we should pray with Psalm 119:33, "Teach me, O LORD, the way of thy statutes; and I shall keep it unto the end."[16] Teellinck saw no dichotomy between theology and spirituality, for, as Arie de Reuver writes, "The Holy Bible is the point of contact with the Holy Spirit."[17]

The divines of the Dutch Further Reformation labored to draw out the implications of doctrine for life. Gisbertus Voetius worked out a Reformed

---

8. William Ames, *The Marrow of Theology*, ed. and trans. John D. Eusden (Grand Rapids: Baker, 1968), 1.1.1.

9. Ames, *Marrow of Theology*, 1.2.1.

10. Ames, *Marrow of Theology*, 2:219–331.

11. Francis Turretin, *Institutes of Elenctic Theology*, trans. George Musgrave Giger, ed. James T. Dennison, Jr. (Phillipsburg, N.J.: P&R, 1992–1997), 2:1–167.

12. John Gill, *A Complete Body of Doctrinal and Practical Divinity* (Paris, Ark.: Baptist Standard Bearer, 1995), 697–851, 973–94.

13. John Brown of Haddington, *Systematic Theology* (repr., Grand Rapids: Reformation Heritage Books, 2016), 450–500. It was originally published as *A Compendious View of Natural and Revealed Religion*.

14. For example, see the catechism expositions of Thomas Vincent, Thomas Watson, James Fisher, John Flavel, Samuel Willard, Thomas Boston, and John Brown of Haddington.

15. Willem Teellinck, *The Path of True Godliness*, trans. Annemie Godbehere, ed. Joel R. Beeke, Classics of Reformed Spirituality (Grand Rapids: Reformation Heritage Books, 2003), 31.

16. Teellinck, *The Path of True Godliness*, 36–37.

17. Arie de Reuver, *Sweet Communion: Trajectories of Spirituality from the Middle Ages through the Further Reformation*, trans. James A. De Jong, Texts and Studies in Reformation and Post-Reformation Thought (Grand Rapids: Baker Academic, 2007), 123.

marriage of knowledge and piety, for he believed that ethics is living out biblical doctrine.[18] Johannes Hoornbeeck wrote, "Theology never teaches one only to speculate but always directs the action of the will."[19]

Petrus van Mastricht said that Christian theology "is neither theoretical only...nor is it practical only," but joins theory and practice as "a knowledge of the truth which is according to piety," as Paul wrote in Titus 1:1.[20] Adriaan Neele says that Mastricht was "one who brought theory and praxis together." Neele writes, "Mastricht defines theology as a doctrine of living to God through Christ and, secondly, as a doctrine that accords with piety (1 Tim. 6:3)."[21] Each chapter of Mastricht's major work of theology has a practical section, and large parts of the book discuss aspects of obedience, godliness, justice and love toward our neighbors, spiritual disciplines, and answers to practical questions.[22]

Brakel's Synthesis of Theology, Ethics, and Christian Spirituality

Nowhere do we see this joining of theology and practice developed more fully than in *The Christian's Reasonable Service*. Brakel covers all the topics of systematic theology in about forty chapters, with each chapter ending with practical instructions to apply that doctrine to the Christian life.[23] As a result, his systematic theology is deeply devotional. However, Brakel went further and gave about sixty more chapters entirely to practical and spiritual topics considered under the doctrine of salvation.[24] Let me outline them by topic to give you a taste of the scope of his practical theology and evangelical ethics.

First, Brakel gave extensive attention to the Ten Commandments, including a chapter on the law in general and then one chapter on each commandment (chaps. 45–55). Brakel explained the meaning of each commandment, the sins

---

18. Joel R. Beeke, *Gisbertus Voetius: Toward a Reformed Marriage of Knowledge and Piety* (Grand Rapids: Reformation Heritage Books, 1999), 25.

19. Johannes Hoornbeeck, *Theologiae Practicae* (Utrecht: Henricus Versteeg, 1663, 1666), 1:7, quoted in Todd M. Rester, introduction to Petrus van Mastricht, *The Best Method of Preaching: The Use of Theoretical-Practical Theology*, trans. Todd M. Rester (Grand Rapids: Reformation Heritage Books, 2013), 10.

20. Petrus van Mastricht, *Theoretico-practica Theologia* (1698), part I, I.i.20, quoted in Rester, introduction to Mastricht, *The Best Method of Preaching*, 12–13.

21. Adriaan Neele, *Petrus van Mastricht (1630–1706), Reformed Orthodoxy: Method and Piety*, Brill's Series in Church History 35 (Leiden: Brill, 2009), 5, 95.

22. Petrus van Mastricht, *Theoretico-practica Theologia*, trans. Todd M. Rester, ed. Joel R. Beeke, vols. 1 and 2 (Grand Rapids: Reformation Heritage Books, 2017, 2019). Volumes 3–7 forthcoming.

23. Brakel, *Christian's Reasonable Service*, chaps. 1–35, 38–40, 44, 99–103. Brakel's book covers the loci of theology in the following order: the doctrine of God (chaps. 1–9), the doctrine of man (chaps. 10–15), the doctrine of Christ (chaps. 16–23), the doctrine of the church (chaps. 24–29), the doctrine of salvation (chaps. 30–99), and the doctrine of last things (chaps. 100–103).

24. Brakel, *Christian's Reasonable Service*, chaps. 36–37, 41–43, 45–98.

it prohibits, and the virtues or duties it requires. Occasionally he also addressed objections, as in the thirty-four-page section defending the practice of the Sabbath today.[25] The result of his studies in the Decalogue is a comprehensive work of ethics that is more than two hundred pages in length.[26] This work breathes the spirit of Psalm 119:14–15, "I have rejoiced in the way of thy testimonies, as much as in all riches. I will meditate in thy precepts, and have respect unto thy ways."

Second, Brakel devoted twenty chapters to exploring the various fruits of the spiritual life that spring from faith in Christ. He offered a chapter on each of the following: spiritual peace, spiritual joy (chaps. 36–37), glorifying God, love toward God, love toward the Lord Jesus, the fear of God, obedience toward God, hope in God, spiritual strength or courage (chaps. 56–62), contentment, self-denial, patience, sincerity or uprightness (chaps. 64–67), love toward our neighbor, humility, meekness, peace, diligence, compassion, and prudence (chaps. 82–88). By themselves these chapters form a treatise on Reformed spirituality that has few equals.

Third, Brakel wrote fifteen chapters on the practice of the spiritual disciplines, both corporate and private. In addition to the treatment he had already given to the doctrine of the church, he wrote a chapter on preparing for, celebrating, and reflecting on the Lord's Supper (chap. 41). He offered a chapter on giving public testimony to Christ and His truth (chap. 63). He treated the subject of prayer at length, including a chapter for each petition of the Lord's Prayer (chaps. 68–74). He wrote a chapter on each of the following spiritual disciplines: fasting, watchfulness, solitude, spiritual meditation, singing spiritual songs, vows, and reflecting on God's providence (chaps. 75–81). This book is a gold mine for anyone desiring practical advice on how to implement the spiritual disciplines that are rooted in biblical doctrine.

Fourth, Brakel devoted several chapters to the battle of faith and unbelief in every believer. He wrote a chapter on living by faith in God's promises (chap. 42) and another warning against mystical spirituality that does not root the believer in the Holy Scriptures or connect believers to the church of God (chap. 43). He commended spiritual growth to believers (chap. 89). He also dealt with the difficult topics of backsliding, spiritual desertion, doubting that God is real, doubting God's Word is true, lack of assurance of salvation, Satan's attacks, the power of indwelling corruption, spiritual darkness, and the experience of spiritual deadness that can come on those who are spiritually alive

---

25. Brakel, *Christian's Reasonable Service*, 3:149–83.
26. Brakel, *Christian's Reasonable Service*, 3:35–242.

(chaps. 90–98). Brakel did not write from an ivory tower of triumphal theology but, like the Good Shepherd, walked with poor Christians through the valley of the shadow of death to show them that even there the Lord is with them.

One can understand why godly Christians of previous generations would read through *The Christian's Reasonable Service* during the long evenings of the winter season.[27] In it they found sound doctrine, warm Christian experience, biblical ethics, Reformed spirituality, disciplines for spiritual growth, and a mixture of idealism, realism, and optimism for the Christian life. The degree to which Brakel integrated these elements into one, unified treatise makes his book an astonishing gift to the church, and we are deeply grateful to God that after almost three centuries it was finally translated into English in the 1990s by Bartel Elshout.

A Practical Sampler of Brakel's Theological Ethics and Spirituality

While it is impossible to sample each of Brakel's sixty or so chapters on ethics and spirituality, we would like to give you a taste of two chapters from different sections of his book. First, we will survey his teaching on the seventh commandment, "Thou shalt not commit adultery" (chap. 52). Second, we will give a brief exposition of his chapter on spiritual growth (chap. 89). On the one hand, we will hear the voice of the law as Brakel unfolds God's condemnation of sin and righteous demands. On the other hand, we will hear the voice of the gospel as he reminds believers that in Christ they are both enabled and obligated to increase in grace.

Brakel on the Seventh Commandment

Brakel's treatment of the seventh commandment in *The Christian's Reasonable Service* opens with a short theology of marriage as God's institution between one man and one woman (Mark 10:8). Brakel wrote, "God instituted marriage and gave His blessing upon it, not only prior to the fall, but He also repeated this after the fall (Gen. 3:16; 9:1). God Himself decrees who one's wife will be and gives her to [a] man (Gen. 24:44). 'A prudent wife is from the Lord' (Prov. 19:14)."[28] Therefore, we must honor marriage (Heb. 13:4), not despise it (1 Tim. 4:1), but give all people, including God's ministers, the freedom to marry (Lev. 1:7; 1 Sam. 8:2; Matt. 8:14; 1 Cor. 9:5). The "ability and inclination to procreate"

---

27. Bartel Elshout, *The Pastoral and Practical Theology of Wilhelmus à Brakel* (Grand Rapids: Reformation Heritage Books, 1997), 6.

28. Brakel, *Christian's Reasonable Service*, 3:205.

in marriage is good and from God, though after the fall sinners often desire the pleasures of sex without the responsibilities of parenting that go with it.[29]

Brakel taught that the commandment "Thou shalt not commit adultery" forbids a number of sins. It prohibits sinful actions, such as:

+ *adultery*, or intercourse of a married person with someone other than his spouse.

+ *desertion* of one's spouse when he or she has not committed adultery (Matt. 5:32; 19:6; 1 Cor. 7:12, 15).

+ *incest*, sexual relations between persons too closely related by blood (Leviticus 18; 20).

+ *sodomy*, sex between two persons of the same gender (Gen. 19:5; Lev. 20:13; Rom. 1:26–27).

+ *bestiality*, sex with an animal (Lev. 18:23).

+ *fornication*, sex between two single persons (Deut. 23:17; Acts 15:20; 1 Cor. 6:9; Gal. 5:19)

+ *personal fornication*, which apparently was Brakel's euphemism for masturbation (Gen. 38:9; Col. 3:5; Gal. 5:19).

+ *polygamy*, the marriage of three or more people (Matt. 19:5; 1 Cor. 7:2).

+ *concubinage*, living together as husband and wife outside of a lawful marriage (John 4:17–18; 1 Cor. 7:9).

+ *premarital intercourse* between persons engaged but not married (Matt. 1:18).[30]

Brakel said that the commandment also forbade sinful gestures, such as lustful looks with the eyes (Matt. 5:28), motions with the body that communicated sexual intent (Ezek. 16:25), kissing and caressing (Prov. 7:13; Ezek. 23:3, 8), and wearing immodest clothing, for clothing reveals the heart. The prohibition extends to lewd stories, words, and books. It condemns lusts and fantasies of the mind (Matt. 15:19).[31]

He spoke against common situations in society that may lead to sexual sin. Dancing, though in its essence consists merely of taking steps in time with music, provokes sexual sin in those observing or participating in it. As to stage plays, he observed that if you removed all the blasphemy, paganism, violence,

---

29. Brakel, *Christian's Reasonable Service*, 3:206.
30. Brakel, *Christian's Reasonable Service*, 3:206–7.
31. Brakel, *Christian's Reasonable Service*, 3:208–9.

sex, and sinful jokes, few people would watch them—a comment also relevant to modern forms of video entertainment. Idleness also corrupts the heart and opens the door for fornication (1 Tim. 5:11, 13), as David's example shows (2 Sam. 11). Similarly one must avoid wild parties (Rom. 13:13), frequent socializing with immoral people (Prov. 13:20), and looking at sexually provocative pictures (Ezek. 23:13–16). Brakel also warned that a troubled marriage leads to immorality, whether caused by marrying someone far older than oneself, resulting in a lack of desire and intercourse between spouses, or from quarrels that alienate husband and wife so that they do not have sex with each other.[32]

Brakel's concern for specific causes of sin did not arise from a legalistic, graceless attitude but from a sincere concern to help people to walk in holiness in their daily lives. He wisely understood that we are sinful people in a sinful world, and life is full of situations where "one's corrupt nature will get the opportunity to manifest itself." Therefore, each person must examine himself "as to how innocent or guilty you are."[33] In any morally questionable gathering, we must not neglect Brakel's call to self-examination. Are you walking in sexual purity? Are you cutting off the offending hand and plucking out the offending eye—that is, are you repenting or turning away from anything that tempts you to uncleanness?

Brakel exhorts us to respond to sexual sin by seriously pursuing holiness, according to the biblical pattern of putting off sin and putting on righteousness. He admonished us to cultivate "in one's heart a hatred and aversion for, and hostility toward all uncleanness of heart and whatever issues forth therefrom" (Amos 5:15; Rom. 12:9; Jude 23).[34] He offered several reasons why believers should hate sexual sin:

- "It is the captain of all sin and is listed first among the works of the flesh" (Gal. 5:19).

- "It runs counter to the indwelling of the Holy Spirit who dwells in believers as in a temple" (1 Cor. 6:18–19).

- "It runs counter to the suffering of Christ, who thereby has redeemed believers and made them His property" (1 Cor. 6:15, 20).

- "It runs counter to the heavenly calling whereby believers have been translated from the kingdom of Satan to the kingdom of Christ" (1 Thess. 4:7).

---

32. Brakel, *Christian's Reasonable Service*, 3:209–10.
33. Brakel, *Christian's Reasonable Service*, 3:210.
34. Brakel, *Christian's Reasonable Service*, 3:212.

✦ "It is a dreadful act of contempt toward God and a provocation against Him." Most people would be ashamed to commit such acts in the presence of another person. How much more should we be ashamed to do such things in the presence of the One who repeatedly threatens His wrath and damnation against those who give themselves to such sins (Heb. 13:4; 2 Peter 2:9–10; 1 Cor. 6:9–10; Eph. 5:5; Rev. 21:8)?[35]

Positively speaking, a believer must "endeavor to have a heart marked by modesty [and] purity" (Matt. 5:8) and to be "chaste in all his actions" (2 Cor. 7:1). The Christian must always keep watch, knowing that "we carry the seed of uncleanness within." He must especially guard his eyes and ears against "all occasions which would stimulate this sin."[36]

Believers must also exercise self-control. Brakel said, "If an unclean motion arises in your heart, immediately shake it off as you would shake off fire. Divert your thoughts immediately to something else." Avoid the company of immoral people. Busy yourself in good, honest work, not just going through the motions but doing your job with joy and mental focus. Exercise moderation in how much you eat, drink, and sleep, for a lack of self-control in one area will make you vulnerable in others. If necessary, "have days of fasting" to help you discipline your body and devote yourself to God. Above all, "arm yourself with fear for God's presence and omniscience." In the light of His holy eyes, which are always upon you, remember that this sin "yields but a brief delight for the flesh and a long and bitter aftertaste for the soul."[37]

Brakel did not mince words when it came to sin. Though a minister of the gospel and an earnest preacher of justification by faith alone, he did not hesitate to call sinners to repentance, to exhort believers to holiness, and to warn that a life of unrepentant sin is headed for hell. At the same time, he had an optimistic view of the Christian life based on the power of God's grace to transform sinners increasingly into the likeness of Jesus Christ.

Brakel on Spiritual Growth

Just as a tree naturally seeks to grow to its proper height and fruitfulness, so "it is natural for a believer to grow," Brakel said, for we are like trees planted in the courts of God (Ps. 92:12–13). Spiritual life is like the dawning of daylight; by its "very nature" it tends to shine brighter as the day progresses (Prov. 4:18). The purpose of God's appointing the means of grace is "the growth of His children"

---

35. Brakel, *Christian's Reasonable Service*, 3:211–12.
36. Brakel, *Christian's Reasonable Service*, 3:212.
37. Brakel, *Christian's Reasonable Service*, 3:213.

(Eph. 4:11–15; 1 Peter 2:2). The Bible constantly exhorts them to growth as their duty: "But grow in grace, and in the knowledge of our Lord and Saviour Jesus Christ" (2 Peter 3:18). The church contains people at all different levels of maturity: spiritual children, youth, and fathers, but "those who do not manifest any growth are not believers."[38]

Brakel offered the following definition of growth: "Spiritual growth is a gracious work of God in the regenerate whereby they increase in both habitual and actual grace."[39] The beginning, preservation, and increase of spiritual life is from the Lord, for apart from Him we can do nothing (John 15:5), but God works in His children both their willing and their doing (Phil. 2:13). Brakel said, "The Lord causes spiritual life to grow by granting an increased measure of His Spirit." He does this by means of His Word, prayer, godly examples, trials and troubles, and experiences of material and spiritual prosperity.[40]

Only the regenerate grow, for "growth presupposes the presence of life." However, among God's children there is great variety in the rate of growth. Some die soon after their conversion and have little time to grow. Some grow quickly to the amazement of those who know them. Others make little progress for various reasons, such as a lack of good teaching, isolation from other believers, or laziness in reading the Bible and praying. Some make steady progress, generally "in the way of strife…and by the exercise of faith" in spiritual conflict. Some grow for a time but then weaken when they get old. Others flourish spiritually to their death (Ps. 92:14).[41]

Spiritual growth does not consist of using one's gifts and abilities to build up others, nor in external, moral improvement without a change of heart, nor in experiences of comfort from the Lord. Spiritual growth, Brakel said, involves a growth of "habitual grace" in the soul, that is, the growth of a settled inclination toward God and holiness created in the heart by His grace.[42] Brakel outlines five dimensions of growth in habitual grace.

---

38. Brakel, *Christian's Reasonable Service*, 4:139–41.

39. Brakel, *Christian's Reasonable Service*, 4:141.

40. Brakel, *Christian's Reasonable Service*, 4:141–42.

41. Brakel, *Christian's Reasonable Service*, 4:142–44.

42. Brakel, *Christian's Reasonable Service*, 4:144. Richard Muller explains the phrase "habit of grace" (*habitus gratiae*) to mean "a divine gift infused into the soul in such a way as to become a part of human nature" (Richard A. Muller, *Dictionary of Latin and Greek Theological Terms: Drawn Principally from Protestant Scholastic Theology* [Grand Rapids: Baker, 1985], 134). Muller notes that the Reformers rejected this terminology because of its association with semi-Pelagianism and justification by inherent righteousness. However, later Reformed divines used the language of *habitus gratiae* or habit of grace while maintaining justification by faith alone. For more on the Reformed use of *habitus*, see Richard A. Muller, *Post-reformation Reformed Dogmatics, Volume 1, Prolegomena to Theology* (Grand Rapids: Baker, 1987), 226–30 (chap. 6.4).

First, spiritual growth consists of greater *spiritual light*, not mere understanding but a light that "has inherent warmth and ignites the soul in love, renders one fruitful, and brings spiritual truths into the soul, so that whatever is true in the Word also becomes true within." The growing Christian sees the beauty of God's attributes more clearly as well as the ugliness of man's sins.[43]

Second, spiritual growth consists of more depth in *fellowship with God*. Brakel wrote of the growing Christian, that "he will pray, yearn for, desire after, and speak with the Lord. His heart will be fixed on the Lord, and he will rest, rejoice in, and glorify Him.... His thoughts will then not gravitate toward earthly things, but to his God."[44] The growing Christian increasingly lives for God.

A third dimension of spiritual growth is increasing *reliance upon Christ*. Brakel said, "Growth which does not center in Christ is no spiritual growth." It is a grand mistake to think that we only need Christ at the beginning of our spiritual lives. Christ is our life (Col. 3:4), and we grow by walking in Him and being increasingly rooted in Him (Col. 2:6–7). He is the Head, and believers are the body (Eph. 4:15–16). He is the vine; believers are the branches (John 15:5). He is the High Priest, and Christians do not dare approach God except by faith in Christ. Therefore, "spiritual growth consists of making use of Christ."[45]

Fourth, spiritual growth consists of greater *holiness of motivation*. As a Christian grows, he becomes more concerned about not just what he does but also why and how he does it. Brakel wrote,

> We shall then find no delight in our conduct if it is not governed by a holy objective; that is, not having ourselves in view, but doing all to the honor of God (1 Cor. 10:31), in the presence of God (Gen. 17:1), in obedient submission to God and His will (Eph. 6:6), in love (1 Cor. 13:1), in the fear of God (Job 31:23), and in believing union with Christ and through Christ with God (Heb. 11:6). We shall thus do everything out of God, for God, and unto God.[46]

The fifth and final dimension of spiritual growth according to Brakel is an increased *display of gracious activity*. Growth in habitual grace in the heart must lead to visible changes in every aspect of our lifestyle. It brings holistic change. The growing Christian fights against both external sins and internal sins and against both sins of commission and sins of omission. Spiritual growth produces fruit that includes virtue, knowledge, temperance, patience, godliness,

---

43. Brakel, *Christian's Reasonable Service*, 4:145.
44. Brakel, *Christian's Reasonable Service*, 4:145.
45. Brakel, *Christian's Reasonable Service*, 4:146.
46. Brakel, *Christian's Reasonable Service*, 4:146–47.

kindness, and love (John 15:5; 2 Peter 1:5–7). Growth is also apparent when we practice Christian virtue with greater perseverance, wisdom, faith, and zeal. We are not so easily shaken by the contempt of other people or the loss of temporal blessings, for we are learning to be "well satisfied to live with God alone."[47]

Brakel challenged every Christian by asking, "Are you growing?" On the one hand, we should not flatter ourselves if we are not. On the other hand, we should not deny our growth. We need to examine ourselves, not just with respect to "a brief time span" but over the course of our lives after our conversion. If there has been no growth or, worse yet, a general increase in sin since one's professed conversion, this is a sign that there is no saving grace in the soul.

However, Brakel also exercised great pastoral caution at this point, for some Christians cannot perceive their own spiritual growth, and others may go through seasons of apparent spiritual barrenness though they are still alive in Christ.[48] Like a tree with many branches, a believer may grow more in one area of life than in another. Like a tree deprived of rain in a dry season, a person may possess true spiritual life yet bear little fruit for a time. Furthermore, as a Christian grows in spiritual illumination and spiritual desire, his increasing frustration with his sins may cause him to think he is regressing rather than progressing.[49] On the basis of Brakel's discussion, we must use wisdom and care in evaluating our own spiritual growth and engage the help of godly friends and pastors to help us discern our true spiritual condition.

Why do true Christians fail to grow as they should? Brakel identified several problems in a believer's soul that hinder growth, such as secret complacency— "I'm saved and going to heaven and don't need to grow"—or a lack of assurance of salvation or discouragement over one's sins or desires after the things of the world.[50] Brakel also put his finger on a major cause of spiritual stagnation when he wrote, "Many are hindered in their walk solely by laziness." He said, "Effort is required here—consisting in prayer, fasting, watchfulness, meditation, and the engagement in spiritual warfare."[51]

Brakel exhorted the children of God to strive after spiritual growth. They have only just begun to walk with God, he said. The only alternative to growth is to remain in their sin. If they grow, they will display more of the image of God and enjoy more communion with God. They will please God more, just as the growth of children pleases a father. Brakel wrote, "God is glorified by our

---

47. Brakel, *Christian's Reasonable Service*, 4:147–49.
48. Brakel called these "spiritual winters" (*Christian's Reasonable Service*, 4:151).
49. Brakel, *Christian's Reasonable Service*, 4:149–52.
50. Brakel, *Christian's Reasonable Service*, 4:153.
51. Brakel, *Christian's Reasonable Service*, 4:154.

growth," for the growth of Christians shows "that He is good, benevolent, faithful, holy, and omnipotent." Furthermore, if they grow, God will cause their joy to grow, for He will draw near to them.[52]

For this reason, Brakel urged believers to press on with "valiant courage" and "joyful willingness," trusting in Christ as their strength and joy. He urged them to engage in the battle against every sin and to practice every virtue. He warned not to let their spiritual wounds and falls into sin discourage them.[53] Instead, Brakel said,

> Continually feed upon the Word of God for by this one grows. Be continually in prayer in order that you might continually be strengthened and supported by the Spirit of the Lord—for you are weak and will not prevail in your own strength. Continually exercise faith so that you may continually be united with Christ and apply the promises to yourself. You will thus purify the heart by faith, overcome the world, and resist the devil. While thus engaged, you will soon experience that you are progressing and increasing in strength.[54]

Brakel's doctrine of spiritual growth exemplifies the practical theology of the Dutch Further Reformation. His book grounds the believer in the assurance of God's sovereign grace. At the same time, it spurs the believer to get up on his feet, shake off his laziness, and run the race that is set before him with his eyes fixed upon Jesus. Brakel's teaching is idealistic in its high demands, realistic in its down-to-earth counsel, and optimistic in its Christ-centered hope. Brakel is thus a model for pastors in every generation.

Conclusion

Brakel's theology is a great resource for pastoral ministry because it is eminently practical theology. *The Christian's Reasonable Service* lives up to its title: it is theology for the worship and service of God. Its extensive exposition of the commandments of God, the fruits of godliness, and the disciplines of the Christian life show how Reformed doctrine must be worked out in our relationships and activities. The book is a sparkling diamond in the crown of the Dutch Further Reformation, a written testimony of a vision for a theology that is theory and practice, doctrine and piety.

Brakel's writings also call us to self-examination. We have surveyed a book that marries truth and obedience, so you must ask yourself, "Am I a man of truth

---

52. Brakel, *Christian's Reasonable Service*, 4:154–55.
53. Brakel, *Christian's Reasonable Service*, 4:156.
54. Brakel, *Christian's Reasonable Service*, 4:156–57.

and obedience?" You confess the truth of Scripture with your mouth. Many of you preach it and teach it. But, is it just a theory to you? Do you live in daily obedience to the teachings of the Bible? Do those who know you say, "There goes a person who has the Bible in his mouth, in his heart, and written across his whole life"? If your personal history were turned into a book, would there be not only chapters on sound doctrine but also chapters on obedience to God's laws, chapters on love and godliness, chapters on the spiritual disciplines, and chapters on spiritual growth by faith—written with the paper and ink of your daily actions and habits?

If your life is missing such a testimony, remember a fundamental truth of Reformed theology: "This is a faithful saying, and worthy of all acceptation, that Christ Jesus came into the world to save sinners; of whom I am chief" (1 Tim. 1:15). Whether God's holy eyes expose you as a hypocrite or as a true believer who has backslidden in some area of life, there is a sense in which the answer to your problem is the same: look to Jesus Christ. Trust in Christ both for justification from the guilt of sin and sanctification from the power of sin. Turn from your sins and draw near to God through Jesus Christ.

If, however, your life is a testimony of how biblical doctrine produces godliness for all of your life, then we say, "Press on, friend, with all humility and faith, in hope of the kingdom of our Lord." You are standing in the aura of the waterfall of grace; stay ever near to it, and bring as many others to its life-giving waters as you possibly can.

Brakel's legacy to us is a doctrine for life. He taught the truth and lived it with integrity. After he died in 1711, these words were written on his tombstone:

> Here rests a man who could not rest
> Until he won souls to Jesus;
> An intercessor for his native land,
> He now is on the other side,
> In the fatherland of Abraham,
> Where he ever follows the blessed Lamb.
> Follow in the way of his doctrine and life,
> And you too shall one day sing Hallelujah![55]

May God grant the grace to be faithful in doctrine and life so that after we pass from this earth, we may receive the same testimony.

---

55. We provide a somewhat better translation here of Brakel's tombstone than is found in the introduction to *Christian's Reasonable Service*, 1:lxxix.

Chapter 19

Images of Union and Communion with Christ

Christ is the great reservoir of blessing, and without Him we have nothing. The great means of salvation's application is union with Christ. In the mind of the apostle Paul, to be "without Christ" is to have "no hope" and be "without God in the world" (Eph. 2:12). John wrote, "And this is the record, that God hath given to us eternal life, and this life is in his Son. He that hath the Son hath life; and he that hath not the Son of God hath not life" (1 John 5:11–12).

John Calvin wrote, "As long as Christ remains outside of us, and we are separated from him, all that he has suffered and done for the salvation of the human race remains useless and of no value for us. Therefore, to share with us what he has received from the Father, he had to become ours and to dwell within us."[1] William Ames said, "Not all are saved by Christ, but only those who are united or engrafted into Christ."[2] Similarly, the Westminster Larger Catechism says:

> Q. 65. *What special benefits do the members of the invisible church enjoy by Christ?*
>
> A. The members of the invisible church by Christ enjoy union and communion with him in grace and glory (John 17:21; Eph. 2:5–6; John 17:24).
>
> Q. 66. *What is that union which the elect have with Christ?*
>
> A. The union which the elect have with Christ is the work of God's grace (Eph. 1:22; 2:6–8), whereby they are spiritually and mystically, yet really and inseparably, joined to Christ as their head and husband (1 Cor. 6:17;

---

1. John Calvin, *Institutes of the Christian Religion*, ed. John T. McNeill, trans. Ford Lewis Battles, The Library of Christian Classics XX and XXI (Philadelphia: Westminster Press, 1960), 3.1.1. The substance of this chapter was given at Grand Rapids Theological Seminary for the Midwest Regional Conference of the Evangelical Theological Society on March 11, 2016.

2. William Ames, *A Sketch of the Christian's Catechism*, trans. Todd M. Rester, Classic Reformed Theology 1 (Grand Rapids: Reformation Heritage Books, 2008), 37. See the Heidelberg Catechism, LD 7, Q. 20.

John 10:28; Eph. 5:23, 30); which is done in their effectual calling (1 Peter 5:10; 1 Cor. 1:9).[3]

Puritan pastor Rowland Stedman (d. 1673) wrote a treatise on mystical union with Christ. He defined it as such: "Union with Christ is that special relation, which believers have to the Lord Jesus, as Mediator of the Covenant of Grace; arising from their close and intimate conjunction with him: whereupon they are accounted as one with Christ, their spiritual state is fundamentally changed, and the benefits of redemption are effectually applied unto their souls."[4]

To open up this rich theme of the Holy Scriptures, in this chapter we will explore the doctrine of union with Christ with respect to various images of union that the Scriptures derive from Adam's first home, the garden of Eden.

We often think of the epistles of Paul as our primary sources for the doctrine of Christ's union with His people, and rightly so, but the building blocks of this doctrine appear as early as the book of Genesis. Before the fall of man into sin, God had prepared types of Christ that would help sinners after the fall to look forward with hope in Christ. As Paul explained in Romans 5, the first and most basic type of the union between Christ and His people appears in the *corporate solidarity* of mankind in Adam.

Christ stands like Adam as the one head of His people. God created the entire human race in a single man so that from him came every other individual in the world, including his wife by a supernatural act of God (Gen. 2:7, 22; 3:20; 1 Chronicles 1). Adam's very name means "Man." This method of creating mankind reveals God's purpose to deal with us as people summed up in one person.

In Luke 3–4, we read that Christ is the Son of God who overcame Satan's temptations in the wilderness and that Christ is descended from Adam, also called a son of God. Luke thus contrasted Adam, the son of God who succumbed to the tempter in a perfect world, to Christ, the Son of God who overcame the tempter in the sorrows of a fallen world (Luke 3:22, 38; 4:1–13). Richard Sibbes wrote, "So then we see we have in Christ, 'the second Adam,' whatsoever we lost in the first root…and more than all we lost, he being God-man."[5]

---

3. James T. Dennison Jr., comp., *Reformed Confessions of the 16th and 17th Centuries in English Translation: 1523–1693* (Grand Rapids: Reformation Heritage Books, 2008–2014), 4:312. Henceforth cited as *Reformed Confessions*.

4. Rowland Stedman, *The Mystical Union of Believers with Christ* (London: by W. R. for Thomas Parkhurst, 1668), 55. Stedman was a Puritan minister of Oakingham (Wokingham) in Berkshire, who was ejected for nonconformity.

5. Richard Sibbes, *The Hidden Life*, in *The Works of Richard Sibbes*, ed. Alexander B. Grosart (1862–1864; repr., Edinburgh: Banner of Truth, 1973), 5:210.

Although we cannot fully understand the union between Christ and His people, God calls His people to embrace this truth with faith, hope, and love. To help us to receive it, God has given us in the Bible a number of delightful pictures of our union with Christ. Though these are fully developed only in the New Testament, all of them are rooted in the account of the garden of Eden, which was the prototype of man's communion with God (Gen. 2). Let's consider six of these images that are traceable back to the garden.

Worshiping as God's Temple

The garden of Eden was the first temple, for in it Adam and Eve experienced God's special presence giving them life, speaking to them, and caring for them. Adam was like a priest in the garden, charged by God to serve and keep (Gen. 2:15), the same two Hebrew words used of the duties of the Levites at the tabernacle (Num. 3:7–8; 8:26). After the fall of man, God gave Israel the tabernacle and the temple as signs that He would dwell with His people again in grace despite the uncleanness of their sins (Ex. 29:42–46; 1 Kings 8:12–13). God designed the tabernacle and the temple with images derived from the garden, such as trees and cherubim.[6] Even after the sins of Israel provoked God to remove His presence from them and destroy His temple, He promised to set up His sanctuary among them forever (Ezek. 37:23–28).

In the new covenant, God has gone far beyond putting a temple among His people; He has made them into His temple by their union with Christ in the Holy Spirit. Paul wrote, "Know ye not that ye are the temple of God, and that the Spirit of God dwelleth in you?" (1 Cor. 3:16). The "ye" translates a plural pronoun, indicating that the church together is God's temple where He dwells.

Paul explained that believers in Christ, regardless of whether they are Jews or Gentiles, are joined to Christ like parts of a temple are joined to its cornerstone, founded upon the truths revealed by the Spirit to the apostles and prophets (Eph. 2:19–22; 3:5). Likewise, Peter, citing the Old Testament, described Christ as the cornerstone upon whom believers are built like living stones into "a spiritual house, an holy priesthood, to offer up spiritual sacrifices" for the glory of Him who called them "out of darkness into his marvellous light" (1 Peter 2:4–9). The hope of believers is that God will dwell with His people, and they will be like a magnificent temple-city which needs no holy buildings because God is there through Jesus Christ (Rev. 21:3, 9–23).[7]

---

6. Compare Gen. 2:8–9; 3:22, 24 with Ex. 25:18–20, 22, 31–33; 26:1, 31; 1 Kings 6:23–35.

7. Note that the description of the New Jerusalem in Rev. 21 is patterned on the temple with its lavish use of gold, cubic most holy place, angels at the gates, and gemstones like those on the high priest's garments.

How can people be God's temple? Believers are joined to the Lord Jesus Christ by the Holy Spirit, and therefore the Holy Spirit dwells in their bodies as God's temple for His glory (1 Cor. 6:17–20). Christ is the temple of God (John 1:14; 2:19–22), for in Him the "fullness" of deity dwells in a bodily form (Col. 2:9). The church in union with Him is indwelt and increasingly filled by His fullness until His glory fills all things in the new creation.[8]

Grant Macaskill writes, "The logic of this image…is that this mediatorial function of Christ involves nothing less than a giving of himself…. The glorification spoken of, then, can only be understood in relational or even personal terms: it is the giving of one person to others, who are thereby glorified by his presence, while remaining distinct from him."[9]

The biblical imagery of a temple teaches us that union with Christ joins believers permanently to Him so that they become the home of God's special presence, to behold His glory and offer up their praises forever. Since He is the cornerstone, believers rest upon Him by faith, and He bears the full weight of God's temple by His wisdom, righteousness, and power.

Bearing Fruit for God's Pleasure

The garden of Eden was an orchard, for "out of the ground made the Lord God to grow every tree that is pleasant to the sight, and good for food," including "the tree of life" (Gen. 2:9). No doubt these trees were for the delight and nourishment of man, as we will discuss shortly. However, Genesis tells us that God also delighted in the goodness of His creation, including fruitful trees (Gen. 1:12). Furthermore, the language of fruitfulness is applied not only to plants but to mankind as well in God's original commission to His image-bearers (Gen. 1:28; cf. 9:1, 7) and is an important part of God's covenant with respect to the multiplication of offspring.[10]

The Holy Scriptures apply this picture of fruitfulness not only to bearing children but also to living in righteousness. In the tabernacle, the golden lampstand had the form of an almond tree (Ex. 25:33), a sign of the fruitful life found through the priestly ministry of Christ (Num. 17:8). The Psalms say that the righteous flourish like trees planted in the house of God to declare His perfection (Ps. 92:12–15). The person who trusts in the faithful love of God is "like a green olive tree in the house of God" (Ps. 52:7). However, idolatrous

---

8. Eph. 1:23; 3:17–19; 4:10–13; cf. Isa. 6:1, 3.

9. Grant Macaskill, *Union with Christ in the New Testament* (Oxford: Oxford University Press, 2013), 151. For his exegesis of the "fullness" texts of Ephesians listed in the previous footnote, see pp. 149–52.

10. Gen. 17:6; 28:3; 35:11; 48:4; Lev. 26:9.

Israel, though once planted by God as "a green olive tree, fair, and of goodly fruit," was shut out of God's house (Jer. 11:15–17). As we noted earlier, these images of trees in the temple allude to the garden of Eden. Surprisingly, we find that in some sayings of Proverbs, the "tree of life" functions as an image of how the righteous produce fruit that blesses other people (Prov. 11:30; 15:4).

God compared Israel to a vine that He had planted and had grown to impressive size but which He gave over to destruction.[11] Like the trees of Eden,[12] the vineyard of Israel was planted by God to bear fruit: the fruit of justice and righteousness (Isa. 5:1–7). The vine of Israel proved corrupt (Jer. 2:21), but God promised that He would bless His vineyard again so that Israel would fill the world with fruit (Isa. 27:2–6). Indeed, the wilderness of Israel would become like the garden of Eden (Isa. 51:3), for the Lord would pour out His Spirit to produce righteousness and peace among a people who acknowledge the Lord (Isa. 32:15–18; 44:1–5). God would heal their backsliding and "be as the dew unto Israel" so that the nation would grow as a beautiful olive tree, for from the Lord comes Israel's fruit (Hos. 14:4–8).

Therefore, when Christ said, "I am the vine, ye are the branches: he that abideth in me, and I in him, the same bringeth forth much fruit: for without me ye can do nothing" (John 15:5), He identified Himself as the true Israel, the fulfillment of what God's people were meant to be. God's judgment was going to fall on the rebellious vineyard again (Matt. 21:33–44; cf. John 15:6). The only way for people to bear fruit pleasing to God is to have a living, organic, abiding union with Christ as branches to a vine. As the branch has no root from which to draw sap unless it is in the vine, so human beings have no spiritual life to produce fruit apart from union with Christ. In Him alone can we be the true Israel of God, the delightful garden of the Lord.

The image of branches on the vine has immense practical significance for the Christian life. Stedman said, "If they have strength and ability to work the works of God, it is imparted through him. For they are branches in him, and he is the vine, so that we have no cause to boast of ourselves, nor is there any ground for self-confidence, or trusting in ourselves. But the whole life that we live, should be by faith on the Son of God."[13]

---

11. Ps. 80:8–19; Ezek. 15:6; 17:6; 19:10.

12. In the Bible, a vine is not sharply distinguished from a tree but is considered as a woody plant "among the trees of the forest" (Ezek. 15:6) and may be depicted as growing to a great height with a mass of branches (Ezek. 19:11).

13. Stedman, *Mystical Union*, 247.

Eating and Drinking in God's Presence

Though the trees of Eden served as pictures of God's fruitful people in union with Christ, in the historic garden they functioned primarily to nourish the life of Adam and his wife. God had given them a place of lush and ample provision (Gen. 2:16), especially in the Tree of Life (Gen. 2:9), which would have sustained life forever (Gen. 3:22). Genesis emphasizes the verdant setting by directing attention to the river that watered the garden before issuing into four great rivers (Gen. 2:10). To the Israelites who had left the Nile to wander in the dry wilderness, this must have been a picture of overwhelming blessing. The first man and woman ate and drank a daily feast in the presence of the Lord God.

Food and drink depict the life-giving communion of God's saints with Him. Israel ate manna, the bread of heaven (Ps. 78:24; John 6:31), in the wilderness (Exodus 16), . The elders of Israel had a taste of table fellowship with God on Mount Sinai (Ex. 24:9–11). Christ appears in Proverbs as the personal Wisdom who is "a tree of life" to all who take hold of Him (Prov. 3:18). Wisdom prepares a rich banquet and calls foolish humanity to come and eat (Prov. 9:1–12). The Lord calls sinners to return to Him so that they may eat and drink without money and without price (Isa. 55:1–2). He is the best of hosts (Ps. 23:5–6) and the fountain of living water who alone can satisfy the thirsty soul (Jer. 2:13; 17:5–8, 13). Feasting on God as one's satisfying food and drink is especially associated with God's temple as the place of God's special presence, a picture of union, which we already discussed.[14] The temple was the location of Israel's feasts, and it was there that Israel ate the meat of the sacrifices (Deut. 12:5–7, 17–18).

Christ drew upon this rich Old Testament background when He compared union and communion with Him to eating and drinking. Christ alone gives the living water that eternally satisfies (John 4:14), the heavenly streams of the Holy Spirit (John 7:37–39). Jesus Himself is the Bread of Life whom we eat by faith (John 6:35). With respect to eating this bread, Jesus shockingly said that we must eat His flesh and blood to have eternal life (John 6:48–58), a reference to the sacrifice of His humanity on the cross. Eating Christ is a metaphor for entering into a deep union with Christ by faith so that the incarnate Mediator becomes your life. Michael Barrett writes, "As we believe Christ and His gospel we receive life and enter into a mutual bond with Christ: 'He that eateth my flesh, and drinketh my blood, dwelleth in me, and I in him' [John 6:56]. We must have a regular, daily diet of eating the Bread of Life and drinking the Living Water if we are going to grow in grace and in the knowledge of God."[15]

---

14. Pss. 36:8; 42:1–4; 46:4–5; 63:1–5; cf. 27:4; 43:3–4; 65:4; 84:1–2.

15. Michael P. V. Barrett, *Complete in Him: A Guide to Understanding and Enjoying the Gospel* (Greenville, S.C.: Ambassador-Emerald International, 2000), 107.

Being Loved as Christ's Bride

One of the most amazing pictures of union with Christ is that of a bride and bridegroom. This, too, is rooted in Eden, where God made the first woman from Adam's side and presented her to him as his wife (Gen. 2:18–25). Just as Christ is the last Adam, so our union with Christ was foreshadowed by the union of the first man and woman in marriage (Eph. 5:31–32). The Bible teaches that marriage is a covenant or solemn promise (Mal. 2:14; cf. Gen. 2:23), so the image of marriage communicates covenantal love and faithfulness.

Through the old covenant prophets, the Lord God repeatedly used the image of marriage to describe His love for Israel and to call her to faithfulness toward Him. God's relationship with His people is a love story, where His undeserved kindness is answered by their infidelity, until His grace breaks their hearts and brings them home to live in covenant with Him (Ezekiel 16). Backsliders in Israel must repent, said the Lord, "for I am married unto you" (Jer. 3:14). Though Israel had committed spiritual adultery, God would renew their marriage covenant based on His own righteousness, faithfulness, love, and compassion (Hos. 2:19–20). The Lord spoke to Israel as to a barren woman, promising her a vast number of children, "for thy Maker is thine husband; the LORD of hosts is his name; and thy Redeemer the Holy One of Israel; the God of the whole earth shall he be called" (Isa. 54:5). This is a surprising twist to the story of Abraham and Sarah, for here the Lord is the husband. The Lord promised to rejoice over His people as a bridegroom rejoices over his bride (Isa. 62:5). Greater love has never been seen than the love between the divine Bridegroom and His beloved bride.

Against this background, we can only consider Christ's reference to Himself as the Bridegroom of His people to be a claim to deity (Matt. 9:15; 25:6). Ministers of the gospel are mere friends of the Bridegroom, and whose hearts long for the church to be fully devoted to Christ (John 3:29; 2 Cor. 11:2). Paul used the marriage of Christ to His church as the basis for his instructions for earthly marriages. Christ gave Himself on the cross because of His husbandly love for the church (Eph. 5:25). A defining mark of the true church is her wifely submission to Christ her Head (Eph. 5:23–24). The spiritual union of the Bridegroom and His bride is compared to the one-flesh union of man and woman (1 Cor. 6:16–17; Eph. 5:31–32; both citing Gen. 2:24). Macaskill writes, "The two do not meld or melt, their beings are not confused. They are, instead, united and any transfer of properties of one to the other must be spoken of in terms of inter-personal communication, not hybridization."[16] The hope of

---

16. Macaskill, *Union with Christ in the New Testament*, 156.

the church is that her covenant betrothal will one day come to fruition at the "marriage supper of the Lamb," and for this she prepares herself by grace by making a wedding dress of righteous deeds (Rev. 19:7–9). Indeed, she can produce good deeds only by her marital union with the risen Lord (Rom. 7:1–6). Joined together as spiritual lovers, Christ and His church live in a union and communion of which the intimacy of sexual union is a faint shadow at best.

Receiving Nurture as Christ's Body

When Adam received his wife from God in the garden of Eden, the Lord added these words to explain the relevance of this for mankind: "Therefore shall a man leave his father and his mother, and shall cleave unto his wife: and they shall be one flesh" (Gen. 2:24). Paul interpreted this according to his inspired Adam-Christ typology, writing, "For no man ever yet hated his own flesh; but nourisheth and cherisheth it, even as the Lord the church: for we are members of his body, of his flesh, and of his bones. For this cause shall a man leave his father and mother, and shall be joined unto his wife, and they two shall be one flesh. This is a great mystery: but I speak concerning Christ and the church" (Eph. 5:29–32).

Therefore, just as a husband and wife are one flesh, so the church is Christ's body, joined to Him as closely as His hands and feet. He is the head of the body.[17] Barrett writes, "The head is the command center for all the operations of life. From the head flow all the impulses and instructions for the body to function. A headless body is lifeless. It is only in union with its head that a body can live."[18]

Christ has great tenderness for His body. Whatever affects them also involves Him, and therefore they must conduct themselves in holiness (1 Cor. 6:13–17). Christ tells His suffering people that whoever touches them touches the apple of His eye (Deut. 32:10; Zech. 2:8). The risen Lord rebukes the persecutors of the church, "Why persecutest thou me?" (Acts 9:4).

Christ's union with His body transcends the union between any earthly husband and wife because He lives in His body by the Holy Spirit (1 Cor. 6:15, 17; 12:12–13). Christ promised to send the Spirit to dwell in His people, and promised, "I will come to you.... Because I live, ye shall live also" (John 14:17–19). Thus it is "the Spirit of Christ" who dwells in those who belong to Christ (Rom. 8:9). Through this spiritual and organic connection, Christ shares His life with His body so that it grows and builds itself up (Eph. 4:15–16;

---

17. 1 Cor. 11:3; Eph. 4:15; 5:23; Col. 1:18; 2:19.
18. Barrett, *Complete in Him*, 108.

Col. 2:19). Though we may perish physically in our afflictions, yet we shall live forever, for already we are joined to Christ in His resurrection and are "his body, the fullness of him that filleth all in all" (Eph. 1:23).

The church is not a collection of isolated individuals but "one new man" in Christ, reconciled to God "in one body" (Eph. 2:15–16). Paul wrote, "so we, being many, are one body in Christ, and individually members of one another" (Rom. 12:5). Though we are diverse, every member of the church belongs to the body, and every member is needed (1 Cor. 12:12–30). We are one body with one Lord and therefore must labor to maintain the unity Christ has given us (Eph. 4:1–6). Union with Christ has massive implications for how we relate to other Christians.

The union of Christ with the church as His body far exceeds anything found in the first Adam. In this regard, we must recognize that the last Adam is more than a man, but the Lord. As God and one person in the Trinity, Christ is one in essence with the Spirit, and therefore is also one with His Spirit-indwelt people in a manner that transcends the types and shadows of the Old Testament and brings us into the most intimate union with God possible for created beings.

Being Clothed by God's Grace

Clothing originated in the garden of Eden. Adam and Eve made puny attempts to cover their shame after the fall (Gen. 3:7). However, God in His mercy clothed them with the skins of animals (Gen. 3:21), which was mankind's first exposure to physical death and a sign of the sacrifices by which their guilt and shame would be covered. In the temple, the priests wore holy garments for beauty and glory so that they would not die in God's holy presence (Exodus 28). Clothing became a symbol of salvation itself: "I will greatly rejoice in the LORD, my soul shall be joyful in my God; for he hath clothed me with the garments of salvation, he hath covered me with the robe of righteousness, as a bridegroom decketh himself with ornaments, and as a bride adorneth herself with her jewels" (Isa. 61:10).[19] Frequently, the Lord puts on clothing when He goes forth to fight for His people: the armor of righteousness, salvation, and judgment (Isa. 59:16–18).

Clothing, too, becomes an image of union and communion with Christ in the New Testament. Paul wrote, "But put ye on the Lord Jesus Christ, and make not provision for the flesh, to fulfil the lusts thereof" (Rom. 13:14). Being clothed with Christ is not only an imperative but also an indicative true of all believers, "For as many of you as have been baptized into Christ have put

---

19. See also Ps. 132:6, 9; Zech. 3:4.

on Christ" (Gal. 3:27). Just as in conversion they have "put off" the "old man" of Adam, so they have "put on the new man" of Christ (Eph. 4:22–24; Col. 3:9–10). Remarkably, their union with Christ is so close that believers may clothe themselves in the very armor of God, for they fight in the strength of the Lord (Eph. 6:10–11).[20] God clothes them with power by the Holy Spirit (Luke 24:49). One day, when the trumpet sounds, they will be clothed with immortality by their union with the risen Lord Jesus (1 Cor. 15:53–54). In all His graces, the Lord Jesus will be as close to them as their own garments.

Conclusion and Application

The union of God's chosen people with Christ arises from His unique office as the last Adam of the new creation. In corporate solidarity with Christ as their Prophet, Priest, and King in the covenant, believers are living stones built upon the cornerstone of Christ in the temple where God dwells; branches abiding in the vine of Christ to bear the fruit of the true Israel; guests eating at God's table where Christ is the bread, meat, and drink received for their life; the beloved bride of the Son of God, who loved them and gave Himself up for them; and the body of Christ, joined to Him as their living Head in the Holy Spirit and clothed with His righteousness and glory. Macaskill summarizes:

> The union between God and humans is covenantal, presented in terms of the formal union between God and Israel. The concept of the covenant underlies a theology of representation, by which the story of the one man (Jesus) is understood to be the story of his people. Their identification with him, their participation in his narrative, is realised by the indwelling Spirit, who constitutes the divine presence in their midst and is understood to be the eschatological gift of the new covenant. Reflecting this covenantal concept of presence, the union is commonly represented using temple imagery. The use of temple imagery maintains an essential distinction between God and his people, so that her glorification is understood as the interpersonal communication of a divine property [glory or fullness], not a mingling of essence.[21]

Since union with Christ is the heart of salvation, we must examine ourselves to see if we are truly united to Him. Paul wrote, "Examine yourselves, whether ye be in the faith; prove your own selves. Know ye not your own selves, how that Jesus Christ is in you, except ye be reprobates?" (2 Cor. 13:5). True religion is not merely a matter of true beliefs, moral behavior, and participation in the

---

20. See also Rom. 13:12; 1 Thess. 5:8.
21. Macaskill, *Union with Christ in the New Testament*, 1.

ordinances of worship, although it includes such. It is a supernatural relationship with Jesus Christ, such as you are in Him and He is in you.

If you are in Christ, then you have much for which to be grateful. The thought that Christ has united Himself so very closely to us should overwhelm Christians with His love for them. God overcame all our enmity and resistance against Him and gave us the Spirit of faith so that we take hold of Him who has taken hold of us. As Owen said, the Christian should exclaim, "What am I, poor, sinful dust and ashes, one that deserves to be lightly esteemed by the whole creation of God, that I should be thus united unto the Son of God, and thereby become his son by adoption?"[22] Our mouths should be full of songs of praise that the almighty Lord would join Himself to such as we are. Our hearts should swell with desire to enjoy intimate fellowship with the God who has so desired to be near to us.

In 1890 at a funeral service for a deacon in his church, C. H. Spurgeon cited the favorite expression of that brother, which was, "Lord Jesus, we are one with thee. We feel that we have a living, loving, lasting union with thee." Said Spurgeon, "Those three words have stuck by me; and ever since he has gone, I have found myself repeating them to myself involuntarily—'a living, loving, lasting union.' He owed everything to that."[23] So also do we.

---

22. Owen, *Hebrews*, 4:149.

23. Charles H. Spurgeon, Sermon 2245, "Living, Loving, Lasting Union," in *Metropolitan Tabernacle Pulpit* (1892; Pasadena, Tex.: Pilgrim Publications, 1969), 38:98.

PRACTICAL THEOLOGY

Chapter 20

Puritans on the Family:
Recent Publications

Post tenebras lux—"After darkness, light." In many ways the Reformation of the sixteenth century was the breaking of divine light through clouds of darkness that had gathered over the church for centuries. The Reformers poured out their lives like oil into a lamp to shine the light of Holy Scripture across Christian belief and practice. By necessity they focused their major writings on the great doctrines of the gospel, summarized by the *solas*: Scripture alone, Christ alone, grace alone, faith alone, and the glory of God alone. When the Puritans arose in the latter half of the sixteenth century, they basked in this light and labored to bring it into practical application for all of human life and society. One area in which the Puritans excelled was the Christian family, and their writings on marriage and parenting continue to be republished today.

A number of classic Puritan writings on marriage and family were reprinted in the last century, including facsimile reprints of William Whately's two small books on marriage[1] and William Ames's book on *Conscience*, which contains several chapters on household life.[2] Richard Baxter's massive tome on Puritan ethics and spirituality, *A Christian Directory*, which I will mention again later in this paper, contains many directions for family life.[3] The republication of *The Works of George Swinnock* brought forth the valuable *Christian Man's Calling*, with sections on conduct in the home.[4] Furthermore, the reprint of the

---

1. William Whately, *A Bride-Bush or A Wedding Sermon* (1617; repr., Norwood, N.J.: Walter J. Johnson, 1975); *A Care-Cloth or the Cumbers and Troubles of Marriage* (1624; repr., Norwood, N.J.: Walter J. Johnson, 1975). I gave this article as an address at the Evangelical Theological Society in Atlanta in November, 2015.

2. William Ames, *Conscience with the Power and Cases thereof* (1639; facsimile repr., Norwood, N.J.: Walter J. Johnson, 1975), 156–59, 196–211 (book 5, chapters 21–22, 35–38).

3. Richard Baxter, *A Christian Directory*, in *The Practical Works of Richard Baxter* (Morgan, Pa.: Soli Deo Gloria, 1996), 1:394–493 (part II: Christian economics, chapters 1–22).

4. George Swinnock, *The Christian Man's Calling*, in *The Works of George Swinnock* (1868; repr., Edinburgh: Banner of Truth, 1992), 1:464–528.

six volumes of *Puritan Sermons* preached at the Cripplegate Morning Exercises included sermons by Richard Adams on the duties of parents and children, Thomas Doolittle on family prayer, and Richard Steele on the duties of husbands and wives.[5]

Though we are presently only two decades into the twenty-first century, twenty more Puritan works relevant to this topic have appeared in print. Let me introduce them to you, organizing them into categories for the sake of convenience.

Puritan Bible Commentaries

First, we must not pass by the commentaries by Puritans who expounded Scripture passages that set forth God's will for the family. Today, people who talk about the Puritans tend to focus on their theological and practical treatises, but the Puritans produced major commentaries on Scripture, as the names Matthew Poole and Matthew Henry still bear witness today. When we think of extended biblical treatments of family life, our minds move quickly to Paul's Epistles to the Ephesians and the Colossians. Three Puritan commentaries on those epistles have been reprinted in the twenty-first century.

Paul Bayne or Baynes (*c.* 1573–1617) succeeded William Perkins as the preacher at St. Andrews, Cambridge. Though not as well-known today as Perkins, Bayne had (according to Ames) a double portion of the spirit of his Elijah-like predecessor. Bayne's commentary on Ephesians, reprinted by Tentmaker Publications, gives twenty-seven large pages to the apostle's instructions to wives, husbands, children, and parents.[6] His comments are sometimes couched in quaint Elizabethan language, but they are full of doctrinal and practical observations. For example, commenting on Ephesians 5:28, Bayne says that the husband who does not love his wife tenderly, despite the fact that she is one flesh with him, is like a man who eats his own liver or becomes his own hangman.[7]

Nicholas Byfield (1579–1622) died in his early forties after terrible suffering from kidney stones, but he published a number of prized books, including

---

5. Richard Adams, "What are the Duties of Parents and Children; and How Are They to Be Managed According to Scripture?" in *Puritan Sermons, 1659–1689* (Wheaton, Ill.: Richard Owen Roberts, 1981), 2:303–358; Thomas Doolittle, "How May the Duty of Daily Family Prayer Be Best Managed for the Spiritual Benefit of Every One in the Family?" in *Puritan Sermons, 1659–1689,* 2:194–272; Richard Steele, "What Are the Duties of Husbands and Wives towards Each Other?" in *Puritan Sermons, 1659–1689,* 2:272–303.

6. Paul Bayne, *An Entire Commentary upon the Whole Epistle of St. Paul to the Ephesians* (1866; repr., Stoke-on-Trent: Tentmaker, 2001), 337–64.

7. Bayne, *Ephesians,* 348.

a commentary on Colossians reprinted by Tentmaker Publications in 2007.[8] John Davenant (1572–1641) represented the Church of England at the Synod of Dort. He wrote a commentary on Colossians reprinted by the Banner of Truth Trust in their Geneva Commentary Series. His commentary is rich in scholarship and devotes over forty pages to family duties.[9] For example, Davenant warns that husbands must not treat their wives like maid or servants but as friends and fellow rulers over the family: "The wife is to be subject to her husband, and directed by him; but as a companion, not a slave"—and specifically forbidding husbands to physically strike their wives.[10]

Though we may not think of the Old Testament prophets as sources of teaching about the family, I mention the commentary by Richard Stock (c. 1569–1626) on Malachi, also reprinted by Tentmaker, which contains twenty pages of exposition on the prophet's rebuke of the sins of husbands against their wives (Mal. 2:13–16).[11]

I encourage scholars to give attention to Puritan commentaries on Scripture. Such expositions offer fertile fields for studies in early Reformed exegesis, hermeneutics, theology, Christian experience, and ethics. In their own time, these biblical commentaries were not the specialized domain of scholars and preachers but influenced all of society from family life to politics and legislation.

Puritan Books with Sections on the Family

Second, I would like to highlight five books reprinted in the twenty-first century that contain significant sections relevant to the family. The Puritans often used the Ramist method of dividing each topic into subtopics, analyzed into further divisions and subpoints. As a result, even a single chapter or sermon often contains a remarkably detailed exposition of its subject. We find such sections on marriage and parenting in books by two Scots, two ministers of the Church of England, and one English Separatist, all recently reprinted.

James Durham (1622–1658) was a Scottish Presbyterian pastor known for his humility and scholarship. Though he died at age thirty-five, he produced an enormous amount of edifying theological writing. Of all the books written by

---

8. Nicholas Byfield, *An Exposition Upon the Epistle to the Colossians* (1866; repr., Stoke-on-Trent: Tentmaker, 2007), 346–61.

9. John Davenant, *Colossians*, trans. by Josiah Allport, A Geneva Series Commentary (1831; repr., Edinburgh: Banner of Truth, 2005), 2:151–95.

10. Davenant, *Colossians*, 2:166–67.

11. Richard Stock, *A Commentary Upon the Prophecy of Malachi*, 168–91. In *Richard Stock and Samuel Torshell on Malachi and Richard Bernard and Thomas Fuller on Ruth* (1865; repr., Stoke-on-Trent: Tentmaker, 2006).

Durham, probably the most popular was his *Practical Exposition of the Ten Commandments*, now carefully edited by Christopher Coldwell and republished by Naphtali Press. In the midst of discussing worship under the Fourth Commandment, Durham's treatment of family worship extends to sixteen pages in length.[12] He directs families to gather in the home to "pray, read, sing psalms," discuss sermons, and have spiritual conversations, for in such times God sweetly draws near and reveals Himself, and the knowledge of God is propagated and increased.[13]

Although the ministry of Thomas Halyburton (1674–1712), followed upon what some scholars would consider to be the end of the Puritan era, he was thoroughly imbued with the spirit of Puritanism, so I include him here. His collected works have been reprinted by the James Begg Society in Scotland. In his book *The Great Concern of Salvation*, he ends with thirty-five pages on family religion. He said that making your home into a place of godliness and worship is a great evangelistic strategy: "It is the way for thee to win souls."[14]

The twenty-first century also saw the reprinting of an early English Puritan known as the "silver-tongued preacher," Henry Smith (1560–1591). Among the collected sermons of Smith is, *A Preparative to Marriage*, a thirty-five page exposition of biblical teaching on matrimony that is full of wisdom and love.[15] He said that for a husband, his wife is "like a little Zoar, a city of refuge to fly to in all his troubles (Gen. 19:20)."[16] Rebuking men inclined to be physically abusive to their wives, he asks, "Doth a king trample his crown?" (cf. Prov. 12:4).[17]

Lewis Stuckley (1621–1687) ministered in the Church of England until ejected by the government on St. Bartholomew's Day in 1662. His book, *A Gospel Glass*, recently reprinted by Ebenezer Publications, is an aid to self-examination with regard to a wide variety of sins. It contains a searching section of fourteen pages on family relationships.[18] For example, Stuckley asked wives if they gossip about their husband's flaws more than they publicly praise their graces.[19]

---

12. James Durham, *A Practical Exposition of the Ten Commandments*, ed. Christopher Coldwell (Dallas, Tex.: Naphtali Press, 2002), 221–36.

13. Durham, *Practical Exposition of the Ten Commandments*, 232, 235.

14. Thomas Halyburton, "The Christian's Duty, with Respect to Both Personal and Family Religion," in *The Great Concern of Salvation*, in *The Works of Thomas Halyburton* (Aberdeen: James Begg Society, 2000–2003), 2:368–403.

15. Henry Smith, *A Preparative to Marriage*, in *The Works of Henry Smith* (repr., Staffordshire: Tentmaker, 2002), 1:5–40.

16. Smith, *Preparative to Marriage*, in *Works*, 1:8.

17. Smith, *Preparative to Marriage*, in *Works*, 1:27.

18. Lewis Stuckley, *A Gospel Glass: Representing the Miscarriages of Professors, Both in Their Personal and Relative Capacities* (1852; repr., Grand Rapids: Ebenezer, 2002), 169–83.

19. Stuckley, *Gospel Glass*, 175.

Lastly in this category, I would note the republication by Sprinkle of the *Works* of English separatist John Robinson (1576–1625), the revered pastor of the Pilgrims in the Netherlands before they went to the New World on the Mayflower. His *Essays* contains two short pieces on marriage and child-rearing.[20]

Let me commend the use of Primo, the discovery system at Puritan Reformed Theological Seminary's William Perkins Library.[21] The librarians have entered the chapter headings of each book which results in unusually fruitful keyword searches. Scholars and interested researchers can enter search terms and then limit by location (PRC Primary) to find what the Puritans wrote on any subject. Another recommendation is the Puritan Studies Database at the seminary. This custom-built database is the only one of its kind specializing in secondary literature for English and American Puritans as well as Dutch Nadere Reformatie divines.

Puritan Booklets Pertinent to Family Life

Third, let me bring to your attention a few booklets relevant to family life recently reprinted from Puritan sources. These are all short, helpful pieces published by Soli Deo Gloria, now an imprint of Reformation Heritage Books.

Arthur Hildersham (1563–1632), though largely forgotten today, was a powerful preacher often persecuted for his refusal to conform to the demands of church and state. His booklet, *Dealing with Sin in our Children*, is an excerpt from a massive folio volume containing 152 sermons on Psalm 51.[22] Given David's statement that he was conceived in his mother's womb in a state of sin (Ps. 51:5), parents should recognize that they have passed original sin along to their children, and strive to lead their children to salvation by the use of their authority, instruction, examples, arrangements for schooling, work, and marriage, and most of all, prayer.

Edward Lawrence (1623–1695) is the author of *Parent's Concerns for the Unsaved Children*, based on Proverbs 17:25, "A foolish son is a grief to his father, and bitterness to her that bare him."[23] He wrote instructions for parents and an

---

20. John Robinson, "Of Marriage," and "Of Children and Their Education," in *New Essays, Or Observations Divine and Moral*, in *The Works of John Robinson*, ed. Robert Ashton (1851; repr., Harrisonburg, Va.: Sprinkle, 2009), 1:236–50.

21. Search Primo (http://prts-primo.hosted.exlibrisgroup.com/primo_library/libweb/action /search.do?menuitem=3&vid=01PRTS) and the Puritan Studies Database (https://prts.edu/ researchtools/#/search)

22. Arthur Hildersham, *Dealing with Sin in Our Children*, ed. Don Kistler (Morgan, Pa.: Soli Deo Gloria, 2004).

23. Edward Lawrence, *Parent's Concerns for Their Unsaved Children*, ed. Don Kistler (Morgan, Pa.: Soli Deo Gloria, 2003).

appeal to wayward children, with his heart heavy with grief for two of his own children who continued to live in rebellious folly.

The last two booklets both come from the pen of Cotton Mather (1663–1728), the warmhearted and rather eccentric but prolix pastor from Boston, Massachusetts. *A Family Well-Ordered* sets forth the responsibility of parents to raise their children in God's ways and the responsibility of children to honor their parents.[24] He taught parents to pray, "Lord, give unto my child a new heart, a clean heart, a soft heart, and a heart after Thy own heart."[25] Mather's other booklet is *Help for Distressed Parents* and actually cites the book by Edward Lawrence just mentioned.[26] Mather offers comfort to the parents of wayward children, calls them to self-examination, and directs them to keep talking to their children about Christ and not give up.

Puritan Books on Marriage and Family

Fourth, let us consider entire books by the Puritans that address Christian marriage or parenting. Seven of them have been reprinted in the twenty-first century.

One of these books appears in two significantly different forms, the treatise by William Gouge (1575–1653) on the duties of husbands, wives, children, and parents—probably the premier Puritan treatise on the subject. Gouge and his wife Elizabeth had thirteen children, eight of whom lived to adulthood. His book, *Of Domestical Duties*, was edited by Greg Fox and reprinted by Puritan Reprints in a single large volume of over five hundred pages.[27] This reprint stays close to the seventeenth-century edition and thus is a valuable resource for scholarly study, though it omits Gouge's original marginal citations. The same book was more thoroughly revised and modernized by Scott Brown and myself and published by Reformation Heritage Books under the title *Building a Godly Home*. It appears in three volumes with these subtitles: (1) *A Holy Vision for Family Life*, (2) *A Holy Vision for a Happy Marriage*, and (3) *A Holy Vision for Raising Children*.[28] While remaining true to Gouge's words, this modernized

---

24. Cotton Mather, *A Family Well-ordered: Or, An Essay to Render Parents and Children Happy in One Another*, ed. Don Kistler (Morgan, Pa.: Soli Deo Gloria, 2001).

25. Mather, *Family Well-ordered*, 19.

26. Cotton Mather, *Help for Distressed Parents*, ed. Don Kistler (Morgan, Pa.: Soli Deo Gloria, 2004). For his citation of Lawrence, see p. 6.

27. William Gouge, *Of Domestical Duties*, ed. Greg Fox (1622; repr., Pensacola: Puritan Reprints, 2006).

28. William Gouge, *Building a Godly Home*, ed. Joel R. Beeke and Scott Brown, 3 vols. (Grand Rapids: Reformation Heritage Books, 2013–2014).

version aims to make him more accessible to readers, defines difficult words, and omits a few sections that may no longer be relevant.[29]

The first part of Gouge's book consists of an exposition of Ephesians 5:21–6:9. While addressing the responsibilities of each member of the household, Gouge also presents a beautiful exposition of the redeeming work of Christ for His church. For example, he exults, "In that the person of Christ, God-Man, was given up, I gather that the price of our redemption is of infinite value. Neither Christ, nor God Himself could give anything greater. Heaven and earth and all things in them are not of similar worth." This gives hope to sinners: "What place can be left for despair in those that know and believe the worth of this ransom?"[30]

The second part of Gouge's book contains an exhaustive treatment of the duties of husbands and wives. Gouge stresses that each spouse must be concerned performing his or her own duties regardless of whether one's spouse is performing those duties. Husbands must love their wives as Christ loves the church no matter how their wives treat them; wives must respect and show submission to their husbands no matter how their husbands treat them. For each virtue required by God, Gouge also sets forth the contrary vice to be avoided. Regarding adultery, though ancient customs and medieval traditions tended to make a woman's adultery a worse crime than a man's, Gouge resolutely insisted that God's Word condemns adultery equally in either case.[31] Throughout, his emphasis is on love: "A loving mutual affection must pass between husband and wife, or else no duty will be well performed."[32]

The third part of Gouge's book develops the mutual responsibilities of parents and children. He examines cases of conscience regarding how a child should honor his parents even if he disagrees with them. As with marriage, he insisted that the "fountain" of all right behavior between parents and children is love.[33] He warned parents against extremes in correcting their children. On the one hand, they should not pamper them and fail to correct their sins so that they run ahead into wickedness; on the other hand, they must not correct them with excessive severity so that their minds are dulled and their hearts hardened. What is excessive correction? Gouge says it is correction for no fault, correction administered in anger and fury, correction that treats young and tender children

---

29. The largest omission from *Building a Godly Home* is Gouge's exposition and application of Paul's instructions to masters and servants (Eph. 6:5–9).

30. Gouge, *Building a Godly Home*, 1:57; cf. *Domestical Duties*, 34.

31. Gouge, *Building a Godly Home*, 2:41; cf. *Domestical Duties*, 159.

32. Gouge, *Building a Godly Home*, 2:48; cf. *Domestical Duties*, 163.

33. Gouge, *Building a Godly Home*, 3:84; cf. *Domestical Duties*, 362.

as if they were older and extremely obstinate, correction for every little thing done wrong, or correction that physically injures the child.[34]

Another recent reprint worthy of our attention is Richard Baxter (1615–1691), *The Godly Home*, published by Crossway.[35] At the beginning of this chapter I mentioned Baxter's *Christian Directory*. This reprint is a substantial (200-page!) excerpt from it, edited by Randall Pederson. Though Baxter deviated from the orthodox Reformed view of the atonement and justification by faith, his practical writings have been greatly treasured through the centuries. His book is a compilation of "directions" to husbands, wives, parents, and children outlining their duties to one another, and indicates what their motives should be in doing them.

One notable feature of the book is a chapter of forty pages containing twenty arguments why families should practice regular worship or devotions together in their homes.[36] Baxter argued that God created the family, owns it as His institution, and rules over it, and therefore, each family owes Him its worship.[37] God revealed His will that the family be dedicated to His worship by His command to Abraham to circumcise his household (Genesis 17), by instituting the Passover as a sacred meal in each household (Exodus 12), by His promise that when the Spirit is poured out "every family apart" will mourn over the death of Christ (Zech. 12:10–14), and by the salvation of entire households in the book of Acts.[38] Baxter also pointed out that the Bible commands heads of households to teach God's Word to those under their authority and care, and commends those that do so (Gen. 18:18–19; Deut. 4:9; 6:7; 11:18–21; Prov. 22:6; Eph. 6:4; 2 Tim. 1:5, 3:15).[39] And he makes many more arguments besides.

Though we may not agree with Baxter on all points, the wisdom and balance of his nearly 350-year-old directions are amazing. For example, he said that parents must not treat young children as either equals or servants but as their dearly loved children. Children are thinkers, and if they only fear your anger, then "fear will make them liars as often as a lie seems necessary to their escape." However, if they see that "you dearly love them and that all your commands, restraints, and corrections are for their good," then they will "obey you more

---

34. Gouge, *Building a Godly Home*, 3:144–46; cf. *Domestical Duties*, 407–408.
35. Richard Baxter, *The Godly Home*, ed. Randall J. Pederson (Wheaton, Ill.: Crossway, 2010).
36. Baxter, *Godly Home*, 57–97.
37. Baxter, *Godly Home*, 65.
38. Baxter, *Godly Home*, 67–69.
39. Baxter, *Godly Home*, 72–73.

willingly," even in your absence.[40] Another example is Baxter's instructions for "sports and recreations." He commended activity for children that served "their health and cheerfulness," particularly stating that whatever "exercises their bodies is best." However, he warned against activities that hinder their schoolwork and chores or tempt them to greed and gambling.[41] These are but samples of Baxter's book.

Daniel Rogers (1573–1652) wrote a treatise based on Hebrews 13:4 titled *Matrimonial Honor*, which was retypeset and published by Edification Press.[42] Rogers was the son of the more famous Richard Rogers, author of the book of practical divinity *Seven Treatises* and a very large commentary on Judges. Like Gouge and Baxter, the younger Rogers expounds the mutual duties of spouses, the specific duties of husbands, and the specific duties of wives. He concluded with sobering warnings of God's judgment against fornicators and adulterers and an exhortation to sexual purity. To those feeling the guilt of their sexual sins, Rogers urged earnest faith in Jesus Christ and brokenhearted repentance toward God. He said,

> Will God judge adulterers? Stoop [bow down] then at his bar; he can save or destroy.... [H]ere is a judge that can damn you to hell forever!... [G]o on, be earnest with God to give you a glimpse of hope in the Lord Jesus, who was made all sin...and has satisfied the wrath of this judge, that he might say, Deliver him, I have accepted a ransom.... Beg of the Lord to turn a terrified heart into a melting one; that it is, which mold an unclean soul, to a clean and chaste one.[43]

This exhortation reminds us that the Puritans addressed practical and ethical matters in the light of the gospel. Eternity weighed heavily on their minds. They dealt with the mundanities of household life, but always with an eye on judgment day, hell, and heaven.

This same spiritual emphasis appears in another, smaller book reprinted by Edification Press, *An Antidote Against Discord between Man and Wife*, whose author we know only by the initials D. B.[44] The *Antidote* diagnoses the root problem of marital conflicts as the inward corruption of original sin, especially inordinate self-love and pride.[45] The author proceeded to describe in very

---

40. Baxter, *Godly Home*, 187.
41. Baxter, *Godly Home*, 192.
42. Daniel Rogers, *Matrimonial Honor* (1642; repr., Warrenton, Va.: Edification, 2010).
43. Rogers, *Matrimonial Honor*, 342–43.
44. D. B., *An Antidote Against Discord Between Man and Wife* (1685; repr., Warrenton, Va.: Edification, 2013).
45. D. B., *Antidote Against Discord Between Man and Wife*, 13–15.

practical terms how the fallen heart of man rages with sinful anger. However, his solution was not a mere list of how-tos but the call to put sin to death by the grace of the gospel. He said that you cannot put sin to death unless "thou art engrafted into Christ by faith," for only then do you have the Spirit of God to enable and empower you to fight against indwelling sin.[46] He went on to give a dozen directions about overcoming sinful anger but said all reformation must be rooted in Christ.

Matthew Henry (1662–1714) is best known for his commentary on the Bible. He also wrote four treatises recently reprinted by Christian Focus Publications under the title *Family Religion*.[47] The first three treatises are *A Church in the House*, *The Catechising of Youth*, and *Christ's Favour to Little Children*. In the last of these, Henry at one point directly addresses children, saying "that the Lord Jesus Christ has a tender concern and affection for you; and that he has blessings in store for you, if you apply yourselves to him, according to your capacity.... Has he thus loved you, and will not you love him?"[48] The entire second half of the book is a treatise on baptism, where Henry shows himself true to his Reformed, covenantal tradition.

George Hamond (*c.* 1620–1705), an English Presbyterian minister and schoolteacher, wrote a book in answer to the question, "Upon what Scripture-grounds and reasons may family-worship be established and enforced?"[49] Soli Deo Gloria has republished it as *The Case for Family Worship*.[50] Hamond drew upon the examples of Abraham, Job, Joshua, the Lord Jesus Christ (with His disciples as His spiritual family), and Cornelius to argue that family worship is an important preparation for public worship on the Lord's Day.

Finally, I have to slip in a book from the Dutch Further Reformation, a movement parallel to and influenced by English Puritanism. The Dutch Reformed Translation Society has overseen the translation of a number of Further Reformation works into English, including *The Duties of Parents* by Jacobus Koelman (1632–1695).[51] This book contains 282 concisely stated principles about rearing children in the Lord, many of which cannot be found in any

---

46. D. B., *Antidote Against Discord Between Man and Wife*, 62.

47. Matthew Henry, *Family Religion: Principles for Raising a Godly Family* (Ross-shire, Scotland: Christian Focus Publications, 2008).

48. Henry, *Family Religion*, 116.

49. George Hamond, *A Discourse of Family-worship* (London: John Lawrence, 1694), title page.

50. George Hamond, *The Case for Family Worship*, ed. Don Kistler (Orlando: Soli Deo Gloria, 2005). The twelfth chapter in this book is not the work of Hamond but of Matthew Barker and was originally an appendix.

51. Jacobus Koelman, *The Duties of Parents*, trans. John Vriend, ed. M. Eugene Osterhaven. Classics of Reformed Spirituality (Grand Rapids: Reformation Heritage Books, 2003).

other books. One striking aspect of the book is Koelman's sensitivity to child development, adjusting expectations according to the child's age.

Conclusion

Puritan writings on the family arose out of the conviction that God's Word is a lamp to our feet and a light to our path (Ps. 119:105). Recent reprints of these books demonstrate that the Puritans were indeed burning and shining lights, and their treatises still shine for us today (cf. John 5:35). There is no denying that their language is quaint—four centuries makes for many changes in the English language. There is also no denying that the Puritans wrote as people of their own culture, sometimes revealing the blind spots of British and European minds in the sixteenth and seventeenth centuries. However, the Puritan expositions and treatises on family life are rich with biblical and practical insights, some of which are seldom found in more modern books. I hope that this brief survey whets your appetite to "take up and read."

Puritans on the Family: Bibliography

This bibliography lists English sources written by the Puritans on marriage and family. In general works, the pages specific to marriage or family are designated. Items marked with an asterisk (*) represent books published in the twenty-first century after being out of print for some time or in a significantly new format, such as publishing a section of a much larger book on its own.

Adams, Richard. "What are the Duties of Parents and Children; and How Are They to Be Managed According to Scripture?" In *Puritan Sermons, 1659–1689*, 2:303–358. Wheaton, Ill.: Richard Owen Roberts, 1981.

Allestree, Richard. *The Whole Duty of Man*, 244–52, 258–64. London: W. Pickering, 1842.

Ambrose, Isaac. "Family Duties." In *The Practice of Sanctification*. In *Works of Isaac Ambrose*, 130–36. London: Thomas Tegg, 1829.

Ames, William. *Conscience with the Power and Cases thereof*, 156–59, 196–211. Book 5, Chapters 21–22, 35–38. 1639. Facsimile reprint. Norwood, N.J.: Walter J. Johnson, 1975.

*B., D. *An Antidote Against Discord Betwixt Man and Wife*. 1685. Reprint. Warrenton, Va.: Edification, 2013.

B., Ste. *Counsel to the Husband; to the Wife Instruction: A Short and Pithy Treatise of Several and Joynt Duties, Belonging unto Man and Wife, as Counsels to the One, and Instructions to the Other; for Their More Perfect Happiness in This Present Life, and Their Eternal Glorie in the Life to Come*. London: by Felix Kyngston, for Richard Boyle, 1608.

Baxter, Richard. *A Christian Directory*, Part II: Christian Economics, Chapters 1–22. In *The Practical Works of Richard Baxter*, 1:394–493. Morgan, Pa.: Soli Deo Gloria, 1996.

*———. *The Godly Home*, edited by Randall J. Pederson. Wheaton, Ill.: Crossway Books, 2010. (Modernized excerpt from *A Christian Directory*)

———. *The Poor Man's Family Book*. In *The Practical Works of Richard Baxter*, 4:165–289. Morgan, Pa.: Soli Deo Gloria, 1996.

Bayly, Lewis. *The Practice of Piety: Directing a Christian How to Walk, that He May Please God*, 143–49. Morgan, Pa.: Soli Deo Gloria, 1994.

*Bayne, Paul. *An Entire Commentary upon the Whole Epistle of St. Paul to the Ephesians*, 337–64. 1866. Reprint. Stoke-on-Trent: Tentmaker, 2001. (Previously reprinted with Thomas Goodwin's commentary, Evansville, Ind.: Sovereign Grace, 1958)

Bolton, Robert. *General Directions for a Comfortable Walking with God*, 262–81. Morgan, Pa.: Soli Deo Gloria, 1995.

Boston, Thomas. "Duties of Husband and Wife." In *The Works of Thomas Boston*, edited by Samuel M'Millan, 4:209–218. Wheaton, Ill: Richard Owen Roberts, 1980.

Bourne, Immanuel. *A Golden Chain of Directions, with Twenty Gold-links of Love, To Preserve Love Firm between Husband and Wife, During Their Lives.* London: by J. Streater for George Sanbridge, 1669.

Bunyan, John. *Christian Behaviour.* In *The Works of John Bunyan*, edited by George Offor, 2:557–62. 1854. Reprint. Edinburgh: Banner of Truth, 1991.

*Byfield, Nicholas. *An Exposition Upon the Epistle to the Colossians*, 346–61. 1866. Reprint. Stoke-on-Trent: Tentmaker, 2007.

Cawdrey, Daniel. *Family Reformation Promoted.* In *Anthology of Presbyterian and Reformed Literature, Volume 4*, 54–73, edited by Christopher Coldwell. 1655. Reprint. Dallas, Tex.: Naphtali, 1991.

[Cooke, Edward.] *The Batchelor's Directory: Being a Treatise of the Excellence of Marriage.* London: Richard Cumberland and Benjamin Bragg, 1694.

*Davenant, John. *Colossians*, translated by Josiah Allport, 2:151–95. A Geneva Series Commentary. 1831; Reprint. Edinburgh: Banner of Truth, 2005.

Dod, John. *A Plain and Familiar Exposition of the Ten Commandments*, 166–86, 199–209. London: Thomas Man, Paul Man, and Jonah Man, 1632.

Dod, John and Robert Cleaver. *A Godly Form of Household Government.* London: Thomas Man, 1612. (First published by Robert Cleaver in 1598, then revised by John Dod)

Doolittle, Thomas. "How May the Duty of Daily Family Prayer Be Best Managed for the Spiritual Benefit of Every One in the Family?" In *Puritan Sermons, 1659–1689*, 2:194–272. Wheaton, Ill: Richard Owen Roberts, 1981.

*Durham, James. "Family Worship." In *A Practical Exposition of the Ten Commandments*, edited by Christopher Coldwell, 221–36. Dallas, Tex.: Naphtali, 2002.

Durham, William. *A Serious Exhortation to the Necessary Duties of Family and Personal Instruction.* London: by Tho. Newcomb, 1659.

Gataker, Thomas. "A Marriage Prayer," "A Good Wife God's Gift," "A Wife in Deed," and "Marriage Duties." In *Certain Sermons*, 2:116–208. London: John Haviland, 1637.

Goodwin, Phillip. *Religio Domestica Rediviva: Or, Family Religion Revived*. London: by R. and W. Leybourn, for Andrew Kemb and Edward Brewster, 1655.

Gouge, Thomas. *Christian Directions, Shewing How to Walk with God All the Day Long*, 131–48. London: R. Ibbitson and M. Wright, 1661.

*Gouge, William. *Building a Godly Home*, edited by Joel R. Beeke and Scott Brown, 3 volumes. Grand Rapids: Reformation Heritage Books, 2013–2014. (Modernized version of *Domestical Duties*)

*———. *Of Domestical Duties*, edited by Greg Fox. 1622. Reprint. Pensacola: Puritan Reprints, 2006.

Greenham, Richard. *A Godlie Exhortation, and Fruitfull Admonition to Virtuous Parents and Modest Matrons. Describing the Holie Life, and Blessed Institution of that Most Honorable State of Matrimonie, and the Increase of Godlie and Happy Children, in Training Them Up in Godly Education, and Household Discipline*. London: N. Ling, 1584.

———. "Of the Good Education of Children." In *The Works of the Reverend and Faithfull Servant of Jesus Christ M. Richard Greenham*, edited by H. H., 159–68. 1599. Facsimile reprint. Amsterdam: Theatrum Orbis Terrarum, 1973.

———. "A Treatise of a Contract before Marriage." In *The Works of the Reverend and Faithfull Servant of Jesus Christ M. Richard Greenham*, edited by H. H., 288–99. 1599. Facsimile reprint. Amsterdam: Theatrum Orbis Terrarum, 1973.

Greenhill, William. *An Exposition of Ezekiel*, 441–43. Edinburgh: Banner of Truth, 1994.

*Halyburton, Thomas. "The Christian's Duty, with Respect to Both Personal and Family Religion." In *The Great Concern of Salvation*. In *The Works of Thomas Halyburton*, 2:368–403. Aberdeen: James Begg Society, 2000–2003.

*Hamond, George. *The Case for Family Worship*. Orlando: Soli Deo Gloria, 2005.

*Henry, Matthew. *Family Religion: Principles for Raising a Godly Family*. Ross-shire, Scotland: Christian Focus, 2008.

Heywood, Oliver. *The Family Altar*. In *The Whole Works of the Rev. Oliver Heywood*. Reprint. Morgan, Pa.: Soli Deo Gloria, 1997.

*Hildersham, Arthur. *Dealing with Sin in Our Children*, edited by Don Kistler. Morgan, Pa.: Soli Deo Gloria, 2004.

Hopkins, Ezekiel. *An Exposition upon the Commandments.* In *The Works of Ezekiel Hopkins,* edited by Charles W. Quick, 1:413–26. 1874. Reprint. Morgan, PA: Soli Deo Gloria, 1995.

*Koelman, Jacobus. *The Duties of Parents,* translated by John Vriend, edited by M. Eugene Osterhaven. Classics of Reformed Spirituality. Grand Rapids: Reformation Heritage Books, 2003.

*Lawrence, Edward. *Parent's Concerns for Their Unsaved Children,* edited by Don Kistler. Morgan, Pa.: Soli Deo Gloria, 2003.

Lye, Thomas. "What May Gracious Parents Best Do for the Conversion of Those Children Whose Wickedness Is Occasioned by Their Sinful Severity or Indulgence?" In *Puritan Sermons, 1659–1689,* 3:153–84. Wheaton, Ill.: Robert Owen Roberts, 1981.

Manton, Thomas. "Sermons Upon Ephesians V." In *The Works of Thomas Manton,* 19:436–76. 1870. Reprint. Birmingham: Solid Ground Christian Books, 2008.

———. "A Wedding Sermon." In *The Works of Thomas Manton,* 2:162–72. 1870. Reprint. Birmingham: Solid Ground Christian Books, 2008.

Maynard, John. *The Beauty of Order of the Creation. Together with Natural and Allegorical Meditations on the Six Dayes Works of the Creation,* 175–84. London: William Gearing, 1668.

*Mather, Cotton. *A Family Well-ordered: Or, An Essay to Render Parents and Children Happy in One Another,* edited by Don Kistler. Morgan, Pa.: Soli Deo Gloria, 2001. (Previously reprinted Bellville, Tex.: Sower's Seed, 1995)

*———. *Help for Distressed Parents,* edited by Don Kistler. Morgan, Pa.: Soli Deo Gloria, 2004.

Norman, John. *Family-governors Persuaded to Family-godliness.* London: by A. Maxey, for Samuel Gellibrand, 1657.

Perkins, William. *Christian Oeconomy.* In *The Work of William Perkins,* edited by Ian Breward, 416–39. Appleford, England: Sutton Courtenay, 1970.

———. *A Golden Chaine,* in *The Workes of that Famous and Worthie Minister of Christ, in the Universitie of Cambridge, M. W. Perkins,* 1:60–61. London: John Legate, 1608.

Petter, George. *A Learned, Pious, and Practical Commentary Upon the Gospel According to St. Mark,* 703–713. London: Printed by F. Streater, 1661.

Reyner, Edward. *Considerations Concerning Marriage: The Honor, Duties, Benefits, Troubles of it. Whereto are added, 1) Directions in two particulars: a. How they that have wives may be as if they had none. b. How to prepare for parting with a dear yoke-fellow by death or otherwise. 2) Resolution of this Case of Conscience: Whether a man may lawfully marry his wive's sister?* London: by J. T. for Thomas Newbery, 1657.

*Robinson, John. "Of Marriage," and "Of Children and Their Education." In *New Essays, Or Observations Divine and Moral.* In *The Works of John Robinson,* edited by Robert Ashton, 1:236–50. 1851. Reprint. Harrisonburg, Va.: Sprinkle, 2009.

*Rogers, Daniel. *Matrimonial Honor.* 1642. Reprint. Warrenton, Va.: Edification, 2010.

Scudder, Henry. *The Godly Man's Choice.* London: Matthew Simmons for Henry Overton, 1644.

Secker, William. "The Wedding Ring, A Sermon," printed with *The Nonsuch Professor in His Meridian Splendour; Or, The Singular Actions of Sanctified Christians,* edited by Matthew Wilks, 245–69. Reprint. Harrisonburg, Va.: Sprinkle, 1997.

*Smith, Henry. *A Preparative to Marriage.* In *The Works of Henry Smith,* 1:5–40. Reprint. Staffordshire: Tentmaker, 2002.

Steele, Richard. "What Are the Duties of Husbands and Wives towards Each Other?" In *Puritan Sermons, 1659–1689,* 2:272–303. Wheaton, Ill.: Richard Owen Roberts, 1981.

*Stock, Richard. *A Commentary Upon the Prophecy of Malachi,* 168–91. In *Richard Stock and Samuel Torshell on Malachi and Richard Bernard and Thomas Fuller on Ruth.* 1865. Reprint. Stoke-on-Trent: Tentmaker, 2006.

Stockton, Owen. *A Treatise of Family Instruction.* London: H. Brome, 1672.

*Stuckley, Lewis. *A Gospel Glass: Representing the Miscarriages of Professors, Both in Their Personal and Relative Capacities,* 169–183. 1852. Reprint. Grand Rapids: Ebenezer, 2002.

Swinnock, George. *The Christian Man's Calling.* In *The Works of George Swinnock,* 1:464–528. 1868. Reprint. Edinburgh: Banner of Truth, 1992.

Taffin, Jean. *The Amendment of Life,* 274–327. London: Georg. Bishop, 1595.

Whately, William. *A Bride-Bush or A Wedding Sermon.* 1617. Reprint. Norwood, N.J.: Walter J. Johnson, 1975.

———. *A Care-Cloth or the Cumbers and Troubles of Marriage.* 1624. Reprint. Norwood, N.J.: Walter J. Johnson, 1975.

Willard, Samuel. "Question LXIV: What Is Required in the Fifth Command-
    ment?" In *A Compleat Body of Divinity in Two Hundred and Fifty
    Expository Lectures on the Assemby's Shorter Catechism*, 598–613. 1726.
    Reprint. New York: Johnson Reprint Corp., 1969.

Willet, Andrew. *Hexapla in Genesin, that is, a Sixfold Commentary upon Genesis,*
    38, 41–44. London: by Tho. Creede, for John Norton, 1608.

Chapter 21

Consider Christ in Affliction:
An Open Letter to True Believers

Dear believer,

I desire to write you about something with which you are well acquainted: *affliction*. Much has been written on affliction by our forebears. A good part of it you have known for a long time. For example, you know that all affliction is ultimately traceable to our tragic fall in Adam. You know, too, the grievousness of affliction. After all, who enjoys suffering?

Yet you also know that all affliction is sent by a wise, fatherly God. Perhaps you even know—as the whole book of Job and the Puritans never tire of teaching us—that the important thing is not the amount of affliction we receive but how we respond to that affliction.

Isn't it just here that your deepest questions about affliction and trial lie? For you want to respond to affliction in a God-glorifying manner, but you feel you often fall inexcusably short. You desire that your entire life may serve God's praise (Isa. 43:21), but somehow when you enter the heat and heart of affliction you find yourself losing grip on your firm intention. To respond rightly to affliction *before* it comes is hard; to look back on it gratefully *after* it is over is harder; but to live Christianly *in* affliction is hardest. Hence you ask yourself again and again: *How may I live through affliction more Christianly—in a way that is more like Christ?* How may I grow in grace while—yes, while—suffering affliction?

You are not alone in such wrestlings. Countless times God's children have been there, begging to be made conformable to the image of Christ through the furnace of affliction. The prayer is simple ("Lord, grant me grace to live through *this* affliction Christianly"); the wrestlings, often agonizing.

Through years of encountering affliction (including times of running from, wrestling with, resolving against, and—by grace—submitting to and bowing under it), I have gleaned a few thoughts on how to live Christianly through affliction. These I wish to share with you. But as you allow me to provide several practical hints on this eminently practical subject, please bear in mind that we are always dependent on the sanctification of the Holy Spirit at every juncture for real spiritual benefit under affliction. Without the Spirit's gracious influences, affliction may readily lead us away from rather than toward God.

I wish to focus my suggestions to you around one major theme that, sad to say, took me many years to learn even in small measure: The most effective means for living Christianly in affliction is to *consider Christ*, the fountainhead of all vital Christianity (Heb. 3:1, 12:3). To live Christianly in any sphere or aspect of life necessitates Spirit-worked faith to look to Him, to feast on Him, to depend on Him—yes, to find both our life in Him (on Calvary's cross) and our death in Him (as exalted Lord, to whom we belong).

Consider Christ—that's the crux of the whole matter of affliction. But *how*, you ask? In what ways must I consider Him? In these seven ways:

The Passion of Christ

First and foremost, consider the *passion of Christ*. What greater source of strength for living through and profiting from affliction can be had than frequent meditation on the sufferings of the Lord Jesus? Think much on these things: If Jesus suffered so much on behalf of His people, shouldn't I be able to endure in His strength the daily afflictions I must bear? What are my afflictions compared to His? Besides, was He not the Sufferer *par excellence* while *wholly innocent*, and am I not, at best, a sufferer in His footsteps while *wholly guilty*?

Moreover (and this may be most encouraging), is there one affliction that I must endure that He has not already endured? Is He not the Breaker to go before His flock both in opening all our paths (Mic. 2:13) and in being tempted in all points as we are, yet without sin (Heb. 4:15)? *All* paths, *all* points. Jesus not only knows your affliction, He has identified Himself with it. He has borne it. And He will sanctify it. "There hath no temptation taken you but such as is common to man: but God is faithful, who will not suffer you to be tempted above that ye are able; but will with the temptation also make a way to escape, that ye may be able to bear it" (1 Cor. 10:13).

The Power of Christ

Second, consider the *power of Christ*. Being infinite God-man, Jesus received power *on earth* to bear infinite sufferings on your behalf. And through the merit of these sufferings, He now receives royal power *in heaven* from His Father to rule and strengthen you in your sufferings (Matt. 28:18). Translated practically relative to affliction, His heaven-earth power reads like this: If He desires to weigh you down with affliction—yes, heavy, seemingly staggering affliction— do not be alarmed, but look to Him for strength.

Nor should you be ashamed. When I worked for my father in early youth, I was advised to carry only half-bundles of shingles up the ladder to the roof, but I anticipated the day of greater maturity and strength when my shoulders could bear full, unsplit bundles as my older brothers could. Similarly, afflicted believer, Jesus Christ tailors your afflictions to you. He has promised to fit your afflictions to your shoulders (1 Cor. 10:13). Neither be proud of slender shoulders nor ask for more affliction, but beg for broader shoulders exercised in the weight room of Jesus's providential leadings.

As you and I realize by grace that the bearing of heavy burdens Christianly is testimony of spiritual maturity and honors the Christ whom we love, our groaning under affliction's "heaviness" will be happily bruised. Isn't this the encouragement that Puritan George Downame intended to convey when he aptly penned: "The Lord does not measure out our afflictions according to our faults, but according to our strength, and looks not at what we have deserved, but at what we are able to bear"?

Oh, how great it is when we may look to the strength of Jesus Christ in all our weakness and apprehend our strength in Him (2 Cor. 12:9)! Then the power of the humiliated and exalted Jesus enables us to sing at times (would to God more heartily and frequently!) in "inner prison" depths with Paul and Silas (Acts 16:25)—yes, to rejoice that we are counted worthy to suffer for the name and sake of the Lord Jesus Christ (cf. 2 Corinthians 6 and 12).

The Presence of Christ

Third, consider the *presence of Christ*. He is at no time absent from you, even when your faith lacks active exercise to grasp Him. Even in your thickest hours of Egyptian darkness, He is close beside you. Only of Him can it be declared, "The darkness and the light are both alike to thee" (Ps. 139:12).

How comforting this is! In all your dark afflictions, your High Priest retains you in His high-priestly eye, preserves you in His high-priestly heart, bears you on His high-priestly shoulders, removes you not from the engravings on His high-priestly hands, and never ceases to remember you in His high-priestly intercessions. "He ever liveth to make intercession for them" (Heb. 7:25).

Oh, what tender love! You are never forgotten by Jesus Christ, despite your negligence toward Him. Your unbrotherliness to Christ never unbrothers this precious Elder Brother from you. From His perspective, He ever remains a friend that sticks "closer than a brother" (Prov. 18:24), even when you cannot see or feel it. Even then He is whispering to you in midnight seasons, "What I do thou knowest not now; but thou shalt know hereafter" (John 13:7).

Take heart. The Jesus who never failed you in *yesterday's* afflictions (did He not rather give you extra tokens of His care?) is still present to give you *today's* strength (Matt. 6:34). Just as waves are cut down to melodious whimpers at shore's reality, so He will break down your waves of *tomorrow's* impossibilities *as* (not *before!*) they break in on the beachheads of your life. Wait on your ever-present Savior. He will not let you down. He is the same yesterday, today, and forever (Heb. 13:8).

The Patience and Perseverance of Christ

Fourth, consider the *patience and perseverance of Christ*. As you know, the form of "Chinese torture" that drips one drop of water at regular intervals on the forehead of a prisoner strapped beneath a faucet gets all its power from the duration of the trial, not from the first one or two hundred drops. Insanity is often the end result.

And so matters might end with you, were it not for Jesus. I know very well that what makes affliction so severe for you is its duration. You often wonder if there will ever be an end and, if so, how you will hang on to the end.

But it is Christ who provides you the strength to bear one more drop, take one more step, live one more day, in the severest of tortures and persecutions. He has earned that provision by enduring His sufferings to their end. Gethsemane, Gabbatha, Golgotha—in each place, He confirmed: "Jesus…having loved his own…he loved them unto *the end*" (John 13:1). Blood drop by blood drop, for six long hours He poured out His life. And never flinched. Never answered His mockers a word. Never yielded to their taunts: "*If* thou be the Christ…."

It's through Jesus's strength that you, too, have endured. Look back at the heaviest of your afflictions, how did you bear them through those long nights, months, and years? How did you retain your silence when persecuted? How did you continue on when many challenged, "*If* you are a Christian…"?

Must you not say, "Only through the perseverance of Christ have I by grace persevered"? Oh, the depth of Paul's confession: "By the *grace of God*, I am what I am" (1 Cor. 15:10)!

Despite your fears of perishing at the hands of "Sauls" through sixteen long years of persecutions as David did, you will not perish. Jesus has done too much, persevered too long (He is still persevering in intercession!) to let you slip through His fingers. "I give unto them eternal life; and they shall never perish, neither shall any man pluck them out of my hand" (John 10:28).

Look more to Christ. Trust more in His promise. Rest more in His perseverance, for your perseverance rests in His. Seek grace to imitate His patience under affliction. Your trials may alarm you, but they will not destroy you. Your crosses are God's way to royal crowning (Rev. 7:14).

The Prayers of Christ

Fifth, consider the *prayers of Christ*. How often He set time apart on earth to pray to His Father, especially in hours of need! How continually He prays in heaven for all His church! How effectual all His prayers are!

You, too, ought to make more use of prayer, especially in combating spiritual depression under afflictions. Bring all your needs steadily to your praying High Priest. Be assured He hears your every whisper.

And when you grow drowsy or sloppy in prayer, pray aloud. Or write down your prayers. Or find a quiet place to walk in the fresh air to pray. Just don't stop praying. Conversation with God through Christ is the antidote that wards off spiritual depression in the thick of affliction.

A *prayerless* affliction is like an open sore, ripe for infection; a *prayerful* affliction is like an open sore, ripe for the balm of Gilead—the healing ointment of Jesus's blood. "Pray without ceasing" (1 Thess. 5:17).

The Purposes of Christ

Sixth, consider the *purposes of Christ*. He lived to do His Father's will, to be sanctified through suffering, to merit salvation for His own, to present His church without spot or wrinkle to His Father. In a word, His life was God-centered.

His God-centered goals are numerous for you, too, in sanctified affliction: Sanctified affliction *humbles* you (Deut. 8:2), teaches you what *sin is* (Zeph. 1:12), and causes you to *seek God* (Hos. 5:15). Affliction vacuums away the fuel that feeds your pride. Bell-like, the harder you are hit, the better you sound. You learn more under the rod that strikes you than through the staff that comforts you. You discover the truth of Robert Leighton's words, "Affliction is the diamond dust that heaven polishes its jewels with."

Sanctified affliction serves to keep you in Christ's communion, close by His side—to conform you to Him, making you partaker of His suffering and image, righteousness and holiness (Heb. 12:10–11). Stephen-like, the stones that hit you only knock you closer to your chief cornerstone, Jesus Christ, opening heaven the wider for you. Affliction rubs the rust off your locked heart and opens your heart's gates afresh to your King's presence-chamber. Yes, the rod of affliction is God's pencil for drawing Christ's image more fully on you.

Sanctified affliction serves to wean you from the world and to *cause you to walk by faith*. A dog bites strangers, not homeowners. Perhaps affliction bites you so deeply because you are too little at home with the Word and ways of God and too much at home with the world. "God," says Thomas Watson, "would have the world hang as a loose tooth which, being twitched away, does not much trouble us." In *prosperity*, you often *talk* of living by other-worldly faith, but in *adversity*, you *live* your talk.

The Plan of Christ

Finally, consider the *plan of Christ*. Highly exalted, there is no name like His. At His name, every knee shall bow (Phil. 2:10). The eternal plan lying behind all His affliction was eternal glory.

Eternal glory—not only for Himself but also for you. He returned to His Father differently than He came. He returned with His blood-bought bride, just as He planned in His eternal covenant with His Father. His church, figuratively speaking, ascended into glory with Him, accepted by the Father in the Beloved (Eph. 1:6). Oh, then think more of God's eternal plan for you and your eternal end in glory if you would be more submissive under affliction and learn to praise God in trial!

Your trials in this life are but for *"ten days."* Your life-to-come glory is *forever.* The "ten days" here are preparation time for glory to come. Affliction elevates your soul to heaven (Heb. 11:10); it paves your way for glory: "For our light affliction, which is but for a moment, worketh for us a far more exceeding and eternal weight of glory" (2 Cor. 4:17).

Your rainy days on earth are nearly over. Don't overestimate them. Think more of your coming crown and your eternal communion with God Triune, saints, and angels. "He that rides to be crowned," John Trapp wrote, "will not think much of a rainy day."

> Light after darkness;
> Gain after loss;
> Strength after weakness;
> Crown after cross;
> Sweet after bitter;
> Hope after fears;
> Home after wandering;
> Praise after tears.
>
> Sheaves after sowing;
> Sun after rain;
> Sight after mystery;
> Peace after pain;

> Joy after sorrow;
> Calm after blast;
> Rest after weariness;
> *Sweet rest at last.*

Remember, you are but renting *here;* your personal mansion is reserved *there.* Expect no heaven on earth (apart from spiritual foretastes by means of sanctified affliction!), but trust that "eye hath not seen, nor ear heard, neither have entered into the heart of man, the things which God hath prepared for them that love him" (1 Cor. 2:9).

Be assured: the Shepherd's rod does have honey at the end. Don't despair. Your afflictions are imposed by a *fatherly* hand of *love* in the context of *grace,* not (as you are too prone to think) by a *punitive* hand of *judgment* in the context of *works.*

Conclusion: Keep Your Eye on Christ

Consider Christ—His passion, power, presence, perseverance, prayers, purposes, and plan. Seek grace to live Christianly *today* through and in your afflictions, and you will soon discover with the apostle, "For me to live is *Christ,* and to die is gain" (Phil. 1:21).

"Wait on the LORD: be of good courage, and he shall strengthen thine heart: wait, I say, on the LORD" (Ps. 27:14).

Warmly, in the Master's bonds,
    Pastor Joel Beeke

Chapter 22

Learning from the Puritans
on Being Salt and Light

Ye are the salt of the earth: but if the salt have lost his savour, wherewith shall it be salted? It is thenceforth good for nothing, but to be cast out, and to be trodden under foot of men. Ye are the light of the world. A city that is set on an hill cannot be hid. Neither do men light a candle, and put it under a bushel, but on a candlestick; and it giveth light unto all that are in the house. Let your light so shine before men, that they may see your good works, and glorify your Father which is in heaven.

—Matthew 5:13–16

The world hates God. Therefore, the world despises godly Christians. Unbelievers often regard Christian humility as weakness of mind, Christian repentance as a pathological lack of self-esteem, Christian holiness as hypocrisy, Christian purity as priggish moralism, and Christian righteousness as the seedbed of hatred and intolerance. To the fervent atheist, Bible-believing Christians are not only deluded but dangerous. In our Western societies driven by rhetoric rooted in atheistic secularism (albeit sometimes comfortably padded with a superficial and rationalized shadow of Christianity), believers face increasing opposition and sometimes even hostility. Our brethren in Asia and Africa, however, know what persecution really is.

But before we become alarmed and fearful, we need to realize that this situation is nothing new. Our Lord Jesus said, "Blessed are they which are persecuted for righteousness' sake: for theirs is the kingdom of heaven" (Matt. 5:10). It does not matter whether we live among people who are predominantly secular, Roman Catholic, Islamic, Hindu, Buddhist, or, as Christ did, Jewish; if we live according to the Word of God, we will be persecuted (2 Tim. 3:12–15).

What, then, are Christians to do? Shall we resign all hopes of influencing the people around us? Shall we retreat and hide from the world until the Lord returns? Shall we relent and conform to the world as much as possible in order to win its smile and avoid its ire?

Contrary to these fearful (and unbelieving!) responses, our Lord speaks a word of hope and issues a call to action. First, He repeatedly declares God's blessing upon the godly in what we call the Beatitudes of Matthew 5:3–12. If we by grace repent of our sins and turn back to God with poverty of spirit, hunger for righteousness, and mercy for hurting people, then no matter how the world may persecute us, we will inherit the kingdom of heaven. In Christ, we shall overcome the world. Second, in Matthew 5:13–16, the Lord Jesus teaches us that godly Christians do indeed have a potent influence on the world, for we are "the salt of the earth" and "the light of the world." However, we act as salt and light not by conquering our persecutors through physical force or hateful rhetoric but precisely by being poor in spirit; mourning for our sins; being meek in the face of anger and aggression; hungering and thirsting for righteousness; and being merciful toward those in need, pure in heart, and peacemakers among men—the kind of people whom Christ blesses in His Beatitudes.

How can we be salt and light in our world so that instead of being "trodden under foot" or "hidden under a bushel" (vv. 13, 15), we can resist evil and do good and move unbelievers to glorify God as our Father in heaven? To answer that question, I will draw from the wisdom of the English Puritans.[1] The eighteenth-century evangelist George Whitefield (1714–1770) observed: "Ministers never write or preach so well as when under the cross. The Spirit of Christ and of glory then rests upon them. It was this, no doubt, that made

---

1. For Puritan sources on Matthew 5:13–16, see William Perkins, *A Godly and Learned Exposition of Christ's Sermon on the Mount*, in *The Works of William Perkins, Volume 1*, ed. Stephen J. Yuille (Grand Rapids: Reformation Heritage Books, 2014), 222–42; Matthew Poole, *Annotations upon the Holy Bible* (New York: Robert Carter and Brothers, 1853), 3:21–22; David Dickson, *Matthew*, Geneva Series of Commentaries (Edinburgh: Banner of Truth, 1981), 49–52; Anonymous (Westminster Divines), *Annotations upon All the Books of the Old and New Testament*, 3rd ed. (London: Evan Tyler, 1657); John Trapp, *A Commentary or Exposition upon All the Books of the New Testament*, ed. W. Webster (Grand Rapids: Baker, 1981), 55–58; Jeremiah Burroughs, *The Saints Happiness…Lectures on the Beatitudes* (Ligonier: Soli Deo Gloria, 1992), 242–60; Richard Baxter, "What Light Must Shine in Our Works," in *Puritan Sermons, 1659–1689, Being the Morning Exercises* (Wheaton, Ill.: Richard Owen Roberts, 1981), 2:460–92; also in *The Practical Works of Richard Baxter* (Ligonier: Soli Deo Gloria, 1991), 4:905–920; Matthew Henry, *Matthew Henry's Commentary on the Whole Bible: Complete and Unabridged in One Volume* (Peabody, Mass.: Hendrickson, 1994), 1630–31; Benjamin Keach, *Preaching from the Types and Metaphors of the Bible* (Grand Rapids: Kregel, 1972), 746–47, 758–59; *Exposition of the Parables in the Bible* (Grand Rapids: Kregel, 1974), 52–61; Jonathan Edwards, "A City on a Hill," in *The Works of Jonathan Edwards, Volume 19, Sermons and Discourses, 1734–1738*, ed. M. X. Lesser (New Haven, Conn.: Yale University Press, 2001), 539–40. This chapter is an expansion of an address I gave at the Aber Conference in Wales in August, 2016.

the Puritans of the last century such burning and shining lights."[2] The Puritans lived under a cross of hostility, opposition, and persecution. Undaunted, they persevered, calling on God, serving Christ as Lord, and walking in the light of God's Word. They have many helpful things to say about how Christians should influence the world as salt and light.[3]

Christians Influence the World Like Salt

Matthew 5:13 says, "Ye are the salt of the earth." Christ was praising and commending His disciples. Though the world may insult and persecute them, true Christians are a precious blessing to the world. Benjamin Keach (1640–1704) noted, "A little salt seasons much meat."[4] Therefore, Christ gives us great encouragement here: though Christians be few and the church small, compared to the wicked world, godly people are precious, needed, and influential in a degree far beyond their numbers. As Keach said, "The saints of God, and the faithful ministers of the gospel, are a great blessing to the world."[5]

Notice the wide reach of our influence. As William Perkins (1558–1602) observed, Christ said that we are not just "salt" but "the salt of *the earth*," implying that His disciples have a commission to make disciples not just in Israel but among all nations (Matt. 28:19).[6] Christ said likewise that we are "the light of *the world*" (Matt. 5:14, emphasis added).

Notice also the calling we have to live in the world, though we are not of the world. Salt does no good until it is mixed with the food we eat. Matthew Henry (1662–1714) notes that the disciples "must not be laid on a heap, must not continue always together at Jerusalem, but must be scattered as salt upon the meat, here a grain and there a grain."[7] We must not hide ourselves in a corner; it is God's will that His servants be scattered abroad among the nations that this salt may benefit many.

---

2. George Whitefield, preface to *The Works of that Eminent Servant of Christ Mr. John Bunyan*, 2 vols. (London: W. Johnston and E. and C. Dilly, 1767), 1:iii.

3. It should be noted that some Puritans, such as Perkins, Dickson, Trapp, Burroughs, and Henry, viewed Matthew 5:13–16 as referring primarily to the apostles and ministers of the gospel. See also George Swinnock, *The Christian Man's Calling*, in *The Works of George Swinnock* (Edinburgh: Banner of Truth, 1992), 1:26. In this regard they followed John Calvin, *Commentaries* (Grand Rapids: Baker, 2003), on Matt. 5:13, 14–16. However, others, like Poole, the Westminster *Annotations*, Baxter, Keach, and Edwards, recognized that in the context of Matthew 5 Christ addressed all true disciples and heirs of God's kingdom, both ministers and all Christians.

4. Keach, *Exposition of the Parables*, 53.

5. Keach, *Exposition of the Parables*, 54.

6. Perkins, *Christ's Sermon on the Mount*, in *Works*, 1:222.

7. Henry, *Commentary*, 1630.

Your Spiritual Saltiness Preserves the World
One of the primary uses of salt is to preserve food from decay. John Ley (1583–1662), a Westminster divine, explains the text this way, "I have chosen you to season and preserve those who are corruptible by sin: as salt suffereth not [does not allow] flesh to corrupt."[8] In a world without mechanical refrigeration, salt was necessary to keep meat and fish from rotting.

As the salt of the earth, God's people exert an influence of righteousness and goodness in a world that is corrupted by sin. Matthew Poole (1624–1679) said, "If it were not for the number of sound and painful ministers, and holy and gracious persons, the earth would be but a stinking dunghill [manure pile] of drunkards, unclean persons, thieves, murderers, unrighteous persons, that would be a stench in the nostrils of a pure and holy God."[9]

Keach wrote, "Salt is very profitable; it keeps and preserves meat from putrefying, which would soon stink, corrupt, and perish, was it not for it…. So the godly are most profitable in all the earth. They keep the world from being totally corrupted by evil and pestilent errors and heresy [and] from being spoiled by profaneness and hellish debauchery…. The world would soon grow much worse than it is, were it not for the saints and people of God." Keach pointed to three examples: ten righteous men would have been enough for God to spare Sodom, and God blessed Laban for Jacob's sake and Potiphar for Joseph's sake.[10]

Your Spiritual Saltiness Requires Grace and Holiness
Our Lord posts a warning for us in Matthew 5:13: "But if the salt have lost his savour, wherewith shall it be salted? It is thenceforth good for nothing, but to be cast out, and to be trodden under foot of men." We dare not assume that just because we name the name of Christ that we are the salt of the earth. It may be that instead of preserving the world, we ourselves are found to be corrupt and worthless.

Christ's parable may puzzle us; how can salt lose its saltiness? Our table salt is 97 percent sodium chloride, which is a stable chemical compound. However, the salts obtained from the Dead Sea in Israel consist of only about 15 percent sodium chloride, and the rest is other minerals. So it is possible for moisture to

---

8. Westminster Divines, *Annotations*, on Matthew 5:13. On the attribution of the Westminster *Annotations* on the Gospels to John Ley, see Richard A. Muller, *Post-Reformation Reformed Dogmatics: The Rise and Development of Reformed Orthodoxy, ca. 1520–ca. 1725* (Grand Rapids: Baker Academic, 2003), 2:91n120.

9. Poole, *Annotations*, 3:21–22.

10. Keach, *Types and Metaphors*, 746.

leach away the sodium chloride from a block of so-called "salt" and leave behind minerals that are more suitable for paving roads than seasoning food.[11]

Christ challenges us, asking, Are you truly salty? Or has the world leached away the Word from your heart? If we lack the marks of saving grace that Christ outlines in the Beatitudes, we have no "saltiness" and are "good for nothing." Henry said, "A wicked man is the worst of creatures; a wicked Christian is the worst of men; and a wicked minister is the worst of Christians."[12]

For example, perhaps you claim to be a Christian, but are you meek, merciful, and a peacemaker? Or are you proud, quick to anger, and divisive in the church? Mark reports Christ as saying, "Salt is good: but if the salt have lost his saltness, wherewith will ye season it? Have salt in yourselves, and have peace one with another" (Mark 9:50). The grace that saves us is what gives us our "saltiness," making us a blessing in the church and enabling us to live and work harmoniously with our fellow Christians.

Perhaps you call yourself a Christian, but you bend and bow as the winds of culture blow. You do not hunger and thirst for righteousness but long just to fit in, and so you change your colors like a chameleon. Saltiness requires us to obey God no matter what other people may think. Poole said, "In our Christian course we are not to trouble ourselves with what men say of us, and do unto us, but only to attend to our duty of holiness, and an exemplary life."[13]

Your Spiritual Saltiness Comes from God's Word

There is a connection between saltiness and wisdom. As Jeremiah Burroughs (c. 1600–1646) relates, an ancient Roman writer said that the Greeks were "the salt of the nations" on account of their wisdom.[14] The Greek verb (*mōrainein*) in Matthew 5:13 translated as "to lose savour" or taste can also be translated "to become foolish."[15] Thus we lose our saltiness when we turn away from the wisdom of God's Word. The apostle Paul also makes this connection when he writes in Colossians 4:5–6, "Walk in wisdom toward them that are without,

---

11. *Holman Bible Dictionary* (Nashville: Holman, 1991), 970; Carson, "Matthew," *Expositor's Bible Commentary*, 8:138. We should not take the parable of salt losing its flavor to imply that true Christians can totally and finally fall away unto damnation. "Where there is true grace in the heart, that will never be lost; but where many truths and gifts come by the gospel, they may be lost." Burroughs, *The Saints' Happiness*, 247.

12. Henry, *Commentary*, 1631.

13. Poole, *Annotations*, 3:21.

14. Burroughs, *The Saints' Happiness*, 243. The statement is attributed to the Roman historian Livy (fl. 25 B.C.).

15. Westminster Divines, *Annotations*, on Matthew 5:13.

redeeming the time. Let your speech be always with grace, seasoned with salt, that ye may know how ye ought to answer every man."

Therefore, if you want to be salty, you must follow the Bible, which makes the simple wise. This is why our saltiness is such a benefit to the world: it savors of God's wisdom. Keach said, "The godly Christian by his wisdom seasons the minds of good men."[16] Salt adds a good flavor to food so that it is desirable and delightful. Job 6:6 says, "Can that which is unsavoury be eaten without salt? Or is there any taste in the white of an egg?" Keach notes that by the salt of a good life, people get a taste of the goodness of God's Word.[17]

But, salt can irritate, even cause pain. John Trapp (1601–1669) said that salt has a "sharpness" to its flavor, and reminded us, "Ye are salt, not honey."[18] We must be willing to stand for the truths that our culture finds most offensive. Only then can our saltiness cleanse away the infection of sin as a spiritual anti-septic (cf. Ezek. 16:4). Perkins noted that salt is "applied to raw flesh, or fresh wounds." In the same way, the law and gospel must be applied to "men's hearts and consciences" so that they feel God's curse against sin, renounce themselves, cry out for salvation, and be healed by grace.[19]

Has the grace of Jesus Christ made you the salt of the earth? As salt, true Christians exercise a powerful influence to hold back moral decay and divine judgment. However, they also provoke strong reactions. If you want to be the salt of the earth, you must be different from the world, not in a freakish or bizarre way, but different because Christ is your King.

Christians Influence the World Like Light

The Lord Jesus Christ also says to His followers, "Ye are the light of the world" (Matt. 5:14). This is all the more striking when we remember that in the previous chapter, Matthew quotes the prophet Isaiah: "The people which sat in darkness saw great light; and to them which sat in the region and shadow of death light is sprung up" (Matt. 4:16; cf. Isa. 9:2). Isaiah saw Christ as a great Light rising in the dark land of Galilee (Isa. 9:1, 6–7). Malachi saw Him as "the Sun of righteousness" arising "with healing in his wings" (Mal. 4:2). Christ Himself says, "I am the light of the world" (John 8:12). Here in Matthew 5, the Lord Jesus says the same thing about His disciples: "Ye are the light of the world."

As Christ dwells in them by His Word and Holy Spirit, Christians reflect and radiate the light of Christ into the world. Ley wrote that we are the light of

---

16. Keach, *Types and Metaphors*, 746.
17. Keach, *Types and Metaphors*, 747.
18. Trapp, *Commentary*, 56.
19. Perkins, *Christ's Sermon on the Mount*, in *Works*, 1:222–23.

the world, "not originally, like the sun, as Christ is (John 1:8–9), but by participation, as the moon…so are ministers (Rev. 1:20; John 5:35), as also are other
Christians (1 Thess. 5:5; Phil. 2:15)."[20] We are "light in the Lord," and through
us, His light penetrates the darkness (Eph. 5:8, 13).

Your Spiritual Light Imparts Knowledge, Understanding, and Joy
Light reveals truth, for with light comes sight—if there are eyes to see. Keach
said, "Light discovers and makes manifest the nature of things to men…. So
the saints of God, by their holy life and doctrine, reveal and make manifest, not
only the works of darkness, but also the excellency of Christ, grace, and divine
things to men."[21]

Just as darkness can symbolize sadness and fear (Isa. 5:30; 8:22), so light
refers to joy and freedom. We read in Ecclesiastes 11:7, "Truly the light is sweet,
and a pleasant thing it is for the eyes to behold the sun." In Psalm 97:11, "light"
is parallel to "gladness." Keach observed, "The word or gospel of Jesus Christ is
very pleasant, and a delightful thing."[22] He also said, "It is a great blessing to
enjoy the company of God's people, to dwell among such whose conversations
shine."[23] "Conversation" here means "manner of life," as it does in the KJV.

Here we see something of the paradox of being salt and light. Both salt and
light can irritate, like salt in a wound or light glaring into the eyes. However, salt
and light also give flavor and joy to life. Are you willing to live that paradox? The
world will not know what to make of you. At times they will praise you; then
they will turn around and attack you.

The key to living this paradox is to remember that you are not salt and
light in yourself, nor according to the world's judgment of you, but only as you
follow the unchangeable Word of God. Never think that you can be spiritual
salt and light apart from the truth of God's Word and the grace of Jesus Christ.
You may sting and irritate, but you will not be a force for good in the world. You
may produce a lot of heat but impart no light. A good flame produces both heat
and illumination; Poole said that we are to be "not only a burning light, burning
with love to God, and zeal for God, and love to and zeal for the souls of others;

---

20. Westminster Divines, *Annotations*, on Matthew 5:13. The ellipsis is "and the stars"; in the
Puritan era the stars included the planets or "wandering stars," as the ancients called them, which
reflected the light of the sun.

21. Keach, *Types and Metaphors*, 758.

22. Keach, *Types and Metaphors*, 527.

23. Keach, *Types and Metaphors*, 758.

but also a shining light, communicating his light to others, both by instruction and a holy conversation."[24]

Your Spiritual Light Should Shine in the Visible Church

Christ observes that "a city that is set on an hill cannot be hid" (Matt. 5:14). Jerusalem was built on Mount Zion, "beautiful for situation, the joy of the whole earth" (Ps. 48:2). The old Rabbis used to say, "He who has not seen Jerusalem in its splendor, has never seen a beautiful city in his life."[25] Christ's disciples marveled at the beauty of the temple buildings (Matt. 24:1). Here Christ says that His church is also a city set on a hill.

Our Lord's point is that God has put us on display for all the world to see. He placards us for His own glory. We are His marketing plan. Ley wrote that, as dwellers in this city on a hill, "you must shew forth good example to others, far and near.... Your lives will be looked on, and scanned by all men; therefore see they be good."[26] Poole said, "The church is often called the city of God.... It is as much as if our Saviour should have said, You had need be holy, for your conversation cannot be hid, any more than a city can that is built upon a hill, which is obvious to every eye. All men's eyes will be upon you."[27]

Perhaps you don't like that. You'd rather that no one notices you. However, it cannot be avoided; every Christian is a billboard for Jesus Christ. Or, as Paul says, we are "epistles of commendation...known and read of all men" (2 Cor. 3:2–3). As a caution to Christians, Henry warns us: "All their neighbours have an eye upon them. Some admire them, commend them, rejoice in them, and study to imitate them; others envy them, hate them, censure them, and study to blast them."[28] Whether people love you or hate you, they will begin to watch you closely as soon as they hear that you profess Christ as your Lord and Savior.

You are not a light alone, however, but as a member of the church. As Jonathon Edwards (1703–1758) recognized, a city on a hill is not the image of an individual person but a "professing society" or group of Christians living in fellowship together.[29] As he exhorted those in his church who professed conversion to Christ, the world was now waiting to see "what a good spirit there appears amongst us; how ready we are to [do] good works; how ready to deny

---

24. Poole, *Annotations*, 3:22.

25. Sukkah 51b, *Babylonian Talmud*, http://www.sefaria.org/Sukkah.51b?lang=en, accessed June 28, 2016.

26. Westminster Divines, *Annotations*, on Matthew 5:14.

27. Poole, *Annotations*, 3:22.

28. Henry, *Commentary*, 1631.

29. Edwards, "A City on a Hill," in *Works*, 19:540.

ourselves; how forward to promote any good design; how charitable, and how public-spirited we be; how ready to lay out our substance for the poor, or for the worship of God, and the like."[30]

Are you a member of a biblical, Christian church? If so, then when outsiders look at you and your church, what do they see? Our Lord said in John 13:35, "By this shall all men know that ye are my disciples, if ye have love one to another." Richard Baxter (1615–1691) wrote that our light shines when our churches are "well-ordered" under God's word, confessing a common faith and promoting relationships of unity and harmony.[31] "Behold, how good and how pleasant it is for brethren to dwell together in unity!" (Ps. 133:1).

Your Spiritual Light Must Be Seen in Your Works

Christ said, "Neither do men light a candle, and put it under a bushel, but on a candlestick; and it giveth light unto all that are in the house. Let your light so shine before men, that they may see your good works" (Matt. 5:15–16). It would be ridiculous to turn on a lamp and then hide it, when its very purpose is to illuminate the room.

Ley wrote, "God intends that his graces given to his ministers or people, should be used for the good of others and not kept for their own good only."[32] Keach said, "Though the saints should do nothing through vain glory, i.e. to be seen of men; yet their good works, and holy walkings should be so done, that others should see them."[33]

God's glory becomes visible in the good works of His children. Baxter quoted Tertullian: "We do not talk great things, but live them."[34] Examine yourself: Is your Christianity mostly talk, or is it the power of God producing good works? As a Christian, are you a great talker or a great doer? Henry wrote, "Those about us must not only *hear* our good words, but *see* our good works; that they may be convinced that religion is more than a bare name, and that we do not only make a profession of it, but abide under the power of it."[35] Talk without action is like much wind without rain—barren, unfruitful, and likely to cause more harm than good.

---

30. Edwards, "A City on a Hill," in *Works*, 19:557.
31. Baxter, "What Light Must Shine," in *Puritan Sermons*, 2:485–88.
32. Westminster Divines, *Annotations*, on Matthew 5:15.
33. Keach, *Types and Metaphors*, 758.
34. "*Non magna loquimur sed vivimus.*" Baxter, "What Light Must Shine," in *Puritan Sermons*, 2:461.
35. Henry, *Commentary*, 1631, emphasis original.

Good works are essential to letting our light shine, but we are not at liberty to do whatever works we please and think that they illuminate the world. Perkins said, "A good work, is a work commanded of God, and done by a man regenerate in faith, for the glory of God in man's good."[36] Here, then, is a litmus test to see if our works truly shine: To be a good work, it must follow the precepts and principles of the Bible; arise from a new, believing heart given by the Holy Spirit; and aim at the good of others so that God is honored.

The Greek word translated "good" (*kalos*) in Matthew 5:16 does not emphasize religion so much as works that are beautiful, useful, helpful, profitable, and productive for men. Baxter said, "Christ here intendeth, that we must abound especially in those good works which the world is capable of knowing to be good, and not only in those which none but Christians themselves approve."[37]

Good works especially means works of practical love. Baxter said, "The dominion of love in the hearts of Christians, appearing in all the course of their lives, doth much glorify God and their religion."[38] He exclaimed, "O, could we learn of the Lord of love, and Him who calleth himself Love itself, to love our enemies, to bless them that curse us, and to do good to the evil, and pray for them that hurt and persecute us, we should not only prove that we are genuine Christians, the children of our heavenly Father (Matt. 5:44, 45), but should heap coals of fire on our enemies' heads, and melt them into compassion and some remorse, if not into a holy love."[39]

Love means not only showing kindness but acting with justice and fairness. George Swinnock (*c.* 1627–1673) said, "True godliness payeth its dues to men, as well as its duty to God.... True holiness will provide things honest, not only in the sight of God, but also in the sight of men."[40] Swinnock observed that Moses came down from Mount Sinai with two tablets in his hands, and the Christian who enjoys communion with God shows it by his concern for both religion toward God and righteousness toward men.[41]

Swinnock also said that we must be careful that our conduct be consistently "righteous, meek, and courteous."[42] Righteous conduct shows a heart to "deal with men as one that in all hath to do with God." In our buying, selling,

---

36. Perkins, *Christ's Sermon on the Mount*, in *Works*, 1:233. Cf. "No good work can be done except [1.] By a child of God [2.] In obedience to his God and Father's command [3.] For the good of men and [4.] For the glory of God." Dickson, *Matthew*, 52.

37. Baxter, "What Light Must Shine," in *Puritan Sermons*, 2:462.

38. Baxter, "What Light Must Shine," in *Puritan Sermons*, 2:469.

39. Baxter, "What Light Must Shine," in *Puritan Sermons*, 2:470.

40. Swinnock, *The Christian Man's Calling*, in *Works*, 2:187–88.

41. Swinnock, *The Christian Man's Calling*, in *Works*, 2:189.

42. Swinnock, *The Christian Man's Calling*, in *Works*, 2:194.

and trading, we must have an eye to what is fair and honest, not seeking to take advantage of people because of their ignorance or desperate situation. We must pay what we promised and promise what is true—not a misrepresentation of the quality or quantity of our product.[43] Baxter said, "He that will glorify his religion and God before men, must be *strictly just in all his dealings*—just in governing, just in trading and bargaining…just in performing all his promises, and in giving every man his right."[44] Swinnock wrote, "In all thy contracts, purchases, and sales, cast an eye upon that golden rule, mentioned by our Saviour, 'Therefore all things whatsoever ye would that men should do to you, do ye even so to them: for this is the law and the prophets' (Matt. 7:12)."[45]

This shows us our duty as Christians, for professing Christians fail to shine forth as light but prove to be stumbling blocks in the darkness, if, as Keach said,

+ They "fail in their morals, i.e., are not just in their dealings between man and man."

+ "They are like the world, and none can discern any great difference between them and others."

+ "They are overcome with scandalous sins, viz., are proud, covetous, backbiters, tattlers, drunkards, etc."[46]

Swinnock also said that Christians must be "courteous" and not "rugged" with people. He counseled, "He that pleaseth all men in all things (indifferent) is the likeliest to save some (1 Cor. 10:33).… We may gain their love by soft words.… Courtesy, like the loadstone [magnet], will draw even iron to it."[47] Courtesy goes with meekness: "Courtesy is a good servant, to wait upon meekness as its master," he said. "The purest gold is soonest melted, and they are usually the best blades that will bend well. The lion of Judah for courage, was a lamb for condescension. The saint must learn of his Saviour to be meek and lowly of heart.… The greatest conquest is to overcome ourselves, and the vilest bondage to be our own slaves (Prov. 16:32)."[48]

Your Spiritual Light Moves People to Glorify God

Christ said that the purpose of letting our light shine in good works is that that they may "glorify your Father which is in heaven" (Matt. 5:16). Ley said, "All

---

43. Swinnock, *The Christian Man's Calling*, in *Works*, 2:194–200.
44. Baxter, "What Light Must Shine," in *Puritan Sermons*, 2:473, emphasis original.
45. Swinnock, *The Christian Man's Calling*, in *Works*, 2:201.
46. Keach, *Types and Metaphors*, 759.
47. Swinnock, *The Christian Man's Calling*, in *Works*, 2:209.
48. Swinnock, *The Christian Man's Calling*, in *Works*, 2:211, 213.

good children seek their fathers' honour,"[49] and so must we, if we are children of God. Poole said, "You are not in your good actions to aim at yourselves, to be seen of men, as Matthew 6:1, nor merely at doing good to others;...but having a primary and principal respect to the glorifying of your Father; for, 'Herein is my Father glorified, if ye bear much fruit' (John 15:8)."[50]

Baxter wrote, "God is not glorified by our adding to him, but by our receiving from him: not by our making him greater, or better, or happier than he is, but by owning him, loving him, and declaring him as he is, that we and others may thereby be wise, and good, and happy. He is his own glory and ours."[51] In order to rightly glorify Him, Baxter concludes,

1. We must so live, that men may see that indeed we take not ourselves to be our own, but God to be our absolute Owner; and that it is not ourselves, but he, that must of right dispose both of us and ours; and that we willingly stand to his disposal. "Ye are not your own" (1 Cor. 6:19).

2. We must so live as may declare that we are not lawless, nor the mere servants of men, but the resolved subjects of God, the Sovereign King of all; and that really we are ruled by his laws and will, and not by our own lusts or wills, nor by the wills of any, but as under him; and that we fear not any hurt to the flesh, or them that can but kill the body, in comparison of that "one Lawgiver" and Judge "who is able to save or to destroy" for ever (Luke 12:4; James 4:12; 1 Cor. 7:23)....

3. We must so live as may declare that God is our grand Benefactor, from whom we have all the good that ever we received, and from whom we hope for all that ever we shall possess; and that he is infinitely good... and that to know him, and love him, and glorify him for ever, is the ultimate end and happiness of man (Pss. 4:7, 8; 63:3; 73:25, 26, 28; Phil. 3:7, 8; Matt. 6:33; 1 Peter 1:5–9; 2 Cor. 5:1).[52]

Why do our good works move men to praise God? You might think that good works can only win praise for us, since we do them. However, Christ assumed here that all our good works come from the grace that God planted in us (Matt. 15:13). Poole said that it is hard to understand how our good works result in men giving glory to God, "if they proceed from mere power and liberty of our own wills, not from his special efficacious grace."[53] As the apostle Paul

---

49. Westminster Divines, *Annotations*, on Matthew 5:16.
50. Poole, *Annotations*, 3:22.
51. Baxter, "What Light Must Shine," in *Puritan Sermons*, 2:462.
52. Baxter, "What Light Must Shine," in *Puritan Sermons*, 2:464.
53. Poole, *Annotations*, 3:22

explained by divine inspiration, "For we are his workmanship, created in Christ Jesus unto good works, which God hath before ordained that we should walk in them" (Eph. 2:10). Henry rightly concluded, "Let them see your good works, that they may see the power of God's grace in you, and may thank him for it, and give him the glory of it, who has given such power unto men."[54]

Your good works are a crucial complement to the preaching of the word. Baxter said, "The good works or lives of Christians is a great means ordained by Christ for the convincing of sinners, and the glorifying of God in the world. Preaching doeth much, but it is not appointed to do all."[55] Henry said, "Let them see your good works, that they may be convinced of the truth and excellency of the Christian religion…. The holy, regular, and exemplary conversation of the saints, may do much towards the conversion of sinners."[56]

What a great responsibility we bear when we take the name of Christian! Baxter reminded us, "The world will judge of the scriptures by your lives, and of religion by your lives, and of Christ himself by your lives!"[57] Who is adequate for these things? Yet we remember that what the world needs to see in us is not perfect people who never did anything wrong but sinners who have been saved by grace, are being saved by grace, and will be saved by grace. They need to see us as pilgrims on the road to the Celestial City, who stumble and occasionally get side-tracked on a by-path, but who press forward until we reach the kingdom of heaven. If we persevere in doing good even under persecution, we will overcome evil with good.

Practical Applications for Us Today
What have we learned about being the salt of the earth and the light of the world, as Christians and as Christ's church on earth? Here are four concluding lessons:

1. *Know what your position is, what your resources are, and where your strength lies.* You must be in Christ by faith and under Him as Lord. The gospel must be "the power of God unto salvation" in your hearts and lives, as Christ works in you by His Word and Holy Spirit. The Word of God must be your rule of faith and life. You must have grace to be gracious. You must have light to be light. Your strength lies in God! "The God of Israel is He that giveth strength unto his people" (Ps. 68:35). Draw strength from Him by the continuous exercise

---

54. Henry, *Commentary*, 1631.
55. Baxter, "What Light Must Shine," in *Puritan Sermons*, 2:490.
56. Henry, *Commentary*, 1631.
57. Baxter, "What Light Must Shine," in *Puritan Sermons*, 2:490.

of faith laboring in prayer: "Trust in him at all times; ye people, pour out your hearts before him" (Ps. 62:8).

2. *Beware, lest your salt lose its savor and the light be hidden under a bushel.* Great pressures are exerted by the world to entice, cow, or coerce us into a situation of compromise with the man-centered values and ways and ends of the world. Our power to influence the world for good lies in our resolve to be faithful to our God and our Savior at all costs. We must fear God and not men. We must obey God and not men. We must be willing to be hated of all men for Christ's sake.

Nor can we bring the light of God's Word to bear on the life of the world if we retreat into a safe place of our own where we hide from the world and preach only to ourselves. The church is not to be a monastic cloister or an underground bunker. Whether we like it or not, Christ has set His city on a hill, to be seen of all men. He bids us lift up the gospel as a candle put on a candlestick, to give light to all the world. We cannot fulfill our mission if we hide ourselves away and talk only to ourselves.

3. *Let your vision for Christian life and witness be as high and holy, as loving and gracious, and as wide and open-handed as the gospel itself.* We cannot call men to faith in Christ if we do not walk by faith in Him. We cannot call men to repentance if we are hardhearted and impenitent. We cannot commend the grace of God to others if we are ungracious and unforgiving in our dealings with them. We cannot proclaim the love of Christ for sinners if we are unloving toward one another. We cannot expect the world to be better than we are or have higher standards than we have set for ourselves as Christians.

4. *The Word preached must become the Word practiced.* Your faith in Christ and love for God must be translated into visible terms. Men must see your good works. These works must be done in obedience to God's Word, out of faith in Him; and done to His glory, out of love for Him. Those who see them will see God's grace at work in you and say, "Blessed be the God whom these Christians serve! He is great and good, and mighty to save!" Many will be gained to Christ by your godly conversation; others will at least be put to shame by their own evil deeds. "The righteous shall see it, and rejoice: and all iniquity shall stop her mouth" (Ps. 107:42).

Chapter 23

Puritans on Marital Love

Edward Taylor (*c.* 1642–1729), a pastor, physician, and poet of Puritan New England, wrote, "A curious knot God made in Paradise.... It was the true-love knot, more sweet than spice."[1] The writings of the Puritans are sprinkled with declarations of the sweetness of marital love.[2] They delighted in the love of God

---

1. Edward Taylor, "Upon Wedlock, and Death of Children," in *The Poems of Edward Taylor*, ed. Donald E. Stanford, abridged ed. (New Haven, Conn.: Yale University Press, 1963), 344. "Sweet" and "sweetness" are used by the Puritans to describe "a pleasant or gratifying experience, possession or state; something that delights or deeply satisfies" (Webster's Dictionary). Portions of this chapter are adapted from Joel R. Beeke, *Living for God's Glory: An Introduction to Calvinism* (Orlando: Reformation Trust, 2008); Joel R. Beeke and James A. LaBelle, *Living for God's Glory in Marriage* (Grand Rapids: Reformation Heritage Books, 2016). This chapter is a slightly expanded version of an address I gave at the Evangelical Theological Society in Atlanta in November, 2015.

2. For Puritan writings on marriage, see Isaac Ambrose, *The Practice of Sanctification*, in *Works of Isaac Ambrose* (London: Thomas Tegg, 1829), 130–33; Richard Baxter, *A Christian Directory*, Part II: Christian Economics, chapters 1–9, in *The Practical Works of Richard Baxter* (Morgan, Pa.: Soli Deo Gloria, 1996), 1:394–449; *The Poor Man's Family Book*, in *The Practical Works*, 4:165–289; Paul Bayne, *An Entire Commentary upon the Whole Epistle of St. Paul to the Ephesians* (Edinburgh: James Nichol, 1866), 337–54; Robert Bolton, *General Directions for a Comfortable Walking with God* (Morgan, Pa.: Soli Deo Gloria, 1995), 262–81; Thomas Boston, "Duties of Husband and Wife; Sermon XXIII," in *The Works of Thomas Boston*, ed. Samuel M'Millan (Wheaton, Ill: Richard Owen Roberts, 1980), 4:209–18; John Bunyan, *Christian Behaviour*, in *The Works of John Bunyan*, ed. George Offor (1854; repr., Edinburgh: Banner of Truth, 1854), 2:557–58, 560–62; John Cotton, *A Meet Help: Or, A Wedding Sermon* (Boston: B. Green & J. Allen, 1699); John Dod and Robert Cleaver, *A Godly Form of Household Government* (London: Thomas Man, 1612); Thomas Doolittle, "How May the Duty of Daily Family Prayer be Best Managed for the Spiritual Benefit of Every One in the Family?" in *Puritan Sermons, 1659–1689* (Wheaton, Ill: Richard Owen Roberts, 1981), 2:194–272; Thomas Gataker, "A Marriage Prayer," "A Good Wife God's Gift," "A Wife in Deed," and "Marriage Duties," in *Certain Sermons* (London: John Haviland, 1637), 2:116–208; William Gouge, *Of Domestical Duties* (Pensacola: Puritan Reprints, 2006); Richard Greenham, "A Treatise of a Contract before Marriage," in *The Works of the Reverend and Faithfull Servant of Jesus Christ M. Richard Greenham*, ed. H. H. (1599; facsimile repr., Amsterdam: Theatrum Orbis Terrarum, 1973), 288–99; George Hamond, *The Case for Family Worship* (Orlando: Soli Deo Gloria, 2005); Matthew Henry, "A Church in the House," in *Complete Works of Matthew Henry* (Grand Rapids: Baker, 1978), 1:248–67; William Perkins, "Christian Oeconomy," in *The Work of William Perkins*, ed. Ian Breward

and in every form of love commanded by God among mankind. In particular, they rejoiced in the love shared by husband and wife and called married couples to love each other romantically, wholeheartedly, and perseveringly.

This may come as a shock to twenty-first-century minds; not many people today would use "Puritan" and "love" in the same sentence. Though evangelicals have become much more aware of the positive heritage of the Puritans, the common cultural perception of the Puritans remains negative, a perception informed only by what the Puritans opposed. One prominent dictionary defines the noun "Puritan" first as "a member of a Protestant group in England and New England in the sixteenth and seventeenth centuries that opposed many customs of the Church of England," and second, "a person who follows strict moral rules and who believes that pleasure is wrong."[3] We are quick to overlook that fact that perhaps the most well-known sentence ever written by the Puritans is "Man's chief end is to glorify God, and to *enjoy* him forever."[4]

The Puritan view of marital love was overwhelmingly positive because it was informed by the Bible, the written word of the God who instituted marriage at the time of our creation and regulated it by His commandments. As J. I. Packer says, "They went to Genesis for its institution, to Ephesians for its full meaning, to Leviticus for its hygiene, to Proverbs for its management, to several New Testament books for its ethic, and to Esther, Ruth and the Song of Songs for illustrations and exhibitions of the ideal."[5] They let the practices, duties, and ethics of marriage flow out of Scripture.

All duties of a married couple were to be performed devotedly, kindly, and cheerfully.[6] In particular, the Puritans emphasized that love was the mutual

---

(Appleford, England: Sutton Courtenay, 1970), 416–39; John Robinson, *New Essays, Or Observations Divine and Moral*, in *The Works of John Robinson*, ed. Robert Ashton (London: John Snow, 1851), 1:236–42; Daniel Rogers, *Matrimonial Honour* (1642; repr., Warrenton, Va.: Edification, 2010); Henry Scudder, *The Godly Man's Choice* (London: Matthew Simmons for Henry Overton, 1644); William Secker, "The Wedding Ring, A Sermon," printed with *The Nonsuch Professor in His Meridian Splendour; Or, The Singular Actions of Sanctified Christians*, ed. Matthew Wilks (repr., Harrisonburg, Va.: Sprinkle, 1997), 245–69; Henry Smith, "A Preparative to Marriage," in *The Works of Henry Smith* (Stoke-on-Trent, England: Tentmaker, 2002), 1:5–40; Richard Steele, "What Are the Duties of Husbands and Wives towards Each Other?" in *Puritan Sermons, 1659–1689*, 2:272–303; William Whately, *A Bride-Bush or A Wedding Sermon* (Norwood, N.J.: Walter J. Johnson, 1975); *A Care-Cloth or the Cumbers and Troubles of Marriage* (Norwood, N.J.: Walter J. Johnson, 1975).

    3. "Puritan," *Merriam-Webster Dictionary*, http://www.merriam-webster.com/dictionary/puritan, accessed October 10, 2015.

    4. Westminster Shorter Catechism, Q. 1, in *The Confession of Faith, and the Larger and Shorter Catechisme* (London: Company of Stationers, 1651), 157, emphasis added.

    5. Packer, *A Quest for Godliness*, 263.

    6. Gouge, *Of Domestical Duties*, 85.

duty of both husband and wife,[7] indeed, the foundational duty of marriage. William Gouge (1575–1653) wrote, "A loving mutual affection must pass betwixt husband and wife, or else no duty will be well performed: this is the ground of all the rest."[8] "As for love," said William Whately (1583–1639), who wrote two books on marriage, "it is the life, the soul of marriage, without which it is no more itself, than a carcass is a man; yea, it is uncomfortable, miserable, and a living death." Whately described marital love as "the king of the heart," so that when it prevails, marriage is "a pleasing combination of two persons into one home, one purse, one heart, and one flesh."[9]

Whately observed, "Love is the life and soul of marriage, without which it differs as much from itself, as a rotten apple from a sound [one] and as a carcass from a living body; yea, verily it is a most miserable and uncomfortable society, and no better than a very living death."[10] Likewise, Henry Smith (1560–1591) declared, "Unless there be a joining of heart and a knitting of affections together, it is not marriage in deed, but in show and name, and they shall dwell in a house like two poisons in a stomach, and one shall ever be sick of another."[11] "Without the union of hearts," George Swinnock (c. 1627–1673) wrote, "the union of bodies will be no benefit."[12] William Secker (d. c. 1681) quipped, "Two joined together without love, are but two tied together to make one another miserable."[13] Henry Scudder (c. 1585–1652) therefore advised those who were married to "love each other as [their] own souls with a Christian, pure, tender, abundant, natural, and matrimonial love."[14] In order to survey Puritan teachings on marital love, we will consider three basic emphases: love must be spiritual, superlative, and sexual.

Marital Love Must Be Spiritual
Love must be rooted in the experience of being equally yoked together spiritually as believers. It must be built with Christ as the foundation and cemented with mutual use of the means of grace. Richard Baxter (1615–1691) said that husbands and wives have the responsibility "especially to be helpers of each other's salvation: to stir up each other to faith, love, and obedience, and good works:

---

7. For an excellent summary by Richard Baxter on the mutual duties of husband and wife, see Packer, *A Quest for Godliness*, 263.

8. Gouge, *Of Domestical Duties*, 163.

9. Whately, *A Bride-Bush*, 7.

10. Whately, *A Bride-Bush*, 31.

11. Smith, *Works*, 1:22.

12. Swinnock, *Works*, 1:472.

13. Secker, "The Wedding Ring, A Sermon," 263.

14. Scudder, *The Godly Man's Choice*, 72.

to warn and help each other against sin, and all temptations: to join in God's worship in the family, and in private: to prepare each other for the approach of death, and comfort each other in the hopes of life eternal."[15] Isaac Ambrose (1604–1664) wrote that they must pray for and with each other.[16]

Although marriage is a universal institution ordained by God for the whole human race regardless of whether they are saved or not, marriage fulfills its deepest purpose and achieves its greatest stability only when grounded in Christian faith and the fear of God. If built on the sandy foundation of physical beauty or exceptional gifts and talents, it can easily be "blown down by some storm," Whately said, adding that "spiritual love, that looks upon God, rests upon his will, yields to his commandment, and resolves to obey it, cannot change itself, because the cause thereof is unchangeable."[17]

Marital love should be profoundly spiritual because, as Gouge observed, Christian marriage should conform to the pattern of Christ and His church. As Christ loves His church, so the husband must love his wife—love her absolutely (Eph. 5:25), purposefully (v. 26), realistically (v. 27), and sacrificially (vv. 28–29). He must exercise a "true, free, pure, exceeding, constant love" to his wife, nourishing and cherishing her as Christ does His gathered people (v. 29).[18] In a wedding sermon, Richard Greenham (c. 1542–1594) charged the groom:

> You, brother, must learn hereby so to love your wife, as Christ Jesus loved His spouse His church. That is to say, even as our Savior Christ is very patient towards it, and by little and little purges, washes, and cleanses away the corruption of it, so must you in like manner in all wisdom use the means (and with a patient mind wait for the amendment of any thing that you shall find to be amiss in your wife) that the graces of God's spirit may daily increase in her. Therefore, I charge you in the sight of God and his angels, and as you will answer unto me and the parents of this my sister, before the judgment seat of Christ, that as you receive her a virgin from her parents, so you neglect no duty whereby her salvation may be furthered, that you may present her pure and blameless, as much as in you lies, unto Jesus Christ when He shall call you to account.[19]

---

15. Baxter, *Practical Works*, 4:234.
16. Ambrose, *Works*, 130.
17. Whately, *A Bride-Bush*, 7.
18. Gouge, *Of Domestical Duties*, 31.
19. Greenham, *Works*, 291–92.

Such Christlike love, said Gouge, will serve "as sugar to sweeten the duties of authority which appertain to a husband," and thereby enable his loving wife to submit more easily to him.[20]

Likewise, the wife's loving submission to her husband is a limited expression of her absolute submission to the Lord Jesus Christ. Robert Bolton (1572–1631) wrote that a wife "ought, like a true [mirror], faithfully to represent and return to her husband's heart, with a sweet and pleasing pliableness, the exact lineaments and proportions of all his honest desires and demands, and that without discontent, thwarting, or sourness. For her subjection in this kind should be as to Christ, sincere, hearty, and free."[21] But conscientious wives must also remember, wrote Ambrose, "that they have a husband in heaven, as well as on earth, betwixt whom there is a greater difference than between heaven and earth; and therefore in case they bid contrary things, they must prefer God before men, Christ before all men."[22]

The love of both husband and wife must be ruled and energized by the fear of the Lord. Whately observed,

> This is the fountain of most disorders in most families: where God is not feared, what can abound but profaneness and impiety in…the whole household; where people are not taught the knowledge and fear of God, how should they know or fear Him? Where these graces are absent, how should anything be found but rudeness, stubbornness, and undutifulness? Now therefore…let all husbands and wives that fear God be of one mind in the Lord, and let them not fail…[to establish] the exercises of religion in their houses.[23]

Mutual love is preserved and increased by religious exercises. Time spent together with God and in the worship of God will help preserve marital love. Let husband and wife pray together, said Whateley; "let them confer with each other of their heavenly country, let them sing a psalm together, and join in such religious exercises; so shall their hearts be knit together fast and firm to God first, and so to each other."[24] For as they do so, he continued, "bright beams of God's image will shine forth, and show themselves in each of them, and that is lovely and alluring, and will make them amiable to each other. These will nourish the spirit of holiness in them, and that kindles love."[25]

---

20. Gouge, *Of Domestical Duties*, 94.
21. Bolton, *General Directions*, 279.
22. Ambrose, *Works*, 133.
23. Whateley, *A Bride-Bush*, 93. Cf. Jer. 10:25.
24. Whateley, *A Bride-Bush*, 49.
25. Whateley, *A Bride-Bush*, 49.

The spiritual implications of marital love should move people to choose their spouses carefully. Secker warned against choosing a wife merely for her beauty: "If a woman's flesh has more of beauty than her spirit has of Christianity, it is like poison in sweetmeats, most dangerous."[26] Concerning riches, he warned: "Take heed, for sometimes the bag and baggage go together…. When Themistocles was to marry his daughter, two suitors courted her together; the one rich, and a fool, the other wise, but poor. And being demanded which of the two he had rather his daughter should have, he answered…I had rather she should have a man without money, than money without a man."[27]

Marital Love Must Be Superlative

A husband and wife are to love each other so dearly that both are persuaded that the other is "the only fit and good match that could be found under the sun for them," Whately writes.[28] Because of parental love, a godly parent would not trade his child for another parent's child, even if that child were better looking and had more ability or gifts; similarly, a godly husband and wife would not trade each other for a better looking and more gifted spouse.[29] Whately concludes: "Marriage-love admits of no equal, but placeth the yoke-fellow next of all to the soul of the party loving; it will know none dearer, none so dear."[30]

Surely, a wife is a man's best companion and friend. Thomas Gataker (1574–1654) suggested that Adam was *truly* happy in Eden, but he was not *fully* happy until God had provided him with a wife, and he was joined to the woman as his closest friend and companion in all of life. Gataker said, "There is no society more near, more entire, more needful, more kindly, more delightful, more comfortable, more constant, more continual, than the society of man and wife."[31] He was convinced that a house was "half unfurnished and unfinished, and not fully happy but half happy, though otherwise never so happy," until it was completed with a wife.[32]

The Puritan ideal of superlative marital love appears in the poems that Anne Bradstreet (1612–1672) wrote to express her longing for her husband when he traveled away from home. She wrote to him,

---

26. Secker, "The Wedding Ring, A Sermon," 266.
27. Secker, "The Wedding Ring, A Sermon," 267.
28. Whately, *A Bride-Bush*, 8.
29. Whately, *A Bride-Bush*, 8.
30. Whately, *A Bride-Bush*, 9.
31. Gataker, *Certain Sermons*, 2:161.
32. Gataker, *Certain Sermons*, 2:161.

> If ever two were one, then surely we.
> If ever man was lov'd by wife, then thee....
> I prize thy love more than whole mines of gold,
> Or all the riches that the East doth hold.
> My love is such that rivers cannot quench,
> Nor ought but love from thee, give recompense.[33]

In another poetic letter, Bradstreet compared her longing for her husband to that of a deer racing through the woods with ears alert to the sound of her mate. She signed it, "Thy loving love and dearest dear."[34]

Husband and wife are to love each other with a fervent and steady love that does not wax and wane with the tide of beauty, dress, or riches, or fluctuate with the emotions and lusts of the flesh. This love, wrote Ambrose, is "loving and tender-hearted pouring out of their hearts, with much affectionate dearness, into each other's bosoms."[35] It is an *entire* love, a full love, a love that pours itself out between spouses constantly and without reservation in a variety of expressions, gestures, looks, and actions. This love, Daniel Rogers (1573–1652) wrote, is not "raised suddenly in a pang of affection, ebbing and flowing...but a habitual and settled love planted in them by God, whereby in a constant, equal, and cheerful consent of spirit they carry themselves [towards] each other."[36] Bolton therefore defined this duty of mutual love as "a drawing into action, and keeping in exercise, [the] *habit* of conjugal affection and matrimonial love."[37] If this mutual love is eclipsed for but a day or even an hour, said Baxter, the husband and wife are "as a bone out of joint; there is no ease, no order, no work well done till they are restored and set in joint again."[38]

Such love is nurtured by guarding each other's honor and reputation instead of complaining and grumbling against each other. Secker put it this way: "Who would trample upon a jewel because it is fallen in the dirt? Or throw away a heap of wheat for a little chaff? Or despise a golden wedge because it retains some dross? These roses [i.e., wives] have some prickles. Now husbands should spread a mantle of charity over their wives' infirmities."[39]

---

33. Quoted in Heidi L. Nichols, *Anne Bradstreet: A Guided Tour of the Life and Thought of a Puritan Poet* (Phillipsburg, N.J.: P&R, 2006), 118.
34. Quoted in Nichols, *Anne Bradstreet*, 122–23.
35. Ambrose, *Works*, 130.
36. Rogers, *Matrimonial Honour*, 137–38.
37. Bolton, *General Directions*, 265, emphasis added.
38. Baxter, *Practical Works*, 1:431.
39. Secker, "The Wedding Ring, A Sermon," 263.

A husband must do his best to see that no one know his wife's faults but himself and God. He should be unwilling to voice them to anyone but God, to pray that she may be pardoned for them and reformed from them. Likewise, a wife must do her best to keep her husband's struggles and sins to herself, as matters of prayer and not gossip. Neither spouse should be surprised by the sins of the other, for each of them is well aware of their own sins. Can it be helpful to uncover faults in public and fling mud in each other's face? Will this help a husband reform or a wife to repent? And which is more displayed in such a case, the spouse's faults and weaknesses or the gossip's unkindness, indiscretion, backbiting, and folly? Does not the family dog behave better than this when it barks at strangers but not at members of the family?[40]

Moreover, if ill speech behind the back of an enemy is a sin, how much more grievous is ill speech behind the back of a spouse, who should be to us as our own flesh? Whateley wrote,

> To hear a husband largely declaiming against his wife, and...aggravating her sins, as if he took delight in nothing so much as in branding her forehead with the black mark of infamy is a testimony of so much hatred, where there should be most love, and of so bitter unkindness, where nature itself requires most tender kindness, that no speeches almost can sound more harsh in the ears of wise men. So again for the woman to be clattering amongst her gossips what a foolish husband she has...and to be...making proclamation of his faults, as if she feared nothing but that they should *not* be known to people...is a most irksome and hateful folly and untrustworthiness.[41]

Love for each other must strive to cover sins much as bandages cover sores so they can heal. Swinnock advised that "to procure a quiet life, the husband must be deaf, and the wife blind. Sure it is, the man must not bear to declare it abroad, nor the wife see to say it among her gossips whatever is amiss at home, if they would live in peace."[42] A breach between a husband and wife is half reconciled when it is kept indoors where love and prayers can be repeatedly administered to it; but if it is announced outdoors in the ears of others, it will be like a festering sore that can hardly be healed.[43]

The common practice of publishing each other's faults must therefore be put far away from every spouse; it is treachery and looks more like the hatred

---

40. Whateley, *A Bride-Bush*, 78.
41. Whateley, *A Bride-Bush*, 77, emphasis added.
42. Swinnock, *Works*, 1:476.
43. Swinnock, *Works*, 1:476.

one might show to an enemy than the love demanded in a marriage. "What mutual love can there be in such?" asked Gouge. "Howsoever their hands have been joined together, surely their hearts were never united, so that it had been better [if] they had never known one another, unless the Lord do afterwards knit their hearts and unite their affections more nearly and firmly together."[44] In extreme cases, it may be necessary to acquaint a close and trusted friend with the faults of one's spouse for the purpose of prayer and sound counsel. But that is far different from publishing little flaws and idiosyncrasies to any company and for no other purpose than murmuring, complaining, and gossiping. "Know therefore, and practice this duty, O husbands and wives," concluded Whateley, "spit not in each other's faces, disclose not each other's faults, but conceal, hide, bury and cover them so much as truth and equity will allow."[45]

Superlative love requires a steady effort to be pleasing to each other. According to Whateley, this "pleasingness" is "a disposition of the will and earnest desire of the heart to give all content [satisfaction] to each other, so far as they may possibly do it, without sinning against God."[46] If husband and wife perform this duty, which 1 Corinthians 7:33–34 commends, with all diligence and faithfulness, then they will experience a great harvest of blessings to the whole family. No good or happiness can be enjoyed by that couple who live as enemies on the field when they are companions in one house and bed. Whateley advises, "Next to the pleasing of God, make your main business to please each other."[47]

Marital Love Must Be Sexual

Marital love must be sexual. Both marital partners should give themselves fully to each other with joy and exuberance in a healthy sexual relationship marked by fidelity. Reformers such as Martin Luther, Ulrich Zwingli, and John Calvin reestablished this aspect of marriage by abandoning medieval Roman Catholic notions that marriage was inferior to celibacy, that all sexual contact between marital partners was only a necessary evil to propagate the human race, and that any procreative act that involved passion was inherently sinful. This negative view was rooted in the writings of the ancient church fathers, such as Tertullian, Ambrose, and Jerome; all these believed that, even within marriage, sexual intercourse necessarily involved sin.[48] This attitude toward sex in marriage held sway among the church's leaders for more than ten centuries and inevitably

---

44. Gouge, *Of Domestical Duties*, 182.
45. Whateley, *A Bride-Bush*, 79–80.
46. Whateley, *A Bride-Bush*, 54.
47. Whateley, *A Bride-Bush*, 59.
48. Packer, *A Quest for Godliness*, 261.

led to the exaltation of virginity and celibacy. By the fifth century, deacons, priests, and bishops were prohibited from marrying.[49] Two classes of Christians emerged: the "religious" (i.e., the spiritual clergy), which included monks and nuns who vowed to abstain from all sexual activity, and the "profane" (i.e., the secular laity), who, being unable to practice the exalted virtues of virginity or celibacy, were conceded the right to marry.

Puritan preachers taught that the Roman Catholic view was unbiblical, even satanic. They cited Paul, who said that prohibition of marriage is a "doctrine of devils" (1 Tim. 4:1–3). Puritan definitions of marriage implied the conjugal act. For example, William Perkins (1558–1602) defines marriage as "the lawful conjunction of the two married persons; that is, of one man and one woman into one flesh."[50] The Puritans viewed sex within marriage as a gift of God and as an essential, enjoyable part of marriage. Gouge said that husbands and wives should cohabit "with good will and delight, willingly, readily, and cheerfully."[51] "They do err," added Perkins, "who hold that the secret coming together of man and wife cannot be without sin unless it be done for the procreation of children."[52]

Perkins goes on to say that marital sex is a "due debt" or "due benevolence" (1 Cor. 7:3) that married persons owe to their spouses. That debt must be paid, he says, "with a singular and entire affection one towards another" in three ways. "First, by the right and lawful use of their bodies or of the marriage bed." Such physical intimacy by "holy usage" should be "a holy and undefiled action (Heb. 13:4)…sanctified by the word and prayer (1 Tim. 4:3–4)." The fruits of God-honoring, enjoyable sex in marriage are the blessing of children, "the preservation of the body in cleanness," and the reflection of marriage as a type of the bond between Christ and His church. Second, married couples must "cherish one another" intimately (Eph. 5:29) rather than having sex in an impersonal way. Third, a couple should be intimate "by an holy kind of rejoicing and solacing themselves each with [the] other in a mutual declaration of the signs and tokens of love and kindness (Prov. 5:18–19; Song 1:2; Gen. 26:8; Isa. 62:7)." In this context, Perkins particularly mentions kissing.[53]

Other Puritans stressed the romantic side of marriage as they compared the love of a husband to God's love for His people. Thomas Hooker (1586–1647)

---

49. Leland Ryken, *Worldly Saints: The Puritans as They Really Were* (Grand Rapids: Zondervan, 1986), 40.

50. Perkins, "Christian Oeconomy," 419.

51. Quoted in Ryken, *Worldly Saints*, 44.

52. Perkins, "Christian Oeconomy," 423.

53. Perkins, "Christian Oeconomy," 423–27.

wrote, "The man whose heart is endeared to the woman he loves, he dreams of her in the night, hath her in his eye and apprehension when he awakes, museth on her as he sits at table, walks with her when he travels and parlies with her in each place where he comes."[54] He also said, "She lies in his Bosom, and his heart trusts in her, which forceth all to confess, that the stream of his affection, like a mighty current, runs with full tide and strength."[55]

Rightfully so, the emphasis on finding romance within marriage (rather than in extramarital relations, as was common in the Middle Ages)[56] has been attributed to the Puritans. Herbert W. Richardson writes that "the rise of romantic marriage and its validation by the Puritans represents a major innovation within the Christian tradition."[57] And C. S. Lewis says, "The conversion of courtly love into romantic monogamous love was largely the work of…Puritan poets."[58] Thus the Puritans emphasized that marital love, in addition to being spiritual love, must also be sexual love. In this way, they embraced God's gift of marriage as the superlative or highest form of human love known on earth.

Conclusion

Though the Puritans honored the sexuality of marriage, they did not reduce marriage to sex. Rather, they maintained a view of marital love as broad as life itself. Whateley and Gouge emphasize other mutual duties in marriage. A husband and wife must be faithful to each other and help each other in every possible way, including seeking each other's spiritual growth, healing each other's faults, and steering each other away from sin. They must pray for each other, compliment each other, appreciate each other, and, together, "keep the unity of the spirit in the bond of peace." They must cultivate true friendship and take an interest in each other. They must be sympathetic to one another in times of distress, sickness, and weakness. They must each promote the other's reputation, never speaking ill of each other in the presence of others. They must be confidential, not revealing each other's secrets. They must be industrious in their callings, working diligently as a team for one another, for their family, and in hospitality to others, especially the poor. For these reasons, they must manage

---

54. Thomas Hooker, *The Application of Redemption…the Ninth and Tenth Books*, 2nd ed. (London: Peter Cole, 1659), 137.

55. Thomas Hooker, *A Comment Upon Christ's Last Prayer* (London: Peter Cole, 1656), 187. I am indebted to Packer, *A Quest for Godliness*, 265, for the last two quotations.

56. William Haller, *The Rise of Puritanism* (New York: Harper, 1957), 122.

57. Herbert W. Richardson, *Nun, Witch, Playmate: The Americanization of Sex* (New York: Harper & Row, 1971), 69.

58. C. S. Lewis, "Donne and Love Poetry in the Seventeenth Century," in *Seventeenth Century Studies Presented to Sir Herbert Grierson* (Oxford: Oxford University Press, 1938), 75.

their money judiciously.[59] Marital love must fill every room of the home and spill out into the world.

The true secret to living happily in marriage is to love—not the exercise of a mere feeling but fulfilling a calling to follow Christ with all that we are and all that we have. Ezekiel Hopkins (1634–1690) wrote, "It is love which ought at first to tie the marriage knot, and it is love alone which can afterwards make it easy."[60]

Though the Puritans lived in a difficult age when plague, persecution, war, and the frequent deaths of children darkened their lives, they nevertheless marveled at the goodness of God in seasoning life with such a sweet spice as the love shared by husband and wife. In our own more prosperous but also more cynical age, we can learn much from them.

---

59. Whateley, *A Bride-Bush*, 11–16; Gouge, *Of Domestical Duties*, 165–90.

60. Ezekiel Hopkins, *The Works of Ezekiel Hopkins*, ed. Charles W. Quick (Philadelphia: Leighton Publications, 1874), 1:414.

PASTORAL THEOLOGY

Chapter 24

God-Centered Adult Education[1]

"Nothing is more important for us to hear than the sermons of God-ordained servants," my dad said to me when I was a child. "Through preaching, we hear what the Holy Spirit wants to teach us personally from God's Book. But it is not enough. We need to buttress that preaching throughout the week with other learning situations.

"Look at it this way, son," Dad went on. "You spend two hours a week hearing the Word of God proclaimed. There are 168 hours in the week. For most of the rest of those hours, the world is trying to teach you its philosophy, tempting you to engage in its carnal pleasures. You need more teaching than you get on Sunday. You need education in sacred things throughout the week. Read your Bible, read good Christian books, take advantage of what the church teaches you during the week, get involved in church ministries, and ask God to make you a teacher of others one day."

My dad put that advice into practice. He helped me build a library and shared my excitement in collecting books. He often asked me what I was reading. He encouraged me as I got involved in the church's educational ministries. Since the mid-1970s, I have had the privilege of preaching and teaching in the church, and I am as excited about it as when I began. I also see its growing importance, and I have attempted to instill the same excitement in my children about learning at church, school, and home.

Let us take a look at the importance of adult education, first by looking at the growing need for it. Then we will look at its purposes, basic components, and primary means. We will examine a model of an adult education program and its various parts. We will look at some areas that need further work and answer some objections people have about becoming involved in adult education. We will conclude with some practical results of such programs.

---

1. This chapter is an expansion of an address given at Ligonier's Pastors' Conference in 2007, in which I was asked to address God-centered adult education in the context of my own congregation.

The Growing Need

In the last five decades, hundreds of books have been written about adult education in the church.[2] There is no end to the advice given to us today on how adults learn and how to set up education programs for them in the church.

Much of this advice is helpful, but unfortunately relatively few of these books operate from a God-centered premise. It is good that, in many churches, adults no longer sit idle while their children attend Sunday school or catechism classes. They go to classes set up for adults. It is good that we no longer assume that adult believers who have made public profession of faith know all that they need to know and that further education is unnecessary. Rather, we realize that we can always learn more about the Bible, the doctrines that developed in church history, and theology that can influence us in practical ways. The desire to learn more about God and His people on a deeper level is sufficient cause in itself to offer an adult education program, but we need to make sure that such a program is God-centered and Bible-based.

The Purposes of Adult Education

The first and primary purpose of adult education is to *enhance God-centered thinking to God's glory*. Only as we think God's thoughts after Him and strive to live to His glory do our lives become truly rich. That is the purpose for which we have been created.

It is critically important to keep all adult education methods Bible-based and God-glorifying. Churches whose programs stray from this purpose will inevitably disintegrate from within, if not quantitatively, then qualitatively. The church can never match the world in entertaining people, nor should it try to do so. The church's business is to supply people with solid, biblical, spiritual food that the Holy Spirit can use to fortify believers with a genuine, scriptural God-centeredness that serves God's glory.[3]

Here is a model to follow to ensure a God-centered education:

---

2. For a quick history of adult education throughout church history, see R. Michael Harton, "Importance of Adult Christian Education," in *A Church Ministering to Adults*, ed. Jerry M. Stubblefield (Nashville: Broadman, 1986), 16–21. For more thorough treatments of recent developments, see Malcolm Knowles, *The Adult Education Movement in the United States* (New York: Holt, Reinhart, & Winston, 1962) and John Elias, *Foundations and Practice of Adult Religious Education* (Malabar, Fla.: Robert E. Krieger, 1982).

3. Edward L. Hayes, "Theological Foundations for Adult Education," in *The Christian Educator's Handbook of Adult Education*, ed. Kenneth O. Gangel and James C. Wilhoit (Wheaton, Ill.: Victor Books, 1993), 36–38.

A God-Centered Basis: The Word of God
A God-Centered Thrust: The Grace of God
A God-Centered Context: The Church of God
A God-Centered Method: The Directives of God
A God-Centered Model: The Christ of God
A God-Centered Aim: The Glory of God[4]

The second purpose of adult education is to *enhance spiritual maturation and formation.* True believers must never stop learning. Every day of our lives we are called to grow "in grace, and in the knowledge of our Lord and Savior Jesus Christ" (2 Peter 3:18). To become more like Christ and to follow Him fully, we need lifelong education in mind and soul, which, in turn, will move our hands and feet. Adult education should expand the head-heart-hand model of Christianity in believers' lives. These maturing believers then set a wonderful example for the generations to follow; they are winsome and contagious as they model the fruits of the Spirit: "love, joy, peace, longsuffering, gentleness, goodness, faith, meekness, [and] temperance" (Gal. 5:22–23).

A third purpose of adult education is to *enhance the communion of saints through fellowship.* Adult education promotes fellowship and interaction among believers; it helps people build relationships that reach beyond superficial carnality. How blessed is the church in which believers love each other, share each other's daily struggles and dreams, and reach out to each other with heart-felt compassion.

Fourth, the purpose of adult education is to *enhance the church.* It helps the church to be faithful and strong, fulfilling its mandate to disciple believers and evangelize unbelievers by the Spirit's grace, to God's glory. Those involved in adult education are usually the same people who do much of the church's work and are usually at the center of nearly every mission endeavor.

A good adult education program also helps the church fulfill its calling to train and establish biblical leaders (1 Timothy 3; Titus 1:5). It helps the church combat heresy, errors, and false practices (Acts 13:9–11; 1 Tim. 1:3; Titus 1:11). As Kenneth Gangel says, we learn from Titus 2 that when an adult education program, under the blessing of the Holy Spirit, is successful, "people will not malign the Word of God" (v. 5), "families will be strong" (v. 4), and "the gospel will be attractive" (v. 10). Students will "reject ungodliness and worldly passions" (v. 11), "live a self-controlled, upright, and godly life" (v. 12), "actively wait for Christ's return" (v. 13), and "eagerly do that which is good" (v. 14).[5]

---

4. I am indebted to my colleague, Dr. Gerald Bilkes, for his help on developing this model.
5. Gangel, "Biblical Foundations for Adult Education," in *Adult Education*, 23–24, 27–28.

Fifth, the purpose of adult education is to *enhance the awareness of common errors in thinking about such programs.* In "Demythologizing Adult Ministry in the Church," C. Ferrish Jordan presents this list of myths:

Myths about Adults
Adulthood is a plateau period
Adults have had their day
Adults are all alike
Adults will not change
Adults are poor prospects for the church

Myths about Adults as Learners
Aging has a negative effect upon learning
Adults are not interested in learning
Adults learn best by listening
Adults will not respond to a variety of learning activities
Adults will tolerate poor teaching

Myths about Adult Ministry
Churches must reach young persons first to assure future ministry
Quality adult religious education is not a priority in building a
    strong church
Young adults are not interested in spiritual things
Middle adults do not need special attention[6]

The Basic Components of Adult Education
Here are some of the basic necessities for developing an effective adult education program:

1. Proper Leadership Training
Pastors and teachers should take the lead in equipping their people for effective ministry and eventual leadership. Just as the church is involved in training its pastors to be pastors through church-supervised seminaries, so the church should supervise the training of elders and deacons to be effective elders and deacons. It should also help train laypeople to become leaders in the adult education program and in the church's outreach ministries.

---

6. C. Ferrish Jordan, "Demythologizing Adult Ministry in the Church," in *A Church Ministering to Adults,* ed. Jerry M. Stubblefield, 256–76.

Leadership training is a major task. Ideally, the church should train leaders for whatever programs it decides to implement. If outside teachers are used for part of this training, those teachers should come under the supervision of church leadership.[7] In all cases, the leadership training should be governed by the kind of God-centered model presented above.

2. Proper Consistorial Supervision

The entire adult education program should be supervised by the pastor(s) and elders—that is, the consistory or presbytery. In larger congregations, consistories or presbyteries can appoint an adult education committee or even subcommittees to oversee the details of the program. Donald Hoekstra says such committees "can help survey the congregation to determine its needs and interests; they can help plan specific courses and classes in response to the congregation's input; they can suggest and help recruit teachers for those classes and courses; and they can help diversify the evaluation of the program by participating themselves and gathering feedback from other students in the classes."[8]

Depending on the amount of activity in a given ministry, committees should regularly submit reports on their activities to update the consistory on how each ministry is doing. Doctrinal concerns and major changes should be referred directly to the church's leaders. At every level of supervision, those in charge of the adult education program should periodically examine the big question: Is our entire adult education program maintaining its mandate to pursue God-centeredness?

3. Proper Biblical Subjects

Adult education should be Bible-based. It must confine itself to subjects that are addressed in the Scriptures. According to Gangel, we should follow the model of adult education Paul used at Crete, addressing home relations (family life issues), human relations (communion of saints and how believers should relate to this world), and heavenly relations (our relationship with God). Anything outside this framework should be eliminated.[9]

---

7. With due caution toward the following author's neo-orthodoxy, ministers who are interested in restoring effective teaching in the church would profit from reading Richard Robert Osmer's *A Teachable Spirit: Recovering the Teaching Office in the Church* (Lousiville: Westminster/John Knox Press, 1990)—especially chap. 6, "Martin Luther's Break with the Roman Catholic *Magisterium*" (84–106), and chap. 7, "The Teaching Office in the Thought and Practice of John Calvin" (107–135).

8. Donald Hoekstra, *Adult Education in the Church: A How to Primer* (Grand Rapids: CRC Publications, 1985), 35.

9. Gangel, "Biblical Foundations for Adult Education," in *The Christian Educator's Handbook of Adult Education*, ed. Kenneth O. Gangel and James C. Wilhoit, 24–25.

We should aim for a nutritious, well-balanced program that includes such subjects as Bible studies, biblical hermeneutics, church history, church creeds and confessions, church worship and liturgy, church polity, biblical archaeology, foundational Christian doctrines (of God, man, Christ, salvation, the church, and the last things), spiritual formation and disciplines, Christian apologetics, Christian polemics, biblical ethics or Christian living, biblical counseling, leadership, missions and evangelism, and Christian family living.[10] Ultimately, all these subjects must begin with God and end in God.

4. Proper Teaching Strategies and Methods

Learning has been defined as "the act or experience of one that learns; knowledge or skill acquired by instruction or study; modification of a behavioral tendency by experience."[11] Such learning is more comprehensive than classroom instruction. Wilbur Parry suggests that adults grow (1) by opening up new areas of knowledge and interest, (2) by becoming a part of a significant enterprise, (3) by developing a real interest in helping others, and (4) by developing a conviction in the practice of the Christian faith.[12]

Adult education programs are usually most effective when they use a variety of teaching strategies and learning activities, such as lecturing, outlining, reading, writing, interacting, listening, reflecting, discussing, brainstorming, debating, demonstrating, interviewing, seeing, experiencing, role-playing, questioning, and testing. Because adults learn in different ways, one approach can reinforce another.

H. Norman Wright charts fifty-seven methods of adult learning, with a purpose and description of each.[13] Such charts must be viewed with discretion since some of these methods would be difficult to implement in a church setting. Also, church leaders should be circumspect in using certain risqué forms of modern media. Nevertheless, some methods, such as field trips, practice teaching, Q & A sessions, sermon discussions, symposiums, and workshops, can enrich an adult program in ways that honor Scripture and enhance learning.[14]

---

10. Hoekstra, *Adult Education in the Church*, 21–25.

11. *Webster's Ninth New Collegiate Dictionary* (Springfield, Mass.: Merriam-Webster, 1983), s.v. "learning."

12. Wilbur C. Parry, *Christian Education for Adults* (St. Louis: The Bethany Press, 1946), 17–27.

13. H. Norman Wright, *Ways to Help Them Learn: The Adult* (Glendale, Calif.: G/L Publications, 1972).

14. For example, see Duane H. Elmer, "Inductive Teaching: Strategy for the Adult Educator," in *The Christian Educator's Handbook of Adult Education*, ed. Kenneth O. Gangel and James C. Wilhoit, 135–47.

Studies by educators such as Malcolm Knowles and Sharan B. Merriam have shown that many adults learn more from class discussions, cell groups, case studies, and personal interviews than they do from lectures.[15] Still, we must not overreact to such studies by abandoning all lecturing in our adult education programs, particularly when the local church has gifted lecturers. Many adults still learn best from an excellent lecturer using a well-constructed outline. They learn more by quietly listening than by actively participating.

Thus, it would be a mistake simply to replace traditional *pedagogy* (in which the teacher lectures and takes full responsibility for determining what is to be learned) with *andragogy* (in which teachers encourage adults to direct and participate in their own learning experiences).[16] On the other hand, we must not turn a blind eye to non-lecturing methods for learning; rather, we should incorporate some andragogical methods into various parts of our programs.

Andragogy is more challenging to implement than pedagogy. Knowles describes these challenges for the adult educator:

a. Helping the learners diagnose their needs for particular learning within the scope of the given situation (the diagnostic function).

b. Planning with students a sequence of experiences that produces the desired learning (the planning function).

c. Creating the conditions that will cause students to want to learn (the motivational function).

d. Selecting the most effective method and techniques for producing the desired learning (the methodological function).

e. Providing the human and material resources necessary to produce the desired learning (the resource function).

f. Helping the students measure the outcomes of the learning experiences (the evaluative function).[17]

---

15. Sharan B. Merriam and Rosemary S. Caffarella, *Learning in Adulthood: A Comprehensive Guide* (San Francisco: Jossey-Bass, 1991).

16. European adult educators coined the term "andragogy" in the mid-twentieth century. It is based on the Greek word *anēr* (with the stem *andr-*), meaning "man, not boy" or adult. It was introduced in 1968 into North American literature by Malcolm Knowles, who first used it for helping adults to learn in contrast to the "pedagogy" of helping children learn. But after teachers reported that some of Knowles's andragogical teaching methods worked effectively for children as well, he began using andragogy as "another model of assumptions about learners to be used alongside the pedagogical model of assumptions" (Malcolm S. Knowles, *Modern Practice of Adult Education* [Chicago: Follet, 1980], 43).

17. Knowles, *Modern Practice of Adult Education*, 26–27.

In sum, adult education programs can profit from becoming more learner-centered.[18] But this approach, too, can be abused. A combined pedagogical/andragogical model may be the most effective for many learning situations.[19] Jane Sygley Mouton and Robert R. Blake make this suggestion in their book *Synergogy*.[20] Richard Patterson summarizes this method:

> Abuses of the pedagogical model were matched by abuses of the andra-gogical model. Some andragogical devotees allowed their belief regarding how adults learn to degenerate into the "blind leading the blind" by foster-ing extensive sharing sessions with no authoritative source for truth. From this abuse syndrome rose yet another adult teaching/learning approach termed *synergogy*. Synergogy attempts to avoid the abuses of some applied andragogy by positioning a truth source in the adult learning experience. It is creative and intriguing and offers considerable promise to the Chris-tian educator.[21]

Some words of caution are in order here. First, preaching the Word, which is the primary form of adult education, should remain just that—preaching the Word. As the Heidelberg Catechism says, "God will have His people taught, not by dumb images, but by the lively preaching of His Word" (Q. 98).

Second, the adult education program should not lean too heavily on para-church organizations. If possible, train people in your own fellowship who are gifted to teach and lead.

Third, though teachers and leaders may be encouraged at times to stretch themselves by using various teaching methods, they should not be forced to use strategies they do not feel comfortable with.

Finally, at no time should any teaching method be tolerated that can't serve the overarching purpose of the entire program to remain God-centered and Bible-based in all its teaching.

---

18. Cf. Maryellen Weimer, *Learner-Centered Teaching: Five Key Changes to Practice* (San Francisco: Jossey-Bass, 2002).

19. Knowles, *Modern Practice of Adult Education*, 43–44. See the updating of his views in Malcolm S. Knowles, "Contributions of Malcolm Knowles," in *The Christian Educator's Handbook of Adult Education*, ed. Kenneth O. Gangel and James C. Wilhoit, 98.

20. Jane Sygley Moulton and Robert R. Blake, *Synergogy* (San Francisco: Jossey-Bass, 1987).

21. Richard Patterson, "How Adults Learn," in *The Christian Educator's Handbook of Adult Education*, ed. Kenneth O. Gangel and James C. Wilhoit, 125–26.

5. Proper Group Divisions

Most of an adult education program can be effectively run for both sexes and adults ages eighteen and up. Growing evidence shows, however, that it is good to provide at least a few classes that are divided according to sex, marital status, and age.

Women often get more out of a Bible study that is limited to women since this allows them to speak more freely than if men are present. Men also often find it easier to open up to each other without women present. Studies have also shown that women and men learn somewhat differently.[22]

Today, more than one-third of American adults are single, which includes those who have never married or are widowed, divorced, or separated. The number of single Americans rose from approximately 30 million in 1940 to 60 million in 1980 to more than 80 million today. A ministry for singles, when governed by biblical teaching and properly handled, can fill a need in people who often feel marginalized and lonely. The divorced and separated, in particular, cope with overwhelming feelings of failure. The "innocent parties" in cases of separation and divorce need special attention. Single parents also need considerable support. Nothing can strengthen singles so much as acceptance and fellowship in the Word, offering hope in Christ Jesus for the future.[23]

Breaking down certain groups in the church by age enables ministries to focus on the needs of that age group. Generally speaking, a church of several hundred members should have at least one class for senior adults, one for middle-aged adults, and one for young adults.

Seniors (age 65 and up) face losses and the fear of losing more. These include the loss of a spouse, relatives, and friends; the loss of intellectual ability; the loss of physical strength; the loss of self-worth; the loss of driving privileges; the loss of a full-size home; the loss of independence, and the loss of health. As many seniors say, "It's not easy being old." Ministering to seniors with these needs is a great challenge.[24]

---

22. Catherine M. Stonehouse, "Learning from Gender Differences," in Gangel and Wilhoit, *Adult Education*, 104–120.

23. Patricia A. Chapman, "Single Adults and Single Parents," in Gangel and Wilhoit, *Adult Education*, 234–46; Jerry M. Stubblefield, "Single Adults: A New Challenge for the Church," in *A Church Ministering to Adults*, ed. Jerry M. Stubblefield, 98–110.

24. Cf. Lucien E. Coleman, "Later Adult Years," in *A Church Ministering to Adults*, ed. Jerry M. Stubblefield, 90–97; Coleman, "Senior Adults: Expanding Opportunities for Ministry/Service," *A Church Ministering to Adults*, 116–21; Robert E. Fillinger, "Teaching Older Adults," in *The Christian Educator's Handbook of Adult Education*, ed. Kenneth O. Gangel and James C. Wilhoit, 223–33; David O. Moberg, "The Nature and Needs of Older Adults," in *Adult Education in the Church*, ed. Roy B. Zuck and Gene A. Getz (Chicago: Moody, 1970), 56–72.

Middle-aged adults (ages 40 to 65) have their own set of fears: the fear of failure, the fear of being passed up for a promotion at work, the fear of stagnation, the fear of drowning in busyness, the fear of physiological changes, the fear of rebellious teens, and the fear of marital degeneration. Middle-aged Baby Boomers who have low levels of loyalty to the church but high expectations of what church should offer are quick to shop around for a "better church."[25] Middle-aged adults, who are often the forgotten group in ministry, need education more than any other group, for they are the backbone of the church.[26]

Young adults (ages 18 to 40) have their struggles too: finding a marital partner and learning to live happily with that partner, starting a family and raising children, managing a home, getting established in an occupation, and facing the challenges of pre-teenage children. R. Michael Harton says, "Young adults are struggling for a sense of stability and moral guidance amid the experimentation so characteristic of this age group. Many are haunted by their insufficiencies as parents, others with the dilemmas of a satisfying, singles lifestyle."[27]

Many volumes have been written on ministering to each of these age groups. For example, *The Handbook of Young Adult Religious Education*, edited by Harley Atkinson, covers the purpose, scope, and principles of young adult religious education; the psychological, sociocultural, religious, and moral characteristics of young adults; educational procedures for educating young adults; reaching various subgroups among young adults, such as the singles, the married, the unchurched, and those in college; and evaluating a young adult religious education program.[28]

Ministers might also read a book or two on generational differences to learn how to better reach out to each generation. For example, Chuck Underwood's *The Generational Imperative* speaks of five generations in the United States:

---

25. Leith C. Anderson, "A Senior Pastor's Perspective on Baby Boomers," *Christian Education Journal* 11 (Autumn 1990):69–70.

26. For a helpful chapter on understanding the needs of middle-adult years, see Wesley R. Willis, "Teaching Middle Adults," in *The Christian Educator's Handbook of Adult Education*, ed. Kenneth O. Gangel and James C. Wilhoit, 211–22; Jerry M. Stubblefield, "Middle Adult Years," in *A Church Ministering to Adults*, ed. Jerry M. Stubblefield, 70–82; H. Norman Wright, "The Nature and Needs of Young Adults," in *Adult Education in the Church*, ed. Roy B. Zuck and Gene A. Getz, 45–55.

27. Harton, "Importance of Adult Christian Education," 27.

28. Harley Atkinson, ed., *Handbook of Young Adult Religious Education* (Birmingham: Religious Education Press, 1995); Fred R. Wilson, "Teaching Young Adults," in *The Christian Educator's Handbook of Adult Education*, ed. Kenneth O. Gangel and James C. Wilhoit, 190–210; Cyril D. Garrett, "The Nature and Needs of Single Adults," in *Adult Education in the Church*, ed. Roy B. Zuck and Gene A. Getz, 73–88.

+ The GIs (born from 1901 to 1926, and numbering 15 million). These are the heroes of the great generation that brought the United States to dominance in the twentieth century.

+ The Silents (born from 1927 to 1945, numbering 45 million). These are conformists. They are patriotic, loyal, marry young, and have an average of 3.3 children.

+ The Boomers (born from 1946 to 1964; numbering 80 million). They are patriotic but will challenge injustices. They are also competitive.

+ Gen-Xers (born from 1965 to 1981, numbering 60 million). They are survivalists who have lost their roots geographically and because of their parents' divorce. They are media-dominated and often settle for mediocrity.

+ The Millennials (born from 1982 to the present, numbering 80 million). This is the most programmed and adult-supervised generation. They are community- and cause-oriented, debt-plagued survivors of brutal competition. They have great spiritual needs, yet they are disengaged from the church (40 percent of them leave the church when they are teens).[29]

Though there are generational differences, it is critical to remember every church attendee has the same fundamental needs. In his *The Struggle of the Soul*, Lewis Joseph Sherrill says that for all age groups, "the church is, above all others, the place where the Word of God is allowed to confront man, speaking its own message undiluted and unscreened. The church can then become spokesman for God to those who know their own inadequacy, who desire the healing of the self down to its deepest foundations, and who are willing to face, not merely the word of man, but the Word of God, with whatever it may promise and whatever it may require."[30] The promotion of Scripture and its God-centeredness must, therefore, be the ultimate cause of every group division in teaching.

6. Proper Gradual Growth

Adult education programs need to grow gradually. Talented teachers and potential leaders need to be trained properly and then encouraged to commit themselves.

Course suggestions usually come from two sources. First, the leaders of the church may see needs to address. For example, if there is a subtle fading of concern about the heinousness of sin or about the all-sufficiency of Christ,

---

29. Chuck Underwood, *The Generational Imperative: Understanding Generational Differences* (North Charlestown, S.C.: BookSurge, 2007).

30. Lewis Joseph Sherrill, *The Struggle of the Soul* (New York: MacMillan, 1951), 146.

church leaders may decide it's time to offer a class on "The Sinfulness of Sin" or on "The Fullness of Christ."

Second, ideas for classes often come from the adults themselves. Many of the classes in our church began not so much with our vision as leaders but with adult members who felt a burden for such a class. Church leaders should pray over such requests and then, providing they meet the purposes outlined above, examine ways that the desire or need might be met.

Of course, a consistory or presbytery cannot satisfy every request. A church can have too many adult programs, resulting in such small cell groups that few people in the congregation know many people beyond their tiny group. Small group discussions are great, but there should also be larger programs that allow people in the congregation to interact with others in various age groups.

Finally, any request for a class that would not promote God-centered, Bible-based teaching should be rejected immediately. The church must avoid becoming a mere social club.

The Primary Means of Adult Education: Preaching

The preaching of God's Word must be the primary form of adult education in the church. Preaching is more than teaching; it is teaching plus application straight from the Bible. Sound preaching can exalt God-centered thinking better than any other part of the adult education program. That God-centered and Word-based thinking is precisely what everyone needs, adults and children alike. In our churches, we use the following methods of promoting God-centeredness in preaching.

1. Expositional Preaching

Preaching expositionally through the books of the Bible is the greatest learning tool. The interested adult listener will come away from such a series of sermons with a great grasp of each Bible book and its implications for God-centered living.

We also place a premium on expository preaching because it explains and applies a particular portion of God's Word in its context. Then, too, a commitment to expositional preaching is important because it gives authority to the preacher. He is bringing God's Word, and such preaching is best suited to moving a church to focus on God Himself and to hear and obey God's Word.

2. Topical Preaching

Topical preaching can also be effective. We in the Reformed tradition find the Heidelberg Catechism effective in helping our people understand the major

truths of Scripture. Each major doctrine of Scripture is preached from different supporting texts approximately every eighteen months. Our experience has
been that adults who sit under God-centered, topical, catechetical preaching
that focuses on one or more summary texts in each message generally have a
better grasp of scriptural doctrines than those who don't. If you have conscience
objections against such preaching, I respect that, but I would advise that you at
least have a mid-week gathering in which you teach—preferably on a confessional basis—the great doctrines of grace on a regular basis. That is a great help
in promoting God-centeredness.

3. Christological Preaching

Though all preaching should be Christ-centered, it is important that we present
series of sermons from time to time that focus on the great Christological acts
of redemption. In some of our traditions, we do that naturally by following an
ecclesiastical calendar that moves from Advent to Pentecost, covering Christ's
birth, sufferings, death, resurrection, and ascension in an orderly way. In our
Dutch tradition, we call this "feast-day preaching," meaning that our people are
taught at least once a year about the major acts of redemption. At the same
time, we refuse to indulge in the commercialization and worldly carnality that
surrounds such feast-day celebrations. However you do it, it is critical that your
congregation be taught well and repeatedly about the historic, redemptive acts
of Christ. You cannot center on God without focusing on His Son.

4. Preaching Beyond Church Walls

Do all you can to promote great God-centered preaching in your church. Nothing will substitute for it. People will learn more from it than from any class.
Then spread the sermons far and wide. We do this in three ways. First, our
own shut-ins and people in the area can listen to Lord's Day sermons on church
phones, and people from around the world can listen through livestreaming on
sermonaudio.com, Facebook, and other modern means. Second, every week,
all our sermons are recorded and made available to our people in various ways.
Through our sermon duplication ministry, sermons are mailed to individuals
and to prisoners throughout the world. Third, all sermons are subsequently
made available on sermonaudio.com.

Through these means, we reach considerably more people with our sermons
than we do the 600 to 700 people who may be actually hearing the sermon in
church. Through these means, all of which involve minimal costs, we educate
many adults beyond our church walls, praying that God-centered theology and
thinking will be the end result.

A God-Centered Model for Adult Education

Let me take some time to tell how we have developed the adult education program in our church, in which every aspect seeks to promote God-centeredness. Perhaps you might glean some helpful ideas for your own churches. Bear in mind that we have a congregation of 700 members, so if your membership is considerably smaller than this, do not think you are falling short if you do not match what we are offering. On the other hand, if your church is larger than this, please do not look down on us for not offering more.

1. Family Living Class

After the Sunday morning worship, we hold catechism classes for our church's children. While those classes are being taught, I teach an adult class called "Family Living." Presently, I am completing a series of about two hundred addresses on Christian marriage and childrearing.

Most lessons focus on one biblical topic, though some lessons are more topical than exegetical. In every case, however, I aim to base all lessons solidly on the Scriptures and provide handouts for each. The goal is to move people to ask in each aspect of marriage and childrearing: What does God want me to be and to do?

There is a great need for this kind of class today. The family is under heavy attack, plagued with such challenges as unbiblical divorces, spousal abuse, non-communicative marriages, and rebellious adolescents. Adult Bible-based classes can be immensely helpful in the midst of crises, but they are also helpful in preventing future problems.[31]

2. Confession of Faith Class

The confession of faith class, or membership class, is a wonderful opportunity to teach young and older adults the God-centered tenets of the faith. I have coauthored a book for this class with my brother, titled *Bible Doctrine Student Workbook*, which presents 500 questions that survey the major doctrines of Scripture. I use a combination of teaching and dialoguing to move through this book in about twenty 90-minute meetings over six months. I give students homework questions and reading assignments along the way. The *Teachers' Guide for Bible Doctrine Student Workbook* contains answers to each question.

---

31. Cf. Zuck and Getz, *Adult Education in the Church*, 239–378; C. Ferris Jordan, "Family Life Education," in *A Church Ministering to Adults*, ed. Jerry M. Stubblefield, 197–205; Nick and Nancy Stinnett, "Family Life Religious Education," *Handbook of Young Adult Religious Education*, ed. Harley Atkinson, 271–90; James R. Slaughter, "Family Life Education," in *The Christian Educator's Handbook of Adult Education*, ed. Kenneth O. Gangel and James C. Wilhoit, 262–77.

Our classes average around twenty students, who range in age from teenagers to seniors. Several nationalities are often represented as well. I also invite people who want to learn more about church doctrine to attend without feeling any pressure to join the church. However, it is not unusual to find that such people become members when the class ends.

3. Bible Study Groups

Our church offers a variety of Bible studies. There are two groups for women: one that meets on weekday mornings and one that meets in the evening. A group for young men meets regularly, and there are also several informal, unsupervised Bible study and fellowship groups that have sprung up spontaneously. All these groups help adults grow in God-centered thinking by studying the Bible and discussing how to put its teaching into practice.

4. Mid-week Class

We used to have a monthly, mid-week, adult class in our church. Each time we complete a subject, I would give the class a choice of five to ten God-honoring topics and ask them to vote for their top three choices, using a point system. We then covered the topic that receives the most points.

We have done a Bible introduction class, a Reformed theology overview class, and a Belgic Confession of Faith class. Other topics that we are considering for the future include a church history overview, an in-depth look at the Reformers and Puritans, Reformed worship, Christian ethics, leadership, and Bunyan's *Pilgrim's Progress*. In every case, we aim to exalt the triune God and His glorious attributes and truths.

5. Family Visitation

Visiting families in their homes is another great opportunity for educating adults in a God-centered way. The goal is for two church leaders (two elders, or a pastor and elder) to visit each family in the congregation one evening each year to instruct them in the faith.

Family visitation is a practical extension of pulpit teaching in three ways. First, it *supplements preaching*. A sermon is a skeleton, which takes on a body in the pulpit. But to have life, that body must move. Family visitation examines that movement; it is a more intimate extension of the proclamation of the gospel.

As P. Y. DeJong states in *Taking Heed to the Flock*, the Reformed churches instituted family visitation "in order that the individual who heard the gospel might be able to examine his heart and life properly in the light of the Word."[32]

Second, family visitation promotes *soul-examination and watchfulness*. Family visitation is shepherding without prying. It stresses that church leaders "must lead and guide, instruct and exhort, warn and comfort all those whom God in His providence has entrusted to their spiritual care."[33] We can truly watch over our flock only if we visit with them in their homes to have an in-depth discussion about spiritual and practical matters.

Finally, family visitation promotes *spiritual growth and encouragement*. As DeJong notes, "Those who care for souls are at their best when they are like a gardener that plants, waters, prunes, fertilizes, and protects his plants, but is not the one who makes the plants to grow, blossom, and bear fruit."[34] In family visitation, we aim to revive the tender plant of faith by personally administering and applying the Word with the help of the Holy Spirit. The goal is that every member might "grow in grace, and in the knowledge of our Lord and Savior Jesus Christ" (2 Peter 3:18).

When properly done, family visitation increases bonds of love in and outside of the church family. It promotes the communion of saints and service to others. It also lovingly examines the fruits of godliness in family life. As Van Dellen and Monsma write, "They [the elders] shall faithfully investigate whether they [the church members] manifest themselves uprightly in walk and conduct, in the duties of godliness, and in the faithful instruction of their households in the matter of family prayers and such like matters."[35]

6. Family Worship

We also teach parents how to conduct family worship in a God-centered way. First, the pastors periodically preach on the need for family worship. Second, every church family receives a booklet on this subject. And third, we as pastors periodically show hospitality to church families with one of the goals being to model for them how to do family worship. We invite church families to

---

32. P. Y. DeJong, *Taking Heed to the Flock* (Grand Rapids: Baker, 1948), 17.
33. DeJong, *Taking Heed*, 18.
34. DeJong, *Taking Heed*, 18.
35. Idzerd VanDellen and Martin Monsma, *The Church Order Commentary* (Eugene, Ore.: Wipf & Stock, 2003), 110.

have dinner with us, after which we have family worship. This is a wonderful opportunity to show them how to lead a family in Bible reading, Bible exposition and dialogue, prayer, and singing.[36]

We do not go as far as Puritan pastors did (though I think it is a good idea), by telling fathers they should invite the pastor and his family over for a dinner meal, after which the pastors would conduct family worship.[37] People learn more about how to do family worship from seeing and hearing it done than from its being preached.

7. Seminary

Our church is in close fellowship with Puritan Reformed Theological Seminary (PRTS, 2965 Leonard N.E., Grand Rapids, Michigan 49525; info@prts.edu; www.prts.edu), which prepares students to serve Christ and His church through biblical, experiential, and practical ministry. The seminary helps our church with God-centered adult education in several ways:

+ Under certain conditions, people can audit several courses in the seminary's various degree programs.

+ Church members are invited specifically to audit courses, such as the evangelism course and Marriage and Family in Ministry.

+ The church is invited to attend various lectures by guest speakers. The seminary also offers mission evenings to keep people informed about the progress of the gospel in various parts of the world.

+ The seminary houses a library of 100,000 volumes, and the Puritan Research Center, a collection of 3,500 volumes by and about the Puritans, which are open to scholars and ministers from around the world as well as to members of the congregation.

8. Literature

We feel strongly that sound, God-glorifying literature is one of the best ways of promoting adult education. We believe that, as Luther put it, "the pen is mightier than the sword." For this reason, we have promoted the following ministries, each of which strives to promote God-centered teaching:

---

36. Joel R. Beeke, *Family Worship* (Grand Rapids: Reformation Heritage Books, 2006), and *Family Worship Bible Guide* (Grand Rapids: Reformation Heritage Books, 2017).

37. See Joel R. Beeke, *Puritan Evangelism* (Grand Rapids: Reformation Heritage Books, 1999), for how the Puritans catechized their own families and churches.

- The seminary houses Reformation Heritage Books (RHB), a non-profit organization that publishes 40 books each year and stores about 4,000 titles of new books from other publishers as well as used books. The publisher also offers books for sale in the church building at steeply discounted prices.

- Several church members are involved in publishing *The Banner of Sovereign Grace Truth*, our denominational periodical, which is family-oriented and strives to educate people at all age levels.

- The Banner of Truth Tract Mission supplies Bibles, booklets, periodicals, and thousands of sermons to prisoners in the United States. It also prints thousands of tracts for distribution in various places around the world.

- The Gospel Trumpet ministry prints contemporary and timely sermons written by Heritage Reformed ministers and broadcasts sermons on various radio stations in America.

- The Inheritance Publishers mails approximately three sermons of our orthodox Reformed forefathers each year to 22,000 people around the world.

9. Mission Outreach

Many of our adults help educate themselves through involvement in teaching opportunities for a variety of mission outreaches, all of which aim to fulfill our church's mission statement: "By the Spirit's grace, discipling believers in Christ and evangelizing unbelievers for God's glory." Here are a few of our mission endeavors:

- Our neighborhood store, Heritage Hills Outreach Mission (HHOM). Here is how one volunteer summarizes the work: "We reach out to the less fortunate in our church neighborhood by providing Bible study, religious books, inexpensive clothing, and most of all, by sharing the gospel. Volunteers who work at HHOM have been stretched spiritually by their fellowship with the neighborhood people and fellow volunteers."

- Active jail and prison ministry programs. A prison worker said of his ministry: "In prison ministry, we meet weekly with about seventy convicted men who are seeking a way out of condemnation. We bring them the Word of the truth of salvation in Christ Jesus and the renewal of life. In the process, we ourselves are taught much about the gospel."

◆ Mission work in Mexico. Many adults join our young people to minister in short-term teams in Mexico. They teach, visit, build or repair houses, mentor people, and learn how to do evangelism more effectively.

For more on getting involved in missions, read "Mission Education and Involvement," by Bruce Powers. His steps for leading adults into missions include learning how discipleship grows, understanding God's call, accepting discipleship, choosing a ministry, and supporting cooperative ministries.[38]

10. Conferences and Youth Groups

The goal of all our adult and youth conferences is to promote God-centered teaching and spirituality. Each year we have a conference for the entire congregation and others connected to our seminary and also host a three-day youth summer camp. Every other year we have a conference for women and a two-day conference camp for men. All these conferences and camps, many of which have been greatly blessed by God, are packed with God-centered topics. The adult organizers and chaperones often confess how much they themselves learn in the process of organizing and running these conferences and camps.

We have a junior youth group (seventh through ninth graders), which meets about once a month for informal events and Bible study in someone's home. Each summer we have a Junior Youth Day that includes study groups, workshops, and activities that aim to move our young people closer to God.

Our senior youth group (tenth graders through college) meets every other Sunday night for Bible study, sermon discussions, or sing-alongs and Q & A sessions. They also meet on weekdays for study, social services, or outings. The young adults group (people in college and their twenties) meets regularly for various studies and times of fellowship. Again, God-centered thinking is the base of the whole, and adults who supervise these groups often feel that they are being ministered to more than they minister!

11. Music Evenings

Our choir offers music evenings that are God-centered, heartwarming, and educational by leading singing of a careful selection of psalms and hymns that glorify God as well as by teaching about the history of their composition.

---

38. Bruce P. Powers, "Mission Education and Involvement," in *A Church Ministering to Adults*, ed. Jerry M. Stubblefield, 188–95.

12. Areas Needing Work

We are doing much to educate adults in a God-centered way, but we need to work harder in several areas that are frequently overlooked in many churches. I would mention just five:

+ Training our leaders and teachers by providing basic teaching tools, such as John Milton Gregory's *The Seven Laws of Teaching*, plus lectures and discussions on how to teach effectively in a God-centered way.

+ Using the teaching gifts of our non-office-bearing members.

+ Learning from the examples of others, for example, the traits of Christian character.

+ Going out and evangelizing under the tutorship of others.

+ Providing more opportunities for sharing our visions and activities and experiences with each other to promote more God-centered convictions.

Objections

Here are a few objections frequently raised by individuals and leaders against developing a good adult education program, together with appropriate responses:

• *I'm too busy to attend.* Today more adults than ever are pursuing some kind of secular continuing education. Shouldn't they have a greater interest in being educated in eternal truths that center on the living God? The church's leaders should encourage adults to set the right priorities in their lives and to get involved in adult education ministries. We encourage potential members to think about what class they would like to take before they join the church. Then, when these potential members meet with the elders, they are asked to state their commitment. This way they truly understand that there is more to membership than simply showing up for church.

• *I'm too old to learn.* No one is too old to learn. Adult education often functions best when its members vary in age, background, sex, status, and education. This diversity encourages better discussions and a more lively group. All that is required is eagerness to learn. And most God-fearing adults want to know how to apply God's truth to their lives.

• *The program doesn't meet my needs or interests.* This objection, often stated by young adults, must be taken seriously. But we must be balanced in our approach to answering it. Some studies segment young adulthood into smaller units, such as Early Adult Transition (ages 18–22), Entering the

Adult World (22–28), Age 30 Transition (28–33), and Settling Down (33–40).[39] I believe that is unrealistic. The main category of Young Adults should be sufficient.

Still, we should heed studies that suggest that churches should offer a variety of cognitive and learning styles in their classes for young adults within a God-centered framework.[40] Such programs should also help adults make a transition from the idealistic world of absolute logic to the realistic world of stress, various life experiences, and other conditions that are less than ideal.[41]

While the church may reflect prayerfully on this advice and adjust its program accordingly, let me stress again that the church must be very careful in its program planning for young adults so that it doesn't lose its God-centered, Bible-based mandate.

‧ *I don't like lectures.* Some people respond better to lectures than do others. For those who don't like them, we can suggest that they pursue other forms of learning and ministry, at least for now. Later on, when they hear others in church express how they enjoy lectures, they may change their minds and try them. They may find, much to their surprise, that they actually like them.

‧ *I'm afraid I'll have to speak or pray in front of everyone.* As ministers who make our living by talking, we are prone to minimize how deeply some people feel about this objection. I respect this by asking for volunteers to ask or answer questions and to pray. That way, no one feels vulnerable. Later, when they feel more comfortable, some may even volunteer to speak in front of others.

‧ *No one will come.* Classes should not simply be offered at the whim of one or two individuals. Some means can be used to evaluate the interest level in the congregation. One approach is to ask adults what would be most beneficial for them.

Despite careful planning and prayer, it is still possible that only a few will attend a given adult class. Some people are busy with other important things and cannot take on any more. We must realize that everyone cannot attend every class that is offered. Also, if even a few earnest people show for a class, Jesus has promised to be in their midst (Matt. 18:20). And it is easier to communicate in a small group.

---

39. D. Levinson, et. al, *The Seasons of a Man's Life* (New York: Knopf, 1978), 56.
40. C. Houle, *The Inquiring Mind* (Madison: University of Wisconsin Press, 1961), 41.
41. Atkinson, ed., *Handbook of Young Adult Religious Education*, 37.

Though we should not pressure adults to attend particular classes, we can encourage them by stressing how solid, biblical teaching is one of God's primary tools to transform us according to His will. God expects us to be learning and growing, to be involved in ministry, and to integrate Christian faith into life. Part of the striving and renewal that God calls us to is given through study and learning. God blesses us with good instruction so that we, in turn, might be a blessing to others (Gen. 12:1–3).

Ultimately, objections to adult education might be rooted in a multifaceted spiritual problem; the objectors might not be born again or are backsliding. They might be spiritually lethargic, live in guilt and fear of God, love the world more than the church, and have no real desire to learn more about God's truth. As ministers, we need to sound the clarion call to repentance and faith.[42]

Conclusion: Practical Uses

Every sermon and every teaching situation is intended to center on God and to change lives. With the blessing of the Spirit, adult education provides an awareness of the need to live all of life *coram Deo*. It promotes conviction of sin, communion with Christ, prayer, gratitude, and various kinds of spiritual growth—all to the glory of God.

Adult education also meets people where they are in life. Sometimes, adults will respond to a class by saying, "If only I had had this instruction when I was newly married; I would have brought up my kids so differently—so much more God-centeredly." Others will say, "Having heard the God-centered, biblical principles involved in disciplining children, I now feel much better equipped to handle my teenage son when he doesn't do his homework."

As ministers, we must be enthusiastic about God-centered adult education programs. We must be zealous to improve them and excited about asking others to join us in this worthy task. Let us press on with adult education, looking to our faithful God for benediction, trusting that their practical results will become evident in due course, or as Ecclesiastes 11:1 puts it, "after many days."

Let us particularly use adult education to focus on Jesus Christ and to enhance our people's knowledge of Him—knowledge about His person, names, offices, states, and natures; knowledge about His relationship to the Father and the Spirit as well as to His adopted brothers and sisters. May our hearts be so moved as we teach about our "altogether lovely" Savior that we might move our people to worship Him in Spirit and truth as they attend our classes. Let us

---

42. James C. Wilhoit, "Christian Adults and Spiritual Formation," in *The Christian Educator's Handbook of Adult Education*, ed. Kenneth O. Gangel and James C. Wilhoit, 58–60.

never forget that we are most near to Christ when we are overwhelmed with a sense of His stupendous love for hell-worthy sinners like us. Then we will be so lost in the wonder of divine love that, with Paul, we will confess that its depth, height, and breadth goes beyond our understanding. This ought to be the hallmark of all our teaching and all our adult education: our delight and confidence in the love of Christ, from which nothing shall be able to separate us (Rom. 8:38–39). Ultimately, the goal of Christian education must be to lead our people, by the Spirit's grace, to find their total salvation in Christ, both here and forever, so that they might cry out from the experiential depth of their souls, with Paul, "For me to live is Christ, and to die is gain" (Phil. 1:21).

Chapter 25

Plain Preaching: Demonstrating
the Spirit and His Power

And I, brethren, when I came to you, came not with excellency of speech or of wisdom, declaring unto you the testimony of God. For I determined not to know any thing among you, save Jesus Christ, and him crucified. And I was with you in weakness, and in fear, and in much trembling. And my speech and my preaching was not with enticing words of man's wisdom, but in demonstration of the Spirit and of power: that your faith should not stand in the wisdom of men, but in the power of God.

—1 Corinthians 2:1–5

Therefore seeing we have this ministry, as we have received mercy, we faint not; but have renounced the hidden things of dishonesty, not walking in craftiness, nor handling the word of God deceitfully; but by manifestation of the truth commending ourselves to every man's conscience in the sight of God.

—2 Corinthians 4:1–2

True preaching is God's brush with which He paints a vivid picture of His Son before the eyes of the soul. By the supernatural grace of the Holy Spirit, Christ is not only pictured in the preached word but also present in the preached word. Spirit-filled, Bible-saturated proclamation brings the hearers into an encounter with Jesus Christ and Him crucified.

The apostle Paul rebuked the Galatian churches, "before whose eyes Jesus Christ hath been evidently set forth, crucified among you," for turning from the truth (Gal. 3:1). The word translated "evidently set forth" (*prographō*) here means to "write or draw something before the eyes of the public."[1] William Perkins said that in this text we "observe the properties of the ministry of the

---

1. Cf. Richard N. Longenecker, *Galatians*, Word Biblical Commentary 41 (n.p.: Nelson, 1990), 100. I delivered an abbreviated form of this address at the Reformed Presbyterian Seminary's annual conference in Pittsburgh on September 8, 2018.

word: The first, that it must be plain, perspicuous, and evident, as if the doctrine were pictured and painted before the eyes of men.... The second property of the ministry of the word is that it must be powerful and lively in operation."[2]

Not all preaching is plain and powerful, and Paul knew that well. The apostle set his own preaching in direct contrast to the oratory that commonly entertains this world. On the one hand, the preaching of the apostles exhibited characteristics distinctly fitting to Christ and His ways; on the other, there is preaching that suits this world and its ways. Though the difference is stark, lack of discernment in this matter can quickly open the church to the wrong kind of preaching. We see this in Paul's words quoted earlier from 1 Corinthians 2 and 2 Corinthians 4, words that should be studied by every preacher and aspirant to the ministry.

Notice the different phrases used of these two kinds of preaching. Apostolic preaching is characterized as: "the testimony of God" (1 Cor. 2:1), concerning "Jesus Christ, and him crucified" (v. 2), the "demonstration of the Spirit and of power" (v. 4), "the power of God" (v. 5), and the "manifestation of the truth" by which the preacher commends himself "to every man's conscience in the sight of God" (2 Cor. 4:2). Worldly preaching is noted by these marks: "excellency of speech or of wisdom" (1 Cor. 2:1), "enticing words of mans wisdom" (v. 4), "the wisdom of men" (v. 5), "hidden things of dishonesty," "craftiness," and "handling the word of God deceitfully" (2 Cor. 4:2).

The difference between these two approaches to preaching is nearly as great as that between Christ and the devil. Yet by nature we crave worldly preaching. Only the grace of the Holy Spirit makes us love spiritual preaching. How can we be sure to follow the right kind of preaching? How can the preacher make sure that he is faithful to his Lord not only in the message but also in his method and manner of delivery? How can a church discern between Christ-honoring, Spirit-empowered preaching, and preaching in the carnal wisdom and power of man? To answer these questions, let us give more specific consideration to the character of plain and powerful Spirit-anointed preaching.

---

2. William Perkins, *A Commentary, or, Exposition upon the Five First Chapters of the Epistle to the Galatians.... Continued with a Supplement upon the Sixth Chapter, by Ralph Cudworth*, in *The Works of William Perkins, Volume 2*, ed. Paul M. Smalley (Grand Rapids: Reformation Heritage Books, 2015), 148. The only explicit reference in the Holy Scriptures to "plain" preaching is "plainness of speech" (2 Cor. 3:12), which may be more precisely translated as "boldness" (*parrēsia*), as will be discussed later in this article. However, the concept of plain preaching resonates through 1 Cor. 2:1–5; 2 Cor. 4:1–2; and 1 Thess. 2:1–6.

The Renunciation Required by Plain Preaching

Plain preaching is not about a style of preaching but the spirituality of the preacher. It grows out of biblical convictions strengthening the heart, the fear of God animating the soul, and faith in Jesus Christ working by love. It is crucified preaching by a crucified preacher—one who has died with Christ to this world, and the world to him (Gal. 6:14). Plain preaching is Christian self-denial applied to the ministry of the Word performed under the direction of the Word. Plain preaching requires the preacher to renounce man's wisdom and carnal ambition.

Renounce Man's Wisdom

Paul wrote to the Corinthians, "And I, brethren, when I came to you, came not with excellency of speech or of wisdom" (1 Cor. 2:1). The word translated "excellency" (*huperochē*) means superiority,[3] and refers to outstanding eloquence or rhetorical skill in speaking.[4] Today we would say the ability to wow an audience. But there was no wow factor in Paul's person or speech (2 Cor. 10:10); he had to work within his own limitations. But more importantly, in the matter of content and method, Paul intentionally chose to preach in such a manner "that your faith should not stand in the wisdom of men" (1 Cor. 2:5).

The first two chapters of 1 Corinthians sharply contrast man's wisdom with God's wisdom.[5] For example, Paul says, "Christ sent me not to baptize, but to preach the gospel: not with wisdom of words, lest the cross of Christ should be made of none effect" (1 Cor. 1:17). God has intentionally designed His plan of salvation to overthrow "the wisdom of the wise" in this world (vv. 19–20; cf. 3:18–20).

What did Paul mean by "wisdom of men" and "wisdom of words"? Let us not twist these phrases into a rejection of all human intelligence and rational argument. Christians have true wisdom. Paul had one of the finest minds of his day. His writings are not rambling streams of consciousness; they are thoughtful arguments and moving rhetoric grounded on Old Testament revelation. Paul did not reject wisdom in itself, but he refused to rely on human wisdom because fallen man cannot find God by the use of human reason: "the world by wisdom knew not God" (1 Cor. 1:21). Paul sought instead to declare God's gospel with what the old divines called perspicuity, which means clarity in thought and meaning. As Henry Smith (1560–1591) said, "To preach simply, is not to

---

3. *Huperochē* can be used for human authority (1 Tim. 2:2). Cf. *huperechō* in Rom. 13:1.

4. Roy E. Ciampa and Brian S. Rosner, *The First Letter to the Corinthians*, The Pillar New Testament Commentary (Grand Rapids: Eerdmans, 2010), 113.

5. 1 Cor. 1:17, 19, 20, 21, 22, 24, 30; 2:1, 4, 5, 6, 7, 13.

preach unlearnedly, nor confusedly, but plainly and perspicuously [clearly], that the simplest which doth hear, may understand what is taught, as if he did hear his name."[6]

What kind of wisdom does Paul then reject? He rejects the so-called wisdom that flatters human pride. In the Hellenistic culture that prevailed in Corinth and throughout the Roman Empire, many Greek-speaking people considered themselves to be "wise" in contrast to the "barbarians" of other nations (Rom. 1:14). The Corinthians had become ensnared by "the speech of them which are puffed up" (1 Cor. 4:19). Paul would have none of it, nor would he embrace the pride of his own Jewish culture. He said, "Where is the wise? Where is the scribe? Where is the disputer of this world?" (1:20; cf. Isa. 33:18). The Greeks had "the wise [man]," that is, the philosopher who by intellectual power was able to reason his way to the truth. In Jewish culture, there was "the scribe," the scholar who claimed to teach God's Word but actually based his doctrine on "the tradition of the elders" (Mark 7:5; cf. Gal. 1:14). There was also "the disputer" (*suzētētēs*), which translates an unusual Greek word and probably refers to someone who engages in witty debates about philosophical topics.[7]

The plain preacher renounces these forms of proclamation, not because reasoning, tradition, and wit are inherently wrong but because God's Word must be the sole basis of Christian proclamation. Unlike the Greek philosopher, the plain preacher will make no claim on people's belief or behavior based merely on human logic. Logic must be the servant of God's Word, not a usurper that seeks to steal the throne. As opposed to the scribes of Judaism, the plain preacher grounds his doctrine on God's Word alone, not what a famous teacher said. Tradition and quotations from past theologians are valuable only insofar as they are faithful to what God says and help make His Word plain to the hearers.

In contrast to the disputer, the plain preacher does not aim to impress and please his hearers with how clever or ingenious he is in his communication. Rhetorical skill and illustrations may be enlisted to press the truth of God home to men's hearts, but they must not betray their commission by taking on a life of their own. Preaching must never be an empty show of oratorical ability.

---

6. *Works of Henry Smith* (Stoke-on-Trent, England: Tentmaker, 2002), 1:337.

7. The word *suzētētēs* is unknown in Greek literature apart from this passage. The related noun *suzētētsis* means "dispute" or "quarrel" but was used by Cicero for delightful conversation with a philosophical friend. Gerhard Kittel, Geoffrey W. Bromiley, and Gerhard Friedrich, eds., *Theological Dictionary of the New Testament* (Grand Rapids: Eerdmans, 1964–), 7:748. See Cicero, *Epistolae ad Familares*, 16.21.4, in *Cicero: The Letters to His Friends, Volume 3, The Letters to Brutus*, trans. W. Glynn Williams and M. Cary, rev. ed., Loeb Classical Library (London: William Heinemann; Cambridge, Mass.: Harvard University Press, 1954), 366–67.

John Flavel (1628–1691) said, "A crucified style best suits the preachers of a crucified Christ…. Words are but servants to the matter. An iron key, fitted to… the lock, is more useful than a golden one, which will not open the door to the treasure."[8]

Renounce Carnal Ambitions

Gospel preachers must repent of the corrupt motives that may lead them to preach man's wisdom. Paul says that he and his comrades in ministry "have renounced the hidden things of dishonesty" (2 Cor. 4:2). The word translated "dishonesty" (*aischunē*) is not about telling lies; rather, it means "dishonor" or "shame." The idea is that a hidden agenda stands behind that kind of preaching that, if exposed, would bring public disgrace to the preacher. Paul's words call us to examine ourselves. If your church could see your motives for preaching, would you slink away in shame, or could you stand before them with a good conscience?

What shameful, hidden agenda might a preacher have? Paul said, "For our exhortation was not of deceit, nor of uncleanness, nor in guile" (1 Thess. 2:3). "Uncleanness" refers to using preaching as a way to win people's affections for the purpose of seducing them into sexual immorality (4:7). Another shameful motive is to win honor from men, or make a name for oneself. Paul says that he speaks "not as pleasing men, but God" (2:4), "nor of men sought we glory" (v. 6). Yet another is greed or covetousness, for Paul said that his words were not "a cloke of covetousness" (v. 5). Sex, fame, and money—these three snares catch and destroy far too many preachers.

Public speaking can be terrifying, but it can also be a thrill to the worldly soul. All eyes are on the preacher in his pulpit, and he drinks up their attention like wine. Afterward, he modestly gives glory to God, but he secretly treasures their compliments like medals of honor. Behind his pious prayers for the advancement of Christ's kingdom are longings for a bigger congregation and the wealth it will bring to him. How despicable are such motives in the soul of the preacher! How we need to watch and pray against temptation! Let us put to death the first motions of these sins by the power of the cross of Jesus Christ. "Wherefore let him that thinketh he standeth take heed lest he fall" (1 Cor. 10:12). Let us aspire to be plain preachers, knowing that this calling requires us to deny ourselves.

---

8. John Flavel, "The Character of a Complete Evangelical Pastor, Drawn by Christ," in *The Works of John Flavel* (1820; repr., Edinburgh: Banner of Truth, 1968), 6:572. The original reads "stile."

The Resolution Required by Plain Preaching

Though plain preaching demands that we say no to the wisdom and lusts of this world, the primary thrust of our calling is positive. The man who fulfills this work must be a man of courage and holy resolve. He has turned his back to the world and lifted his eyes to heaven. Plain preaching requires that the preacher resolve to declare God's Word to inform the mind concerning Jesus Christ and convince the conscience before God.

Resolve to Declare God's Word

Instead of preaching with "excellence of speech or of wisdom," Paul commends declaring "the testimony of God" (1 Cor. 2:1). The word translated "testimony" (*martyrion*) suggests that the word preached by the apostle possessed the solemn authority of a legal or covenantal document (Deut. 6:17; Ps. 25:10 LXX), such as the Ten Commandments (Ex. 32:15; 34:29 LXX). The Word of God bears inherent authority infinitely greater than that of man. John says, "If we receive the witness of men, the witness of God is greater" (1 John 5:9). David declares that "the testimony of the LORD is sure, making wise the simple" (Ps. 19:7).

Christian preachers are commissioned "before God, and the Lord Jesus Christ" only to "preach the word" (2 Tim. 4:1–2). Indeed, as God's covenant messengers, faithful preachers dare not add or subtract from God's Word but proclaim and apply only what the Lord has said. Plain preaching is fundamentally the exposition of the meaning of the Holy Scriptures, the faithful drawing out of their sound doctrines, and the experiential and practical application of those doctrines to daily life.

The problem with preaching man's wisdom is not just what we say but what we neglect to say. Paul says, "We speak the wisdom of God" (1 Cor. 2:7). Though men often despise God's Word as foolishness, "the foolishness of God is wiser than men" (1:18, 23, 25). God's wisdom is the gold, silver, and gemstones fit to build a temple of eternal glory; man's wisdom is wood, hay, and stubble that will burn up and be lost forever (3:12–15). Which would you rather use to build the church? Shall we pass by what is solid, durable, and precious in order to seek to grasp what will ultimately prove to be a mere vapor of smoke?

The inestimable privilege of the Christian preacher is to declare God's Word. Preachers, resolve with all your heart to be like Ezra, who set his heart to study God's Word, to put it into practice, and to teach it to God's people (Ezra 7:10). Like the faithful priests of ancient Israel, may your lips guard knowledge, and may people seek God's Word from your mouth, for you are the messenger of the Lord of hosts (Mal. 2:7).

Resolve to Inform the Mind Concerning Jesus Christ

Paul goes on to say, "For I determined not to know any thing among you, save Jesus Christ, and him crucified" (1 Cor. 2:2). Note the simplicity of Paul's resolution: his sermons all brought his hearers to the person and work of Jesus Christ. Paul says, "God forbid that I should glory, save in the cross of our Lord Jesus Christ, by whom the world is crucified unto me, and I unto the world" (Gal. 6:14). To proclaim that a man killed as a criminal is the Lord and Savior is offensive to the world (1 Cor. 1:17), yet it is the heart of the Christian gospel (15:3).

Let us not confuse simplicity in preaching Christ with oversimplification. Paul did not preach the same sermon over and over again. Paul preached "Jesus Christ, and him crucified" because he understood that all the many streams of divine grace meet in Christ and flow to us through Christ, whom God has made to us "wisdom, and righteousness, and sanctification, and redemption" (1 Cor. 1:30). At times he preached Christ as our Prophet, "in whom are hid all the treasures of wisdom and knowledge" (Col. 2:2). Never did our Prophet reveal the will of God for our salvation more clearly and powerfully than when He suffered the shame of the cross. At other times Paul's preaching focused on Christ the Priest, who offered Himself "a propitiation through faith in his blood," to glorify God's righteousness "that he might be just, and the justifier of him which believeth in Jesus" (Rom. 3:25–26). On the basis of His atoning death, that same Priest intercedes at God's right hand for His people—which fueled Paul's assurance that nothing can separate us from the love of God (8:33–35). Paul sometimes preached Christ as our King, who "spoiled principalities and powers," triumphing over Satan's forces by the cross (Col. 2:15). Having won the victory once and for all at Calvary, the Lord Christ is now risen from the dead to share His power and victory with the church that lives in union with Him (Eph. 1:19–23). Paul did not preach a bland, formulaic, repetitive message but, rather, "the unsearchable riches of Christ" (3:8).

We also should not conclude that Paul always preached the doctrine of Christ explicitly. He preached the whole counsel of God (Acts 20:27). If Paul preached the doctrine of God, he proclaimed the God and Father of our Lord Jesus Christ (2 Cor. 1:3). If Paul preached the doctrine of sin, it was to show that we need the righteousness of God in Christ (Rom. 3:10–26). If Paul preached obedience to God's law, he did so in the context of the new man created in Christ Jesus (Eph. 4:22–24). Everything brought him back to Christ, for it is God's will that Christ be everything to the believer. Roy Ciampa and Brian Rosner comment, "For Paul, *Christ crucified* is more than just the means of forgiveness and salvation; rather, it informs his total vision of the Christian life and ministry."[9]

The preaching of Christ and Him crucified shows us that plain preaching is not sentimental but doctrinal (2 Tim. 4:2). Our aim is not merely to generate emotion but to inform the mind with the clear light of the truth. Paul called his preaching the "manifestation of the truth" (2 Cor. 4:2), where "manifestation" (*phanerōsis*) means "clear and open display."[10] He compared it to the shining of light, "the light of the glorious gospel of Christ," which is so plain to see that only those "blinded" by Satan can fail to apprehend it (vv. 3–4).

Plain preaching aims to set forth in clearest and simplest terms the doctrinal truths of the Holy Scriptures so that ordinary men, women, and children can see Jesus Christ, their need of Him, and what it means to trust in Him and to follow Him. The preacher must indeed dig into the deep mines of exegesis and theology as he prepares for his sermon. But he does not bring to the congregation raw ore out of those mines; he brings refined gold and silver and gemstones already cut and polished—ready to adorn God's living temple. He considers whether to discuss the meaning of a Hebrew or Greek word or to present a theological term and its definition or to quote some theologian of the past, and weighs it not in the worldly scale of whether it will impress his hearers with his scholarship but in the balance of the sanctuary as to whether it will make the message of God's Word plain and clear to them. Cotton Mather said of John Eliot, a Puritan missionary to the Native Americans, that his "way of preaching was very plain; so that the very *lambs* might wade into his discourses on those texts and themes, wherein *elephants* might swim."[11]

Resolve to Convince the Conscience before God

Plain preaching not only teaches doctrine, however, but also calls for the response of "faith" (1 Cor. 2:5). Therefore, Paul says, faithful preachers are always "commending ourselves to every man's conscience in the sight of God" (2 Cor. 4:2). When Paul speaks of "commending ourselves," he is not seeking men's praises

---

9. Ciampa and Rosner, *The First Letter to the Corinthians*, 114.

10. The noun *phanerōsis* appears in the NT only in 2 Cor. 4:2 and 1 Cor. 12:7. The cognate verb *phaneroō* means to visibly "appear" (Mark 16:12, 14) or metaphorically to "become plain" (Rom. 3:21; Eph. 5:13) and is the opposite of to "hide" (Mark 4:22; 1 Cor. 4:5). Compare *phanerōs* in Mark 1:45; John 7:10. Ralph Martin renders *phanerōsis* as "open declaration." Ralph P. Martin, *2 Corinthians*, Word Biblical Commentary 40 (Nashville: Thomas Nelson, 1986), 78.

11. Cotton Mather, *The Great Works of Christ in America: Magnalia Christi Americana*, Book 3 (London: Banner of Truth, 1979), 1:547–48.

but persuading men's hearts that he is a faithful messenger of God and that his message has divine authority.

To appeal to men's consciences, the preacher must be absolutely convinced concerning the truth of what he preaches and earnestly moved by its reality. Such conviction and earnestness comes from the fear of God and an awareness of preaching in the presence of God. Paul says, "Knowing therefore the terror of the Lord, we persuade men; but we are made manifest unto God; and I trust also are made manifest in your consciences" (2 Cor. 5:11).

Nothing is so tragic as a preacher whose mode of preaching breathes an air of unreality. It is said that in the seventeenth century, Archbishop William Sancroft (1617–1693) asked the actor Thomas Betterton (c. 1635–1710) why actors can move their audiences with imaginary things when preachers declare real things but people in church treat them as imaginary. Betterton replied, "I don't know, except it is that we actors speak of things imaginary as if they were real, while you in the pulpit speak of things real as if they were imaginary."[12] May this never be said of us!

Convinced in his own conscience, the preacher aims to convince the conscience of his hearers. He reminds them that they, too, are in the presence of God and presses upon them their sins against God and their duties to God. As Paul says, he preaches "to every man's conscience in the sight of God" (2 Cor. 4:2). He proclaims the truth as a true messenger of God, addressing those who shortly must appear before God's judgment seat. Increase Mather (1639–1723) said of his father, Richard Mather (1596–1669), "His way of preaching was plain, aiming to shoot his arrows not over his people's heads, but into their hearts and consciences."[13]

The faithful preacher must invest significant thought in the application of the text to his own life and the lives of his hearers. The Westminster *Directory for the Public Worship of God* says, "He is not to rest in general doctrine, although never so much cleared and confirmed, but to bring it home to special use, by application to his hearers." The directory acknowledges that this may be "a work of great difficulty to himself, requiring much prudence, zeal, and meditation, and to the natural and corrupt man will be very unpleasant," but says he must do it so that "his auditors may feel the word of God to be quick and powerful, and a discerner of the thoughts and intents of the heart." In the directory, the Westminster divines identified six kinds of application:

---

12. *The Tatler: A Daily Paper of Literature, Fine Arts, Music, and the Stage*, no. 131 (February 3, 1831): 523.

13. Increase Mather, *The Life and Death of that Reverend Man of God, Mr. Richard Mather* (Cambridge, Mass.: S.G. and M.J., 1670), 31–32.

(1) instruction in doctrinal implications for the Christian worldview; (2) refutation of errors presently threatening the people; (3) exhortation to obey God's commands and make use of the means God provides to flourish spiritually; (4) "dehortations," or warnings against particular sins and their consequences; (5) comfort for believers to strengthen them to keep fighting the good fight; and (6) help in self-examination by giving marks from God's Word to determine one's spiritual condition.[14]

Applied preaching is possible only by the fear of God. This was the case for the faithful Levitical priest, of whom the Lord said, "He feared me, and was afraid before my name. The law of truth was in his mouth, and iniquity was not found in his lips: he walked with me in peace and equity, and did turn many away from iniquity" (Mal. 2:5–6). Such was the great principle behind the book of Ecclesiastes, summed up in its final words: "Fear God, and keep his commandments: for this is the whole duty of man. For God shall bring every work into judgment, with every secret thing, whether it be good, or whether it be evil" (Eccl. 12:13–14).

Such holy resolutions are essential to plain preaching, but they are not natural to our souls. They require us to crucify the flesh by the death of Christ and to live unto God by His resurrection life. Plain preaching requires that the preacher resolve to declare God's Word to inform the mind concerning Jesus Christ and convince the conscience before God.

The Results God Gives through Plain Preaching

We cannot produce results, but we do desire results for the glory of God and the good of our hearers. Therefore, we pray for and labor to bring forth spiritual children. We may do so in confidence. Plain preaching is God's ordinary means to exercise spiritual power, not by human manipulation but by the Holy Spirit who gives faith.

God's Ordinary Means to Exercise Spiritual Power

The Word plainly preached is a powerful tool in the hands of God. Paul says he preaches Christ in this plain manner "that your faith should not stand in the wisdom of men, but in the power of God" (1 Cor. 2:5). He heartily believed that the gospel was "the power of God unto salvation" (Rom. 1:16). Yes, "the word of the cross is folly to those who are perishing," and they scoff at it; but to those "who are being saved it is the power of God" (1 Cor. 1:18).

---

14. *Westminster Confession of Faith* (Glasgow: Free Presbyterian Publications, 1994), 380.

Are we satisfied merely by the dissemination of information if the power of God is not present to change lives? May it never be so. We must not mistake Paul's emphasis upon teaching the truth for merely educating the mind. Paul says, "For the kingdom of God is not in word, but in power" (1 Cor. 4:20), and we find him rejoicing that "our gospel came not unto you in word only, but also in power" (1 Thess. 1:5). The faithful preacher does not shrug and say, "Whether or not anyone is saved or sanctified through my preaching, it does not matter to me." No, his heart's cry is for the power of God to come flaming from heaven and strike the altar so that the people turn back to God and declare, "The LORD, he is God!" (see 1 Kings 18:37–39).

Nor is the power of God divorced from the preacher and his manner of preaching. Hear me carefully on this point. I am not saying that the preacher provides the power nor that he merits God's blessing. All is of sovereign grace. However, when God sends power *through* the preacher, He generally sends power *to* the preacher. When Paul and Barnabas preached in Iconium, Luke reports that they "so spake, that a great multitude...believed" (Acts 14:1). The manner of their preaching impacted their hearers. How did they preach? Luke goes on to say that they were "speaking boldly" (*parrēsiazomai*). Paul likewise says, "We were bold in our God to speak unto you the gospel of God with much contention" (1 Thess. 2:2). When Paul says of his ministry, "We use great plainness of speech" (2 Cor. 3:12), the Greek text may be literally translated, "We use boldness [*parrēsia*]" (cf. KJV mg.). This is characteristic of Spirit-filled preaching—a supernatural boldness, freedom, and authority (Acts 4:8, 13, 31).

Powerful Christian preaching is not human boldness or proud self-confidence. It is boldness rooted in God and in His Word and is entirely consistent with preaching "in weakness, and in fear, and in much trembling," as Paul says (1 Cor. 2:3). Spirit-empowered boldness humbles man and exalts God alone. Paul's "fear" and "trembling" have sometimes been explained as the consequence of his personal problems or the challenges of the ministry, but it may well be that he preached with fear and trembling precisely because he spoke as one who knows that he speaks in the presence of the living God.[15] In other words, a sense of your own weakness and unworthiness mingled with the fear of God may be a sign not of poor preaching but preaching in the fullness of the Spirit.

---

15. Ciampa and Rosner, *The First Letter to the Corinthians*, 115–16. See the use of "fear" (*phobos*) and "trembling" (*tromos*) in Ex. 15:16; Ps. 2:11; Isa. 19:16 LXX; Phil. 2:12.

Not Power by Human Manipulation

This spiritual power is not the natural influence that a skillful speaker can exercise over a crowd. Paul says, "My speech and my preaching was not with enticing words of man's wisdom" (1 Cor. 2:4). The word translated "enticing" (*peithos*) means "persuasive."[16] The idea here is that the faithful preacher does not rely on techniques of persuasion to motivate people apart from their sincere belief and conviction of the truth. The plain preacher is "not walking in craftiness, nor handling the word of God deceitfully" (2 Cor. 4:2). Instead he is relying on the power of God while he faithfully preaches the truth to the minds and consciences of his hearers.

Speech writers understand that there are certain methods that often succeed in getting people on your side and motivated to do what you want them to do. For example, a speaker might talk in a way that moves people to say, "He's one of us. I like him. He's a really impressive person. He can help us get what we want." But, Paul says, "We preach not ourselves, but Christ Jesus the Lord; and ourselves your servants for Jesus' sake" (2 Cor. 4:5).

Another method of human manipulation is the emotional appeal. Even if truth is not on a speaker's side, he can often stir people up with appeals and stories that keep them laughing or play on their fears or incite their anger. Demetrius the silversmith caused a riot in Ephesus with a speech like that, and the angry mob was ready to attack Christians though they hardly understood why (Acts 19:24–41). In contrast, Paul appealed to the emotions of his hearers only as he "reasoned with them out of the scriptures" (Acts 17:2). Affections must stand on truth. If we cannot move people with the truth of God, we have no alternative.

God made people to be motivated by hope (cf. Prov. 13:12), but a preacher can manipulate his hearers by giving them false hope of salvation without repenting of their sin. In Jeremiah's day, people in Jerusalem assured one another that they were safe because "the temple of the LORD" was with them—while neglecting to turn from injustice, oppression, and bloodshed to keeping God's commandments (Jer. 7:1–15). Paul refused to use "flattering words" that stroked the pride of his hearers and boosted their self-confidence instead of calling them to faith in Christ (1 Thess. 2:5). Paul also warned Timothy that people "will not endure sound doctrine; but after their own lusts shall they heap to themselves teachers, having itching ears" (2 Tim. 4:3). The faithful preacher will not scratch people where they itch or stoop to gratify their pride and sinful desires.

---

16. *Peithos* is *hapax legomena* in the NT and not attested in other Greek literature. It is an adjective related to "persuade" (*peithō*).

Spiritual power flows from Christ and Him crucified and thus bears the character of the cross. It is power to embrace the truth that offends us and humbles us. It is power to love what is good and hate what is evil, even though what is evil resides in our own hearts. It is power to hope in the glory that we cannot see and to have no regard for what we can see. Such power is not an effect produced by human manipulation. It is the power of God, speaking in His Word and speaking through His faithful servant.

Power by the Holy Spirit Who Gives Faith

Paul says, "My speech and my preaching was…in demonstration of the Spirit and of power: that your faith should not stand in the wisdom of men, but in the power of God" (1 Cor. 2:4–5). The power of plain preaching is the supernatural work of the Holy Spirit, using the preaching of the gospel to create and nurture faith in Jesus Christ. There is no substitute for the work of the Spirit. There is no safety net or fallback position for the preacher if the Holy Spirit does not do His work. All depends on His gracious influence. Such preaching is a fulfillment of Zechariah's prophecy that God's temple will be built "not by might, nor by power, but by my spirit, saith the LORD of hosts" (Zech. 4:6).

The word translated "demonstration" (*apodeixis*) means an exhibition or proof.[17] Among the ancient Greeks, the word could be used of logical proofs or arguments, such as in the philosophy of Aristotle.[18] Paul uses the word in direct contrast to the persuasive words of human wisdom. The "demonstration of the Spirit" refers to the Holy Spirit's powerful work to convince the hearts of men that God's preached Word is true so that they trust in Him.

How does the Holy Spirit work this "demonstration"? It cannot refer to miracles, signs, and wonders worked by the Holy Spirit, for Paul has just said that "the Jews require a sign" and consequently reject the message of "Christ crucified" (1 Cor. 1:22–23).[19] His point there is that God's saving message is not one of outward power but apparent weakness (v. 25). The "demonstration of the Spirit" is the inward, secret work of effectual calling by which God makes people into believers (v. 24). Paul tells us in the second chapter of his first epistle to the Corinthians that the Spirit gave the words of God to the apostles (1 Cor. 2:9–13). Now the Spirit enables us to receive the apostolic words as

---

17. *Apodeixis* is *hapax legomenon* in the NT. The cognate verb *apodeiknumi* means to display, exhibit, or prove to be genuine (Acts 2:22; 25:7; 1 Cor. 4:9; 2 Thess. 2:4).

18. Henry George Liddell and Robert Scott, comp., *A Greek-English Lexicon*, rev. Henry Stuart Jones and Roderick McKenzie (Oxford: Clarendon, 1996), 196.

19. Ciampa and Rosner, *The First Letter to the Corinthians*, 118. They comment, "*Power* here is about moral conviction, not miraculous display."

true wisdom. The person who does not have the Holy Spirit "receiveth not the things of the Spirit of God: for they are foolishness unto him: neither can he know them, because they are spiritually discerned" (v. 14). The power at work is the Spirit acting through the preaching of the Word that He inspired.

The greatest demonstration or proof of God's Word, and the only proof sufficient for saving faith, is the inner demonstration when the Holy Spirit opens our eyes to see the truth of God. When the Holy Spirit exercises His power through the preached Word, then the message comes with "much assurance," a strong inward conviction of the reality of unseen spiritual things (1 Thess. 1:5). John Calvin (1509–1564) says, "If we desire to provide in the best way for our consciences…we ought to seek our conviction in a higher place than human reasons, judgments, or conjectures, that is, in the secret testimony of the Spirit."[20] He explains, "For truth is cleared of all doubt when, not sustained by external props, it serves as its own support."[21]

This, then, is the power of the Holy Spirit: not visible or outward display of power but an inward demonstration or proof by which the Spirit convinces the heart of the gospel's truth so that the person intelligently and willingly cannot but trust in Christ. Faith may not seem like an impressive result in the eyes of this world. However, saving faith in Christ is the effect of "the exceeding greatness" of God's power, power no less than that which raised Christ from the dead and exalted Him to the right hand of God (Eph. 1:19–20). Faith unites a poor sinner to a rich Christ, so that all the benefits purchased by Christ's death on the cross are now his (John 1:12). Such faith conquers this evil world (1 John 5:4). By faith, God saves us and will bring us to eternal glory. Truly, the gift of faith is a work of sovereign power, and its preservation and growth a cause for glorifying God forever.

Though God could exercise His power to create faith through whatever means He chooses, it is very fitting that faith in Christ is worked through plain preaching. Plain preaching requires the preacher *to renounce man's wisdom and carnal ambitions*. Faith likewise is turning from our own understanding to trust in the Lord with all our hearts (Prov. 3:5). Faith in Christ trusts Jesus to save us from our sins and therefore is incompatible with the reign of sinful ambitions and desires in the heart. Plain preaching requires that the preacher *resolve faithfully to declare God's Word*, and faith rests entirely upon the testimony of God as true and trustworthy. Plain preaching aims to *inform the mind concerning*

---

20. John Calvin, *Institutes of the Christian Religion*, ed. John T. McNeill, trans. Ford Lewis Battles, Library of Christian Classics 20–21 (Philadelphia: Westminster, 1960), 1.7.4.

21. Calvin, *Institutes*, 1.8.1.

Jesus Christ and Him crucified, and that is precisely the great object of saving faith and the only confidence of the believer. Plain preaching aims to *convince the conscience before God*, and faith arises from a wounded conscience seeking healing by the blood of Christ, so that the sinner finds peace in the presence of a righteous God whose justice is satisfied once and for all by the finished work of Christ. How wise it was for our God to choose plain preaching as His primary means to exercise spiritual power unto faith!

Conclusion

Ministers of God, will you be plain preachers? Members of churches, will you pray that your ministers would be plain preachers? If you or your pastor will persevere in plain preaching, it will require more than an understanding of what it is. Plain preaching is only sustainable by faith in Christ and the fear of the Lord.

It takes faith to preach with plainness and boldness, especially when crowds of people are not flocking to hear you but are swarming about popular, worldly preachers. It requires faith to believe that plain preaching is God's method to bring many sons and daughters to glory. Even as the preacher calls his hearers to faith in Christ, he, too, must exercise faith in Christ that the Word preached is the power of God for salvation.

The pressure to employ worldly methods to bolster your ministry will be intense at times. Who among us is not tempted to please people? However, the fear of the Lord can deliver us from this snare. Let us remember that we are messengers of the King. Both we and our hearers will stand before His judgment seat one day. Let the preacher preach as a dying man to dying men with the world behind his back and the glory of God before his eyes.

Plain preaching is contrary to the nature of fallen mankind. It is ignored, derided, and scorned. Yet the plain preaching of God's Word is exceedingly precious. This is the box in which God brings the wedding ring of faith to His bride. Far from being boring, plain preaching in the power of the Holy Spirit is a beam of heavenly glory touching this sin-darkened earth.

Therefore, let us devote ourselves to prayer for the ministry of the Word, that it may be plain and powerful. Let the preacher make his study into his prayer closet and read and write with continual petition and praise. Robert Traill (1642–1716) said, "Many good sermons are lost for lack of much prayer in study."[22] May it never be said of our preaching, "Ye have not, because ye ask not" (James 4:2). Rather, may our preaching be a continual testimony to the

---

22. Robert Traill, "By What Means May Ministers Best Win Souls?," in *The Works of the Late Reverend Robert Traill* (Edinburgh: J. Ogle et al., 1810), 1:246.

promise, "Ask, and it shall be given you; seek, and ye shall find; knock, and it shall be opened unto you" (Matt. 7:7). And as we pray, let us labor to conform our preaching as much as possible to the gospel-pattern exemplified by the apostle Paul, who preached "not with enticing words of man's wisdom, but in demonstration of the Spirit and of power" (1 Cor. 2:4).

Chapter 26

How to Evaluate Your Sermons

Who then is Paul, and who is Apollos, but ministers by whom ye believed, even as the Lord gave to every man? I have planted, Apollos watered; but God gave the increase. So then neither is he that planteth any thing, neither he that watereth; but God that giveth the increase. Now he that planteth and he that watereth are one: and every man shall receive his own reward according to his own labour. For we are labourers together with God: ye are God's husbandry, ye are God's building. According to the grace of God which is given unto me, as a wise masterbuilder, I have laid the foundation, and another buildeth thereon. But let every man take heed how he buildeth thereupon. For other foundation can no man lay than that is laid, which is Jesus Christ. Now if any man build upon this foundation gold, silver, precious stones, wood, hay, stubble; every man's work shall be made manifest: for the day shall declare it, because it shall be revealed by fire; and the fire shall try every man's work of what sort it is. If any man's work abide which he hath built thereupon, he shall receive a reward. If any man's work shall be burned, he shall suffer loss: but he himself shall be saved; yet so as by fire.

—1 Corinthians 3:5–15

In the 2010 Winter Olympics, speed-skater Sven Kramer was poised to win a second gold medal. He pressed forward in the last eight of twenty-five laps in the grueling 10,000-meter race. He had a six-second lead on the men behind him, and victory seemed sure. But then Kramer's coach shouted, "Inner lane!" Kramer hesitated, then changed lanes, finishing the race for what he believed was a sure win.

His race earned him nothing, as Olympic officials ruled that Kramer's cross into the wrong lane disqualified him from the race. The loss was far worse for his coach. "This is the worst moment of my career," he said.[1] What a tragedy for those highly skilled men after years of training!

It is far worse for a servant of the Lord to cross the boundaries of his calling, thereby losing some of the heavenly reward that might have been his. The Bible reminds us that an athlete does not receive the victor's crown unless he competes according to the rules (2 Tim. 2:5). This tragedy is not limited to scandalous falls and apostasies that bring open shame to ministers of the gospel. It is also evident in the quiet lane changes by which godly preachers of the Word operate outside their Lord's will. These errors do not disqualify a man's pastoral ministry, but they do compromise his calling and will ultimately cost him some reward.

As preachers, we are like spiritual athletes who need to keep growing and developing our skills. We also function as spiritual coaches to Christ's church. Our sermons seriously affect those under our care; our responsibility is great. It is especially frightening for a preacher to press forward with energy and satisfaction, realizing how he erred only after reaching the finish line.

We must regularly evaluate our preaching to know if we are growing as preachers. Charles Spurgeon (1834–1892) said to his ministerial students, "I give you the motto, 'Go forward.' Go forward in personal attainments, forward in gifts and in grace, forward in fitness for the work, and forward in conformity to the image of Jesus." Spurgeon went on to say, "If there be any brother here who thinks he can preach as well as he should, I would advise him to leave off altogether."[2]

How do you evaluate yourself as a preacher? A preacher's view of his own messages can be an emotional roller-coaster ride driven by his moods and the responses of the congregation. We dare not evaluate ourselves by measurable results such as increased attendance or new members joining the church, for people often flock to false teachers like flies to manure. Nor can we gauge our effectiveness by a brother who shoots out of a worship service like a bullet out of a rifle while a woman gets misty-eyed and emotional in shaking your hand after a sermon. For all you know, the brother was suddenly taken ill, and the sister received bad news yesterday about a distant relative. Neither response necessarily has anything to do with your preaching. My father was once so moved by a child's

---

1. http://sportsillustrated.cnn.com/2010/olympics/2010/writers/alexander_wolff/02/23/kramer.netherlands/index.html, accessed 11-10-10. I thank Paul Smalley for his assistance on this chapter, which is an address I gave in Homiletics I at Puritan Reformed Theological Seminary, November 16, 2010.

2. C. H. Spurgeon, "The Necessity of Ministerial Progress," in *Lectures to My Students* (1881; reprint, Pasadena: Pilgrim, 1990), 2.23, 28.

intense listening that he questioned her about what she found so important. She responded, "I was trying to figure out if you had shaved this morning."

This does not mean we should plow forward without reflection, however. We need standards for self-evaluation. Our habitual standard should be *to evaluate our preaching as a servant anticipating our Master's evaluation.* In 1 Corinthians 1, the apostle Paul addresses the issue of division within the church, specifically in people's preference for one teacher over another, such as Paul or Apollos or Peter (1 Cor. 1:10–12). Chapter 3 opens with Paul accusing the Corinthians of petty, childish bickering. He says in 1 Corinthians 3:4, "For while one saith, I am of Paul; and another, I am of Apollos; are ye not carnal?" This sets the stage for 1 Corinthians 3:5–15, in which Paul tells the church how to evaluate teachers of the Word. The text has huge implications for how pastors and Bible teachers should view their own ministry. In telling us that we must each evaluate our preaching as a servant anticipating his master's evaluation, this text suggests five questions to ask ourselves about our preaching. Each question provides both a motivation and a method for evaluating your sermons.

1. Did I preach as God's servant?

The apostle says in 1 Corinthians 3:5–8, "Who then is Paul, and who is Apollos, but ministers by whom ye believed, even as the Lord gave to every man? I have planted, Apollos watered; but God gave the increase. So then neither is he that planteth any thing, neither he that watereth; but God that giveth the increase. Now he that planteth and he that watereth are one: and every man shall receive his own reward according to his own labour."

The word *ministers* (in Greek, *diakonoi*) refers to household servants under the authority of a master or lord (*kurios*, cf. Luke 12:37). No matter what their tax forms say, ministers are not self-employed. We are not independent agents free to do as we please; we are servants of the King. The Lord assigns to us our vocation, and He rewards us accordingly. Though the Lord gives us different gifts, different placements, and different degrees of fruitfulness, we are one in our calling as His servants. Instead of evaluating our work by comparing it to other preachers, we should evaluate it in comparison to the Lord's commands.

We are also farmers who plant and irrigate our fields but cannot make the seeds grow. Cornfields often have signs posting what kind of seed the farmer planted, such as Pioneer, Agrigold, or DeKalb. The signs remind us that much depends on the life within the seed, not the farmer. A thousand factors determine the yield of a crop, almost all of which God directly controls. How much more, then, are ministers dependent on the work of God the Holy Spirit to save and sanctify people by the life-giving seed of His Word? We can do nothing by ourselves. Charles Hodge (1797–1878) said in his commentary on this text, "Ministers are mere instruments in the hands of God. The doctrines which they preach are not their own discoveries, and the power which renders their preaching successful is not in them."[3]

As a servant under the Lord's authority, a preacher should evaluate his sermons based on their fidelity to Holy Scripture. First Corinthians 4:1 tells us that we are "stewards of the mysteries of God." You are God's delivery man to bring His message to others; you are not the author of the message. A messenger who rushes off without first listening to his Master's words exposes himself to great shame.

So evaluate your sermons with what I am calling *humble exegesis*, with the criteria of a humble servant, asking yourself if you:

+ Approached the Scripture with a willingness to be taught and corrected by God or assumed that you already knew what the Scripture said;
+ Spent enough time and energy to study that Scripture text and let God speak to you through it;
+ Read the commentaries of godly and wise teachers to check your interpretation;
+ Derived the main idea and points from the clear statement of a Scripture text;
+ Spent time explaining what the text meant so your listeners could better understand it;
+ Based applications of your sermon on the Scriptures, not just on your vision for the church;
+ Preached a message that was faithful to the text's meaning in its context;
+ Demonstrated to your hearers that your sermon came from God's Word instead of your own ideas, thoughts, or opinions.

Since your ministry depends on God's power, you should also evaluate your preaching in prayers of *humble dependence*. Without the Holy Spirit you are no more useful than an unplugged power saw. So ask yourself as a servant of the Savior if you:

+ Planned this series and this specific sermon, prayerfully asking God for wisdom;
+ Enlisted your congregation to pray for your preaching;

---

3. Charles Hodge, *A Commentary on 1&2 Corinthians* (1857–1859; reprint, Edinburgh: Banner of Truth, 1994), 51.

- Studied the Scripture text on your knees, with fervent pleas for illumination;
- Prepared the sermon in the context of regular, private prayers for the church;
- Cried out to God prior to the worship services for the Spirit's anointing;
- Cried out to God after the services for divine application;
- Gave God all the glory for any good that resulted from your efforts.

Do you feel an urgent need for the anointing of the Holy Spirit? One of the greatest preachers of the last century, Martyn Lloyd-Jones (1899–1981), wrote,

> Do you always look for and seek this unction, this anointing before preaching? Has this been your greatest concern?... It is God giving power, and enabling, through the Spirit, to the preacher in order that he may do this work in a manner that lifts it up beyond the efforts and endeavors of man to a position in which the preacher is being used by the Spirit and becomes a channel through which the Spirit works.[4]

You must ask yourself, "Did I preach as God's servant?" Evaluate your sermons for any hint that you stood in the pulpit as a lord and savior instead of a humble servant and messenger whose authority comes solely from God.

2. Did I preach to build God's church?

Paul goes on to say in 1 Corinthians 3:9, "For we are labourers together with God: ye are God's husbandry [farm], ye are God's building." The Greek text stresses that this entire project belongs to God when it says: "*God's* workers... *God's* field... and *God's* building."[5] The metaphor shifts from agriculture to construction as God tells His servants to build the people of the church, which verse 16 says is "the temple of God."

God is the architect of His temple. He is also the general contractor and the glorious Being who inhabits this house. Ministers are laborers whom God hires to build His house, a building not made of wood, brick, stone, or steel, but of "living stones," the people of God. "Ye are God's building," our text says. Therefore the construction metaphor communicates the love of our covenant God who wants to dwell in eternal intimacy with His people. The Lord aims not only to make His home among us but also to make us His home.

---

4. D. Martyn Lloyd-Jones, *Preaching & Preachers* (Grand Rapids: Zondervan, 1971), 305.

5. In each of the three clauses of 1 Cor. 3:9, the word "God's" (*theou*) is pushed to the beginning. See Gordon D. Fee, *The First Epistle to the Corinthians* (Grand Rapids: Eerdmans, 1987), 134.

The purpose of preaching, then, is not to produce a work of theological or rhetorical art abstracted from human need. It is to build up God's living and holy temple—men, women, and children—in Christ. Preaching the Word is the divinely appointed means to bring God and His people together in eternal, mutual love. J. I. Packer writes, "Christianity, on earth as in heaven, is…fellowship with the Father and with His Son Jesus Christ, and the preaching of God's Word in the power of God's Spirit is the activity that…brings the Father and the Son down from heaven to dwell with men."[6]

This means your preaching must be helpful to people. So ask in preparing your sermons, did you:

- Write your sermon with an eye to your flock and their needs?
- Labor hard and long on this sermon out of love, or were you lazy?
- Organize the message to make listening easier for people?
- Begin with an introduction (either before or after giving out your text) to engage people's minds and lead them to the main idea?
- Clearly state the main idea of the message?
- Highlight the main points so that listeners recognized them?
- State your main idea and points so succinctly that a twelve-year-old boy and a seventy-year-old woman could write them in their notes?
- Help people understand ancient culture and customs foreign to their world?
- Limit your time and content to what your hearers can profitably absorb?
- Illustrate each major point to engage their imagination and affections?
- Craft your illustrations to make them helpful for understanding and applying the gospel?
- Make specific applications throughout the sermon relevant to people's lives?
- Conclude the sermon by pressing the main idea home to listeners?
- Express the loving heart of the Father who calls prodigals home?
- Call the unsaved to repentance and faith in Christ?

Love for the congregation must also motivate us to consider the spiritual variety of our listeners. William Perkins reminds us that our people have different spiritual capacities and needs. The preacher is like a housewife preparing a meal for a family ranging from a diabetic grandpa to voracious teenagers to a

---

6. J. I. Packer, "Introduction: Why Preach?" in *The Preacher and Preaching: Reviving the Art in the Twentieth Century*, ed. Samuel T. Logan, Jr. (Phillipsburg: Presbyterian & Reformed, 1986), 2.

toddler. You must preach law and gospel in the right proportion to a group of people with various needs. Ask yourself, did you:

+ Rebuke unbelievers who are ignorant and unteachable?
+ Offer basic catechetical truths to unbelievers who are ignorant but teachable?
+ State the terms of the law to people with knowledge but who are not yet believers?
+ Offer the gospel call and comfort of Christ to unbelievers humbled by sin?
+ Explain the doctrines of grace and the rule of life to believers?
+ Stress the doctrines of repentance and hope to backsliding believers?[7]

No sermon can do everything, but if your sermons consistently address only some people or certain topics, you may be neglecting the spiritual needs of a significant number of your hearers.

Nothing can replace a burning love in the heart when we actually deliver the sermon. A match cannot start a fire until it is flaming. So, ask yourself, did I preach with warm love, affection, and kindness to my hearers? Thomas Murphy (1823–1900) wrote, "Preaching should be with tenderness."[8] The wife of Jonathan Edwards said to her brother after George Whitefield (1714–1770) preached in Northampton, Massachusetts, "It is wonderful to see what a spell he casts over an audience by proclaiming the simplest truths of the Bible.... He speaks from a heart all aglow with love."[9] When evaluating your preaching, ask yourself whether you preached with a burning love for God that made you long to see His church built up on earth. God loves His church with an everlasting love. If you love God, your preaching must be full of love for God's church. If you serve God, your preaching must serve His church. Did you preach to build God's church?

3. Did I preach Christ as the only foundation?

Paul says in 1 Corinthians 3:10–11, "According to the grace of God which is given unto me, as a wise master builder, I have laid the foundation, and another buildeth thereon. But let every man take heed how he buildeth thereupon. For other foundation can no man lay than that is laid, which is Jesus Christ." Without

---

7. William Perkins, *The Art of Prophecying*, ch. 7, in *The Workes of...William Perkins* (London: John Legatt, 1612–1613), 2:752–56.
8. Thomas Murphy, *Pastoral Theology* (1877; reprint Audubon: Old Paths, 1996), 194.
9. Iain H. Murray, *Jonathan Edwards: A New Biography* (Edinburgh: Banner of Truth, 1987), 162.

a solid foundation, a building cannot withstand harsh winds and rain. Over time, or perhaps in a single climactic storm, it will collapse (Matt. 7:24–27). A compromised foundation will cause the building's walls to shift, crack, and ultimately to fall. Jonathan Edwards (1703–1758) experienced this when a spring thaw shifted his old church meeting house in 1737. A gallery full of people fell upon those sitting in the pews below. By God's remarkable grace, no one was killed.[10]

The context of our text makes it clear that Christ is the church's only sure foundation, so we must preach Christ crucified for the faith of His called ones (1 Cor. 1:18, 22–24). Verse 10 says that Paul laid this foundation in Corinth in his preaching.[11] Paul writes in 1 Corinthians 2:2, 5, "For I determined not to know any thing among you, save Jesus Christ, and him crucified…that your faith should not stand in the wisdom of men, but in the power of God." By God's sovereign will, Christ is everything to the believer: our wisdom, righteousness, sanctification, and redemption (1 Cor. 1:30). Christ is not only the door into salvation, He is the entire road on which we must travel to glory.

Matthew Henry (1662–1714) wrote, "The doctrine of our Saviour and his mediation is the principal doctrine of Christianity. It lies at the bottom, and is the foundation of all the rest. Leave out this, and you lay waste all our comforts, and leave no foundation for our hopes as sinners."[12] Ministers must therefore ask themselves whether they are preaching Christ crucified, Christ risen, and Christ all-sufficient for His people. If you fail in this, you fail to feed people the Bread of life. Their souls will starve without Christ. So ask yourself, did I:

+ Write this sermon in the confidence that Christ, in His offices of Prophet, Priest, and King, has in Himself the fullness of wisdom, grace, and power that everyone needs?

+ Write this knowing that Christ is the Bible's main character and fulfillment of its every theme?

+ Connect this text to Christ so that people will be encouraged to lean on Him in trust?

+ Thoughtfully consider how this text points to Christ?

+ Seek to display men's need for grace and Christ's full provision of grace?

---

10. Murray, *Jonathan Edwards: A New Biography*, 148–49.

11. If the laying of the foundation in this context referred to the person and atoning work of Christ, then only God could be said to have laid the foundation (Isa. 28:6; 1 Peter 2:6). Since Paul laid the foundation, then Christ must function as the foundation through the preaching the gospel of Christ. Hodge, *1&2 Corinthians*, 55.

12. Matthew Henry, *Commentary on the Whole Bible: New Modern Edition* (Peabody, Mass.: Hendrickson, 1991), 6:418.

+ Press upon hearers their obligation to keep God's law as well as seek justification before God by faith alone in Christ alone?

+ Direct people to obey by faith out of the sanctifying grace of Jesus Christ?

+ Explain that the gospel is both for the salvation of the lost and for the lives of the saved?

+ Preach Christ not only as useful to us but as gloriously beautiful and worthy of our worship?

+ Preach with an eye on Christ, depending on Him to grant me the wisdom, grace, and power I need as a Christian and as a preacher?

The last question deserves special attention. While evaluating your preaching, you will soon find yourself convicted of many sins. This is humbling and can be terrifying. How dreadful are the words of James 3:1–2, "My brethren, be not many masters, knowing that we shall receive the greater condemnation. For in many things we offend all."[13] Lest your conscience overwhelm you, you must always evaluate your preaching in the presence of the Lamb who was slain. Depend on His illumination so that you can rightly evaluate your ministry. Rely on His atonement to cover your shortcomings. Lean on His sovereign power to overcome your sins and change you. Evaluate your sermons, not as a condemned sinner who is under law but as God's child who is under the grace of Christ.

Christ is the only foundation for preaching the Word. He is the foundation of eternal life, the church, and Christian ministry. William Perkins said the "sum of the sum" of his instructions for preachers is "Preach one Christ by Christ to the praise of Christ."[14]

4. Did I build my sermons with the precious materials of Reformed experiential preaching?

Paul says in 1 Corinthians 3:12–13, "Now if any man build upon this foundation gold, silver, precious stones, wood, hay, stubble; every man's work shall be made manifest: for the day shall declare it, because it shall be revealed by fire; and the fire shall try every man's work of what sort it is." Earlier, Paul warned us to be careful how we build upon the foundation (v. 10). Now he elaborates this point by telling us what materials we are to use. The contrast between them is

---

13. Or as the ESV puts it, "Not many of you should become teachers, my brothers, for you know that we who teach will be judged with greater strictness. For we all stumble in many ways" (James 3:1–2a).

14. Perkins, *Workes*, 2:762.

not one of strength, like steel versus paper, but of value and beauty, as marble and gold differ from wood and straw; the building under construction is the Lord's glorious temple, not a man's wooden house.[15] The Lord will test our materials by fire on the last day. Fire often symbolizes the presence and glory of the Lord, who dwelled in His temple in a pillar of fire and will come again in fire "on the day of the Lord."

Paul speaks here about the day when our Lord Jesus will come with flaming fire to judge each person's works and glorify His saints.[16] These verses have been taken out of context to support the Roman Catholic doctrine of purgatory, which is an imaginary place where fire burns sin out of Christians before they can enter heaven, a place of temporal punishment for sin and purification from sin.[17] But this concept is not found in Scripture and counters the full forgiveness that Christ's finished work grants believers.

Note that this text speaks of testing, not punishment. Materials, not people, are placed in the fire. Within its context, this verse speaks of Christ's judgment of His servants' teaching ministry. Christ will evaluate the materials they used in ministering to the church.

The gold, silver, and precious stones as well as wood, hay, and stubble represent the efforts of preachers such as Paul, Apollos, and others. The contrast between gold and hay does not symbolize the difference between gospel and heresy, for Paul says in verse 12 that men "build upon this foundation," that is, they all preach Christ and not some false gospel.

Rather, the contrast between gold and straw symbolizes God's wisdom versus man's wisdom. Paul begins describing this difference in 1 Corinthians 1:17 and develops it through 1 Corinthians 3. Thus, God's wisdom is the precious treasure by which the preacher builds and adorns God's temple. Paul calls himself a "wise master-builder" (v. 10) who builds the church by laying its foundation of the gospel of Christ, then adding the gold, silver, and precious stones of divine wisdom.[18]

---

15. "Precious stones here mean stones valuable for building, such as granite and marble. Gold and silver were extensively employed in adorning ancient temples, and are therefore appropriately used as the symbols of pure doctrine. Wood, hay, and stubble are the perishable materials out of which ordinary houses were built, but not temples. Wood for the doors and posts; hay [*chortos*], dried grass mixed with mud for the walls; and straw [*kalame*], for the roof. These materials, unsuitable for the temple of God, are appropriate symbols of false doctrines." Hodge, *1&2 Corinthians*, 56.

16. Rom. 2:5, 16; 13:12–13; 1 Cor. 1:8; 5:5; 2 Cor. 1:14; Eph. 4:30; Phil. 1:6, 10; 2:16; 1 Thess. 5:2, 5, 8; 2 Thess. 2:2.

17. *The Catechism of the Catholic Church* (Mahwah: Paulist Press, 1994), 268–69, 370–72 [sec. 1030–1032, 1472, 1479].

18. Hodge, *1&2 Corinthians*, 56; Fee, *The First Epistle to the Corinthians*, 136–42.

John Gill said that Paul uses the metaphors of wood, hay, and stubble to describe "not heretical doctrines, damnable heresies, such as are diametrically opposite to, and overturn the foundation...but empty, trifling, useless things... such as fables, endless genealogies, human traditions, Jewish rites and ceremonies...the wisdom of the world, the philosophy of the Gentiles."[19]

Divine wisdom is thus the only acceptable building material that preachers can use. The first two chapters of 1 Corinthians explain that God's wisdom is *biblical*, coming only from words of divine revelation, not from fallen human reasoning (1 Cor. 2:10–13). His wisdom is also *doctrinal*, granting a definite knowledge of God's graces, such as justification and sanctification (1 Cor. 1:30; 2:9–10). This wisdom is Christ-centered (1 Cor. 1:17, 22–24; 2:2), going beyond the foundation of the gospel to build up the church's faith and life. The wisdom of God is *experiential*, granted by the Holy Spirit to work in our inner person to overcome the spirit of the world and create in us the mind of Christ (1 Cor. 2:12, 14–16). And this wisdom is eminently *practical*, for in it we encounter the power of God that changes how we live (1 Cor. 1:18, 24; 2:4, 5; 4:19–20; cf. 6:9–11). These are the hallmarks of Reformed experiential preaching, which is biblical, doctrinal, experiential, and practical.[20]

So before Christ evaluates your sermons, take time to throw out the straw or stubble in them and replace them with nuggets of gold. A temple worthy of God must be built of the sturdiest, purest, and most precious material. Test your sermons by asking, "Did I build these with the precious materials of Reformed experiential preaching?"

We have already considered questions that evaluate how *biblical* your sermon was. You must also test your sermon to see how *doctrinal* it was. Thomas Murphy wrote,

> It is taken for granted that the sermon in which there is much doctrine must necessarily be dry, unspiritual, full of sectarianism and almost necessarily incomprehensible.... In fact there can be no preaching without doctrine.... The attributes of God, the mysteries of the Trinity, the fall of our race, the incarnation, life, death, and ascension of Christ, salvation by his blood, faith, conversion, the Church, the resurrection, judgment, heaven and hell—what are all these but doctrines?[21]

---

19. John Gill, *Exposition of the Old and New Testaments* (1809; reprint, Paris, Ark: Baptist Standard Bearer, 1989), 8:617.

20. See "Applying the Word," in Joel R. Beeke, *Living for God's Glory: An Introduction to Calvinism* (Orlando: Reformation Trust, 2008), 255–74.

21. Murphy, *Pastoral Theology*, 175–76.

When asking yourself whether you built your sermons with the precious materials of Reformed experiential preaching with respect to doctrine, ask specifically, did I:

- Approach the Bible to find directions for success or to listen and learn the truth?
- Refer to the confessions, catechisms, and theology of the church?
- Present clear teaching about God that flowed naturally from the biblical text?
- Show how that same doctrine is taught in other parts of the Bible?
- Express the truths of theology in terms that are clear to ordinary believers?
- Help people to understand classic doctrinal terms such as *justification?*
- Connect the doctrine of your Scripture text to related biblical doctrines?
- Base every application on doctrinal truths drawn from a specific text of Scripture?

In addition, ask yourself how *experiential* your sermon was. Did your sermon communicate to people that Christianity must be experienced, tasted, enjoyed, and lived in the power of the Holy Spirit? In its three main divisions, the Heidelberg Catechism suggests three dimensions of Christian experience. Ask yourself, did I:

- Speak of the experience of the misery of sin due to its great evil in God's eyes?
- Speak of the experience of deliverance, our glad confidence in Christ's salvation and sufficiency?
- Speak of the experience of gratitude, stirred in our renewed hearts by God's love, to love and obey Him?

Experiential preaching is like a sergeant on the battlefield who sets tactical goals, recognizing that war is a mess yet offers hope through strategic victory. Ask yourself, did I:

- Talk about how the Christian life *ought to go*—a lofty ideal for a lifelong pursuit?
- Talk about how the Christian life *does go* in reality—encouraging them in their defeats to look to Christ?
- Talk about how the Christian life *will ultimately go*—pointing them to hope in the final victory in glory?

Experiential preaching also uses the keys of the kingdom to draw lines of demarcation so that each listener can evaluate his spiritual position. Ask yourself, did I:

+ Distinguish between the children of God and children of the world?
+ Distinguish between Christian experience and the counterfeit graces of hypocrites?
+ Distinguish among the different levels of Christian maturity?

Furthermore, you should ask how *practical* your sermon was. Application should not be given like a big bang at the end of the message. Each point of the sermon should be applied. The Westminster *Directory for the Public Worship of God* includes a chapter titled "Of the Preaching of the Word," which presents several kinds of application. So ask yourself, did I use a variety of applications such as:

+ Instruction—to shape the mind and worldview with God's truth?
+ Confutation—to expose and refute the doctrinal errors of our day?
+ Exhortation—to press God's people to obey God's laws by the means He provides?
+ Dehortation—to rebuke sin and stir up hatred for it?
+ Comfort—to encourage believers to press forward in the fight of faith?
+ Trial—to present the marks of a true believer for self-examination?
+ Exultation—to help people see the beauty and glory of God so that they might love Him, fear Him, and praise Him with affection?[22]

God's wisdom is worth more than gold, silver, and precious stones. It brings all of life under the counsel of God for our wholehearted happiness. The wisdom of the Scriptures is the only material worthy of use in God's holy temple. Therefore, do not build your sermons with the materials of man, which will perish in God's flaming glory. Give your listeners golden words.

5. Did I preach for the Master's reward?

The apostle says in 1 Corinthians 3:14–15, "If any man's work abide which he hath built thereupon, he shall receive a reward. If any man's work shall be burned, he shall suffer loss: but he himself shall be saved; yet so as by fire." Though you and your hearers may have long forgotten the specifics of what you preached, the Lord will judge every sermon. Every sermon will have one of two

---

22. *The Westminster Directory of Public Worship*, discussed by Mark Dever and Sinclair Ferguson (Ross-Shire, Scotland: Christian Focus, 2008), 95–96.

outcomes on judgment day: it may be found precious in God's sight and receive His approbation, or it will be judged unworthy and the fire of God's glory will consume it.

What a waste it is to build a sermon not of the eternal materials of God's wisdom in Christ but on man's flimsy, cheap wisdom. If you build your sermons in part on your own wisdom, you will lose some of your reward though not your salvation, for that is built upon the foundation of the gospel of Christ. Nevertheless, you will forfeit the reward that you might have enjoyed for all eternity. As Gordon Fee writes in his commentary,

> Paul's point is unquestionably warning. It is unfortunately possible for people to attempt to build a church out of every imaginable human system predicated on merely worldly wisdom, be it philosophy, "pop" psychology, managerial techniques, relational "good feelings," or what have you. But at the final judgment, all such building…will be shown for what it is: something merely human, with no character of Christ or his gospel in it.[23]

A servant must work for his Master's reward by doing his Master's will. Jesus did not think it wrong to seek a reward but encouraged His disciples to live daily with an eye on the Father's reward (Matt. 6:1–21). We must labor to express our love for God and to please Him. The anticipation of judgment day should motivate us to evaluate our ministries today out of the glad hope of hearing the Lord say, "Well done, good and faithful servant!" You cannot undo the errors of the past, but you can find forgiveness with God and grow in faithfulness for the future.

Hoping for the positive evaluation of our Master will release us from catering to the tastes of people. How many sermons have been corrupted by people-pleasing! After denouncing the preacher of a false gospel as under God's curse, Paul asks in Galatians 1:10, "Do I seek to please men? for if I yet pleased men, I should not be the servant of Christ." Which master are you trying to please, the harsh slave-master of popular opinion, or the gracious Master who died for your sins? To help find out, ask yourself some more questions about your sermons. Ask yourself, did I:

+ Add or subtract anything from my sermon to win the approval of people?
+ Preach with the boldness of a clear conscience before God or in fear of my listeners?
+ Preach with a profound sense of reverence, fear, and awe of God?

---

23. Fee, *The First Epistle to the Corinthians*, 145.

+ Preach with gladness that the Lord will honor me if I honor Him, or with the frustration of wanting more honor among people?
+ Preach ultimately for the pleasure of the audience of One?

Regarding the teaching office of the Old Testament priest, Malachi 2:5–7 says, "My covenant was with him of life and peace; and I gave them to him for the fear wherewith he feared me, and was afraid before my name. The law of truth was in his mouth, and iniquity was not found in his lips: he walked with me in peace and equity, and did turn many away from iniquity. For the priest's lips should keep knowledge, and they should seek the law at his mouth: for he is the messenger of the LORD of hosts." Pastors, as messengers of the Lord of hosts, speak with holy fear. Do not be a court jester but a herald of the King.

Preach with your eyes upon Jesus, who is seated at the right hand of God and will come with glory. Remember what Paul says to Timothy, "I charge thee therefore before God, and the Lord Jesus Christ, who shall judge the quick and the dead at his appearing and his kingdom; preach the word" (2 Tim. 4:1–2).

Conclusion: Preach Toward the Finish Line

Until four young American skiers went to the 2010 Winter Olympics, the United States had never won a medal in the Nordic Combined. The Nordic Combined involves individual ski-jumping and cross-country skiing for six miles and team competition in a ski relay race for twelve miles. The American team won one gold and three silver medals in three Nordic Combined events.[24] After winning the gold medal, one team member gave a gold ring to his girlfriend, asking her to marry him. She said yes![25] What a way to celebrate!

How much greater will be the joy of the faithful preacher when his Master rewards him in the everlasting kingdom! He will look into the smiling face of the Lord Jesus, the great Bridegroom who loved His church and laid down His life for her. He will receive honor and commendation from the King of Kings. He will look upon the men, women, and children whom he served from the pulpit, many of whom will now be clothed with the glory that shines brighter than any earthly gold. Surely that will be worth every drop of energy we put into preaching the Word. If our Lord will reward us for offering a cup of water to people in His name, how much more He will reward us for the hours we spend preparing, preaching, and evaluating our sermons.

---

24. http://vancouver2010.com/olympic-nordic-combined, accessed 11-10-10.
25. http://today.msnbc.msn.com/id/35600802/ns/today-today_in_vancouver, accessed 11-10-10.

So evaluate your preaching as a servant anticipating his master's evaluation. Regularly ask yourself these five questions: Did I preach as God's servant? Did I preach to build God's church? Did I preach Christ as the only foundation? Did I build with the precious materials of Reformed experiential preaching? Did I preach for my Master's reward?

Make every effort to grow as a preacher. Eternity will prove it time well spent.

SERMON EVALUATION CHART
[Copy for repeated use.]
Evaluate your preaching as a servant anticipating his
master's evaluation (1 Cor. 3:5–15).

1. Did I preach as God's servant?

a. The test of *humble exegesis*. Ask, did I:

+ Approach the Scripture with a willingness to be taught and corrected by God, or did I assume that I already knew what the Scripture said?

+ Spend enough time and energy to study that Scripture text and let God speak to me through it?

+ Read the commentaries of godly and wise teachers to check my interpretation?

+ Derive the main idea and points from the clear statement of a Scripture text?

+ Spend time explaining what the text meant so my listeners could better understand it?

+ Base applications of my sermon on the Scriptures, not just on my vision for the church?

+ Preach a message that was faithful to the text's meaning in its context?

+ Demonstrate to my hearers that the sermon came from God's Word and not my ideas?

b. The test of *humble dependence*. Did I:

+ Plan this series and this specific sermon, prayerfully asking God for wisdom?

+ Enlist my congregation to pray for my preaching?

+ Study the Scripture text on my knees, with fervent pleas for illumination?

+ Prepare the sermon in the context of regular, private prayers for the church?

+ Cry out to God prior to the worship services for the Spirit's anointing?

+ Cry out to God after the services for divine application?

+ Give all the glory to God for any good that resulted from my efforts?

2. Did I preach to build God's church?

a. The test of *helpfulness*. Ask yourself, did I:

+ Write my sermon with an eye to my flock and their needs?

+ Labor hard and long on this sermon out of love, or was I lazy?

+ Organize the message to make listening easier for people?

+ Begin with an introduction to engage their minds and lead them to the main idea?

+ Clearly state the main idea of the message?

+ Highlight the main points so that listeners recognized them?

+ State my main idea and points so succinctly that a twelve-year-old boy and a seventy-year-old woman could write them in their notes?

+ Help people understand ancient culture and customs foreign to their world?

+ Limit my time and amount of content to what my hearers can absorb profitably?

+ Illustrate each major point to engage their imagination and affections?

+ Craft my illustrations so as to make them helpful for understanding and applying the gospel?

+ Make specific applications throughout the sermon relevant to people's lives?

+ Conclude the sermon by pressing the main idea home to my hearers?

+ Express the loving heart of the Father who calls the prodigal to come home?

+ Call the unsaved to repentance and faith in Christ?

b. The test of *spiritual needs*. Ask, did I:

+ Rebuke unbelievers who are ignorant and unteachable?

+ Offer basic catechetical truths to unbelievers who are ignorant but teachable?

+ State the terms of the law to unbelievers with knowledge but who are not yet believers?

+ Offer the gospel call of Christ to unbelievers humbled by sin?

+ Explain the doctrines of grace and the rule of life to believers?

- Stress the doctrines of repentance and hope to backsliding believers?

c. The test of *love*. Did I preach with affection and kindness to my hearers?

3. Did I preach Christ as the only foundation?

a. The test of *the Bread of life*. Ask yourself, did I:

- Write this sermon in the confidence that Christ, in His offices of Prophet, Priest, and King, has in Himself the fullness of wisdom, grace, and power that everyone needs?

- Write this knowing that Christ is the Bible's main character and fulfillment of its every theme?

- Connect this text to Christ so that people will be encouraged to lean on Him in trust?

- Thoughtfully consider how this text points to Christ?

- Seek to display men's need for grace and Christ's full provision of grace?

- Press upon hearers their obligation to keep God's law as well as to seek justification before God by faith alone in Christ alone?

- Direct people to obey by faith out of the sanctifying grace of Jesus Christ?

- Explain that the gospel is both for the salvation of the lost and the lives of the saved?

- Preach Christ not only as useful to us but as gloriously beautiful and worthy of our worship?

- Preach with an eye on Christ, depending confidently on Him to grant me the wisdom, grace, and power I needed as a Christian and as a preacher?

b. The test of *preaching under grace*. Am I evaluating my preaching trusting in the Lamb who was slain?

4. Did I build with the precious materials of Reformed experiential preaching?

a. The test of *biblical* preaching. (See #1 above)

b. The test of *doctrinal* preaching. Ask, did I:

- Approach the Bible to find directions for success or to listen and learn the truth?

- Refer to the confessions, catechisms, and theology of the church?

- Present clear teaching about God that flowed naturally from the biblical text?

- Show how that same doctrine is taught in other parts of the Bible?

- Express the truths of theology in terms that are clear to ordinary believers?

- Help people to understand classic doctrinal terminology like *justification*?

- Connect the doctrine of my Scripture text to related biblical doctrines?

- Base every application on doctrinal truth drawn from a specific text of Scripture?

c. The test of *experiential* preaching.

i. The three dimensions of Christian experience (Heidelberg Catechism). Did I:

- Speak of the experience of the misery of sin due to its great evil in God's eyes?

- Speak of the experience of deliverance, our glad confidence in Christ's salvation and sufficiency?

- Speak of the experience of gratitude, stirred in our renewed hearts by God's love, to love and obey Him?

ii. The battlefield mentality. Did I:

- Talk about how the Christian life *ought to go*—a lofty ideal for life-long pursuit?

- Talk about how the Christian life *does go* in reality—encouraging them in their defeats to look to Christ?

- Talk about how the Christian life will go ultimately—pointing them to hope in the final victory in glory?

iii. The keys of the kingdom. Did I:

- Distinguish between the children of God and children of the world?

+ Distinguish between Christian experience and the counterfeit graces of hypocrites?

+ Distinguish among the different levels of Christian maturity?

d. The test of *practical* preaching. Did I use a variety of applications like:

+ Instruction—to shape the mind and worldview with God's truth?

+ Confutation—to expose and refute the doctrinal errors of our day?

+ Exhortation—to press God's people to obey God's laws by the means He provides?

+ Dehortation—to rebuke sin and stir up hatred for it?

+ Comfort—to encourage believers to press forward in the fight of faith?

+ Trial—to present the marks of a true believer for self-examination?

+ Exultation—to help people see the beauty and glory of God so that they might love Him, fear Him, and praise Him with affection?

5. Did I preach for my Master's reward? Did I:

+ Add or subtract anything from my sermon to win the approval of people?

+ Preach with the boldness of a clear conscience before God or in fear of my listeners?

+ Preach with a profound sense of reverence, fear, and awe toward God?

+ Preach with gladness that the Lord will honor me if I honor Him or with the frustration of wanting more honor among people?

+ Preach ultimately for the pleasure of the audience of One?

Chapter 27

Practical Application in Preaching

Today, much of what is preached on Sunday mornings falls short of biblical preaching. We hear academic lectures, colorful storytelling, or moralistic lessons but not true, biblical preaching. J. I. Packer once said that preaching consists of two elements: teaching *plus* application. Where those two elements are missing, "something less than preaching occurs."[1]

In *Why Johnny Can't Preach*, T. David Gordon estimates that in Reformed and Presbyterian churches "less than 30 percent of those who are ordained to the Christian ministry can preach an even mediocre sermon."[2] The failure to preach well is particularly evident in preachers' application of Scripture to people's lives. And, as Geoffrey Thomas says, "Preaching that lacks application is the bane of the modern Reformed pulpit."[3]

Many preachers who are called to Christ's work in His church are misguided about applicatory preaching. Because of this, we need to seriously reflect on applicatory preaching. When we fail to apply what we preach in a biblical way, our people are left starving for the truth. Sinclair Ferguson writes, "We live in an age when the primary need is for our people to be instructed in the teaching and application of Scripture."[4]

In this chapter, we will explore what applicatory preaching is, why the church needs applicatory preaching, prerequisites to applicatory preaching, general principles for applicatory preaching, basic subject matter for application, and forms and methods to use in applicatory preaching.

---

1. J. I. Packer, "Introduction: Why Preach," in Samuel Logan, ed., *The Preacher and Preaching* (Phillipsburg, N.J.: P&R, 1986), 3. Thanks to Kyle Borg for research assistance on this chapter.

2. T. David Gordon, *Why Johnny Can't Preach* (Phillipsburg, N.J.: P&R, 2009), 11.

3. Geoffrey Thomas, in Logan, *The Preacher and Preaching*, 380.

4. Sinclair Ferguson, "Exegesis," in Logan, *The Preacher and Preaching*, 195.

What Applicatory Preaching Is

To explain what applicatory preaching is, we must first recognize the difficulty of answering this question. An effective sermon is like a multi-faceted jewel. All of a sermon's parts work together to give it richness, beauty, and completeness. A sermon cannot be complete without expository preaching, doctrinal preaching, Christ-centered preaching, experiential preaching, and practical preaching. But we must limit ourselves in this address to examine just one diamond-like facet of a sermon—its applicatory element. William Perkins (1558–1602), the great Puritan of Cambridge, defines sermon application as "the skill by which the doctrine which has been properly drawn from Scripture is handled in ways which are appropriate to the circumstances of the place and time and to the people in the congregation."[5] More simply, application is the process by which God's Word is brought into the lives of listeners, enabling them, by the Spirit's grace, to put Christianity into practice.[6]

Jay Adams's definition of sermon application is even more specific: "Application is the...process by which preachers make scriptural truths so pertinent to members of their congregations that they not only understand how these truths should effect changes in their lives but feel obligated and perhaps even eager to implement those changes."[7] Like the Puritans, Al Martin puts more focus on the conscience, saying, "Application is the arduous task of suffusing the sermon with pointed, specific, and discriminating force to the conscience."[8]

Application is the process by which the unchanging principles of God's Word are brought into life-changing contact with people who live in an ever-changing world.[9] Building on these definitions, we would say that applicatory preaching takes place when the unchanging truths, principles, and doctrines of God's Word are brought to bear upon people's consciences and every part of their lives to increasingly transform them into Christ's likeness.

In one sense, these definitions seem obvious. However, some preachers think that once they have explained the meaning of a Scripture text, their work is done. They make little attempt to determine what the text means to people today. Exegesis thus becomes merely a scholarly exercise detached from real life.

---

5. William Perkins, *The Art of Prophesying* (Edinburgh: Banner of Truth, 2002), 54.

6. Jay Adams, *Truth Applied* (Stanley, N.C.: Timeless Texts, 1990), 17.

7. Adams, *Truth Applied*, 17.

8. Al Martin, Quoted in David Murray, *How Sermons Work* (Darlington, England: Evangelical Press, 2011), 107–108.

9. David Murray, lecture in Homiletics I, Puritan Reformed Theological Seminary (October 2010).

Other preachers want to connect Scripture with practical living but believe that application is the Holy Spirit's job, not theirs. They say, "We explain the text; the Spirit applies it." This tends to leave listeners at the mercy of their own subjective inclinations. Douglas Stuart talks about the unfairness of this approach, saying, "The exegete leaves the key function—response—completely to the subjective sensibilities of the reader or hearer, who knows the passage least."[10]

What is more likely is that listeners will do nothing at all. John Calvin writes, "If we leave it to men's choice to follow what is taught them, they will never move one foot. Therefore, the doctrine of itself can profit nothing at all."[11]

Why the Church Needs Application

Is application an indispensable element of biblical preaching? Should we agree with John Bettler, who says, "The essence of preaching is application"?[12] Many advocates of redemptive-historical preaching argue against personal application. Bill Dennison, for example, says that "[g]ood preaching does not apply the text to you, but applies you to the text. The preacher is not drawing the text into your world; he is drawing you into the world of the text. The preacher ought not add to his preaching text subjective applications to a supposed objective historical text. Rather, the preacher as a herald of God's living Word should proclaim the Word...and allow the Spirit to use it as He wills."[13]

Preaching without application often focuses on history to the exclusion of ethics. It emphasizes the indicative at the expense of the imperative. Geerhardus Vos's sermons, *Grace and Glory*, are an example of this.[14] There you will find beautiful and instructive sermons with little application. They leave application to the reader or listener.

Scripture justifies and warrants application. Here are just a few of the many examples of application that we find in the Bible:

+ In Matthew 19:16–22, Christ applies the law to a rich young ruler.

+ Peter, in Acts 2:22–27, applies the prophecies of the Old Testament to his generation (vv. 25–28; 34–35). His intent is to change his hearers. Notice how often he uses the second person (vv. 22, 23, 29, 33, 36) to

---

10 Douglas Stuart, *Old Testament Exegesis* (Louisville: Westminster, 2001), 27–28.

11. John Calvin, *Sermons on the Epistles to Timothy and Titus* (Edinburgh: Banner of Truth, 1983), 2 Timothy 4:1–2.

12. John F. Bettler, "Application," in Logan, *The Preacher and Preaching*, 332.

13. Bill Dennison, http://www.banneroftruth.org/pages/articles/article_detail.php?119 (accessed August 22, 2010).

14. Geerhardus Vos, *Grace and Glory* (Edinburgh: Banner of Truth, 1994).

call people to action (vv. 38, 39). By the Spirit's grace, such preaching prompts this question in listeners: "What shall we do?" (v. 37).

+ In his first letter to the Corinthians, Paul says the history of Israel was written as an example and admonition to later generations (10:11).

Our Reformed and Puritan forefathers were united in emphasizing the need for applicatory preaching. William Gouge (1575–1653) writes, "Ministers are herein to *imitate God*, and, to their best endeavour, to instruct people in the mysteries of godliness, and to teach them what to believe and practise, and then to stir them up in act and deed, to do what they are instructed to do."[15] Puritan preachers stressed the need to inform the mind, to prick the conscience, then to bend the will, believing that a sermon must connect with the people and by the Spirit's grace transform them and their wills. That is the heart of applicatory preaching.

In his classic *The Christian Ministry*, Charles Bridges (1794–1869) powerfully promotes applicatory preaching. He says, "For this end we must show them [our hearers] from first to last, that we are not merely saying good things in their presence; but directing what we say to them personally, as a matter which concerns them beyond expression."[16] Likewise, the great preacher Charles Spurgeon (1834–1892) stresses the necessity of application in saying, "Where the application begins, there the sermon begins."

Well-known twentieth-century preachers also agree with the need for application in preaching. John Stott writes,

> This was an essential element in the classical understanding of public speaking. Cicero had said in The Orator that "an eloquent man must so speak as to teach (*docere*), to please (*delectare*) and to persuade (*flectere* or *move*)." Augustine quoted Cicero's dictum and applied it to the responsibility of Christian preachers to teach the mind, delight or inspire the affections and move the will. "For," he went on, "to teach is a necessity, to please is a sweetness, to persuade is a victory." Our expectation, then, as the sermon comes to an end, is not merely that people will understand or remember or enjoy our teaching, but that they will do something about it. "If there is no summons, there is no sermon."[17]

In ongoing conversations today about the issue of application, many say that the very character of Scripture teaches the need for application since the

---

15. William Gouge, *A Commentary on the Whole Epistle to the Hebrews* (Edinburgh: James Nichol, 1866), 2:195 (emphasis added).

16. Charles Bridges, *The Christian Ministry* (Edinburgh, Scotland: Banner of Truth, 2006), 269.

17. John Stott, *Between Two Worlds* (Grand Rapids: Eerdmans, 1987), 246.

indicatives of Scripture are never divorced from its imperatives. The apostle Paul says, "For whatsoever things were written aforetime were written for our learning, that we through patience and comfort of the scriptures might have hope" (Rom. 15:4). The Holy Spirit and the human authors of the Bible agree that God's Word is never to remain an abstraction.

This indicative-imperative pattern abounds throughout the epistles and sermons of the apostles. They continually connect the truth of God with real-life situations and real people because the gospel message is connected with the people who hear it. This truth sets a pattern for our preaching, which is to take those truths forged in God's divine counsel and proclaim them to men. The message is God's message, not man's message (Gal. 1:11), and since God has not left His truth in abstraction, neither can we when we preach those truths.

Prerequisites to Applicatory Preaching

There are many prerequisites for applicatory preaching, but let us examine three important ones.

First, to be sound applicatory preachers, we must first have personal, experiential knowledge of the doctrines we preach. In Robert Murray M'Cheyne's memoir, Andrew Bonar says of M'Cheyne, "From the first he fed others by what he himself was feeding upon. His preaching was in a manner the development of his soul's experience. It was a giving out of the inward life. He loved to come up from the pastures wherein the chief Shepherd had met him—to lead the flock entrusted to his care to the spots where he found nourishment."[18]

True, applicatory preaching cannot be learned in seminaries or through textbooks unless preachers have studied in Christ's school and fed on the manna of the Word. If we endeavor to preach on the intercession of Christ, we will fail to apply it adequately if we are not personally acquainted with its reality and riches. As under-shepherds of Christ, we feed the flock with the nourishment our Shepherd gives us. If we would have our congregants know how to live, we ourselves must walk in the footsteps of our Master. Charles Spurgeon notes, "The truth as it is in Jesus must be instructively declared, so that the people may not merely hear, but know, the joyful sound."[19]

Second, to be sound in application as preachers, we must cultivate personal closeness with God. Fellowship with God makes Christianity real and personal; a man cannot, consequently, be a great preacher if he lives distant from the Lord.

---

18. Andrew Bonar, *Memoir and Remains of Robert Murray M'Cheyne* (Grand Rapids: Baker Books, 1978), 59.

19. Charles Spurgeon, *Lectures to My Students* (Grand Rapids: Zondervan, 1954), 70.

In 2 Corinthians 2:17, the apostle Paul explains the contrast between true and false preachers. A true minister of the gospel is sincere, Paul says; he cannot fake nearness to the Lord. Like children who listen to every word and observe every move of their parents, true children of God are always listening to their preacher, looking at him, and examining the way he lives. If he is not living close to God, his preaching and counsel will eventually expose any falseness and hypocrisy. Richard Baxter says, "Pride makes many a man's sermons; and what pride makes, the devil makes." Likewise, what hypocrisy makes, the devil makes.[20]

How is this closeness to be cultivated? God reveals Himself to us in His Word, in prayer, and in other spiritual disciplines. A minister's solemn duty *and* joyful privilege, then, is to labor tirelessly in private prayer and to be a diligent student of the Bible. In regard to prayer, Spurgeon says, "Prayer will singularly assist you in the delivery of your sermon; in fact, nothing can so gloriously fit you to preach as descending fresh from the mount of communion with God."[21] Prayer must be the lifeblood behind the sermon, for you need divine assistance, first, as you prepare for the sermon and, second, as you deliver the sermon. As for studying Scripture, Geoffrey Thomas observes, "We will not be affected by the Scriptures, we will not tap the power that is in them, unless we read, read, read, and read them yet some more."[22] We should also consult teachers of the Bible who will help give us clarity and insight into the mysteries of the gospel. In this our Reformed forefathers and the Puritans can be of immense value—whether it be Owen's majestic eloquence, Sibbes's Christ-centeredness, or Flavel's simple style.

A third prerequisite for applicatory preaching is to understand human nature. If you want to connect your message with people, you must know people's natures and personalities, especially those in your own flock. The heart is the throne of natural corruptions, fears, weaknesses, and sin. A preacher must strike a balance between how things are and how they ought to be. A medical doctor must know how the body ought to operate before he can diagnose an ailment. You trust his prescriptions, or even his scalpel, because he has proven himself to be an expert of the human body. Likewise, the pastor must discern from the Scriptures how things are and ought to be as well as how biblical remedies should be applied. You must be a master of the human soul so that your people can trust what you prescribe.

---

20. Richard Baxter, *The Practical Works of Richard Baxter* (Morgan, Pa.: Soli Deo Gloria, 2000), 4:403.

21. Spurgeon, *Lectures*, 45.

22. Thomas, "Powerful Preaching," in Logan, *Preacher and Preaching*, 373.

Principles for Applicatory Preaching

There are many principles of application. Here are ten of them:

1. Applications are derived from rightly preaching a text. It may seem obvious to say that applications in a sermon should be based on the Bible, particularly the text being preached. However, we need this emphasis because, today, many churches increasingly set aside the Bible to make space for moving stories and personal anecdotes from which the pastor draws morals or inspiration. The faithful preacher must instead base his application on God's Word, particularly on the passage from which he is preaching. Douglas Stuart says: "An application should be just as rigorous, just as thorough, and just as analytically sound as any other step in the exegesis process. It cannot be merely tacked on to the rest of the exegesis as a sort of spiritual afterthought. Moreover it must carefully reflect the data of the passage if it is to be convincing. Your reader needs to see how you derived the application as the natural and final stage of the entire process of careful, analytical study of your passage."[23]

To rightly apply a text, we must first understand the text rightly, both in its context and in the broader context of all Scripture. Sound hermeneutics paves the way for sound application. Charles Bridges warns: "The solid establishment of the people may be materially hindered by the Minister's contracted statement, crude interpretations, or misdirected Scriptural application."[24] We must be careful not to base a doctrine or practice on an isolated or obscure text without first ensuring that the doctrine is consistent with Scripture as a whole.

We may be tempted to preach right application from the wrong text. Thankfully, the Word itself directs us in application. The divine author has intended, through Scripture, to accomplish specific purposes in every generation.[25] In determining this, we learn another crucial lesson in interpreting Scripture. "It is absolutely critical to determine the purpose of a text if I am not going to pervert it and compromise the integrity of Scripture," writes Bettler. "The application must be that of the text."[26]

Application that does not emerge from "the purpose for which God himself gave his Word [will] lack credibility and power to motivate hearers," adds Dennis Johnson.[27] If we rightly understand our text, the heart of its application has already been given to us. So we must labor to discern the mind of the Spirit in

---

23. Douglas Stuart, *Old Testament Exegesis* (Louisville: Westminster, 2001), 27–28.
24. Bridges, *Christian Ministry*, 28 (emphasis added).
25. Dennis Johnson, *Him We Proclaim* (Phillipsburg, N.J.: P&R, 2007), 13.
26. Bettler, "Application," in Logan, *Preacher and Preaching*, 339.
27. Johnson, *Him We Proclaim*, 14.

our interpretation. In short, getting the text right paves the road to applying it correctly.

2. Determine the primary application. We must not draw applications from the accidental, incidental, or coincidental parts of a passage but from its essentials. This is especially important when preaching from historical narratives or parables. Often parables make one main point, so we must not found a doctrine or practice on one of its incidental points. Or, as an old Baptist minister used to tell young preachers, "Don't turn a monopod into a centipede."

One of the best ways of finding the primary application of a particular passage is to ask, "What was the application to the original audience at the original time of writing?" Jay Adams says, "The truth God revealed in Scripture came in an applied form and should be reapplied to the same sort of people for the same purposes for which it was originally given. That is to say, truth should be applied today just as God originally applied it."[28]

3. Make applications throughout your sermon. Although at times it may be appropriate to put most applications at the conclusion of a sermon, it is usually best to offer them throughout. Bridges highlights the persistent application of history and doctrine throughout the book of Hebrews and concludes: "The method of perpetual application, therefore, where the subject will admit of it, is probably best calculated for the effect of applying each head distinctly."[29] Of course, we should avoid the clinical method of inserting precisely one application after each exegetical or doctrinal point of a sermon, as that makes the sermon appear contrived.

We must also remember that application is not an epilogue to the sermon. John Broadus says, "The application in a sermon is not merely an appendage to the discussion or a subordinate part of it, but is the main thing to be done."[30] Right application is what Bridges calls "perpetual application."[31] Listeners must realize that all of a sermon is useful; all its doctrines, historical circumstances, and its prophecies are for our advantage, not just the last part of a sermon. Bridges likens a good sermon to a portrait, saying, "A good portrait... looks directly at all, though placed in different situations, as if it were ready to

---

28. Adams, *Truth Applied*, 17.
29. Bridges, *Christian Ministry*, 275.
30. John Broadus, *On the Preparation and Delivery of Sermons* (New York: Harper Collins, 1979), 210.
31. Bridges, *Christian Ministry*, 275.

speak to each—'I have a message from God unto thee.'"[32] So a sermon should address a congregation in various situations so that individual listeners know that in every word, God is speaking to them.

Adams speaks of applicatory introductions as well as conclusions, saying, "It [application] should begin with the first sentence and continue throughout."[33] We must not think that listeners have the natural capacity to make all the applications of a sermon, nor that we should leave this task for the Holy Spirit. To be sure, the Holy Spirit will make applications during or after a sermon that we may not have considered, for which we praise God, but His normal way is to use preacher-spoken applications.

Bettler says that all preaching is application. That goes a bit too far, but he is right that a preacher must keep application in mind from choosing a text to post-sermon discussions. He should think of applications throughout the preparation, preaching, and post-delivery discussion of a sermon.

4. Prepare and pray for applications. While many preachers spend hours on the exegesis of a text, they often spend little time on application. Sometimes this is for theological reasons. The preacher cites texts such as Matthew 10:19, which says the Spirit will provide the words in accord with His promise. However, such promises of the Spirit's help in speaking without preparation were given to disciples facing arrests, court trials, or other dangers, not to ordinary preachers in their pulpits. Remember what Stuart says: "An application should be just as rigorous, just as thorough, and just as analytically sound as any other step in the exegesis process." Failing to prepare applications in a sermon usually results in repetitive and ineffectual applications, as the preacher, who is mentally tired after the exertions of explaining his text, resorts to the well-worn lines of application that he has used in the past.

One of the best ways to prepare applications is to pray over a sermon, asking God to show you how to apply it. God's Spirit knows the hearts of listeners better than you do, and He can reveal people's needs to you by His Spirit.

All this does not mean that you need to stick rigidly to prepared applications while preaching. A prayerful spirit while preaching can also result in God guiding you to speak to specific needs in your hearers that you did not contemplate during your sermon preparation. What an early theological instructor said about preaching as a whole is particularly true of making good applications:

---

32. Bridges, *Christian Ministry*, 273.
33. Adams, *Truth Applied*, 119.

"We need the Holy Spirit twice in every sermon—first, in the study, and then on the pulpit."[34]

Finally, because the fear of man can ensnare and disable applications, we must pray for constant deliverance from such sinful fear, particularly in applying a text. John Brown says that proper fear, which is esteeming the smiles and frowns of God to be of greater weight than the smiles and frowns of men, should prevail.

5. *Make up-to-date applications.* There is no point in simply taking the applications made by early Puritans and Reformers and repeating them verbatim to people today. Their applications were up-to-date when written, but some of them are now well past due. Others may be used but need to be translated into contemporary language and freshened up. One of the greatest helps in finding applications is to keep informed about the people we preach to and the world in which they live. We must know our people's troubles, struggles, problems, and needs to preach to them.

Another way to improve applications is to go through your congregation, describing each person in a word or two that characterize his or her spiritual condition. You will then have a ready-made checklist of various kinds of listeners in your congregation on which to focus your applications. To get you started, some broad categories of listeners include: Christian / non-Christian, Old / Young, Rich / Poor, Parents / Children / Singles, Employer / Employee, Government / Citizen, Male / Female, Atheist / Agnostic / Persecutor. More specific categories of people in the broader categories include: sick, dying, afflicted, tempted, backslidden, hypocritical, immoral, discouraged, worried, tired, salvation-seeking, doubting, proud, bereaved, brokenhearted, and convicted.

6. *Make applications personal.* Daniel Webster once said, "When a man preaches to me, I want him to make it a personal matter, a personal matter, a personal matter!" His point is that application starts with a preacher's application of God's Word to himself. Al Martin says: "Here is the main reason why there is so little applicatory preaching. Men are not applying the Word to their own hearts. A minister's life is the life of the minister."[35]

What we want to focus on here is the importance of second-person application. That is not to say that other applications are wrong or out of place. Application may sometimes work well with first-person singular or plural

---

34. Jan C. Weststrate, class lecture, September, 1974.
35. Quoted in Murray, *How Sermons Work*, 113.

pronouns. When the preacher wishes to personally identify with the application, he uses terms such as "*We* must," "He died for *us*," or "*Our* privilege is…" (e.g., Heb. 4:1, 11, 14, 16). Application may also include the third-person approach. For example, a sermon preached to a congregation including singles on the duties of husbands or wives may include terms such as "*Husbands* will," "When *wives* are," or "*She* usually knows." An application about the errors of false religions and the cults may also include the third-person approach, "*They* wrongly believe and teach" (e.g., Titus 1:10–16; John 3:5).

While first-person and third-person applications are both scriptural and, at times, appropriate, the majority of applications are better off using second-person pronouns, such as "*You* must," "*You* should understand," or "*Your* experience will be" (e.g., John 3:7; Rom. 12:1). This does not exclude the preacher from his own application. However, it does reflect that the preacher holds an office and so is not preaching in his own right but as an ambassador of God sent to deliver a message to the people of God. He therefore speaks in Christ's stead, or as Christ would speak, were He present. This practice avoids this difficulty described by Al Martin: "Many sermons are like unaddressed, unsigned letters which if one hundred read them would not think the contents concerned them."[36]

Sermon listeners must know they are personally and individually being addressed. As Charles Bridges says, "Preaching, in order to be effective, must be reduced from vague generalities, to a tangible, individual character—coming home to every man's business, and even his bosom."[37]

The editor of the *Brooklyn Eagle* newspaper kept a notice on his desk saying, "Always remember that a dog fight in Brooklyn is more important than a revolution in China." The point is that what happens at home is more important than what happens far away. Go through your congregation one by one, and ask how to apply your message to each person.

7. *Make application pointed.* It is not enough just to draw a general principle out of a passage, such as, "You should be holy." This general principle must be broken down so it applies to specific, concrete, everyday situations. Only by answering the questions of who, when, what, where, how, and why of holiness does an application become pointed. David Veerman puts it this way: "Application is answering two questions: 'So what?' And, 'Now what?' The first

---

36. Quoted in Murray, *How Sermons Work*, 114.
37. Bridges, *Christian Ministry*, 271.

question asks, 'Why is this passage important to me?' The second asks, 'What should I do about it today?'"[38]

We should not expect listeners to make precise applications for themselves. As Bridges says, "We must not expect our hearers to apply to themselves such unpalatable truths. So unnatural is this habit of personal application, that most will fit the doctrine to anyone but themselves."[39] Massillon, a famous French preacher, used to say, "I don't want people leaving my church saying, 'What a wonderful sermon, what a wonderful preacher.' I want them to go out saying, 'I will *do* something.'"[40]

One way of sharpening the point of our sermons is to make each application specific. John the Baptist preached the necessity of fruit-bearing repentance but then specified exactly what fruit each group should bring forth (Luke 3:10–14).

Another way of making our sermons pointed is by directing most of our applications within an overall application rather than offering a disparate disconnected series of exhortations. This should culminate at the very end of a sermon. Bryan Chapell says, "The last sixty seconds are typically the most dynamic moments in excellent sermons. With these final words, a preacher marshals the thought and emotion of an entire message into an exhortation that makes all that has preceded it clear and compelling. A conclusion is a sermon's destination. Ending contents are alive—packed with tension, drama, energy, and emotion."[41]

Our sermons must also point to the main issue. We must insert the knife of God's Word into the parts of people's lives that are especially putrid. We must lance the boils. John Stott tells about Alexander Whyte, who experienced a crisis towards the end of his ministry in Edinburgh. He knew that some people regarded him as little short of a monomaniac about sin, and he was tempted to muffle that note in his preaching. But one day while walking in the Highlands, he heard what he deemed a divine voice speaking with all-commanding power in his conscience. Whyte says,

> He said to me as clear as clear could be: "Go on, and flinch not! Go back and boldly finish the work that has been given you to do. Speak out and fear not. Make them at any cost to see themselves in God's holy law as in a glass. Do you that, for no one else will do it. No one else will so risk his life and his reputation as to do it. And you have not much of either left to

---

38. David Veerman, "Sermons: Apply Within," *Leadership* (Spring 1990), 121.
39. Bridges, *Christian Ministry*, 270.
40. Cited in Murray, *How Sermons Work*, 115.
41. Bryan Chapell, *Christ-centered Preaching* (Grand Rapids: Baker, 2005), 254.

risk. Go home and spend what is left of your life in your appointed task of showing my people their sin and their need of my salvation."[42]

When God's Word is pointedly applied to people's hearts, it will bring friction that causes pain and heat. When we apply the sword of truth, we can expect action and reaction!

8. Strive for balance in application. We must vary our applications. Some preachers condemn while preaching a text such as "Comfort ye, comfort ye my people." Others comfort when preaching, "Flee the wrath that is to come." Such preachers are unbalanced in their applications. We achieve balance first by preaching from Scripture passages that allow us varied applications and, second, by applying the Word in a varied way. John Stott illustrates this point by saying,

> Anthony Trollope in *Barchester Towers* very evidently despised his character, the Rev. Obadiah Slope, for this very thing. Although "gifted with a certain kind of pulpit eloquence," yet, Trollope wrote, "in his sermons he deals greatly in denunciations." Indeed, "his looks and tones are extremely severe…. As he walks through the streets, his very face denotes his horror of the world's wickedness; and there is always an anathema lurking in the corner of his eye…. To him the mercies of our Saviour speak in vain…. In a neat phrase of Colin Morris, he used the pulpit "to purvey Good Chidings rather than Good Tidings."[43]

Following our Master and the apostle Paul, we must call sinners to behold both the goodness and truth of God in our applications.

Most preachers have a bias that they should be aware of, lest they become unbalanced. Some are great comforters and some are great disturbers. Stott concludes: "Every preacher needs to be both a Boanerges (having the courage to disturb) and a Barnabas (having the charity to console)."[44]

9. Be passionate in application. No part of a sermon requires more of a preacher's emotional involvement than application. The arguments have been made; now is the time for persuasion. Robert L. Dabney writes, "To produce volition, it is not enough that the understanding be convinced; affection must also be aroused."[45]

The preacher's emotions should reflect the nature of the application. If his application issues a warning, the preacher should be solemn; if it calls for

---

42. John Stott, *Between Two Worlds* (Grand Rapids: Eerdmans, 1987), 310.
43. Stott, *Between Two Worlds*, 312.
44. Stott, *Between Two Worlds*, 315.
45. Robert L. Dabney, *Lectures on Sacred Rhetoric* (Edinburgh: Banner of Truth, 1979), 234.

worship, the preacher must show devotion; if it offers a promise, the preacher should show confidence; if it offers comfort, he should show tenderness; if it commands something, the preacher should show authority. Dabney explains:

> The preacher's soul should here show itself fired with the force of the truth which has been developed, and glowing both with light and heat. The quality of unction should suffuse the end of your discourse, and bathe the truth in evangelical emotion. But this emotion must be genuine and not assumed; it must be spiritual, the zeal of heavenly love, and not the carnal heat of the mental gymnastic.... It must disclose itself spontaneously and unannounced, as the gushing of a fountain which will not be suppressed. What can give this glow except the indwelling of the Holy Ghost? You are thus led again to that great, ever-recurring deduction, the first qualification of the sacred orator, the grace of Christ.[46]

This emotional connection with the Word is related to what our forefathers referred to as Spirit-given unction. It is better caught than taught, better experienced than explained.

10. Be Christ-centered in application. Holy passion must be peculiarly manifest when preachers speak about the beauty and glory of Christ Jesus, our Immanuel. Samuel Rutherford speaks of the need to preach a "felt Christ." Today, one of our greatest needs in preaching is for more Christ-centered applications. Christ-centered applications help God's people fall more in love with their perfect Bridegroom. They simultaneously deliver preachers from moralization and legalism.

For example, if a sermon is based on biblical history, Christ-centered application will show how history prefigures and points to Christ, or eventually leads to Him. If a sermon is based on a psalm, Christ-centered application will show how the Psalms help us worship Christ. If the sermon is based on Proverbs, Christ-centered application may show how Christ is ultimately the Wisdom of God. If the sermon is based on the prophets, Christ-centered application will show how prophecy predicts Christ. If preaching is from the law, Christ-centered application will show how the law points to our need of Christ. If preaching practical duties, Christ-centered application will show how to practice obedience by loving Christ. If preaching Christ's words, Christ-centered application will show how what we say can magnify Christ. If preaching on suffering, Christ-centered application will show how suffering brings us into fellowship with Christ's sufferings. If preaching duty, Christ-centered

---

46. Dabney, *Lectures on Sacred Rhetoric*, 176.

application may show how Christ forgives our failings in the line of duty. If preaching about love, Christ-centered application may stress the example of Christ. If preaching about sin, Christ-centered application may reveal Christ as the only Savior from sin. Let all applications bring us to the feet of Christ.

Subject Matter for Applications

Here are some suggestions on the basic truths of God that we should communicate to listeners through applicatory preaching:

First, to apply truth in preaching, you must preach the truth about *God*. As obvious as this seems, let me ask how often you have preached about God in His holiness, sovereignty, compassion, and mercy in the past few months. Have you poured out your heart to your congregation like Thomas Watson who says, "His mercy is His darling attribute"?[47] Have people felt who God really is through your preaching? Or are you caught up with so many social issues and other things in your preaching that the focus is really not on God? It is critical that your focus remains on the Lord. The greatest goal of all sermons is to bring people closer to the great and wonderful, holy and terrible, majestic and merciful God. Let people, through your text, feel the character of the living God; apply His attributes to inform their mind, penetrate their conscience, move their affections, and bend their will.

At times, provide applications specifically for children. I have used the following illustration when preaching on the omniscience of God:

> Two little girls were asked to bring cookies to their grandma about a mile away. Their mother told them, "Make sure you don't eat any on the way!" Well, on the way, Cindy got tired and hungry. She set the cookies down, looked around, and whispered to Julie, "Is anyone looking?" Not waiting for an answer, she opened the lid and began reaching for a cookie.
>
> Julie grabbed her by the arm, saying, "Wait! Someone is looking!"
>
> "Who?" asked Cindy, looking all around.
>
> Julie pointed up, saying, "God is looking! He sees all that we do."
>
> The lid quietly went back on the basket. Every cookie made it safely to Grandma's house.
>
> Dear boys and girls, do you live like Julie, knowing that God knows and sees everything—not just what you say or do but even what you think? God knows everything!

Second, preach the truth about *man*. We cannot afford to shy away from the truth of man's sin at the risk of sounding offensive. Preach, dear brothers,

---

47. Thomas Watson, *A Body of Divinity* (Edinburgh: Banner of Truth, 2008), 93.

about how sinful and depraved we are apart from divine grace. Compel listeners to reckon with their corrupt natures and the strength and vileness of their inner sin. John Owen told his listeners, "Every unclean thought or glance would be adultery if it could; every covetous desire would be oppression, every thought of unbelief atheism, might it grow to its head."[48] You do people a favor when you expose their sins because you can then, by the Spirit's grace, draw or drive them to Christ to find sufficiency in Him. Sometimes the best way to make unpleasant applications is to use an illustration. Here is an illustration that I have used to personalize depravity:

> Martin Luther became so weary of his inward corruption that he turned to his wife one day and complained that his heart was like his beard. Every day he tried to clean himself up by shaving his beard, but the next morning inward depravity would spring out again, much like his beard. Have you ever felt that, no matter what you do to uproot it, sin keeps growing in you every day? Does this knowledge drive you to Jesus Christ, who is the only remedy for sin?

Third, preach the need for *true repentance*. The apostles never left their hearers comfortable in sin; they preached to incite people to action. Paul thus writes, "I testified to you publicly and from house to house repentance toward God, and faith toward our Lord Jesus Christ" (Acts 20:20–21). Let us never forget that though repentance is the work of grace, not nature, it is through the means of applying imperatives to repent and believe that the Spirit works genuine repentance in sinners' hearts.

Preach repentance experientially as well. Show people that repentance involves searching out sin, grieving over sin, confessing sin, forsaking sin, bowing under sin's just punishment, and taking refuge in Christ.

Fourth, preach *Christ*. William Perkins summarizes his entire book on preaching this way: "Preach one Christ, by Christ, to the praise of Christ."[49] You must press Christ, in all of His offices, states, natures, person, and benefits, on the souls of saints and sinners. There is no end to the preaching of Christ. Preach Him as the grand remedy for the great malady of our sinfulness. Preach how He meets the needs of undeserving sinners like us. Preach Him as Savior and as Lord. Preach His crucifixion, His righteousness, and His beauty. Preach Christ as chief among ten thousand and the One who is altogether lovely. Preach Him in such a way that your congregation knows that you wish with all your heart that they would know Jesus and live out of Him.

---

48. John Owen, *The Works of John Owen* (Edinburgh: Banner of Truth, 2000), 6:12.
49. Perkins, *The Art of Prophesying*, 79.

"Preaching is not Christ," however, as Samuel Rutherford says.[50] Preaching is never the end; Christ is. Preach to make listeners feel that they do not need a sermon as much as the Christ proclaimed in the sermon. The sermon is the lowly means of bringing souls to the greater Truth. Oh, preach Jesus Christ— let Him be the diamond that shines in the bosom of your every sermon![51] Preach this Savior of men and let people know that He loves souls more than people love their own souls.

Fifth, preach the truth about *salvation*. Teach people that salvation means to be delivered from the greatest evil, sin, and brought into supreme good, fellowship with the Father and the Son by the Spirit. Teach them that this glorious salvation is essential, available, free, and has lifelong, yes, eternal, consequences.

Dear colleagues in the ministry, if people do not hear about this salvation from you, who will they hear it from? Consider the world around us; in more than a thousand ways, people are being told they have no need of salvation and are sufficient in themselves. We therefore must reject the enemies' arrows and arm ourselves with more powerful strategies than he uses. Our strategies, thank God, are more powerful, because they are motivated by eternal love. With an unrelenting spirit and great urgency, we must compel people to come to Christ. Preach with such conviction that it may seem that you have the ability to draw them to Christ, yet realizing that you have no ability to do so, for that is ultimately the Spirit's domain.

Sixth, preach the *truth about the Christian*. The Christian always finds himself in the dilemma of the apostle Paul in Romans 7: "The good that I would I do not: but the evil that I would not I do." Do not gloss over the ups and downs of the Christian life, but openly and honestly preach about the inward struggles against indwelling sin, the frustrations of sanctification, and the struggles of consistent use of the spiritual disciplines. Set before others the challenges of being Christ's disciples. Geoffrey Thomas writes, "In applicatory preaching, the implications of Christian discipleship are made very plain to distinguish between believers who are walking in the spirit and those who in some area of their lives are walking in the flesh."[52] But also preach the infallible hope of every Christian, that one day every Christian will be perfectly conformed to the image of Christ.

Finally, preach the *whole counsel of God* to the conscience. Have you ever considered that the preaching of the apostle Peter, especially on the day of

---

50. Samuel Rutherford, *The Letters of Samuel Rutherford* (Edinburgh: Banner of Truth, 2006), 202.

51. Bridges, *Christian Ministry*, 258.

52. Thomas, "Powerful Preaching," in Logan, *Preacher and Preaching*, 379.

Pentecost, thrust "that sword relentlessly into their hearts, and he would not stop while they rejected the Lord Jesus"?[53] The people "were pricked in their heart," says Acts 2:37. So do not be afraid to preach the reality of hell and damnation, warning people of the impending judgment of the soul. Pierce their consciences with these weighty truths.

In short, preach the whole counsel of God to the whole man. Whether you preach God, Christ, the nature of man, salvation, or hell, do so with convicting and heartfelt power. In 1 Corinthians 2:4, Paul reminds the church at Corinth that his preaching "was not with enticing words of man's wisdom, but in demonstration of the Spirit and of power." The demonstration of the Spirit and power must be evident in all of our preaching.

"Whether the matter of preaching is a doctrine or a word of reproof or practical application it is to be done powerfully," says Thomas.[54] We confess with Romans 10:17 that the preaching of the Word causes change, so let us preach with the power of this life-changing Word. Let us apply the Word as people who have been mastered by its immortal truths, conquered by its supreme wisdom, captivated by its content, and enthralled with its message. Let us preach it as the Word of life.

Methods of Applicatory Preaching

Applicatory preaching has many forms. Let us briefly summarize twenty methods of using Scripture in a life-changing way. We will briefly explain each method, provide an example from Scripture to justify that method, then give an example of the method at work.

1. Declaration

"Christianity begins with a triumphant indicative," says J. Gresham Machen.[55] One type of applicatory preaching, then, is an authoritative declaration of divinely inspired facts. The preacher communicates vital information from the all-knowing God to ignorant human beings. This process of replacing ignorance with knowledge and falsehood with facts is, in itself, the first application of God's Word. It is a potentially transforming experience for the hearer as his ignorance and prejudices are replaced with knowledge and truth. By announcing God's Word with authority, the preacher is saying, "It is vital that you know these facts." He is not in the business of suggestion but of declaration, assertion,

---

53. Thomas, "Powerful Preaching," 377.
54. Thomas, "Powerful Preaching," 370.
55. J. Gresham Machen, *Christianity and Liberalism* (Grand Rapids: Eerdmans, 1977), 47.

and affirmation. This first application of God's Word changes lectures into sermons. Authoritative declarations of the truth establish and confirm the faith of God's people.

+ *Scriptural Example*: In Acts 17:22 and following, Paul preaches the knowledge of God to ignorant, prejudiced listeners. He announces and declares life-changing historical and theological facts.

• *Sermon Example*: A sermon on "God is love" (1 John 4:8) benefits listeners by replacing misunderstanding about God's love with accurate knowledge of it. This transformational knowledge is, in itself, an application of God's Word.

2. Exclamation

Information becomes more memorable when a preacher expresses his approval or disapproval of what he is saying. Spurgeon says a preacher should pepper his sermons with many "Ohs." An exclamatory phrase may also begin with "What a great Savior!" or "How great God is!" Though such exclamatory phrases should not be overdone, they can help listeners realize the preacher's appreciation or deprecation ("Woe!") of what is being preached. They also prepare people for what is coming. Exclamatory words appeal to the heart as well as the head.

+ *Scriptural Example*: The Psalms abound with exclamation (Pss. 8:1, 9; 73:19; 104:24). After explaining the awesome sovereignty of God, the apostle Paul exclaims, "O the depth of the riches both of the wisdom and knowledge of God! how unsearchable are his judgments, and his ways past finding out!" (Rom. 11:33). Matthew 23 is an example of Christ's seven woes as He denounces the Pharisees.

+ *Sermon Example*: When preaching on the beauty of Christ, instead of simply stating, "Christ is beautiful," a preacher might exclaim, "Oh, the beauty of Christ!" This applies the truth of feelings and inflames the heart.

3. Interrogation

Having given information and invited the congregation to enjoy it, the preacher may then challenge listeners with questions about their relationship to these truths.

+ *Scriptural Example*: Interrogation abounds in Romans. For example, in Romans 2:21 Paul asks, "Thou therefore which teachest another, teachest thou not thyself? thou that preachest a man should not steal, dost thou steal?" Notice also the prophet's use of rhetorical questions in Isaiah 40:12–14.

+ *Sermon Example*: A preacher could conclude a sermon on doing religious things only to be seen and applauded by men (Matt. 6:1–6) by asking: "Why do you come to church—to be seen of men or to see God? Why do you pray—so that others will hear or so that God will hear?"

4. Obligation

A preacher presents the truth, then gives his congregation commands that follow logically from that truth. W. E. Sangster recommends that we do not just say, "Do this or that," however. He says, "In ethical preaching, it [the point] is to make the people thrill over a particular virtue or grace, and not merely to thrill about it, but to long for it and study to secure it in their own hearts; or, conversely, to make them loathe a particular vice, turn from it, and scheme to become its master."[56] But is this not being moralistic? Many advocates of redemptive-historical preaching confuse morality, which is biblical and Christ-honoring, with moralism, which is Christ-less and unbiblical; they end up condemning both. Biblical morality requires ethical change empowered by thankfulness for Christ's forgiveness and prayer for Christ's power. Moralism is simply legalism; it sets out God's requirements and requires obedience. It fails to point the believer to Christ as the reason, basis, and power for obedience. While we should shun moralism in applicatory preaching, we must promote morality and its Christ-centered basis. It is wrong to set up a false dichotomy between biblical history on the one hand and ethics or morality on the other.

+ *Scriptural Example*: In Exodus 20, God says, I redeemed you (vv. 1–2); therefore, obey Me (vv. 3–17). Paul concludes the doctrinal part of Romans (chaps. 1–11) with a number of imperatives in chapter 12.

+ *Sermon Example*: A sermon on the lukewarm church of Laodicea (Rev. 3:16) may be permeated with imperatives such as "Be zealous… committed…serious…wholehearted…single-minded."

5. Exhortation

Exhortation is somewhat less confrontational than imperative application. It often uses the hortatory "Let us…." Through exhortation the preacher takes more of a sympathetic stance in motivating listeners to do something.

+ *Scriptural Example*: The apostle Paul addresses converted Jews in his letter to the Hebrews with a number of mutual exhortations, such as, "Let us therefore come boldly unto the throne of grace" (Heb. 4:16; cf. 4:1; 4:11; 6:1).

---

56. W. E. Sangster, *The Craft of the Sermon* (Philadelphia: Westminster, 1960), 137.

+ *Sermon Example*: In a sermon on the condescension of Christ in His incarnation (Phil. 2:5–11), a preacher may conclude the apostle's application with exhortations to peace, unity, and humility (2:3) in imitation of Christ (2:5).

6. Motivation

Sometimes a preacher adds to these first five methods of applicatory preaching by stressing their motivation, accenting motives for information, exclamation, interrogation, obligation, and exhortation. He thus increases the likelihood of listeners receiving the information, joining him in exclamation, answering interrogation, binding themselves to the obligation, and agreeing with the exhortation, by giving the scriptural motives for doing so.

+ *Scriptural Example*: In 1 Corinthians 15:34, the apostle commands listeners, "Awake to righteousness, and sin not," then adds the motivating reason, "for some have not the knowledge of God: I speak this to your shame."

+ *Sermon Example*: When informing a congregation about the deceitful and desperately wicked nature of the human heart (Jer. 17:9), a preacher may motivate listeners to respond by explaining the vital importance of understanding our disease in order to seek the right cure.

7. Imitation

Advocates of redemptive-historical preaching cannot deny that the Old and New Testaments contain examples of exemplary preaching. Richard Gaffin highlights how "a subordinate, even incidental, aspect of the Old Testament narrative is taken by James and used to encourage New Testament Christians to continue patiently in praying." He says, "James knew that Elijah was a prophet with a role in the history of redemption, but he also knew that he was a man just like us, a sinner saved by grace, who battled to pray aright."[57] In Corinthians, Paul draws a straight line from Old Testament examples to his readers, showing how they should and should not act in present circumstances (1 Corinthians 10; Hebrews 12).

+ *Scriptural Example*: After highlighting parts of Israel's history, Paul says to the Corinthians, "Now these things were our examples, to the intent we should not lust after evil things, as they also lusted" (1 Cor. 10:6; cf. v. 11).

---

57. http://www.banneroftruth.org/pages/articles/article_detail.php?119 (accessed May 15, 2008).

+ *Sermon Example*: A sermon on David's courage when facing Goliath in God's strength (1 Samuel 17) might go on to urge the same response in modern Christians as they face ungodly powers with God's help.

8. Illustration and metaphor

Sometimes the best way to apply a truth is with an illustration, metaphor, story, or picture. W. E. Sangster suggests using illustration to nail down the concluding application of the sermon. He says, "The people are a little tired, maybe, from thirty minutes of serious thinking, and yet one cannot part from them without gathering it all up for its final reception into their believing hearts. Put it in an illustration. Hold up a picture that will both recapitulate and apply all that is in your mind. Having given the illustration, end. Make the illustration so good that it is utterly unnecessary to add more than a concluding sentence or two afterward—and be glad when it does not even require that."[58]

Below are examples for story, then illustration.

+ *Scriptural Example*: In applying the teaching of "Love your neighbour as yourself," Jesus tells the story of the Good Samaritan (Luke 10:29–37).

+ *Sermon Example*: In a sermon on Christ's substitutionary death, a preacher could show the gratitude and love that should result by telling how, as a teenager, he became indebted to his father who took his son's large credit card bill and paid it for him.

+ *Scriptural Example*: Instead of warning His disciples to be on their guard lest hypocrisy gradually and imperceptibly encroach on them, Jesus uses a vivid baker's metaphor and says, "Take heed and beware of the leaven of the Pharisees and of the Sadducees" (Matt. 16:6).

+ *Sermon Example*: When a preacher wants to emphasize the importance of "keeping the heart" (Prov. 4:23), he might use the illustration of a computer's hard drive and how it impacts everything else.

9. Quotation

A preacher may apply Scripture by quoting from the sayings and writings of others. These may help buttress and emphasize the lessons in the sermon. There are many examples of biblical authors using previously written Scripture in this way. However, there are also examples of biblical authors using secular writers to help apply the truth.

---

58. Sangster, *The Craft of the Sermon*, 145.

+ *Scriptural Example*: Apart from frequently quoting the Old Testament, Paul quotes a Greek poet to support one of his points during his sermon in Athens (Acts 17:28).

+ *Sermon Example*: Quoting the words of John Calvin or Charles Spurgeon may support a pastor's preaching and make his listeners more receptive. Or a preacher may use the words of famous non-Christians to show the despair and meaninglessness in successful, worldly people. Such quotes can have a dramatic impact on unconverted hearers.

10. Conversation

One of the best ways to get a congregation's attention is to set up a dialogue or conversation between two people. For example, it may be a debate between the preacher and an opponent or between the preacher and a genuine seeker after the truth.

+ *Scriptural Example*: In Romans, Paul frequently set up dialogues between himself and an opponent to apply the truth (Rom. 3:1–9; 6:1–3).

+ *Sermon Example*: In a sermon on creation (Gen. 1:1), a preacher may apply the truth by carrying on a hypothetical conversation between himself and an evolutionist, answering the evolutionist's questions and challenging him in return.

11. Condemnation

Once you teach the truth, it may be necessary to highlight and condemn distortions and denials of the truth.

+ *Scriptural Example*: Most of Jude's epistle exposes and condemns false teachers in the churches of Christ.

+ *Sermon Example*: A sermon on the uniqueness and sufficiency of Christ's death (Heb. 10:14) may conclude with the teaching of the Roman Catholic Church regarding the ongoing sacrifice of Christ in the Mass, which a preacher may then prove is both a blasphemous and dangerous doctrine.

12. Invitation

Having set Christ forth, it is incumbent upon the preacher to call sinners to Him.

+ *Scriptural Example*: In Psalm 2, the psalmist concludes his description of the Messiah's ultimate victory over his foes with, "Kiss the Son, lest he be angry, and ye perish from the way" (Ps. 2:12).

+ *Sermon Example:* No sermon on Christ as the Good Shepherd (John 10:14) should be concluded without calling listeners to follow Christ and be fed by Him.

13. Demonstration

Sometimes it is not enough for preachers to simply urge their hearers to do something; they must show exactly how to do what they have heard.

+ *Scriptural Example:* When the Ten Commandments are given in Exodus 20, the following chapters give concrete examples of how to obey them.

+ *Sermon Example:* A preacher who urges listeners to evangelize the lost on the basis of "Ye shall be witnesses unto me" (Acts 1:8) may spend a large part of his sermon on the practicalities of how to evangelize in specific situations.

14. Adoration

A preacher should quite naturally feel adoration welling up within his heart as he preaches the truth. As his devotional spirit is excited, he may let out expressions of worship or send brief petitions heavenward. Such spontaneous responses to the truth bring its reality and importance home to listeners.

+ *Scriptural Example:* In the Psalms, writers often move from third-person narratives about God to second-person expressions of praise to God (Ps. 106:4, 47).

+ *Sermon Example:* When preaching on the everlasting destruction of sinners, a preacher may occasionally turn from his congregation to God, saying things such as "Lord Jesus, Thou art merciful.... Gracious Lord, save us all from hell...."

15. Admonition

The congregation may need to be rebuked or admonished before it is led to true confession.

+ *Scriptural Example:* Isaiah 1–39 sets forth God as the only hope for Israel. In light of that, the prophet repeatedly rebukes God's people for turning away from God to ask ungodly nations to save them (Isaiah 30).

+ *Sermon Example:* Someone preaching on "Love not the world..." (1 John 2:15) may go on to rebuke his listeners' worldliness, then lead the congregation in confessing, "Holy God, we have loved the world, we have copied the world, we have followed the world, we have admired the world. Turn us, and we shall be turned."

16. Consolation

There are times when a congregation needs the comfort and encouragement of the truth.

+ *Scriptural Example*: In Isaiah 40–66, Isaiah turns from rebuke to comfort. His prophecies assume that Israel is captive in Babylon, so the prophet encourages people to put their trust in God and look forward to restoration in their land (Isaiah 40).

+ *Sermon Example*: A sermon on the Lord's pursuit of Peter after his denial (John 21) may be used to encourage backsliders not to despair but to return to an all-merciful and all-forgiving God.

17. Examination and Discrimination

When preaching on the internal marks of a true Christian, a preacher may impress on listeners the need to examine their hearts to discover whether they have these marks. He may then explain how a true Christian thinks and feels in certain situations and how that differs from the reactions of unbelievers.

Some redemptive-historical preachers emphasize the importance of determining a single meaning in a portion of Scripture. This is commendable and confessional. Nevertheless, by deducing from a single meaning the imperative for only a single application, they often confound two separate ideas. They argue against discriminatory preaching that applies the text's single meaning to different kinds of listeners. As Sidney Greidanus says, "One message throughout the sermon…implies that a multiple application which would address a separate word to different categories of people is out of the question…. The preacher is to proclaim to all alike the Word of God as given in his text. It is one Word that is spoken, but this Word has a dual effect: it calls up faith here, hardens hearts there; it equips for greater service here, increases resistance there; it saves here, condemns there."[59]

Greidanus then favorably quotes Holwerda, who says: "Let the preacher preach the gospel to *all*! Only then does he swing the ax of Christ. Woe to the preacher who *presupposes* divisions in the church and directs the word of text to only one group. He must preach it to all and by that means Christ shall make the divisions."[60]

---

59. Sidney Greidanus, *Preaching Christ from the Old Testament* (Grand Rapids: Eerdmans, 1999), 166.

60. Sidney Greidanus, *Sola Scriptura* (Toronto: Wedge, 1970), 100.

- *Scriptural Example*: In Luke 6:20–26, Jesus describes the blessed identifying marks of the true Christian, then contrasts this with the characteristics of the unbeliever.

- *Sermon Example*: In a sermon on "The joy of the Lord is your strength" (Neh. 8:10), a preacher may distinguish the joy of the Christian from the joy of the non-Christian by examining the object of each joy, the nature of each joy, the duration of each joy, and the end of each joy. Listeners may then be encouraged to search their hearts to see what joy is their strength and to derive comfort on discovering true spiritual joy.

18. Reconciliation

One important part of sermon application is to reconcile the truth of a preached passage with modern science, with human experience, or even with the rest of Scripture.

- *Scriptural Example*: In Romans 9, the apostle Paul shows that the doctrine of human responsibility is not incompatible with divine sovereignty (Rom. 9:19–23).

- *Sermon Example*: In a sermon on God's leaving Hezekiah (2 Chron. 32:31), a preacher may show how this leaving is consistent with the promise that God will never leave nor forsake His people (Heb. 13:5). He may then explain how the leaving was not objective but subjective.

19. Anticipation

Many Scripture passages anticipate Christ's person and work. They may have a primary reference to Israel and its experiences; however, subsequent Scripture shows they have a further significance.

- *Scriptural Example*: Prophetic anticipation (Hos. 11:1; Matt. 2:15), typological anticipation (Exodus 25; Heb. 9:24), and analogical anticipation (Jonah 2; Matt. 12:39–40) all point to Christ.

- *Sermon Example*: Few sermons on David would be complete without showing how his life and character anticipate Christ, the Son of David.

20. Modernization

The Bible addressed the problems of an ancient people in ancient times. The preacher, therefore, must contemporize when preaching on many passages of Scripture. He must explain what the people were like when a Scripture passage was written, what problems they were struggling with, and why God gave them this message. Having done that, the preacher can deduce a timeless principle for application.

+ *Scriptural Example:* In Deuteronomy 25:4, Moses instructs the children of Israel to allow the ox that is treading corn to eat the corn. In 1 Corinthians 9:9 and 1 Timothy 5:18, the apostle Paul takes the principle behind this verse—the one who labors should be supported by those for whom he labors—and uses it to justify financial, congregational support of ministers.

+ *Sermon Example:* Proverbs 20:23 says, "Divers weights are an abomination unto the Lord; and a false balance is not good." Although few Christians use balances and weights today, a preacher may take this text, extract the principle of fairness and justice in buying and selling, then use this principle to exhort present-day Christians to practice honesty, fairness, and truthfulness, both in business and everyday life.

Conclusion

Let us conclude by returning to Perkins's definition of application as "the skill by which the doctrine which has been properly drawn from Scripture is handled in ways which are appropriate to the circumstances of the place and time and to the people in the congregation."[61] Applicatory preaching faithfully connects a sermon with people who listen to it. It tells them, "God has a Word for *you.*" We must continually show people that the living and active Word speaks to every struggle, circumstance, and situation (Heb. 4:12).

Numerous books on preaching make the process of application so difficult that many preachers give up on trying to apply the Word. However, if God gives us scriptural warrant for our methods of application, it really does not matter what academics and professors say in opposition. Let the Word of God free you to apply Scripture with life-changing power to your listeners.

Every Lord's Day as people file out of church, they go back to a world of danger, temptation, and sin. Lectures that merely inform the mind of God's truths are not sufficient to help people stand in the day of trial. Let us be faithful to our calling in applying God's Word to every person's conscience, feeding them even as our Chief Shepherd feeds us with the nourishment of His Word.

---

61. Perkins, *The Art of Prophesying,* 54.

Chapter 28

Authentic Ministry:
Servanthood, Tears, and Temptations

Ye know, from the first day that I came into Asia, after what manner I have been with you at all seasons, serving the Lord with all humility of mind, and with many tears, and temptations.

—Acts 20:18b–19[1]

In 1688 conflict erupted between the city authorities of Rotterdam in the Netherlands and the Reformed minister Wilhelmus à Brakel (1635–1711). The government paid the salary of ministers and had a role in confirming their calls.[2] When the civil magistrate refused to approve an otherwise duly called pastor, Brakel preached a sermon entitled "The Lord Jesus Declared to be the Only Sovereign King of His Church."

The government responded by prohibiting Brakel from preaching and suspending his salary. Brakel believed the government had no right to exercise such control over the ministers of Christ, so he ignored his suspension and kept on preaching. For some weeks he lived outside the city, commuting to Rotterdam to fulfill his ministerial duties. He said he would rather face exile, even death, rather than stop preaching the Word of Christ. However, when Brakel's consistory asked his permission to let another minister preach until the controversy cooled, Brakel submitted to the authority of the elders. In so doing, he demonstrated that he was not a revolutionary. Yet it took the influence of William of Orange (Willem III) to prevent Brakel from being sent into exile.[3]

---

1. This chapter is a slightly expanded version of an address I gave at the URC Ministers' Conference at Puritan Reformed Theological Seminary, Grand Rapids, Michigan on May 12, 2011.
2. "Church Order of Dort," in *Doctrinal Standards, Liturgy, and Church Order*, ed. Joel R. Beeke (Grand Rapids: Reformation Heritage Books, 1999), 179 (Art. 4).
3. W. Fieret, "Wilhelmus à Brakel," in Wilhelmus à Brakel, *The Christian's Reasonable Service*, trans. Bartel Elshout, ed. Joel R. Beeke (repr., Grand Rapids: Reformation Heritage Books, 2010), 1:lxxi–lxxiv.

Brakel later said of the ministry, "There must be self-denial, that is, a willingness to sacrifice one's honor, goods—yes, even one's life.... The servant of Christ...should let Paul be his example."[4] Today we can learn from Paul's description of his ministry in Acts 20:19 that the Lord calls pastors to do His will with lowliness of mind and heart, compassion, and faithfulness.

Just as Jesus Christ set His face toward Jerusalem to fulfill His Father's will (Luke 9:51), the apostle Paul knew that he, too, must go to Jerusalem, and knew what it would cost him (Acts 20:22–23).[5] He gathered the Ephesian elders, his dear friends, around him for one last meeting (vv. 17, 25, 38). Luke refers to Paul's audience as elders and overseers, the men called to shepherd the flock of God (vv. 17, 28).

Paul spoke to the elders as a veteran minister addressing fellow servants in the Lord. He bids them to follow him as he followed the Lord (1 Cor. 11:1). The first thing he says about his ministry in Acts 20:19 is to serve the Lord "with all humility of mind, and with many tears, and temptations."

The heart of this Scripture is "serving the Lord." Literally the Greek text says, "serving as a slave of the Lord."[6] "Slave" and "Lord" indicate a relationship of authority and submission, or one man doing the will of another. We do not serve according to our own will; rather, the Lord calls pastors to do His will in a life of obedience to His holy Word. We are not masters or owners, only stewards entrusted with the revealed mysteries of God and the care of the blood-bought church of Christ. Matthew Henry (1662–1714) said of Paul, "He had made it his business to serve the Lord, to promote the honour of God and the interest of Christ and his kingdom among them. He never served himself, nor made himself the servant of men, of their lusts and humours...but he made it his business to serve the Lord."[7]

Are you serving the church in an attitude of prostration before the throne of Christ? Do you work with the heart of a servant? Are you serving with your eye on His pleasure and His promised reward? Does your ministry echo the first three petitions of the Lord's Prayer: "Hallowed be Thy name. Thy kingdom come. Thy will be done"? What does this look like in practice?

---

4. Brakel, *The Christian's Reasonable Service*, 2:134.

5. "In his journey to Jerusalem and Rome, Paul mirrors Jesus' journey to Jerusalem and the way he prepared his disciples for his absence in Luke 9–19." Darrell L. Bock, *Acts* (Grand Rapids: Baker Academic, 2007), 623.

6. The verb "serving" (δουλευων) is cognate to "slave" (δουλος). "He literally calls himself a slave." Simon J. Kistemaker, *Acts* (Grand Rapids: Baker, 1992), 725.

7. *Matthew Henry's Commentary* (Peabody, Mass.: Hendrickson, 2003), 6:211.

Paul gives us three words about authentic ministry: *humility, tears,* and *temptations.* Let us thus examine what it means to serve Christ in these three ways, drawing from Paul's entire speech in Acts 20:18–35.

Serving God in Humility

Humility is not an outward show of wearing old clothes or walking around with eyes on the ground. Humility is "lowliness of mind."[8] It is a quality of the heart, a mind-set, an attitude, a perspective. Ministers in particular need to hear Paul's words in Romans 12:1–3, "I beseech you therefore, brethren, by the mercies of God, that ye present your bodies a living sacrifice, holy, acceptable unto God, which is your reasonable service. And be not conformed to this world: but be ye transformed by the renewing of your mind, that ye may prove what is that good, and acceptable, and perfect, will of God. For I say, through the grace given unto me, to every man that is among you, not to think of himself more highly than he ought to think; but to think soberly, according as God hath dealt to every man the measure of faith."

True humility is giving all you are to doing the will of your Savior, having a sober and just estimate of yourself and your abilities as a minister, while remembering that anything you have of real value or use is a gift from God. John Dick wrote of Paul, "Elevated to the highest rank in the Christian Church, more learned than any of his brethren, and possessed of great natural talents, and of miraculous powers, he was not elated with an idea of his superiority, nor haughty and overbearing in his intercourse with others."[9] Paul is a model for us all, for humility is the heartbeat of service in the kingdom of God (Matt. 18:1–4). Augustine (354–430) said the first matter of importance in the Christian life is humility; the second, humility; and the third, humility.[10] The humility of Christ's slave is evident in Acts 20 in the following ways:

---

8. The Greek term is ταπεινοφροσυνη, literally "low mindedness." "It is sometimes rendered lowliness (Eph. 4, 2) or *lowliness of mind* (Phi. 2, 3)." J. A. Alexander, *Acts* (Edinburgh: Banner of Truth, 1984), 241.

9. John Dick, *Lectures on the Acts of the Apostles,* 2nd ed. (New York: Robert Carter, 1845), 320.

10. "In that way the first part is humility; the second, humility; the third, humility: and this I would continue to repeat as often as you asked for direction, not that there are not other instructions which may be given, but because, unless humility precede, accompany, and follow every good action which we perform...pride wrests from our hand any good work on which we are congratulating ourselves.... Wherefore, as that most illustrious orator, on being asked what seemed to him the first thing to be observed in the art of eloquence, is said to have replied, Delivery; and when he was asked what the second thing, replied again, Delivery; and when asked what was the third thing, still gave no other reply than this, Delivery; so if you were to ask me, however often you might repeat the question, what are the instructions of the Christian religion, I would be disposed to answer always and only, 'Humility.'" Letter CXVIII (AD 410), Augustin to Dioscorus, 3.22, in *Confessions and Letters of St.*

1. He loves obedience more than life. Rather than being puffed up with his own importance, the slave of Christ is satisfied to do his Master's will. Paul says in Acts 20:22–24, "And now, behold, I go bound in the spirit unto Jerusalem, not knowing the things that shall befall me there: save that the Holy Ghost witnesseth in every city, saying that bonds and afflictions abide me. But none of these things move me, neither count I my life dear unto myself, so that I might finish my course with joy, and the ministry, which I have received of the Lord Jesus, to testify the gospel of the grace of God."

Paul did not consider his life as precious or "of great value."[11] When he understood that it was necessary for him to go to Jerusalem to glorify God, he did not protest, saying, "But Lord, they want to kill me there. I have an important ministry among the Gentiles. The churches in Asia and Greece need my theological wisdom and my practical guidance. Surely someone else could go." Instead, Paul saw himself as a servant for Jesus's sake (2 Cor. 4:5). Nothing was more precious to him than to submit to the will of God. Nothing was more important than completing the work that the Lord Jesus gave to him. Thomas Manton (1620–1677) said, "Life is only then worth the having when we may honour Christ by it.... Paul loved his work more than his life, and preferred obedience before safety."[12]

In this way Paul denied himself, took up his cross and followed Christ, who, "being found in fashion as a man,...humbled himself, and became obedient unto death, even the death of the cross" (Phil. 2:8). Christ is God; yet Christ is also God's servant *par excellence*. If He, whom we rightly call Lord and Master, washed the feet of His disciples, how much more should we be willing to undertake lowly and difficult tasks? Henry wrote of Paul, "He was willing to stoop to any service, and to make himself and his labours as cheap as they could desire."[13]

Gisbertus Voetius (1589–1676), a leading theologian of the Dutch Further Reformation, wrote voluminous theological disputations in Latin, while seeking to reform the church and society of the Netherlands. Voetius has been compared to the English Puritan John Owen in stature and influence, yet Voetius took time every week to teach catechism to orphaned children.[14] He did

---

Augustin with a Sketch of His Life, A Select Library of the Nicene and Post-Nicene Fathers, Volume 1 (repr., Edinburgh: T&T Clark, 1989), 446.

11. Greek τιμιαν.

12. Sermon I on Philippians 1:21, "For to me to live is Christ, and to die is gain," in *The Complete Works of Thomas Manton* (London: James Nisbet, 1870–1875), 20:184.

13. *Matthew Henry's Commentary*, 6:211.

14. Joel R. Beeke, *Gisbertus Voetius: Towards a Reformed Marriage of Knowledge and Piety* (Grand Rapids: Reformation Heritage Books, 1999), 15.

not regard that work as something too lowly for someone of his standing but gladly obeyed the Bible's call to care for widows and orphans (James 1:27).

Brothers in ministry, whose feet are you washing? How do you exhibit the humility of a slave of the Lord who loves obedience more than life?

2. *He delights in giving more than in receiving.* Paul says in Acts 20:33–34, "I have coveted no man's silver, or gold, or apparel. Yea, ye yourselves know, that these hands have ministered unto my necessities, and to them that were with me." As apostle to the Gentiles, Paul started many churches in centers of wealth, but not with the idea of making himself rich in the process. He gladly preached the gospel for free, earning his own way as a tentmaker if no one was able or willing to support him. He was willing to spend his own money on these churches, much as parents support their children (2 Cor. 12:14–15). So Paul could say to the Ephesian elders, "I have shewed you all things, how that so labouring ye ought to support the weak, and to remember the words of the Lord Jesus, how he said, It is more blessed to give than to receive" (Acts 20:35). How precious these words are from Christ's earthly ministry, "It is more blessed to give than to receive."

Proud people are like black holes in outer space. They think they deserve glory, honor, and power for what they do, but whatever they manage to get simply disappears into their darkness, for they are never satisfied. They are like Haman who was a great prince in the Persian empire but was "full of wrath" when one man refused to bow to him (Est. 3:1–5). By contrast, people of humility are like the sun. They constantly shine forth light and warmth, blessing those around them. They do not covet glory and honor for themselves; they give freely, willing to "spend and be spent" for Christ's sake. In doing so, they attract people as the sun does with its gravitational pull, and create beautiful, ordered families, churches, and societies.

Are you the man in Jesus's parable who tries to get the best seat at a banquet? Or do you try to honor others rather than to seek it for yourself? Do you preach against this world while still coveting what's in it? Does your heart lust after praise and recognition, wealth and riches, or any other form of glory or praise from men? Beware, for the love of the world will leave you groveling at the feet of the devil. Rather, "let this mind be in you, which was also in Christ Jesus" (Phil. 2:5), that is, the true humility, or lowliness of mind, of one who is the slave of God.

The Tears of the Slave of the Lord

It may seem strange to hear Paul talking about tears in ministry as an essential component of serving the Lord. Aren't we supposed to be serving the Lord in the strength of His might? God calls us to be men of valor, not cry-babies, right? First Corinthians 16:13 commands us to "stand fast in the faith, quit you like men, be strong." So what does biblical masculinity look like?

There are times when life's pain wrenches tears from our eyes and groans from our souls. Christ Himself "offered up prayers and supplications with strong crying and tears unto him that was able to save him from death" (Heb. 5:7). What's more, the Holy Spirit groans within us as we await our redemption from all evil (Rom. 8:23, 26).

However, the Bible does not condone pity parties or self-centered whining for sympathy. Paul was far from saying, "Poor me. I'm going to Jerusalem. Isn't it horrible?" In Acts 20:24, Paul says, "But none of these things move me, neither count I my life dear unto myself, so that I might finish my course *with joy*, and the ministry, which I have received of the Lord Jesus, to testify the gospel of the grace of God." Paul ran his race in life with the elevated joy of a runner headed for the finish line and the victor's crown (1 Cor. 9:24–25). Like Eric Liddell (1902–1945), the missionary to China and Olympic champion, Paul ran hard feeling God's pleasure in sacrificial and zealous obedience.

So then, why should we run with tears? Acts 20:31 tells us, "Therefore watch, and remember, that by the space of three years I ceased not to warn every one night and day with tears." Paul did not shed tears for himself; he wept for the precious souls whom he called to repent and believe in the Lord Jesus Christ.[15] Charles Simeon (1759–1836) said, "With this humility of mind he had blended compassion for their souls; so that…he had wept much on their account, both in his addresses to them, and in his supplications in their behalf."[16]

In this, Paul was an authentic representative of his Lord. When Jesus carried His cross to Calvary in weariness, pain, and misery, and shed His blood, He did not pity Himself, nor did He ask it of others. He said to the women around Him, "Weep not for me, but weep for yourselves," knowing that God's severe judgment would fall on Jerusalem (Luke 23:28). Yet when His friend Lazarus died, "Jesus wept" (John 11:35). Christ was not a stoic; He was ruled by love.

When Paul speaks about tears in ministry, we see that ministers of Christ must be people of heartfelt compassion for God's people and for those not yet saved. Let us look at how that works in more detail.

---

15. "His tears were expressive of his tender concern, for the souls of men, of the compassion with which he regarded those who were perishing in their sins, and as well as of his sympathy with the disciples, in their common afflictions, and in their sufferings for religion. He was not a man of stern unfeeling temper; but in him a tender heart was conjoined with a vigorous understanding." Dick, *Lectures on the Acts of the Apostles*, 320.

16. Charles Simeon, *Expository Outlines on the Whole Bible* (1847; repr., Grand Rapids: Baker, 1988), 14:506.

1. We weep for God's people. Paul says in 2 Corinthians 2:4, "For out of much affliction and anguish of heart I wrote unto you with many tears; not that ye should be grieved, but that ye might know the love which I have more abundantly unto you." Paul had to confront some difficult problems in the Corinthian church. He did so boldly, but not coldly. Many of his epistles were stained with tears. Do you weep for your people as you write your sermons? Are you moved with compassion as you preach and pray for your people? We are not talking about a mere rhetorical device here; we are talking about a heartfelt love for the flock of God. We are one body in Christ. When one member suffers, all suffer, says 1 Corinthians 12:12, 26. Are you attached or detached in your ministry to the people of God? The Holy Spirit commands us in Romans 12:15, "Rejoice with them that do rejoice, and weep with them that weep." He does not say, "Have a measure of sympathy." He says, "*Weep.*"

We may feel that such emotion is not appropriate for a minister, but Paul says in 2 Corinthians 6:11, "O ye Corinthians, our mouth is open unto you, our heart is enlarged." A minister's heart must be open so the church may see the affections of Christ moving us to action. We are not making a display of ourselves; we are displaying the humanity and compassion of Christ to His people, His sense of our great need and His sorrow for our sins. Because of our union with Christ, Christ's sufferings and death abound in us, so that His life is manifested in us and brings comfort to others in their sufferings (2 Cor. 1:3–6; 4:8–12). The display of Christ's suffering in us as ministers is a profound mystery, but it is also powerfully real. Is it possible that what hinders us from weeping is not our dignity as men but our lack of conformity to Christ?

A man once visited the church of Robert Murray M'Cheyne (1813–1843) when M'Cheyne was not there. The visitor asked a member of the church what the secret of M'Cheyne's power in ministry was. The church member walked the visitor to the pastor's study. He then said to the visitor, "Kneel down by the pastor's chair. Bow your head. Fold your hands. Now weep." Then he took the man to the pulpit and said, "Now stretch out your hands and weep." May God grant us tears in our secret prayer and in public preaching.

2. We are brokenhearted for the lost. In Philippians 3:18–19, Paul says, "For many walk, of whom I have told you often, and now tell you even weeping, that they are the enemies of the cross of Christ: whose end is destruction, whose God is their belly, and whose glory is in their shame, who mind earthly things." It is horrible to hear men speak of sin and judgment and hell with utter detachment. Paul grieved and wept over the lost, even the enemies of Christ.

In Romans 9:1–3 Paul says, "I say the truth in Christ, I lie not, my conscience also bearing me witness in the Holy Ghost, that I have great heaviness and continual sorrow in my heart. For I could wish that myself were accursed from Christ for my brethren, my kinsmen according to the flesh." The Holy Spirit inspired Paul to teach the truths of divine election and reprobation, but not without "great heaviness and continual sorrow" for his unsaved Jewish relatives and countrymen. Likewise, our Lord Jesus wept over Jerusalem (Luke 19:41). The Savior willingly traveled the way of suffering and death to fulfill God's eternal plan. He did all according to "the determinate counsel and foreknowledge of God" so that, as the church later prayed to God, the people would "do whatsoever thy hand and thy counsel determined before to be done" (Acts 2:23; 4:28). The Savior wept over Jerusalem! How can we be like Him?

George Whitefield (1714–1770), one of the greatest evangelists of all time, was immersed in the writings of the Puritans. God used Whitefield's preaching to revive the church and to save thousands of sinners. Tears were a significant aspect of his preaching. He said, "You blame me for weeping, but how can I help it, when you will not weep for yourselves, although your immortal souls are on the verge of destruction."[17] Francis Schaeffer (1912–1984) said, "We must proclaim the message with tears and give it with love."[18]

The Christian life is not just marked by tears. We are asked to be "sorrowful yet always rejoicing" (2 Cor. 6:10). If your heart is cold and your eyes too dry, pray for God to fill you with the Spirit of Jesus, who both fills us with the compassionate love of God (Rom. 5:5) and imparts that joy in the Lord that makes us strong in His service (Rom. 14:17).

The Temptations of a Slave of the Lord

Ministers are mortal, so they must daily battle temptation and trial in the form of attacks from the world, the flesh, and the devil. Daily devotions, self-denial, and personal discipline, and the love and prayers of a supportive family and the elders of the church, are the best resources for fighting temptation, but so is the wisdom of the Puritans, who offer a full armory of weapons with which to fight the three-headed enemy.

---

17. Joseph Belcher, *George Whitefield: A Biography* (New York: American Tract Society, [1857]), 507.

18. Francis A. Schaeffer, *Death in the City* (Downers Grove, Ill.: Inter-Varsity, 1972), 71. Interestingly, Schaeffer wrote this as an act of public repentance for the kind of militant, angry fundamentalism he had earlier embraced in the 1930s. He had learned that the Lord's work must be done in a different way.

Paul seemingly had a specific temptation in mind in Acts 20:19–20, speaking about "temptations, which befell me by the lying in wait of the Jews: and how I kept back nothing that was profitable unto you, but have shewed you, and have taught you publickly, and from house to house." J. A. Alexander said Paul speaks of "temptations, not in the restricted sense of allurements or inducements to commit sin, but in the broader sense of trials that include troubles or afflictions that are a test of character."[19] In other words, Paul is referring to temptations that rise out of opposition to the Word of God. The apostle could say that he had held back nothing profitable to his hearers, rather than modify his message to appease such opposition. John Chrysostom (d. 407) said that in so doing, Paul is a model of "love and bravery...both generosity and resoluteness."[20]

Experienced ministers of the gospel understand the weight of the words of Proverbs 29:25, "The fear of man bringeth a snare: but whoso putteth his trust in the LORD shall be safe." The fear of man, and a correspondingly weak faith in the Lord, is a snare that has caught the foot of too many preachers. Paul writes in Galatians 1:10, "For do I now persuade men, or God? or do I seek to please men? for if I yet pleased men, I should not be the servant of Christ." People-pleasing has ruined many slaves of the Lord (Eph. 6:6), for it strikes at the heart of our allegiance. We must ask, are we the slaves of the Lord or slaves of men? We cannot serve two masters.

Acts 20 describes three things that tempt God's servant: opposition from the world, from the church, and from our own souls.

1. Opposition from the world. In Acts 20:19, Paul speaks of "temptations, which befell me by the lying in wait of the Jews." The Holy Spirit told Paul that "bonds and afflictions" waited for him in Jerusalem (Acts 20:23). Likewise, throughout the world today, preachers face persecution from militant Hindus, Muslims, Orthodox Jews, Buddhists, and Communists. Indeed, we also face hostility from nominal Christians. Just as Judaism and early Christianity seemed to be branches of the same religion, so Christian ministers today face opposition from groups claiming to be Christian while holding to a fundamentally different gospel. These include Roman Catholics as well as liberal Protestants, not to mention sects and cults, such as Mormonism and the like.

The temptation here is for gospel ministers to soft-pedal or be silent about offensive elements of biblical truth, to curry favor with one's hearers. But Paul

---

19. Alexander, *Acts*, 242.

20. John Chrysostom, *Homilies on the Acts of the Apostles*, 44, quoted in *Ancient Christian Commentary on Scripture, New Testament, Volume 5, Acts*, ed. Francis Martin (Downers Grove, Ill.: InterVarsity, 2006), 250.

says in Acts 20:26–27, "Wherefore I take you to record this day, that I am pure from the blood of all men. For I have not shunned to declare unto you all the counsel of God." Some parts of God's revelation will offend your listeners. Knowing that, will you preach the whole counsel of God? Will you speak out against the sins of our time and place? Satan will tempt you to pass quietly over the controversial points or to reshape them so they do not offend rebels against God. The devil wraps this temptation in fine words such as *sensitivity* and *tolerance*. Those are fine words but not excuses for failing to preach the whole counsel of God. In the end, the question is whether we preach everything God has revealed for the good of our hearers' souls or only what seems to promote our prosperity.[21]

It should also be said that ministers should avoid the opposite temptation, which is to substitute controversial axe-grinding and hobby-horse riding for the preaching of the gospel. Paul's concern was to preach what was profitable for his hearers. Is a steady diet of "what's wrong with our country today," or "this week in American politics," truly profitable for our people? Paul's aim was to preach Christ and Him crucified as the very heart and soul of the whole counsel of God. We should be willing to brook any amount of criticism or opposition if we are truly preaching Christ.

2. *The temptation of opposition in the church.* Paul says in Acts 20:28–29, "Take heed therefore unto yourselves, and to all the flock, over the which the Holy Ghost hath made you overseers, to feed the church of God, which he hath purchased with his own blood. For I know this, that after my departing shall grievous wolves enter in among you, not sparing the flock." This echoes what Jesus says in Matthew 7:15, "Beware of false prophets, which come to you in sheep's clothing, but inwardly they are ravening wolves." Ravening wolves are out to destroy the flock of God, not to build it up, maintain it, and protect it from harm (John 10:11–15). Many false prophets are guilty of making insignificant items to be as important as the true fundamentals of the faith.

The devil, who embeds these wolves in the flock, whispers in your ear, "These men are part of the church. Look at the good they are doing and the souls they are winning. They love the Lord Jesus. Look how orthodox they are in other doctrines. So do not destroy the peace of Christ's church by opposing

---

21. "Those who are influenced by selfish considerations are in constant danger of forsaking the path of rectitude. Instead of preaching those doctrines which would be profitable to others, they are tempted to preach such only as are profitable to themselves." Dick, *Lectures on the Acts of the Apostles*, 322.

what they say." The love of peace and unity in the gospel has caused many good men to brush heresy under the rug.

Alexander Whyte (1836–1921) was a godly Scots Presbyterian, a preacher of vibrant orthodoxy. But when so-called Higher Criticism of the Bible began to undermine biblical authority in the Free Church of Scotland, Whyte actually defended the right of those who held such views to teach at Presbyterian schools. Though it is true that these men cloaked their new ideas in a dress of piety, speaking of "Believing Criticism," Whyte was strangely blind to the devastating effects this doctrine would have on the faith and saw it merely as "a new theological method" that should be permitted in the spirit of progress.[22] The churches reacted by no longer requiring men to subscribe to their confessions except in the most general way.[23]

Thomas M'Crie (1772–1835) had warned against such liberalism as early as 1820, saying, "A vague and indefinite evangelism…[will] degenerate into an unsubstantial and incoherent pietism, which after effervescing [or bubbling up] in enthusiasm will finally settle into indifference; in which case, the spirit of infidelity and unbelief…will achieve an easy conquest."[24] Thomas Carlyle (1795–1881), though not really evangelical or orthodox himself, offered his own assessment, saying, "Have my countrymen's heads become turnips when they think they can hold the premises of…unbelief and draw the conclusions of Scottish evangelical orthodoxy?"[25] So stand firm, brothers, against the temptation to overlook heresy in the church. Preserving peace at the cost of truth will only destroy the real unity in the gospel, which is "the unity of the faith" (Eph. 4:13). Perhaps one of the greatest heresies we face today is that many think that careful definition and exposition of Christian doctrine is not relevant to the needs of the times in which we live.

3. *The temptation of opposition from our own soul.* The most sobering temptation is implied in Acts 20:30, "Also of your own selves shall men arise, speaking perverse things, to draw away disciples after them." Imagine the horror that the

---

22. Michael A. G. Haykin, "The Piety of Alexander Whyte (1836–1921)," in *A Consuming Fire: The Piety of Alexander Whyte*, Profiles in Reformed Spirituality (Grand Rapids: Reformation Heritage Books, 2006), 8–10.

23. K. R. Ross, "Declaratory Acts," in *Dictionary of Scottish Church History and Theology*, ed. Nigel M. de S. Cameron (Downers Grove, Ill.: InterVarsity, 1993), 237–38.

24. John Macleod, *Scottish Theology in Relation to Church History* (repr., Edinburgh: Banner of Truth, 1974), 314–15.

25. N. M. de S. Cameron, "Believing Criticism," in *Dictionary of Scottish Church History and Theology*, 69. The omitted words are "German" and "Scottish"! His contrast may not be racial so much as Lutheran versus Reformed.

Ephesian elders must have felt when Paul said that. It was the same when Jesus said to His disciples, "One of you shall betray me" (Matt. 26:21). It would be like standing in a meeting of pastors and saying, "Some of you will fall away from the faith and draw others away from Christ." Brothers, the greatest opposition to the Word of God that we must fight is opposition arising from our own souls. Therefore, Paul's exhortation to the elders in verse 28 begins, "Take heed to yourselves."

Let us be honest. Within us all remains what Paul called "flesh" in Romans 7 and Galatians 5. The essence of flesh, according to Romans 8:7, is "enmity [or hatred] against God." John Owen (1616–1683) said long ago, "As every drop of poison is poison, and will infect, and every spark of fire is fire, and will burn; so is every thing of the law of sin, the last, the least of it—it is enmity, it will poison, it will burn.… 'God is love' (1 John 4:8). He is so in himself, eternally excellent, and desirable above all.… Against this God we carry about us an enmity all our days."[26]

Part of us will always recoil at sound doctrine, for biblical truth glorifies God and humbles man. John Calvin (1509–1564) said of Paul, "Knowing his own infirmity, he did mistrust himself."[27] The temptation is to assume that we will always be faithful to the Word, which is only another form of trusting in ourselves that we are righteous. Over a long ministry, we shall often be tempted, even inclined, to compromise, to sell out, to betray the gospel for the sake of personal advantage. Oh brothers, how necessary it is to obey Paul's instruction in 1 Timothy 4:16, "Take heed unto thyself, and unto the doctrine; continue in them: for in doing this thou shalt both save thyself, and them that hear thee."

We must serve the Lord with humility, for we are only sinners saved by the grace of our Lord Jesus. We also have good reason to serve with tears of compassion, for we ourselves are brands plucked from the burning by the pierced hands of our Savior. The frailty of our own human nature compels us to be watchful, to examine ourselves, and by grace, to keep ourselves in the faith of Christ and the love of God.

Conclusion

The Lord calls pastors to do His will with lowliness of mind, compassion, and faithfulness. He calls us to serve Him in humility, tears, and temptations. That

---

26. "The Nature, Power, Deceit, and Prevalency of the Remainders of Indwelling Sin in Believers," in *The Works of John Owen*, ed. William H. Goold (New York: Robert Carter & Bros., 1851), 6:177.

27. John Calvin, *Commentary upon the Acts of the Apostles, Volume 2* (repr., Grand Rapids: Baker, 1996), 241.

is what we learn from Paul's words in Acts 20:19. We have this calling from a glorious Lord who is worthy of our faith and of such faithful service.

Let us conclude with the encouraging words of Paul in Acts 20:32, "And now, brethren, I commend you to God, and to the word of his grace, which is able to build you up, and to give you an inheritance among all them which are sanctified." Cling to the Word, brothers. The Bible will be light in your darkness and a well of salvation in your dryness. You have a high calling, but it is attainable because God gives us what we need to do what He commands. Do you need to grow in humility or compassion or the determination to fight against temptation? Meet with God daily in prayer and in meditation on His Word. Look constantly to Christ as the author and finisher of our faith. Seek ever to be filled with the Spirit and to walk in the Spirit.

> God our heavenly Father, who hath called thee to His holy ministry, enlighten thee with His Holy Spirit, strengthen thee with His hand, and so govern thee in thy ministry that thou mayest decently and fruitfully walk therein to the glory of His Name and the propagation of the kingdom of His Son Jesus Christ.... Bear patiently all sufferings and oppressions as a good soldier of Jesus Christ, for in doing this thou shalt both save thyself and them that hear thee. And when the chief Shepherd shall appear, thou shalt receive a crown of glory that fadeth not away.[28]

---

28. "Form of Ordination of the Ministers of God's Word," *Doctrinal Standards, Liturgy, and Church Order*, 143.

Chapter 29

Children in the Church

*When all Israel is come to appear before the LORD thy God in the place
which he shall choose, thou shalt read this law before all Israel in their hearing. Gather the people together, men, and women, and children, and thy
stranger that is within thy gates, that they may hear, and that they may
learn, and fear the LORD your God, and observe to do all the words of this
law: and that their children, which have not known any thing, may hear,
and learn to fear the LORD your God, as long as ye live in the land whither
ye go over Jordan to possess it.*

—Deuteronomy 31:11–13

Few subjects are as important as children in the church, for they represent its
future. Matthew Henry (1663–1714) said God has "appointed that parents
should train up their children in the knowledge of his law...that, as one generation of God's servants and worshippers passes away, another generation may
come, and the church, as the earth, may abide forever, and thus God's name
among men may be as the days of heaven."[1] Very soon we who are adults will
be gone. Who then will praise God on the earth? Who will be His salt and
light in our cities, towns, and nations? Christ has guaranteed the church will
continue by His divine power and faithfulness; yet He accomplishes this by
human means, often through our ministry to children.

Our topic is also of critical significance for the future of our children.
Henry wrote to Christian parents, "Consider especially what they [the chil-
dren] are designed for in another world: they are made for eternity. Every child
hath a precious and immortal soul, that must be for ever either in heaven or
hell, according as it is prepared in this present state,—and perhaps it must

---

1. *Matthew Henry's Commentary* (reprint, Peabody, Mass.: Hendrickson, 1991), 3:434 [Ps.
78:1–8]. This chapter is an expansion of an address I gave for the Philadelphia Conference of Reformed
Theology (PCRT) in Portland, Oregon (Feb. 26, 2011); Byron Center, Michigan (March 19, 2011);
and Greenville, South Carolina (April 2, 2011).

remove to that world of spirits very shortly."[2] This is true not only of our own dear children but also of the children in our neighborhood and non-Christian friends whom we invite to church with us. They, too, have souls; they, too, need the Savior. Do our churches care for these tender and impressionable souls whom God has entrusted to us?

At the same time, we must acknowledge that caring for children in the church involves both laughter and tears. Simonetta Carr shared one woman's impression of working with children:

> With small children, we find, more often than not, that we're happy when we barely slide through the sanctuary door before the elders file in, all the while firmly telling four bustling, noisy little ones, "Shhh, we are in worship!" Then, we squeeze into the last three remaining seats in the sanctuary for our family of six, with all four children complaining much too audibly that they are squished, or one of them yelling out to me that I promised that this week he or she could sit next to Mommy. Then the service begins, and before we can even sing the last note of the first hymn, one, two, three, or possibly four suddenly have an urgent need to go to the bathroom.[3]

The sublime and the ridiculous often meet in ministry to children. How can we deal with this responsibility in a Christ-honoring way? Let's begin first with how we view children in the church. After that, I will offer some practical guidelines on how to minister to them.

How to View Children in the Church

The children and young people who grow up in the fellowship of the church enjoy tremendous privileges through God's covenant of grace. We may say of them, as Paul said of ancient Israel in Romans 3:2, "Unto them were committed the oracles of God." They grow up reading the Word of the covenant, singing the Word of the covenant, absorbing the preaching of the Word of the covenant, praying the Word of the covenant back to God, and seeing the Word of the covenant made visible in the sacraments, the signs and seals of the covenant.

We might say that children growing up in a biblical church are embraced by the arms of the covenant Word of promise, nursed on the milk of the covenant Word of instruction, and buckled in by the covenant Word of command for safety as they begin their journey in life. What an amazing privilege it is

---

2. Matthew Henry "A Church in the House, A Sermon concerning Family Religion," in *The Complete Works of the Rev. Matthew Henry* (1855; reprint, Grand Rapids: Baker, 1979), 1:253.

3. Simonetta Carr, "Children Worshiping God," *The Outlook* 61, no. 1 (Jan.–Feb. 2011): 9.

for children to grow up in the church! While we grieve over the church's failings, let us never forget the unspeakable blessings that belong to children in a true church of Christ, as opposed to the lot of those who grow up "having no hope and without God in the world" (Eph. 2:12). Paul wrote in 1 Corinthians 7:14, "For the unbelieving husband is sanctified by the wife, and the unbelieving wife is sanctified by the husband: else were your children unclean; but now are they holy." Never begrudge a child his place in the meetings of the church. God calls your children holy because when God saves a parent, He puts His hand of blessing and consecration on the entire family.[4]

But covenant privileges do not negate or diminish the need each child has for God's particular grace to make him a living, spiritual member of the church. We have every reason to believe that David was circumcised on the eighth day and raised in a pious home. Boaz and Ruth were his godly great-grandparents (Ruth 4:21–22). His father, Jesse, participated in daily sacrifices, honored God's prophet, and sent his sons to fight for God's anointed king (1 Sam. 16:5; 17:13). Nevertheless, David confessed in Psalm 51:5, "Behold, I was shapen in iniquity; and in sin did my mother conceive me." Since the fall of man, sin and its doleful effects have been a plague on every child born into the world (Rom. 5:12). As the Belgic Confession of Faith (Art. 15) says:

> Through the disobedience of Adam original sin is extended to all mankind, which is a corruption of the whole nature and a hereditary disease, wherewith infants themselves are infected even in their mother's womb, and which produceth in man all sorts of sin, being in him as a root thereof; and therefore is so vile and abominable in the sight of God that it is sufficient to condemn all mankind. Nor is it by any means abolished or done away with in baptism, since sin always issues forth from this woeful source as water from a fountain.[5]

Covenant children must be born again. Our Lord Jesus Christ said in John 3:3, "Verily, verily, I say unto thee, Except a man be born again, he cannot see the kingdom of God." He said this to a man who had participated in all the external forms of the covenant in force at the time. He was a renowned teacher of Israel (John 3:10). But in order to "enter the kingdom of God" (3:5), this teacher still needed to be "born of the Spirit" (3:8). In faithfulness to Scripture, we must

---

4. The perfect "sanctified" does not refer to moral purification but the fact that the family is already set apart or claimed by God for Himself. W. Harold Mare, "1 Corinthians," in *The Expositor's Bible Commentary*, ed. Frank E. Gaebelein (Grand Rapids: Zondervan, 1976), 10:230.

5. *Doctrinal Standards, Liturgy, and Church Order*, ed. Joel R. Beeke (Grand Rapids: Reformation Heritage Books, 2003), 12.

view our children as "heirs of the kingdom of God and of His covenant,"[6] who nonetheless were born in sin and need a supernatural rebirth from God in order to come into full personal possession of their inheritance.

We must therefore view our children as sinners who need to hear the gospel and respond to it with faith. God's usual way of saving the seed of His church is through the call of the gospel. Certainly God may regenerate a soul in the womb, as He did with John the Baptist (Luke 1:15, 41–44), but God's ordinary manner of working faith in our hearts is through the preaching of the Word as well as by the faith, example, nurture, and prayers of believing parents.

Peter described true Christians in 1 Peter 1:23 and 25 as "being born again, not of corruptible seed, but of incorruptible, by the word of God, which liveth and abideth for ever.... And this is the word which by the gospel is preached unto you." So Paul writes in Romans 10:17, "Faith cometh by hearing, and hearing by the word of God."

The Westminster Confession of Faith (7.3) says that in the covenant of grace, God "freely offereth unto sinners life and salvation by Jesus Christ, requiring of them faith in Him, that they may be saved."[7] Reformed Christianity is evangelistic Christianity, and Reformed evangelism begins with our own children.

Reformed Christians sometimes fall into the trap of thinking that we may presume that covenant children, being members of the church by baptism, are regenerated by the Holy Spirit unless they openly reject the covenant.[8] In this way, the promise and the sign of the covenant become poor substitutes for its requirement of saving faith in Jesus Christ as the only ground of justification and salvation. When the covenant is abused in such a way, parents and children alike are often lulled into a false sense of security, and any serious effort to call little ones to conversion is given up.

On the contrary, the covenant demands the conversion of all to whom its promises are made, parents and children alike. "Therefore are we by God through baptism admonished of, and obliged unto new obedience," the Reformed Liturgy says, "namely, that we cleave to this one God, Father, Son, and Holy Ghost; that we trust in Him, and love Him with all our hearts, with all our souls, with all our mind, and with all our strength; that we forsake the world, crucify our old nature, and walk in a new and holy life."[9] How, then, can we assume that a child is born again without these evidences of that life?

---

6. "Form for the Administration of Baptism to Infants of Believers," *Doctrinal Standards*, 127.

7. *Westminster Confession of Faith* (Glasgow: Free Presbyterian Publications, 1994), 42.

8. This view is associated with Abraham Kuyper (1837–1920), Dutch theologian, journalist, and statesman.

9. "Form for the Administration of Baptism," *Doctrinal Standards*, 126.

So it is necessary to affirm the blessings and privileges of covenant children while insisting on the need to respond to the covenant with faith in Christ and repentance from sin. On the one hand, we must not treat our children as if they were so many "little heathens" who have no rightful place in our well-ordered church services. They belong there. On the other hand, we must not assume they are saved simply because they have been born into Christian homes, have been received into the church by baptism, and are being instructed in the doctrine of salvation. With faith in God's promises, we must use all the means of grace, seeking the regeneration, justification, and sanctification of our covenant children. In particular, we must pray for the conversion of our children.

Listen to how Alexander Whyte (1836–1921), a Scottish divine, prayed for children:

> O Almighty God, our Heavenly Father, give us a seed right with Thee! Smite us and our house with everlasting barrenness rather than that our seed should not be right with Thee. O God, give us our children. Give us our children. A second time, and by a far better birth, give us our children to be beside us in Thy holy covenant. For it had been better we had never been betrothed; it had been better we had sat all our days solitary unless our children are to be right with Thee.... But Thou, O God, art Thyself a Father, and thus hast in Thyself a Father's heart. Hear us, then, for our children, O our Father.... In season and out of season, we shall not go up into our bed, we shall not give sleep to our eyes nor slumber to our eyelids till we and all our seed are right with Thee.[10]

Practical Guidelines for Ministry to Children in the Church

Let us consider next how the church should minister to children in our midst. We will not focus on Christian parenting so much as the church's ministry, although that ministry has many implications for Christian parents, since they have a unique task in their children's lives as their first evangelists, teachers, and guides. I will attempt to be brief rather than comprehensive in these guidelines.

Include the Children

Children should attend public worship with their parents to experience the corporate life of the body of Christ. They should learn how to worship by watching others worship. Don't discourage mothers from bringing young children into worship (Luke 18:15–16). The prophet Joel included "the children, and those that suck the breasts" in the call to sacred assembly (Joel 2:16). Encourage

---

10. Alexander Whyte, *Bunyan Characters* (London: Pickering & Inglis, 1902), 3:289–90.

families to bring their children to worship. You might reserve a section in the back or in the balcony for families with very young children. If they need an early exit, this can be done without distracting or disturbing other worshipers.

The Scriptures teach us to view the assemblies of the church as gatherings of the household of faith. God's children are called to be brothers to each other. When Moses commanded that the law be read publicly every seven years, he said, "Gather the people together, men, and women, and children, and thy stranger that is within thy gates, that they may hear, and that they may learn, and fear the LORD your God, and observe to do all the words of this law" (Deut. 31:12). When the Israelites celebrated the feasts of the Lord, the law required them to come to the sanctuary as "households," including sons and daughters and even servants (Deut. 12:7, 12).[11]

Children were also present in the synagogues where Christ taught (Matt. 18:2; 19:13–15). Paul assumed that children would be present when his letters were read in the churches, and he even addressed the children directly (Eph. 6:1–3; Col. 3:20). Jeremy Walker writes, "The constant presumption of Scripture is the children were present in the worship of the people of God."[12] Don't separate children, teenagers, and adults into different worship compartments; bring them together as members of one family, and encourage them to sit together as families so that parents can make good use of the situation to train their children in godliness.

Including the children will influence how ministers of the Word prepare for public worship. When you offer public prayer in the worship service, include the children. Pray specifically for children and young people. Intercede for God to grant them Spirit-worked submission to their parents, regeneration, faith, repentance, and spiritual growth. If a child is sick, pray for him by name. Encourage them to sing by making frequent use of songs the children already know and love—and encourage parents, in teaching the children at home, to give priority to the songs used in the worship of the church.

In preaching, labor to speak with plainness and simplicity but also with color and vitality, in the way of a good storyteller, to interest even your youngest hearers in the sermon. If it is necessary to speak "over their heads," stop and address the children directly, giving them explanations or applications at the level of their own understanding. Nothing is more off-putting than to have a preacher tag a statement with "boys and girls" and then go on to say things

---

11. Cf. Josh. 8:35; 2 Chron. 20:13; Joel 2:16.

12. Jeremy Walker, "Attendance of Children in Public Worship Services," *Banner of Truth* (http://www.banneroftruth.org/pages/articles/article_detail.php?142), accessed February 15, 2011.

that no boy or girl could understand or care about. Likewise, with regard to the length of the service, think of the children, and take care not to prolong sermons or prayers to the point that they cease to edify and only become a trial to be endured.

Teach the Children

Jesus said in Matthew 19:14, "Suffer little children, and forbid them not, to come unto me: for of such is the kingdom of heaven." We bring our children to Christ by presenting them for baptism and by bringing them to public worship; but we must also teach them the truths of the Christian faith, bringing them up in the nurture and admonition of the Lord. In hearing the words of Scripture, little lambs of the flock hear the voice of the Good Shepherd, who thereby calls them by name to follow Him (John 10:3).

Our children should be catechized. The Heidelberg Catechism presents biblical truth with warm spirituality; the Westminster Shorter Catechism and Larger Catechism offer rich biblical teaching in brilliantly condensed form. With such great resources at our disposal, it is a shame that many evangelical Christians fear that the word *catechism* implies Roman Catholicism. What a joy it is for many Christians now today to rediscover the beauty of Reformed catechisms! The question-and-answer format is ideally suited for children.

As G. I. Williamson writes, a catechism is like a map for a road trip. Someone might say, "Why bother with a map? Why not just start driving to find where things are?" The answer, of course, is that you'll likely waste a lot of time speculating how far you have to drive to places or what route to take, and perhaps get lost. Other people carefully study roads and maps. No map is perfect, but they are generally accurate. So it is with catechisms. The Bible contains the riches of Christ. It is clear but also very deep. While we must read our Bibles, it is wise to use the maps others have provided to guide us through Scripture.[13]

Make sure that your catechism teachers are well-trained members of the church, preferably office-bearers who uphold solid, confessional Reformed teaching with hearts aflame with the fear and love of God. Children under ten years old should memorize answers to questions, while children ten and over should be pressed to explain what they have been learning. Use a good curriculum, such as that produced by Great Commission Publications[14] or the

---

13. G. I. Williamson, *The Heidelberg Catechism: A Study Guide* (Phillipsburg, N.J.: P&R, 1993), 2.
14. A ministry of the PCA and OPC (www.gcp.org).

Bible Doctrine workbooks written by James W. Beeke or G. I. Williamson's study guides to the Westminster and Heidelberg Catechisms.

Catechism in the church should be supplemented by Christian education, whether at a Christian day school or by godly homeschooling. Never underestimate the impact of school teachers and textbooks on your children. Your child's education is not just about his future career in the world; a Christian education can have a profound influence on whether your sons and daughters persevere as active members of a biblically faithful church when they grow up.

Train the Parents

Ephesians 4:11–12 says the glorified Christ gives pastors and teachers to His church to equip its members. Verse 16 envisions the church as a body in which every member performs its God-designed function. Since the function of parents is to nurture their children in the Lord, the ministry of the church must equip them to do so. How should the church train them?

1. Train parents to *lead as prophets, priests, and kings*. Teach parents how, by faith in Christ, we share in Christ's anointing by the Spirit and, in a limited way, are images of His offices and bearers of His authority.[15] Train parents to be prophetic teachers of truth to their children. Call them to be priests who lift up intercessions for their families and lay down themselves as loving sacrifices. Remind them of their authority as servant-kings to defend their families from ungodly influences and to discipline them under the rule of Christ.

2. Train parents to *bring their children to Christ*. Just as parents brought their little ones to Jesus in Mark 10:13, we must continually bring our children to Christ. Doing so requires that we believe our children need more than polite behavior and an outward form of godliness—they need Christ, or they are lost forever! Bringing children to Christ also requires us to understand that conversion is not the mere recitation of a prayer. God must give every sinner a new heart so that he may know Him, love Him, and walk with Him.

3. Train parents to *conduct family worship*. In one way, family worship is a child's daily training for public worship. In another, something special and unique happens between fathers and mothers and sons and daughters when they open their Bibles and pray together. For how to conduct family worship, you might

---

15. Acts 2:17; Rom. 12:1; Heb. 13:15–16; 1 Peter 2:5, 9; 4:11; 1 John 2:27; Rev. 1:6; 5:10; 20:6. Cf. Heidelberg Catechism (LD 12, Q. 32).

want to obtain James W. Alexander's *Thoughts on Family Worship*, Matthew Henry's *Family Religion*, and my *Family Worship*.[16]

4. Train parents to *lead their families during public worship.* When parents are in the pews, they are both worshipers toward God and leaders to their children. Parents need to explain to their children the importance of sitting together as a family. One mother said to her sons, "It is much harder to pay attention to God when you want to pay attention to your friend. You will have time later to be with your friend; right now Jesus wants all of your attention because he has something to say to us."[17] Make public worship a rich family time.

Children should be taught that worship is not playtime. Children should not be allowed to turn the pew into a race track for a Hot Wheels toy, a library for reading secular books, or a nursery to play with toys. Teach your children, as God says, to "be still and know that I am God." If children cannot be quiet in church, remove them discreetly, discipline them, and then return them to the service. Give them a pen and paper to take sermon notes. Help the early elementary-age children to copy key words or sentences from your own notes. To encourage attentive listening, discuss sermons afterward. Ask your children questions and listen to their responses. Knowing they will be questioned later will encourage your children to listen better now.[18]

Talk to your children before going to services and explain your expectations. To pay attention, they must sit straight and look at the minister or the page of the songbook or Bible to which the minister is referring. Talk to them in a quiet whisper during the worship service if they need further exhortations. Encourage them to be respectful and considerate of other people sitting nearby.

Leading children in public worship is more than a matter of their outward behavior, however. Worship is about meeting with God! Build a sense of anticipation by praying together on Saturday night for God to visit His people through His means of grace. Talk to your children about the wonderful privilege that through Christ we are entering into God's glorious, holy presence.

---

16. James W. Alexander, *Thoughts on Family Worship* (1847; repr., Morgan, Pa.: Soli Deo Gloria, 1998); Matthew Henry, *Family Religion: Principles for Raising a Godly Family* (repr., Ross-shire, U.K.: Christian Focus, 2008); Joel R. Beeke, *Family Worship* (Grand Rapids: Reformation Heritage Books, 2009).

17. Robbie Castleman, *Parenting in the Pew: Guiding Your Children into the Joy of Worship* (Downers Grove, Ill: InterVarsity, 2002), 56.

18. For more on listening to sermons, see Joel R. Beeke, *The Family at Church: Listening to Sermons and Attending Prayer Meetings* (Reformation Heritage Books, 2008).

Teach them to view worship as entering into the house and presence of God to appear before His throne of grace.

5. Train parents to *cultivate sober-mindedness in their families.* Titus 2:4 and 6 says we are to cultivate sober-mindedness. To be sober-minded is to be steady, like a ship with its anchor deep in the ocean floor, so that tides and currents cannot drag the ship to destruction. Cultivate this by talking to your children at an early age about what is in their heart. Talk to them of God, Christ, sin, the devil, heaven, and hell as awesome realities. Encourage self-discipline by limiting their use of various forms of media. Train them in personal and family devotions. Let them have times to play, but also engage them in serious tasks where you labor together for an important cause. Beware of letting them view life as an amusement park that exists for their entertainment; rather, give them something worth living and dying for.

6. Train parents to teach their children how to *build a sound, biblical library of great books.* Many families have vast collections of toys, clothing, DVDs, and music. But how many parents invest in solid Christian books for their children? Fill your shelves with good reading material. Some of the same publishing houses that produce Puritan writings like Cumberland Valley or Christian Focus Publications or Reformation Heritage Books also sell high quality children's books. Read them. Give them to your children to read. Take time to enjoy these books by reading them aloud as a family. As your children get older, introduce them to modern renderings of the Puritans, such as *Living by God's Promises* or *Stop Loving the World,* and then the easier Puritans such as Thomas Watson or John Flavel. If you want to know why we are experiencing a resurgence of Reformed theology and piety, one reason is the republishing and renewed reading of old Reformed and Puritan books. Do you want your children to share in this blessing?

7. Train parents to *teach their children to pray.* John Calvin (1509–1564) considered prayer as a holy and intimate conversation with God, our heavenly Father.[19] Calvin said we should cast our "desires, sighs, anxieties, fears, hopes, and joys into the lap of God."[20] We are "permitted to pour into God's bosom the difficulties which torment us, in order that he may loosen the knots which we

---

19. John Calvin, *Commentaries of Calvin* (Grand Rapids: Eerdmans, 1948–50), on Psalm 10:13.
20. Calvin, *Commentary* on Psalm 89:38–39.

cannot untie."[21] Therefore, an excellent way to train children to pray is by putting them in Daddy's lap. Begin when the child is about three years old, gently setting him in your lap during family worship, whispering a few words at a time, and having him repeat those after you, so that he, too, can take his turn in praying on behalf of the family. Walk him through a very simple version of ACTS: Adoration, Confession, Thanksgiving, and Supplication. This helps children to avoid getting stuck in supplication, which is natural, given their selfishness and immaturity. When a child is four, tell him to try a few sentences on his own. If he gets stuck, he can give Daddy a poke so that you can return to whispering and repeating. By about age seven, a child should be able to pray on his own. Children naturally view their fathers as an image of God, so it is beautiful to associate prayer with sitting on Daddy's lap.

8. Finally, remind parents that the teaching and training of their children begins with and depends on *their own example* as children of God, followers of Christ, and members of His church. "Do as I say, but not as I do," is no part of the law of Christ for His disciples.

Pastors and elders, if you want to reach the children in the church, train the parents. Parents who conscientiously implement spiritual training of their children are usually those who experience God's blessing of rearing stalwart sons and daughters for the church of Jesus Christ. Proverbs 22:6 then proves to be the norm, not the exception: "Train up a child in the way he should go: and when he is old, he will not depart from it."

Involve the Children
Involve the children in the whole life of the church. Many Christian parents worship as a family on the Lord's Day but do not bring their children to other church meetings during the week. Of course, some meetings would not be appropriate for children, but consider the prayer meeting. Corporate prayer is the lifeline of the church; in Acts, the members of the church devoted themselves to prayer meetings.[22] They were serious about the calling of the church to be "an house of prayer" (Isa. 56:7). Shall we exclude our children from this most essential dimension of our church's life? Bring your children to prayer meetings.

Bring the children to other ministry opportunities too. Note the talents and interests of the children and teach them to use those gifts while they are young. Recruit children to stuff envelopes for mailings. Ask them to make cards for the

---

21. Calvin, *Commentary* on Genesis 18:25.
22. Acts 1:14, 24; 2:42; 3:1; 4:23–31; 6:4; 12:5, 12; 13:1–4; 14:23; 16:16, 25; 20:36; 21:5.

sick or residents of nursing homes. Take them on visits to shut-ins. One minister I know has several children who are gifted singers. He and his wife and family often visit nursing homes and move from room to room to sing to their church folk and other residents. The people love it. Put their gifts to work! Young men and women who can sing should glorify God in sacred concerts. Girls can join their mothers in making blankets for the poor or in cooking meals for the sick. Boys can help their fathers rake leaves or shovel snow for elderly people. Bring them with you when you visit a mission or work in a church nursery. Children will learn much about ministry by doing it with their parents. As soon as your children are old enough, involve them in one or more ministries in the church.

Talk to the Children

Don't just ignore children as you walk through your church building. Greet them. The Bible commands us to greet one another with warmth and brotherly affection.[23] Would you ignore your nephews and nieces or grandchildren at a family reunion? The assembling of the church is a sacred family reunion. People who stand at the door greeting people as they come in should be trained to welcome children with the same kind of warmth. We should all greet the children around us. Stoop down to their level and look them in the eye. Learn their names. Ask them what they are learning in school or what they did this week.

Try to put in a good word for the Lord when you talk to children. Lift up Christ. Let them see your joy in serving the Savior. Remind them that the Bible is the best of books for it tells us about the Lord Jesus. Talk to them about the sermon. Parents will appreciate this as well. Here's a short email I received from a mother a few weeks ago:

> Pastor, I just wanted to tell you I think our son got a kick out of your questions to him and his friend about the sermon last Sunday. He was quite proud that he knew all the answers (at least he said he did). Thank you for questioning them. I think it's a good thing to do. Thanks for your truly pastoral spirit and attitude!

Let the children of the church see your joy in knowing and serving this wonderful Savior.

Love the Children

To sum it up, God calls us to love children in the church. Children are very sensitive to emotions and attitudes. Don't be sour or stiff with them. Let your

---

23. 1 Cor. 16:20; 2 Cor. 13:12; 1 Thess. 5:26; 1 Peter 5:14.

heart be warm and your face aglow for them. We have an elder in our church who makes it a point to speak with young children after every service. He gets down on their level, asks them what they learned from the sermon, helps them understand it better, and then gives them a piece of candy. Love permeates all that he says and does. No wonder the children love him!

Christ loves children. So should we. Why not befriend a teenager in your church and shower him with Christlike love? It can be very rewarding. I take a young man in our church out to lunch periodically. He now opens up to me with his most profound fears and deepest questions and asks my advice on all kinds of important matters. We can speak plainly about sex and other areas of danger and temptation. At our last meeting, he asked me, "How can I get through college without falling into temptation?" and "What do you think are the most important qualities to look for in a future wife?" I love this young man and enjoy our meetings immensely.

Pastors, loving pastoral care is particularly important for you to show to children, teens, and college-age youth. You need to do more than preach to the rising generation and teach them one catechism lesson per week. Get close to them. Ask them questions. Show them you care. Challenge them to godly living in a positive manner both from the pulpit and in private. Curb the tendency to be negative about young people in your preaching and private conversations.

Elders, you have a special calling to love the baptized members of God's flock. If you love them habitually as they grow up, if the time comes that they may not be walking worthy of their baptism, you will be able to exercise effective, loving discipline in their lives even when they have not yet made public professions of faith. We must love our young people so much that we dare not allow their status as non-communicant members to exempt them from the loving admonition of the church.

Parents and church members, we all need to build close relationships with our children so that when we talk, they will listen, and so that when they talk, we will be sure to listen carefully. Be more ready to hear than to speak or act, especially if anger is present (James 1:19–20). Hold children accountable for their conduct in the house of God in a fair, balanced, and loving way. We must love them without catering to them; but neither do we want to crush the life out of them, turning the experience of worship into an endless succession of rebukes and exactions for every offense.

Church officers, members, and parents all need to work together and stand together in our work with children and youth. We must watch out for their bodies and their souls. We must be diligent to protect our children from sexual abuse and other forms of exploitation and predation in the church. Above all, we must be diligent to protect our children from spiritual abuse, seeking to inculcate in their minds hatred against sin, love for Christ, and a longing to live wholly and solely for God and His glory.

Conclusion: Don't Give Up on the Children!

Sometimes Christian parents become discouraged about their children. You glance down the pew during the service, and perhaps one of your children is asleep. Perhaps another is looking at everyone except the pastor. Perhaps one has escaped and is heading down the aisle! It's easy to start asking, "What am I doing wrong?"

Don't give up. Galatians 6:9 says, "Let us not be weary in well doing: for in due season we shall reap, if we faint not." Keep waiting on the Lord and persevere in the paths of righteousness for His name's sake. Be faithful in doing your duty and keep trusting the Lord. Bringing our children to Christ, bringing them up in the nurture and admonition of the Lord, and seeking their conversion to eternal life are long-term endeavors of faith and the obedience of faith. Hebrews 10:38–39 says, "Now the just shall live by faith: but if any man draw back, my soul shall have no pleasure in him. But we are not of them who draw back unto perdition; but of them that believe to the saving of the soul."

Persevere in prayer for the children in the church. Remember when you were a child; did not God hear the prayers of your parents and your pastors for your spiritual well-being? He can do the same for your children. When teens go through troubles, intercede for them in prayer with the persistence of the importunate widow with the unjust judge. God will hear your prayers. Remind God of His promises to us. Our Lord Jesus spoke of all our conversions when He said in Matthew 19:26, "With men this is impossible; but with God all things are possible."

Chapter 30

The Minister's Helpmeet

Likewise must the deacons be grave, not double-tongued, not given to much wine, not greedy of filthy lucre; holding the mystery of the faith in a pure conscience. And let these also first be proved; then let them use the office of a deacon, being found blameless. Even so must their wives be grave, not slanderers, sober, faithful in all things. Let the deacons be the husbands of one wife, ruling their children and their own houses well. For they that have used the office of a deacon well purchase to themselves a good degree, and great boldness in the faith which is in Christ Jesus.
—1 Timothy 3:8–13

The wife of a pastor has a high calling. In some respects this calling is like that of any other Christian wife. God says in Genesis 2:18, "It is not good that the man should be alone; I will make him an help meet for him." Drink in those words: your husband needs you. You are God's specially designed "help" for him, crafted to be "meet" or fitting, that is, corresponding to him as a man and his calling in the world. You must therefore fit your life to his as his helper. This is the calling of every wife.[1]

Yet, in other respects, a minister's wife has a special calling because of the special nature of her husband's calling. He bears special gifts, responsibilities, and honor within the church. If he serves well, he will receive a special crown of glory from the chief Shepherd (1 Peter 5:5). Thus your calling as his wife engages you in special responsibilities and special honor. You are called to be his helpmeet in spiritual character and supportive care. The heart of this is based on 1 Timothy 3:11. Though you as a Christian's wife are called to many things, we will focus specifically on your calling as a minister's helpmeet.

---

1. This chapter is an edited version of an inaugural address I gave in 2011 for the Ministry Wives' Fellowship (MWF) of Puritan Reformed Theological Seminary. I wish to thank Paul Smalley for his assistance.

You may find it odd that I prefaced this article with a passage of Scripture that speaks about deacons. Don't misunderstand; I'm not nominating any women for the office of deacon. Nor am I saying that a pastor is a deacon, for the Bible clearly teaches that the role of pastor or shepherd belongs to the category of elders or presbyters (Acts 20:17, 28; 1 Peter 5:1–2). Pastors are teaching elders, a sub-class of elders or bishops who are called to labor in preaching and teaching the Word. They, together with ruling elders who rule well, are worthy of double honor (1 Tim. 5:17).

But let us go back to 1 Timothy 3:8–13. In the midst of a description of men who are qualified to serve as deacons is a statement that specifically relates to their wives: "Even so must their wives be grave, not slanderers, sober, faithful in all things." I realize there are different translations and interpretations of this verse. Though "wives" could also be translated "women," the Greek original shows this category is distinct from deacons and does not refer to female deacons.[2] Also, these women are not officers in the church, for Paul's reference to them is brief and sandwiched into his discussion of deacons (vv. 8–10, 12–13). It is consistent with Paul's teaching in 1 Timothy 2:12 that women should not teach or have authority over men in the church. The same word for wife appears in 1 Timothy 3:12, which refers to "husbands of one wife." So it is best to view verse 11 not as a generic statement about women in ministry but as a statement that a deacon's wife must have certain spiritual characteristics.[3]

Paul offers no comparable statement about the wives of bishops in the early part of 1 Timothy 3. But surely if a deacon's wife must have these qualities, how much more must a pastor's wife have them?

Therefore verse 11 sets forth the spiritual character of an office bearer's wife: gravity, confidentiality, sobriety, and faithfulness. The spiritual beauty of a godly woman is like a lovely bed of flowers, each of which has certain characteristics. A flower garden does not grow from seed to full blossom in a day; growth takes time and effort plus the blessings of rain and sunshine. Thus, I urge you, in dependence on the Holy Spirit, to put on the graces of a godly woman, investing the needed time and effort and seeking the blessing of Jesus Christ, who gave Himself to redeem you from all lawlessness and to make you His own.

---

2. Just as the category of deacons is introduced with "likewise" (*hōsautōs*), distinguishing them from the bishops, so also the wives are distinguished with the same word (translated "even so"), distinguishing them from the deacons.

3. See George W. Knight III, *Commentary on the Pastoral Epistles*, New International Greek Testament Commentary (Grand Rapids: Eerdmans, 1992), 170–72.

The Gravity of a Pastor's Helpmeet

The word translated *grave* means honorable or "worthy of respect."[4] It suggests a person who is serious and earnest about living in accord with God's moral law.[5] If a wife is a flower, gravity is the stem of the flower. Pastor's wives may be beautiful and delicate in some respects, like the petals of a flower, but they also need strong spines. That does not mean you must be stiff; but you must be strong. Trials and temptations will require this of you, not to mention the demands of your life in the home and at church.

A woman worthy of honor, according to Proverbs 31:30, is "a woman that feareth the LORD." The text goes on to say, "She shall be praised." This woman sees something of God's infinite glory, and her heart delights to serve Him with fear and trembling. She sees heaven and hell as ultimate realities, which gives her a serious, or "grave," commitment to doing God's will in all things.

Do not think the word *gravity* suggests a pastor's wife has had the nerves to her lips cut so that she can't smile anymore, much less kiss her husband. True gravity is consistent with laughter and love. Remember Proverbs 17:22, "A merry heart doeth good like a medicine: but a broken spirit drieth the bones." The more you fear the Lord, the less you will fear others and rather become a woman of hope.

Solid, reverent hope will enable you to make the sacrifices necessary for ministry as well as daily Christian life. Don't expect your husband to work only forty hours a week; few men of any vocation do. You may long for more of his time and attention. I am not suggesting that you sacrifice your marriage before the idol of ministry; God does command you to develop your marriage. But being a helpmeet will involve sacrifice. If you view the sacrifices of ministry through the lens of the fear of the Lord, you can rejoice. If you have gravity of soul, the ministry of the gospel will have a glorious weight that will make the day's pain seem light and momentary.

Gravity of character will also help you honor your husband. Ephesians 5:22 says, "Wives, submit yourselves unto your own husbands, as unto the Lord." You must honor and submit to your husband, even though he is a sinful and imperfect human being, because his authority and what he is called to do reflect the perfect righteousness and infinite majesty of God. "A virtuous woman is a crown to her husband: but she that maketh ashamed is as rottenness in his

---

4. Knight, *Commentary on the Pastoral Epistles*, 168.

5. The related noun means "dignity, seriousness, and connotes moral earnestness." Knight, *Commentary on the Pastoral Epistles*, 118.

bones" (Prov. 12:4). Sara Leone writes, "Remember that your husband is judged in part by your behavior—be an asset, not a liability to him."[6]

The Confidentiality of a Pastor's Helpmeet

Wives must not be "slanderers," says 1 Timothy 3:11. Slander suggests evil speaking or malicious gossip. Remarkably, this word is normally translated "devil," for the devil is the accuser of the brethren. Wives who carelessly or maliciously spread secrets are more like the devil than they realize. Here again the wives of pastors must be like flowers. Tulips close at night when it grows cold but open in the morning of warm sunshine. Likewise, Christian wives should have mouths like tulips that know when to close to protect people and when to open in the warmth of love. A pastor's wife has access to many secrets and bits of private information about people in the congregation. You must close your mouth on these secrets. Proverbs 11:13 says, "A talebearer revealeth secrets: but he that is of a faithful spirit concealeth the matter." Too much talking may dangerously undermine your husband's trustworthiness in the church. Let your love for people be like a blanket that covers the nakedness of their shame. Proverbs 17:9 says, "He that covereth a transgression seeketh love; but he that repeateth a matter separateth very friends." One schoolteacher put a sign in her classroom to discourage gossip by asking students to consider three simple questions before saying something about someone else: "Is it true? It is kind? Is it necessary?"[7]

You must also respect the privacy of your husband. People are curious about their pastor, sometimes in an unhealthy way. So take care not to relate things that are personal to him, and never criticize him in public. Proverbs 31:11 says, "The heart of her husband doth safely trust in her." Be worthy of his trust. That does not mean you cannot share anything about your husband; there are innocent things that your husband does not mind if you share. For example, I don't mind if my wife tells others that I am a poor singer. But never criticize your husband or broadcast details of his personal life in public.

My mother used to say that you can talk about people all you want as long as you say good things about them. So show deep respect for your husband in your words. That can lift him up in the eyes of the congregation as well as be a role model for other women in how to show respect to their husbands.

---

6. Sara J. Leone, *Her Husband's Crown* (Edinburgh: Banner of Truth, 2007), 44.
7. Leone, *Her Husband's Crown*, 31.

The Sobriety of a Pastor's Helpmeet

Paul told Timothy that the wife of an office bearer must be "sober." This rules out drunkenness or drug abuse, of course, but it also refers more broadly to exercising clear thinking and self-control.[8] A pastor's wife must be ruled by the wisdom of the Holy Spirit, not her passions and desires. She must be watchful and vigilant (2 Tim. 4:5; 1 Peter 5:8). The Bible associates this clear-headed sobriety with the hope that Christ will return (1 Thess. 5:6, 8; 1 Peter 1:13; 4:7).

Sobriety is the root of the flower, from which the stem grows and by which the whole flower is nourished. It is a mind-set and attitude shaped by the doctrines of the Bible, especially the doctrines of God's grace in Christ manifested in His past death on the cross, His present work in sanctifying our lives, and His future coming in glory (Titus 2:11–14).

As a pastor's wife, you should cultivate your mind in communion with Christ. You should read God's Word, meditate on His truth, and have daily personal devotions. You should also read good books. I understand that your schedules are full from dawn to dusk. But if you can read an edifying or useful book just fifteen minutes a day, you will be surprised how many books you complete over the years, for fifteen minutes a day adds up to ninety hours in a year. By reading and growing theologically, you will also increasingly become one with your husband, who, by gifts and calling is a reader, thinker, and communicator. You will enter his world by reading solid books. Also, consider listening to good preaching and teaching while you go about your daily duties.

By cultivating a sober, biblical mind, you will also become more deeply rooted so that you may be equipped to handle the times of discouragement that will come. There are many precious, sweet experiences of serving as a pastor's wife here on earth, but there are also times of darkness and difficulty. A survey of evangelical pastors' wives revealed that 41 percent experienced frequent emotional ups and downs, 35 percent thought they needed help with overcoming discouragement or depression, and 17 percent said they were close to burnout.[9] For your own sake, you should be rooted and grounded in the faith and in the love of Christ (Eph. 3:18; Col. 2:7–8).

Sobriety will help fortify your attitude to your husband in countless ways. For example, consider your attitude toward his books. Sobriety tells us that a minister is called to labor in knowledge and words. He trades in knowledge and crafts words. He is a servant of the word of truth, the gospel of our salvation.

---

8. Knight, *Commentary on the Pastoral Epistles*, 159, 172.

9. Lynne Dugan, "National Association of Evangelicals Survey of Ministers' Wives: Executive Summary," in *Heart to Heart with Pastors' Wives*, comp. Lynne Dugan (Ventura, Calif.: Regal, 1994), 163, 165.

God has called him to this. Therefore, do not resent the number of books your husband has or make him feel guilty about buying more. He needs books the same way a carpenter needs tools. Some tools are only used once or twice a year, but when the time comes, they are sorely needed. So don't expect your husband to read every book he buys cover to cover; some are reference works. Help him set a budget for books as part of your financial planning. When he is excited about a new book, share his joy. Consider, too, that you will benefit from his books through his preaching. View his books and studies and his entire ministry with a sober mind-set that is informed by the Word of God.

The Fidelity of a Pastor's Helpmeet

Our text goes on to say that wives should be "faithful in all things." We have established that gravity or a serious commitment to holiness is the stem of the flower of a pastor's helpmeet. Confidentiality closes this flower's petals at night. Sobriety roots the flower, supporting and sustaining it with a clear, biblical mind-set. Faithfulness, then, is the fragrance of the flower. It is the sweet aroma of a freshly blooming rose. Just as a flower's fragrance fills the space around it, so a pastor's wife should be "faithful in all things," bringing the fragrance of Christ to every aspect of life. Three aspects of this faithfulness in action are prayer, constructive criticism, and love.

Colossians 4:2–4 commends prayer for a helpmeet's ministry, saying, "Continue in prayer, and watch in the same with thanksgiving; withal praying also for us, that God would open unto us a door of utterance, to speak the mystery of Christ, for which I am also in bonds: that I may make it manifest, as I ought to speak." By saying "continue in prayer," the text implies steady perseverance or faithfulness in a daily ministry of prayer. If the duty of members is to pray for their ministers, how much more should wives pray for their minister-husbands? Pray with your husband. Pray for him. Pray for church members. When your husband hears you praying for the church, he will know that you care about the ministry as much as he does.

Constructive criticism is another aspect of faithfulness. Proverbs 27:5–6 says, "Open rebuke is better than secret love. Faithful are the wounds of a friend; but the kisses of an enemy are deceitful." If you refuse to give your husband feedback on his preaching, teaching, and leadership, you will rob him of valuable insights that could help him grow. Of course, that doesn't mean hitting him with a sledgehammer on Sunday nights! There are better times and better approaches to the task. Think of constructive criticism as a sandwich. Start with a layer of praise for something that he did well. Then give him a layer of suggestions on how he could have done better. Top this with another layer of praise. He will most likely swallow the entire sandwich without complaint.

In addition, be aware of when your husband is most willing to eat this sandwich. For some pastors, perhaps very few, this is right after the service. For others it is best to wait until Tuesday! Also, offer your suggestions respectfully and submissively, as you would to any leader. Mary Somerville writes, "Do you constantly catch yourself evaluating your husband as a speaker instead of seeking to have God speak to your heart through His Word?... I shouldn't be thinking about how people are responding to his preaching rather than concentrating on my own life in relation to the Word of God. Just think of how much more our husbands will be built up when we share how his preaching impacted our lives!"[10] Forget about what others may be thinking; it is enough to ask whether you yourself correctly understood what was said and whether it was helpful to you as a Christian.

A third aspect of faithfulness, and the most important for you as helpmeet of your husband, is conjugal love. The Scripture says that an office bearer should be a "husband of one wife." If married, he must be a one-woman man, implying that an exclusive marital bond between him and you is central to his ministry. Therefore, investing in your relationship with your husband will bless not only the two of you but also the church you both serve. One of the most significant ways you can help your husband in his ministry is to cultivate an intimate and godly union with him.

Stay best friends with your husband. When Titus 2:4 says, "[T]each the young women...to love their husbands," it literally means "be [their] husbands' friend."[11] Friends are more than two people who are nice to each other. Friends are joined together. Proverbs 18:24 says, "There is a friend that sticketh closer than a brother." Friends stick together throughout the hardships of life. Proverbs 17:17 says, "A friend loveth at all times, and a brother is born for adversity." Friends support each other because they share life together. Ecclesiastes 4:9–10 says, "Two are better than one; because they have a good reward for their labour. For if they fall, the one will lift up his fellow: but woe to him that is alone when he falleth; for he hath not another to help him up." Therefore work to be a faithful friend to your husband so that your lives may be joined together through thick and thin. Your husband needs you, for "[i]t is not good that the man should be alone" (Gen. 2:18).

---

10. Mary Somerville, *One with a Shepherd: The Tears and Triumphs of a Ministry Marriage* (The Woodlands, Tex.: Kress Christian Publications, 2005), 114.

11. It is a compound noun formed of "friend" (Greek *philos*) and "man" or "husband" (Greek *aner* or *andros*).

Loneliness in the ministry is a common problem that makes your friendship with your husband very important. A study done by *U.S. News and World Report* showed that the ministry was the second loneliest job out of a hundred occupations. The first was a night watchman! Why is the ministry so lonely? Even though a pastor is around people all the time, the nature of his work makes it difficult for him to open up his heart and share his burdens with the congregation. People expect their shepherd to be strong. They also need to feel that the pastor loves all members equally. This expectation limits how close he can get to any one person in church. As a result, much of a pastor's social fulfillment must come from his family, especially his wife.

Feed and water your relationship with your husband. Talk with him, especially at night when your work is done. Sit together, talk together, and read together. Ask about his day. Listen to him. Discuss decisions that need to be made. Do so with love and submission. Be careful how you disagree with each other. As Somerville says, "One evening as Bob and I were having a heated discussion over an issue that we were working through, our son called from the bedroom and asked us to stop arguing. Bob responded, 'We aren't arguing, we're discussing.' To which Daniel retorted, 'Then can you discuss a little quieter?'"[12] This story is a reminder that your children have a need to be shielded from many of the pressures and difficulties of life in the ministry. A true home is a refuge and place of safety.

Do things together too. My wife and I regularly take a bike ride in the morning and a walk together in the evening. Keep romance alive. Do what you can to look good for him. Enjoy physical intimacy with him. And don't forget to compliment him. If he has beautiful eyes but a nose like the Goodyear blimp, tell him he has beautiful eyes! Focus on the positive. There will be men and women complimenting your husband; why let him get praise from another woman but not from you? Whatever he does for you, from the pulpit to the kitchen to the bedroom, take note and thank him. Be positive so that home is his favorite place to be.

Support your husband through conjugal love. One purpose of a flower is to attract bees and butterflies to its sweetness. Be a flower that attracts your husband and keeps him coming back for more.

Conclusion

If you have already begun to be women of gravity, confidentiality, sobriety, and fidelity, you mean so much to your husbands. When John Calvin's wife Idelette

---

12. Somerville, *One with a Shepherd*, 123.

died in 1549, he wrote to a friend, "I have been bereaved of the best companion of my life, of one who, had it been so ordered, would not only have been the willing sharer of my indigence [or poverty], but even of my death. During her life she was the faithful helper of my ministry. From her I never experienced the slightest hindrance."[13] That is a remarkable statement when one considers that it must not have been easy to be the wife of a man like John Calvin!

Godly pastors' wives are like a garden full of flowers, a veritable Eden of beauty and fragrance. Your blossoms will beautify more than just your marriage and family, for you are the helpmeets of the servants of the Lord. You are God's garden planted to refresh the spirits of the preachers of Christ. Your fragrance is the fragrance of Christ, and when your husbands go to the pulpit or classroom or meeting room, they carry the heavenly scents that they have absorbed from you to the world.

Therefore, labor in your flowerbeds. Survey every quality named in 1 Timothy 3:11, and consider how you can grow more plentiful and beautiful flowers. Pick one area where you are weak, and start there. Pray. Put sin to death and put on the deeds of the new man. Talk to your husband. Enlist the help of another godly woman. Read a book on the subject. Keep praying. And in all things, rest in Jesus Christ as your Savior from sin. Do not tackle spiritual growth without faith in the full forgiveness and reconciliation accomplished by Christ's shedding of His blood. And do not attempt to grow as flowers without being watered by the Holy Spirit sent down from heaven by the exalted Christ.

May God grant that the faithfulness of you and your husbands over a lifetime of ministry will result in the flowering of our churches, fulfilling the prophecy of Isaiah 35:1–2, "The wilderness and the solitary place shall be glad for them; and the desert shall rejoice, and blossom as the rose. It shall blossom abundantly, and rejoice even with joy and singing: the glory of Lebanon shall be given unto it, the excellency of Carmel and Sharon, they shall see the glory of the LORD, and the excellency of our God."

---

13. Letter CCXXXVIII, April 7, 1549, in *Letters of John Calvin*, ed. Jules Bonnet (Philadelphia: Presbyterian Board of Publication, 1858), 2:216.

Chapter 31

Unprofessional Puritans and Professional Pastors: What the Puritans Would Say to Modern Pastors

Edward Dering became a rising star in church ministry and academic scholarship, though still only a young man.[1] The University of Cambridge selected him to deliver an oration in Greek to Queen Elizabeth. He was widely sought after as a preacher. On February 25, 1570, he preached before the royal court. But, to the surprise of his audience, he publicly rebuked the bishops of the church for their sins and complacency. Then he looked at the queen, who by law was the supreme governor of the Church of England, and said to her, "And yet you sit still and are careless, and let men do what they will." The queen suspended him from preaching for a year, but he continued to lecture on the Scriptures. His sermon to the queen was printed sixteen times in the next thirty-three years.

His lectures on the epistle to the Hebrews fed the souls of many godly people in London. God was answering his prayer, "O Lord God, which hast left unto us Thy holy Word to be a lantern unto our feet, and a light unto our steps, give unto us all Thy Holy Spirit, that out of the…Word we may learn what is Thy eternal will, and frame our lives in all holy obedience to the same, to Thy honor and glory, and increase our faith, through Jesus Christ our Lord."

Dering returned to preaching, but a few years later he received a summons to appear before the dreaded high court of the Star Chamber for his criticisms of the bishops. He was acquitted of all charges. However, his health soon declined, and he died in 1576, only thirty-six years old. Some of his last recorded words were "Dally not with the Word of God, make not light of it; blessed are they that use their tongues well when they have them."

Dering's life reminds us that the Puritans were not professional pastors seeking a successful career in this world. They were faithful servants who lived

---

1. On Edward Dering see Patrick Collinson, "A Mirror of Elizabethan Puritanism: The Life and Letters of 'Godly Master Dering,'" in *Godly People: Essays on English Protestantism and Puritanism* (London: Hambledon, 1983), 288–323. This chapter is slightly expanded from an address I gave at Desiring God Pastor's Conference in 2013.

and died for the Lord who had bought them with His blood. The Puritans would not want us to be unprofessional in the sense of being lazy, rude, undisciplined, disorganized, careless, or having no regard for the honor of our Lord. However, they would object to a wicked professionalism that arises from the love of the world. They viewed such professionalism as a form of the lust of the flesh, the lust of the eyes, and the pride of life. The love of the Father is not in it. Nor is such professionalism beneficial to our vocation. On the contrary, it is a trap for the pastor, candy-coated poison for the lost, and a whip laid on the backs of the godly.

One of the great motives driving the Puritans was the need to raise up ministers who imitated Christ. Luke 6:40 says, "The disciple is not above his master: but every one that is perfect [fully trained] shall be as his master." I would lay before you seven points in which the Puritans called pastors to take up their crosses and follow Jesus Christ so as to be better disciple-makers.[2]

1. Invest Precious Time in Prayer

Professionalism makes prayer into a formality, a ceremonial way to open and close meetings. Longer prayers can serve to broadcast to other people how intelligent and spiritual we are. But for Christ, prayer was a tearful cry to God for deliverance for Himself and us (Heb. 5:7). The Bible says that in Gethsemane Christ "fell on the ground, and prayed," calling out with the language of a child, "Abba, Father!" (Mark 14:35–36).

The Puritans saturated all their pastoral ministry in prayer. They were great preachers only because they were also great petitioners who wrestled with God for His blessing. They understood the urgency of Paul's request, "Finally, brethren, pray for us, that the word of the Lord may have free course, and be glorified, even as it is with you: and that we may be delivered from unreasonable and wicked men: for all men have not faith" (2 Thess. 3:1–2).

Richard Baxter said, "Prayer must carry on our work as well as preaching; he preacheth not heartily to his people, that prayeth not earnestly for them. If we prevail not with God to give them faith and repentance, we are unlikely to prevail with them to believe and repent."[3] And Robert Traill wrote, "Some ministers of meaner [lesser] gifts and parts are more successful than some that are

---

2. Some parts of this chapter are adapted from Joel R. Beeke and Mark Jones, *A Puritan Theology: Doctrine for Life* (Grand Rapids: Reformation Heritage Books, 2012).

3. Richard Baxter, *The Reformed Pastor*, in *The Practical Works of the Rev. Richard Baxter*, ed. William Orme (London: James Duncan, 1830), 14:125.

far above them in abilities; not because they preach better, so much as because they pray more. Many good sermons are lost for lack of much prayer in study."[4]

The church today desperately needs preachers whose private prayers season their pulpit messages. The Puritan pastors jealously guarded their personal devotional time. They set their priorities on spiritual, eternal realities. They knew that if they ceased to watch and pray they would be courting spiritual disaster.

2. Depend Radically on the Holy Spirit

Professionalism manages resources in order to manipulate apparent spiritual results. It fishes for men and then "offers a sacrifice to its net" (Hab. 1:14–16), that is, claims success for its programs or skills. Jesus Christ came preaching in the power of the Holy Spirit, and His spiritual authority amazed people used to skillful but non-supernatural ministry (Luke 4:14; Mark 1:22). Now Christ calls us to be fishers of men (Mark 1:17) but says that we cannot do it without being "endued with power from on high" (Luke 24:49).

The Puritans showed a profound dependence on the Holy Spirit in everything they said and did for and in disciple-making. They felt keenly their inability to bring anyone to Christ. Baxter wrote, "Conversion is another kind of work than most are aware of. It is not a small matter…to have the very drift and bent of his life change so that a man renounces that which he took for his happiness, and places his happiness where he never did before."[5]

The Puritans were convinced that both preacher and listener are totally dependent on the work of the Spirit to effect regeneration and conversion when, how, and in whom He will. The Spirit brings God's presence into human hearts. He persuades sinners to seek salvation, renews corrupt wills, and makes scriptural truths take root in stony hearts. Thomas Watson wrote, "Ministers knock at the door of men's hearts, the Spirit comes with a key and opens the door."[6]

They also felt their complete dependence on the Spirit to build up the saints in holiness and mature discipleship. They knew that apart from Christ, Christians can bear no spiritual fruit (John 15:5). John Owen said, "The Lord Christ…sends his Holy Spirit into our hearts, which is the efficient cause of all holiness and sanctification—quickening, enlightening, purifying the souls of his saints."[7]

---

4. Robert Traill, "By What Means may Ministers Best Win Souls?" in *The Works of Robert Traill* (Edinburgh: Banner of Truth, 1975), 1:246.

5. Baxter, *A Call to the Unconverted*, in *Works*, 7:370.

6. Thomas Watson, *A Body of Divinity* (Edinburgh: Banner of Truth, 1965), 221.

7. John Owen, *Communion with God*, in *The Works of John Owen* (Edinburgh: Banner of Truth, 1965–1968), 2:199.

The church needs men who know God's sovereignty not just in theoretical pronouncements from the pulpit but in the private prostration of their souls before the throne of grace. Despite our affirmations of God's sovereignty, we are quick to puff ourselves up when we see success, and easily deflated and downcast when we harvest little. The Puritans would remind us that men's hearts will receive God's Word only when Christ writes it in them with the ink of the Spirit of the living God (2 Cor. 3:3).

3. Embrace the Thorns of Affliction

Professionalism views weakness and pain with contempt and fear. To the victor belong the spoils; to losers belongs the agony of defeat. However Jesus Christ willingly received a crown of thorns upon His head, pressed into His bloody brow by mocking soldiers (Matt. 27:29–30). How will we respond when a thorn pierces our flesh and God leaves it there despite all our prayers for its removal (2 Cor. 12:7–9)?

The Puritans teach us to groan in God's presence. Do not pretend that ministry doesn't hurt. Perhaps you have seen your plans and disciple-making come to nothing. You have poured your life into people only to suffer unfair criticism and rejection. Perhaps you feel like a child who built sandcastles by the sea, only to watch your labors on behalf of the church be swallowed up by the inevitable rising tides of human sin, whether your own or someone else's.

George Hutcheson said that to be "mournful under affliction…is very consistent with a patient and meek frame of spirit under trouble."[8] If we try not to feel the pain, we may harden our hearts, and fail to profit from affliction. Hutcheson said the best way to manage grief is to "run to God with all that grieves us," with much humility and self-abasement.[9]

Let us sweeten our groaning, however, with abundant praises to God. There is a difference between moaning and murmuring. Thomas Manton said, "Murmuring is an anti-providence, a renouncing of God's sovereignty."[10] How horrible it is when men whose mouths preach the gospel of God then complain with the same mouths about what God has done, or apparently failed to do! Watson wrote, "Our murmuring is the devil's music."[11] Satan likes nothing better than to get men to curse God, even if they do it under their breath. Let us

---

8. George Hutcheson, *An Exposition of the Book of Job* (London: for Ralph Smith, 1669), 14.

9. Hutcheson, *Job*, 14–15.

10. Thomas Manton, *A Treatise of Self-Denial*, in *The Complete Works of Thomas Manton* (London: James Nisbet, 1873), 15:249.

11. Thomas Watson, *The Art of Divine Contentment*, ed. Don Kistler (Morgan, Pa.: Soli Deo Gloria, 2001), 65.

learn rather to say, "The LORD gave, and the LORD hath taken away; blessed be the name of the LORD" (Job 1:21).

Praising God in pain requires us to submit our limited minds to God's incomprehensible ways. Why do we think we can judge God? Owen was one of the greatest Christian thinkers of all time. But he wrote, "All our notions of God are but childish in respect of his infinite perfections."[12] As children of God, we must not criticize our Father but trust His will and His timing. John Flavel said God's timing is always "precise, certain, and punctual," but "the Lord doth not compute and reckon his seasons of working by our arithmetic."[13]

4. Cultivate Personal Holiness

Professionalism is resumé-driven. It glories in credentials, measurable results, upward career moves, and financial rewards. Each church is a stepping stone to a yet more prominent ministry. Christ's meat was to do the will of His Father (John 4:34). His career moves were all downward: "he humbled himself, and became obedient unto death, even the death of the cross" (Phil. 2:6). Now He calls us to work out our salvation with fear and trembling (Phil. 2:12), and to "cleanse ourselves from all filthiness of the flesh and spirit, perfecting holiness in the fear of God" (2 Cor. 7:1).

The Puritans taught that the core duty of our calling is to walk with Christ by faith on the pathway of holiness. Flavel wrote, "The soul is the life of the body, faith is the life of the soul, and Christ is the life of faith."[14] Hebrews 12:1–2 commands us to cast off sin and to run the race set before us, "looking unto Jesus." Isaac Ambrose said that this looking to Christ is not a bare, intellectual knowledge but an inward and experiential "looking unto Jesus, such as stirs up affections in the heart, and the effects thereof in our life…knowing, considering, desiring, hoping, believing, loving, joying, calling on Jesus, and conforming to Jesus."[15]

If we desire Christ to walk with us in our public ministry, then we must walk with Christ in our private lives. Traill said to ministers, "Take heed unto thyself, that thou be a lively thriving Christian. See that all thy religion run not in the channel of thy employment."[16] These words capture the essence of unholy and unhealthy professionalism. As David resolved in Psalm 101:2, so we too must

---

12. Owen, *Of the Mortification of Sin in Believers*, in *Works*, 6:65.

13. John Flavel, *The Mystery of Providence*, in *The Works of John Flavel* (Edinburgh: Banner of Truth, 1968), 5:472.

14. Flavel, *The Method of Grace*, in *Works*, 2:104.

15. Isaac Ambrose, *Looking unto Jesus* (Harrisonburg, Va.: Sprinkle Publications, 1986), 28.

16. Traill, "By What Means May Ministers Best Win Souls?" 1:241.

say, "I will walk within my house with a perfect heart." This is not sinless perfection but sincere godliness, as opposed to hypocritical religion, where all is done to be seen of men. John Trapp wrote, "Follow hypocrites home to their houses, and there you shall see what they are."[17] Matthew Henry said, "It is not enough to put on our religion when we go abroad and appear before men; but we must govern ourselves by it in our families. Those that are in public stations are not thereby excused from care in governing their families; nay, rather, they are more concerned to set a good example of ruling their own houses well (1 Tim. 3:4)."[18]

In Psalm 101:3 David wrote, "I will set no wicked thing before mine eyes: I hate the work of them that turn aside; it shall not cleave to me." Trapp paraphrased David, "I will not gaze upon forbidden objects, nor venture upon a temptation to or an occasion of sin."[19] So we are called to do battle for the purity of our minds. Matthew Poole wrote, "If any ungodly or unjust thing shall be suggested to me…I will cast it out of my mind and thoughts with abhorrency."[20]

5. Digest the Bible One Verse at a Time

Professionalism takes every thought captive to the wisdom of the world. It follows with bated breath the latest trend, newest book, and most popular cultural events, for these, it thinks, hold the secret code to unlock the minds of men. By contrast, Christ was a man of the Book. He is the preeminent Psalm 1 man who rejects "the counsel of the ungodly," but "his delight is in the law of the Lord; and in his law doth he meditate day and night" (Ps. 1:2). Whether fasting in the wilderness of temptation or teaching in the temple, the mind, heart, and mouth of Jesus were filled with Scripture.

The Puritans taught that we, too, must meditate on the Word (Josh. 1:8). What is meditation? Thomas Hooker said, "Meditation is a serious intention of the mind whereby we come to search out the truth, and settle it effectually upon the heart."[21] In meditation your mind hovers over a truth like a bee over a flower to draw out all its sweetness.

The Puritans abounded in practical directions on how to meditate on the Word. First, pray for the Holy Spirit to help you. You might use the words of

---

17. John Trapp, *A Commentary on the Old and New Testaments* (London: Richard D. Dickinson, 1868), 2:624.

18. *Matthew Henry's Commentary* (Peabody, Mass.: Hendrickson, 1991), 3:503 [Ps. 101].

19. Trapp, *Commentary*, 2:624.

20. Matthew Poole, *A Commentary on the Whole Bible* (Peabody, Mass.: Hendrickson, n.d.), 2:154.

21. Thomas Hooker, *The Application of Redemption by the Effectual Work of the Word, and Spirit of Christ, for the Bringing Home of Lost Sinners to God. The Ninth and Tenth Books* (London: Peter Cole, 1657), 210.

Psalm 119:18, "Open thou mine eyes, that I may behold wondrous things out of thy law." Second, read a portion of the Scriptures. Don't read so much that you have no time to meditate. Third, focus on one verse or doctrine, something clear and applicable to your life. Repeat the verse or doctrine to yourself several times to memorize it. Fourth, analyze it in your mind by its various names, properties, causes, and effects, together with illustrations, comparisons, and opposites. Be careful not to speculate over matters left unspoken. Fifth, preach the truth to your own soul to stir up your faith, love, desire, hope, courage, grief, gratitude, and joy in the presence of God. Examine your life and make detailed application. Sixth, resolve with prayer to grow in grace. Seventh, praise the Lord with thanksgiving. So to meditate is to pray, read, focus, analyze, preach to yourself, resolve with prayer, and praise God in a manner that revolves around a single truth of Scripture.

Meditation will feed your soul. Thomas Manton wrote, "Faith is lean and ready to starve unless it be fed with continual meditation on the promises."[22] Beware of a professional approach to the Bible. Traill warned, "When we read the word, we read it as ministers, to know what we should teach, rather than what we should learn as Christians. Unless there be great heed taken, it will be found, that our ministry, and labour therein, may eat out the life of our Christianity."[23]

6. Feel the Momentous Dignity of Ministry

Professionalism is essentially materialistic and focused on this world. Therefore, if it values pastoral ministry at all, it does so by reducing it to an earthly pursuit requiring only skill, organization, and technique. The goal, frankly, is customer satisfaction! But Christ refused to submit His mission to an earthly agenda (Luke 12:14; John 6:15). Why should He? Christ knew that He was sent by the Father to do an eternally significant work, and He set Himself apart to do it. He said to His ministers, "As my Father hath sent me, even so send I you" (John 20:21).

The Puritans stood in awe that a mere man could be the ambassador of the almighty, triune God (2 Cor. 5:20). William Gurnall said, "The Word of God is too sacred a thing, and preaching too solemn a work, to be toyed and played with."[24] They also felt the amazing privilege of being called to serve Christ as an under-shepherd. Richard Sibbes said, "This is a gift of all gifts, the ordinance of preaching. God esteems it so, Christ esteems it so, and so should we esteem

---

22. Manton, "Sermons on Genesis 24:63," in *Works*, 17:270.

23. Traill, "By What Means May Ministers Best Win Souls?" 1:242.

24. William Gurnall, *The Christian in Complete Armour* (Edinburgh: Banner of Truth, 1964), 2:286.

it."[25] Thomas Goodwin wrote, "The work of the ministry is the best work in the world; God had but one Son in the world and He made Him a minister."[26]

Our secular society has dramatically downgraded the value of pastoral ministry because secularism demeans the spiritual and the eternal. The Puritans, however, saw our calling as the glorious responsibility to prepare people to stand before God on judgment day and to receive an everlasting kingdom. "There is not a sermon which is heard, but it sets us nearer heaven or hell," wrote John Preston.[27]

Therefore pastors should take up their work with joy, dignity, sobriety, and hope. This is a work worthy of our life's labors. Flavel caught the ethos of Puritan ministry when he wrote:

> How many truths we have to study! How many wiles of Satan and mysteries of corruption, to detect! How many cases of conscience to resolve! Yea, we must fight in defense of the truths we preach, as well as study them to paleness, and preach them unto faithfulness: but well-spent: head, heart, lungs and all; welcome pained breasts, aching backs, and trembling legs; if we can all but approve ourselves Christ's faithful servants, and hear that joyful voice from his mouth, 'Well done, good and faithful servants'![28]

7. Love the Triune God and His People

Professionalism is focused on the bottom line. It views God's people and God Himself according to how useful they are to fulfill its agenda. But while viewing God as useful, it fails to see Him as beautiful. Christ rejoiced in worshiping the Father (Luke 10:21). He lived in constant intimacy with God (John 1:18). Zeal for God's house consumed Him (John 2:17). And Christ's compassion fills Him with warm feeling when He sees people in their brokenness and misery (Luke 7:13; John 11:35; Heb. 4:15).

The Puritans practiced Christlike ministry with a heart full of affection. They stirred themselves up to zeal. Oliver Bowles said zeal "is a holy ardor kindled by the Holy Spirit of God in the affections, improving a man to the utmost for God's glory, and the church's good."[29] Yet their zeal was not proud and harsh but sweet and gentle. Jonathan Edwards wrote,

---

25. Richard Sibbes, *The Fountain Opened*, in *Works of Richard Sibbes* (Edinburgh: Banner of Truth, 1978), 5:509.

26. Thomas Goodwin, *An Exposition of the First Chapter of the Epistle to the Ephesians*, in *The Works of Thomas Goodwin* (Grand Rapids: Reformation Heritage Books, 2006), 1:563.

27. John Preston, *Riches of Mercy to Men in Misery* (London: by J. T., 1658), 288.

28. Flavel, *The Character of a True Evangelical Pastor*, in *Works*, 6:569.

29. Oliver Bowles, *Zeal for God's House Quickened* (London: Richard Bishop for Samuel Gellibrand, 1643), 5.

> As some are mistaken concerning the nature of true boldness for Christ, so they are concerning Christian zeal. 'Tis indeed a flame, but a sweet one; or rather it is the heat and fervor of a sweet flame. For the flame of which it is the heat, is no other than that of divine love, or Christian charity; which is the sweetest and most benevolent thing that is, or can be, in the heart of man or angel.[30]

Zeal is indeed the heat of a flame, but the flame is the fire of love. Therefore we should avoid the destructive wildfire of pride, selfishness, and divisive partisanship, on the one hand, and on the other hand, avoid coldness, lethargy, laziness, and deadness. Let us burn with love!

William Ames said that love for our neighbors means that we desire their good "with sincere and hearty affection" and "endeavor to procure it."[31] He also wrote that ministers "ought so to behave themselves towards the congregation as servants, and not lords." Though they "do all things with authority" as "Christ's delegates," still "they are the servants of all men."[32]

Since I speak at a number of conferences, I have the opportunity to talk with numerous Christians, both pastors and church members. Many times someone will start telling me about his pastor, that he is a good teacher, preacher, and leader and yet there is something missing. He does not feel a personal connection with his pastor, a sense that his pastor truly loves him. Brothers, as a pastor myself, I understand both the demands of ministry and the unrealistic expectations of many church members. But I also know how easy it is to begin to view people merely as tools we use to attain our ministerial goals—goals often driven, sadly, by human pride and selfish ambition.

Our Lord taught us that love for God as our supreme end and love for our neighbor as ourselves are the most important ingredients in all our duties. So it is too with ministry. Owen said that "zeal for the glory of God and compassion for the souls of men" are "the life and soul of preaching."[33] That means that preaching without love is lifeless and soulless.

And it is not just preaching. Owen wrote that a pastor's responsibilities include being "ready, willing, and able, to comfort, relieve, and refresh, those that are tempted, tossed, wearied with fears and grounds of disconsolation, in times of trial and desertion." Pastors must resemble Christ as the great High

---

30. *The Works of Jonathan Edwards, Volume 2, Religious Affections*, ed. John E. Smith (New Haven: Yale University Press, 1959), 2:352.

31. William Ames, *Conscience with the Power and Cases Thereof* (1639; facsimile repr., Norwood, N.J.: Walter J. Johnson, 1975), 5.7.4 [Rr recto].

32. Ames, *Conscience with the Power and Cases Thereof*, 5.24.1 [Xx2v].

33. Owen, *The True Nature of a Gospel Church*, in *Works*, 16:77.

Priest.[34] Our duties also include "a compassionate suffering with all the members of the church in all their trials and troubles, whether internal or external"; Owen remarked that nothing in pastors "renders them more like unto Jesus Christ" than this.[35]

How beautiful is a disciple-making pastor with a heart of warm love for God and genuine tenderness toward people! His heart truly streams out toward others with living water from the Lord, sometimes in tears and sometimes in shouts of joy.

Don't treat people as tools or obstacles for your professional advancement. Love them!

Conclusion

The Puritans didn't just talk about pastoral ministry; they did it. They not only were used by God for the conversions of thousands of people but were equally used for the maintenance and growth of those people in genuine and maturing discipleship. Before he died, Richard Baxter could say of his decades of ministry in Kidderminster that he didn't know of one soul of the hundreds converted under his ministry who had slidden back to the world. That is not just a tribute to God's amazing, preserving grace. It is also a tribute to Baxter's constant discipleship of believers, ever aiming for their full conformity to Christ.

In 1665 the plague, or "black death," swept through London. At its peak, over seven thousand people were dying every week. So many people died that they carried the bodies off in carts and buried them in mass graves. Historians estimate that the plague killed between seventy-five thousand and one hundred thousand people in London in those times—far more than the coronavirus in our day.

The "professional" pastors fled the city, fearing for their lives. But the Puritan ministers stayed in the city to care for the sick and bereaved and to bring them the gospel. To make and strengthen disciples, they risked their lives and followed the Good Shepherd, who laid down His life for the sheep. They were men like Thomas Vincent. Vincent had been expelled by the government from his church ministry in London in 1662 by the Act of Uniformity. But he stayed in the city as a schoolteacher. When the plague came, Vincent chose to remain. He believed that those dying from the plague needed true spiritual comfort, and he could think of no greater opportunity for ministry.

---

34. Owen, *The True Nature of a Gospel Church*, in *Works*, 16:85.
35. Owen, *The True Nature of a Gospel Church*, in *Works*, 16:87.

Fearlessly he visited the homes of the infected. Though he had no official pastorate, he preached every Lord's Day. It is said that he never preached a sermon during this period without someone being affected powerfully by the Word. The danger was real; seven persons died in the very house where Vincent was staying. But God preserved Vincent and continued to uphold him as he suffered through another thirteen years of official persecution before he died.[36]

Someone has said, "Those of us who minister *for* Christ should strive to minister *like* Christ."[37] It is easy for us to fall into the trap of ministerial professionalism. It comes naturally. If we would follow Christ, then we must strive and labor against our greatest opponent: *ourselves*. If, however, Christ is in us, then we have the Spirit's grace to deny ourselves and press forward.

Let us begin, brothers, by humbling ourselves in the presence of the Good Shepherd, lamenting our worldly professionalism, and calling on God to give us more of graces of His Holy Spirit. Let us begin with prayer and dependence on God.

Preston wrote, "The love of God is peculiarly the work of the Holy Ghost.... Therefore the way to get it is earnestly to pray.... We are no more able to love the Lord than cold water is able to heat itself...so the Holy Ghost must breed that fire of love in us, it must be kindled from heaven, or else we shall never have it."[38]

---

36. "Life of the Author," in Thomas Vincent, *The True Christian's Love of the Unseen Christ*, ed. Don Kistler (Morgan, Pa.: Soli Deo Gloria, 1993), viii–ix.

37. Warren W. Wiersbe, *On Being a Servant of God*, rev. ed. (Grand Rapids: Baker, 2007), 58.

38. John Preston, *The Breastplate of Faith and Love*, 2 vols. in one (1634; facsimile repr., Edinburgh: Banner of Truth, 1979), 2:50.

Chapter 32

Catechism Preaching

In 1562, Frederick III, elector of the Palatinate, commissioned the writing of a catechism that he hoped would unify the church's confession and practice in his realm. One year later, on January 19, 1563, Frederick sent the new catechism to the publisher.[1] More than 450 years later, as part of the one, holy, catholic and apostolic church, through our Lord and Savior Jesus Christ, we commemorate the publication of the Heidelberg Catechism (1563) as a remarkable fruit of the sixteenth century Reformation. Some say this catechism is the most widely distributed book ever written besides the Bible and *Pilgrim's Progress*.

Although the production of a new catechism was not original to the Palatinate church,[2] what is unique to the Heidelberg Catechism (HC) is that it was originally intended to be *preached*. In his analysis of Frederick's preface to the Heidelberg Catechism, Lyle Bierma notes three distinct purposes for creating this document:

---

1. For more on the historical background and theology of the Heidelberg Catechism see the essays included in Lyle Bierma with Charles D. Gunnoe Jr., Karin Y. Maag, and Paul W. Fields, *An Introduction to the Heidelberg Catechism: Sources, History, and Theology*, Texts & Studies in Reformation & Post-Reformation Thought, gen. ed. Richard Muller (Grand Rapids: Baker Academic, 2005), 15–133. See also the various essays in *The Church's Book of Comfort*, ed. Willem van't Spijker, trans. Gerrit Bilkes (Grand Rapids: Reformation Heritage Books, 2009). Also useful is W. Verboom, *De theologie van de Heidelbergse Catechismus: twaalf themas: de context en de latere uitwerking* (Zoetermeer: Boekencentrum, 1996); Bard Thompson, et. al., *Essays on the Heidelberg Catechism* (Boston: United Church Press, 1963); Otto Thelemann, *An Aid to the Heidelberg Catechism*, trans. M. Peters (Grand Rapids: Douma, 1959), 447–509; M. A. Gooszen, ed., *De Heidelbergsche Catechismus: Textus Receptus met Toelichtende Teksten* (Leiden: E.J. Brill, 1890); Frank H. Walker, *Theological Sources of the Heidelberg Catechism* (n.p., 2003). This chapter is a slightly expanded version of an address delivered at the Canadian Reformed Theological School's annual conference in Hamilton, Ontario; it is also an abridged version of two chapters in Jon D. Payne and Sebastian Heck, eds., *A Faith Worth Teaching: The Heidelberg Catechism's Enduring Heritage* (Grand Rapids: Reformation Heritage Books, 2013), 35–78.

2. R. Scott Clark notes that between 1523 and 1675 the Reformed produced, on average, "a significant confessional document every six years." R. Scott Clark, *Recovering the Reformed Confession: Our Theology, Piety, and Practice* (Phillipsburg, N.J.: Presbyterian & Reformed, 2008), 159.

Frederick wanted this new catechism first of all, then, for the instruction of the children in sound doctrine. However, it is not only that the youth may be trained in piety, it is "also that the Pastors and Schoolmasters themselves may be provided with a fixed form and model, by which to regulate the instruction of youth, and not, at their option, adopt daily changes, or introduce erroneous doctrine." All such instructors should thankfully accept this catechism, diligently explain it to the youth in the schools *and the common people in the pews*, and act and live in accordance with it.... The preface suggests, therefore, that Elector Frederick had at least three objectives for his new catechism: that it serve as a *catechetical tool* for teaching the children, as a *preaching guide* for instructing the common people in the churches, and as a *form for confessional unity* among the several Protestant factions in the Palatinate.[3]

Today, the need for a confessional document such as the HC is being challenged, even in some Reformed circles. The cry of "No creed but Christ" (which may sound pious, but, as Dorothy Sayers eloquently states, leads to nothing but chaos) is also sounded in Reformed churches.[4] But of Frederick's three aims for the catechism, the greatest objections are made against the validity and profitability of catechism preaching, that is, using a catechism as a guide and source for preaching. This chapter will show how catechism preaching is vital for the life of the church. I will argue *for* the revival of catechism preaching in Reformed churches, and I will also illustrate principles by which the HC may be biblically and soundly preached. In short, the church of the twenty-first century has much to learn from the careful exposition and preaching of the HC. Let us consider 1) the development of catechism preaching, 2) the decline of catechism preaching, 3) objections to catechism preaching, 4) strengths of catechism preaching, 5) approaches to catechism preaching, and 6) the practical aspects of catechism preaching.

---

3. Lyle Bierma, "The Purpose and Authorship of the Heidelberg Catechism," in *An Introduction to the Heidelberg Catechism*, 51. Cf. Daniel R. Hyde, "The Principle and Practice of Preaching in the Heidelberg Catechism," *Puritan Reformed Journal* 1:1 (January 2009): 97–117; Donald Sinnema, "The Second Sunday Service in the Early Dutch Reformed Tradition," *Calvin Theological Journal* 32 (1997): 298–333; N. H. Gootjes, "Catechism Preaching," in *Proceedings of the International Conference of Reformed Churches, September 1–9, 1993* (Neerlandia, Alba.: Inheritance, 1993), Part 1: 136–52; Part 2: 153–66. http://www.spindleworks.com/library/wcf/catech.htm# (accessed June 11, 2011).

4. See, for example, Dorothy Sayers's essay "Creed or Chaos?" as found in *The Whimsical Christian: 18 Essays* (repr., New York: Macmillan, 1978), 34–52.

The Development of Catechism Preaching

Throughout church history, catechetical preaching, that is, instruction in the basic truths and norms of the Christian faith, has often taken the form of sermons on the Apostles' Creed, the sacraments, the Ten Commandments, and the Lord's Prayer.[5] Hughes Oliphant Old has shown us that such catechetical preaching is nearly as old as Christianity. It has a long history in the Christian church, as seen in the *Didache*, the sermons of Cyril of Jerusalem (313–386), John Chrysostom (347–407), Theodore of Mopuestia (350–428), and Augustine of Hippo (354–430).[6]

In the Middles Ages, the importance of catechetical preaching was periodically acknowledged. In 789, bishops were charged to make sure that the priests preached on the Lord's Prayer, and in 852, every priest was requested to study how the orthodox fathers expounded the Lord's Prayer and the Apostles' Creed, then to preach a series of sermons on what they learned.[7] Four centuries later, in England, the Synod of Lambeth charged priests in 1281 to preach on the Ten Commandments, the two "great commandments," the Apostles' Creed, the seven works of mercy, the seven deadly sins, the seven cardinal virtues, and the seven sacraments of the church.[8] In 1294, priests in the Netherlands were ordered to preach regularly in their local language and at a popular level on the Lord's Prayer and the Apostles' Creed and at least three times a year on the Ten Commandments and the church's seven sacraments.[9] Still, the vast majority of preachers in the Middle Ages neglected catechetical preaching.

The Protestant Reformers revived the practice of catechetical teaching and preaching. Martin Luther (1483–1546) only slightly exaggerated when he said, "We have the catechism on the pulpit, something which did not happen for a thousand years."[10] Luther preached on the church's catechism even prior to 1517.[11] In April 1529, he published his *Large Catechism* (originally called the *German Catechism*) as a synopsis of sermons he had preached on the Ten

---

5. For parts of this section, I have gleaned from N. H. Gootjes, "Catechism Preaching, Part 1," in *Proceedings of the International Conference of Reformed Churches*, 136–52.

6. Hughes Oliphant Old, *The Reading and Preaching of the Scriptures in the Worship of the Christian Church* (Grand Rapids: Eerdmans, 1998), 1:255–65; 2:5–18, 196–202, 224–28, 382–85.

7. J. C. L. Gieseler, *Lehrbuch der Kirchengeschichte*, 3rd ed. (Bonn: Adolph Marcus, 1831), 2.1.71.

8. A. Troelstra, *De toestand der catechese in Nederland gedurende de voor-reformatorische eeuw* (Groningen: J. B. Wolters, 1901), 108.

9. Troelstra, *Der catechese in Nederland*, 114.

10. Martin Luther, *Table Talk*, no. 4692, cited in M. B. Van't Veer, *Catechese en catechetische stof bij Calvijn* (Kampen: Kok, 1942), 153n16.

11. Van't Veer, *Catechese en catechetische stof bij Calvijn*, 169.

Commandments, the Apostles' Creed, the Lord's Prayer, and the sacraments.[12] The purpose of these sermons was to show ministers how to teach catechetically so they would learn to preach the basic doctrines of Christianity on a regular basis. The following month, Luther published his *Small Catechism* for the daily reading and instruction of children.

The Zwinglian Reformation also emphasized catechetical preaching in general and preaching from a particular catechism. In 1532, Leo Jud (1482–1542) and Heinrich Bullinger (1504–1575) drafted *Predicantenordnung*, a set of rules for the preachers of Zurich, which included the stipulation that ministers should preach on an article of the Apostles' Creed every Sunday afternoon.[13] The following year, Leo Jud's catechism became the basis for catechism preaching.[14]

Catechism preaching became common not only in Lutheranism and Zwinglianism but also in Calvinism. Gootjes summarizes Calvin's efforts this way:

> Calvin wrote two catechisms, one before he was expelled from Geneva, and one after his return. The second, which used a question-and-answer form much like the Heidelberg Catechism, was published in French (1542) and Latin (1545).
>
> Calvin drafted his second catechism to comply with the 1541 church order rules Geneva had drafted for preaching. The church order prescribed that three services should be held on each Sunday, of which the middle one, which began at noon, was to be the catechism service.[15]

Catechism preaching took a major step forward in the Reformed faith with the publishing of the HC, partly because it was designed from the very beginning for preaching. Zacharias Ursinus (1534–1583), the primary author of the HC, wrote in 1563 that the authorities asked him to preach the catechism at the Sunday afternoon service, as his co-author, Caspar Olevianus (1536–1587), had already done.[16] Then, too, in the preface to the HC's first edition, dated

---

12. For the Large Catechism, see *The Book of Concord: The Confessions of the Evangelical Lutheran Church*, trans. and ed. Theodore G. Tappert (Philadelphia: Fortress, 1959), 357–461. For the sermons on which the *Large Catechism* are based see *Luther's Works, Vol. 51: Sermons*, trans. and ed. John W. Doberstein (Philadelphia: Fortress, 1959), 133–93.

13. Gootjes, *Proceedings of the International Conference of Reformed Churches*, 141.

14. Klaas Dijk, *De dienst der prediking* (Kampen: Kok, 1950), 406.

15. Gootjes, *Proceedings of the International Conference of Reformed Churches*, 139. For Calvin's second catechism, see *Calvin: Theological Treatises*, trans. J. K. S. Reid, vol. 22 of the Library of Christian Classics (Philadelphia: Westminster Press, n.d.), see esp. 62, 69, 88–90.

16. W. Hollweg, *Neue Untersuchungen zur Geschichte und Lehre des Heidelberger Katechismus* (Neukirchen: Neukirchener Verlag, 1961), 137.

January 19, 1563, Frederick urged preachers to inculcate knowledge of the HC in the common people from the pulpit.[17]

In November 1563, ten months after the original publication of the HC, Frederick included the catechism in the Church Order of the Palatinate. Frederick divided the catechism into fifty-two portions and implemented three ways the catechism was to be used in worship. First, a portion of the catechism was to be read each Sabbath so that its entirety would be read aloud every nine weeks. Second, the questions and answers of the HC were to be asked and answered responsively; the minister would pose the question, and the catechumens would answer in the presence of the entire congregation. Third, the questions were to be expounded in the preacher's afternoon (second) sermon, and after one year of such sermons, the preacher was to start over again.[18]

Preaching the HC soon spread beyond the Palatinate; as early as 1566 the practice of preaching from the catechism entered the Netherlands via Pieter Gabriël (d. 1573), a field preacher. He used the Dutch translation of the catechism's third German edition made by Petrus Dathenus (c. 1531–1588), a former book publisher but now a court preacher and tutor to Frederick III's children.[19] Dathenus included his 1566 translation in the back of his metrical version of the Psalms.[20] Thus, early on there was a close connection between the HC and the Dutch Reformed Church's liturgical manual (*kerkboek*).

In the 1570s and 1580s, several Reformed churches in the Netherlands, such as Delft, Dort, Naaldwijk, and Amsterdam, regularly heard preaching

---

17. J. N. Bakhuizen van den Brink, *De Nederlandse Belijdenisgeschriften*, 2nd ed. (Amsterdam: Ton Bolland, 1976), 151.

18. As quoted in G.I. Williamson, *The Heidelberg Catechism: A Study Guide* (Phillipsburg, N.J.: P&R, 1993), xi–xii. Cf. the more explicit instructions as quoted in Theleman, *Aid to the Heidelberg Catechism*, 505–6.

19. For a brief synopsis of Dathenus's life see my introduction in Petrus Dathenus, *The Pearl of Christian Comfort*, trans. Arie W. Blok (Grand Rapids: Reformation Heritage Books, 1997), v–xii; Herman Hanko, *Portraits of Faithful Saints* (Grandville, Mich.: Reformed Free Publishing, 1999), 216–21.

20. Teunis M. Hofman, "The Heidelberg Catechism in the Netherlands: Ecclesiastical Recognition of the Catechism (Part B)," in *The Church's Book of Comfort*, 154–55. Cf. Karin Y. Maag's brief article outlining the many German, Dutch, Latin, French, and English translations and printings of the HC. Maag includes an impressive list (65 in total) of the earliest editions and printings (1563–1663). As she notes, it was the Dutch who were "among the most prolific translators of the Catechism," producing in 1566 alone six separate editions. See her article "Early Editions and Translations of the Heidelberg Catechism" in *An Introduction to the Heidelberg Catechism*, 103–117 (the quotation is from 107). For a fuller bibliography of the HC editions and commentaries and sermons based on it in different languages, see Eric D. Bristley, "Bibliographica Catechismus Heidelbergenis: An Historical Bibliography of Editions, Translations, Commentaries, Sermons and Historical Studies of the Heidelberg Catechism 1563" (unpublished paper, Westminster Theological Seminary, 1983).

from the Heidelberg Catechism in their second Lord's Day services. Other churches taught the catechism during weekday services. By 1583, the Classis of Dort required theological students to deliver two practice sermons at each classis meeting, one of which had to be based on the catechism.[21]

In 1586, twenty years after the introduction of catechetical preaching in the Netherlands, the Synod of Den Haag (The Hague) made it mandatory that all ministers of the gospel preach from the HC during the second worship service on Sunday.[22] However, many ministers and churches resisted this mandate for decades. The major Dutch assemblies spoke out against the resistance. One provincial synod acknowledged that a catechism in question-and-answer form is not prescribed in Scripture, but then affirmed, "having and teaching a summary of the fundamental articles of the Christian religion is an apostolic custom (Heb. 6:1) [that] has always been maintained in the church and has great usefulness."[23]

Objections against catechism preaching were later raised by Arminian ministers in the early seventeenth century. These men were followers of Jacobus Arminius (1560–1609). They became known as the "Remonstrants" because they presented their objections to the Reformed faith in a document called the *Remonstrantia* ("remonstrance" or "protestation"), laid before the assemblies of the churches. They also questioned some of the catechism's content. At the Conference of Delft in 1613, some Remonstrant ministers were asked if they agreed with a number of statements from the catechism. They responded that they could not.[24] In 1618, Isaac Frederici, a Remonstrant minister of Noordwijk, presented his objections to catechism preaching at the Synod of Dort.[25] Among the objections to catechetical preaching were the multi-parish responsibilities of some ministers, the people's negligence in attending catechism services, and the government's failure to compel Sabbath-keeping.[26]

The international Synod of Dort (1618–1619) reinforced the 1586 decision of the Synod of Den Haag to promote catechism preaching during Sabbath

---

21. Willem Jan op 't Hof, "The Heidelberg Catechism in Preaching and Teaching: The Catechism in Preaching (Part A)," *The Church's Book of Comfort*, 187.

22. Before the Synod of The Hague (1586) the Heidelberg Catechism was recognized in the Dutch churches by the Convent of Wezel (1568) and various synods: Emden (1571), Dort (1574), Dort (1578), and Middelburg (1581). See Hofman, "Ecclesiastical Recognition of the Catechism," in *The Church's Book of Comfort*, 163–67.

23. Gootjes, *Proceedings of the International Conference of Reformed Churches*, 148. Cf. 1 Tim. 3:16, 2 Tim. 1:13.

24. I. D. De Lind Van Wijngaarden, *De Dordtsche Leerregels of de Vijf Artikelen tegen de Remonstranten*, 2nd ed. (Utrecht: Ruys, 1905), 52–57.

25. Op 't Hof, "The Catechism in Preaching," *The Church's Book of Comfort*, 188.

26. Daniel R. Hyde, "The Principle and Practice of Preaching in the Heidelberg Catechism," *Puritan Reformed Journal* 1, 1 (2009): 116.

afternoon services. Despite varying customs respecting catechism preaching, delegates from Great Britain, Germany, Switzerland, and the Netherlands affirmed the validity and profitability of catechetical preaching and concurred with the synod's draft of Article 68 of the Church Order of Dort, which states, "The Ministers everywhere shall briefly explain on Sunday, ordinarily in the afternoon service, the sum of Christian doctrine comprehended in the Catechism which at present is accepted in the Netherland Churches, so that it may be completed every year in accordance with the division of the Catechism itself made for that purpose."[27]

Catechism preaching was thus considered essential to the well-being of the churches. The Synod of Dort produced the following rules to encourage and protect the practice of catechism preaching:

1. The Synod reiterated the 1586 synodical decision, asserting that ministers who failed to comply in preaching the catechism would be censured.

2. Catechism sermons should be brief and understandable; doctrine must be presented at the layperson's level so that even children could understand it.

3. If the attendance at the second service is small (even if only the minister's family was in attendance), the minister should proceed with his catechism sermon, a good example to the people.

4. Appeal ought to be made to the government to curb labor, sports, drinking parties, etc., so that people may attend church regularly and keep the Sabbath day holy.

5. Every church, as much as possible, ought to have its own minister rather than have one minister serving two or more churches; the intent here was to allow for two sermons, one from the catechism, on each Lord's Day in each congregation.

6. Church visitors were to take particular note whether the preaching of the catechism was done regularly. Censure of both minister and

---

27. *Doctrinal Standards, Liturgy, and Church Order*, ed. Joel R. Beeke (Grand Rapids: Reformation Heritage Books, 1999), 187. Article 68 follows almost exactly the wording of the 1586 Synod of The Hague. Cf. Ronald Cammenga, "The Homiletical Use of the Heidelberg Catechism: An Examination of the Practice of Systematic Preaching of the Heidelberg Catechism in the Dutch Reformed Tradition," *Protestant Reformed Theological Journal* 41, 1 (Nov. 2007): 5–7; Arie W. Blok, "A Heidelberg Catechism Survey" (Chatham, Ont., 1988; unpublished manuscript), 9–10. For a helpful summary of the opinions of the Synod's delegates from individual states and countries, see Gootjes, *Proceedings of the International Conference of Reformed Churches*, 149–52.

confessing members ought to be applied to those unwilling or delinquent in practice or attendance respectively.[28]

Change often comes slowly in churches, so it wasn't until the second half of the seventeenth century that most churchgoers in the Netherlands, particularly those living in cities, began faithfully to attend the Sunday afternoon catechism sermon.[29] Certain Dutch "Further Reformation"[30] ministers, most notably Jacobus Koelman (1631–1695), resisted synodical laws that required catechism preaching. He also opposed the use of various forms in worship services, such as those for administering the sacraments. He referred to catechism sermons as "worn-out form sermons" that promoted laziness in ministers who seldom referred to the Scriptures when preaching them.[31] By the 1680s, some Reformed church members were objecting to the abstract nature of catechism preaching and its apparent lack of connection to Scripture. Though these objectors were a minority, David Knibbe (1639–1701), pastor and theological teacher in Leiden, addressed their concerns in his homiletics textbook, *Manuductio ad Oratorium Sacrum*. Knibbe offered several guidelines for preaching the Heidelberg Catechism:

+ Before the sermon is preached, a Scripture text or texts are to be announced; the sermon should be grounded in those texts.

+ The structure and outline of the sermon should be developed according to the same rules that govern other kinds of preaching.

+ The words and sentences of the catechism must not be too minutely and scrupulously explained, except in cases where prevalent errors compel such detailed work.

+ The points of doctrine must be exposited from the Scriptures rather than from other theological works, though the preacher may consult such works in preparing his sermon.

+ Whenever the questions and answers deal with polemical issues, such as the Mass or free will, the opponent's position must be stated fairly,

---

28. Idzerd Van Dellen and Martin Monsma, *The Church Order Commentary: Being A Brief Explanation of the Church Order of the Christian Reformed Church*, 3rd ed. (Grand Rapids: Zondervan, 1964), 278–79. Cf. Blok, "A Heidelberg Catechism Survey," 10–11.

29. Wim Verboom, "Catechism Teaching from the Late Middle Ages," in *The Church's Book of Comfort*, 137; op't Hof, "The Catechism in Preaching," *The Church's Book of Comfort*, 190.

30. *Nadere Reformatie* refers to a movement promoting further or "closer" reformation in the Dutch churches, similar to and having many links with English Puritanism.

31. Op 't Hof, "The Catechism in Preaching," *The Church's Book of Comfort*, 192–96. Koelman was not opposed to referring to the Catechism in preaching, but supported William Ames (1576–1633) who taught that Scripture must be the starting point for catechism preaching (ibid., 194–95).

perhaps even quoting his own words, as the preacher must not strike at straw men in his sermons.

+ When the section on the Ten Commandments is preached, the minister should give a short exposition of the commandment, then list some of the particular virtues and vices related to the commandment, after which he should explain the spiritual character of the commandment.

+ After expounding a doctrine, the minister should show the necessity and use of this doctrine in relation to other doctrines.

+ The minister must also never neglect to stress the practical uses of holiness lest he be accused of vain speculation.[32]

Throughout the eighteenth and early nineteenth centuries, weekly preaching from the HC remained strong in Dutch Reformed churches. G. D. J. Schotel describes how eagerly these sermons were received:

> Never, never was the church so crowded as in the afternoons; then you not only met the average citizenry there, as now, but also the nobility and the patricians. William I and Charlotte of Bourbon, Louise de Coligny, Maurice, Frederick Henry, and William III and William IV were generally not absent then. And rather than anxiously causing their sons and daughters to be absent when Lord's Day 41 was preached [on the seventh commandment], parents especially made sure their children were present then! In those centuries, people were not ashamed to hear about sin, but they were afraid to commit sin.[33]

Numerous ministers published their catechism sermons, which were read by thousands of Dutch Reformed Christians. Some of the most famous catechism sermons were written by Bernardus Smytegelt (1665–1739), Johannes Beukelman (1704–1757), and Johannes VanderKemp (1747–1811). VanderKemp's sermons, which abound with experiential and practical applications, were translated and published in English in 1810 and reprinted in 1997.[34]

---

32. David Knibbe, *Manuductio ad Oratorium Sacram* (Lausanne: David Gentil, 1682). Knibbe also wrote a well-known volume of sermons on the Catechism: *De Leere der Gereformeerde Kerk, Volgens de order van de Heydelbergse Katechismus* (Leyden: Samuel Suchtmans, 1718).

33. G. D. J. Schotel, *De openbare Eeredienst der Nederlandse Hervormde Kerk in de 16e, 17e en 18e eeuw* (Leiden: Sijthoff, 1870), 427; cited in W. Verboom, *Hulde aan de Heidelberger: Over de waarde van leerdienst en catechismuspreek* (Heerenveen, The Netherlands: Groen, 2005), 13. I wish to thank Adam Slingerland for translating Verboom's book into English.

34. Johannes VanderKemp, *The Christian Entirely the Property of Christ, in Life and Death, Exhibited in Fifty-three Sermons on the Heidelberg Catechism*, trans. John M. Harlingen, intro. Joel R. Beeke, 2 vols. (Grand Rapids: Reformation Heritage Books, 1997).

The Decline of Catechism Preaching

While catechism preaching enjoyed a kind of golden age during the seventeenth, eighteenth, and early nineteenth centuries, it has declined since then. In 1831, the Synod of the Nederlands Hervormde Kerk (NHK, at that time, the national or state church in the Netherlands) rejected a request to replace Sunday catechism sermons with Scripture readings, but in 1860 the Synod of the Hervormde Kerk made Sunday catechism sermons non-compulsory. Though that decision produced so much opposition that it was rescinded the following year, it was reinstated in 1863 in a different form, namely, that catechism preaching was optional for each minister, but each minister had to respect his congregation's wishes. Not surprisingly, catechism preaching declined throughout the NHK into the twentieth century. It remained strong in the churches that seceded from the national church in 1834 (known as the *Afscheiding* or "Secession"), however. The Gereformeerde Kerken in Nederland (GKN), rooted in the 1886 secession (the *Doleantie,* a word meaning the state of being aggrieved or offended, that is, by acts or decisions of the national synod of the NHK), retained catechism preaching until the mid-twentieth century, though in 1905, the synod of the GKN decided that ministers did not have to preach through the entire catechism each year.[35]

While we should be careful about making generalizations, it is interesting to note that the decline of catechetical preaching in America is more pronounced in Reformed denominations that have existed the longest on American soil.[36] Though various factors may account for this, it is evident that North American culture does not support the profitability or even the validity of doctrinal preaching. Many find doctrinal preaching tedious or difficult to follow. Many seminaries undermine the value of doctrine and systematic theology; candidates for the ministry from such institutions find it next to impossible to preach doctrinally, let alone to preach from the catechism. With this in mind, it is not surprising that catechism preaching has declined.

In 1985, Peter Y. De Jong lamented, "Today such sermons are sometimes regarded as little more than a pious tradition which need not be taken seriously. Often in churches which still profess commitment to the Reformed faith

---

35. Op 't Hof, "The Catechism in Preaching," *The Church's Book of Comfort,* 199. Though the 1905 decision can be viewed as a diminishing of commitment to the catechism, it can also be viewed in a positive way, so that ministers are not bound to preach catechism sermons on "feast-day" Sundays such as Easter nor are bound to give only one sermon for each Lord's Day each time they preach through the catechism.

36. Arie W. Blok, "Preaching with the Heidelberg Catechism Today" (Holland, Mich., 1988; unpublished manuscript), 5.

it [catechism preaching] is neglected for months on end."[37] Preaching regularly from the HC, however, is still the practice of more conservative Reformed denominations that have their roots in the Netherlands, including the Canadian Reformed, Free Reformed, Heritage Reformed, Netherlands Reformed, Protestant Reformed, and United Reformed Churches.

Objections to Catechism Preaching

Before considering the strengths, methods, and proper practice of preaching from the catechism, let us examine some major objections to it.[38] Here are four of them:

1. *Catechism preaching "biblicizes" the confession.* The first and most serious objection to catechetical preaching is that it is based on a derivative document rather than on the Word of God. Objectors to preaching the catechism assert that using the HC as a source of preaching supplants Holy Scripture with a man-made document. Eugene Heideman summarizes this objection: "Many have been suspicious of formal catechetical preaching because they have feared that such sermons would in actuality subordinate the Scriptures to the doctrines of the church. Systematic theology would overpower biblical exposition."[39]

Certainly such fears are warranted if the catechism is equated with Scripture (have you really ever met anyone who believed that?) or wrongly preached. Nevertheless, proper catechism preaching is first and foremost biblical. The Reformed churches have always confessed that Scripture is the "norming norm" (*norma normans*), or the supreme standard, to which all other standards are subordinate, and by which all other standards are to be interpreted. A "biblicizing" objection to preaching the catechism usually fails to understand that when the catechism is preached rightly, its *material principle* remains the Scriptures while its *formal principle*, that is, the organization of the sermon's material, is primarily based on the catechism. Let us remember that systematic theology and topical preaching that seek to glean all that Scripture says on a particular

---

37. Peter Y. De Jong, "Comments on Catechetical Preaching," *Mid-America Journal of Theology* 1, 2 (1985): 155. Speaking from within a CRC context, De Jong notes that anyone who challenges the current perception of catechetical preaching is simply labeled a "troublemaker" (155–56).

38. D. Martyn Lloyd-Jones provides a succinct list of his objections to catechism preaching in *Preaching & Preachers* (Grand Rapids: Zondervan, 1972), 187–88.

39. Eugene Heideman, "Catechetical Preaching," chap. 3, p. 6, in "Four Chapters Prepared for the Course CM432 *Preaching as a Teaching Ministry*, at Western Theological Seminary, Holland, Michigan, 1978" (unpublished).

doctrine are no less biblical than biblical theology and expository preaching that examine one aspect of a certain doctrine from a particular text.

Then, too, let us remember that though the HC and other doctrinal standards do not possess the authority of Scripture and are subject to revision, they nonetheless do possess ecclesiastical authority.[40] Scripture alone has complete authority while the church's confessions have only a derived authority, but that authority, should not be denigrated. Confessions are not mere man-made, abstract statements but the living confession of the Reformed churches; in them, the Reformed churches speak in unity. In a confessional statement the church says, "By the Spirit's gracious leading of the church into all truth [John 16:13], this confession or catechism is what we believe and understand to be Scripture's teaching of its foundational truths."[41]

In practice, faithful preaching of the HC does not displace the Bible but preserves the Scriptures and their supremacy.[42] As Johannes Hoornbeeck (1617–1666) wrote, "Ultimately, the catechism is not about the catechism, but about the Word of God."[43] Edward J. Masselink went on to say, "Sometimes fear has been expressed that the Heidelberg Catechism may take the place of the Bible. The contrary is true. The catechism has never displaced the Bible on the pulpit. In many churches where the truths of the catechism have been neglected, the Bible has been displaced, but never where the catechism has been faithfully followed."[44]

2. *Catechism preaching is boring and repetitious.* Catechism preaching may indeed be boring in some churches, admits Peter Y. De Jong. He wrote, "It cannot be denied that some sermons of this kind are dull, pedantic, even boring to the extreme. They may be so poorly structured or preached that no one really knows what is being said."[45] Then, too, if ministers preach the same sermons

---

40. Belgic Confession, Articles 30–32; Westminster Confession, 31.3.

41. Willem Verboom, *Hulde aan de Heidelberger*, 84.

42. Verboom points out that the supremacy of Scripture was evident in the Reformed church of the Netherlands in the seventeenth century even in the hat-wearing of the male members. When the Bible was read, they removed their hats out of respect for Scripture's supreme authority as the very Word of God; when the Catechism was read, they put their hats back on (Verboom, *Hulde aan de Heidelberger*, 82–83)!

43. Cited in Hoekstra, *Gereformeerde homiletiek*, 228: "Non ex catechismo, ut scripto canonico; verum ille laudabiliter etiam explicatur, probatur, pro concione tractatur, sed ex scriptura."

44. Edward J. Masselink, *The Heidelberg Story* (Grand Rapids: Baker, 1964), 12.

45. Peter Y. De Jong, "Comments on Catechetical Preaching," *Mid-America Journal of Theology* 2, 2 (1986): 156. For helpful answers against objections to catechetical preaching, see the whole of De Jong's second article, 149–70.

repeatedly and do not grow in their own understanding of the catechism, people will understandably find their sermons repetitious, dull, and unedifying.

Yet, this second argument against catechetical preaching is in itself a logical fallacy; a boring sermon based on the catechism does not prove that the catechism itself is boring, nor does it prove that preaching from the catechism lends itself to boring sermons. Rather, the fault is due to either the preacher or the listener; either the preacher has made the catechism dull by simply repeating the same platitudes each year, or the listener has convinced himself that nothing more can be gleaned from the catechism because it has already been said.

3. Catechism preaching misreads or distorts the true meaning of the catechism. De Jong notes there are "two serious misrepresentations" of the HC: some treat the catechism to be a closely reasoned and overly intellectual presentation of impersonal scholastic propositions, while others see it as little more than an experiential handbook demonstrating the steps of despair and despondency that one must take before seeing the faint light of deliverance.

Obviously, a preacher's preconceptions will influence how he preaches the catechism; an intellectual minister will preach the catechism in a scholastic manner, whereas a minister who embraces *experientialism* (i.e., an experiential emphasis that goes beyond the Scriptures) will adopt an equally objectionable manner. But as with the previous objection, the misrepresentations or distortions of particular preachers do not prove that catechetical preaching ought to be rejected. The catechism itself has often been commended for its generous balance of doctrinal truth and experimental emphasis.

4. Catechism preaching is based on an outdated, time-conditioned document. Considering the historical context of the writing of the HC and the pertinence of the issues of baptism and the Lord's Supper in the sixteenth century, some might question whether it is necessary to devote so much time preaching on these matters today. Furthermore, one may question whether preaching on historical controversies such as the Roman Catholic Mass (Q. 80) is still relevant.[46] What is more, critics of catechetical preaching will say that elaboration on necessary doctrines such as eschatology, predestination, missions, and evangelism is largely passed over when undue emphasis is placed on sixteenth-century debates.

---

46. It should be noted that Question 80 was not included in the first edition of the HC. Only after the express urging of Olevianus did Frederick include this question in later editions. See Lyle Bierma, "The Sources and Theological Orientation of the Heidelberg Catechism," in *An Introduction to the Heidelberg Catechism*, 78–79.

It might be observed in passing that one never knows when these historic debates on the nature and efficacy of the sacraments will suddenly become matters of urgent contemporary concern. For example, the nature and efficacy of infant baptism is at the heart of the present controversy over "Federal Vision" theology, and likewise, the current debate over whether covenant children should be allowed to partake of the Lord's Supper without making a personal profession of faith in Christ.

Nonetheless, as with the preceding objections, this criticism is a valid warning for today's church, but also one sufficiently answered by *proper* preaching of the catechism. We need to remember two things. First, just as every minister who preaches from the Scriptures must cross the bridge from Old Testament Israel and first-century Ephesus to the situation of Christians living in today's world, so the catechism preacher must cross the bridge from sixteenth-century Reformed theology to the needs and concerns of persons living in a twenty-first century culture. Actually, the latter is the easier task, for the bridge from the sixteenth century is much shorter than the bridge from Bible times to today, though in both cases it is possible to exaggerate the real length of the bridge one needs to build. Like Dr. Martyn Lloyd-Jones, we ought never tire of pointing out that in many respects nothing important about fallen man has ever changed in all of history.

Second, it is remarkable how little sound, biblical, Reformed doctrine needs to be adjusted for today, for all the major doctrines have remained constant. We today must still be made experientially aware of our sin and misery to find deliverance or salvation in Christ by grace alone through faith and to live in gratitude to God, for His glory alone. All this is taught in Scripture and faithfully summarized in the HC.[47]

Strengths of Catechism Preaching

Having considered some objections to catechism, let us now turn to the strengths of catechism preaching.

1. Catechism preaching is biblical in content. A close and inseparable connection exists between the HC and Scripture. Commenting on this relation, Van Baalen wrote, "There is much Scripture crowded into its [the HC] few pages."[48] Properly understood, the catechism's intent is to present a summary of biblical

---

47. Cf. Shinji Matsuda, "The Heidelberg Catechism and Preaching" (ThM thesis, Western Theological Seminary, 1987), 65–66.

48. Van Baalen, *The Heritage of the Fathers*, 4.

teaching; as stated in the opening paragraph of the Palatinate church order, the three-fold structure[49] of the catechism is itself a summary of Scripture: "The Word of God aims to direct doctrine primarily so that first it brings people to awareness of their sin and misery; subsequently it instructs them in how they can be delivered from all sin and misery; and in the third place it shows how grateful they must be to God for this deliverance."[50] Thus, not only is the HC replete with scriptural quotations and accompanied by numerous proof-texts but even in its structure, the HC conforms to Scripture.

The catechism, however, does not only quote Scripture in its answers. As was the case with most catechisms and confessions of the sixteenth century, the HC expounds the the Ten Commandments (LD 34–44) and the Lord's Prayer (LD 45–52).[51] Preaching from the last twenty Lord's Days needs no justification because these questions and answers explicate specific passages of Scripture, the Ten Commandments (Ex. 20:1–17) and the Lord's Prayer (Matt. 6:9–13). In short, the HC is biblical because it is founded upon Scripture, conforms to the pattern of Scripture, exegetes Scripture, and summarizes Scripture teaching.

2. Catechism preaching is doctrinal. By promoting a teaching ministry, catechism preaching encourages doctrinal stability and growth within the church. As the catechism gleans its teaching from Scripture and presents its findings in condensed, practical summaries, preaching through it ensures that ministers preach the entire system of biblical truth, or "all the counsel of God" (Acts 20:27). The very nature of a summary requires selectivity and arrangement, so the HC does not cover every doctrine that is found in Scripture. Nevertheless, in dependence

---

49. The three parts or divisions of the HC are: (1) "Of the Misery of Man;" (2) "Of Man's Deliverance;" and (3) "Of Thankfulness."

50. See Willem van't Spijker, "The Theology of the Heidelberg Catechism," in *The Church's Book of Comfort*, 96. The HC itself is patterned after the Epistle to the Romans framework of misery, deliverance, and gratitude.

51. For example, Calvin's first edition of his *Institutes* (1536) was catechetical in nature elaborating the Law, the Creed, and the Lord's Prayer. See Richard Muller, *Post-Reformation Reformed Dogmatics*, vol. 1: *Prolegomena to Theology* (Grand Rapids: Baker, 2003), 2.3 (B), 1. Calvin's catechism also outlines and explains these three common sources for early Reformed confessions. Cf. I. John Hesselink, *Calvin's First Catechism: A Commentary: Featuring Ford Lewis Battles' translation of the* 1538 Catechism, Columbia Series in Reformed Theology (Louisville, Ky.: Westminster John Knox Press, 1997). It is noteworthy that the order Calvin followed (Law, Creed, Lord's Prayer) is not used by the HC (Creed, Law, Lord's Prayer). While this is not evidence of a significant change in theology, it does indicate a different emphasis especially on the use of the law. Nevertheless, the HC's emphasis on the third use of the law is not so great that it obliterates any sense of the law's evangelical use; as already evident from Lord's Day 2, the HC upholds that the law is a schoolmaster that drives us to Christ. For more on the three uses of the law, see Joel R. Beeke, "The Didactic Use of the Law," in *Puritan Reformed Spirituality* (Grand Rapids: Reformation Heritage Books, 2004), 101–124.

on the Reformed tradition preceding it, the authors compiled the HC focusing on the primary doctrines of the gospel, the things "necessary for a Christian to believe" (Q. 22).

Proper catechism preaching also maintains doctrinal balance within a congregation. All too often churches err by emphasizing one particular doctrine over another, whether this is the extent of one's misery, one's experience of gracious redemption, or the cultivation of holiness. By contrast, the catechism teaches the whole counsel of God: human misery, divine redemption, and the believer's sanctification. The HC includes all the major *loci* of systematic theology: theology proper (LD 9–10), anthropology (LD 3–4), Christology (LD 6, 11–16), soteriology (LD 7, 23–24), ecclesiology (LD 21), and eschatology (LD 22).

In an age when doctrine is disparaged and neglected, catechism preaching is especially needed.[52] Using the catechism to inform, structure, and ground the sermon offers the Christian church a summary of doctrine and practice in a straightforward manner that will promote maturity, faithfulness, and fruitfulness in its members.

3. *Catechism preaching is pastoral.* Doctrinal preaching need not be pedantic or dry. Rather, a significant strength of catechism preaching is that it is pastoral, a way of nurturing and caring for the flock of God. The personal language of the catechism ("I," "me," or "mine") encourages immediate application, helping the hearers, by the Spirit's grace, to apply Christ's benefits to themselves. The aim is not simply to promote a vague "spirituality" in the hearers but, rather, to lead them to Christ and to help them find the comfort they need in Him and in His salvation.

Lord's Day 1 sets the tone for the pastoral character of the HC: "What is thy only comfort in life and death?" In the answer, the believer confesses that he or she belongs "with body and soul, both in life and death" to Jesus Christ and, being united to Him, participates in all the glorious blessings given freely by a heavenly Father, through the indwelling Holy Spirit. In the application of Christ's benefits, the Christian finds strength and courage to combat sin and the devil, to forsake the world, to deny the lusts of the flesh, and to live a life consecrated to the service of Jesus Christ.[53]

---

52. Peter De Jong shows that whenever the Christian church has been biblical and solid, it has emphasized a teaching ministry ("Comments on Catechetical Preaching (2)," *Mid-America Journal of Theology* 1, 2 [1985]: 155–87).

53. De Jong, "Comments on Catechetical Preaching (2)," *Mid-America Journal of Theology* 1, 2 (1985): 184–85.

4. Catechism preaching is pedagogically sound. A further strength of catechetical preaching is its question-and-answer method. The value of this pedagogical method can hardly be overstated. Socrates, Augustine, Anselm, Aquinas, and Erasmus, to name only a few of the great teachers of history, all used this method. The catechism also provides concise, well-formulated statements, easily memorized and recalled, thereby making the rank-and-file church member conversant with the foundational truths of Christianity.[54]

5. Catechism preaching is experiential. The HC not only emphasizes sound theology but also displays on every page the nature and value of Christian experience. Christianity is presented as a "head, heart, and hand" religion, which encapsulates the entire person in his life experience. James I. Good wrote, "The combination of head-and-faith in the Heidelberg, of intellectual faith and personal experience, has been one of the most striking peculiarities of our catechism."[55] Eugene Osterhaven put it this way, "One of the characteristics of the Heidelberg Catechism often noted is its experientialism. No cold, abstract statement of theology, it is a warm personal confession which, while sophisticated in outline, sequence, and theological substructure, lures the learner to embrace its teaching with graceful, artistic simplicity."[56]

6. Catechism preaching is practical. Linked to the experiential quality of the catechism is its practicality. I. John Hesselink writes that in the catechism "we have no speculation or theoretical discussions of abstract problems but rather the character of a handbook of practical religion. The Heidelberg Catechism seeks to help men face the problems and questions of daily living. There is no interest here in bare doctrine. Rather, the practical aspects of Christian living are dominant."[57] Catechism preaching is typical of good Reformed theology,

---

54. On this point see the helpful short essay by Scott R. Clark, "Why We Memorize the Catechism," *Presbyterian Banner* (August, 2003). Cf. Dorothy L. Sayers, "The Lost Tools of Learning," *National Review* 31, 3 (1979): 90–99.

55. James I. Good, *The Heidelberg Catechism in its Newest Light* (Philadelphia: Publication and Sunday School Board of the Reformed Church in the United States, 1914), 297.

56. M. Eugene Osterhaven, "The Experientialism of the Heidelberg Catechism and Orthodoxy," in *Controversy and Conciliation: The Reformed and the Palatinate 1559–1583*, ed. Derk Visser (Pittsburgh: Pickwick, 1986), 197.

57. I. John Hesselink, "The Heidelberg Catechism: Its Structure and Distinctive Characteristics," in *Shingaku to Bokkai* (Theology and Pastoralia), no. 1, ed. Takeshi Takasaki (Oyama, Japan: Kitakanto Theological Institute, 1982), 28.

Hesselink concludes, which is "doctrine with a purpose."[58] True catechetical preaching gives hands and feet to orthodox Reformed doctrine.[59]

Christians are asked in numerous questions of the catechism what profit, advantage, comfort, benefit, admonition, or assurance a particular doctrine provides them. Questions 28, 36, 43, 45, 49, 51, 52, 57, 58, 59, 69, and 75 make clear that doctrinal truths are not to be divorced from practical ends, namely, the direction, help, and comfort for Christian living in a tumultuous world.

7. *Catechism preaching is contemporary.* By God's grace, preaching the catechism can reach today's postmodern generation in many ways. According to Stan Mast: (1) Postmoderns are woefully ignorant of the basic doctrines of Christianity; but the HC provides a clear, uncluttered systematic summary of the Christian faith, including an exposition of the Apostles' Creed, the Ten Commandments, and the Lord's Prayer, universally considered to be essential knowledge for every Christian. The HC is a crash course in Basic Christianity 101. (2) Having embraced relative truth and blurred morality, postmoderns often have a naïve respect for different traditions. The HC can tell the story of the Reformed tradition in a warm and winsome way, a tradition rooted firmly in the older tradition of the ancient church. (3) Postmodernism is pragmatic ("Does it work?"), personal ("What can it do for me?"), and experiential ("How can I experience it?"). The catechism abundantly addresses practical, personal, and experiential concerns better than any other Reformed doctrinal standard. Just read the questions, and these things will jump out at you. The catechism is intensely relational toward both God and one's fellow human beings. The catechism is a remarkable fit for contemporary man.[60]

8. *Catechism preaching is doxological.* The catechism repeatedly calls the believer to live for God's praise and glory. The third part of the catechism is devoted to teaching us how to express our gratitude to God for our deliverance in Christ.[61]

Various Approaches to Catechism Preaching
To understand how catechism preaching should be done, let us examine various approaches given in the past. Although more representatives could be

---

58. I. John Hesselink, *On Being Reformed* (Ann Arbor, Mich.: Servant Books, 1983), 106–108.

59. Cf. *Reformatorisch Dagblad*, June 10, 2011, http://www.refdag.nl/opinie/commentaar /commentaar_tweede_dienst_waardevol_1_528109 (accessed June 11, 2011).

60. Stan Mast, "Preaching the Heidelberg to Postmoderns," *CTS Forum* Summer 2006): 11–12.

61. De Jong, "Comments on Catechetical Preaching (2)," *Mid-America Journal of Theology* 1, 2 (1985): 186.

studied, this section will focus on various approaches found in the writings of Theodorus L. Haitjema, Klaas Dijk, Peter Y. De Jong, and Paul Zylstra. They present us with three traditional approaches, to which I will add three more.

1. The traditional synthetic approach. Theodorus Lambertus Haitjema (1888–1972) proposes that it is most suitable for preachers, especially young preachers, to preach systematically through the catechism once a year. However, this does not mean a preacher must scrupulously adhere to the fifty-two divisions (Lord's Days).[62] Haitjema advocates a synthetic or thematic approach to preaching, in which the preacher's sermon title and outline are synthesized, "put together" from the biblical and confessional material before him, in a manner not directly bound to the form of that material. The synthetic method does not slavishly follow the material or text being expounded but looks for the overarching theme and expounds that. The danger of the synthetic method is that the preacher can fasten on a subject and then, if not watchful, abandon the text or the catechism material to pursue his own ideas.

Like Haitjema, Klaas Dijk (1885–1968) advocates a synthetic method of catechism preaching. He writes, "It is better to take together the subject matter with which one works and work out the theme and the divisions, especially since this preaching returns repeatedly."[63] Dijk further cautions against transgressing outside the bounds of the Lord's Day under consideration. In other words, the divisions set by the catechism are to be maintained. This allows the minister to focus on a particular topic while avoiding needless repetition (or worse, overemphasis). For example, Dijk advises that a sermon on Question 5, "I am prone by nature…," which presents the frowardness or perversity of fallen man, should not focus on the extent or totality of human depravity because this topic is presented in Question 8.

2. The traditional analytic approach. The analytical method adheres more strictly to the form of the HC portion, viewing it as the preacher's text, so that the minister expounds it word by word, phrase by phrase, and sentence by sentence. The strength of this type of preaching is that it is easy for the congregation to follow. Its weakness is that it often presents no overarching theme with clarity; it can easily lose the forest because it is too closely examining each tree.

---

62. For example, Haitjema thought it best for a minister in our day to combine the polemical Lord's Days concerning the sacraments into one sermon. Haitjema, "De prediking als catechismusprediking," 2:304.

63. Klaas Dijk, *De Dienst der Prediking* (Kampen: Kok, 1954), 413.

Scripture texts and catechism questions lend themselves to different approaches. It should be noted that Haitjema was not entirely opposed to using the analytical method (see below). He advised that this method be used at times to increase the variety of catechism sermons, but he believed the synthetic method to be the most valuable.

Peter Y. De Jong (1915–2005) also promoted catechism preaching that uses the catechism as a text. In a series of articles, De Jong argues that since the catechism is a summary or digest of Scripture, we need not add a single verse "to serve as apology or even a basis for such a message."[64] Agreeing with Abraham Kuyper (1837–1920),[65] De Jong believes that a catechism sermon based on a single Scripture verse or select passage, rather than advancing the catechism sermon, which summarizes all that Scripture says on the topic being presented, actually does injustice to the intention of the Lord's Day. He writes, "Such preaching, when done as its composers intended, shows more clearly than sermons based on a single verse or passage far more of the length and breadth and depth of the treasures displayed on the sacred page."[66]

3. The traditional Scripture-as-text approach. Paul Zylstra argues against De Jong's method, saying that such an approach "interposes the catechism between the text and the sermon."[67] Instead, Zylstra advocates the "Scripture text" method.[68] Zylstra says the catechism must not be front and center in the sermon. The sermon must be an exegetical treatment based on a single text of Scripture.[69] According to Zylstra, catechetical preaching "involves the use of a biblical text as that which governs the structure, direction, and content of the sermon, with the Heidelberg Catechism material for the day being employed in the

---

64. De Jong, "Comments on Catechetical Preaching (2)," *Mid-America Journal of Theology* 1, 2 (1985): 160.

65. Verboom, *Hulde aan de Heidelberger,* 17.

66. De Jong, "Comments on Catechetical Preaching (2)," *Mid-America Journal of Theology* 1, 2 (1985): 160.

67. Paul C. Zylstra, "A Preferred Method for Preaching on the Heidelberg Catechism: The Advantages of the Biblical Text-Method Over the Catechism-Text Method" (ThM thesis, Calvin Theological Seminary, 1985), 47.

68. For a summary of these two models (Catechism-text and Scripture-text) see Randal S. Lankheet, "Two Ways to Write a Catechism Sermon," *The Outlook* (October 1987): 4–5. Lankheet also advocates the "Scripture-text" method. Cf. the response by Nelson Kloosterman in his "Assumptions and Methods in Catechism Preaching," *The Outlook* (Jan. 1988): 13–15. See also C. L. Stam, "Catechism Preaching," *The Clarion* 35, 23 (Oct. 20, 1987): 505–507, who, against Lankheet, argues that "Scripture-text" catechism sermons "will not save the catechism preaching…but will, instead, devalue it" (507).

69. Zylstra, "A Preferred Method," 38–39.

service of such biblical exposition."[70] The catechism must always remain in the background. Zylstra's view has become increasingly popular today, particularly among those who would prefer to phase out catechism preaching altogether.

4. *The "text first, then catechism" approach.* This approach selects a Scripture text that illustrates the most important doctrine presented in the Lord's Day. The preacher preaches on that text for ten to fifteen minutes as an introduction to the catechism questions. He then proceeds to expound the catechism portion. It seems to me that this approach may work well with certain Lord's Days, but I would be hard pressed to use it for an entire series of catechism sermons because the preacher must often expound more than one text in the body of a sermon to explain what the catechism is saying.

5. *The "tailor-made" or combination approach.* Perhaps some of the debate about the method of catechetical preaching—whether the catechism-as-text or Scripture-as-text approach, or shades of both, can be eased by adopting the method that best fits the given Lord's Day to be preached on, hence, the "tailor-made" approach. In this way, the minister varies his approach, depending on the Lord's Day. The catechism-as-text approach may be appropriate for one Lord's Day, whereas the Scripture-as-text approach may be better for the next.

Some Lord's Days may require a judicious combination of both approaches. A combination of exegetical (that is, exegesis of Scripture) and topical preaching is a natural fit for Lord's Days 34–44, on the Ten Commandments, and Lord's Days 46–52, on the Lord's Prayer. Since these Lord's Days focus on particular texts of Scripture, they lend themselves both to exegesis and a topical treatment. When applying this combination of approaches, however, the preacher must take care to cover the catechetical material. Exegesis should not so overpower the topical material that the catechism's statements are not addressed.

Some Lord's Days, however, do not lend themselves to a concentrated approach; for example, Lord's Days 10, 12, and 21 are topical summaries of multiple Scripture passages. In such cases the preacher might introduce his sermon by informing the congregation of one or two pertinent texts that will be emphasized in his sermon (which, if changed yearly, will keep the sermon fresh), but that his message also relies on other Bible passages as well.

The problem with *always* requiring that catechism preaching be based on an individual text of Scripture is that textual analysis may have to be manipulated to fit the topical content. When the preacher attempts to juggle both a

---

70. Zylstra, "A Preferred Method," 18.

given text and a Lord's Day (one that does not lend itself to a combination method), the result is that neither the text nor the catechism is expounded well. The sermon may come across as jumbled and disorganized, leaving the congregants confused. Actually, the minister is trying to preach two sermons at once, forcing the text and the catechism together.[71]

In the final analysis, one particular method of catechism preaching should not be dogmatically asserted; rather, the text of the catechism should guide us to the most appropriate method. In long-term ministry, say, ten years or more, a preacher may find it helpful periodically to preach a topical series on a burning issue of the day. This will help him gain more diversity in catechism preaching. Such a series would expand the scope of the catechism material, and preaching on it would tend to become more exegetically based than more typical catechism preaching. For example, I once preached twenty-nine sermons based on LD 20 in which I explained from Scripture the work of the Holy Spirit in salvation, covering effectual calling, regeneration, faith, repentance, justification, sanctification, assurance, and perseverance. Another time, I preached nine sermons based on LD 35 on worship, covering private worship, family worship, and public or corporate worship. I have found that a congregation greatly appreciates a series that is clearly rooted in both Scripture and the catechism.

Finally, let me add a practical thought that is overlooked in the literature I have surveyed: *Each minister should ascertain his own gifts in catechism preaching and allow that to influence his approach.* For example, some of my colleagues in the ministry feel that their gifts are best exercised using a traditional synthetic approach with a strong emphasis on one Scripture text, whereas I, having taught seminary-level systematic theology for three decades, feel more comfortable expounding the catechism portion or Lord's Day as a comprehensive biblical statement of the doctrine it presents. Though we may vary our approaches according to the particular Lord's Day in hand, we may tend to gravitate toward those approaches we feel more gifted to use.

The Practical Aspects of Catechism Preaching

If catechism preaching is to be maintained as a vital part of the church's worship, we must in this final section address some practical questions about how it must be done.[72] Here are several helps:

---

71. W. Verboom, *Hulde aan de Heidelberger*, 92.

72. For this section, I have gleaned the most help from Peter Y. De Jong, "Comments on Catechetical Preaching (3)," *Mid-America Journal of Theology* 3, 1 (1987): 89–134.

First, catechism preaching must remain sermonic, that is, it must contain both *kerygma* (proclamation) and *didache* (instruction).[73] *Kerygma* is derived from the Greek *kerussein*, which means to proclaim as a herald. As a herald announces his lord's will with the authority invested in him, so the preacher proclaims God's Word with the authority invested in him by the Lord Jesus Christ as Head of the church. *Didache,* from which we derive "didactic," focuses on content, or instruction, in a sermon. As the assembly of Christ's disciples, the church is to be a learning community. Hence, every sermon must be preached with authority, and every sermon ought to instruct believers in the way of Christ. This is true of catechism sermons as well. De Jong writes, "For every catechetical sermon the *sine-qua-non* is that it shall be a 'sermon.'"[74] This caution may seem obvious; nevertheless, the tendency of a catechetical sermon is to be simply a theological exercise or doctrinal discourse. While instruction is important, the catechism preacher is far more than a teacher. He must speak as one sent from God, as the Lord's official representative. Preaching from the catechism is first and foremost preaching the whole counsel of God, in the name of Christ, and in the power of the Spirit.

Second, catechism preaching must be consistent. It must be thoroughly biblical, truly evangelical, warmly catholic, and distinctly Reformed. As indicated previously, catechism sermons are to declare the whole counsel of God given in Scripture. Such sermons, then, must not rely only on a select few texts or books of Scripture but must be grounded in the entire Word of God. Of course, every sermon cannot cover every text of Scripture or every doctrine in Scripture, yet regular, systematic preaching through the catechism relies on all sixty-six books of God's Word.

Third, catechetical preaching must be confrontational; it must challenge the listener experientially and practically. As I have written elsewhere, experiential preaching "aims to apply divine truth to the whole range of the believer's personal experience, including his relationships with his family, the church, and the world around him."[75] Preaching that stops at the expository or doctrinal level is not really preaching at all; it is mere lecturing. The truths gleaned from the catechism must be applied directly to listeners, whether they are believers or unbelievers. Catechism preaching must instruct, refute, rebuke, encourage, and comfort listeners, challenging them to live holy and Spirit-filled lives, for Christ's sake.

---

73. Cf. W. Verboom, *Hulde aan de Heidelberger,* 93–97.

74. Peter Y. De Jong, "Comments on Catechetical Preaching (3)," *Mid-America Journal of Theology* 3, 1 (1987): 90.

75. See my chapter "Applying the Word," in *Living for God's Glory,* 255–74 (quotation from 256).

Fourth, good catechism preaching must be structured. First, it must have a unified message. The preacher must set certain parameters for himself each time he preaches from the catechism. He should formulate a concise thematic statement that summarizes the message of the sermon, which he then successively unpacks and expands throughout the sermon. In addition, an effective sermon must have discernible progression rather than circling around a theme with endless repetition of statement. The theme of the sermon should be developed point by point. Such development was once called the "argument" of the sermon. The catechism sermon must also be focused and coherent. All parts of the catechetical sermon must be logically related.

Conclusion: Delight and Comfort in the Whole Counsel of God

Having preached the Heidelberg Catechism since 1978, I am convinced more than ever that good catechism preaching promotes the church's intellectual health, enhances its spiritual comfort, and increases the fruitfulness of the lives of its members. In light of its famous first question on the believer's comfort in life and death and its contents that repeatedly apply that comfort, the HC has understandably been called "the book of comfort" by Reformed believers. The authors of the HC have bequeathed to today's church a well-ordered summary of Reformed, biblical doctrine. As churches that recognize this document as a doctrinal standard, we ought to treasure this teaching, holding dear its valuable contents and faithfully transmitting it to the rising generation.

When our people hear the major doctrines of the Reformed faith expounded in sermons every twelve to twenty-four months, they will be better informed of their faith than those who sit under preaching where such teaching does not take place. In churches where catechetical preaching is not practiced, some doctrines may not be touched upon (depending on the pastor) for several years or even decades, whereas good catechetical preaching ensures the periodic repetition of nearly every major doctrine of the Bible.

Familiarizing our congregations with the Heidelberg Catechism need not breed contempt. Rather, good catechetical preaching should be: 1) varied, that is, approached from a different angle each time the preacher returns to a given Lord's Day; 2) fresh, due to further study that is put into a Lord's Day every time it is preached; 3) faithful, because it is preached biblically, doctrinally, practically, and experientially; 4) fervent, because motivated by the glory of God, and the love of God; and 5) relevant, preached in a way that it challenges the twenty-first century audience. Those of us who preach the catechism must do so as believers, students, theologians, pastors, and teachers, as instruments in

God's hand, seeking our own eternal welfare, as well as that of our flock.[76] If such catechetical preaching by such preachers were the norm today, the HC would never be disparaged as a document stuck in the distant past.

The Heidelberg Catechism, now more than 450 years old, has stood the test of time. It has comforted, instructed, exhorted, and matured countless Christians. It is our duty as heirs of God's covenant and the Reformed faith, to pass on to our children the truths conveyed so clearly in this confessional statement as a faithful summary of the "whole counsel of God." Let us delight in delivering and receiving this counsel through catechism preaching. Let us say to our children what Hermann Kohlbrugge (1801–1875) said on his deathbed, "The Heidelberger, children, the simple Heidelberger, hold to it firmly."[77]

---

76. W. Verboom, *Hulde aan de Heidelberger*, 171–80.

77. P. A. van Stempvoort in *H. F. Kohlbrugge*, cited in Verboom, *Hulde aan de Heidelberger*, 31–32.

Chapter 33

A Life in the Word

If you drew a picture of the ideal pastor, what would he look like? We have one such picture drawn for us by John Bunyan in *The Pilgrim's Progress*. Christian comes to the house of Interpreter, where he sees a picture on the wall. It shows a person who "had his eyes lifted up to heaven, the best of books in his hand, the law of truth was written upon his lips, the world was behind his back. [He] stood as if [he] pleaded with men, and a crown of gold did hang over [his] head."[1]

There is a glory about being called to preach the Word of God. As preachers, we are messengers of the Lord of hosts. We speak of heavenly and eternal realities. We proclaim the truth as ambassadors of the King of the angels.

At the same time, a preacher must bear the cross as he follows the Lord Jesus. Our calling is not to tickle men's ears with entertainment or doctrines that tolerate their lusts. We are evangelists in the City of Destruction. We call sinners to love the very God whom they by nature hate and to hate the very sins that they love. That inescapable conflict causes us to suffer both inwardly and outwardly. It can wear a man down and even tear him apart.

The glory and the cross of proclaiming God's Word is apparent in the calling of Ezekiel (Ezekiel 1–3). The book of Ezekiel opens with a majestic vision of God. The Lord appears as a man-like figure of burning fire, riding a heavenly chariot attended by mysterious cherubim resembling men, lions, oxen, and eagles all mixed together. What a glorious calling that was to speak for a glorious Lord! However, the Lord sent Ezekiel to prophesy to "impudent and stiffhearted" people (Ezek. 2:4). The opposition to his ministry was frightening.

---

1. John Bunyan, *The Pilgrim's Progress*, in *The Works of John Bunyan*, ed. George Offor (1854; repr., Edinburgh: Banner of Truth, 1991), 3:98. The pronouns in brackets originally were "it" or "its," referring to the portrait. Many thanks to Paul Smalley for his research assistance. I delivered a shortened form of this chapter to pastors and their wives at an NCFIC luncheon at Ridgecrest, North Carolina in 2014.

So was God's warning to Ezekiel that "briers and thorns" would be with him and he would "dwell among scorpions."

In the context of such a glorious but difficult ministry, God called Ezekiel to live in His Word and feed on His Word. This calling is stated concisely in Ezekiel 2:8, "But thou, son of man, hear what I say unto thee; be not thou rebellious like that rebellious house: open thy mouth, and eat that I give thee."

Although the calling of pastors today is not based on a supernatural vision of God, nevertheless, like Ezekiel, pastors and church members alike are called to live in the Word and to feed on the Word. We can discern three imperatives of this calling in Ezekiel 2:8: hear the Word, don't rebel against the Word, and eat the Word.

Hear the Word

We are to listen and learn from God through our reading and studying of Holy Scripture. Samuel modeled such a commitment when he responded to God's call by saying in 1 Samuel 3:9, "Speak, for thy servant heareth." Since we are not prophets or apostles, we do not hear God speak directly to us through new or immediate revelations. However, we do hear God speak every time the Bible is opened. We must thus listen to the Word. We must listen with understanding, interpreting the Bible according to what we call sound hermeneutical principles. *Hermeneutics* is a rather fancy word that simply means interpretation, or the science of interpretation. So, by sound hermeneutical principles we mean that when we hear or read the Bible we need to use proper means of interpreting it. What follows are seven principles for interpreting the Bible as we move through our three imperatives.

We must also listen with reverence, fear, love, and delight. Hearing the Word is no easy task for sinful people in a fallen world. God's specific words to Ezekiel teach us much about what it means to hear.

Hear the Word as a Son of Adam

The Lord addresses Ezekiel as "son of man" more than ninety times in this book. We may tend to think of the "Son of man" in terms of Daniel's vision of a glorious figure receiving all authority and dominion, which points us to Christ (Dan. 7:13–14). Here, however, the term has the lowly sense of Psalm 8:4, "What is man, that thou art mindful of him? And the son of man, that thou visitest him?" Quite literally, God called Ezekiel a "son of Adam," reminding us of our sinfulness and weakness, our inability and insufficiency. The Lord was reminding the prophet and us of who we are by nature: created, human, fallen, sinful mortals.

Here we see our first hermeneutic—our first principle of interpretation—that we must use in studying the Bible: the hermeneutic of *humility*. We must sit at Jesus's feet and wait on Him to teach us from the Word. Psalm 25:4–5 says, "Shew me thy ways, O LORD; teach me thy paths. Lead me in thy truth, and teach me: for thou art the God of my salvation; on thee do I wait all the day." This prayer is supported by God's promises in verses 8–9, "Good and upright is the LORD: therefore will he teach sinners in the way. The meek will he guide in judgment: and the meek will he teach his way." When you open the Bible, do you do so with an attitude that says, "Lord, I need Thee to teach me"? One test to determine that is how much time you spend praying for your studies in Scripture. Humility moves us to ask God, "Open thou mine eyes, that I may behold wondrous things out of thy law. Teach me, O LORD, the way of thy statutes; and I shall keep it unto the end" (Ps. 119:18, 33).

God speaks to us all through our text: "But thou, son of man, *hear*." Listen. Study. Think. Pray. Learn. That is especially true for office-bearers or teachers. William Greenhill wrote, "Those who are to teach others, must first hear and be taught themselves; they must hear Christ, and learn of him."[2]

We must read the Bible as sons of Adam. Do not read the Word as if you were somebody special but as a sinful human being created by God to serve Him. Let the Word master you. Seek to grasp its plain, literal meaning. That implies a second hermeneutical principle, which is *to interpret Scripture according to its literal sense*. If we are good listeners, we must pay attention to the words and sentences in their redemptive-historical contexts. We are sons of Adam, and God speaks to us in human language that follows the ordinary rules of grammar and communication. The Bible is not written in some kind of mysterious code. One of the great advances of the Reformed and Puritan hermeneutic over medieval Roman Catholicism was that the Reformers rejected the so-called fourfold sense of Scripture, which said the Bible not only has a literal meaning but also three more layers of spiritual meanings.[3] The result was often a neglect of the literal sense of the Word in favor of fanciful interpretations. In some respects, that created confusion between the primary meaning of the text and its many applications. We must not select the applications we want to make before we do the hard work of studying the text.

---

2. William Greenhill, *An Exposition of the Prophet Ezekiel*, ed. James Sherman (Edinburgh: James Nichol, 1864), 92.

3. The other three meanings were allegorical (Christ), tropological (morality), and anagogical (heaven). For a discussion of Puritan hermeneutics, including several of the principles mentioned in this article, see Joel R. Beeke and Mark Jones, *A Puritan Theology: Doctrine for Life* (Grand Rapids: Reformation Heritage Books, 2013), 27–40.

Our first calling is to listen, to learn, to allow God to teach us His Word and His agenda, and then to put it into practice. We must be like Ezra the scribe, who, as Ezra 7:10 says, "had prepared his heart to seek the law of the LORD, and to do it, and to teach in Israel statutes and judgments." We must live in the Word. Luke 8:18 says, "Take heed, therefore, how ye hear" the Word.

This ought to greatly impact how we come to church. Come prepared. Come hungry. Come with expectant faith. Come with a sense of the importance of what is about to take place, knowing that you are about to hear God's Word, and that every sermon counts for eternity. Enter the sanctuary knowing that you are entering a battlefield. Satan will do all he can to keep this Word from being applied to your soul.

Then, under the sermon, listen with a tender, understanding conscience. Listen attentively, not as a spectator but as a participant. Respond with repentance, resolution, or praise. Listen with submissive faith—with humility and self-examination. Ask after each sermon: How does God want me to be different after hearing this sermon?

Then, go out and practice the preached Word. Strive to retain it, and pray over what you have heard. Talk to your loved ones about what you have heard. Encourage your children to take notes with you, if that will help you and them to retain the message. Leaning on the Holy Spirit, strive to put the sermon into action. Do what you have heard. Obey the Word of God.

We must hear God's Word because we, the sons and daughters of Adam, were created to be God's servants. We must therefore approach the Bible saying with the psalmist, "O LORD, truly I am thy servant; I am thy servant" (Ps. 116:16).

Hear the Word as the Word of God

The Lord said to Ezekiel, "But thou, son of man, hear what *I* say unto thee." We must never forget who is speaking to us in Scripture: the Lord. This point would not have been lost on Ezekiel, who had just gotten up off his face before a Being so glorious that even His angelic servants were like flashes of lightning (Ezek. 1:14, 28). His presence was overwhelming. In Ezekiel 2:4, this Glorious One called Himself "the Lord GOD." The placing of "GOD" in capitals indicates His divine name, so "the Lord GOD" means Lord Jehovah, or the Sovereign Master who is I AM (cf. Ex. 3:14).[4] The book of Ezekiel uses that title 210 times; more than 70 percent of its usage in the Old Testament stresses God's Lordship.

---

4. The Hebrew is *Adonai Yahweh*.

The Lord Jehovah says to His servant, "Hear what I say unto thee." Therefore, a third hermeneutical principle is *the fear of the Lord.* "The fear of the LORD is the beginning of knowledge," says Proverbs 1:7. Whether we are reading the Bible in personal devotions or while preparing a sermon, we must always open the Bible with the perspective of Isaiah 66:1–2 in mind: "Thus saith the LORD, The heaven is my throne, and the earth is my footstool: where is the house that ye build unto me? And where is the place of my rest? For all those things hath mine hand made, and all those things have been, saith the LORD: but to this man will I look, even to him that is poor and of a contrite spirit, and trembleth at my word."

To fear God, John Brown said, is to value the smiles and frowns of God to be of greater weight and value than the smiles and frowns of men. That is how we should hear and read the Bible. Our consciousness of God profoundly shapes how we hear and read the Word. If we are big and God is small, then our words and actions will be full of man's wisdom and man's works. We will distort the God-centered message of the Bible into nonsense, such as the therapeutic, moralistic, pragmatic deism that characterizes too much of contemporary American religion.[5] If our hearts are impressed with God's holiness and majesty, then our lives will be full of God's glory and Christ's grace, which is the true message of the Scriptures.

The Westminster divines said, "The holy Scriptures are to be read with an high and reverent esteem of them, with a firm persuasion that they are the very word of God, and that he only can enable us to understand them; with desire to know, believe, and obey the will of God revealed in them; with diligence, and attention to the matter and scope of them; with meditation, application, self-denial, and prayer" (Larger Catechism, Q. 157).

Believing that all Scripture is inspired of Holy God will motivate us to believe and obey all that Scripture reveals. We will not meditate only on our favorite themes or quietly pass over those biblical teachings that make us uncomfortable. Old Testament scholar Daniel Bock translates "hear what I say unto thee" as "listen to *whatever* I declare to you."[6] May God grant us such a hearty and wholesome fear of Him that we can say at the end of our lives what Paul said of his ministry in Acts 20:27, "I have not shunned to declare unto you all the counsel of God." Expository preaching through books of the Bible helps

---

5. Michael Horton, "Are Churches Secularizing America?," *Modern Reformation* 17, no. 2 (March/ April 2008): 42–47, http://www.modernreformation.org/default.php?page=articledisplay&var1 =ArtRead&var2=917&var3=main (accessed October 3, 2014).

6. Emphasis added. Daniel I. Bock, *The Book of Ezekiel, Chapters 1–24,* The New International Commentary on the Old Testament (Grand Rapids: Eerdmans, 1997), 122n51.

us to do this, for it forces us to consider topics that we might not otherwise choose but will do so in the fear of God.

Hearing preaching that embraces the whole counsel of God includes a fourth hermeneutical principle, what the Westminster Confession of Faith calls *good and necessary consequence*, that is, whatever "by good and necessary consequence may be deduced from Scripture."[7] God's revealed will is not limited to what the Bible explicitly says but also includes what it clearly implies. The Bible itself teaches us to do this. For example, Jesus silenced the Sadducees by proving the resurrection of the dead by a logical deduction from God's statement, "I am the God of Abraham" for "God is not the God of the dead, but of the living" (Matt. 22:31–32). This principle is based on recognizing that God is the author of all Scripture, and, since He is "the all-wise God," as Ryan McGraw writes, "unlike human authors, God is aware of all of the consequences of His words."[8] Thus we must think about the logical implications of biblical teaching and how its doctrines fit together, for this too is part of what God reveals to us.

The fear of the Lord will also help develop our hermeneutical skills in a fifth way, most commonly described as *the analogy of Scripture*, that is, interpreting each part of Scripture in the light of the rest of Scripture. We must compare Scripture with Scripture, interpreting texts that are less clear or written in symbols and figures of speech with texts that are more literal. Though Scripture was written by many human authors, it had only one divine author, who does not contradict Himself. God is not a liar or a fool. We should not spin some bizarre interpretation from a text or passage that contradicts the teachings of the Bible as a whole.

The fear of the Lord will also help us to avoid being trivial in our preaching and our listening. We should speak and listen as those standing on tiptoes looking into the windows of heaven to see the glory of God. Since the great message of the Bible is the glory of God, all our preaching and listening should aim to reflect His glory. Martin Lloyd-Jones said,

> I can forgive a man for a bad sermon, I can forgive the preacher almost anything if he gives me a sense of God, if he gives me something for my soul, if he gives me the sense that, though he is inadequate himself, he is handling something which is very great and very glorious, if he gives me

---

7. Westminster Confession of Faith (1.6), in *Westminster Confession of Faith* (Glasgow: Free Presbyterian Publications, 1994), 22.

8. Ryan M. McGraw, *By Good and Necessary Consequence, Explorations in Reformed Confessional Theology* (Grand Rapids: Reformation Heritage Books, 2012), 27, 32.

some dim glimpse of the majesty and the glory of God, the love of Christ my Saviour, and the magnificence of the Gospel.[9]

The Lord of the universe has sent a message to the human race and has charged preachers to be His messengers and His people to be students of the Word. You and I must thus know His Word. As the great Puritan preacher William Perkins wrote in the flyleaf of his books, "Thou art a minister of the Word; mind thy business."[10] But that can also be said of church members: You are members of Christ's church, mind your business of hearing, studying, knowing, and loving His Word. Obey the Word of God to Ezekiel: "Son of man, hear what I say unto thee."

Be Not Rebellious

The second imperative in Ezekiel 2:8 is "Be not thou rebellious like that rebellious house." The essence of rebellion is rejecting the Word of God as the binding rule for life (1 Sam. 15:22–23; Neh. 9:16–17; Isa. 30:9–10). Ezekiel 20:13 says, "But the house of Israel rebelled against me in the wilderness: they walked not in my statutes, and they despised my judgments." We will consider this command both in its individual focus and in its social implications.

Be Not Rebellious in Your Fallen Condition

When the Lord said to Ezekiel, "Be thou not rebellious," He was warning His prophet to keep watch against the sinful corruption of his soul and its resistance to the Word of God. He was also telling Ezekiel to put this corruption to death. The fundamental problem that preachers and all believing church members face is not the intellectual difficulty of interpreting and applying the Word to ourselves and to each other, although that is hard work. Our main problem is the sin that dwells within us, which fights against the very Word that we are called to preach or to hear. Our sin blinds us to the true meaning of the Word and its implications for our lives and stirs up unbelief and resentment against the doctrines revealed by God, as well as turns us away from our task of clearly applying the Word to ourselves and to others.

We must approach the Bible conscious both of our fall and of Christ's work of redemption. This brings us to a sixth hermeneutical principle of biblical interpretation, which is to recognize continually in our Bible study the two overarching covenants of the Bible: *the covenant of works* and *the covenant of*

---

9. D. Martyn Lloyd-Jones, *Preaching and Preachers* (Grand Rapids: Zondervan, 1971), 98.

10. Ian Breward, "The Life and Theology of William Perkins, 1558–1602" (PhD diss., University of Manchester, 1963), 35.

grace. Adam broke the covenant of works in the garden of Eden, and Christ established the covenant of grace upon the cross. Believers of all ages have rested by faith in that covenant of grace, first revealed as the promise in Genesis 3:15, and then in subsequent historical covenants. We must constantly remember that we by nature are covenant-breakers who by grace must learn from Christ to be covenant-keepers.

It is relevant here, too, that God addressed Ezekiel as "son of Adam." We all read the Bible as sons or daughters of Adam who have fallen into sin and misery through Adam's rebellion. We are not neutral, independent observers of the text. Even when by grace we have been born again into a sincere love for God, we still find the dilemma of Romans 7:14–25 true of each of us experientially. The law of God provokes the remaining sin in us to further rebellion, and the same law condemns the sins within us. On the one hand, believers delight greatly in the Word of God, while on the other hand, we discover to our horror that studying the Word exacerbates our inward struggle with sin and guilt. We must pray for grace that we may win the battle against sin by persevering in faith and self-denial.

The alternative to internal combat is hypocrisy. Rebellion need not be a scandalous crime or blatant rejection of the faith; it can merely be selective obedience (1 Sam. 15:1–23). When God commanded Ezekiel, "Be thou not rebellious," most likely Ezekiel was not in danger of completely rejecting the Lord and turning to idol worship but, rather, shrinking back from fully declaring the revealed will of God. Greenhill said,

> We think it must be some great, notorious thing that makes a rebel or rebellious; but there is great difference between the judgment of men and judgment of God. If Ezekiel should be difficult and backward to his work he called him unto, he would count it rebellion; if he would not hear and do what God bid him, he should be numbered among the rebellious…. If there should be a crossing of God's will in anything, in the least thing, in refusing to hear or do, it should be before him rebellion.[11]

How can we live in the Word when we as heirs of Adam are rebels by nature? The only answer is that we must rely on the covenant of grace. By faith we must grasp hold of the promises of Jesus Christ. When the Bible impresses upon us the guilt of our sins, we must flee to the blood of Jesus Christ as our only righteousness. When we find ourselves secretly rebelling against the very

---

11. Greenhill, *Ezekiel*, 93.

Word that we must preach or listen to being preached, we must seek the Spirit of holiness through Jesus Christ.

Ezekiel's obedience to the Word was only possible through the power of the Spirit. We see that visually demonstrated in Ezekiel 2:1–2, which says, "And he said unto me, Son of man, stand upon thy feet, and I will speak unto thee. And the spirit entered into me when he spake unto me, and set me upon my feet, that I heard him that spake unto me." God spoke the Word, and the Spirit empowered Ezekiel to obey the Word. Just as the dry bones came to life in chapter 37, Ezekiel became a living example of how the Lord puts His Spirit in people, and those cast down in death rise up to live for the Lord (Ezek. 37:14). We also hear this principle proclaimed later in Ezekiel 36:27, "And I will put my spirit within you, and cause you to walk in my statutes, and ye shall keep my judgments, and do them." Iain Duguid writes that Ezekiel is a "model of Spirit-infused submission," a prime "member of a new community, empowered by the infusion of the divine Spirit to a life of radical obedience."[12]

As those fallen under the covenant of works and redeemed under the covenant of grace, we must study the Word prayerfully. John Owen said he who desires to study the Scriptures with confidence to avoid serious error and find true spiritual knowledge must "abide in fervent supplications, in and by Jesus Christ, for supplies of the Spirit of grace, to lead him into all truth." On the other hand, Owen warned that any man who undertakes to interpret any portion of Scripture without praying to God for the Holy Spirit to instruct him greatly provokes God, for he acts in pride and ignorance.[13] That does not mean we should wait passively for some mystical experience to show us what the Bible means. We must fully engage our minds and hearts to interpret the Bible, reading the text, meditating on its meaning and application, reading a good study Bible, good commentaries and theological books—all in utter dependence on the supernatural work of the Spirit to illumine our minds.[14] Remember Johann Bengel's dictum: "Apply thy whole self to the [study of] the text; apply the whole matter of it to thyself."[15]

---

12. Iain M. Duguid, *The NIV Application Commentary: Ezekiel* (Grand Rapids: Zondervan, 1999), 69.

13. John Owen, *The Causes, Ways, and Means of Understanding the Mind of God as Revealed in His Word*, in *The Works of John Owen*, ed. William H. Goold (1850–1853; repr., Edinburgh: Banner of Truth, 1967), 4:204–5.

14. See Beeke and Jones, *A Puritan Theology*, 38–40.

15. *Te totum applica ad textum; rem totam applica ad te;* from the preface of his *Handbook for the Greek New Testament*, 1734.

God rightly warns the prophet as well as preachers of the Word, "Be thou not rebellious," for we must live in the Word with a profound awareness of our fallenness and need for God's grace and Holy Spirit.

Be Not Rebellious in a Fallen World

God said to Ezekiel, "Be not thou rebellious like that rebellious house." The Lord specifically addressed Ezekiel as "thou" in contrast to the people around him,[16] for Ezekiel's prophecy refers to Israel as a "rebellious house" thirteen times.[17] Israel was the visible church at that time, yet it stubbornly resisted God's Word (Ezek. 2:3–4). But God sent the prophet to Israel. Ezekiel's fellow Jews would oppose him with scornful words and hateful resentment, but he had to continue preaching the Word of God to them (Ezek. 2:6).

Preachers are under constant pressure to please people. Greenhill said the "example of others is like a mighty torrent that carries down all before it."[18] Flood waters have immense force to move boulders, uproot trees, and destroy buildings and bridges. Scientists tell us that a mere six inches of fast-moving flood water can knock over an adult.[19] When preachers attempt to stand against popular tastes, prejudices, preferences, or practices, we are like men trying to wade upstream through a flood.

When we realize that preaching the Word may offend people in our community or our congregation, our natural tendency will be either to conform to men's customs and expectations or to break out against the world with the pride of man-made zeal. Both of these reactions are rebellion.

We must speak the truth in love (Eph. 4:15), and our people must receive it in love. Paul wrote in 2 Timothy 2:24–25, "The servant of the Lord must not strive; but be gentle unto all men, apt to teach, patient, in meekness instructing those that oppose themselves; if God peradventure [perhaps] will give them repentance to the acknowledging of the truth." How is this possible? Verse 1 says, "Thou therefore, my son, be strong in the grace that is in Christ Jesus." Like Ezekiel, we must gaze upon the glory of Jesus Christ and find strength in Him.

Greenhill imagined how Christ might answer our fears about preaching the truth in the face of opposition. We might say, "Lord, if I preach this I will lose my friends," but Christ would answer, "I am your friend, your best friend." We might say, "I will alienate my family from me," but Christ replies, "I am your

---

16. In Hebrew, "but thou" (*ve-attah*) appears at the very beginning of Ezek 2:8 for emphasis.

17. Ezek. 2:5, 6, 8; 3:9, 26, 27; 12:2, 3, 9, 25; 17:12; 24:3.

18. Greenhill, *Ezekiel*, 93.

19. National Weather Service, "Turn Around, Don't Drown," http://www.nws.noaa.gov/os/water/tadd/tadd-intro.shtml (accessed October 6, 2014).

Kinsman, for I took your very nature to suffer for you and make you a child of God." We might say, "Great and powerful men will become my enemies," but Christ says, "I am greater than they, and my throne is above all thrones."[20]

The Lord later promised Ezekiel that He would make his face "harder than flint" to confront the rebels of Israel (Ezek. 3:8–9). That same spirit characterized Jesus Christ: for all His compassion and tenderness of heart, He set His face as flint in suffering and death to fulfill His calling (Luke 9:51). Isaiah 50:5–7 says, "The Lord GOD hath opened mine ear, and I was not rebellious, neither turned away back. I gave my back to the smiters, and my cheeks to them that plucked off the hair: I hid not my face from shame and spitting. For the Lord GOD will help me; therefore shall I not be confounded: therefore have I set my face like a flint, and I know that I shall not be ashamed." Christ can make us tough as rock, too, for His truth, since His Spirit dwells in those who believe.

Therefore, we ministers must preach what God tells us to preach. Greenhill said, "Do not make the manners of the world the rule of your life, nor the worship of the world the rule of your worship, but look higher."[21] The Lord says, "Be not thou rebellious like that rebellious house." By the grace of the Spirit of Jesus Christ, fight the good fight and finish the race.

Eat the Word

The third imperative of our calling is found in the closing words of Ezekiel 2:8: "Open thy mouth, and eat what I give thee." That is a strange command, but it fits with the many symbolic visions and actions in the book of Ezekiel. The prophet saw the Lord holding in His hand a scroll, written on the inside and outside with sad words of judgment. God told Ezekiel to eat the scroll, and when he ate it, it was sweet as honey (Ezek. 2:9–3:3). What does this vision mean for us?

Eat the Word with an Open Heart of Faith

The Lord says to us, "Open thy mouth." Often in Scripture opening one's mouth is an expression for someone preparing to speak (Ezek. 3:27).[22] The mouth or speech of God's servant must be consecrated to Him, as we see by Isaiah's lamentation of unclean lips and his experience of purging (Isa. 6:5–8), and God's touching Jeremiah's mouth and saying that the Lord has put His words in the prophet's mouth (Jer. 1:9). However, Ezekiel's mouth must also

---

20. Adapted from Greenhill, *Ezekiel*, 93.

21. Greenhill, *Ezekiel*, 93.

22. See also Num. 22:28; Judg. 11:35–36; Job 3:1; 33:2; 35:16; Pss. 35:21; 38:13; 39:9; 51:15; 78:2; 109:2; Prov. 31:26; Matt. 5:2; 13:35; Acts 8:35; Eph. 6:19; etc.

be open to receive food. Before he can speak forth the truth with his mouth, he must eat the truth. As God's messenger, the words that he speaks must not be his own but the Lord's.

So open your mouth with desire to eat the truth, whether you are a minister, a teacher, or a lay person. Come to the Bible with hunger and thirst (Job 29:23). Psalm 119:131 says, "I opened my mouth, and panted: for I longed for thy commandments." Beware of approaching the Bible with a lack of appetite for the Bible. If you are not hungry for it, confess your sinful indifference and pray for God's Spirit to fill you with hunger and thirst for righteousness.

Come to the Word with faith, and expect that God will bless you spiritually. Psalm 81:10–11 says, "I am the LORD thy God, which brought thee out of the land of Egypt: open thy mouth wide, and I will fill it. But my people would not hearken to my voice; and Israel would none of me." The Lord is a faithful covenant God and the redeemer of His people. He does not tell people to seek Him in vain, so we must take Him and His Word with the open mouth of faith.

Read the Scriptures with a particular hunger for Christ, for Christ alone is the bread of life for our souls. John 6:35 says Christ promises, "I am the bread of life: he that cometh to me shall never hunger; and he that believeth on me shall never thirst." When we study the Bible, we must remember that the great theme of all Scripture is Christ. The Lord Jesus said in John 5:39, "Search the scriptures; for in them ye think ye have eternal life: and they are they which testify of me."

No hermeneutical principle is more important than this seventh one: *the centrality of Jesus Christ in all Scripture*, both the Old and New Testaments.[23] The Old Testament contains many promises of the coming Messiah and many types of Christ. They include divinely designed people, institutions, or events that imperfectly but truly foreshadow Jesus Christ. Thus, Jesus indicated that the angels ascending and descending on Jacob's ladder foreshadowed Him as the mediator between heaven and earth (Gen. 28:12; John 1:51). Israel finding healing by looking at the bronze serpent on the pole also foreshadowed the crucified Christ (Num. 21:8–9; John 3:14–15).

The Bible offers the food and drink of life eternal through Christ. Thomas Adams said, "This blessed Christ is the sole paragon of our joy, the fountain of life, the foundation of all blessedness. He is the sum of the whole Bible.... Christ

---

23. Luke 24:27, 44; Acts 3:18; 1 Cor. 2:2; 2 Tim. 3:15.

is the main, the center whither all these lines are referred."[24] To receive Christ with an open heart of faith, we must study the Bible to feed upon Christ.

Eat the Word with the Digestion of Meditation

The Lord also said to Ezekiel, "Eat what I give thee." The picture is of taking something into your mouth, chewing it and swallowing it. What is more, Ezekiel 3:3 speaks of not just eating with the "mouth" but also with the "belly" and "bowels." The picture here is of complete digestion and assimilation so that what is eaten enters every part of your being and becomes incorporated into who you are. It implies more than a superficial contact with the Word; it is a process of thinking about the Word, engaging in it with one's affections and will, and repeatedly putting it into practice to form habits of godliness.

This process of spiritual digestion is what we call meditation. Greenhill explained, "Digest the truths thou hearest, by serious meditation, and by faith that they may become thy nutriment, and thou mayst feel the power and efficacy of them in thy heart, and act accordingly."[25]

Meditation on the Word is much neglected today, but the Puritans offer some helpful principles to get started.[26] They said to begin by asking the Holy Spirit for assistance. As Edmund Calamy wrote, "I would have you pray unto God to enlighten your understandings, to quicken your devotion, to warm your affections, and so to bless that hour unto you, that by the meditation of holy things you may be made more holy, you may have your lusts more mortified, and your graces more increased, you may be the more mortified to the world, and the vanity of it, and lifted up to Heaven, and the things of Heaven."[27]

The Puritans said that the next step is to read the Scriptures, then select a verse or doctrine on which to meditate. Choose relatively easy subjects to meditate on at the beginning, they advised. In addition, select subjects that are most applicable to your present circumstances and will be most beneficial for your soul. For example, if you are spiritually dejected, meditate on Christ's willingness to receive poor sinners and pardon all who come to Him. If your conscience troubles you, meditate on God's promises to give grace to the penitent. If you

---

24. Thomas Adams, *Meditations upon Some Part of the Creed*, in *The Works of Thomas Adams* (1861–1866; repr., Eureka, Ca.: Tanski, 1998), 3:224.

25. Greenhill, *Ezekiel*, 96.

26. The following section is adapted from Beeke and Jones, "The Puritan Practice of Meditation," in *A Puritan Theology*, 897–99.

27. Edmund Calamy, *The Art of Divine Meditation* (London: for Tho. Parkhurst, 1634), 172.

are financially afflicted, meditate on God's wonderful providences to those in need.[28]

Now, memorize the selected verse(s), or some aspect of the subject to stimulate meditation, to strengthen faith, and to serve as a means of divine guidance. Then, fix your thoughts on the Scripture or a scriptural subject without prying further than what God has revealed. Like Mary, ponder these things in your heart. Think of illustrations, comparisons, and opposites in your mind to enlighten your understanding.

Next, stir up affections such as love, desire, hope, courage, gratitude, zeal, and joy, to glorify God. Taste the goodness of God in the text (1 Peter 2:2–3). Ezekiel found when he ate the Word that "it was in my mouth as honey for sweetness" (Ezek. 3:3). Jeremiah 15:16 says, "Thy words were found, and I did eat them; and thy word was unto me the joy and rejoicing of mine heart: for I am called by thy name, O LORD God of hosts."

Now, stir your soul to do your duty by holy resolutions and plans. Ask practical questions. Greenhill said, "The word of God should be in our hearts, in our heads, in our lips, in our lives."[29] Reflect on the past and ask, "What have I done?" Look to the future, asking, "What am I resolved to do, by God's grace?" Follow Calamy's advice, "If ever you would get good by the practice of meditation, you must come down to *particulars*; and you must so meditate of Christ, as to apply Christ to thy soul; and so meditate of Heaven, as to apply Heaven to thy soul."[30]

Conclude with prayer, thanksgiving, and psalm singing. "Meditation is the best beginning of prayer, and prayer is the best conclusion of meditation," wrote George Swinnock.[31] Thomas Watson said, "Prayer fastens meditation upon the soul; prayer is a tying a knot at the end of meditation that it doth not slip."[32]

Joseph Hall found much comfort in closing his meditations by lifting up his "heart and voice to God in singing some verse or two of David's Psalms — one that answers to our disposition and the matter of our meditation. In this way the heart closes up with much sweetness and contentment."[33] Thomas Cranmer composed a prayer that might well be used by us every day to study God's

---

28. Calamy, *The Art of Divine Meditation*, 164–68.

29. Greenhill, *Ezekiel*, 97.

30. Calamy, *The Art of Divine Meditation*, 108.

31. George Swinnock, *The Christian Man's Calling*, in *The Works of George Swinnock* (1868; repr., Edinburgh: Banner of Truth, 1992), 1:112.

32. Thomas Watson, *A Christian on the Mount, or A Treatise Concerning Meditation*, in *Discourses on Important and Interesting Subjects* (1829; repr., Ligonier, Penn.: Soli Deo Gloria, 1990), 269.

33. Joseph Hall, *The Art of Meditation* (Jenkintown, Penn.: Sovereign Grace, 1972), 26–27.

Word: "Blessed Lord, who hast caused all holy Scriptures to be written for our learning; Grant that we may in such wise hear them, read, mark, learn, and inwardly digest them, that by patience and comfort of thy holy Word, we may embrace, and ever hold fast, the blessed hope of everlasting life, which thou hast given us in our Saviour Jesus Christ. Amen."[34]

God promises to bless the believer who meditates regularly on Scripture (Josh. 1:8). Psalm 1:1–3, which describes a tree flourishing and bearing fruit by a continual source of life, is a metaphor for the true believer:

> That man is blest who, fearing God, from sin restrains his feet,
> Who will not stand with wicked men, who shuns the scorners' seat.
>
> Yea, blest is he who makes God's law his portion and delight,
> And meditates upon that law with gladness day and night.
>
> That man is nourished like a tree set by the river's side;
> Its leaf is green, its fruit is sure, and thus his works abide.[35]

All this, of course, is particularly true for a pastor. The messenger of God must digest a message before he can deliver it. Greenhill said, "When ministers and messengers of God have eaten and digested the truths of God, then they are fit to go and preach them to the people of God."[36] Preachers are less like chefs who prepare meals for other people than like nursing mothers (1 Thess. 2:7–8). Greenhill said that if a mother does not eat and digest her food, she will not have nutritious milk to feed her baby.[37] Therefore, we must not merely arrange the Word into sermons. We must eat the Word.

"But," perhaps you say, "that's just my problem. I'm not a minister. Finding my life in the Bible and reading it every day, and eating it by faith, and meditating on it—that all is so difficult for me. I know I should do it, but when I try, I often get nothing out of it. Can you give me some practical helps how to do this?"

Practical Helps for Reading the Bible

You're not alone. Let me say first of all: If we are going to be successful in attempting to read the Bible, we must discipline ourselves. Lots of people have had good intentions for reading the Bible but have ultimately given up on it. We need God's grace if we are to make any progress in Bible reading, and we

---

34. "Collect for the Second Sunday in Advent," *Book of Common Prayer*.

35. *The Psalter with Doctrinal Standards, Liturgy, Church Order, and Added Chorale Section*, rev. ed. (Grand Rapids: Eerdmans, 1965), 1.

36. Greenhill, *Ezekiel*, 96.

37. Greenhill, *Ezekiel*, 97.

certainly need it if we are going to benefit from our reading. Reading the Bible isn't a goal in itself; the goal is communion with God. If reading the Bible doesn't bring you into communion with God, then it's a failure. The goal is communion, not completing a checklist of passages read. It takes God's grace to truly read the Bible profitably. But the Bible itself is a channel of grace! It's a blessed circular system. You need grace for reading the Word, but grace comes through the Word. So get into the Word!

Grace is primary, but there are some very practical things you can do to help yourself read the Bible regularly and profitably:

Commit to a Time

The first and most important thing to do is to set a time. There are so many things that we have to do and so many things that we like to do that, unless we plan carefully, we'll never have any time left for reading our Bibles. So we need to plan. If reading the Bible is at the bottom of our priority lists, if we plan to do that after we've done everything else, we won't do it at all. Think about your day, and pick a time for reading your Bible. Read your Bible at that time, and don't let anything else crowd into it.

Find a Place

The second thing to do is to think of the best place to read your Bible, a place with no distractions. Don't try to read your Bible while sitting next to your son who's playing a video game. It won't work; you'll be hopelessly distracted.

Develop a Plan

Third, set a plan. A reading plan helps you know what you've read and what you haven't. If you just randomly flip open your Bible every day, there will be many portions of Scripture that you will never read. If you have no plan and you're wondering what to read one day, how likely are you to flip to Lamentations or 3 John? Not very. But if you don't read all the parts of the Bible, you will never develop a sense for its grand, overarching story. There are lots of Bible-reading plans you can use, but a good one to start out with is a plan that takes you through the entire Bible in a year. A through-the-Bible plan makes sure that you read every part of Scripture. Did you know that you can read through the entire Bible in one year by spending only fifteen minutes reading each day? There are 1,440 minutes in one day. If you use only fifteen of those minutes every day to read the Bible, which is about 1 percent of your time, you can read through the whole Word of God in one year. So plan your Bible reading. You'll never have to wonder what to read next; you'll always know what you've read and what you haven't.

How to Read

But how should we read? One of the most helpful little books on reading the Scriptures was penned by the Puritan Richard Greenham (ca. 1535–1594) under the title *A Profitable Treatise, Containing a Direction for the Reading and Understanding of the Holy Scriptures*. He gives us eight helps for how to read the Bible, each of which can be summarized in one word. Here they are:

Diligence

Diligence must be pursued in reading the Scriptures more than in doing anything secular. We ought to read and study our Bibles with more diligence than men dig for hidden treasure, Greenham says. Diligence makes rough places plain, makes the difficult easy, makes the unsavory tasty.

Wisdom

Wisdom must be used in the choice of matter, order, and time. Though we must read all the Bible, as we have seen, it is not wise to spend most of our reading time on the hardest parts of Scripture. In terms of order, Greenham agrees that we should have a system that helps us get through the whole Bible, since only a whole Bible will make a whole Christian. As for time, no day should pass without reading the Bible.

Preparation

Proper preparation is critical. Without it, Scripture reading is seldom blessed. Preparation involves three things. First, we must approach Scripture with reverence, determined like Mary to lay up God's Word in our hearts (Luke 2:19). Second, we must approach Scripture with faith in Christ, looking to Him as the Messiah who can open our hearts just as He did for the disciples traveling to Emmaus (Luke 24:27). Third, we must approach Scripture with a sincere desire in our hearts to be taught by God (Prov. 17:16) and with a longing to study it in detail. Martin Luther said he studied the Bible in the same way he gathered apples: "First, I shake the whole tree that the ripest may fall. Then I shake each limb, and when I have shaken each limb I shake each branch and every twig. Then I look under every leaf."[38]

---

38. Blanchard, *Complete Gathered Gold*, 60.

Meditation

Read slowly, thoughtfully, and meditatively. Some portions of Scripture—the book of Proverbs, for example—need to be read extra slowly to allow time for meditating on each verse. It is better to read five verses from Proverbs with meditation and prayer than one hundred without them.

Meditating on what we read in the Bible is critical. You can read diligently, but the reading will bear no fruit if you don't stop to think about and study what you have read. Reading may give you some breadth of knowledge, but only meditation and study will give you depth. The difference between reading and meditation is like the difference between drifting and rowing toward a destination in a boat. If you only read, you will drift aimlessly; if you meditate and pray over what you read, you will have oars that will propel you to your destination.

Fellowship

Greenham actually calls this "conference," but he means that you should fellowship with others about what you read in the Bible. You should especially talk with other believers about the truths of the Bible. That will help you grow in knowledge. Proverbs 27:17 says it this way: "Iron sharpeneth iron: so a man sharpeneth the countenance of his friend."

Faith

Our Scripture reading must be mixed with faith. Faith is the key to getting real profit from reading the Bible (Heb. 4:2); without it, it is impossible to please God (Heb. 11:6). "To read without faith is to walk in darkness," said Luther. It is to read in vain. By faith, as Horatius Bonar said, "we must not only lay the Bible up within us, but transfuse it through the whole texture of the soul."[39]

Practice

The fruit of faith must be practice; the read Word must be done. Dr. Martyn Lloyd-Jones wrote, "It is a good thing to be a student of the Word, but only in order to be a practiser and experiencer of the Word."[40]

We must read the Word with the goal of obeying it. We must prayerfully aim for believing obedience, willing obedience, submissive obedience, loving obedience, wholehearted obedience, prayerful obedience, dependent obedience, and childlike obedience. The more we put the Word into practice in the daily obedience of faith, the more God will increase our gifts for His service and for

---

39. Blanchard, *Complete Gathered Gold*, 59.
40. Blanchard, *Complete Gathered Gold*, 60.

additional practice. When the Spirit sheds light upon our conscience that we are "doing" the read Word, we also receive the great benefit of being assured that we possess faith.

This means that we must examine ourselves by what we read. For example, if you read Proverbs 3:5, "Trust in the LORD with all thine heart; and lean not unto thine own understanding," pause to ask yourself: Am I, by grace, trusting in the Lord? What areas of my life am I not surrendering to Him? In what areas am I not putting this text into practice but, instead, leaning to my own understanding? Then repent of these things, and turn to God in prayer for forgiveness and for strength to change.

Prayer

Prayer is essential throughout our reading of Scripture, for we are dependent on the Holy Spirit to enlighten us, to give us understanding, and to apply the Word to our souls and lives. Pray before you read the Bible, while you read it, and after you read it. In public reading of Scripture, it is not possible to pause and pray after each verse. In private reading, feel free to salt Scripture constantly with short, pungent, applicable petitions suggested by the particular verses being considered.

If we pray for nourishment from our physical food at every meal, shouldn't we pray much more for spiritual nourishment from every Bible reading? If we do not dare touch our food and drink before we pray, how do we dare touch God's holy Book—our spiritual food and drink—without prayer?

If the Bible is to get into us, we must get into it. Charles Spurgeon said, "Backsliders begin with dusty Bibles and end with filthy garments."[41] Read and study the Bible to be wise; believe it to be safe; practice it to be holy. Lay hold of it until it lays hold of you.

Practical Helps for Studying the Bible

I've already implied that your reading of the Bible will be greatly enhanced if you study the Bible as you read it. But how should you study it? Here are a few helpful hints:

Study one book of the Bible at a time

Read a good introduction to each book. These introductions provide introductory material on each Bible book, showing you its major themes, purposes, and outline. Read this first. Then, read the Bible book, along with the study notes,

---

41. Blanchard, *Complete Gathered Gold*, 62.

so that you get a good grasp of the book's outline, flow, and themes. Ask yourself questions like these: Are there words or phrases that keep reappearing? What do they mean? For example, in Ephesians you notice the frequency of the phrase "in Christ"; in Philippians, it is the word *joy*. As you read the text and the notes together, apply what you are discovering to your own heart and life. Returning to Philippians for a moment, you cannot help but notice that Paul has great joy even as he writes this epistle from prison. The message is clear: true Christians can triumph over adversity. Ask yourself: Am I doing that right now in my life? How could I do it better?

Then, read through the Bible book once more, this time with a few good commentaries by your side, or perhaps a series of sermons, and go slowly, prayerfully, and meditatively. Purchase and use John Calvin's, Matthew Henry's, and Matthew Poole's commentaries on the whole Bible as well as the best commentaries on individual Bible books that your financial means will allow. They can be of great help to you. Speak to others about your study or, better yet, join a Bible study group that is seriously studying this book.

Study one chapter at a time
Here are ten questions to ask of every chapter of Scripture:

1. *What does this chapter teach me about God?* Look for teaching about His attributes, attitudes, and actions.

2. *Specifically, what does this chapter reveal about Christ?* Look for Christ in all the Scriptures, including the Old Testament. He is the key to and the message of the entire Bible (Acts 10:43).

3. *What doctrines are taught in this chapter?* Make a list of them with relevant quotations from the chapter and any cross references you may know.

4. *Who are the leading characters?*

5. *What are the main events?*

6. *What sins and follies are stated or implied?* Examine your heart in the light of this list. Which things in the list, or suggested by it, do you need to confess and forsake?

7. *What are the virtues evidenced in this chapter that I should seek after and cultivate?*

8. *What new thing have I seen, and what old truth has the Lord brought with fresh blessing to my heart?*

9. *What are the key words and phrases that call for further study?*

10. *What two or three things may I remember this chapter by, and how may I apply them to my life?* Given your background, your circumstances, and your challenges, ask yourself: What are these particular words and this particular verse saying to me in a practical way today? Can I grow in my knowledge of a particular doctrine from this verse? Does the study of this verse prompt me to see some guidance for my daily life—perhaps something to be thankful for or some change that must be made, by the strength of the Spirit? Is there some sin exposed here that I must fight more earnestly, some righteousness that I must pursue more aggressively, some promise that I must embrace more fully? What should I experience from studying this verse? How should I feel concerning this passage? Should I respond with joy, sorrow, or a mixture of the two?

Study individual words and verses
We grow in depth in our Bible study when we look carefully at individual words and verses in their biblical context. Assuming you have not studied Old Testament Hebrew or New Testament Greek, the best way you can do this is by purchasing three books: *Strong's Concordance; Theological Wordbook of the Old Testament (TWOT)* by Harris, Archer, and Waltke; and *Vine's Expository Dictionary of Biblical Words.* Begin by looking up key words of a text in *Strong's,* then use the number just to the right of the word entry to look up the fuller meaning of that word in the back, as well as in *TWOT* for Old Testament words and in *Vine's* for New Testament words.

Then make a list of the word in its contexts. Study the contexts for clues to its meaning. Find clear passages to illustrate the senses you have seen in the word. This may seem a bit tedious at first, but if you persist, you will soon find it stimulating and exciting.

As you study, ask questions. Given the meaning of these words, what is the text saying? What is God's particular message in this particular verse located in this particular chapter? What is the doctrine being explained? What experience of believers is being opened up?

Study various subjects in the Bible
There are thousands of exciting subjects to study in the Bible. Many of them are doctrines—such as the sovereignty of God or the intercession of Christ. Others are practical topics, such as how Christians should cope with suffering. Or you might want to study an individual Bible character, such as Noah, Elijah, or Peter. Above all, don't forget to make Jesus Christ, the Living Word, your

supreme object of study. Study Christ in His person, offices, states, natures, and benefits. Study His character. Study His parables and miracles.

Conclusion

Hearing, reading, and eating the Bible by faith can be hard work, but it is definitely worth the effort. There are so many reasons to do so. It's the Word of God Himself! Read the Bible because it can give you, with the Spirit's blessing, real truth, real joy, and real wisdom. It can make you wise to life eternal. Listen to it, read it, and pray for grace to drink it in even when you don't feel like it. By the grace of God in Jesus Christ, you will find joy in that Word—a world of joy. The Bible is able not only to give you a world of joy and a life of joy but also an eternity of joy.

Know your Bible, search your Bible, meditate on your Bible, love your Bible, obey your Bible, live your Bible. It will bless you abundantly, both for this life and for a better life to come. I pray to God that you will find your life, put your life, and live your life in the Word of God. Hear the Word, do not rebel against it, and eat it spiritually by faith.

Chapter 34

Why You and Your Family Should Go to Church:
Biblical Answers to "Churchless Christianity"

Since ancient times, God's people have gathered for worship and service under leaders appointed by God (Gen. 4:26). God ordained these assemblies in the tabernacle, priesthood, and feasts of Israel, and later in the temple.[1] When the Lord Jesus came in the flesh, He said, "I will build my church, and the gates of hell shall not prevail against it" (Matt. 16:18).

The universal church throughout the world manifests itself in local congregations, which Scripture calls "the churches,"[2] such as "the churches of Galatia," "the churches of Asia," or "the churches of Judea."[3] The New Testament assumes that every true disciple of Jesus will participate in a local church and be subject to its discipline (Matt. 18:17). Notice how Paul addresses the Philippians: "To all the saints in Christ Jesus which are at Philippi, with the bishops [elders] and deacons" (Phil. 1:1). This statement reflects the New Testament pattern: The apostles "ordained elders in every church" (Acts 14:23) and organized believers into congregations under their leadership. Acts 2 says that the Lord added converts to the church when He saved them (Acts 2:40, 47). When Christ saves a sinner, He does not leave the sinner alone but adds him to the church. Thus from beginning to end, God wills that His people are gathered into the fellowship of local churches.

---

1. Over time, the Jews increasingly organized their gatherings around the synagogues, local assemblies for prayer and instruction (cf. Ps. 74:8). Christianity started in the synagogues as Jesus Christ preached to His fellow Jews (Luke 4:15–16). When the Pharisees put Christ's disciples out of the synagogues, the disciples formed assemblies of their own. James uses the Greek word συναγωγή when describing the "assembly" of Christians (James 2:2).

2. Acts 9:31; 15:41; 16:5; Rom. 16:4, 16; 1 Cor. 7:17; 11:16; 14:33; 2 Cor. 8:1, 18–19; 11:28; 1 Thess. 2:14; 2 Thess. 1:4; Rev. 1:4; chs. 2–3. The substance of this chapter was given as an address for the Christian Home Educators of Washington in Ocean Shores, Washington, on October 11, 2014.

3. 1 Cor. 16:1, 19; Gal. 1:2, 22. See Paul's salutations in 1 Cor. 1:2; 2 Cor. 1:1; Gal. 1:2; Phil. 4:15; Col. 4:16; 1 Thess. 1:1; 2 Thess. 1:1.

A number of people today, however, advocate what they call "churchless Christianity."[4] This phenomenon can arise from various points of view and motivations. First, it may come from people who seek personal spirituality while rejecting authority, organization, and historic Christianity. One popular book portrays Jesus as saying, "I don't create institutions; that's an occupation for those who want to play God."[5] Second, some people believe that the local church has failed to fulfill its divine mission so we need a "revolution" that will "redefine the church" as a lifestyle instead of as "a specific group of believers."[6] Third, other people are deeply concerned about the inroads of unbiblical teachings and practices in churches and wonder if it is wiser and safer just to worship as a family or meet with a few friends rather than with the compromised church in their community.

Why do our families need the local church? How do we find a healthy church? This chapter will address these questions by looking at characteristics of the God-honoring assembly as stated in Nehemiah 8. As we see what God intends for the assembly of His people, we will also see why it is important to be a part of a church and how to discern what kind of church to look for. We will look at Nehemiah 8 with some help from the New Testament epistle to the Hebrews.

The Church Enables Us to Follow Christ's Appointed Leaders

Nehemiah 8 says that the assembly was led by "Ezra the scribe" at the people's request (v. 1). Gerald Bilkes explains that Ezra's role as a scribe "means that he was highly skilled in understanding the law that God had given to His people through Moses."[7] Ezra was a man of God's Book. The text says that "all the people gathered themselves together as one man" (v. 1) to listen to this Book. Raymond Brown writes, "However diverse their individual likes and dislikes, this common desire to listen to the message of Scripture took precedence over

4. For a critique, see Timothy C. Tennent, "The Challenge of Churchless Christianity: An Evangelical Assessment," *International Bulletin of Missionary Research* 29, no. 4 (October 2005): 171–77.

5. William P. Young, author of *The Shack*, cited in Susan Olasky, "Commuter-driven bestseller," *World Magazine* (June 28, 2008), http://www.worldmag.com/2008/06/commuter_driven_bestseller /page2 (September 17, 2014). See also Annette J. Gysen, "Looking for God in William Paul Young's *The Shack* — A Book Review," *The Outlook* 59, no. 3 (March 2009): 26–31, also available at http://www .reformedfellowship.net/articles/gysen-the-shack-mar09v59-n3.htm (September 17, 2014).

6. George Barna, *Revolution* (Carol Stream, Ill.: Tyndale, 2005), x, cited in Kevin DeYoung and Ted Kluck, *Why We Love the Church: In Praise of Institutions and Organized Religion* (Chicago: Moody, 2009), 165.

7. Gerald M. Bilkes, *Memoirs of the Way Home: Ezra and Nehemiah as a Call to Conversion* (Grand Rapids: Reformation Heritage Books, 2013), 54.

everything else."[8] Ezra was also a priest (v. 2), ordained to perform the rites of God's holy worship. He was both equipped and authorized to lead God's people through God's Word.

What does it mean to follow the leaders of the church? God commands us to follow them in three ways.

We Imitate Their Faith in Christ

Why did the people ask Ezra to lead their assembly (Neh. 8:1)? The man does not appear earlier in the book of Nehemiah, but we are introduced to him in Ezra 7, where we learn that "the hand of the LORD his God [was] upon him" (Ezra 7:6, 9). Ezra 7:10 explains why: "For Ezra had prepared his heart to seek the law of the LORD, and to do it, and to teach in Israel statutes and judgments." He was not only gifted to teach the Bible but was personally devoted to obey the Bible. He was not a leader who had to tell people, "Do as I say and not as I do" (cf. Matt. 23:3); rather, he could say with Paul, "Be ye followers of me, even as I also am of Christ" (1 Cor. 11:1).

The Lord Jesus gives us not only words to follow but living examples of godly people to emulate as they follow Christ. Hebrews 13:7–8 says, "Remember them which have the rule over you, who have spoken unto you the word of God: whose faith follow, considering the end of their conversation." This command assumes that each Christian is under the "rule" or authority of spiritual leaders. These leaders are not celebrities off in the distance, like a face on a TV screen or a picture on a website. Verse 24 says, "Salute all them that have the rule over you"—or, greet them personally. God's people should personally know these pastors and elders and see them regularly.

Why is it important that Christians have personal relationships with spiritual leaders in a local church? This text says believers must "follow" the faith of their leaders. The Greek word literally means to imitate or mimic.[9] The text does not call us to imitate their personal mannerisms and idiosyncrasies, much less their sins, but to imitate their faith in Christ and the holy conduct it produces. Listening to audio recordings and going to conferences is good, but it is no substitute for the example of a living, breathing, godly pastor.

---

8. Raymond Brown, *The Message of Nehemiah*, The Bible Speaks Today, Old Testament, ed. Alec Motyer (Nottingham, Eng.: Inter-Varsity Press, 1998), 128.

9. Greek μιμέομαι. See 2 Thess. 3:7, 9.

We Obey Their Teaching of the Word

Ezra not only provided the people with a good example; he also brought them the Book of God (Neh. 8:1–3). Standing on a wooden pulpit or platform (v. 4),[10] he and other Levites read and expounded the Word. This meeting lasted "from the morning until midday" (v. 3). Nehemiah 8:8 says, "So they read in the book in the law of God distinctly, and gave the sense, and caused them to understand the reading." God blesses the reading and sound preaching of the Word. William Greenhill, alluding to Acts 8, said, "It was not the eunuch's reading, but Philip's preaching, that [worked] faith in him."[11]

These leaders administered the Word of God to the gathered families of the church. According to verse 2, they preached "before the congregation both of men and women, and all that could hear with understanding." This appears to answer Moses's instructions in Deuteronomy 31:12–13:[12]

> Gather the people together, men, and women, and children, and thy stranger that is within thy gates, that they may hear, and that they may learn, and fear the LORD your God, and observe to do all the words of this law: and that their children, which have not known any thing, may hear, and learn to fear the LORD your God, as long as ye live in the land whither ye go over Jordan to possess it.

Moses had instructed parents to teach the Word to their children in their daily lives (Deut. 6:7), but in this passage he says that the family also needs to assemble with the larger body of God's people to hear the Word of God. Family worship and public worship do not compete with each other; they complement and reinforce each other. Thus every Christian needs to be part of a good church where men of God preach the Word of God (Heb. 13:7, 17). Insofar as they preach the Word of God, these leaders must be listened to and obeyed.

Since the preaching and teaching of the Bible is so central to the life of a church, we should be careful to choose a church that faithfully confesses the truth of God. Hebrews 4:14 and 10:23 call us to "hold fast" to our confession of faith in the Lord Jesus. Titus 1:9 reminds us that an elder must hold fast "the

---

10. The Hebrew of Neh. 8:4 literally says "tower" (see KJV margin).

11. William Greenhill, "To All Lovers of Divine Truths," in *An Exposition of the Prophet Ezekiel*, ed. James Sherman (Edinburgh: James Nichol, 1864), vii. The original reads "wrought," not "worked."

12. The command in Deut. 31:12 applies to the Feast of Tabernacles in the sabbath year (v. 10), which began on the fifteenth day of the seventh month (Lev. 23:34). The great assembly under Ezra took place on the first day of the seventh month (Neh. 8:2), the day of blowing trumpets (Lev. 23:24), and it led into the Feast of Tabernacles (Neh. 8:14–18). This correspondence in the calendar strengthens the link between the texts. "The occasion described in Ne. 8 vividly recalls the teaching in Dt. 31:9–13." Brown, *The Message of Nehemiah*, 137n19.

faithful word as he hath been taught, that he may be able by sound doctrine both to exhort and to convince the gainsayers." Ask for the church's confession or statement of faith. Is it sound in doctrine? Does it reflect the great biblical truths rediscovered in the Reformation of Scripture alone, Christ alone, faith alone, grace alone, and the glory of God alone? Furthermore, ask how the pastors teach and defend the doctrines of their confession so that it does not become a forgotten document. Remember that what the pastors of the church preach and teach will powerfully shape your family for generations.

Your elders who "watch for your souls," as Hebrews 13:17 says, also speak the Word of God in a personal and private way to members to encourage their faith and rebuke sin. As Paul reminds the Ephesian elders, "I kept back nothing that was profitable unto you, and have taught you publickly, and from house to house" (Acts 20:20). That is a tremendous help to Christians and Christian families. Church members can go to an elder for wise counsel when they face a difficult issue in their family life. If a family member falls into sin, the family can appeal to the elders to exhort the sinner and, if necessary, use church discipline to call him to repentance. If the family faces some tragedy or crisis, the elders can provide comfort and guidance. What will you do if you do not have a good church? You will face these problems alone. Many burdens that the family bears can be lightened by the spiritual leadership of men who will speak the Word in love.

We Experience the Power of the Spirit
When Ezra and the Levites proclaimed the Word to the gathered families of Israel, a remarkable thing happened. Nehemiah 8:9 says that "all the people wept, when they heard the words of the law." Why did they weep? God's Spirit was convicting them of the ways they and their fathers had broken God's holy law and brought God's judgment on their nation (Psalms 78, 106). A short time later, the people confessed their sins and God's righteousness in judging them (Neh. 9:2, 33). William Bridge reminds us that the Bible is a spiritual mirror to help us see invisible, spiritual realities (James 1:23), saying, "There is God seen especially, and Christ seen; there also you see yourself, and your own dirty face."[13] The preaching of the Word reveals the ugliness of our sins, which is cause to weep.

When Nehemiah saw the people in tears, he encouraged them not to weep but to rejoice in God's grace, reminding them that "the joy of the LORD is your strength" (Neh. 8:10). So the people went out to feast, and twice the text tells

---

13. William Bridge, *Scripture Light the Most Sure Light*, in *The Works of the Rev. William Bridge* (London: Thomas Tegg, 1845), 1:411.

us that they did so with great gladness (vv. 12, 17). How did their sorrow turn to such great joy? Verse 12 explains, "Because they had understood the words that were declared unto them." The preaching of God's Word in the power of the Holy Spirit produces strong affections.

The Word of God is powerful. Hebrews 4:12 says, "For the word of God is quick, and powerful, and sharper than any two-edged sword, piercing even to the dividing asunder of soul and spirit, and of the joints and marrow, and is a discerner of the thoughts and intents of the heart." Reading the Bible in private devotions and family worship is powerful. However, the Scriptures indicate that God sends His power especially through the preaching of the Word by ministers of the Word. "How then shall they call on him in whom they have not believed? And how shall they believe in him of whom they have not heard? And how shall they hear without a preacher?... So then faith cometh by hearing, and hearing by the word of God" (Rom. 10:14, 17). God's ordinary means, though not His exclusive means, of bringing people to faith is the preaching of God's Word. We are born again "by the word of God," that gospel that "is preached unto you" (1 Peter 1:23, 25). Though God's preachers are only vessels of clay, God has willed to fill them with treasure: the power of the gospel (2 Cor. 4:7).

Christians have historically recognized that preaching is God's primary means of calling sinners to Christ and making believers holier (1 Cor. 1:21–24; Eph. 4:11–13). As the Larger Catechism says, "The Spirit of God maketh the reading, but especially the preaching of the word, an effectual means of enlightening, convincing, and humbling sinners; of driving them out of themselves, and drawing them unto Christ; of conforming them to his image, and subduing them to his will; of strengthening them against temptations and corruptions; of building them up in grace; and establishing their hearts in holiness and comfort through faith unto salvation" (Q. 155; cf. Shorter Catechism, Q. 89).

Why do you need to join a church? First, because God puts men such as Ezra in His church, who are committed to studying the Word, obeying the Word, and preaching the Word, and the Spirit of God is with them. They are Christ's gift to the church to build up the saints (Eph. 4:11). So imitate their faith, hear and obey their public teaching and personal counsel, and receive the ministry of the Spirit as He works through their faithful ministry of the Word. If you do not participate in a local church, you are cutting yourself and your family off from the primary means by which God saves sinners, builds His church, and blesses His people.

To determine what kind of church, you should ask these questions: Is this church led by men who are examples of sincere godliness before God and men? Is this church an assembly where the pastors and elders teach the Word of

God and call people to obedience? Is the preaching of this church marked by the work of the Holy Spirit to convict people of sin and give them joy in God?

The Church Enables Us to Worship God as His Holy Temple

The families of Israel who assembled before Ezra and the Levites came not only to hear preaching; they also "worshipped the LORD" in truth (Neh. 8:6). Verse 13 says the leaders of the families met on the second day with the priests and Levites to study the Scriptures more deeply. They discovered that God had also commanded Israel to celebrate the Feast of Tabernacles (vv. 14–15). The result was a reformation in public worship. One commentator writes that because of years of neglect, parts of God's revealed will for His people had been obscured, but "the freshly studied Scripture, like a cleaned painting, now revealed some long-forgotten colours."[14] Nehemiah 8:17 says that the people recovered the biblical way of worship, "and there was very great gladness."[15] Biblical preaching leads to joyful worship according to the will of God.

One reason why the Son of God became a man was to lead His church in worship. Hebrews 2:11–12 says, "He is not ashamed to call them brethren, saying, I will declare thy name unto my brethren, in the midst of the church will I sing praise unto thee" (cf. Ps. 22:22). Christ is our chief Prophet to teach us how to worship, our great High Priest to lead us into the presence of God as the worshiping people of God, and our enthroned King to receive our sacrifices of praise, giving thanks to His name (1 Peter 3:18; Rev. 1:13, 20; Heb. 13:15).

We Are God's House in Christ

Hebrews 3 speaks of Christ as the Son over God's "house." God's house is not an earthly tabernacle or temple but a spiritual house built of living stones, that is, the people with whom He dwells. Moses was a servant in that house. Hebrews 3:6 says, "But Christ as a son over his own house; whose house are we, if we hold fast the confidence and the rejoicing of the hope firm unto the end." Although we often speak of going to the house of God, the New Testament tells us that we who are true believers are the house of God because we are joined to Christ by true faith.

---

14. Derek Kidner, *Ezra and Nehemiah*, Tyndale Old Testament Commentaries, ed. D. J. Wiseman (Downers Grove, Ill.: Inter-Varsity Press, 1979), 108.

15. Nehemiah 8:17 notes, "For since the days of Jeshua the son of Nun unto that day had not the children of Israel done so." Other Scriptures indicate that the Feast of Tabernacles had been celebrated since Joshua (1 Kings 8:2; 2 Chron. 5:3; 8:13; Ezra 3:4). The text may mean that previous celebrations could not compare to the joy of this one, that the practice of dwelling in booths had lapsed in the feast, or that aside from a few notable exceptions this feast had been generally neglected in Israel's history.

Though each believer in Christ is indwelt by the Holy Spirit (1 Cor. 6:19), the emphasis of Scripture is that the church is the temple (1 Cor. 3:16–17; 2 Cor. 6:16; Eph. 2:20–22). Thus Peter wrote in 1 Peter 2:5, "Ye also, as lively stones, are built up a spiritual house." God joins believers together in the church to form a spiritual temple in which He dwells by His Spirit. A solid building is constructed of stones closely cemented together. Joseph Hall said, "There is no place for any loose stone in God's edifice."[16] Therefore, we should not neglect or forsake assembling together but come to church to worship God (Heb. 10:25). Meeting with other believers in corporate worship, we experience the highest privileges of the saints on earth.

We Draw Near to God through Christ

The Feast of Tabernacles was a time to remember God's great work of salvation in redeeming Israel from slavery (Lev. 23:33–44). In the same way, the church's worship revolves around our salvation in Jesus Christ. Hebrews 10:19–22 invites us to "draw near" to God, entering "into the holiest by the blood of Jesus." Verse 21 says we draw near through the mediation of "an high priest over the house of God," again emphasizing that we are God's temple because we are joined together in Christ. Verse 25 rounds out the passage with the exhortation not to forsake "the assembling of ourselves together, as the manner of some is." Hebrew Christians were tempted to abandon the Christian church and return to Old Testament worship, but this epistle tells them that New Testament worship is far superior because the Son of God has come. Through faith in Jesus Christ, the church's worship brings us into the Holy of Holies, and we are welcome there because Christ died for our sins and intercedes for us in heaven.

The worshiping congregation can draw near to God and experience communion with Him. What an amazing privilege! Paul speaks of this privilege in terms of access: "For through him we both have access by one Spirit unto the Father" (Eph. 2:18). The context in Ephesians 2 is the church that consists of Jews and Gentiles united in Christ, "builded together for an habitation of God through the Spirit."

Our attitude should be like that of David, who sings in Psalm 122:1, "I was glad when they said unto me, Let us go into the house of the LORD." God inhabits this house to hear the praises of His people (Ps. 22:3). One day in God's courts is better than a thousand spent anywhere else (Ps. 84:10). If God's presence in the earthly temple on Mount Zion was the joy of believing Israel,

---

16. Joseph Hall, *Holy Raptures*, in *The Works of the Right Reverend Joseph Hall*, ed. Philip Wynter (Oxford: Oxford University Press, 1863), 7:154.

how much more should the public worship of God's church be the joy of believers today? Psalm 87:2 says, "The LORD loveth the gates of Zion more than all the dwellings of Jacob." No doubt many prayers and psalms of praise rose up to God from the homes of the Israelites, but God's special delight was the worship of God's assembled people.

We Enjoy a Foretaste of Heaven with Christ

The Feast of Tabernacles reminded Israel of the days when they camped in the wilderness on their way to the promised land. Gerald Bilkes says, "It was…a visible reminder of their pilgrim life."[17] This was a poignant lesson in Ezra's day, for the people had recently returned home after being exiled in Babylon.[18] Having just rebuilt the walls of Jerusalem (Neh. 6:15; cf. Ps. 51:18), living for a week in makeshift tabernacles reminded them that their hope was not in walls of stone on earth but in the Lord and the heavenly city whose builder and maker is God (Heb. 11:10, 16).[19]

Public worship reminds us that we are strangers in this world and pilgrims on our way to heaven. Public worship also gives us a foretaste of heaven. "Ye are come unto Mount Sion, and unto the city of the living God, the heavenly Jerusalem, and to an innumerable company of angels" (Heb. 12:22). The Greek verb translated "ye are come" is the same word for "let us draw near" (Heb. 10:22), and refers to worship (Heb. 10:1).[20] When we assemble as the church on earth, in the communion of saints, we are one with the heavenly church in the presence of God and with "Jesus the mediator of the new covenant" (12:23–24).

Public worship is the appetizer on the menu of heaven. When we worship with God's church, we stand on the threshold of heaven. Our voices mingle with the praise of the angels and the spirits of righteous men made perfect. We offer up ourselves and our praise to the God of heaven. We receive the grace mediated to us by Christ, who is seated at God's right hand in heaven.

Do you thirst for God? Do you long for Him as for water in a dry land? If so, you will seek His power and glory "in the sanctuary" (Ps. 63:1–2). In the public worship of God's church, the Lord sends out His light and His truth and leads people into His presence "unto God my exceeding joy" (Ps. 43:3–4). Psalm 65:4 says, "Blessed is the man whom thou choosest, and causest to approach unto thee, that he may dwell in thy courts: we shall be satisfied with the goodness of thy house, even of thy holy temple."

---

17. Bilkes, *Memoirs of the Way Home*, 138.
18. Kidner, *Ezra and Nehemiah*, 109.
19. Brown, *The Message of Nehemiah*, 139.
20. Greek, προσέρχομαι.

How can you know a church is healthy? A healthy church loves to worship God. It delights to fear His holy name. It glories in His glory. Its worship services are not a display of human wisdom, nor do they cater to human appetites for entertainment; the worship of a healthy church celebrates God's glory according to God's revealed will. In Nehemiah 8, the Israelites realized that their worship was not fully biblical and needed to be changed. We dare not invent our own worship. A healthy church listens to what God's Word says about worship and obeys it because it worships for God's pleasure.

The Church Enables Us to Serve One Another

It is easy to overlook this third great lesson about the assemblies of God's people, but it is crucial to the church. To be a church requires not spectators or auditors but active participants. We will focus on two ways that illustrate how every Christian and his family should actively engage in the life of the church.

We Share God's Gifts with Others

The Feast of Tabernacles was a time of rejoicing with lots of good food from the gathered harvest (Ex. 23:16; 34:22), not just for the rich but also for orphans and widows (Deut. 16:13–14; cf. 14:28–29). This required the people to send portions of their food to others so that all would have enough. Nehemiah 8:10 says that the people must eat delicious food and "send portions unto them for whom nothing is prepared." "And all the people went their way to eat, and to drink, and to send portions, and to make great mirth [rejoicing]" (Neh. 8:12).

People in church sometimes wonder how to do ministry if they are not called to preach or teach the Word. Though some are gifted to speak, others are gifted to serve (1 Peter 4:11). When Tabitha died, people did not remember her for her worldwide conference speaking but for the many coats and garments she had sewn for local widows: she was "full of good works" (Acts 9:36, 39). By regularly meeting together, we get to know each other's needs. That opens doors for us to use our resources to help one another. God is pleased with this ministry and rewards it. "For God is not unrighteous to forget your work and labour of love, which ye have shewed toward his name, in that ye have ministered to the saints, and do minister" (Heb. 6:10).

The Lord calls us to care for others in the church family that is bigger than our biological families. Hebrews 13:1 says, "Let brotherly love continue." Hebrews 13:16 actually classifies acts of practical help and mercy as acts of worship: "But to do good and to communicate forget not: for with such sacrifices God is well pleased." Here "communicate" means to share your possessions or abilities with others. Too often we come to church asking, "What's in it for me and my family?" Instead, we should come asking, "How can we serve?" We should not seek high profile positions but opportunities to wash the feet of the saints through practical acts of kindness.

Do not over-spiritualize fellowship, as if people were souls without bodies. Although Christian fellowship is grounded upon sharing the Spirit of Christ, it overflows into all of life. Conrad Mbewe says, "Hence, in your fellowship with other believers...share with them what God has blessed you with, and be sincere enough to share with them your physical and social needs as well."[21] We need to serve each other and be served in countless ways.

We Speak God's Truth to Others
Nehemiah 8:15 says that by studying the Scriptures, the Israelites learned their duty was to "publish and proclaim in all their cities" the need for everyone to gather material for making booths for the Feast of Tabernacles. Many people needed to go out from Jerusalem to spread the word, exhorting their fellow Israelites to do their duty. While there are not a large number of teachers in the church, many are needed to speak the truth in love to one another.

Hebrews 3:13 says, "But exhort one another daily, while it is called Today; lest any of you be hardened through the deceitfulness of sin." Hebrews 10:24–25 says, "And let us consider one another to provoke unto love and to good works: not forsaking the assembling of ourselves together, as the manner of some is; but exhorting one another: and so much the more, as ye see the day approaching." One reason not to forsake meeting with the church is that if we do, we will lose touch with others and thus cannot encourage and exhort each other.

The church is God's means for holy fellowship, which promotes holy living. Henry Scudder said we should "highly esteem" and "much desire" Christian fellowship with fellow believers. Psalm 16:3 says that "all my delight" is in "the saints that are in the earth." First Peter 2:17 commands us to "love the brotherhood." Psalm 119:63 tells us, "I am a companion of all them that fear thee, and of them that keep thy precepts."[22] By meeting regularly with the church of Christ, we help each other to flee from our lusts and pursue righteousness, faith, love, and peace with those who call upon the Lord from a pure heart (2 Tim. 2:22).

Do not isolate yourself and your family by staying away from church. You will miss out on so much of God's blessing, including being a blessing to others.

---

21. Conrad Mbewe, *Foundations for the Flock: Truths about the Church for All the Saints* (Hannibal, Mo.: Grand Ministries Press, 2011), 9.
22. Henry Scudder, *The Christian's Daily Walk* (repr., Harrisonburg, Va.: Sprinkle, 1984), 118.

You might be asked to do something as simple as mowing the grass and raking the leaves for an elderly couple or babysitting for a single mother. Participating in the church joins you to a network of relationships in which you begin to know one another. As a result, service is not an impersonal act of charity but an act of brotherly love in the context of mutual friendship.

When you look for a church for yourself and your family, look for a church that is more than a preaching station; look for godly fellowship. Do the people rush out of the building after the service like anonymous shoppers leaving the mall? Or do they linger with each other, talking as good friends? Are the people involved in each other's lives, interconnected as one body? Do they "send portions" to one another like the Israelites did in Ezra's day, caring for each other's practical needs? Do they encourage each other to love and do good works? That is the kind of church you should join.

Conclusion

In Nehemiah 8, we have seen three very good reasons why you and your family should join and actively participate in a local church. First, God has given us pastors and elders to follow as leaders of the church. By gathering with the church, you bring your family under the influence of godly men who preach the Word in the power of the Holy Spirit. Second, God has made the church His temple, where we are fitted together as living stones to draw near to Him in worship and to experience a foretaste of heaven in His presence. Third, the church is the body of Christ, where each member serves others in practical ways and encourages people to glorify God as He commands in the Word. Of course, there is more to the life of the church, for we have not spoken of evangelism, missions, or corporate prayer. However, we have chosen to focus here on why we should join a church. Historic Christianity that is rooted in Scripture and the Reformation has long recognized this and called people to become members of local churches.[23] We need the church, and it is our duty before God to join its membership, submit to its leaders, and serve in its ministries.

---

23. The Belgic Confession (Art. 28) of the Reformed Churches in the Netherlands affirmed in 1561, "We believe, since this holy congregation is an assembly of those who are saved...all men are in duty bound to join and unite themselves with it; maintaining the unity of the church; submitting themselves to the doctrine and discipline thereof; bowing their necks under the yoke of Jesus Christ; and as mutual members of the same body, serving to the edification of the brethren, according to the talents God has given them" (*Reformed Confessions of the Sixteenth and Seventeenth Centuries in English Translation, Volume 2, 1552–1566*, ed. James T. Dennison, Jr. [Grand Rapids: Reformation Heritage Books, 2010], 441). The English Baptists similarly affirmed in their Confession of 1677/1689 (26.5) that those whom Christ calls to Himself through the gospel, He also "commands to walk together in

At this point someone might say, "I agree with all this. I desire to do it. However, what if I cannot find a good church within an hour of my home?" In answer to this question, let me address three possible situations in which you might find yourself.

1. *Churches with Fundamental Problems.* These are churches that promote false teachings or ignore sins, which are great mountains that we cannot cross. Their teaching is full of errors that break up the foundations of the faith. For example, they might include the following:

+ Denial of basic Christian orthodoxy, such as contradicting the Trinity, the deity of Christ, His physical resurrection from the dead, or the inerrancy of Scripture.

+ Rejection of one or more of the evangelical essentials formulated at the Reformation, such as giving divine authority to human tradition or modern prophets and apostles instead of Scripture alone, looking to someone other than Christ alone as the mediator of grace, or contradicting the principles of salvation by grace alone, justification by faith alone, and for the glory of God alone.

+ Refusal to teach or enforce church discipline for flagrant sin violating the Ten Commandments, or publicly endorsing sin.

+ A spirit of legalism, pride, and hyper-separatism instead of Christlike love, humility, and graciousness toward other sinners with a deep awareness of our own sins.

+ A practice of worship that is plainly idolatrous, ignores or grossly perverts God's ordinances of baptism and the Lord's Supper, or is ruled by human teachings to entertain and please men instead of being regulated by the Holy Scriptures for the pleasure of God.

We must separate ourselves from participation in such churches. Second Corinthians 6:16–17 says, "And what agreement hath the temple of God with idols? For ye are the temple of the living God; as God hath said, I will dwell in them, and walk in them; and I will be their God, and they shall be my people. Wherefore come out from among them, and be ye separate, saith the Lord, and touch not the unclean thing; and I will receive you." If you cannot find a basically healthy church near you, you might tune into Sermon Audio (www.sermon audio.com) to listen to good sermons at home, pray for God to start a faithful

---

particular societies, or churches, for their mutual edification, and the due performance of that public worship which He requires of them in the world" (*Reformed Confessions*, 4:563).

church in your town, and seek fellowship with likeminded believers. Do not be proud of separating from churches with false teachings, but grieve and long for Christ to build a true church in your community.

2. *Churches with Significant Problems.* The errors of these churches do not break up the foundation of the faith but introduce false doctrines or practices of less importance that nevertheless concern you. If this is the best church in your area, view these problems not as an impassable mountain but as a hill to climb. Both the Westminster Confession of Faith (25.5) and the Second London Baptist Confession (26.3) recognize that "the purest churches under heaven are subject to both mixture and error."[24] In your family devotions, when you come across a point of disagreement with the church, teach your children according to your conscience. Then go to the church, and if they can accept you with your point of view, be accepting of its leaders without endorsing their errors. Romans 15:7 says, "Wherefore receive ye one another, as Christ also received us to the glory of God." When your children are old enough to understand, talk to them about your differences with the church and open the Bible to show them why you take this stand. Do this with a gracious, humble spirit, however; explain to them that we are not to approach fellow believers with a critical spirit. Thank God for your church often in family worship, and privately pray that God would give the elders and pastors further illumination.

3. *Churches with Minor Problems.* If the first category was a mountain and the second a hill, then the third is a molehill. Do not get hung up on technical points of doctrine that few Christians understand or with disagreements about specifics of methodology, style, and preference. Shower your relationship with the church with abundant grace. Remember that the church is the assembly of redeemed sinners, and we all are saved by grace alone. Turn your disagreements into prayers, and be willing to be taught by others, because you might be wrong.

---

24. *Reformed Confessions*, 264, 562. The Baptist Confession omits "both."

CONTEMPORARY AND
CULTURAL ISSUES

Chapter 35

Handling Error in the Church:
Martin Downes Interviewing Joel Beeke

As you reflect back to your days in seminary and early years in the ministry, were there men who started out with evangelical convictions who later moved away from the gospel? How did you cope with that?[1]

I can only think of a few men with whom I had some personal acquaintance who have fallen from evangelical convictions. Initially, these rare situations shook me—particularly one Reformed brother with whom I studied at Westminster Seminary who embraced Roman Catholicism. Praying for their awakening and return, and for myself that I might not stumble nor look down haughtily upon them, has helped me cope. Then, I suppose, so have the daily challenges of the ministry that press me to keep my hand on the plow and not become overly distracted by an erring brother or two.

I know far more ministerial colleagues—numbering well into the hundreds—who have moved from non-evangelical positions to a solid evangelical and Reformed stance. Many of them suffered greatly, losing large portions, if not all, of their congregations in the process. I have often been profoundly encouraged by their courageous stance to contend earnestly for the faith that was once delivered unto the saints (Jude 3).

Have you ever been drawn toward any views or movements that time has shown to have been unhelpful or even dangerous theologically?

By the grace of God, no.

How should a minister keep his own heart, mind, and will from theological error?

---

1. *This chapter is adapted from Martin Downes, ed.,* Risking the Truth: Interviews on Handling Truth and Error in the Church *(Fearn, Ross-shire: Christian Focus, 2009), 165–176. Twenty other ministers are similarly interviewed in this book, including Carl Trueman, Michael Horton, Mark Dever, Derek Thomas, Tom Ascol, Conrad Mbewe, Geoffrey Thomas, and Ligon Duncan.*

+ Keep yourself deeply immersed in the Scriptures, and pray daily to be willing to surrender all to their inerrant truth.

+ Surround yourself with sound, godly colleagues and laypeople who love you sufficiently to be honest with you so that iron will sharpen iron.

+ Read the best, sound, scriptural, classic books, especially those by the Reformers and Puritans, that address your mind with clarity, convict your conscience with poignancy, bend your will with conviction, and move your feet with passion.

+ Meditate on those truths preached that do your people the most good; in every case, you will discover that they are biblical truths.

+ Develop the hide of a rhinoceros so that you won't be tossed about with every criticism and wind of doctrine, while maintaining the heart of a child so that you will be a tender undershepherd to the needy.

Calvin said that ministers have two voices. One is for the sheep, and the other for warding off the wolves. How have you struck the right balance in this regard in your pulpit ministry?

I suppose that one can never be absolutely certain that he is striking the right balance on this critical subject, but here are four guidelines that I find helpful:

+ Pray daily for biblical balance in all areas of ministry.

+ Love your sheep. Love has a way of balancing out our often imbalanced personalities. Those in error can receive much more from a minister who obviously loves them than from one who comes across as combative.

+ Be patient with your sheep. Be willing to teach them the same truth repeatedly, just as the Lord has done with you (cf. Phil. 3:1; 2 Peter 3:1–2).

+ Let your "voice for the sheep" always receive the primary accent of your ministry. Truth must ultimately be positive in nature to win the day with a congregation. Many ministers have focused too much on polemical and apologetical theology, often setting up and then beating down straw men in their congregation to the detriment of the flock. Polemics and apologetics must have their proper place of a minor accent in the ministry so that no error is left unexposed. But the minister must expose error wisely, forthrightly, humbly, compellingly, not by lording it over the sheep (2 Tim. 4:1–2; 1 Peter 5:2–3).

Why do old heresies persist today? Why do men possessed of fine intellectual gifts end up embracing and believing significant theological errors?

Heresy is the product of the mind of "the natural man," as Paul puts it in 1 Corinthians 2:14, that is, "the unrenewed man" (Charles Hodge), who must necessarily receive and understand Christian truth without the illumination of the Holy Spirit and without a renewed mind. As a stranger to "the wisdom of God" revealed in the gospel, he must also consult and depend on "the wisdom of this world" (1 Cor. 1:19–24). Compounding the problem is the vanity of his mind, his darkened understanding, his ignorance and blindness of heart (Eph. 4:17–18). Such a man can have at best only a shallow, imperfect, distorted view of the truth, and it is not surprising that he conceives and propagates a multitude of errors and falsehoods.

The root of our English word *heresy* is the Greek word *hairesis*, meaning "choice" or "opinion." Note that the word implies the activity of both the mind and the will of man. Having come to a misunderstanding of the truth or having concocted or embraced a falsehood in its place, the natural man cleaves to his errors and zealously asserts and advances them precisely because they are his own opinions.

Nor is it surprising that when a false prophet or teacher begins to proclaim his erroneous views to others, many are willing to receive and embrace them. Fallen men are hostile to the truth of God and prefer to believe a falsehood rather than submit to that truth. The wonder is not that there are many heretics but that there are not many, many more.

Because the mind of the natural man is finite, there are only so many erroneous or heretical views it can conceive or embrace. Because that mind is corrupt and the corruption is inherited by succeeding generations, there is a tendency to resurrect or reproduce the errors of the past. After two thousand years, it is only to be expected that the errors and heresies of the present day all seem to have their historical antecedents, often reaching back to the earliest history and experience of the ancient church.

Ignorance always serves the cause of error. Christians who do not know what the Bible says and have no knowledge of the history of Christian doctrine find themselves unequipped to detect and refute these resurrected errors and heresies of the past. As a result, it is all too easy for false teachers "to creep in unawares" (Jude 4) and launch campaigns to subvert congregations and denominations that historically embraced the apostolic Christian faith.

In America, wealth and business acumen have also been called upon to advance some of the most ancient and obvious falsehoods and errors. The Church of Latter-Day Saints, better known as the Mormons, is a huge and highly profitable business enterprise devoted to promoting polytheism on a scale that rivals Hinduism, a "gospel" of salvation by works righteousness, continuing revelation, "baptism for the dead," "eternal marriage," and a secret temple *cultus* modeled on Free Masonry.

Finally, we must reckon with the activity of Satan as "the father of lies" (John 8:44). Wherever men call into question the truth and trustworthiness of God's Word, handle the Word of God deceitfully, and love and make a lie as a substitute for the truth of God's Word, we can see the hand of the enemy of souls at work.

How can a minister discern between those who are thinking their way through doctrines on the way to greater depth and clarity, and those who are questioning doctrines in a way that could lead to significant error?

First of all, we must follow the example of Christ and the apostles, who openly invited and urged their hearers to prove or test the truth and worth of what they proclaimed and taught. Reformed Christians have asserted and maintained the liberty of the Christian and the liberty of conscience. "The requiring of an implicit faith, and an absolute and blind obedience, is to destroy liberty of conscience, and reason also" (Westminster Confession of Faith, 20.2).

Every minister must learn to defend the faith without being defensive or combative. "The servant of the Lord must not strive; but be gentle unto all men, apt to teach, patient, in meekness instructing those that oppose themselves" (2 Tim. 2:24, 25). We should encourage our people to "prove all things" (1 Thess. 5:21). Rather than rebuking someone for asking questions, we should devote our energy to finding answers to those questions from God's Word. The ecumenical creeds and Reformed confessions, and the vast theological literature connected with them, are also great helps to a right understanding of faith and practice.

On the other hand, as those who watch for the souls of God's people, we must be alert to any sign of straying from the truth. We must warn against embracing any notion or doctrine that requires one to set aside the clear testimony of Scripture. We must resist efforts to reinterpret Scripture to accommodate sinful practices or lifestyles. We must expose the sinful tendency of the fallen man to exalt himself and make himself a judge of God's Word, rather than submitting to its judgment.

We must use discernment. A true Christian will gladly receive faithful instruction from the Word of God. A man who is merely dabbling in theology or looking for an intellectual sparring partner deserves to be rebuked. And "a man that is an heretic after the first and second admonition reject; knowing that he that is such is subverted, and sinneth, being condemned of himself" (Titus 3:10–11).

How do you cope with men who are sound in many ways, and whose ministries have been beneficial, but who, nonetheless, have held harmful views?

One of the consequences, or benefits, of being known as a Reformed Christian who adheres consistently to the teaching of Scripture as summarized in the Reformed confessions is that one is seldom put in such a position. Such men as you describe in your question seem to find the Reformed faith to be a pill they can't or won't swallow—perhaps because for all their strengths, these men are generally pragmatists and averse to consistency.

Even so, our people often find something attractive in the ministries of such men, and we need to take time to know their positions—both strengths and weaknesses—so that we can speak intelligently and helpfully about them. The difficulty is that these men and their ministries, broadcasts, and books are many and various. There is almost always one big name at a given moment, the man whose sayings and doings and nostrums are being widely discussed and hotly debated. We should beware of being drawn into endless and useless debates. These men come and go and have surprisingly little impact over the long term.

It should be a rule with us to have nothing to do with any man or ministry that errs in regard to the way of salvation in Jesus Christ. Whatever good a man may do along other lines, he has done the greatest conceivable harm if he errs at this point. "It were better for him that a millstone were hanged about his neck, and that he were drowned in the depth of the sea" (Matt. 18:6).

Many Christians would be surprised to learn that major heretics like Pelagius and Faustus Socinus were known for scrupulously moral living, when perhaps they would have expected them to be openly immoral. How did Paul's assertion that false teaching leads to ungodliness manifest itself in the lives of these false teachers?

It is a misreading of Paul to suggest that false teaching must always lead to ungodliness or immorality, although it often does. Paul was keenly aware of the life he had lived as a Pharisee, so zealous to observe the traditions of the elders that he claimed to be "touching the righteousness of the law, blameless" (Phil. 3:6). He likewise bears record of his fellow Jews that "they have zeal of God, but not according to knowledge. For they being ignorant of God's righteousness, and going about to establish their own righteousness, have not submitted themselves unto the righteousness of God" (Rom. 10:2–3). It is simply a fact of human experience that men often do the right things for the wrong reasons.

It is therefore essential to the Christian notion of ethics to consider motive or "the thoughts and intents of the heart" (Heb. 4:12), as well as outward appearance or conduct, when determining whether one's works are good or not. That which is not done out of true faith, in obedience to God's Word, and for the glory of God, is not, in the most important sense, a good work (Heidelberg Catechism, Q. 91). According to the Word of God, Pelagius and Faustus Socinus were both "as an unclean thing," and all their good works were "as filthy rags" (Isa. 64:6).

However much these men may have lived an outwardly moral life, Scripture describes them in very different terms: as "grievous wolves…speaking perverse things, to draw away disciples after them" (Acts 20:29–30). In the balance of Scripture, the sins of the mind and heart are more heinous than the sins of the flesh. It is gross wickedness to mislead others concerning the way of salvation, to destroy faith in the truth of God's Word, and to corrupt the worship of God.

At the same time, many Christians are guilty of failing to "adorn the doctrine of God our Saviour in all things" (Titus 2:9)—that is, by a consistent Christian manner of life and conduct. Because of the depravity that still cleaves to us, there must always be a gap between our profession and our conduct. We are called upon nonetheless to crucify the old nature, to walk in newness of life, and, in dependency on the Holy Spirit, to make every effort to narrow the gap between profession and conduct, for the sake of Christ and the gospel (cf. Romans 8).

What would you consider to be the main theological dangers confronting us today, and how can we deal with them?

Some dangers have been with us for a long time, and some are just beginning to loom on the horizon. "The Battle for the Bible" has been with us for more than one hundred years, and it has proven to be a great setback for the cause of Christ in the world. The apostasy of the Protestant churches in Europe and Great Britain; the disorder and corruption of evangelical churches in North America; the extension of much of that disorder and corruption to newly planted churches in Latin America, Africa, and Asia; the resilience of corrupt bodies such as the Church of Rome and the sway it holds over so many millions; the propagation of cults of many kinds—all this may be attributed in very large measure to ignorance, false views, and rank unbelief concerning the unique character, content, and authority of Holy Scripture as God's written Word.

In the community of Reformed churches, we must deplore the rise of what can be called "boutique" versions of the Reformed faith: little groups centered around some novel idea or practice, such as paedo-Communion, that sets them apart from other Reformed Christians. Equally distressing is the widespread defection from the faithful observance of the second commandment regarding the regulation of the content and manner of Christian worship; many Reformed Christians have forgotten that the Reformers were as much concerned to regulate Christian worship according to Scripture as they were determined to establish Christian doctrine from the Word of God. Rightly understood and practiced, Christian worship is profoundly theological, spiritual, and practical.

Nothing, however, is more astonishing than contemporary denials or disclaimers concerning faith as the sole instrument of our justification before God. Nothing was more basic to the Reformation, and nothing is more essential to the gospel, than justification by faith alone. Scripture acknowledges only one way of salvation, and it has nothing to do with covenant status, church membership, sacramental administration, Christian education, or progressive sanctification to acquire salvation. "Believe on the Lord Jesus Christ, and thou shalt be saved" (Acts 16:31).

Almost as disturbing is the rise of the postmodern school of thought or mind-set and the inroads it is making among Christians in North America. As the name implies, postmodernism is a reaction to the modernism so dominant in Europe and America in the last decades of the nineteenth century and the first decades of the twentieth. One would think this rejection of modernism would work in favor of the historic Christian faith, but that is not the direction postmodernism has taken. Fundamental to postmodernism is the rejection of rational systems of thought and any kind of meta-narrative. Reformed Christianity has a rational system of thought, summarized in its historic creeds and confessions; its meta-narrative is nothing less than the witness of Holy Scripture to the history of redemption in Christ, and its summary in the gospel.

It is open to question whether there is any such thing as postmodernism, at least anything that can be expressed in positive terms. Even so, there are many important self-identified postmodern thinkers, writers, and shapers of popular culture. Their blend of radical skepticism, unbelief, eclecticism, and nihilism is making its impact on our world and the people to whom we must preach the gospel. It must also be admitted that these trends in the culture around us often have a profound and often destructive impact on the Christian church. We ministers should be alert to the ways in which the young people in our own churches, much more attuned to and involved in popular culture than we may like to think, may be embracing the stances and ways of postmodernism.

Knowledge is power, and we need to know and understand the world we live in and the churches we serve. Even more important, we need to grow in our knowledge and practice of the things taught and commanded in Holy Scripture. The man who knows the Scriptures well is "throughly furnished unto all good works" (2 Tim. 3:16), including in particular the good work of proclaiming the great truths of the Christian faith, wielding God's Word as a mighty spiritual weapon, "casting down imagination, and every high thing that exalteth itself against the knowledge of God" (2 Cor. 10:5)—in order to save both himself and his hearers and to build up the church of Christ unto all generations.

It is natural that a younger generation can find it harder to navigate the theological currents in the church. With all your ministerial experience, what advice would you give to younger ministers as they assess and handle various movements today?

Younger ministers are sometimes the victim of the particular bent of their theological training. Since the rise of the so-called church growth movement, there has been an increasing emphasis on technique and methodology at the expense of the disciplines that once were the "meat and potatoes" of seminary education, namely, biblical languages, exegesis, systematics, apologetics, church history, and the history of Christian doctrine.

Where this shift in emphasis has taken place, the seminary graduate will not have the tools he needs to use Scripture effectively and to wield it with ever-increasing knowledge and skill as "the sword of the Spirit." He will not have sufficient access to the Scriptures themselves, nor the comprehensive and analytical grasp of Christian truth, to be a true minister of the Word in today's world. He will find himself captive to the winds of the moment. As a preacher, he will be reduced to repeating the ideas of other men, gleaned from commentaries and popular books.

The minister who finds himself in this unhappy position should take action to make up for this deficit of knowledge and skill. He can go back to seminary and make a better choice of a place to train. He can seek advice and direction from other ministers and enter on a course of self-study. The important thing is for him to realize what he doesn't know and needs to know, and for him to seek out the best kind of books and study helps. Conferences and seminars are also helpful, and the guidance and encouragement of older and better-equipped ministers of the Word will be invaluable.

In sum, here are three short guidelines:

- Become and stay well versed in the Scriptures, in confessional Reformed theology, and in the great classics of Reformed, experiential theology.

- Summarize the errors of various movements succinctly from the pulpit when the scriptural text you are expounding pertains to them. Enlarge upon your exposure of error, perhaps, in catechism classes (because young people are the church's future) or weekday classes (because those who attend have, in general, greater appreciation for apologetics than does your average Sabbath attendee and because your teaching situation is less formal).

+ Remember that you cannot study every false movement in depth, nor should you. Study in depth for yourself those that directly affect your congregation. Otherwise, read the best book from an evangelical perspective that refutes a particular error. In some cases, reading one good article may suffice.

Younger ministers should beware of being so caught up with the trends, debates, and crises of the present that they neglect to reinforce their knowledge of Christian history and Christian doctrine. It is important that they know what they are up against in terms of the challenges of today, but it is even more important that they know precisely what the Christian faith is at its roots, what the authentic gospel of Jesus Christ is, and how it is to be proclaimed, according to its Author. God does not change, His Word cannot change, His mercy is from everlasting to everlasting, and His Son, our Savior Jesus Christ, is the same yesterday, today, and forever.

Chapter 36

Practical Lessons for Today from the Life of Idelette Calvin[1]

John Calvin was devoted to Scripture and the church. He emphasized God's sovereignty and Christian living in his preaching and writing, and he was surrounded by many loyal Christian friends. Not surprisingly, he also had a very happy marriage. Yet finding a suitable marriage partner had proved to be a daunting task for Calvin. Many of his well-meaning friends and family members had attempted to play matchmaker for him, and each time Calvin had been disappointed. Eventually he nearly resigned himself to celibacy.[2] When Calvin's friend Guillaume Farel wrote to tell of yet another possible life mate, Calvin responded, "I do not belong to that foolish group of lovers, who are willing to cover even the shortcomings of a woman with kisses, as soon as they have fallen for her external appearance. The only beauty that charms me is that she is virtuous, obedient not arrogant, thrifty, and patient, and that I can expect her to care for my health."[3]

When Calvin finally married Idelette van Buren, he found the one thing needful for which he was looking: a sincere and obedient heart of piety toward God. For Calvin and Idelette, such piety was key to braving the difficulties and challenges of married life.

While we know little of Calvin and Idelette's home life, from all indications it was serene and godly despite its many tragedies and hardships. As we examine Idelette's life with Calvin, let us focus on several lessons that we can learn from her godly example. For in Idelette we see what can be called the blueprint for Christian marriage. It is the pattern of holy living that Colossians 3:12 says includes "kindness, humbleness of mind, meekness, longsuffering; forbearing

---

1. This chapter was first delivered as an address on October 31, 2009, to a breakout session for women at the 17th Annual Audubon Bible Church Reformation Celebration, Laurel, Mississippi.

2. John Calvin, *Tracts and Letters* (repr., Edinburgh: Banner of Truth, 2009), 4:191.

3. Machiel A. van den Berg, *Friends of Calvin*, trans. Reinder Bruinsma (Grand Rapids: Eerdmans, 2009), 125 (cf. *Tracts and Letters*, 4:141).

one another, and forgiving one another." These ingredients, which permeated John and Idelette's marriage, still offer us today a variety of helpful ways to enrich and bless our marriages.

Courtship

Calvin's duties as a pastor and Reformer were too much for his health. He contracted so many diseases under his heavy load that his friends persuaded him that he needed a helpmeet to relieve some of the burdens of domestic life. Calvin had several students living with him, a few retirees (pensioners), and a surly housekeeper and her son. Calvin's good friend Guillaume Farel attempted twice to find Calvin a spouse who would match his biblical ideal.

Eventually Martin Bucer suggested the widow Idelette van Buren (possibly from Buren in the Dutch province of Gelderland) as a suitable candidate. By this time, Calvin was ready to remain single for the rest of his life. After contemplating Bucer's suggestion, however, Calvin realized that Idelette indeed appeared to have the character that he sought.

Idelette was a young widow with two young children. Her former husband, Jean Stordeur, a cabinet maker from Liège (one of "those cities of the Netherlands in which the awakening had been most remarkable," D'Aubigne writes),[4] contracted the plague in 1540, a little more than a year after Calvin's arrival there, and died within a few days. The Stordeurs lived in Strasburg, which was a refuge for Christians fleeing Roman persecution. They were Anabaptists who were rejected by Roman Catholics, Lutherans, and the Reformers alike. It is possible that Idelette was the daughter of a famous Anabaptist, Lambert van Buren, who in 1533 was convicted of heresy, had his property confiscated, and was banished from Liege.[5]

In addition to not believing in infant baptism, the Anabaptists embraced several teachings that differed from those of the Reformed faith. For example, the Anabaptists believed they should not participate in government or fight in wars. They also believed they should never swear an oath, even in court. In some cases, Anabaptists tried to separate themselves from the world by establishing their own communities. Though Jean and Idelette did not belong to the radical wing of the Anabaptists, generally speaking, the Anabaptists were radical compared with other faith expressions of the Reformation. Some Anabaptists stressed spiritual life at the expense of Scripture and sound doctrine. Others took

---

4. J. H. Merle D'Aubigne, *History of the Reformation in Europe in the Time of Calvin* (repr., Harrisonburg, Va.: Sprinkle, 2000), 6:508.

5. D'Aubigne, *History of the Reformation in Europe*; cf. Philip Schaff, *History of the Christian Church* (repr., Grand Rapids: Eerdmans, 1985), 8:415.

radical measures to promote their beliefs, even to the point of violence. Interestingly, Calvin helped suppress Anabaptism by his writings and by supporting the imprisonment and banishment of some of its more radical members.[6]

When Calvin and Farel were expelled from Geneva in 1538, Calvin began preaching in the French church in Strasburg, where Jean and Idelette attended services. How curious they must have been to hear Calvin, who was already well known for writing the *Institutes of the Christian Religion*. Convinced of the Reformed truth, Jean and Idelette soon left the Anabaptists and joined Calvin's church. There they acquired a love for Scripture and its central place in worship. They also enjoyed the clear preaching, pastoral care, and warm friendship of their leader.[7]

At this time Idelette was already exhibiting a strong commitment to Christ and a teachable spirit. Instead of resenting Calvin's stern policy against the Anabaptists, she read the *Institutes* and learned to appreciate Calvin's devotion to the Word of God. She and her husband attended many of Calvin's daily Bible lectures. They were also very hospitable to Calvin. Calvin enjoyed their friendship and considered them, as they called themselves, his disciples. He admired "the simplicity and sanctity of their lives."[8]

Jean Stordeur's death was a profound blow to Idelette. Not only did she miss her dear husband, with whom she was united in so many ways, but she had no way to support herself and her children as a widow.

Shortly after Stordeur's death Bucer asked Calvin, "What about the gentle Idelette?" Though Calvin had formerly thought of Idelette as a dear sister in Christ, he now began to reconsider that relationship. While working hard to expand the *Institutes* from six chapters to seventeen, he must have periodically heard the echo, *Why not Idelette?* After all, the woman was godly, kind, and intelligent. Though she was a few years older than Calvin, she was strikingly young and attractive. Machiel van den Berg noted that "the extroverted Farel expressed his astonishment that she was such a pretty woman!"[9] Ultimately, though, it was the evident fruit of Colossians 3:12 in Idelette's life that impressed Calvin, who pursued godliness in every aspect of his life.

Calvin had enjoyed Idelette's hospitality both before and after her first husband had died. Those visits increased when Calvin formally began to court

---

6. Willem Balke, *Calvin and the Anabaptist Radicals*, trans. William J. Heynen (Grand Rapids: Eerdmans, 1981).

7. J. H. Alexander, *Ladies of the Reformation: Short Biographies of Distinguished Ladies of the Sixteenth Century* (repr., New York: Westminster, 2002), 88.

8. Alexander, *Ladies of the Reformation*, 89.

9. Van den Berg, *Friends of Calvin*, 129.

Idelette. A few months later, on August 17, 1540, Calvin married Idelette, taking her and her children (a son and daughter) into his home. Friends came from near and far to attend Calvin's wedding.[10]

> *Lesson #1:* One of the first lessons we can learn from Calvin's new wife is the importance of having a full allegiance and humble submission to the Scriptures as well as a teachable and hospitable spirit. Too often today people are governed more by tradition than by Scripture. They do not study the Word for themselves or seek to learn and grow under the faithful expositional ministry of the Word. What about you? Are you humbly submitting to the Scriptures? Do you demonstrate a teachable spirit? Are you hospitable and warm to others?

Character

Idelette was quiet, unassuming, cheerful, and yet sober.[11] Theodore Beza, Calvin's first reliable biographer, called her a most choice woman—"a serious-minded woman of good character."[12] Although she was petite and suffered from poor health, Idelette devoted all her strength to educating her children.[13] Idelette's faithfulness within the hardships she faced indicated her meekness and humility. These responses did not mean that she was weak or fearful, however. Following Christ on the path of suffering takes great strength and courage, and Idelette submitted patiently to God's various providences.

To make room for Idelette and her children in his little home in Strasburg, Calvin had to let two of his renters go. Letting these sources of revenue go was a significant sacrifice for Calvin, considering his meager salary, but he appears to have made it gladly. Only weeks after he was married, he wrote to Farel about how pleased he was with his new wife. As van den Berg writes, Calvin "clearly found marriage a special experience of joy." Van den Berg goes on to say that their "marriage was more than simply a rational agreement; it became a true and solid bond of love and loyalty. The quiet and patient Idelette was an exceptionally suitable friend-in-marriage."[14]

Shortly after he married Idelette, Calvin went to Regensburg to attend a theological debate. While he was gone, the plague hit Strasburg. One of Calvin's closest friends, Claude Feray, died from it. Calvin worried about Idelette,

---

10. D'Aubigne, *History of the Reformation in Europe in the Time of Calvin*, 6:509.

11. Schaff, *History of the Christian Church*, 8:416, Farel recalled her disposition as "grave."

12. Theodore Beza, *The Life of John Calvin* (Darlington, U.K.: Evangelical Press, 1997), 35; cf. Edna Gerstner, *Idelette* (Morgan, Pa.: Soli Deo Gloria, 1992).

13. Schaff, *History of the Christian Church*, 8:415.

14. Van den Berg, *Friends of Calvin*, 130.

who took refuge outside of the city. He wrote, "Day and night my wife is in my thoughts, now that she is deprived of my counsel and must do without her husband."[15] Eventually Calvin could not take the worry anymore; he left the debate early to return to Idelette.

Idelette and Calvin stayed in Strasburg for less than a year before Calvin was called back to Geneva to continue his great work as a Reformer. The stress of this decision weighed heavily on him. Calvin's letters from this period indicate that he was very happy in Strasburg and did not wish to return to Geneva. He wrote to Farel, "I dread throwing myself into that whirlpool I found so dangerous."[16] While we have no account of Idelette's thoughts and feelings at that time, the couple decided to move to Geneva in response to the will of God. Idelette's daughter, Judith, accompanied them, while her son remained in Strasburg with relatives.

> Lesson #2: The second lesson we learn from Idelette is that true spiritual growth and resignation to God's will are nearly always inseparable. When is the last time that you patiently submitted to God's will even when you did not feel like doing it? How did you feel after you placed your will under God's will by the Spirit's grace?

While the Genevan city council provided a beautiful parsonage for Idelette and Calvin at the top of the Rue de Chanoines—it had a little garden and a magnificent view of Lake Leman and the Jura mountains on one side and the Alps on the other—Calvin only received a salary of about $200 per year, twelve measures of corn, and two casks of wine. Though the resources at her disposal were very modest, Idelette gladly opened up her home to numerous refugees and frequently extended hospitality to Calvin's friends, such as Farel, Beza, and Viret, who all highly respected her.

Idelette was a wonderful wife and companion for Geneva's most prominent pastor. When Calvin's work as a pastor, writer, and civil servant threatened his health, Idelette proved to be a much needed confidant, counselor, and sounding board. She tended to his downcast spirit and his fragile health and visited the sick in his place. She also went out of her way to assure Calvin that she respected him for remaining true to God and Scripture, no matter what the cost. Idelette was willing to share with him whatever burdens he carried and assured him that he should never be tempted to shrink from his duties for the sake of her ease and comfort. She was deeply committed to Calvin's ministry as

---

15. Van den Berg, *Friends of Calvin*, 131.
16. Alexander, *Ladies of the Reformation*, 91.

a preacher and teacher as well as to his organization of a form of church-state government founded on the principles of Scripture.[17]

After Idelette's death in 1549, Calvin wrote to a friend, "I have been bereaved of the best companion of my life, of one who, had it been so ordered, would not only have been the willing sharer of my exile and poverty, but even of my death. During her life she was the faithful helper of my ministry. From her I never experienced the slightest hindrance."[18]

> *Lesson #3:* Another lesson a Christian woman can learn from Idelette is that a marriage will be greatly blessed if the wife is committed to being a faithful helpmeet for her husband and if her goals, vision, and passion are similar to his. Do not marry someone you are not committed to helping or someone whose vision and goals differ from your own. Such a marriage will only cause division later on.

Perhaps the crucial point of Calvin and Idelette's marriage is that God's wisdom shines brightest in poor, earthen vessels. A woman Calvin considered marrying prior to marrying Idelette was very wealthy. Although she could have provided a substantial dowry, she did not speak his native French.[19] Can you imagine trying to carry out the world-changing, church-shaping task of providing spiritual direction for the people of God during one of the most challenging times in history with a spouse who did not speak the French language? When we seek God's will first for our lives, we obtain the blessing, says Colossians 3:24. Calvin and Idelette did not seek riches, status, or worldly gain for themselves. They are a beautiful example of believers who united together as spouses to do God's work in a humble yet magnificent way.

> *Lesson #4:* Learn from what Idelette had to offer Calvin that when you look for a spouse for life, do not let wealth or the lack of it be a significant issue. Rather, focus on this question: Are both of us deeply committed to using our talents to provide spiritual direction and health for the church and kingdom of God?

Trials and Perseverance

Soon after their return to Geneva, Idelette prematurely gave birth to a little boy they named Jacques. The baby died a month later in August, 1542. "The Lord has certainly inflicted a severe and bitter wound by the death of our infant son," Calvin wrote to Viret. "But He is himself a Father and knows what is necessary

---

17. Alexander, *Ladies of the Reformation*, 91–92.
18. Schaff, *History of the Christian Church*, 8:419.
19. She spoke German, which Calvin did not know well.

for His children."[20] In the same letter Calvin noted that Idelette was too grief-stricken to write, though she was submitting to God in her affliction. She had also nearly lost her life in the delivery of their baby. Calvin wrote to Viret that she had been in "extreme danger."

Idelette recovered, but sorrow followed upon sorrow. Two years later, she gave birth to a daughter on May 30. Calvin wrote to Farel, "My little daughter labors under a continual fever," and days later she, too, died.[21] Sometime later it seems that a third child was stillborn. In the midst of Calvin's overwhelming duties and pressures, the grief of losing children was most profound, particularly for Idelette. Yet she and Calvin pressed on, submitting to the Lord and putting their trust in Him.

> *Lesson #5*: Idelette's life, which included considerable suffering, shows us the beauty of submitting to God in grief rather than denying or rebelling against it. Her submission teaches us that genuine Christianity bows under God, trusting Him as the greatest friend even when He seems to be our greatest enemy. The end result of such trust is what the Puritans called "the rare jewel of Christian contentment." We might all ask for a greater portion of this Christlike submission.

Insult was then heaped upon sorrow as some Roman Catholics wrote that since sterility in marriage was a reproach and a judgment, the childless condition of Calvin and Idelette must be God's judgment against Calvin.[22] One writer, Baudouin, even wrote, "He married Idelette by whom he had no children, though she was in the prime of life, that the name of this infamous man might not be propagated."[23]

Calvin later said the profound affliction of his childlessness was lifted only by meditating on God's Word and through prayer. He wrote privately to his close friend Pierre Viret that he also found comfort in knowing that he had "myriads of sons throughout the Christian world."[24]

> *Lesson #6*: Just as Idelette, together with her husband, took refuge in God's Word and in prayer in their time of need, we ought to find relief in the midst of life's trials by turning in prayer to the Word-based means of grace. Have you, too, discovered that the Bible is an amazing book of comfort and that prayer gives us solace quite unlike anything else?

---

20. Alexander, *Ladies of the Reformation*, 93.
21. *Tracts and Letters*, 4:420.
22. Schaff, *History of the Christian Church*, 8:418–419.
23. Alexander, *Ladies of the Reformation*, 93.
24. Alexander, *Ladies of the Reformation*, 93.

More heartbreak followed. Around this time the plague struck people all over Geneva. It spread all over Europe, displacing hundreds of thousands of people from their cities and homes. From a letter (April 1541) to his father, we learn that Calvin sent Idelette and the children to Strasburg for safety. The separation from Idelette was unbearable. Though Calvin was deeply anxious about his wife's safety,[25] he was also unwavering in his confidence in Christ. We should learn from this that nothing on earth bound Idelette and Calvin together as strongly as their bond of love anchored in Christ.

> *Lesson #7:* Learn from Idelette, together with her husband, that love for truth that is grounded in unwavering confidence in Christ is what holds a marriage together even in times of prolonged absence and great suffering. We need to cultivate loving trust in each other in good times, when we are not under trials or absent from each other, so that we have much on hand to draw from when the trials and absences do impact our lives.

In 1545, hundreds of persecuted Waldensians took refuge in Geneva. Idelette was at Calvin's side during that time, working hard to provide lodging and employment for them. They were so tireless in their devotion to the immigrants that some Genevans accused them of being more helpful to strangers than to friends.

> *Lesson #8:* Learn from Idelette not to expect everyone to praise you, even when you are doing good. Criticism is an unavoidable reality of life. Learn to accept it, to turn it over to God, and to walk forward with biblical integrity and humility.

John and Idelette Calvin experienced joyous times as well as many heartaches. In our day, when so many psychologists and therapists promise help for marriages based on secular thinking, it is tempting to dismiss Scripture as insufficient for telling us what married life should be. Yet Calvin and Idelette offer a striking example of how a Scripture-based, Christ-centered marriage can function in the midst of challenging circumstances. Losing children and friends, uprooting from one community to another, facing an incredibly demanding schedule, and adjusting to a new marriage are just some of the trials that faced this couple. Yet, they were blessed with a peaceful and joyous marriage and family life.

Calvin and Idelette attributed the success of their marriage to the grace of God. God was their source of forgiveness, compassion, mercy, tenderheartedness, patience, and contentment through all their difficulties. By God's grace, these gifts and principles do not change with the times but remain stable in Christ for believers who pursue God-glorifying marriages. When we live by

---

25. Schaff, *History of the Christian Church,* 8:421.

these principles in union with Christ, our marriages can know a joy that far exceeds worldly happiness.

> *Lesson #9:* Learn from Idelette, together with her husband, that patterning our marriage after Ephesians 5:21–33, then giving God the glory for any success and joy we encounter in marriage, is a sure way to increase our joy until the day we are finally wedded forever to Jesus Christ, the perfect Bridegroom, in the glory of heaven.

Idelette's Death

Idelette's health steadily worsened during her nine years with Calvin. She suffered from fever during the last three years of her life. By March 1549, she was bedridden. At that same time, Calvin was being hounded by powerful enemies in Geneva, not knowing that they would be defeated in six years' time. For the moment, it seemed that everything in his life was crashing down upon him. The city appeared to be rejecting him, his reforms were failing, and his precious wife was dying. Yet, through it all, God sustained His servant.

Idelette's last earthly concern was for her children. Calvin promised to treat them as his own, to which she replied, "I have already commended them to the Lord, but I know well that thou wilt not abandon those whom I have confided in the Lord."[26]

"This greatness of soul," Calvin later wrote, "will influence me more powerfully than a hundred commendations would have done."[27]

At the close of her earthly life, Idelette prayed, "O God of Abraham and of all our fathers, the faithful in all generations have trusted in Thee, and none have ever been confounded. I also will hope."[28] She passed on to glory April 5, 1549. Calvin was at her side, speaking to her of the happiness they had enjoyed for nine years and about the joy she would soon have in "exchanging an abode on earth for her Father's house above."[29]

> *Lesson #10:* Learn from Idelette that those who, by grace, live well, usually die well. Idelette had a sweet, submissive death, despite the pain that preceded it. When we surrender everything to God, both in life and death, we will not only worry less in this life but we will also not be confounded even when difficulties loom before us. Our comfort in Christ and His salvation is good for both life and death, and for all eternity.

---

26. James I. Good, *Famous Women of the Reformed Church* (repr., Birmingham: Solid Ground Christian books, 2002), 29.
27. Alexander, *Ladies of the Reformation*, 97.
28. Good, *Famous Women of the Reformed Church*, 29.
29. Alexander, *Ladies of the Reformation*, 97.

Calvin's letters shortly after Idelette's death expressed his grief over losing his dearest companion, who he said was a rare woman without equal.[30] Even on her deathbed "she was never troublesome to me," he wrote.[31] That made Calvin's sorrow even more profound. This trial shows us that submitting ourselves to the will of God does not exclude us from hardship.

Calvin was only forty when Idelette died. Like Hezekiah, fifteen years would be added to his life, but they would be years without his precious wife. He wrote to his friends that he could scarcely continue with his work, yet he steeled himself to do so. His enemies charged Calvin with being heartless for working so diligently, but Calvin was anything but heartless. He wrote to a friend, "I do what I can that I may not be altogether consumed with grief. I have been bereaved of the best companion of my life; she was the faithful helper of my ministry.... My friends leave nothing undone to lighten, in some degree, the sorrow of my soul.... May the Lord Jesus confirm you by His Spirit, and me also under this great affliction, which certainly would have crushed me had not He whose office it is to raise up the prostrate, to strengthen the weak, and to revive the faint, extended help to me from heaven."[32]

Conclusion

Our culture has a cynical view of marriage and promiscuity. A recent report on the rising rate of divorce shows that it is highest among people ages twenty-five to thirty-five. While some of this rise in divorce may be due to the economy, one contributing factor is the wedding day itself. So much time and money are spent planning for the wedding day that little time is spent preparing for the marriage! A society that emphasizes only the wedding day tends to breed cynicism about marriage.

The biblical view of marriage is quite different. Scripture teaches us that sin has deeply disfigured God's intentions for marriage, but Christ has lovingly restored it.[33] True joy in marriage results when a husband strives to love his wife the way Christ loves the church and when the wife strives to respect her husband the way the church respects Jesus Christ. John and Idelette Calvin knew that joy. One of the most amazing things about their relationship is that

---

30. Michael Haykin, "Christian Marriage in the 21st Century: Listening to John Calvin on the Purpose of Marriage," in *Calvin for Today* (Grand Rapids: Reformation Heritage Books, 2009), 218–24.

31. Schaff, *History of the Christian Church*, 8:419.

32. Alexander, *Ladies of the Reformation*, 97.

33. Haykin, "Christian Marriage in the 21st Century: Listening to John Calvin on the Purpose of Marriage," 15.

they exuded joy even in the most traumatic circumstances. They knew what it meant to rejoice in God in the midst of persecution. They found joy in the fear of God as they strove to glorify Him. They found joy in their salvation, joy in their fidelity to each other, joy in each other's love and companionship, and joy in service to their neighbor. In short, Idelette was a genuine, joyous helpmate to her husband.

> *Lesson #11*: Learn from Idelette, together with her husband, that true joy is not found in living for one's self; it is only found in serving God as number one, serving our spouse as number two, and serving ourselves as number three. That is the essence of the blueprint for a truly joyous marriage and joyous life that Paul has outlined for us in Colossians 3:12–17.

Chapter 37

Rediscovering the Laity: The Reformation in the Pew and in the Classroom[1]

Read 2 Timothy 3:1–4:5

The Reformation revived the role of the laity. Prior to the Reformation, church members were reduced to an audience watching a priest do the Mass and listening to choirs of monks sing in Latin. But the Reformation revived the priesthood of the laity as commanded in the Scriptures. Peasants learned from the gospel to draw near to the holy God through faith in Christ's blood and intercession. Soldiers and printers participated in worship by singing the Scriptures back to God. Bakers, carpenters, and milkmaids took up their work as sacred ministries through which they served God according to His Word. None of this undermined the pastoral ministry but exalted it as spreading the Word to equip the saints.

The Reformers dreamed of Word- and Spirit-filled men, women, and children of all social and educational levels. William Tyndale devoted himself to translating the Scriptures into the vernacular of the English people. Tyndale once told a priest, "If God spare my life, ere many years pass, I will cause a boy that driveth the plough to know more of the Scriptures than thou dost." His dream came true as his translation paved the way for every parish church in England to offer an English Bible to all its members. Tyndale paid for that Bible with his life.[2]

I praise God that the Holy Spirit is stirring a renewed interest in the Reformation today. This, then, is the topic before us now: "Rediscovering the Laity: The Reformation in the Pew and in the Classroom." The question we must answer is: How may we bring the Reformation to people in the pews today?

---

1. This chapter was delivered as an address for a conference held at Southern Baptist Theological Seminary in Louisville, Kentucky, on September 28, 2010.

2. John D. Woodbridge, ed., *Great Leaders of the Christian Church* (Chicago: Moody, 1988), 202–203, 205.

Our rule for reformation, as well as for all matters of faith and obedience, is the Holy Scriptures. In 2 Timothy, the apostle Paul warns his young friend, Timothy, of present and future perils that besiege the church. False teachers are already spreading errors like a deadly disease among believers (2 Tim. 2:16–18; 3:6–9; 4:3). The church is swimming in a rising tide of wickedness (3:1–4). And people are embracing external religion without true spirituality, "having a form of godliness, but denying the power thereof" (3:5). Such people have no appetite for sound doctrine but seek teachers who will scratch them where they itch (4:3–4). How should Christian leaders respond to these problems in the church? Let us examine three suggestions Paul offers in 2 Timothy 3 and 4.

Remember the Fathers of the Church

We read in 2 Timothy 3:10–11: "But thou hast fully known my doctrine, manner of life, purpose, faith, longsuffering, charity, patience, persecutions, afflictions, which came unto me at Antioch, at Iconium, at Lystra; what persecutions I endured: but out of them all the Lord delivered me." In this passage, Paul is urging Timothy to remember the Christ-shaped pattern in Paul. Paul is not boasting of his own merits but reminding Timothy of how God uses one part of the body to strengthen the rest. Paul is a spiritual father to Timothy, so Timothy is called to meditate on his example and teachings.

This principle is expanded in Hebrews 13:7–8, which says, "Remember them which have the rule over you, who have spoken unto you the word of God: whose faith follows, considering the end of their conversation. Jesus Christ is the same yesterday, and today, and forever." Christ shines in the conversation of the church fathers, that is, in their lives. Remembering the fathers was a conviction of the Reformers, who sought to return to the biblical, Christ-centered simplicity of the church fathers. How should we introduce the laity to the fathers of the Reformation?

Teach Them about the Reformers

Whenever you preach or teach, speak to the church about the Reformers, great and small. Do not offer an academic lecture on these fathers; tell their stories. Summarize their teachings in contemporary language. Beware of using long quotes in outdated language. Help people to see Christ in these men and in their teachings.

Take advantage of historic dates to do this. For example, October 31 is the date on which Martin Luther nailed his ninety-five theses to the Wittenberg church door. I use this date as an opportunity to preach on the life of a Reformer or principles of the Reformation, grounding it in a scriptural text that best exemplifies God's work of grace. For example, I have preached about God's grace in the lives of Martin Luther, Ulrich Zwingli, John Calvin, Theodore Beza, and William Tyndale.

You might also offer a class for adults on Reformed doctrine. I taught a class of about two hundred people over a period of five years, moving from prolegomena to eschatology, covering the whole field of systematic theology from a Reformed perspective.[3] I was amazed at how eager people were to learn.

Encourage People to Read about the Reformers

Introduce believers to great Christian leaders through books about the Reformers. For example, Reformation Heritage Books is publishing a series of books titled *Profiles in Reformed Spirituality*. Each book profiles a significant Reformed leader, such as John Calvin, George Swinnock, Thomas Goodwin, or Jonathan Edwards. After a brief sketch of each man's life and spirituality, each book offers selections of the person's writings or letters. The books offer easy-to-read, devotional writing broken into selections that are only a few pages long. Hopefully, these short books will encourage people to go on to read larger works written by the Reformers and Puritans themselves.

People welcome such books if they are hungry for the Word. For example, a pastor received a free copy of *John Calvin: A Heart for Devotion, Doctrine, & Doxology*, edited by Burk Parsons. The pastor gave it to a factory worker who had a love for Christ. The factory worker later brought the book to his Bible study group to share with others.

If you are a pastor, you might encourage your congregation to read the works of Reformers or books about them. I did that for years when I taught a mid-week adult class. I would suggest some material on the life of a Reformer or Puritan, then invite people to sign up to buy a book or two. Often I sold up to two hundred copies of a particular book to our local church. I often followed up these sales by talking to the people about these books when I came to their homes for a pastoral visit.

Promote God Glorifying Websites on the Reformation

The worldwide web has revolutionized the way we receive information. We should not reject the internet, but we do need great discernment in mining the valuable things found on it. Promote a wide range of useful websites among your congregants. Directory sites like Google Books, Monergism, A Puritan's

---

3. The workbook used for the class is *Bible Doctrine Student Workbook* (Grand Rapids: Reformation Heritage Books, 1993).

Mind, Christian Classics Ethereal Library, Puritan Library, and many more can be useful for devotional or theological study. There are tens of thousands of articles, journals, magazines, and books available at these sites. YouTube can be used, with a lot of caution, to view videos, debates, forums, or brief biographies about Reformation people and theology. Scores of Reformed blogs and hundreds more websites from churches and other ministries can be utilized to better understand how and where the Lord is promoting the Reformed faith throughout the world. For sermons, sermonaudio.com is incredibly helpful.

iTunes continues to shape the way we receive audio output; iTunes-U offers lectures from many universities, including several Reformed universities, with free downloads for laypeople to listen and learn from. Puritan Reformed Theological Seminary has a vast collection of their classes online that can be listened to via mp3s. Facebook offers users opportunities to plug into different groups, from their favorite Reformed authors to publishing companies to their favorite Reformed or Puritan theologians, where they are socially connected with like-minded people throughout the world. Promote good and God-glorifying uses of the internet among your people.

Instruct Children in the Church

Second Timothy 3:15 says, "And that from a child thou hast known the holy scriptures, which are able to make thee wise unto salvation through faith which is in Christ Jesus." Instructing little ones in the Scriptures lays a foundation for reformation in troubled times.

Jesus is the Apostle and High Priest of our profession, says Hebrews 3:1. No seminary professor or author or pastor has had a higher calling than our Lord. Yet, contrary to the culture of His day, Jesus invited small children to come to Him (Matt. 19:13–15). He gave them His precious time. Should not we also serve our children?

Use the Catechisms

In his preface to the Catechism of the Church of Geneva (1545), John Calvin writes, "It has always been a matter which the Church has held in singular commendation, to see that little children should be instructed in Christian doctrine." His catechism begins by stating, "What is the chief end of human life? To know God. Why do you say that? Because He created us and placed us in this world to be glorified in us…. What is the sovereign good [or chief happiness] of man? The same thing."[4]

Churches of the Reformation produced many beautiful catechisms for the church. Find a catechism that reflects the richest biblical truths of your theological stream, and teach it to your children. Turn off the TV, let the computer hibernate, and teach the catechism. Be creative when you do so. Jim Scott Orrick composed *The Baptist Catechism Set to Music* so that preschoolers can sing by heart such truths as, "God is a spirit, infinite, eternal, and unchangeable, in his being, wisdom, power, holiness, justice, goodness and truth." Music is a wonderful way to catechize children.

Promote the Writing of Sound Books for Children
R. C. Sproul has written several gripping children's books, some of which are now available as audio books. For example, *The King without a Shadow* is a delightful tale about a king and a little boy who are both learning about God. He also wrote *The Prince's Poison Cup*, a moving parable for children about substitutionary atonement. Christian Focus Publications has published many short biographies on Christians, such as Robert Murray M'Cheyne, written by Irene Howat. What a joy it is to introduce such a godly man to a grade-school child!

Check out Sinclair Ferguson's efforts in Reformed truth for children, such as *Big Book of Bible Truths, Books 1 and 2*; *The Plan: How God got the world ready for Jesus*; and *Jesus Teaches Us How to Pray*. Or read James W. Beeke's seven-volume series on Reformed Theology, which includes *Bible Doctrine for Younger Children, Books A and B* (for grades 4–5), *Bible Doctrine for Older Children, Books A and B* (for grades 6–7), and *Bible Doctrine for Teens and Young Adults, Books 1–3*. Teacher workbooks are provided for this unique set of books.

Reformation Heritage Books offers a coffee-table style book that is beautifully illustrated for children ten years old and up, titled *Reformation Heroes*, which presents illustrated stories of forty Reformers. The goal of this book is to teach young people about real Reformation heroes rather than Hollywood or sport heroes. It is also suitable for use in Christian schools or home education. Many adults are reading the book to learn more about men such as Henry Bullinger, Peter Martyr Vermigli, and Martin Bucer. The book offers a detailed

---

4. James T. Dennison, Jr., ed., *Reformed Confessions of the 16th and 17th Centuries in English Translation: Volume I, 1523–1552* (Grand Rapids: Reformation Heritage Books, 2008), 468. Where the French reads, "the sovereign good" (*le souverain bien*), the Latin reads *summum bonum*. An old English translation renders it, "the chief felicitie." Benjamin. B. Warfield, *The Westminster Assembly and Its Work* (Grand Rapids: Baker Book House, 1991), 382.

bibliography on each hero in the back of the book to help people who wish to read more about the Reformers.

Reformation Heritage Books is also working with Simonetta Carr to produce a series of books about John Calvin, John Owen, and other Reformers. The series is for children, ages seven through ten, and includes many beautiful illustrations.

Preach the Scriptures to the Church

Paul writes in 2 Timothy 3:16–4:2, "All scripture is given by inspiration of God, and is profitable for doctrine, for reproof, for correction, for instruction in righteousness: that the man of God may be perfect, thoroughly furnished unto all good works. I charge thee therefore before God, and the Lord Jesus Christ, who shall judge the quick and the dead at his appearing and his kingdom; preach the word; be instant in season, out of season; reprove, rebuke, exhort with all longsuffering and doctrine."

The Bible is the key to the sixteenth-century Reformation and to reformation in the church today. More and more the church seems to be moving back to its pre-Reformation condition. The royal priesthood of the laity is being reduced to observation rather than participation. Biblical ignorance abounds. The church needs men who will preach the Word as the Reformers did centuries ago.

Paul reminds us in 2 Timothy 3:15 that Scripture is the means through which we must preach Christ. We need preachers who will powerfully and winsomely set forth Christ's beauties and fullness of grace as our Prophet, Priest, and King. Nothing will move Christ's people further towards biblical reformation than helping them taste the sovereign sweetness of their Savior. Expository, doctrinal, experiential preaching on God's Word is the greatest means for biblical reformation and spiritual revival.

Promote Books That Preach the Bible

Some of the best books of all time are compilations of sermons. Wilhelmus à Brakel, a Dutch pastor and theologian, wrote:

> [The preacher's] life generally is of short duration, during which his preaching reaches but a few and he himself is consumed while illuminating others.... God has wonderfully compensated for both the brevity of the minister's life as well as the limited scope of his audience, by having given man the wisdom to become acquainted with the art of printing....

Now a single minister, even centuries after his death, is capable of preaching to an entire nation, yes, even to the entire world.[5]

Brakel's great work is still preaching the Bible more than three hundred years after he wrote it. How can we measure the value of such Bible-saturated books and their usefulness in the hands of the Holy Spirit?

A truck driver was asked to teach a Sunday school class on the topic of sanctification. He noticed a book in the church library titled *The Gospel Mystery of Sanctification*, written by Walter Marshall, a Puritan, and put into modern language. The truck driver's Sunday school class was treated to a wonderfully sweet exploration of our union with Jesus Christ, who is our sanctification.

Sing Songs That Preach the Bible

One of the most powerful means to train laypeople in biblical truth is through singing. Colossians 3:16 says, "Let the word of Christ dwell in you richly in all wisdom; teaching and admonishing one another in psalms and hymns and spiritual songs, singing with grace in your hearts to the Lord." Poorly chosen songs in worship will negatively impact the theology of the laity, no matter how good the preaching is. But solid, biblical worship fortified by Scripture-based singing can enrich biblical faith and godliness for many generations.

Sing the Scriptures; what better way is there to bring reformation to the heart? Sing the Psalms. God did not give us the book of Psalms just to study them. Psalms are to be sung! Much of the Reformation revolved around worship, and Reformed worship revolves around the Psalms. Calvin said,

> That which St. Augustine has said is true, that no one is able to sing things worthy of God except that which he has received from him. Therefore, when we have looked thoroughly, and searched here and there, we shall not find better songs nor more fitting for the purpose, than the Psalms of David, which the Holy Spirit spoke and made through him. And moreover, when we sing them, we are certain that God puts in our mouths these, as if he himself were singing in us to exalt his glory.[6]

If you want children to memorize Scriptures, why not teach them to sing Bible passages? Many CDs have been made of Bible songs. So urge parents to sing the Scriptures in their family devotions and at the bedsides of their beloved

---

5. Wilhelmus à Brakel, *The Christian's Reasonable Service*, trans. Bartel Elshout, ed. Joel R. Beeke (Grand Rapids: Reformation Heritage Books, 1999), 1:cxiv.

6. John Calvin, "Preface" to the *Genevan Psalter*, quoted by W. Robert Godfrey in *The Worship of God* (Ross-shire: Christian Focus, 2005), 45.

children. If you teach someone to sing the Bible, they will remember God's Word every time they hear or sing verses of the Word of God set to music.

So, to reform the laity, teach them to remember the fathers of the church. Teach the children in the church. And preach the Scriptures to the church. Preach God's Word with your mouth, with books, and with spiritual songs. Preach the Word.

Conclusion: Prayerful Patience in Reformation

Two words in 2 Timothy 4:2 are a fitting conclusion to this teaching on reforming the laity: "all longsuffering." Patience is a key element in the education of the laity. In 2 Timothy 2:24–25 Paul exhorts Timothy, "The servant of the Lord must not strive; but be gentle unto all men, apt to teach, patient, in meekness instructing those that oppose themselves; if God peradventure will give them repentance to the acknowledging of the truth."

Do not rush at the laity with Reformation truth to trample them underfoot. Impatience will discredit our ministry, for it savors of pride rather than the meekness of Christ. Reformation is a spiritual work, requiring God's supernatural gifts of enlightenment and repentance. It summons us to labor on our knees, praying for laypeople. If only God can bring reformation, then men of prayer are true reformers.

But reformation also summons us to be patient, for God works in His time. Luther did not quickly learn to say, "Doctrine is heaven." He learned it by living the truths of Scripture. He learned it through meditation, affliction, and prayer. We, too, must not expect our churches to become thoroughly reformed overnight.

We should also be wary of forcing people into a mold. We are to be the mouth of Jesus Christ whereby the sheep hear the voice of their Shepherd calling them forward. This is indeed a work of long-suffering. This work takes a long time and may mean suffering along the way. It may even cost us our lives, as it did with William Tyndale. But in our suffering we can show the laity the love of the Good Shepherd, who laid down His life for the sheep.

Chapter 38

In Commemoration of the Heidelberg Catechism's 450th Anniversary: The Heidelberg Catechism as a Confession of Faith

But why art thou called a Christian?
Because I am a member of Christ by faith, and thus am partaker of His anointing; that so I may confess His name, and present myself a living sacrifice of thankfulness to Him....

—Heidelberg Catechism, Q. 32

What is a confession of faith? How is it related to the truth revealed in God's Word? Scotland's Robert Shaw (1795–1863) provides this definition:

A Confession of Faith...is a declaration of the manner in which any man, or number of men—any Christian or any Church—understands the truth which has been revealed. Its object is, therefore not to teach divine truth; but to exhibit a clear, systematic, and intelligible declaration of our own sentiments, and to furnish the means of ascertaining the opinions of others, especially in religious controversies.... The question is not, therefore, one respecting God's truth, but respecting man's truth—not respecting the truth of the Bible, but respecting man's apprehension of that truth.[1]

In other words, a confession of faith is not simply a summary of statements taken from Scripture. Nor is it an exercise in exegesis, the science of drawing the precise meaning out of a Scripture text. The exegesis of Scripture is the necessary, but preliminary, work that furnishes the foundation of biblical truth on which the confession is based.

A confession of faith is an exercise in hermeneutics, the science of interpreting and applying the results of sound exegesis or "searching of the Scriptures" (John 5:39; Acts 17:17). Exegesis answers the question of "What precisely does

---

1. Robert Shaw, *The Reformed Faith: An Exposition of the Westminster Confession of Faith* (1845; repr., Inverness: Christian Focus, 2008), "Introductory Essay," 11, 13. Shaw was professor in the Associate Presbytery's Divinity Hall at Whitburn, W. Lothian, from 1817 until his death.

the text say?" Hermeneutics answers such questions as "What does it mean to us? How do we understand it and apply it?"

The most important truth revealed in Scripture is the way of salvation in Christ. What precisely is the good news, the gospel? How are sinners saved? What does it mean to be a Christian? Hence the remarkable starting point for the Heidelberg Catechism is its statement of the Christian's only comfort in life and in death.

Unique among all confessions of faith, ancient and modern, the Heidelberg Catechism begins with the good news that Christ has fully satisfied the price of all our sins with His precious blood and delivered us from all the power of the devil. Those who belong to Christ are justified, emancipated, preserved, adopted by God as His children, indwelt by the Spirit, sanctified, assured of eternal life, and made "willing and ready henceforth" to live for Christ.[2]

Other Functions of a Confession of Faith

Shaw goes on to identify other functions of a confession of faith. A confession of faith is the church's united affirmation of the truth: "Since she has been constituted the depository of God's truth, it is her duty to him to state, in the most distinct and explicit terms, what she understands that truth to mean. In this manner she not only proclaims what God has said, but also appends her seal that God is true."[3] The confession thus becomes the church's "Yea and Amen" (2 Cor. 1:20) to God's Word, affirming its truth and trustworthiness and its inerrant and infallible authority as "given by inspiration of God to be the rule of faith and life."[4]

As a witness to how the church understands the truth of God in Scripture, and as an affirmation and commendation of that truth, a confession of faith also serves as a standard of teaching and interpretation for the church's ministers of the Word, a bond of union for the members of the church, a term of admission for others who ask to be received as members of the church, and finally, a common testimony to the wider church and to the world at large.

Doxology: The Ultimate End of a Confession of Faith

The Heidelberg Catechism says a Christian partakes of Christ's anointing "that so I may confess His name, and present myself a living sacrifice of thanksgiving

---

2. Heidelberg Catechism, Q. 1 [hereafter: Catechism]. Citations from the catechism are taken from the version printed in *The Psalter* (Grand Rapids: Reformation Heritage Books, 1999).

3. Shaw, xiii. See also John 3:33.

4. *Westminster Confession of Faith* (Glasgow: Free Presbyterian, 1994), 1.2.

to Him."[5] The third commandment regulates our use of God's name, "so that He may be rightly confessed and worshipped by us, and be glorified in all our words and works."[6] The ninth commandment requires of the believer that "I love the truth, speak it uprightly and confess it."[7] Thus the ultimate end of a confession of faith is to praise God for the truth and grace that shine together in His most holy and divine Word.[8]

Evaluating the Catechism as a Confession of Faith

In the light of the nature and functions of a confession of faith, how well does the Heidelberg Catechism fulfill these purposes?

1. As an explanation of the way of salvation
2. As a statement of the church's understanding of the system of biblical truth in general
3. As an affirmation of the truth and trustworthiness of God's Word
4. As a guide to the application of that Word to the believer's faith and life
5. As a doxology, or ascription of praise to God.

Let's examine each of these individually.

As an Explanation of the Way of Salvation

The Heidelberg Catechism is unique among all the confessions and catechisms of the Reformation in its starting point, the Christian's "only comfort." The catechism thus begins its explanation of the truth of God with a summary of what the gospel means to a believer.

The way of salvation is presented in the most personal terms. Salvation is found in self-denial, self-renunciation, and committing all to the hands of our faithful Savior, Jesus Christ, knowing that He has paid for our sins with His precious blood and delivered us from all the power of the devil—that is, from condemnation, death, and hell.

This succinct but satisfying summary of the gospel opens the way for the next six Lord's Days to be devoted to our creation and fall, our helpless condition as sinners, and our need for a Mediator and Deliverer. Step by step, we are brought face to face with the Lord Jesus Christ, our Mediator, the incarnate

---

5. Catechism, Q. 32.
6. Catechism, Q. 99.
7. Catechism, Q. 112.
8. *The Psalter*, No. 381 (Psalm 138).

Son of God, "who of God is made unto us wisdom, and righteousness, and sanctification, and redemption."[9]

At this juncture, the catechism asks, "Are all men then, as they perished in Adam, saved by Christ?" Answer: "No; only those who are ingrafted in Him, and receive all His benefits, by a true faith."[10] "True faith" is one of the recurring themes of the catechism, referred to many times and explained in various places.

The term is meant to be a reminder that, as Christ teaches in the parable of the sower (Matt. 13:3–9, 18–23), there is more than one kind of faith. True faith endures, and it bears much fruit. Its counterfeit versions endure only for a time, if at all; are easily overwhelmed by life's circumstances; and although they may show promise at the first, in the end bear no real or lasting fruit. Thus the catechism states:

> True faith is not only a certain knowledge, whereby I hold for truth all that God has revealed to us in His Word, but also an assured confidence, which the Holy Ghost works by the Gospel in my heart, that not only to others, but to me also, remission of sin, everlasting righteousness and salvation are freely given by God, merely of grace, only for the sake of Christ's merits.[11]

The Marrow Men of Scotland could not have written a better description of faith taking hold of Christ for salvation, as He is freely offered in the gospel. Over many generations, Reformed Christians have cherished this description of true faith, and some have asked that it be expounded at their funerals as their witness to the living.

Much more could be said. The contents of the gospel—what they mean to the believer, how they are experienced in Christ, and what it should mean for our lives—is another recurring theme of the catechism. True faith is revisited in connection with the substantial account of justification by faith alone in Lord's Days 23 and 51. It could justly be said that the catechism as a whole is an explanation and commentary on the way of salvation in Christ.

As an Explanation of the System of Biblical Truth

The catechism is not narrowly focused on one aspect of revealed truth. Rather, adhering to the ancient custom of explaining the Twelve Articles of the Apostles' Creed, the catechism explains the whole system of truth revealed in the Bible, including the being of God; the trinity of persons in the Godhead; creation and providence; the incarnation of the Son; His names and titles; His work in the

---

9. 1 Corinthians 1:30, cited in Catechism, Q. 18.
10. Catechism, Q. 20.
11. Catechism, Q. 21.

state of humiliation to accomplish redemption, including suffering, crucifixion, death, and burial; His exaltation to God's right hand; His subsequent work in applying redemption through the work of the Spirit in the life of the church and the believer; and His coming again to judge the world.

At each point the catechism does several things at once. It demands explanations and definitions, asking the questions time and again, "What dost thou mean by that? What believest thou when thou sayest that?" It often follows up an answer by asking another question or raising an objection, compelling the respondent to reason with the truth and examine its implications. And finally, it addresses the matter of application: "What advantage is it to us? What profit dost thou receive? What further benefit do we receive? What comfort is it to thee?"

As an explanation of how Reformed believers understand the foundational truths revealed in Scripture, the catechism cannot be faulted. It excels beyond other Reformed confessions of faith by teaching the believer to reason from Scripture to those "good and necessary consequences" cited by the Westminster Divines, which are also held to be part of the whole counsel of God.[12]

As an Affirmation of the Truth of God's Word

No section of the Heidelberg Catechism is devoted to the doctrine of Scripture; certainly, there is nothing like the first chapter of the Westminster Confession, or Articles 2 through 7 of the Belgic Confession.

This deficiency is covered by the catechism's definition of true faith as in part, "a certain knowledge whereby I hold for truth all that God has revealed to us in His Word."

This statement has the ring of childlike faith in the truth of Scripture, and that is not to be despised. Furthermore, the catechism makes good on this assertion of faith in the truth and trustworthiness of the whole of Scripture:

+ The believer knows his misery "out of the law of God" (Q. 3).

+ He knows that Christ is the Mediator "from the holy gospel, which God Himself first revealed in Paradise, and afterwards published by the patriarchs and prophets, and represented by the sacrifices and other ceremonies of the law; and lastly has fulfilled it by His only begotten Son" (Q. 19).

+ He holds that it is necessary for a Christian to believe "all things promised us in the gospel" (Q. 22).

---

12. Westminster Confession of Faith, 1.6.

- He believes in the Trinity "because God has so revealed Himself in His Word" (Q. 25).

- He believes that Christ, as King and Head of the church, builds His church and governs us "by His Word and Spirit" (Q. 31, 54).

- He believes that the Holy Ghost "works faith in our hearts by the preaching of the gospel" (Q. 65), and that such preaching is one of "the keys of the kingdom" (Q. 83).

- He believes that infants are to be baptized because they "are included in the covenant...and since redemption from sin by the blood of Christ, and the Holy Ghost, the author of faith, is promised to them no less than to the adult" (Q. 74).

- He expects Christ to feed and nourish believers with His body and blood in the sacrament of Holy Communion, because He has promised to do so "in the institution of the holy supper" and because "this promise is repeated by the holy apostle Paul" (Q. 77).

- He knows that good works must be "such as are performed according to the law of God...and not such as are founded on the imaginations or institutions of man" (Q. 91).

- He believes that he must "pray to the one true God only, who hath manifested Himself in His word, for all things He has commanded us to ask of Him" (Q. 117).

It is clear from this chain of evidences that the inerrant truth and infallible authority of Scripture as God's inspired rule of faith and life is everywhere assumed, believed, and acted upon in the catechism, even though an explicit statement of the doctrine of Scripture is missing. The situation is succinctly described in the Westminster Confession:

> By this faith, a Christian believeth to be true whatsoever is revealed in the word, for the authority of God himself speaking therein; and acteth differently upon that which each particular passage thereof containeth; yielding obedience to the commands, trembling at the threatenings, and embracing the promises of God for this life and that which is to come. But the principle acts of saving faith are, accepting, receiving and resting upon Christ alone for justification, sanctification and eternal life.[13]

---

13. Westminster Confession of Faith, 14.2.

As a Guide to the Application of Scripture to Faith and Life
In passing, note that other doctrinal topics are highlighted in confessions of faith that receive scant or no attention in the catechism. It offers only the barest essentials of the doctrines of election, the church, and the covenant of grace. It does not mention church polity, the civil magistrate, or the Christian commonwealth. For statements on these topics, Reformed believers may consult the Belgic Confession, the Liturgy of the Reformed Churches, including the Forms for Baptism and the Lord's Supper, and at a later date, the Canons of Dort.

But as a guide for the application of the truth of Scripture to faith and life, the catechism is unsurpassed. We have already noted how, in explaining the Articles of the Creed, the catechism constantly presses the believer to know and experience the practical side of each doctrinal truth, driving all home with the final demand: "But what doth it profit thee now that thou believest all this?" (Q. 59). So the truths of Scripture, rightly understood, are applied to the faith and comfort of the believer, one by one.

The lessons regarding the application of Scripture to life are presented in the form of an explanation of each of the Ten Commandments of the moral law. Unlike Westminster's Larger Catechism, the Heidelberg does not major on the details of all the specific duties required or on the numerous particular sins forbidden. Rather, the basic requirement of the commandment is stated in a memorable form, full of implications for the believer to draw out for himself.

There are exceptions along the way, of course, such as Question 98, which specifically asks if "images may be tolerated in the churches as books for the [illiterate] laity," as the Roman Catholic Church had taught. The answer is "No, for we must not pretend to be wiser than God, who will have His people taught, not by dumb images, but by the lively preaching of His Word."

The original German text of Lord's Day 38, devoted to the fourth commandment, made no reference to the Christian Sabbath as such. That deficiency was covered by the fathers at Dort, by adding the words, "especially on the Sabbath, that is, on the day of rest." Otherwise, the text paints a vivid portrait of church-going in the sixteenth century.

Lord's Day 41 reminds believers that purity and self-control are as obligatory for married persons as for singles. The seventh commandment is said to teach "that all uncleanness is accursed of God; and that therefore we must with all our hearts detest the same, and live chastely and temperately, whether in holy wedlock or in single life" (Q. 108).

But the explanation of the commandments comes to a somewhat bittersweet end in Lord's Day 44, where the believer is told that "even the holiest men, while in this life, have only a small beginning of this obedience; yet so, that with a sincere resolution they begin to live, not only according to some, but all the commandments of God" (Q. 114). Our sanctification will never be perfect or even very substantial in this life. The Christian life is a life of repentance, sorrowing over our sins, seeking pardon for them from God, and striving to be conformed to the image of the Son; but we shall reach that goal when we are safe on the other side, "at the perfection proposed to us in a life to come" (Q. 115).

The final section of the catechism is devoted to the practice of prayer and to the understanding and profitable use of the Lord's Prayer. Each of the six petitions of the Lord's Prayer is explained, not by objective statement but by expanding the simple words of the petitions into six prayers for the believer to use in private or family worship. The extreme aversion to "form prayers" that sprang up among the more radical Puritans was unknown to the Reformers.

This treatment of the Lord's Prayer means that as the catechism comes to an end, instruction ceases and gives way to worship in an extended time of prayer to our God and Father in heaven (Q. 122–129). In terms of application, what could be more thorough than to cease from hearing and get on to the doing of the truth?

As Doxology: Praising God for His Truth and Grace

One final dimension in which the Heidelberg Catechism exceeds other Reformed confessions of faith is the way in which doxology, or the ascription of praise to God, is woven into its very fabric. One reason is the decision to discuss the Christian life under the heading of "Thankfulness." No less than twenty-one Lord's Days (32–52) are devoted to the theme of "how I shall express my gratitude to God for such deliverance," and so "enjoying this comfort, may live and die happily."[14]

But the catechism does not wait until Lord's Day 32 before introducing notes of praise to God for His truth and grace. At the very outset, in Question 1, the believer testifies to a great change of heart, declaring that Christ by His Holy Spirit has made him "willing and ready, henceforth to live unto Him." The heart has been redirected from self to Christ. This redirection is necessary as a precondition for offering acceptable worship, praise, and thanksgiving to God.

In Question 6, we are reminded that man was created with the capacity to "know God his Creator, heartily love Him and live with Him in eternal happiness to glorify and praise Him." This is the Heidelberger counterpart to the famous dictum of Westminster's Shorter Catechism that "Man's chief end is to

---

14. Catechism, Q. 2.

glorify God, and to enjoy Him forever."[15] This capacity was lost to man in the fall in paradise but recovered, as we have seen, in redemption.

Question 32 tells us that the Christian partakes of Christ's anointing "that so I may confess His name, and present myself a living sacrifice of thankfulness to Him." Question 43 states that by virtue of the death of Christ on the cross, our old man is crucified with Him, "that so the corrupt inclinations of the flesh may no more reign in us, but that we may offer ourselves unto Him a sacrifice of thanksgiving." Question 58, on the life everlasting, anticipates the joys of heaven, where salvation is perfected in glory, as the final state of the believer in which he shall "praise God therein for ever."

Refuting a common objection to justification by faith alone, Question 64 declares that "it is impossible that those, who are implanted into Christ by a true faith, should not bring forth fruits of thankfulness." Or, as the Westminster Confession says, "Faith…is the alone instrument of justification; yet is it not alone in the person justified, but is ever accompanied with all other saving graces, and is no dead faith, but worketh by love."[16]

Doxology is more fully explained in the third part of the catechism, "Of Thankfulness," beginning with Lord's Day 32. Question 86 says we must still do good works, "that so we may testify, by the whole of our conduct, our gratitude to God for His blessings, and that He may be praised by us." Question 91 insists that those works are only good if "performed…to His glory."

Question 94 says the first commandment enjoins us "to love, fear and glorify" God with our whole heart. Question 99 states that the third commandment requires us to "use the holy name of God no otherwise that with fear and reverence, so that He may be rightly confessed and worshipped by us, and be glorified in all our words and works."

Finally, the first petition of the Lord's Prayer, "Hallowed be Thy name," is explained as the believer's heartfelt plea that "we may so order and direct our whole lives, our thoughts, words, and actions, that Thy name may never be blasphemed, but rather honored and praised on our account" (Q. 122). Concluding the prayer with the doxology "For Thine is the kingdom, the power, and the glory for ever," the believer professes that he has asked all things "because Thou, being our King and almighty, art willing and able to give us all good; and all this we pray for, that thereby not we, but Thy holy name may be glorified forever" (Q. 128).

---

15. Westminster Shorter Catechism, Q. 1.
16. Westminster Confession of Faith, 11.2.

From the first steps we take in the Christian life until our feet are firmly planted in the halls of heaven, the catechism teaches us that our first and great duty is to love God, to praise Him, to give thanks to Him always, and to glorify Him in all that we say and do. This is the end for which we were created. This is the end for which we have been redeemed in Christ. This is why we have been given His Word. This is why we have been indwelt by the Holy Spirit. And this is why we have been appointed a place in the Father's house on high, to dwell with God forever.

Conclusion

By now you will have discerned my bias in favor of the Heidelberg Catechism as a confession of faith. Along the way, I have tried to take note of its deficiencies in regard to important doctrines that receive little or no attention. However, some of the most important Reformed confessions have been criticized for similar defects and omissions.

For example, the Westminster Confession of Faith has been critiqued for its scant reference to the love of God[17] and its failure to devote a specific chapter to the person and work of the Holy Spirit or to include a chapter on the gospel. Early in the twentieth century, zealous efforts were made to remedy those perceived defects. That is why some Presbyterian denominations have a few more chapters in their versions of the Westminster Confession of Faith beyond the usual thirty-three.

I am happy to belong to a denomination that holds not only to the three Westminster standards but also the Heidelberg Catechism together with the Belgic Confession and the Canons of Dort as "Three Forms of Unity." Together, these "subordinate standards" provide a more complete testimony than any one offers on its own. But if I were pressed to choose which one of these doctrinal standards I would take as the confession of faith of the church I love, and as my own personal confession of faith, the Heidelberg Catechism would be my first choice.

---

17. In fact, there are only three brief references to the love of God in the Westminster Confession of Faith: in 2.1, where God is described as "most loving"; in 3.5, where election is ascribed to "his mere free grace and love"; and in 17.1, where saints are identified as "they whom God hath accepted in the Beloved."

Chapter 39

How to Battle Hostility and Secularism

The topic before us today involves two powerful forces at work in our world: hostility and secularism.[1] These forces are different in character but nonetheless related to each other. Since they are universal in human experience, we ought not be surprised to find them even in the church, both in America and in Korea. The hostility and secularism that pastors encounter on any given day in California and in Korea are essentially the same, differing only in the cultural garb these forces may wear or the current way in which they are manifesting themselves. We shall consider each of these forces in turn, showing what they are and how they are related and how we as the followers of Christ should respond to them as they come to expression in our world today.

Hostility: The Enmity That Is in the World

What do we mean by hostility? The biblical word for hostility is *enmity*, a word first heard from the mouth of God when He pronounced His punishment upon fallen humanity and specifically cursed the tempter who had enticed Adam and Eve into the trap of sin: "I will put enmity between thee and the woman, and between thy seed and her seed" (Gen. 3:15). This enmity is imposed on the parties involved by the very word and command of Almighty God.

We don't have long to wait to see how this enmity will express itself in human experience. As the human family begins to grow, two sons, Cain and Abel, are born to our first parents. In time both men bring their offerings to the Lord, but the Lord accepts the offering of Abel and spurns that of Cain. "Cain was very wroth" (Gen. 4:5), bitterly resenting that his offering was rejected. He is angry with God, who warns him of where such anger may lead. Heedless of the warning, "Cain talked with Abel his brother: and it came to pass when they were in the field, that Cain rose up against Abel his brother, and slew him" (4:8).

---

1. This chapter was originally an address before Korean pastors in May of 2014 in California on how to battle hostility and secularism in Korean churches.

So began the endless conflict between the children of the promise and the children of this world. The former are the true offspring of believing Adam and Eve; these people live by faith, trusting in God's promise of salvation, and doing what pleases Him. The latter children are truly "the seed of the serpent," Satan's slaves who share his hatred of God and God's handiwork, and live only to do Satan's bidding. They are held in his power and under the dominion of sin.

So there are several kinds of enmity at work in our world. First and foremost, there is the wrath of God against sin. God has declared Himself to be the greatest enemy of unbelieving, unrepentant sinners. "The wrath of God is revealed from heaven against all ungodliness and unrighteousness of men" (Rom. 1:18).

Second, there is the wrath of human beings against God, against each other, and against Christ and all who belong to Him. By nature, fallen man is prone to hate God and to hate his fellow human beings. Sin has a terrible estranging power, alienating man from God and setting every man's hand against his fellows. Men are even estranged from themselves, since they are creatures made in the image of the God they hate. Thus we have wars and conflicts, brutal assaults and murders, and finally, suicide, all of which are the outworking of the enmity that lives as hatred in the hearts of fallen men.

This same enmity lived in the world before Christ came, in the hostility between Jew and Gentile that existed under the law. The law of Moses erected a wall of partition, enclosing the seed of Abraham within the circle of its promises, commands, and protection and shutting out the other nations of the world. "He hath shewed his word unto Jacob, his statutes and his judgments unto Israel. He hath not dealt so with any nation: and as for his judgments, they have not known them" (Ps. 147:19–20). So deep was this enmity between Jew and Gentile that it could only be slain by the death of Christ (Eph. 2:13–16). "The handwriting of ordinances that was against us" as Gentiles was blotted out and taken out of the way, when it was nailed to the cross of Christ (Col. 2:14).

This human enmity or hostility came into sharpest focus with the coming of Christ into the world as the incarnate Son of God. David foresees it all with the perfect clarity of prophetic vision in Psalm 2:1–3:

> Why do the heathen rage, and the people imagine a vain thing? The kings of the earth set themselves, and the rulers take counsel together, against the LORD, and against his anointed, saying, Let us break their bands asunder, and cast away their cords from us.

So fallen humanity hates and opposes God and the kingdom of His Son, saying, "We will not have this man to reign over us" (Luke 19:15). That's why it was only to be expected that Christ should be despised and rejected of men, and finally, be taken, and by wicked hands be crucified and slain.

This hostility or enmity of fallen mankind was directed at Christ during all the time of His life on earth. It was first manifested in Herod's ruthless endeavor to destroy the infant Jesus. "Herod…was exceeding wroth, and sent forth and slew all the children that were in Bethlehem, and in all the coasts thereof, from two years old and under" (Matt. 2:16). From that time until the hour of His death, Christ was constantly assaulted by men and devils.

Hostility and the Christian

At the end of His earthly life and work, Christ had much to tell His disciples about this enmity or hatred in fallen mankind and the world they have made for themselves. "If the world hate you, ye know that it hated me before it hated you. If ye were of the world, the world would love his own: but because ye are not of the world, but I have chosen you out of the world, therefore the world hateth you. Remember the word that I said unto you, The servant is not greater than his lord. If they have persecuted me, they will also persecute you,…but all these things will they do unto you for my name's sake, because they know not him that sent me" (John 15:18–21).

So no Christian should be the least surprised to encounter hostility, tribulation, and persecution. Rather, we should expect to encounter it—in fact, if we submit to the authority of Christ, rejoice in it and be exceeding glad, as Matthew 5:12 says, for great is our reward in heaven. Whatever we may lose by the world's hostility will be more than compensated by the glory laid up in store for us as "an inheritance incorruptible, and undefiled, and that fadeth not away, reserved in heaven" for us (1 Peter 1:4).

That teaching notwithstanding, we should recall the plain but pointed words of the apostle Peter when he writes, "Let none of you suffer as a murderer, or as a thief, or as an evildoer, or as a busybody in other men's matters" (1 Peter 4:15). If as a Christian, you commit crimes and are punished; if you do evil to your neighbors and suffer retaliation; if you poke your nose into matters that are none of your concern and get it bloodied, you cannot claim to be suffering for righteousness' sake. You are receiving the due reward of your wrongdoing, and you are being chastened by the Lord and called to repentance.

It is a saying as old as Shakespeare that "men should be what they seem." Scripture says there should be no disjunction between the heart, character, and life of a man who is called to proclaim God's Word and the content of the message he proclaims: "Take heed unto thyself, and unto the doctrine; continue in them: for in doing this thou shalt both save thyself, and them that hear thee"

(1 Tim. 4:16). In other words, there should be no gap or inconsistency between what we are privately and what we appear to be in public. Anything else is hypocrisy. As ministers we are called to be as holy in our private relationship with God, in our role as husbands and fathers in our families, and as shepherds among our people as we appear to be on the pulpit. We should live by the Word we preach; we should be transcripts of our sermons. Our churches should uphold the standards of the Bible for the daily life and conduct of officers and members. It is so easy to cultivate a pious image; it is much more difficult but much more profitable to sanctify the Lord God in our hearts and serve Him with fear and trembling. Personal integrity is a discipline of true godliness.

Presbyterian church polity can help us here. It is a basic principle of that polity that the authority given by Christ to church officers is joint authority that is exercised by officers assembled together in church courts. A minister or elder by himself is simply another member of the church and should also be subject to church discipline like any other member. By contrast, the pre-Reformation church had succumbed to "one man rule," with popes and bishops and even parish priests lording it over others. A Presbyterian minister must be accountable to his fellow office bearers, locally and in the higher courts. To act independently of the courts of the church is to usurp and abuse your authority.

When authority is abused, the world has every right to be hostile toward us. Today in America—and no doubt Korea as well—many ministers have forgotten this. They act as if elders and deacons are just there to serve their wishes. They have abandoned the whole concept of biblical, servant leadership. And once they abandon servant leadership, they make themselves vulnerable to all kinds of temptations, such as inappropriate sexual advances and adultery, sermon plagiarism, man-pleasing, power-grabbing, and financial abuse. The list of spiritual and moral failures in both the American and Korean church is embarrassingly long. And sadly, ministers who perpetuate these abuses, instead of being disciplined and deposed, often receive little admonition and stay in power far too long.

All this shames the church in the eyes of the world. The world has every right to expect the church to act like the church. When the church loses its saltiness in the world and increasingly acts like the world rather than like the church, we ought not be surprised when the world despises the church's hypocrisy since the world is living in that hypocritical environment continually and knows what it is like. Are we exercising humble servant leadership together with godly piety so that the world around us is moved to respect us rather than to despise us? Can your family, your church, your denomination, and your church testify of you that your talk and walk resembles that of our Savior's? Are you meek and lowly of heart, seeking to minister to others rather than being ministered to by others?

Likewise, we must guard against enmity and anger in our own hearts and in the midst of our churches. James warns us that "the wrath of man worketh not the righteousness of God" (James 1:20). The apostle Paul commands us to "[l]et all bitterness and wrath, and anger, and clamour, and evil speaking, be put away from you, with all malice" (Eph. 4:31). The Heidelberg Catechism teaches regarding the requirement of the sixth commandment, "Thou shalt not kill," that "in forbidding murder, God teaches us, that He abhors the causes thereof, such as envy, hatred, and desire of revenge; and that He accounts all these as murder" (Q. 106). As the children of God, we should be peacemakers and a force for unity and reconciliation wherever God has placed us. Have you gained a reputation for being a peacemaker in the church of Jesus Christ so that even the world must say of the church, "Behold, how they love one another"?

This is not to say that the world will always respond positively to the church and its ministers when they walk in a godly, humble way. Sometimes the world despises godliness as much as it despises ungodliness. Godliness often convicts the world's conscience and moves the world to find fault with the church, no matter how godly the church may be. What a dark picture appears before our eyes! Our world has become a seething cauldron of hostility of all kinds. God is hostile toward fallen mankind because of sin, and all are by nature children of wrath. Fallen men are likewise hostile to God, opposing His kingdom and rejecting His anointed King. They are also hostile one to another, so they quarrel and fight and wage war against one another on battlefields, on blogs, and in families. And it seems the only way they can put aside the quarrels among themselves is to unite in fighting against Christ and all who belong to Him.

We must expect persecution and opposition from the world, as Jesus told us. But we must give the world no just reason for that persecution and hostility.

Secularism: Living in the World on Our Own Terms

The second great force that shapes the life of this present world is what we call secularism, from the Latin word *saecula*, meaning this present age, or the fashion of the world around us. Secularism is rooted in hostility of fallen man toward God. Since God has cast sinners out of Paradise and cursed them to live in a hostile world, fallen man is determined to live his life without regard to God.

This secularism is both a state of mind and a way of life. It began with the original sin, when our first parents rejected God's law for their life in this world and began to walk by another law of wickedness and sin. Having sinned this way at the beginning, fallen men and women have persisted ever since in a desperate bid to live in the world on terms of their own choosing rather than to live in submission to God and His law.

As a state of mind, secularism begins with the refusal to glorify the Creator as God (Rom. 1:21), and proceeds to exchange knowledge of the true God for lies and vain imaginings (1:25). Speaking through David as His prophet, God confronts such people, saying, "O ye sons of men, how long will ye turn my glory into shame? how long will ye love vanity and seek after leasing?" (Ps. 4:2). To "love vanity" is to serve idols, gods that are no gods, and to "seek after leasing" is to prefer the lies of false religion to the truth of God. Fallen men and women do not "like to retain God in their knowledge" (Rom. 1:28). Describing the secular mind of a wicked man, David says that "God is not in all his thoughts" (Ps. 10:4), and "there is no fear of God before his eyes" (Ps. 36:1).

In ancient times, secularism took the form of old-fashioned pagan idolatry, the worship of images "made like unto corruptible man, and to birds, and four-footed beasts, and creeping things" (Rom. 1:23). Christians in America sometimes forget that there is plenty of this old-fashioned paganism in the world today. Millions still bow down to man-made images of wood or stone. No one in Latin America, Africa, or Asia would say that paganism has gone out of style or lost its hold on the minds and hearts of fallen humanity. In the so-called Western world, the modern secularist has simply dismissed the very idea of God and has made man a law unto himself. Anything religious, that is, related in any way to God, is dismissed as at best a personal and private matter or at worst a menace to human understanding, cooperation, and progress. Zealous efforts are made to exclude religion from the public sphere and even from the field of human knowledge. It begins with the theory of evolution, which attempts to explain the origin of all things without reference to God, and it goes on to affect every aspect of human life, including marriage and family life, education, economics, politics, social life, ethics, recreation, and entertainment.

In this way, the mind of secularism is translated into a way of life. Fallen men tell themselves that they can live without God. They can eat and drink without asking His blessing or acknowledging His mercies. They can marry and be given in marriage, rear their children, labor at their trades and conduct their businesses, and perform their social and civic duties with no thought of God, no regard for His law, no consulting of His wisdom, no claiming of His promises, and no trembling at His commands.

Above all, and most fatally, they imagine that they can transgress God's law with no fear of the consequences. God Himself addresses such wicked men, saying, "These things hast thou done, and I kept silence; thou thoughtest that I was altogether such an one as thyself" (Ps. 50:21). The psalmist confirms this verdict, quoting the wicked as saying, "The LORD shall not see it, neither shall the God of Jacob regard it" (Ps. 94:7).

Do you see the logic of the secularist mind? First, the secularists call in question whether there be any such being as God. Then they go on to posit that if such a God exists, He must view sin as they do and overlook their wrongdoing, assigning no significance to it. In this way, secularism seeks to sever any ties that bind us to God and oblige us to keep His commands.

Ultimately, then, secularism or worldliness is human nature without God. Someone who is secular is controlled by worldly pursuits: the quest for pleasure, profit, and position. Pleasure, profit, and position are the secular man's trinity. A secular person yields to the spirit of fallen mankind—the spirit of self-seeking and self-indulgence—without regard for God.

The goal of worldly people is to move forward rather than upward, to live horizontally rather than vertically. They seek after outward prosperity more than inward holiness. They burst with selfish desires rather than heartfelt supplications. If they do not deny God, they marginalize Him, or else use Him for selfish ends.

Secularism, the Christian, and the Church

If secularism were only the state of mind and way of life of the children of this world, that "seed of the serpent" we spoke of earlier, we could leave the matter there. But the fact is, this same mind-set and way of life are found in the church of Jesus Christ among those who profess the truth of the Christian religion. Hypocrisy is natural to all fallen human beings, and so it is entirely possible to hold the form of religion while denying the power of it; that is, to give lip service to a creed, and live on in sin.

So the apostle Paul warns Christians not to be "conformed to this world" (Rom. 12:1, 2). He is warning against secularism, warning us not to think as the world thinks or do as the world does. In this context, secularism is just another word for worldliness. Since we were born in this world and have lived in it all our days, it is easy for us to be conformed to it more than we may realize, even as followers of Christ.

Right away it needs to be said that in Europe and North America, some Christians have made a serious mistake with regard to worldliness. They have taken a page out of the wisdom of the Pharisees and put certain practices under the ban on the assumption that if we stay free of these practices we are not being conformed to the world. At one time or another, Christians have banned such things as the reading of novels, wearing certain kinds of clothing, using cosmetics, cutting hair in a certain style, and the like. Those who observe such prohibitions are regarded as good Christians and commended as models of Christian conduct. Where does this approach go wrong? We err in thinking that if we cleanse the outside of the cup, its contents will be pure, the very error of the Pharisees condemned by our Lord (Matt. 23:25, 26). Conforming out-wardly to manmade rules of conduct does not change the inner man. Washing the hands does not cleanse the heart.

Worse still, keeping man-made rules leads to self-righteousness and pride, to looking down on those who don't keep these rules. Remember the Pharisee who prayed, "God, I thank thee, that I am not as other men!" (Luke 18:11). He was impressed with his own moral standards and conduct and didn't mind saying so. There are too many of us who perform our duties and do our good works in front of a mirror!

Finally, while we obsess over our little rules for conduct and reinforce our natural self-righteousness and pride, we fail to keep watch over our own hearts and to keep ourselves from the idols of the day. We will do anything we have to do to succeed in business, to amass wealth, and to win the approval of men.

Paul rejects such an approach as unworthy of true Christians. "If ye be dead with Christ from the rudiments of the world, why, as though living in the world, are ye subject to ordinances, (Touch not; taste not; handle not; which are all to perish with the using;) after the commandments and doctrines of men?" (Col. 2:20–22). He urges us to seek change at a much deeper level. "Be ye transformed by the renewing of your mind, that ye may prove what is that good, and acceptable, and perfect, will of God" (Rom. 12:2). We must cease to think as the world thinks before we can cease to do as the world does.

Paul repented of all his old beliefs and practices as a Pharisee. His frank assessment was that his fellow Jews, "being ignorant of God's righteousness, and going about to establish their own righteousness, have not submitted them-selves to the righteousness of God" (Rom. 10:2). He turned his back on all his attainments as a Pharisee "that I may win Christ, and be found in him, not having mine own righteousness, which is of the law, but that which is through the faith of Christ, the righteousness which is of God by faith" (Phil. 3:8–9).

It should be apparent by now that secularism is the way in which fallen man seeks to shut God out of his life and world because of the enmity of his sinful heart against God. To live without consulting the will of God, to dispense with praying for the guidance and help of God, to do anything in our own strength without drawing on and relying upon the grace of God in Christ, forgetting God and living carelessly, heedless of the consequences, is secularism—thinking as the world thinks and doing as the world does. Even if we claim to be Christians!

Nothing is more worldly in a professing Christian than to forget God, trust in his own understanding and ability, follow his own instincts, and devise his own ways and ends. No matter how orthodox the creed we subscribe to, if we can live without God in the affairs of daily life, we are secularists.

I fear that worldliness and secularism abound in Christians and, therefore, in the Christian church today worldwide. Nearly every aspect of the secularization of American churches is transpiring in Korean churches today—and sometimes even in a heightened way, I fear, due in part to the largeness of mega-churches. Korean churches experienced a record-breaking growth in a short period of time, and several of its mega-churches are among the largest in the world. But that blessing has side effects as well, side effects that often reveal themselves in worldly models of success, of health and wealth, and of teaching more of man's words than God's Word. Ministers can fall into sin by living for this world's trinity: pleasure, profit, and position. Once secularism takes control in the church, the church spins out of control. Churches lose their principles and become more interested in quantitative growth than qualitative growth. Then ministers become more interested in consolidating their power than in seeing genuine conversions and glorifying God. In the end, churches then become modern towers of Babel.

In Korea and in America, man-made towers need to fall, man-centered power needs to be broken, man-focused ministry needs to yield to God. Reformation and revival is the great need of the day. But how should the church battle against the enmity in the world and the secularism in the church?

How Should We Battle the Enmity That Is in the World?

There is a great danger in the very idea of battling hostility. The danger is that we will stoop to using the weapons and tactics of our enemies. We will become like them, which is just another way of being conformed to the world. Church history has many a page stained with the record of how Christians seized upon the opportunity to avenge themselves and punish their enemies, repaying them wrong for wrong in flagrant disobedience to the law of Christ and His kingdom.

Christ puts very different weapons into our hands. Let me just mention three kinds of weapons. First, if the world hates simply because we belong to Jesus Christ, love Him sincerely, and hate sin, we are to use the weapon of love. Jesus commands us, "Love your enemies, bless them that curse you, do good to them that hate you, and pray for them which despitefully use you, and persecute you" (Matt. 5:44). Paul expounds this teaching, saying, "Recompense no man evil for evil. Provide things honest in the sight of all men. If it be possible, as much as lieth in you, live peaceably with all men. Dearly beloved, avenge not yourselves, but rather give place unto wrath: for it is written, Vengeance is mine; I will repay, saith the Lord. Therefore if thine enemy hunger, feed him; if he thirst, give him drink: for in so doing thou shalt heap coals of fire on his head. Be not overcome of evil, but overcome evil with good" (Rom. 12:17–21).

The world sneers at the very idea that we should battle hostility with love, blessings, good deeds, and prayer. The worldly-minded man says, "Fight fire with fire." You can only survive by adhering to the old *lex talionis*, "An eye for an eye, a tooth for a tooth." You must get down and get dirty or the enemy will walk all over you.

We have seen in the United States what happens when Christians take such an approach to politics, adopting the ways and means of secular politicians. We yield to the temptation to out-spend, out-promise, out-publicize, out-misrepresent, and out-mudsling the opposition. We try to provoke public outrage, circulate known falsehoods, and manipulate statistics and polling data to our advantage. All of which serves to destroy public confidence in government officials and respect for the offices they hold, without changing in the least the corrupt or mistaken policies they are pursuing.

Second, we are to use the weapons of godliness and good works, which glorify God. The apostle Peter joins with Christ and Paul in commending a very different approach to battling the hostility of the world. "Dearly beloved, I beseech you as strangers and pilgrims, abstain from fleshly lusts, which war against the soul; having your conversation honest among the Gentiles: that, whereas they speak against you as evildoers, they may by your good works, which they shall behold, glorify God in the day of visitation" (1 Peter 2:11–12).

Again, Peter says, "Sanctify the Lord God in your hearts: and be ready always to give an answer to every man that asketh you a reason of the hope that is in you with meekness and fear: having a good conscience; that, whereas they speak evil of you, as of evil doers, they may be ashamed that falsely accuse your good conversation in Christ" (3:15–16). To overcome hostility and silence opposition, Peter commends the use of powerful spiritual weapons: faith in God, the fear of God, a well-grounded hope, a good conscience, meekness of spirit, and finally, a godly "conversation," that is, a manner of life that is consistent with what we believe and teach as followers of Christ.

Third, if the world hates us because we live a hypocritical life, our weapons are to be reformation and repentance. How desperately the church today—both in America and Korea—needs to repent of its worldliness, lukewarmness, institutionalized corruption, lack of self-discipline and church discipline, corruption and infighting, bribery, man-centered worship, and hypocrisy! How desperately the church needs to discipline those who are corrupting Christ's bride from within rather than punishing those who are exposing the church's secularism!

This reformation and repentance needs to begin with ministers themselves. Such has nearly always been the case with true revival in the past. True revival normally does not begin with lay people but with God's people—especially with God's ambassadors. The world desperately needs hundreds and thousands of gospel ministers who serve the church humbly, daily repenting of its sins, calling the church to beseech the Holy Spirit to send reformation and revival.

Using these very weapons—love, godliness and good works, reformation and repentance—the ancient church endured persecution and commended its Lord to the world of its day by its unshakeable faith in God, its love for Christ, its daily repentance, the rejoicing of its members in the face of suffering and death, and its persistence in doing good to all men. In the end, the ancient Roman Empire was conquered by the power of the gospel of Christ. And who can say what may happen if Christians in America and Korea were to pursue the same course of spiritual combat, using such spiritual weapons in the name of Christ?

How Should We Battle the Secularism in the Church?

As for secularism, the remedy is spiritual and inward, not carnal or external. As we have said already, setting up an array of man-made prohibitions and requiring Christians to conform to them will not transform minds and hearts or keep the ways of the world out of the church or keep the mind-set of secularism out of the Christian.

This is not to say that we have nothing to fear from secularism. The sad history of the false church under both the Old and the New Testaments bears compelling and heartbreaking testimony to the evils that result from being conformed to the world. The prophets confronted Israel for its unfaithfulness in adopting the ways of the nations around them. The Belgic Confession is famous for its succinct account of the marks of the true church; less attention has been paid to its account of the false church:

> As for the false Church, she ascribes more power and authority to herself and her ordinances than to the Word of God, and will not submit herself to the yoke of Christ. Neither does she administer the sacraments as appointed by Christ in his Word, but adds to and takes from them, as she thinks proper; she relieth more upon men than upon Christ; and persecutes those who live holily according to the Word of God, and rebuke her for her errors, covetousness, and idolatry. (Art. 29)

The authors of the confession were clearly thinking of the sad state of the Christian church in Europe on the eve of the Reformation. What had gone wrong? How did this great historic church become false?

+ By adopting the world's contempt for the authority of God's Word;

+ by refusing, as the world does, to submit to Christ's yoke;

+ by adopting the world's way of picking and choosing for ourselves what we like from among the ordinances of Christ and doing with them as we please;

+ by relying on the power of the sword wielded by Vatican-friendly kings and princes and intruding into the politics of the day while ignoring the truly spiritual concerns and moral issues of the day;

+ by despising, as the world does, the example and counsel of those who labored for its reformation and silencing them with the heavy hand of persecution, and

+ by persisting, as the world does, in its worst besetting sins.

In sum, the pre-Reformation church had sunk to the level of being largely conformed to the world, thinking as the world thinks and doing as the world does—not to mention the well-attested fact that as the institutional church sank into conformity to the world, so did its ministers and members.

On almost every page of the New Testament we can find exhortations to doing the things that prove to be the remedy for secularist thinking and secularist living. The most potent remedy and the surest antidote to the love of the world is prescribed in the epistle of Jude: "But ye beloved, building up yourselves on your most holy faith, praying in the Holy Ghost, keep yourselves in the love of God, looking for the mercy of our Lord Jesus Christ unto eternal life" (vv. 20, 21).

Jude gives us a fourfold directive:

First, to build on our most holy faith. That is, to look at our core beliefs as Christians as a platform or foundation to build on, by living in obedience to Christ to make our life as consistent as possible with what we profess to believe. We as ministers must seek grace to build the house of God with two hands: the hand of sound preaching and doctrine as well as with the hand of a sanctified life. Our doctrine must shape our life, and our life must adorn our doctrine. "He doth preach most who doth live best," wrote John Boys. We must be what we preach and teach, not only applying ourselves to our texts but applying our texts to ourselves. Our hearts must be transcripts of our sermons.[2] Otherwise, as John Owen warned, "If a man teach uprightly and walk crookedly, more will fall down in the night of his life than he built in the day of his doctrine."

To build ourselves up in the most holy faith, we must seek to have a large, varied, and personal acquaintance with God that is realized primarily by prayerful use of the spiritual disciplines for our own souls and lives. Every day we need to be reading the Scriptures for ourselves, engaging in personal prayer and meditation, and fellowshipping with believers. We build ourselves up also by exercising God-honoring Sabbath-keeping, reading and listening to other preachers' sermons, evangelizing and serving others, exercising good stewardship of our time and money, and aiming to walk in the King's highway of holiness in every area of our lives.

Second, to pray in the Holy Ghost. That is, to enter into the heart of what it means to trust in God, to live in union and communion with Christ, and to open our hearts to receive the Spirit in His fullness and power as the Spirit of Christ and to rely on His guidance and sustaining power as the Spirit of prayer. Our Puritan forefathers are a notable example of this. They developed a profound dependence on the Holy Spirit in both their personal lives and for their ministry. They felt keenly their inability to bring anyone to Christ as well as the magnitude of what true conversion is. As Thomas Watson wrote, "Ministers knock at the door of men's hearts, the Spirit comes with a key and opens the door."[3] This realization made the Puritan ministers great wrestlers with God, men who habitually prayed in and by the Holy Spirit. The Puritan Robert Traill stressed that the main reason some pastors with ordinary gifts were used more of God than some pastors with extraordinary gifts is because they prayed more "in the Holy Ghost." Traill then concluded: "Many good sermons are lost for lack of much prayer in study."[4]

Third, to keep ourselves in the love of God. That is, to live as captives to that love as ever under the Father's watchful eye, shielded by the power and might of our Savior, Jesus Christ, and comforted by the shedding abroad of the love of God in our hearts by the Holy Ghost given unto us. Like Paul, the love of Christ must constrain us in our personal lives and in our preaching and pastoring (2 Cor. 5:8–15). The love of God must be our greatest motivator in life. It must

---

2. Gardiner Spring, *The Power of the Pulpit* (Pelham, Ala.: Solid Ground Christian Books, 2009), 154.

3. Thomas Watson, *A Body of Divinity* (Edinburgh: Banner of Truth, 1957), 154.

4. Robert Traill, *Works of Robert Traill* (Edinburgh: Banner of Truth, 1975), 1:246.

fill our souls, our mouths, our lives. It must be the engine that moves us to do whatever we do.

Fourth, to look for the mercy of our Lord Jesus Christ unto eternal life. Mercy is a biblical synonym for God's grace, love, and compassion. We begin the Christian life by the mercy of God, and we press on in the Christian life by the mercy of God. "He that shall endure to the end, the same shall be saved" (Matt. 24:13). In the face of the most determined enmity, we go on hoping that, in due time, God will arise and His enemies will be scattered (Ps. 68:1). He has given us the victory through our Lord Jesus Christ and access into the grace we need to stand and rejoice in hope of the glory of God.

When, by God's grace, we make the truth of God as revealed in His Word the foundation of our faith and our rule of life and devote ourselves to prayer in the power of the Holy Spirit, keeping ourselves full of a sense of the greatness and wonder of God's love for us and His mercy toward us in Christ, we will have nothing to fear from the hostility of the world. Trusting in God, hoping in His Word, walking according to His commandments, we will be transformed, renewed in our minds and made fruitful in our lives and showing ourselves to be the children of God and the followers of Christ in the sight of the whole world.

Chapter 40

Busy but Fruitful:
How to Manage Time

See then that ye walk circumspectly, not as fools,
but as wise, redeeming the time, because the days are evil.
—Ephesians 5:15–16

Therefore, my beloved brethren, be ye stedfast, unmoveable, always abound-
ing in the work of the Lord, forasmuch as ye know that your labour is not
in vain in the Lord.   —1 Corinthians 15:58

It is early springtime, and you are traveling through the country to visit friends on a farm.[1] You turn on to an unpaved road. The ruts in front of you tell you that the road is not in good shape; between the lingering frost of winter and the plentiful rains of spring, the ground beneath your tires is muddy and slushy. And then it happens—you slow down for an intersection, slide a bit, and find yourself stuck with no help in sight. You push on the accelerator repeatedly; the engine roars and the tires spin, but you are going nowhere. You are accomplishing nothing except to coat your car with mud and dig yourself in deeper. So you groan and reach for your cell phone.

Have you ever felt in your ministry that you are just spinning your wheels, struggling mightily? You exhaust yourself, but nothing is accomplished. You seem to be going two steps forward and three steps back. Nothing is so frustrating as being busy but not fruitful. Sometimes you feel you are stuck in the mud when you are actually doing exactly what God has called you to do. Other times you feel trapped in fruitless activism. You feel like you're squandering time through disorganization, inefficiency, or laziness.

Many pastors keep busy with legitimate activities of which few hold eternal significance. Some think that the solution to this problem is to avoid busyness

---

1. This chapter is the substance of an address given to ministers at a conference near Detroit, Michigan, in 2010.

altogether. Busyness seems so unspiritual, they say. Often we associate spiritu-ality with a contemplative kind of life, such as a quiet retreat in the woods. We admire Isaac Ambrose, who went four weeks in the woods to meditate every year. I understand that admiration.

Others think that spirituality means following the impulse of the moment: "God told me to do this this morning" or "God told me to do that." Every action all day long is an imperative from God that He lays on their heart. Instead of making a sustained effort in one direction, they are pulled in dozens of direc-tions, responding to the feelings of the moment. Still others ask, when it comes to busyness, can it be God's will if it seems so hard and requires so much of us?

The example of our Lord Jesus Christ doesn't fit any of these molds. It is true that Jesus often did seek solitude for prayer, but those moments of solitude in Jesus's life were punctuated with a life that was packed with activity from morning until night. Every day, Jesus set His face in the direction of doing His Father's will. He was a people person. He embraced little children; He touched and healed the eyes of blind people. He was constantly dealing with people, working with crowds as well as individuals. He spent a great deal of His time training twelve disciples, but He also organized a group of seventy. He sent out thirty-five teams to prepare the ground in the cities and places He planned to visit. Christ did all of these things—and much more. John says the world can-not contain the books that could be written about what He did. He did it all in the midst of constant travel and without any of the time-saving devices of modern technology. There was no computer, no car, no cell phone, no fast food restaurant. Undeniably, Jesus Christ was both deeply busy and deeply spiritual, and His efforts were abundantly fruitful. So Christ Himself knew all about the tyranny and the urgency of time.

In John 9:4–5, Jesus talks about the coming night when He would no lon-ger be in the world: "I must work the works of him that sent me, while it is day: the night cometh, when no man can work. As long as I am in the world, I am the light of the world." Jesus says, "I must work *now*." He teaches us that God has allotted each of us a certain amount of time in this world to work. He knew that He Himself had a limited time, and He had much to do. That is the way we are to view our lives as well.

The Bible speaks a lot about time. David Murray, to whom I am indebted for several thoughts in this article, gives us a thumbnail sketch of a biblical the-ology of time in these six thoughts:

+ God gives us time (James 1:17)
+ God gives enough time (John 11:9)

+ God gives limited time (Ps. 90:10)
+ God judges our use of time (Rom. 14:12)
+ God commands us to redeem time (Eph. 5:16)
+ God offers eternal life to those who have abused time (Rom. 6:23)

We must view our time as God's gift to us. The older I become, the more I feel that time is short. Time is far more precious than money. Every minute matters to me, and more and more I understand the significance of Jesus's teaching of the importance of things that last, that have eternal value. But how do you actually handle your time in a practical way? That can be a pressing problem in the ministry, particularly when you manage your own time and when people expect all kinds of time commitments of you.

I want to look at two things with you. First, true gospel busyness—that is, what does it mean to be busy in a good sense of the word? We will look at that from 1 Corinthians 15:58. Second, in conjunction with Ephesians 5:15–16, I will give you thirteen ways to redeem time so that by God's grace you can make it more fruitful. So I have two thoughts to lay before you: how to redeem time through gospel busyness and how to redeem time in practical ways.

Redeeming the Time through Gospel Busyness
"Therefore, my beloved brethren, be ye stedfast, unmoveable, always abounding in the work of the Lord, forasmuch as ye know that your labour is not in vain in the Lord" (1 Cor. 15:58). "Always abounding"—Paul is talking about very busy people here. He is describing plentiful activity as well as fruitfulness, for, he says, "ye know that your labour is not in vain in the Lord." So what does gospel busyness look like? I have three thoughts from this text for you.

Stay Rooted in Gospel Truth
Paul begins, "Be ye stedfast, unmoveable." He is talking about men who are always moving and full of activity. This seems almost ironic or paradoxical. Be abounding, be moving, but yet be unmovable. Well, the greatest movers are often those who move the least. That may seem odd, because we are told that we should be dynamic and flexible and creative in responding to our culture. But Paul uses the Greek word translated "stedfast" here, which can also be translated as "settled." In Colossians 1:23, for example, he tells us to continue in the faith, "grounded and settled, and be not moved away from the hope of the gospel." That is what he means here in 1 Corinthians 15 as well. He is saying to ministers—fruitful men who are busy and abounding in God's work: "You must be rooted and settled in, not budging from the truth of the gospel." He

says earlier in this chapter, stay firm in the gospel "which I have preached unto you...and wherein ye stand."

One of the greatest temptations of Christian activity, Christian busyness, is to neglect the truth. So many "busy" Christians are pushing the edge of the envelope in their churches, wanting to abandon the old paths of Scripture for new ideas that compromise biblical, sovereign grace gospel. But Paul says, "No, no. You need to stand firm in the gospel that I have preached to you." Don't get so busy serving the Lord in so many different ways, spreading yourselves so thin, that you are tempted to start looking for new things. Don't try to turn yourself into a Martha where you are always busy but never have time to sit at the feet of the Lord like Mary. Be steadfast and unmovable, first of all, in the doctrines of God's Word. This is crucial for three reasons.

First, we are not spiritual civilians operating in the safety and freedom of peacetime prosperity; *we are called to serve as soldiers of Christ* in a war against the powers of darkness. Paul says in Ephesians that we are waging war against principalities and powers. Therefore, put on the whole armor of God and stand; take your stand upon the truth.

Second, we must stay rooted in the truth *so that we don't fall.* Too many pastors become too self-confident in the ministry. Only when we are grounded in the truth will we remain standing. The minute we let down our guard against the devil, we expose ourselves to the grave dangers of moral temptation and doctrinal error. If we don't stay firm in the truth, our busyness will take us into scores of different directions. We may be very active in the church, but we won't be cultivating depth of soul. That shortfall will leave us open for temptations and falls.

I had a dear friend, a seasoned pastor in South Africa, who spent a great deal of time counseling younger ministers. He said to me, "There isn't a single fallen minister that I have counseled over the years who was still maintaining at the time of his fall a daily life of prayer and Scripture reading." Whatever you do in the ministry, make sure you do not neglect your time alone with God every day. Be in the Word; be grounded and be steadfast in the truth.

Third, we need to be steadfast in the truth *for the unity of the church,* flowing out of the unity we experience with the Lord Jesus Christ. People often say today, "Doctrine divides." But the truth is that the reason we need doctrine—the reason the church needs a statement of what it believes—is to unite! Be steadfast so that you can be united in one truth as one people, serving one Lord. So that's the first thing Paul tells us: in terms of gospel busyness, we need to remain unmovable, rooted in gospel truth.

Aim at Gospel Abundance

Second, Paul speaks of "always abounding" in the work of the Lord, that is, in the gospel. The point is not merely to do good works but to fill our days with them. As we come to know Christ better day after day, the Bible says that streams of living water will flow from us to others. We must treasure that; we must seek, by God's grace, to bring forth the fruit of the Spirit of joy, peace, longsuffering, gentleness, goodness, faith, meekness, and temperance. We must strive and agonize to press on in the work of the Lord. We must be busy for God because God is busy in us, working in us both to will and to do of His good pleasure.

In all true gospel work, there is a beautiful twin dynamic: God's grace and our labor are both operative. All our worthwhile labor is by God's grace. That is why Paul said, "But by the grace of God I am what I am: and his grace which was bestowed upon me was not in vain; but I laboured more abundantly than they all: yet not I, but the grace of God which was with me. Therefore whether it were I or they, so we preach, and so ye believed" (1 Cor. 15:10–11). So in gospel busyness you are acutely aware that in order to do everything you do, you are dependent on God's grace.

Persevere in Hope

Third, Paul speaks of hope in the midst of gospel busyness when he says, "For as much as ye know that your labour is not in vain in the Lord." That is, our labor is not empty or futile. It will not be thrown away. It won't go unrewarded. We labor in hope.

This hope is not just subjective optimism, but it is the objective reality of God's promise that He *will reward His people graciously to all eternity for genuine gospel busyness.* That is a beautiful thing. I can't tell you how many times that has helped me. When I have been downcast or persecuted or overwhelmed, I pray, "Lord, help me to press on, knowing that if I labor on in the Lord, it will all one day bear fruit and be made right." All the wrongs will be made right. Everything will be corrected. God will reward us in glory far more than we deserve. So, brother, don't give up; don't *resign* from the Lord's work, but *re-sign* in the Lord's work and persevere in it. Don't be a hireling. The hireling abandons the sheep, but a faithful pastor keeps on keeping on, in hope, persevering in the work of the Lord.

Paul tells us in 1 Corinthians 15 that we know our gospel busyness won't be fruitless because of Christ's resurrection. In this chapter, verse 58 can seem so out of place at first glance. The first fifty-seven verses speak of the resurrection, and then suddenly, you get this one verse about working tacked on the end. What Paul is saying is this: because Jesus is resurrected, because Christianity is valid, because our preaching is not in vain and our faith is not in vain, because death has lost its sting and the grave has been conquered—therefore abound, beloved brethren, in the work of the Lord, knowing it is not in vain, because Christ is alive. He lives at the right hand of the Father. If He were not resurrected, then it would all be in vain. There would then be no use for gospel busyness. Everything would then depend upon you, which would be hopeless. The difference is that Jesus Christ is alive and He is the resurrected Lord of glory at the right hand of God.

You will not always see the fruit of gospel busyness right away. Sometimes it may take years. But persevere. Fill your life with holy gospel busyness, not knowing what shall prosper, either this or that, as we read in Ecclesiastes 11, or whether both alike may be fruitful. But press on doing what God has called you to do, doing it diligently, expectantly, abounding in the work of the Lord, knowing that your labor will not be in vain in the Lord. Believe that. Do not let doubt and discouragement sap your strength.

Thomas Boston put it beautifully: "I made a vow to God that whatever I did in my ministry, I would always leave the savor of Christ behind." That's the way to minister. Every home you visit, every sick person you see, every time you teach, and every time you have social contact with someone, be resolved to leave behind the savor of Christ. That's gospel busyness.

Redeeming the Time

How do you put gospel busyness into practice so that you truly redeem the time? Here are a dozen practical ways to redeem time.

Price

Redeeming something implies that what is to be redeemed is precious. Time is indeed precious; it is of high price. Proverbs 18:9 says, "He also that is slothful in his work is brother to him that is a great waster." The sad reality is that we all waste a lot of time. We often use lack of time as an excuse for leaving so much of our work undone. But the judgment day clock will speak against us. J. Oswald Sanders said, "Our problem really is not too little time but better use of the time we have." Jonathan Edwards said, "Time is a thing that is exceeding precious"; to grasp its preciousness, Edwards has an entire message on "redeem the time," which can be summarized in six points: (1) eternal happiness or misery depends on the good use of time; (2) time is very short and scarcity multiplies the value of any commodity; (3) we don't know how much time we have left; (4) time is valuable because once it has passed, it is gone forever—it cannot be recovered;

(5) we are accountable to God for our time; (6) we have already lost and wasted so much time. Every second counts. Elsewhere, Edwards states in his famous resolutions, "Resolved never to lose one moment of time, but improve it the most profitable way I possibly can" (no. 5).

A world-class athlete knows that the difference between a performance and a winning performance is measured in fractions of a second. In the men's 400-meter freestyle swimming event at the 2008 Summer Olympics, the difference between the gold medalist and the silver medalist was one half of a second after they had swam more than the length of four football fields. Athletes, therefore, understand that wasted time results in victory lost. Businessmen understand that time is money. Christians should invest and value time wisely as well, though not legalistically. Too often we are prone to say, "If I don't pray or meditate for fifteen minutes now, God is going to be against me." That is not what I mean. But use your time wisely, redeem it, count it valuable. Don't fritter it away. So time management begins, first of all, with this concept of price, of valuing time. What are we doing with our time? Do we treasure every minute as if it were of great price?

Peace

If you would live at peace with God and your fellow Christians, begin each day by spending some time alone with God. Start each day with Scripture reading, meditating, and praying, getting grounded afresh in God's precious truth. Put the shoes of the gospel of peace on your feet so you have a firm footing to stand on for today's battles. This will help you start each day with a peaceful sense of spiritual equilibrium.

That time—however long you spend at morning devotions—is time well spent. It will anchor your soul in the grace and peace of God that pass understanding. Grace is God's free, de-merited favor; peace is the condition that results from receiving grace. And this inner peace will keep you at peace with God and others when your life throughout the day may seem to be going to pieces.

Plan

The Greek word for "redeem" in Ephesians 5:16 literally means "buy up the time." Before buying something, you give thought to it. You think about its potential use. "Buy up the time," therefore, is a Pauline imperative that we must think about our time. You can't buy up your past; it is gone forever. You can only purchase the future as it enters the present. But think of time as a box of items brought to the platform for an auction. Before you bid on something, you first inspect it; otherwise, you are forced to act on the spur of the moment, and you will spend too much on three old cookbooks, an alternator, a shirt, or whatever. So it is with our time: We must carefully consider the future. Knowing my set of gifts, knowing my circumstances and my calling, is it a fitting use of my time? Maybe what we are doing is perfectly legitimate, but is it the best thing to do? Is it the most fitting thing to do? That is the question we need to ask.

My wife bought me a shirt recently. It was the right size, so she had no doubt it would fit me, and she put it in the washing machine so I could wear it. I put it on, and it was too tight. I asked if she could return it, but she couldn't now. So that was fifty dollars wasted. Now that's not such a tragedy; it's only a shirt. But if you stop wasting time every day on things that don't "fit" you well— thirty minutes here, an hour there—it is amazing how many more profitable things you could accomplish.

During my lecture to my theological students in Grand Rapids on the value of time, I say, "As a minister, you've got to put on a tie quite often. I generally put on two ties a day—one in the morning for work, and one in the evening for church events. It takes a minute and a half to put on a tie every day, twice. That's three minutes a day; multiplied by 365, you have enough time to write two more sermons in a year just with the time you use to put on your tie. So what you need is a clip-on tie like this!" Then I pull off my old clip-on tie, and they all burst out laughing. They remember that more than anything else in the lecture. My point is that I do want them to think about the smallest things they do in life and whether they are just a waste of time.

Part of that planning is having a master calendar and looking at it each day to know exactly what you are going to do that day. Divide your work carefully. If you have new tasks and new events, you need to ask, "Can I fit it in this day or not?" Ninety percent of the things in ministry can wait one more day. I try not to overload a single day, trying to leave at least 10 percent of the day open for what I call "white space."

There are going to be other things that come my way during that day, such as phone calls or people stepping into my office briefly. If I pack everything full, when people come by or phone me, I am trying to overstuff my day, and what is going to happen? I'm going to be short with those people. And they wonder, "What's wrong with him? Doesn't he have any time for me?" I have learned that I need at least 10 percent extra time to fit those unexpected things in. I don't call them interruptions anymore, as I used to when I was first in the ministry. I realized that is my real work; that is my calling: to minister to people. So plan your days wisely, and give adequate time for each task.

Sunday arrives before you know it, and we all know the tyranny of time in terms of finding time to prepare for the pulpit. The most important thing you do in the world, besides prayer, is to stand up before God's people and bring them the Word of God. Plan time for study to prepare your sermons, and make that time nonnegotiable. You cannot prepare a sermon adequately on a Saturday night. If you realize your time is dissipating and the weekend is approaching, you may need to call up a few people you had planned to visit on Friday and say, "My friend, I am so sorry, I am not able to make it. I haven't had enough time for sermon preparation this week. Can I come and see you next Monday?" Your people will be happy that you did that! They don't want your sermons to suffer; no one wants to hear a lousy, unprepared preacher on Sunday.

So plan the best you can, marking off items as you complete them. I keep a list on my computer, and right now there are about hundreds of items that I really should be doing, plus dozens of backlogged emails that need time. But those hundreds of items are organized by importance and time sensitivity. Each day I look at the top ten or fifteen things, decide which order I will do these in, and plan my day accordingly.

Another helpful exercise, if you really want to use your time better, is to record every fifteen minutes of your day for a week or two as to how you spent your time. At the end of that two weeks, consider how much time you could have used more wisely.

Planning was begun by God. He planned to create the world in a beautiful, wise, and well-ordered manner. His plan stretches forward throughout history. Ephesians 1 says God "worketh all things after the counsel of his own will." We are to be His image bearers, so we are to plan like Him, but we operate within limits. Therefore, intentionally planning how we will use our time can further His kingdom as we strive to be profitable servants.

Pass

By pass, I mean pass the baton on and delegate. More often than not, the best thing a quarterback can do is to pass the ball to someone else. Ask God, "Show me, Lord, not only what is most important but also what I can do best," and then put your best energies and your gifts to bear in those areas. Seek to delegate the other things.

We usually have two or three ministers in our church of 750 people, so the elders sit down with us and ask us, "Where do you think you are most gifted and least gifted? Let's work together to use each minister in his strongest areas, and in his weakest areas we will try to use him minimally." The work is then delegated out. That is a great way of managing time. As president of a seminary, I have learned that the more that crosses my desk from people doing first drafts of a project, and I approve it or tweak it and send it on, the more I accomplish. I accomplish much more when I delegate much to the staff.

You can do that in your family as well. You can have your household econ-omy. In the divine economy, God the Father has certain tasks, God the Son has certain tasks, and the Holy Spirit has certain tasks. Yes, there are areas of overlap, but the Trinity's divine economy works well this way, so it should work that way in your family as well. Everyone in your family should know his chores and should do them. Implement a system, and delegate as much as you can.

In his book, *The Effective Pastor*, Peter White says his approach to paper-work is "dump, delegate, and deal." I took that from him about ten years ago, and I like that principle a lot. So let's put this into practice. An email comes in, and I realize by the second paragraph that it is too big for me to handle right now, so I stop reading it and put it with other emails that are opened but not done, and take care of them later at a scheduled point in my week. That's what it means to "deal." You deal with things as much as possible at first glance.

To dump means you look at something, read it a quarter way through, and you say, "I really don't want to do anything with this at all," and you hit the delete button. If you aren't sure whether or not you'll need it later, consider printing out a hard copy and keeping it in a file, arranged by date. If a response comes later, you'll be able to find it in the pile. And once a year, throw away the previous year's pile without looking at any of it. If you didn't use it within the year, throw it away.

To delegate means you look at it and say, "Is there anyone else who can do this for me? They might take twice as long to do it or may not be able to do it quite as well, but maybe I still need to delegate it. How important is this item? Then I'd better do it myself. Or maybe it is extremely important, but I have someone very gifted on my staff who can do it maybe as well as I can." Then delegate it.

An important factor in this is hiring wisely. Sometimes you can delegate things to people who end up making more work for you, and you could have better done it yourself in the first place. Be careful whom you hire and to whom you delegate. Give people opportunity to prove themselves bit by bit with small jobs before entrusting greater responsibilities to them. If they prove very effec-tive, you'll be able to entrust larger jobs to them in the future.

Prepare

Prepare adequately, especially for your most important tasks. That applies par-ticularly to speaking engagements. You need to research and meditate; your message needs to be ruminating in your mind.

Putting things off until the last minute is not good organization or good use of time. We have to learn from the ants. Solomon said the ants are exceedingly wise. They are not strong, yet they prepare their meat for the winter in the summer. Organization is key.

Keep records. It takes a little time to do it, but to stay organized is absolutely paramount in the ministry, and keeping records helps one stay organized and prepared. Every book in my library is subject filed, so if I'm going to write an article on abortion, I can immediately look up that section and pull out my thirty or forty sources on abortion. Every text is filed for anything five pages or more on a particular text. So when I preach on a particular text, I have all the resources at my fingertips. That takes time, but it is time well spent. You need to be organized if you are going to prepare well.

Prioritize

You can't do everything. To do all the things you are supposed to do, you would need forty-eight hours a day. I told my wise wife one time when I was frustrated and overwhelmed, "I just wish there were forty-eight hours in the day." She replied, "Well, I think God knew what He was doing when He gave us twenty-four hours." And I said, "Yes, you're right; I take that back. Delete it." God doesn't want us to do everything.

What you need to do is put things in your mind in three piles:

+ *What you must do.* The necessary pile. I must do this today; I must do this by tomorrow; and I must do that by next week, etc. That's one list.

+ *What you should do.* This pile consists of what you really should do and what would help you if you did do it, but it is not yet urgent.

+ *What you like to do.* These are things you are intrigued by, perhaps subjects you would like to study or books you would like to read.

At this point in my life, I seldom get to the "like to" list. Different life stages hold different opportunities. But if you spend a whole evening doing the "like to" list when you've got some pressing things on the "necessary" list that are going to suffer, your priorities are mixed up. Plenty of people are *efficient* with their time, but they are not *effective* with their time. The efficient person can accomplish a lot of things and say, "Wow, look at that," but were they all very important? The effective person does the right thing in the right order, and ultimately enjoys all three piles!

Pick

Pick a task, and then focus fully on that task. Don't keep your email handy at the same time; don't go back and forth frequently with email and the sermon you are writing. Prepare for the future, in other words, but live in the present. Jesus said, "Take…no thought for the morrow, for the morrow shall take thought for the things of itself. Sufficient unto the day is the evil thereof." He is not advocating the lack of foresight and preparation, in contradiction to Proverbs. What He is saying is that you shouldn't allow anxiety to overwhelm you and keep you from focusing on the people and the task before you.

I once had a man say to me, "You know, I like you as a person, but sometimes when I look at you, you give me eye contact, but it looks like you are thinking about something else. You haven't given me your full attention." I said, "Really? I'm so sorry; I don't want to be that way at all!" That really convicted me. When you are organized and give time to someone or to something, you can relax and focus. Exercise complete present-tense commitment to the glory of God now. That's the way to live. Pick what you need to do, and give your all to it.

One of my theological students said to me, "I can do five things at once." But I don't think if you do five things at once you do any of them that well. You need uninterrupted, total devotion to the task at hand.

Purge

Get rid of every single time waster in your life. Let me share with you how I do that. First, we don't have a TV, so I don't waste any time there. Second, I never surf the internet. I know what I'm going on there for, find it, and am done. Third, I try to purge from my life as much as possible those things that don't have any abiding value. I try to think of what will last when I'm gone. I try to stamp the reality of death and eternity on my time. Jonathan Edwards put it this way in his seventh resolution: "Resolved never to do anything that I should be afraid to do if it were the last hour of my life." And his fiftieth resolution is "I will act so as I think I shall judge would have been best and most prudent when I come into the future world."

I purge so that I can expand on things that will outlive me. For example, God has called me to write. I love to bring God's truth through the printed page, knowing that if Christ tarries, the printed page will outlast me. So, I'm going to find time to do that. But that means I have to sacrifice other things that I like to do so I can fulfill the calling God has given me.

You have to know yourself, but generally speaking, far too many of us spend too much time watching TV, surfing the internet, text messaging, doing Facebook, watching professional sports, and reading frivolous books. There is no longevity to these things. Paul said, "All things are lawful unto me, but all things are not expedient: all things are lawful for me, but I will not be brought under the power of any" (1 Cor. 6:12).

Does that mean that I should have no recreation? Of course not. But it means that when you have times of recreation, those, too, are for the purposes of rejuvenation and reenergizing. Plan your vacations and your entertainment that way.

Protect

Remove temptation and distractions from your environment. We can be challenged a thousand times a day, can't we? But we need to somehow protect ourselves. Consider posting office hours. That is perfectly legitimate. Don't submit to the tyranny of the text message, email, Twitter, or phone.

Don't check your email ten times a day. Email could easily become my full-time job. But I'd never get anything done in the church or in the seminary. I can only allot a few hours a day at most to responding to emails. So I delegate a number of emails to different people, and some I just can't answer.

Learn to protect yourself. Learn to protect even the amount of time you spend talking to people. When I visit or counsel people, I usually schedule the visits to last one hour. I have found that the quality of visits usually suffers after an hour. But what do you do if you can't get your visitor to stop talking? Simply say to them, to wind down the conversation, "Well, I appreciate talking with you. Maybe we can pick this up the next time we talk. Meanwhile, why don't we pray together." They get the hint, and they appreciate your prayers for them. You don't mean any ill will, but it is just a measure of balancing your life, and they will understand that.

Pause

Even machines need time to cool off, or they will break down. Don't run yourself ragged; it will not help you. You will grow weaker and less productive. You need breaks. Pause to exercise—it will actually save you time! Research has shown that exercise increases cognitive function, creativity, and productivity. Pause to take one day off in seven—or to take a few hours off on different days, depending on what works best for you. And pause to sleep. Sleep actually boosts your memory. Be sure to get enough of it.

Know yourself. Know how much exercise and sleep you need to work at your maximum. And know how long you can study effectively. Some men in the ministry can study only for one hour at a time before they need a five-minute break. Their mind bursts with energy when they come back. They need to go for a short walk and think their thoughts, and then come back. I'm not that way. I'm much better if I can have eight or ten hours straight to study. I'm a plodder. That's the way God has made me. You have to know your own body, and what it is saying to you about your mind and your weariness. For me, when I get weary, a five- to ten-minute nap does wonders, and I can keep on going. For you, that may not work at all. Know yourself, and accept the way God has made you.

Persevere

You must persevere for the Lord Jesus who persevered for you to the end. Cast your bread upon the waters, and you will find it after many days. It will bear fruit. When we persevere, a certain holy habit develops in our lives that enables us to continue to persevere. When perseverance becomes a normal mode of discipline, whether it is your daily devotions or your work, and you truly labor and abound in the work of the Lord, perseverance becomes a holy habit. Keep hoping, trusting, and believing.

Conclusion

Let me close by returning to the image of spinning your wheels in the mud. After your call for help, your farmer friend tows you out of the muck with his tractor. Then he hoses off the dirt from your car and gently reminds you that if you had just called ahead of time for directions, you never would have ended up on the dirt road, for there was a solid paved road farther up. "Well," he says, "enough of that," and he invites you to his house, where he offers you a cup of coffee and a piece of apple pie. Eventually you're back on the highway again, but you have lost hours because of your own foolishness. You could have taken your GPS with you. You could have asked someone for directions, but you were too proud. You could have called your friend for help. But you instead thought, "I'll just figure it out myself." That is often the problem. We need to ask for help. Ask God for help; ask others for help. We need to use alternatives available to us to help us manage our time wisely.

So don't live frenetically. Don't fall into the trap of thinking you have to perform at a certain level to be acceptable to God. But run the race set before you faithfully, planning your time, looking to Jesus, the Author and Finisher of your faith. And then with fresh vigor you can take the shortest way home in order to serve Him with all your might for the rest of your life and ministry.

Dear brother in the ministry, you are a marked man, living a summoned life, called to engage in the most important calling in the world as an ambassador of Jesus Christ. In eternity past before time began, God determined to save you and call you to the ministry, and portioned out so much time for you to use for His kingdom. Since He will not give you any more time than what He has portioned, you are to do for God what must be done within the time He has given to you. And that clock is ticking at this very moment. The impact of your life on time and eternity hinges on the wise use of your time. If you use your time wisely, with the Spirit's blessing, you will be used by God in a substantial way. Let your daily prayer be "Take my life and let it be / consecrated Lord to Thee / Take my moments and my days / let them flow in ceaseless praise."

For whatever time you have left in your ministry and in your life, I urge you to make Jonathan Edwards's 52nd resolution your own: "Resolved, I frequently hear persons in old age say how they would live if they were to live their lives over again. Resolved, that I will live just so as I can think I shall wish I had done, supposing I live to an old age."

When you come to the end of your life, may you not be filled with regret because of time wasted. Rather, when you stand before the Savior on the judgment day, may you be deeply humbled to hear Him say, "Well done, thou good and faithful servant. By grace, you invested the time that I allotted to you wisely for My glory. Enter thou into the joy of thy Lord."

Chapter 41

Nurturing Intimate Communication
with Your Spouse

There is a friend that sticketh closer than a brother.
—Proverbs 18:24

This is my beloved, and this is my friend.
—Song of Songs 5:16

Rejoice with the wife of thy youth…let her breasts satisfy thee
at all times; and be thou ravished always with her love.
—Proverbs 5:18–19

Next to new life in Christ, close friendship is life's greatest gift. That is particularly so in marriage. I am privileged to be engaged in a number of ministries, but friendship with my wife is worth more to me than any of them. Her friendship is priceless to me.

There's something deep and mysterious about this bond of Christian friendship, because it reflects the very nature of God. We might define it as the personal bond of shared life. Typically the bond of true friendship can take months to build and lasts for years. It is not an accidental connection; it is a mutual bond of faithfulness. Friendship is not just any bond or relationship but a bond of shared life. Deuteronomy 13:6 makes a passing reference to "thy friend, which is as thine own soul." This implies that losing such a friend would be like death. Your lives are so bound together that whatever touches your friend touches you. You are like two strings on a well-tuned guitar: When one is plucked, the other string vibrates in harmony.

God created marriage as a relationship uniquely designed for intimate friendship. Thomas Gataker (1574–1654) said, "There is no society [relationship] more near, more entire, more needful, more kindly, more delightful, more comfortable, more constant, more continual, than the society of man and wife."[1] By the grace of God, such friendship between husbands and wives is possible and practical and should be our priority.

This chapter will first study the foundation of friendship in marriage, followed by a consideration of five key ways to cultivate friendship in marriage.

The Foundation of Friendship in Marriage

Marriage was instituted by God at the dawn of human history. Both the sweet possibilities and bitter tragedies of marriage are rooted in the Bible's description of God's dealings with our first father and mother in Genesis 1–3. Indeed, marriage is rooted in God Himself. In Genesis 1:26, the Lord said, "Let us make man in our image, after our likeness." The divine image in man is the reflection of the divine "us"—that is, the three persons of the Godhead, one in substance and equal in power and glory, living together in unity and eternal love. The three persons constantly commune with one another and cooperate as one God in all they do (John 5:19–20). The Son delights to do the Father's will (John 4:34), and the Spirit delights to glorify the Son (John 16:14). This is beyond our comprehension, but by faith we believe that authentic friendship in Christ is rooted in the relationship of the three persons of the Trinity with each other.

The triune God has chosen to display His glory in our common humanity, our gender differences, and our relationships with each other. "So God created man in his own image, in the image of God created he him; male and female created he them" (Gen. 1:27). There is but one humanity, shared by both men and women as creatures made in the image of God; yet there are two sexes, male and female, each distinct from the other. The purpose of marriage is more than emotional satisfaction or the fulfillment of physical desires. The purpose of marriage is to reveal the glory of the triune God. Alan Dunn says, "Marital intimacy is something more wonderful than mere biological mechanisms or animal urges.... Our inclination to intimacy is essential to our being: we are creatures made in the image of God."[2]

God's intent for marriage is clarified in the way He created woman. In Genesis 2:18, we read, "And the LORD God said, It is not good that the man should be alone; I will make him an help meet for him." He then showed the man that

---

1. Quoted in J. I. Packer, *A Quest for Godliness: The Puritan Vision of the Christian Life* (Wheaton, Ill.: Crossway, 1990), 262. I thank Paul Smalley for his research assistance on this article. The substance of this chapter was given as an address for the Christian Home Educators of Washington in Ocean Shores, Washington, on October 11, 2014.

2. Alan Dunn, *Gospel Intimacy in a Godly Marriage: A Pursuit of Godly Romance* (North Bergen, N.J.: Pillar and Ground Publications, 2009), 17.

no mere animal would fit that description. Man's well-being depended on having a companion who could come to his aid in time of need and unite with him in doing God's will in the world. He needed someone "meet," or suitable, to who and what he was. This was a true friend.

So the Lord formed woman out of man's side. Genesis 2:23–25 says, "And the man said, This is now bone of my bones, and flesh of my flesh: she shall be called Woman, because she was taken out of Man. Therefore shall a man leave his father and his mother, and shall cleave unto his wife: and they shall be one flesh. And they were both naked, the man and his wife, and were not ashamed." This is a remarkable description of God's design for marriage, which includes oneness, separation into a special and unique relationship, mutual commitment to one another, and total openness.

Sadly, our first parents sinned, and their corruption had dire effects on their marriage. We see this in Genesis 3. Paradise ended even before the man and woman left the garden of Eden; the loss of original righteousness severed their relationship with God and damaged their marriage bond. Their openness gave way to shame, guilt, and covering their nakedness with aprons of fig leaves. As for mutual commitment, when God confronted them, the man tried to shift blame to the woman, knowing full well that the penalty of sin was death. God told the woman that the result of her sin was that her desire would be to conquer her husband, but he would continue to rule over her, resulting in conflict, anger, and bitter estrangement. If you wonder why friendship in marriage can be difficult, the short answer is: original sin.

But God also showed grace to the couple. In Genesis 3:15, God declared that He would turn the hearts of the woman and her offspring against the devil. One day a descendant of the woman would crush the serpent's head and by His redemptive suffering bring deliverance to fallen mankind. This is the promise of Jesus Christ. They believed God's promise, so the man gave his wife a new name. He did not call her mother of the dead, though death was now due to the race because of sin. Instead, he repented of having blamed her for his own sin and called her "Eve; because she was the mother of all living" (Gen. 3:20). He blessed her with a name of hope. He used his authority over woman to bless her, not to curse! By calling her "mother," he also recommitted himself to his wife and the mother of their children. Thus, by the grace of God revealed in the gospel, their relationship as husband and wife was renewed.

We learn from the first three chapters of the Bible that friendship in marriage has a theological foundation. Married persons are to be friends in the best and deepest sense of the term. Such friendship glorifies the triune God by realizing the full, God-given potential of the marriage bond. Marriage is rooted in the basic facts of our creation; we were made to have communion with each other, and the closest possible communion is that between husband and wife. The beauty of this communion was marred by the fall and obscured by the curse of sin, but friendship in marriage can be restored and renewed by faith in the promise of a Savior.

We could go on. We might speak of the law and how marriage must be regulated by the commandments of God, such as, "Thou shalt love thy neighbor as thyself" (Lev. 19:18), "Thou shalt not commit adultery" (Ex. 20:14), and "Thou shalt not covet thy neighbor's wife" (Ex. 20:17). We could delve into the mystery of how marriage reflects Christ's relationship to the church (Eph. 5:22–33). As you know, there is a wealth of teaching in the Bible that is relevant to marriage. But let us pass by those topics and come to our second point.

The Cultivation of Friendship in Marriage
Cultivation is rooted in farm work. Seed is sown, and tender plants spring up. They cannot flourish if they are not cultivated. Cultivation is rewarding work, for it results in an abundant harvest, when God gives the increase. But it is hard work. Nobody wakes up one morning and is pleasantly surprised to discover that, without any effort on his part, a field of ripe corn has appeared on his property.

Likewise, cultivating friendship in marriage is hard work—yet most rewarding. Many people in our culture think that love is something you fall into and then somehow fall out of. That might be true of passing emotions, but true friendship relies on cultivation: uprooting bad attitudes, planting daily seeds of love toward one another, pulling out weeds, eliminating pests that threaten to choke the relationship, watering the tender plants with daily prayer, and then taking time to reap a harvest of love and enjoyment in each other's company.

We must resist the laziness and ingratitude that often creep into marriage. Before you were married, didn't you invest a lot in each other? You couldn't wait to be together, and you made time for each other. You sent each other notes and talked often on the phone together. You paid each other compliments, brought each other gifts, showed each other affection, and shared each other's daily joys and trials. If you stop doing such things after you marry, what will happen to your friendship? The tender plant of friendship will languish and die away. Friendship does not persist, deepen, and grow automatically.

We should strive in our marriages to say of each other what Christ's bride says of Him in Song of Songs 5:16: "This is my beloved, and this is my friend." We must work to build true Christian fellowship with our spouses. The Greek word translated *fellowship* in the New Testament actually means *sharing* or communing with each other: sharing each other's joys, bearing each other's burdens, and being involved in each other's lives. Fellowship is one of the goals of the gospel. First John 1:3 says, "That which we have seen and heard declare we unto you, that ye also may have fellowship with us: and truly our fellowship is with the Father, and with his Son Jesus Christ." The same gospel should increase our love for each other as husband and wife, and our longing to have fellowship with each other.

Let us explore several aspects of cultivating friendship in marriage under the theme of sharing.

1. Cultivate Friendship by Sharing Yourselves

The Lord describes His closeness with His people in terms of friendship. Exodus 33:11 says, "And the LORD spake unto Moses face to face, as a man speaketh unto his friend." God is a Spirit (John 4:24), so this verse does not refer to physical closeness or seeing any physical form or face of God. It refers to an immediacy of spirit to spirit. God sent messages to His other prophets in dreams and visions, but spoke His Word directly to Moses (Num. 12:6–8). In the new covenant, this kind of spiritual intimacy is extended to true believers who yearn to walk with God (Eph. 2:18; 3:12). God compares this closeness to what friends should be to each other: "as a man speaketh unto his friend." Jesus also called His disciples "friends" because He shared His mind and heart with them (John 15:15), and He commands us to love each other as He loved us (John 13:34; Eph. 5:2).

A woman once told me that when her husband was gone for four or five hours, she would ask him, "Where were you? What did you do?" He said, "I don't ask you what you did today, do I? Don't ask me what I did today." A man who treats his wife that way has a servant in his house, not a friend. Richard Baxter (1615–1691) wrote this about marriage:

> It is a mercy to have a faithful friend, that loveth you entirely, and is as true to you as yourself, to whom you may open your mind and communicate your affairs, and who would be ready to strengthen you, and divide the cares of your affairs and family with you, and help you to bear your burdens, and comfort you in your sorrows, and be the daily companion of your life, and partaker of your joys and sorrows.[3]

When you marry, the Lord says you enter into a covenant of companionship. Malachi 2:14 says, "The wife of thy youth" is "thy companion, and the wife of thy covenant." You promise to walk together all the way through the pilgrimage of

---

3. Richard Baxter, *The Christian Directory*, 2.1, dir. 9, in *The Practical Works of the Rev. Richard Baxter*, ed. William Orme (London: James Duncan, 1830), 4:30.

life. One couple I know uses the five Ts to remember what companionship is: giving each other time, thought, talk, tenderness, and touch.

There is no substitute for spending time together. Friendship cannot be warmed up by thirty seconds in the microwave. So much today is instant; friendship is not. It costs something. It costs you yourself, your commitment, and your vulnerability. There are no rush orders in friendship. It must be baked slowly, gently, and continually if we want the flavor we are looking for.

One aspect of sharing your minds and hearts is discussing major decisions together and waiting until you have unity before moving ahead. Any decision that significantly affects your time or money or that involves a major change for your family's life, home, work, or church, should be made only after talking together about it, praying together, and coming to a point of unity. Although the husband is the head of the household, a godly man should not—with rare exceptions—lead his family against his godly wife's desires. As William Gouge (1575–1653) said, "Though the man be as the head, yet is the woman as the heart."[4] Listen to her thoughts and feelings on a regular basis so that she knows she is an important part of your life.

2. Cultivate Friendship by Sharing Your Faith

The deepest fellowship is spiritual fellowship, in which you share your life with a dear friend in the presence of the living God. It is remarkable how few Christians actually enjoy spiritual fellowship with their spouses. I'm not talking about having family devotions, though that is a crucial spiritual discipline. I'm talking about sharing your faith with each other.

Obviously that assumes that you both have a living faith in Christ. Paul warns us in 2 Corinthians 6:14, "Be ye not unequally yoked together with unbelievers: for what fellowship hath righteousness with unrighteousness? And what communion hath light with darkness?" Spiritual fellowship is impossible unless Christ lives in both people in a marriage. For this reason Paul says in 1 Corinthians 7:39 that if a woman's husband dies, "she is at liberty to be married to whom she will; *only in the Lord.*"

If you are a Christian who is single, do not enter a romantic relationship with a person who does not love the Lord Jesus Christ and is not walking with God. Don't settle for someone who goes to church but has a questionable profession of faith. The minimum standard for dating or courtship should be a faith that is producing good works through love.

---

4. William Gouge, *Building a Godly Home: Volume 2, A Holy Vision for Marriage*, ed. Scott Brown and Joel R. Beeke (Grand Rapids: Reformation Heritage Books, 2013), 98.

If you are a Christian and are married to an unconverted person who is willing to live with you, do not leave your spouse (1 Cor. 7:12–13). But do not try to nag your spouse into the kingdom! Be the best husband or wife that you can possibly be so that you might win your spouse's heart with your godly conduct (1 Peter 3:1–2). Similarly, if your spouse professes to be saved but resists talking about spiritual things, give yourself to private prayer and serve your spouse with true love.

But if you are both Christians, then share your spiritual experiences. Share your spiritual concerns, frustrations and triumphs, your pilgrimage and your progress. Talk about how the Lord is working in your life by His Word and Spirit.

Most importantly, share your faith as a couple by praying together. I realize that praying out loud can be intimidating for some Christians, and we should be patient with each other in this. But there is nothing like spending time each day as a couple, offering thanksgiving together for the day's blessings and petitioning God for the grace you need. Moreover, don't put off prayer if your spouse asks you to pray together at some point during the day when you don't normally pray together. Men, put down the book, set aside your tools, turn away from the screen, and pray. Women, turn off the stove, put down your phone, and pray. Baxter said, "It is a mercy to have so near a friend to be a helper to your soul."[5]

3. Cultivate Friendship by Sharing Your Trust

The traditional wedding vow includes the phrase, "I plight thee my troth," which means "I pledge my trustworthiness and fidelity to you." We need more "troth" in our marriages. Proverbs 18:24 says, "There is a friend that sticketh closer than a brother." Cultivate with your spouse a commitment that is more intimate and enduring than blood relations. Superglue your hearts together in an unbreakable bond.

Don't be a fair-weather friend. Proverbs 19:6 says, "Every man is a friend to him that giveth gifts." Before you married, you probably lavished gifts and attention on each other. But will you keep your troth when the fervor of first romance wears off? Let your spouse know through consistent faithfulness that you can be relied on in good times and bad. Wives, don't be resentful if your husband's job takes him away from you more than you like. Husbands, don't be disappointed if your wife isn't as slim and cheerful as she was before having three children. Don't give way to such resentments. Love each other with loyalty, and your trust will deepen.

---

5. Baxter, *Christian Directory*, 2.1, dir. 9, in *Works*, 4:30.

Trustworthiness nurtures trust. Trust develops over time as your relationship matures. You trust each other more and more as you learn to feel comfortable and confident with each other. Both of you should refrain from flirting with members of the opposite sex and should offer no reason for suspicion. Over time you should be drawn together in a deeper sense of troth, which binds you in friendship. You will feel comfortable when you see each other. That is what happens in a good marriage.

So whatever you can do to cultivate mutual openness and confidence to build a sense of trust will build your friendship. Let me warn you here against things that tear down trust. First is lack of discretion and confidentiality. Proverbs 17:9 says, "He that repeateth a matter separateth very friends." You should also be slow to believe rumors that you hear about each other. Rumors are very divisive, even if they have no basis in fact. "A froward man soweth strife: and a whisperer separateth chief friends" (Prov. 16:28). I'm not suggesting that you ignore any signs that your spouse may be involved in a sinful behavior; there are times when a wayward spouse must be confronted, if need be, with the help of your pastor. But realize that you can't take seriously all that you hear, especially when it is contrary to what you know about a person's character.

Proverbs 31:11–12 says of a virtuous woman, "The heart of her husband doth safely trust in her, so that he shall have no need of spoil. She will do him good and not evil all the days of her life." Strive to be worthy of the trust that every man should place in his wife, every wife in her husband.

4. Cultivate Friendship by Sharing Your Joy

A sour and negative disposition discourages people and relationships. A sense of humor, smiles, warmth, and optimism are important ways to encourage each other. So develop a joyful spirit. "A merry heart doeth good like a medicine: but a broken spirit drieth the bones" (Prov. 17:22). Laughing together is a sweet way to refresh your spirits and draw closer together.

Your children and your own human foibles should provide plenty of material for humor. Of course, God, sin, heaven, and hell are not laughing matters; we must never respond to the truths of God with levity. But there is much in life that we should not take so seriously. Learn to laugh at situations that are not inherently weighty. It's a way of saying, "The Lord is with us despite our idiosyncrasies."

Cultivate joy that does not depend on physical circumstances. "Be of good cheer" (Matt. 9:2; 14:27). Proverbs 15:15–16 says, "All the days of the afflicted are evil: but he that is of a merry heart hath a continual feast. Better is little with the fear of the LORD than great treasure and trouble therewith. Better is a dinner of herbs where love is, than a stalled ox and hatred therewith." If you have each other's love and fear the Lord, you can feast on inward joys even if you have nothing but peanut butter sandwiches for supper.

Learn how to please your spouse. We read in 1 Corinthians 7:33–34, "But he that is married careth for the things that are of the world, how he may please his wife," and "she that is married careth for the things of the world, how she may please her husband." Pleasing someone (without compromising your faith) is a mark of friendship. Baxter wrote, "When husband and wife take pleasure in each other, it uniteth them in duty, it helpeth them with ease to do their work, and bear their burdens; and is not the least part of the comfort of the married state."[6]

Don't be so super-spiritual that earthly things don't matter. Wesley said that cleanliness is next to godliness, and he was not far off the mark.[7] Personal hygiene is a must when two people live in close proximity. Grooming and dress are also important. Find out what your husband or wife likes, and do it. Baxter said, "Avoid therefore all things that may represent you unpleasant or unlovely to each other.... Whatever is loathsome in body or mind, must be shunned as temptations which would hinder you from that love, and pleasure, and content, which husband and wife should have in one another."[8] When my wife and I first married, I thought I was a careful driver, but my wife saw it differently. What to me seemed a safe distance between my car and the one ahead to her seemed dangerously near. I had to be willing to sacrifice my ideas about driving in order to make her feel safer in the car with me.

Sharing your joys also means sharing activities that you both enjoy and that glorify God. Look for areas of common interest and invest in them. If your spouse enjoys something that is not your favorite activity, learn to enjoy it, or learn to enjoy your spouse's enjoyment. The more your lives overlap, the closer your friendship will become.

5. Cultivate Friendship by Sharing Your Sexuality

Marriage is unique among human relationships because in it God blesses a "one flesh" bond of sexual intimacy. The Bible calls us to enjoy sex with our spouses. Proverbs 5:18–19 commands the husband to "rejoice with the wife of thy youth," and adds, "let her breasts satisfy thee at all times; and be thou ravished always with her love."

This may surprise you. Too often we view sex much like what someone might say about a piece of double chocolate cake: "It's so good, it must be sinful."

---

6. Baxter, *Christian Directory*, 2.7, dir. 4, in *Works*, 4:122.

7. John Wesley, "On Dress," in *The Works of the Reverend John Wesley*, ed. John Emory (New York: T. Mason and G. Lane, 1840), 2:259.

8. Baxter, *Christian Directory*, 2.7, dir. 4, in *Works*, 4:122.

Nurturing sexual intimacy with your spouse requires seeing sex in the perspective that God created all things very good. Paul warned in 1 Timothy 4:1–5 against "doctrines of devils" that forbid people to marry, for, Paul said, all that God created should be received with thankfulness and "sanctified by the word of God and prayer."

Sexual love in marriage is like fire in a fireplace. If the fire breaks through the boundaries of the fireplace and ignites other parts of the house, it can destroy your property, kill your family, and end your life. Likewise, sex outside of its God-ordained boundaries destroys and kills. What the world considers sexual freedom is really death. "Whoso committeth adultery with a woman lacketh understanding: he that doeth it destroyeth his own soul" (Prov. 6:32). But we would not want to harbor such a fear of fire that we could never again enjoy the dancing flames in a fireplace. A blazing hearth is warm and beautiful. Likewise, sex within marriage is a warm and beautiful way to be close to the one you love.

We must reject the remnants of medieval tradition that cling like barnacles to our view of Christian sexuality. The Reformed and Puritan tradition has a healthy, God-glorifying, marriage-honoring perspective on sexual intimacy in marriage. Matthew Henry (1662–1714) wrote of being "always ravished with the love of a faithful virtuous wife."[9] In biblical thinking, passion and purity go together.

The doctrine of creation also reminds us that sex is not just about passions and hormones but two people relating to each other in the image of God. Genesis 1:27 says, "So God created man in his own image, in the image of God created he him; male and female created he them." Our gender and sexuality are dimensions of an entire person created in God's image. Human sexuality is the coming together of two people, male and female, who were made for each other; and both were made to serve God. The best sex springs from a relationship in which we honor each other throughout life.

Scripture furthermore implies that sex thrives in an environment of personal communication. Men and women were made in the image of God as a result of communication among the three persons of the Godhead, who agreed to the proposal, "Let us make man in our image" (Gen. 1:26). Gary Chapman writes, "Sexual intimacy is the result of a relationship, and relationship is fostered by communication.... If we do not have time to talk, then we don't have time for sex."[10]

---

9. *Matthew Henry's Commentary on the Whole Bible* (Peabody, Mass.: Hendrickson, 1991), 3:671 [Prov. 5:15–23].

10. Gary Chapman, *Covenant Marriage* (Nashville: Broadman and Holman, 2003), 190.

However, that does not mean that married couples can delay having a sexual relationship for a year until they develop better communication. God commands you to make love regularly with your spouse if it is physically possible. Paul wrote in 1 Corinthians 7:3, "Let the husband render unto the wife due benevolence: and likewise also the wife unto the husband." The Greek words translated "due benevolence" communicate the idea of a debt of love.[11] William Gouge wrote, "As it is called 'benevolence' because it must be performed with good will and delight, willingly, readily and cheerfully; so it is said to be 'due' because it is a debt which the wife owes to her husband, and he to her."[12]

It is God's will that married couples regularly have sexual relations, physical and medical conditions permitting, out of love for each other. This does not mean that one spouse has the right to demand sex every night regardless of how tired the other spouse is. Nor must a spouse demand a certain kind of sexual activity if the other is uncomfortable with it. We should reject our culture's obsessions with increasingly bizarre forms of sex that seem to make sex an end in itself. However, even with these caveats, husband and wife are to live as one flesh.

I understand that our sexuality has been corrupted and complicated since the fall of mankind into sin and misery. Yet the grace of Jesus Christ has the power to progressively heal us from our sins and comfort us in our wounds. I spend more than forty pages in my book *Friends and Lovers* talking about how biblical truth applied through Spirit-worked faith can lead to greater sexual freedom and joy in marriage.[13]

My point here is that God has given us sexual intimacy as a means to enhance the overall intimacy of our marriages. As Gouge said, making love serves a three-fold purpose: to guard us from immorality, to produce children, and "for linking the affections of the married couple more firmly together."[14] Make love as best friends. Forget about the rest of the world, and stop obsessing with how you look or how you perform. Just love each other. As Gary Thomas says, "Give what you have."[15]

Conclusion

Intimate friendship in marriage is a gift from God. As we saw from Genesis, it originates in the nature of God and expresses itself in us as creatures made in

---

11. Greek, την οφειλομενην ευνοιαν. Some Greek manuscripts omit "benevolence" but retain "duty."

12. Gouge, *Building a Godly Home*, 2:44.

13. Joel R. Beeke, *Friends and Lovers: Cultivating Companionship and Intimacy in Marriage* (Adelphi, Md.: Cruciform, 2012), 45–88.

14. Gouge, *Building a Godly Home*, 2:44.

15. Gary Thomas, *Sacred Marriage* (Grand Rapids: Zondervan, 2000), 218.

His image. Therefore, a good friend should be cherished, especially when that friend is your spouse. Pray for friendship in Christ, and seek God's blessing on your marriage so that your spouse would be your best friend on earth. And when God grants that request, give Him thanks.

At the same time, don't expect too much of this or any other friendship. Be realistic. Your spouse is not God. Friendship with your spouse cannot meet all your needs or ensure that your marriage will be trouble-free. Your spouse is not sinless, nor are you. You will have to bear with faults and foolishness all your days together.

Finally, remember that ultimately we stand alone before God. Neither your wife nor husband nor any other friend can stand in for you in your relationship with God. You are responsible to Him for "the things done in the body" (2 Cor. 5:10). Even if you try to ignore the Lord, He is still there, always watching and always working. Every other person is of no significance in comparison to Him. Make your marriage into a means of nurturing intimacy with Jesus Christ, and you will never be disappointed. If you are joined to Christ by faith, then He loves you as His own flesh and bones and will nourish and cherish you to eternal life.

Subject Index